DATE			

KAFKA

K

KAFKA
THE YEARS OF INSIGHT

REINER STACH

TRANSLATED BY SHELLEY FRISCH

PRINCETON UNIVERSITY PRESS
Princeton and Oxford

Originally published in Germany as *Kafka—Die Jahre der Erkenntnis*

Published by Princeton University Press, 41 William Street, Princeton, New Jersey 08540
In the United Kingdom: Princeton University Press, 6 Oxford Street, Woodstock, Oxfordshire OX20 1TW

press.princeton.edu

Jacket photograph: Detail of a portrait of Austrian writer Franz Kafka (1883–1924) as a young man, c. 1910. Photo © Hulton Archive. Courtesy of Getty Images.

Library of Congress Cataloging-in-Publication Data
Stach, Reiner.
[Kafka, die Jahre der Erkenntnis. English]
Kafka, the years of insight / Reiner Stach ; translated by Shelley Frisch.
pages cm
Includes bibliographical references and index.
ISBN 978-0-691-14751-2 (hardback : alk. paper) 1. Kafka, Franz, 1883–1924. 2. Authors, Austrian—20th century—Biography. I. Frisch, Shelley Laura, translator. II. Title.
PT2621.A26Z886313 2013
833'.912—dc23
[B]
2012042048

British Library Cataloging-in-Publication Data is available

The translation of this work was funded by Geisteswissenschaften International—Translation Funding for Humanities and Social Sciences from Germany, a joint initiative of the Fritz Thyssen Foundation, the German Federal Foreign Office, the collecting society VG WORT and the Börsenverein des Deutschen Buchhandels (German Publishers & Booksellers Association)

This book has been composed in Mensch and MVB Verdigris Pro

Printed on acid-free paper. ∞

Printed in the United States of America

10 9 8 7 6 5 4 3 2 1

For Leo

CONTENTS

KAFKA

PROLOGUE

The Ants of Prague

In the geographical heart of the European continent lies a forested region, far from the oceans and seas, with an unwelcoming climate and no natural resources to speak of. Repeatedly devastated by wars and epidemics, and fragmented over the centuries into politically insignificant parcels of land, it is a poor, empty center.

Rarely, and for only brief periods of time, the force field of power extended beyond its own borders. Decisions had always been handed down from elsewhere regarding the resources of the world, as had new, more efficient forms of economy and political rule. Even so, the residents of this region were able within a few generations to attain a level of wealth that was well above average for the scale of the world economy. At the threshold of the twentieth century, after a phase of hectic industrialization, the German Reich and Austria-Hungary were prosperous states with oversized armies, which trumpeted their newfound self-confidence. It took these parvenus a long time to realize that such a rapid upsurge would upset the global balance and exact a political price.

Suddenly they were encircled and threatened by covetous and malevolent neighbors. The leaders in Germany and Austria took too long to recognize that the older, most established Great Powers were using their edge in diplomatic skill and had no intention of standing aside in silence. They had likely already reached an agreement to occupy and exploit the emergent center together—and the evidence to justify this suspicion kept mounting. In the East, Russia, a volatile colossus, prepared to send millions upon millions of slaves into a war of conquest. In the West, an envious France and British profiteers extolled the virtues of civilization while looking out for their bottom lines. And in the South, an opportunistic Italy, an ambitious satellite state, which despite its repeated promises to form alliances would clearly side with the majority. The circle was virtually closed; it was a strangulation that August 1, 1914, finally brought to a halt. That is how it was reported in the press, anyway. Within days, all those in the center wrapped their minds around a new, interesting-sounding notion: *world war.*

Dr. Kafka, a thirty-two-year-old unmarried Jewish official at the Workers' Accident Insurance Institute in Prague, had yet to set eyes on the war a year later. A tall, slender, lanky man, who despite his youthful appearance was plagued by nervousness, headaches, and insomnia but was deemed fit for military service; back in June 1915, his fitness had been certified after a brief physical. But the insurance institute—most likely his superiors, Pfohl and Marschner, who were kindly disposed toward him—claimed that he had indispensable legal expertise, and the military authorities granted their petition. Kafka's name was entered onto the muster roll of some auxiliary unit pro forma, but with a stipulation that the man in question was "excused indefinitely."

Not long before, when the war was still young, yet the patriotic fervor had already faded, Dr. Kafka took a brief trip to Hungary and the supply center of the Carpathian front. There were officers in German uniforms, field chaplains, Red Cross nurses, hospital trains, cannons ready for shipment in accordance with regulations, and, above all, refugees—whole columns of ragged refugees from Poland and Galicia who had just escaped from the advancing Russians and were now streaming toward the visitor. He observed the preparations for events of enormous proportion that loomed ahead, and he saw where they would lead. But what about the essence, the great battle, the great liberation? The movies and newsreels tilted their coverage away from the wretched, mundane details.

Kafka was not alone with his doubts. People back home learned from newspapers and a limited number of silent and unrevealing newsreel images about the exciting, adventurous dynamic of the war, the use of the latest technology, the camaraderie, and the impressive ability of the troops to hold their ground. In their own everyday lives, civilians experienced a scarcity of food—and what little could be had was of poor quality—and a lack of heat in their homes. There was also rampant inflation, censorship, harassment from the authorities, and militarization yet neglect of the public space. The press called this area the "home front," but the lie of this concept was all too apparent, and no one took it seriously. Only those on the *actual* front experienced anything, while people back home were condemned to passive endurance, the origin and meaning of which they had to infer from overblown military progress reports. The yawning abyss between these reports and the situation at home made for a potentially perilous discontent.

Presentation was one of the modern and still-unfamiliar pressing issues facing politicians as the war dragged on: if it could not be won soon, it would have to be "sold" more effectively. It was thus a welcome, if somewhat obvious and propagandistic, idea to give the civilian population a taste of the real war, so as to bring them into close fellowship with the troops. The idea was to replicate the war at home, but not in the form of those unspeakable exhibits of weapons and flags that mummified the battles of the nineteenth century and put historical showpieces on a par with antiquated natural history collections. Instead, urban dwellers—even with their dulled senses—would be offered something they could ponder and tell stories about for a long time to come.

Just after the onset of the war, seized weapons were paraded through the cities in triumph, and the much-vaunted Leipzig International Trade Fair for Books and Graphic Arts (which Dr. Kafka, who was interested in literature, had of course already seen) opened its own war division featuring a cheap thrill that was gratefully embraced by the public: four wax enemy soldiers brandishing weapons and staring down visitors. Back in the fall of 1914, no one had come up with the idea that people could actually reenact the war instead of remaining mere spectators from afar. War was pictured as an extensive, explosive, and expansive movement incapable of replication. It was only when the war got bogged down that the key role of the trenches—long predicted by military experts—opened up the possibility of actually playing at war. Burrowing in the earth could be done anywhere, so why not at Reichskanzlerplatz in the west end of Berlin? In the summer of 1915, the inquisitive got a chance to climb into a dry, clean-swept, wood-paneled "model trench."[1]

It is difficult to understand today why these archaic-looking, purely defensive trenches were being put on display as though they were technical wonders, and why they so quickly became all the rage with the masses and were soon duplicated in other cities. Hiding under the earth like moles and spending weeks or even months lying in wait for the opponent was not the virile, gallant battle that people had painted in glowing colors, and the promised quick victory certainly could not be achieved with means like these. But the propaganda and the physicality of the presentation gradually persuaded people that they were part of a grand scheme. They learned about complex meandering or zigzagging trench systems that were equipped with inhabitable dugouts, listening-post passageways, telephones, wire obstacles, and steps to repel future assaults. All of that could be experienced up close or viewed on newsreels. High-society ladies decked out in fashionable hats and floor-length gowns and escorted by uniformed gentlemen could be seen climbing down into the trench to gain some impression of the war.

Naturally people wanted to see something like that in Prague, as well, and an unused area accessible by public transportation was quickly identified: the long and narrow Kaiserinsel, which divided the river for miles in the north of the city and the tip of which was located across from Stromovka Park, a spacious park noted for its trees and flowers. In the summer, this was the recreational area for the people of Prague who could not afford country retreats of their own, and it was easy to see why adding a trench replica to the outdoor cafés, playgrounds, and sunbathing lawns would offer a most welcome new form of entertainment.

The project was a spectacular success. Although it began to pour just after the trench's opening ceremonies, and the sun did not peek out for weeks to come, the Number 3 streetcar could barely accommodate the crush of visitors. On September 28 alone—the Bohemian legal holiday of St. Wenceslas Day—ten thousand people crowded through the turnstiles of the model trench, while beer barrels rolled next door and the Imperial Infantry Regiment No. 51 Band braved the squalls of rain to perform for the crowds. This was no longer a supplement to Stromovka Park; this was a fairground in its own right. And the nicest part was that one could enjoy oneself here with a clear conscience; the admission fee went to benefit "our wounded warriors." Even the Prague suffragan bishop donated fifty kronen to support the show.

The *Prager Tagblatt* assured its readers that "neither wind nor inclement weather could cause the least damage to any part of the grounds," but this claim did not hold up. Pelting rain made the Vltava River rise so rapidly that it inundated the island, and with it the trench that had been so painstakingly constructed. It took weeks to clear out the mud and debris. But eventually, in early November, came the proud announcement that the people of Prague would be offered an improved version: in addition to the newly reinforced trench there was a covered refreshment area featuring Pilsener beer and sausages, and military marches would be played every Sunday.

Kafka may not have been musically inclined, but he *was* curious. He almost missed out on this sensation because he was dog-tired, his temples were pounding, and he had no desire to stand in line dodging dripping umbrellas and whining children. A film of the opening ceremony had already been shown in Prague, picture postcards were selling briskly, and every elementary school child was talking about the trench. There was no need for him to subject himself to all this bother to keep informed. But maybe now was just the right time to take a closer look. A good deal was now being said about the war once again, reports of victory had come to dominate the headlines day after day following a long silence, and for the first time in months, discussions at the office and on the street began to focus on how things would proceed when it was all over.

Kafka, who in his civil service capacity sidestepped political discussions whenever he could, got caught up in an unaccustomed, almost disturbing state of excitement. Of course, he had plans. He wanted to get away from Prague, and longed for the Western urbanity he had come to know in Paris and Berlin, which made the old Prague, his hometown, seem suffocatingly provincial. His parents, sisters, and friends knew of his longing—although he rarely spoke of it—but no one took it very seriously. It was a pipe dream that failed to mask the increasingly wretched daily reality and pervasive sense of dread. Kafka had two brothers-in-law at the front. If they eventually came home alive, he might be able to think about Berlin.

But it was the state itself that was now highlighting the question of the future. The Austro-Hungarian monarchy offered its populace a wager: if you bet on victory and won, you would get 5½ percent annual interest and a subsequent return of principal; if you lost, you would lose it all. Of course, it would have been unseemly to make explicit mention of a wager and the possibility of a military defeat; that topic that was taboo even for the technocrats of the war. The wager took the form of "war bonds." The purchaser lent the state money so that the state could continue the war and make a big haul, and a certain percentage of this net profit would be distributed among the millions of creditors. Everyone would emerge from the war a winner. From this perspective, the transaction seemed far more appealing. And since no one could imagine that there might not be a bond issuer left when the bonds matured, two rounds of donations had already poured in. The success of the most recent issue, the "3rd Austro-Hungarian war bond," wound up surpassing even the most optimistic predictions. More than five billion kronen were exchanged for scrip adorned with double eagles, Jugendstil ornaments, official seals, and signatures, promising the moon and an ironclad guarantee until 1930.

Kafka found the idea of high long-term interest rates enticing as well, especially when he pondered his plans for Berlin. He had no more doubts about the integrity of the offer than his colleagues at work had; after all, even the Workers' Accident Insurance Institute considered it an act of patriotism to invest a substantial portion of its precious reserve funds—six million kronen to date—in war bonds. Nevertheless, Kafka hesitated for quite some time, understanding full well the consequences of his decision. In order to make his dream of breaking away from his profession, his parents, and Prague a reality, he had to count on the two annual salaries he had now saved up, about six thousand kronen, being available at the crucial moment. Then again, the interest rate might one day yield the extra income he would need to feed a family.

Kafka made his way to the registration office. It was Friday, November 5, 1915; he was running out of time because the next day at noon the counter would close and his chance to invest would slip away. He had just read in the *Prager Tagblatt*, "Everyone should ponder the question of what assets have ever achieved such a high yield. Use the final remaining hours to complete the purchasing formalities." That sounded reasonable, but how much should he wager? Kafka stood in front of the office, turned on his heel and strode home, turned around again and headed back to the registration office frantically, but he could not bring himself to enter this time either. Once he was back home and realized that he had frittered away the afternoon, his only option was to ask his mother to complete the purchase because he had to work on Saturday morning and could not run around town. He instructed her to invest one thousand kronen in his name. No, maybe that was too cautious—make it two thousand kronen.

On the afternoon of the following day—his savings now in the best of hands[2]—Kafka decided he would finally have a look at the trench on the Kaiserinsel in Prague. Why now? Did he sense a connection? Did he feel a sense of responsibility because of his financial stake in the war? His one rather odd remark about this experience provides no clue: "*Sight of the people swarming like ants in front of and inside the trench.*" A hollow in the ground with many living creatures squeezed together was really all that could be seen.

Kafka joined the swarm, then headed back to the city to visit the family of Oskar Pollak, a childhood friend with whom he had exchanged almost intimate letters more than ten years earlier. Pollak had been a supporter of the war right from the start and, five months ago, had become a casualty at the Isonzo while serving as an officer cadet. The time for Kafka to express his condolences was long past, and today he would do so, on the way home from the trench, nearly too late, as always.

CHAPTER ONE

Stepping Outside the Self

Strange what a feeling of solitude there is in failure.

—Karel Čapek, *Povětroň*

Don't write like that, Felice. You are wrong. There are misunderstandings between us which I, at any rate, certainly expect to be cleared up, although not in letters. I have not changed (unfortunately); the balance—of which I represent the fluctuations—has remained the same, but only the distribution of weight has been modified a bit; I believe I know more about both of us, and have a tentative goal. We will discuss it at Whitsun, if we can. Felice, don't think that I don't consider the inhibiting reflections and worries an almost unbearable and detestable burden, that I wouldn't love to shed everything and prefer a straightforward approach, and that I wouldn't rather be happy now and at once in a small natural circle, and above all give happiness. But this isn't possible, it is a burden I am forced to bear, I shiver with dissatisfaction, and even if my failures should stare me in the face, and not only my failures but also the loss of all hope, and my need to keep turning over all encumbrances in my mind—I most likely couldn't hold back. Incidentally, Felice, why do you think—at least it seems as though you do at times—that life together here in Prague might be possible? After all, you used to have serious doubts about it. What has erased them? This is something I still don't know.[1]

In 1999, Cynthia Ozick published an essay in the *New Yorker* called "The Impossibility of Being Kafka."[2] Her title is both baffling and enlightening because it invokes the familiar portrait of a neurotic, hypochondriac, fastidious individual who was complex and sensitive in every regard, who always circled around himself and who made a problem out of absolutely everything. It is the image that has long been engraved so deeply in the cultural foundations of the Western world that Kafka ultimately became the prototype and paradigm of a self-devouring introspection out of touch with reality.

He himself had smilingly and unhesitatingly endorsed the claim that it was impossible to be Kafka. "Impossible" was one of Kafka's signature adjectives. He invoked it in a surprising array of contexts and invariably imbued it with hidden layers of meaning, seemingly unconcerned that it aroused suspicions of notorious exaggeration and invariably set friends and family against him. He did not accept the difficulties of life lying down, which would have been the natural thing to do according to the logic of his own complaints (assuming that these ought to be taken at face value). Instead, he consistently accomplished to everyone's satisfaction things he had just deemed impossible, at times even of his own accord and without having to be pressured. He displayed a pragmatic and sometimes even ironic relationship to the impossible, and anyone who knew him even slightly could easily conclude that he was bent on making himself more difficult than he already was. "[O]ne must not prostrate oneself before the minor impossibilities," Kafka rationalized this contradiction, "or else the major impossibilities would never come into view."[3] That made sense. But did he mean it?

Even Max Brod, who had known Kafka from their earliest student days, was ultimately incapable of understanding him on this point. Countless times he had proved his mettle in listening patiently to Kafka's lamentations and enduring his wavering will and the steady barrage of misgivings that gnawed at him in making even the most ordinary decisions. Brod's patience stemmed from his growing awareness that all the obstacles his friend amassed were not simply hypochondriac delusions; they arose from an overpowering will to perfection that could not be toned down. Kafka sought perfection, in matters large and small, and perfection was *impossible*. Brod could neither dispute nor dismiss outright his friend's utopian desire as unrealistic or antagonistic. But to throw a manuscript into the fire because it is not perfect? To abandon a profession, a journey, a woman because one is imperfect? That was indefensible, Brod felt, and unreasonable by strict moral principles. Kafka's rigidity would ultimately work against him; it was self-destructive because it rendered even the easiest things impossible.

But Kafka did live, so it was quite illogical to reduce his friend's unrelenting literary, social, and above all erotic problems simply to his need for perfection. If that were truly the source of all unhappiness, Brod argued, why didn't this will to perfection render everything else impossible—everyday life, work at the office, even eating? "That is correct," Kafka replied dryly. "Although striving for perfection is only a small part of my big Gordian knot, in this instance every part is the whole and so what you are saying is correct. But this impossibility actually does exist, this impossibility of eating, etc.; it is just not as blatantly obvious as the impossibility of marriage."[4] Yes, that was Kafka. There was no getting at him. And perhaps Brod recalled while reading these placid, unhappy lines that he had scarcely read any text by his friend in which the impossible did *not* occur.

Her former fiancé had changed, Felice Bauer concluded in the spring of 1915. The change in her own situation seems to have made her see the issue more clearly. She was no longer the "childish lady" that she had once jauntily presented herself as to Kafka, and her usual optimism had eroded under the pressure of family catastrophes. Her beloved (and only) brother, who had fled to America after embezzling funds, did not get in touch very often. Would she ever see him again? Her father, who had had a weak character but a consoling presence, had succumbed to a sudden heart attack at the age of fifty-eight, and the grief Felice and her sisters experienced certainly ran deeper than their mother's. Moreover, Felice had forfeited her executive position at Lindström A.G. in Berlin, of which her fiancé had been as proud as if it were his own. She had given notice because the wedding was planned for the fall of 1914, and she wanted to begin a new life in Prague, a life without an office, in accordance with the conventions of marriage. Now that all her plans had gone up in smoke, she was lucky to find employment with a new company called Technical Workshop, a small supplier of precision machinery. This company had no need of an elegant woman to represent its products at German trade fairs. Kafka showed little interest in her new job.

His waning curiosity about what was happening in Felice's life, the details of which he had pleaded for and inhaled like a drug as recently as the previous year, was far from the only striking change that she glumly noted amidst all her other distress. In January they had met in the border town of Bodenbach, hoping to come to an understanding and perhaps even achieve a reconciliation, but Kafka kept his distance, avoided any physical contact, and asked probing questions that she could not answer. Their correspondence dragged on intermittently; sometimes entire weeks would go by without a letter—a mere trickle compared to the flood of letters that Kafka had churned out after their first encounter in the fall of 1912. Even so, he claimed not to have changed, while nearly every line of his letters bespoke the opposite.

In the past, Felice's mother and her sister Toni had had no compunction about reading bits and pieces of his letters in secret, until there was a little family uproar, and the letters were safely tucked away. But *this* letter—a meta-lament completely incomprehensible to outside observers—could lie open; her inquisitive mother would not be able to puzzle out even the outward status of this wretched relationship. It was as if Kafka were furnishing just the bare outlines of his emotional state, scattered traces made up of thousands of sighs, in the expectation that the recipient would flesh out the details on her own. He had never steered clear of ambiguity and intimation before, but this letter was the first to be pieced together, sentence by sentence, from ciphers and ellipses. Its mental shorthand evoked many of their recurring discussions without offering the recipient a single clue as to whether she was on the right track in puzzling it out.

Kafka wrote "There are misunderstandings between us"—but what were they? "The distribution of weight has been modified a bit"—what weight, and modified how? "I believe I know more about both of us"—what did he know? "[A]nd have a tentative goal"—what was it? All "inhibiting reflections and worries" are "unbearable" and even "detestable"—what reflections, what worries? "[I]t is a burden I am forced to bear"—what burden? "I shiver with dissatisfaction"—dissatisfaction with what? "[A]nd even if my failures should stare me in the face . . . I most likely couldn't hold back"—from doing what? If Kafka had numbered his complaints of the previous years and simply recorded the numbers here, the letter would be less dry and more comprehensible.

Kafka appears not to have noticed the latent comic aspect of this "discourse," but he was aware that his own increasing gravitation to anemic, overcautious formulations was casting an eerie light on the correspondence. He knew that he was opening himself up to additional reproaches, but as usual he was mounting a preemptive defense because he knew what he was doing, although his reflexive alertness, his overwhelming, neverending, glaring consciousness of self, did not enable him to steer the urges to flee that it registered so meticulously, so his defense of vagueness had to remain just as vague as everything else:

> Look here, Felice, the only thing that has happened is that my letters have become less frequent and different. What was the result of those more frequent and different letters? You know. We must start afresh. That "we," however, does not mean you, for you were and are in the right where you alone were concerned; that "we" refers rather to me and to our relationship. But for such a fresh start, letters are no good; and if they are necessary—and they are—then they must be different from the way they were before.

Different, of course. But he does not say what that difference would be, and the formulaic abbreviations he chooses are hardly conducive to presenting Felice with a convincing, let alone enticing model of a future love correspondence. Although she certainly enjoyed and admired Kafka's rhetorical skills, she had always sensed that they were ultimately a highly sophisticated means for him to maintain his silence, and although he kept vehemently contesting and denying the existence of unspoken obstacles, he provided new cause for suspicion in the same breath with his evasions, invented images, and quotations instead of direct speech. It was as though his letters were circling around a dark center that concealed something inexpressible.

It is quite likely that Felice Bauer, who had herself failed to reveal quite a bit about her family, pictured these unspoken obstacles in terms that were too concrete and external: parental objections, financial woes, a love affair in Prague, an ailment he did not want to mention, or something of that sort. There were certainly hints to this effect, and Kafka had once even made such a pressing issue out of his fear of impotence—he stopped just short of putting a name to it—that she must have thought that this one issue might be the key to soothing his tormented conscience, and things would fall into place on their own once they were living together. She was wrong.

But she was absolutely right to suspect that despite any protestations on his part, he was withholding something crucial. Kafka *had* changed. And we know the exact date this change occurred: July 12, 1914, the day the engagement was dissolved at the Hotel Askanischer Hof in Berlin, in the presence of Felice's sister Erna and her close friend Grete Bloch—a date that Kafka henceforth considered a catastrophe. He had been caught unawares at his most sensitive spots, assailed in the core of his psyche, in front of witnesses, no less. He had probably not experienced an exposure of this magnitude since childhood, and he was horrified by the fact that all his defensive instincts had let him down. Like being slapped in the face in public, this scene stung him, and he must have played it out in his mind's eye countless times. Back then in the hotel, he had not known how to reply, and he ultimately fell silent—which was certainly awkward but may have spared him further humiliation, as he now saw it. Far worse was that he could not get over this experience, neither by reflection nor by self-recriminations, which now set in almost as a matter of routine. No, he could not forgive her. For the first time, Kafka must have felt hatred for Felice Bauer, without being able to put it into words. He could not tell her this; not *this*.

However, he could not prevent this hatred from seeping out and settling in the pores of his texts. Felice Bauer did not yet know *The Trial*, and he had good reason to keep this manuscript away from her. She would have been horrified to see the cold portrayals of herself and of Grete Bloch. All she got from him was a series of self-justifications.

He had heard things in the Askanischer Hof, he wrote to her, "that ought to have been almost impossible for one person to say to another," "childishly nasty words," and nearly two years later, in the spring of 1916, Kafka could not help reminding Felice one last time of that disastrous tribunal and relegating it once and for all to the realm of evil: "Basically, the same primitive accusations are always being leveled against me. The highest representative of this form of accusation, which comes right from my father, is of course my father."[5]

She was well aware that Kafka was bristling, but she could not coax a satisfactory explanation out of him. His stated mistrust of letters—which was paradoxical because who has ever relied more heavily on letters?—was an outgrowth of his profound and fundamental skepticism about the efficacy of language, and this skepticism had been confirmed and intensified by the incident in the Askanischer Hof. Kafka simply no longer believed that something essential or true could be conveyed or clarified by means of explanatory statements if it was not seen, felt, or recognized. This applied to his literary texts—which he consistently refused to elucidate—but even more so to human relationships, which, according to his now-unshakable conviction, lived not from words but from gestures. Maybe it would have been best if Kafka had not bothered to send his ex-fiancée that faded letter wallowing in sober laments and decided instead to tear a page out of his diary and send it to Berlin. He had probably penned these remarks *the same day*, and they revealed the core of his unhappiness in surprisingly simple language, devoid of any metaphorical extravagance:

> Reflection on other people's relationship to me. Insignificant as I may be, there is no one here who understands me in my entirety. To have someone with such understanding, a wife perhaps, would mean to have support from every side, to have God.
>
> Ottla understands some things, even a great many; Max [Brod], Felix [Weltsch], some things; others, such as E. [?], understand only individual details, but with appalling intensity; F. [Felice Bauer] may understand nothing at all, which, because of our undeniable inner relationship, places her in a very special position. Sometimes I thought she understood me without realizing it; for instance, the time she waited for me at the subway station; I had been longing

> for her unbearably, and in my passion to reach her as quickly as possible almost ran past her, thinking she would be upstairs, and she took me quietly by the hand.[6]

She may not have understood a word. It was so hard for Kafka to commit this thought to paper that at first he left out the all-important "nothing" and had to insert it later, as though hesitating to sign a devastating indictment. If he were not altogether mistaken, more than 350 letters had been written to no avail, and the woman who once was to enter the innermost sphere of human intimacy with him was in reality no closer than his own family, whose closeness was gradually coming apart while he was still lingering as a rigid observer. That his parents understood nothing—nothing whatsoever—he had confirmed at least to his mother in so many words; it was so obvious and irrefutable that he *had* to express his mortification. The very idea of continuing to hope for understanding from them struck him as so misguided that he did not even include his parents on his social balance sheet. Yet he had an "undeniable inner relationship" even with them, despite their dismaying lack of understanding. Kafka could not help wondering whether Felice Bauer had a "special position" in his life after all.

It is one of the odd, unfortunate coincidences that characterized Kafka's life as a whole that the two catastrophes that thwarted any remaining hope of a new beginning, both mentally and materially, befell him at virtually the same time: the "public" tribunal in the Askanischer Hof, and—a mere three weeks later—the beginning of World War I. "Germany declared war on Russia—Swimming in the afternoon," Kafka noted. The unintentional humor of this diary entry—which has resulted in an overabundance of quoting—does seem to indicate that Kafka was still far too preoccupied with the debacle in Berlin to take note of the more extensive catastrophe. It has led many readers to conclude that Kafka's constitution was far more powerful than anything that came at him from without, that his development adhered exclusively to a psychological rhythm deep within him, and that consequently neither his life nor his work would have taken an essentially different course if he had been spared the suffering of that war.

This extremely enticing and clearly comforting image of the soul of the genius as a rock amidst a chaotic and brutal world is, unfortunately, a mere fantasy, which Kafka interpreters are all too happy to share with Kafka readers. The humanities, which tend to disdain biographical readings, became the arbiters of Kafka's work and thus the stewards of his fame. Even the most astute methodological humanities scholar is secretly pleased to establish that the life and work of a classic European author form an "intellectual unity" subject to autonomous laws—and "intellectual autonomy" is the loftiest title of nobility that can be bestowed here. If this author himself indicates that the world of "hard" facts does not interest him or at least fails to sway him, the temptation becomes overwhelming to accept this as true and to identify social, political, and economic circumstances as no more than background material, as props on the stage of a singular consciousness, particularly when these props go up in flames while the author, seemingly unaffected, remains rooted to his manuscript pages.

Actual life adheres to a different logic. It forces decisions that can run counter not only to emotional needs but to an individual's entire mental makeup, and Kafka's situation in July 1914 offers what may well be one of the most stunning examples of this type of decision making in literary history. He had expended all his willpower on not succumbing to depression, and he was even able to derive productive and "autonomous" benefits from the separation from Felice Bauer. Now he was determined—and never in his life had he been *so* determined—not to repair the partly collapsed structure but instead to tear it down and rebuild it from the ground up: give notice at the Workers' Accident Insurance Institute, leave his parents' apartment, move to Berlin, write full-time. Every literary fortune and erotic misfortune that had befallen him virtually required this decision. The plan was finally crafted, committed to writing, and divulged to his parents in the form of a long letter. Then came the world war.

We have to keep in mind, and Kafka needed only a few days to realize this himself, that the termination of his engagement and the onset of war—private and public misfortune—not only coincided chronologically but dug into the same wound. Both were catastrophes that severed precious human ties and left him solitary in a moment of hope; these were catastrophes of loneliness. Kafka soon transformed his desperate longing for intimacy and the touch of a beloved and understanding person into the image of an isolated accused man who—tormented by his trial, in irrepressible lust, "like a thirsty animal"—kisses the face of a woman who is indifferent to him. This longing now existed in an empty echo chamber. "Complete solitude," he noted. "No longed-for wife to open the door." And he added a "terrible saying," one that Felice Bauer may have thrown in his face at the Askanischer Hof: "Now you've got what you wanted."[7]

That was unfair, and Kafka was quite certain that he had *never* wanted emptiness like this. But he dared not hope for a revision of that judgment, and the path to the court of appeal was blocked for the foreseeable future. The Great War signaled the triumph of an anonymous power of disposition that Kafka had known only as a threat and that affected him within a matter of hours, as it did everyone else. He had *felt* caged up in Prague for years, and now he actually *was*. He despaired of ever being able to communicate in letters things that truly mattered—the essentials, himself—and that was now completely impossible because all letters abroad, even to the German Reich, were opened and read by censors. When the weekend approached, he had often toyed with the idea of jumping on a train to Berlin spontaneously and without advance notice, but put off the trip while pondering the what-ifs; now travel plans were canceled and the borders closed for men who were deemed "fit for military service." And there was the telephone: Kafka had hated this jangling presence, which counted out conversations by the minute; never was there time to take back an awkward statement or to clear up a misunderstanding. The telephone had required painstaking caution—but now that it was his last remaining way of achieving sensory closeness, the Austro-Hungarian war ministry decided that letting its own subjects make phone calls across national borders was too risky, and this connection was severed as well.

The war separated face from face, voice from voice, skin from skin. Although that was problematic, this was an era in which mobility was far from a basic right, and people were used to waiting stoically and coping with long separations. But beyond this sphere of physical closeness, the war severed the fabric of *all* social connections and in a matter of days destroyed what Kafka had initiated over the course of months and years, groping his way beyond the borders of his stamping ground in Prague. His publisher, Kurt Wolff, went to serve at the Belgian front as an officer. He could no longer look after his authors, and handed over the business (for what he thought would be a brief period) to an obliging and energetic publisher who was not especially sensitive to literary matters—a nonreader. And Robert Musil, who had indicated a willingness to pave Kafka's way to Berlin, now had to pack his own suitcases; three weeks after the war began he was assigned to Linz, Austria, as a lieutenant, and his contact with Kafka broke off. Ernst Weiss—the only friend of Kafka's outside the incestuous group in Prague on whom Kafka could lean in literary matters—was in the same spot as Musil; he too had to leave Berlin and head to Linz. Weiss was a doctor and thus indispensable for keeping the war machinery going.

Smarting over these dashed hopes, Kafka shied away from his friends in Prague. He had caught sight of the longed-for fulfillment of his desires from afar; now that he could not have it, he no longer enjoyed his daily routines. He felt defiant and totally out of place in a situation that made nearly everyone resort to crude self-interest. It was both understandable and inevitable that in the tumult of a world war, no one had the patience to listen to the grievances of a rejected suitor or nonwriting writer.

Max Brod and Felix Weltsch were deemed unfit for military service, so they could count on being spared the worst. The same was true of the blind writer Oskar Baum, whose contact with the war had been limited to a patriotic soundscape and looming financial hardships. But everyone had family or friends who had to "enlist," and the sudden, overwhelming proximity of a mortal danger narrowed the range of what people thought and felt. Even Kafka's own mother wrote, "Naturally, the situation with Franz has taken a back seat."[8] Just a few days earlier she had been tearing her hair out about the canceled marriage and her unhappy son's plans to leave Prague—and now all of a sudden she had to comfort her daughters Elli and Valli, whose husbands were risking their necks somewhere in the east.

Kafka suddenly had to hold back even with Ottla, his youngest sister and confidante. A rival had come upon the scene. Ottla had had a boyfriend for quite some time now, and although Kafka's notes do not mention the disclosure of this secret, it is not difficult to imagine its highly ambivalent significance for him. Ottla was the first and only one of the sisters who—without the knowledge of her parents, of course—had taken up an erotic relationship of her own accord, with a man who was neither German nor Jewish nor, for that matter, well-to-do. He was a Czech *goy*, a bank employee whose only asset was his professional ambition. Undoubtedly this triple proof of Ottla's resolute independence stirred Kafka's pride. He himself had not missed an opportunity to foster her will to independence, which started as rebellion and grew increasingly purposeful, and now she was the one furnishing the proof that a free decision, maybe even a true escape, an escape from the "the herd at home," was possible.[9] Kafka's respect and awe in light of this accomplishment surely contributed to his desire to seek a friendly understanding right away with Ottla's future husband.

But jealousy must have been an issue as well. The poignant daydreams of Gregor Samsa, the hapless hero of "The Metamorphosis," give us some indication of the difficulty involved in loosening his exclusive bond with Ottla to embrace a socially open relationship more in line with his sister's needs. The more that Gregor, who has been degraded to a base animal, is pushed out of his social sphere and thrown back on his creaturely existence, the better his sister looks to him. What Gregor longs for from her is not really understanding, any more than a drowning man seeks understanding, or yearns for God. Gregor wants his life saved by symbiosis. But his sister refuses to go along with him and crosses over to the enemy—a threat that always loomed in Kafka's mind and was his express incentive for writing "The Metamorphosis."[10] This threat intensified as Ottla's sphere of action widened and she devoted herself to social issues outside the family:

> [H]er thoughts are not on the shop, but solely on the institute for the blind, where for the last few weeks, and especially in the past two weeks, she has had a few good friends and a very best friend. He is a young basket maker; one of his eyes is closed, and the other is hugely swollen. That is her best friend; he is gentle, understanding, and devoted. She visits him on Sundays and holidays and reads to him, preferably funny things. I must say that this is a somewhat perilous and poignant pleasure. The blind use their fingers to ex-

> press what others communicate with their eyes. The blind touch her dress, take hold of her sleeve, stroke her hands, and this big strong girl, who unfortunately has been led a bit astray by me, though it was not my fault, calls this her greatest delight. As she says, she only knows that she wakes up happy when she remembers the blind.[11]

That was in the summer of 1914. The tone is that of a concerned brother who is not entirely comfortable with bucking conventions; he is clearly mortified. Now, however, after the unexpected appearance of a serious suitor, Kafka suddenly understood that he was no longer the one who defined this girl's "proper path." She had made a decision without asking him for advice. She had done the right thing. She was an adult, of course, and it was just a matter of time until her parents showed up with the old familiar marriage broker. And yet, when Kafka rented his own room in the spring of 1915, why did it take *weeks* for his sister to finally visit him there, even though it was just a few minutes away from their parents' shop? He found that hard to swallow, and he informed her curtly, "The only thing you can say in response is that I pay little attention to your things (but there is a particular reason for that) and that you are in the shop all day long. I admit that that makes us somewhat even."[12] His legalistic tone showed how hurt he was. Kafka was now grouping his beloved sister with all the others who had left him and were preoccupied with their own problems. But it was not hard to figure out that the "particular reason" was a Czech man named Josef David, who went by "Pepa." His name could not, of course, be mentioned in a family in which everyone read everything.

It took months for Kafka to fully grasp that it was in fact not symbiosis or exclusivity that would rescue him but understanding, "understanding for me as a whole." And he placed his greatest hopes in Ottla because he began to see that she could give back in human devotion what she had to withdraw from him in whispered, regressive intimacy. Besides, the experiences that she now had beyond the old familiar family bonds were the only substratum that maintained those bonds. Would Kafka have been able to somehow make his unsuspecting sister understand the erotic unhappiness he had experienced in Weimar, in Riva, and eventually in Berlin? We do not know whether he tried to, but it seems out of the question that he could have gotten more than sympathy. Now, however, in the spring of 1915, the young Ottla also had some insight into longing and the pain of separation. The man she loved was in uniform and had boarded one of those unscheduled trains with an unknown destination, crowded into a railroad car with laughing, chattering soldiers telling dirty jokes and smoking despondently, knowing full well how the soldiers looked when they *returned* in the same railroad cars. Ottla had seen all this, and she too returned transformed.

It is difficult to determine the extent to which Ottla was able to fill the new and challenging role her brother ascribed to her. The documentation is scanty. We know about some excursions they made to the country, the books they read together, and their growing interest in Zionism and the fate of the eastern European Jewish refugees who were stranded in Prague. All these shared times and interests shed light on the new degree of closeness they had achieved. It is striking that Ottla's letters to Josef David lack any ironic language or resentment of her difficult brother. That "evil," ethnologically distanced eye that Kafka tended to cast on his own family was not in Ottla's nature, and the reservoir of patience that she revealed as an adult woman seemed boundless. It is highly doubtful—although this cannot be verified, of course—that Kafka would have survived the isolation of the first years of the war emotionally or physically without this last foothold. But Ottla could not offer him more than a foothold, and she could not anticipate, understand, or avert the fateful psychological dynamic that Kafka now set in motion to spare himself further wounds. No one could.

> I seek out a good hiding place and train my eye on the entrance to my house—this time from the outside—for days and nights on end. Even if it might be called foolish, it gives me untold pleasure, and what is more, it soothes me. At these times I feel as though I am standing not in front of my house but in front of myself while I am sleeping, and had the good fortune to sleep deeply and at the same time to be able to keep a close watch over myself. I am privileged, in a way, to see the ghosts of the night not only in the helplessness and blind trust of sleep but also to encounter them in

> reality with the full power of calm judgment that comes with wakefulness. And I find, strangely enough, that I am not in as bad a shape as I have often thought and as I will probably think again when I go back down into my house.

One of those linguistically straightforward yet deeply cryptic passages from Kafka's story "The Burrow," compelling in its unparalleled blend of image and logic. Attentive readers typically feel bound to expand on the paradoxical implications of this scenario. A badger-like animal goes to extreme lengths to build himself a subterranean labyrinthine fortress, but instead of staying there quietly and enjoying the security he worked so hard to attain, this unfortunate creature goes out to guard the entrance *from the outside*. There is a touch of insanity here. It is like constructing a magnificent mansion, then camping next to it.

Still, isn't an idea that makes perfectly good sense and is even somewhat touching just being brought to its logical extreme? The functionality of a villa can be experienced only from the inside, but the material unity of form and function—in other words, its beauty—is left to someone observing it from the outside. The animal in its cave experiences "security." But the delight in one's own achievement of having wrested from life a maximum of security, that "untold pleasure," requires the broader view that comes with distance. It is the pleasure in reflection, in stocktaking, in fathoming what one has accomplished, a pleasure that is human to the extent that instant gratification, even the realization of one's wildest dreams, always comes up short.

> It got to the point that at times I was seized by the childish desire never to go back to the burrow at all but rather to settle in here near the entrance and spend my life watching the entrance and find my happiness in realizing all the time how the burrow would keep me secure if I were inside it.[13]

This repeated use of the conditional brings the narrator and readers back to their senses. The price is too high after all, and it would be literal insanity to jeopardize one's own survival for nothing but the luxury of being able to observe this very survival as a performance, as well. And so the animal finally returns to the burrow and thenceforth can enjoy its functional beauty *imaginatively*—such as by telling himself stories about it.

Kafka wrote this text in late 1923, when he could look back on nearly a decade of his own intense burrowing. It is the diligent and neverending work on oneself required of anyone who regards security as the highest priority; it is, in other words, the joy and sorrow of the defensive, which Kafka depicts with a perceptiveness and vivid precision that would be just as compelling if we knew *nothing* about the autobiographical crux of the story. But this crux can be pinpointed in time.

The foundation had been laid ages ago, but Kafka began constructing the walls on October 15, 1914. On that day he received a letter from Grete Bloch, who evidently felt compelled to explain once again why she had to meddle in the hot-and-cold relationship between Kafka and Felice Bauer. Her interference had resulted in a confrontation and temporary separation that gradually threatened to become permanent. Felice was unhappy about it, but her pride was too wounded to reach out to him. That Kafka was also unhappy was easy to guess, and easy to verify indirectly by asking the garrulous Max Brod and his wife, Elsa. This twofold unhappiness was more than Grete Bloch was prepared to shoulder the responsibility for, so she decided to blunt the force of her earlier meddling by meddling yet again. "You must hate me," she wrote to Kafka, to give him a little signal that he ought to set her mind at ease. Although she knew a thing or two about him, she could not divine the rebuff that would come her way a few days later.

> It is a strange coincidence, Fräulein Grete, that I received your letter just today. I won't say with what it coincided; that concerns only me and the thoughts that were in my head tonight when I went to bed at about three o'clock.
>
> Your letter truly surprises me. It doesn't surprise me that you write to me. Why shouldn't you write to me? You say that I hate you, but that isn't true. Even if everyone were to hate you, I don't hate you, and not merely because I don't have the right to. You did sit in judgment over me at the Askanischer Hof—it was awful for you,

for me, for everyone—but it only looked that way; in reality I was sitting in your place and have not left it to this day.

You are completely mistaken about F. I am not saying that to draw details out of you. I can think of no detail—and my imagination has so often chased back and forth across this ground that I can trust it—I say I can think of no detail that could convince me that you are not mistaken. What you imply is absolutely impossible; it makes me unhappy to think that for some inexplicable reason F. might be deceiving herself. But that too is impossible.

I have always regarded your interest as genuine and unsparing of yourself. And it was not easy for you to write this last letter.

Thank you kindly for it.

Franz K[14]

This letter is a series of defensive gestures. My thoughts with which your letter has coincided are none of your business. Go ahead and write to me—no one can stop you. The details of Felice's life with which you try to draw me in don't interest me. You are mistaken about my hatred, but maybe you are hated in Berlin? You are mistaken about Felice, as well. And you overestimate your capabilities if you think you can pass judgment on me. I know that it was hard for you to bring yourself to write to me, but that is of no help to you.

The acknowledgment of genuine interest was the only part likely to flatter the recipient; Grete Bloch promptly marked this sentence—and *only* this one—in red.

This astonishing belligerence, barely tempered by conventional politeness, was something new and without parallel in the whole of Kafka's correspondence. He made little or no effort to rein in his aggression; indeed, he stepped it up with an undertone of condescension, even of arrogance. Kafka was capitalizing on his superiority, and he knew it; it was the moral superiority of someone who no longer needs judgments from others because he has become his own most merciless judge.[15] But the central message was "Stay away from me."

Kafka had his reasons for refusing to tolerate these kinds of interruptions. Every night for the past two months, he had been experiencing a spurt of swift and excessive yet exceedingly controlled writing. He spent even the precious vacation days he was still entitled to for 1914 at his desk, and even if there was no more hope that the eerie state of emergency in which Prague, Austria, and the whole planet now found itself would end any time soon, he still wanted to be prepared to emerge with a major text and thus try once again to escape the drudgery of life as a civil servant. And this major text, *The Trial*, was rapidly taking shape.

Just a few hours before Grete Bloch's letter arrived, Kafka had once again pondered the resort of suicide, and he had experimented with drawing up a list of final instructions he would send to Max Brod if he went through with it—this was the "strange coincidence" that he was not able to divulge to the woman from Berlin. But this time it was not despair that drove him to ideas of this kind. "Two weeks of mainly good work," he noted in his diary, "full grasp of my situation." High self-praise, by his standards, but above all a sign of how bound up Kafka's successful writing was with sweeping and realistic self-knowledge. Although this realization was bitter, even devastating—"I know I am intended to remain alone," he continued—breaking through to this level of clarity brought him a moment of happiness that he was utterly incapable of distinguishing from the pleasure in linguistic triumph. He certainly would not have wanted to die, especially not on this day when he so clearly envisaged the remaining options for his life.

But this clearsightedness made him acutely aware of his own neediness, of that longing to put an end to the continuous tension and let go, if not toward death, then into the arms of a person: "[I]n spite of everything," Kafka noted after replying to Grete Bloch's letter, "in spite of everything, the unending temptation is setting in again. I played with the letter throughout the evening, and my work has stalled." After writing this harsh response in his diary from memory, almost verbatim, he added this cryptic postscript:

> What has this accomplished? The letter appears unyielding, but only because I was ashamed, because I considered it irresponsible, because I was afraid to be compliant, and not because I didn't want to comply. That was actually exactly what I wanted. It would be best

> for all of us if she didn't reply, but she will reply and I will wait for her reply.[16]

Vacillation, ambiguity, dogged maneuvering, and a litany of complaints where decisions were needed. Those were the charges that had cost him the engagement, and he could not dismiss these "primitive accusations" out of hand, because they were intended as a flexible system of defense with which he had hoped to avoid hurtful confrontations without having to shut down altogether. It had not worked, and Kafka was now determined not to give cause for accusations of this sort any more.

Kafka's letter to Grete Bloch is his earliest extant document that is a masquerade from beginning to end, an invented role play that facilitates free aggression, even a kind of triumph, yet stands in complete contrast to the significance of the moment. If Kafka's own emphatic concept of truth is applied, this letter is a lie, and signals a radical shift of strategy. Thus far, Kafka had only been playing with the conventional polite gestures of dissociation and had only hinted at preparing to do battle—not as a threat, but as a plea not to force him to take emergency measures. Now, however, he was getting serious. He was no longer defending his own fluid self, but a position, a place, a *burrow*. Kafka began to dig in. And he was aware of the significance of this beginning, because he copied the letter like a hefty corporate charter and kept it in his own files.

Felice Bauer noticed the change, although Kafka denied it for the time being and conceded only that from now on, his letters would "different from before." Different in what way? Could something of that sort be specified, planned, foreseen? Certainly not. But Kafka now knew what he *no longer* wanted, and he let go of the dream of symbiosis, of a free, unreserved, downright irresponsible opening of his body and soul, a universal toleration and all-encompassing forgiveness. Kafka recalled the almost childlike, plaintive cries he had once sent Felice when she had forgotten about him for a few days during her business trip. That would not happen again.

> Do you recall the letters I wrote you when you were in Frankfurt about two years ago, perhaps in this very month? Believe me, I'm

> basically close to the point of writing them again right now. They are lurking at the tip of my pen. But they will not be written.[17]

And he held to that. There would be no more undignified laments, and those ironic, charming, and sometimes witty self-accusations with which he once had courted her and she had come to associate with him came to a halt as well. Kafka gritted his teeth, exercised self-control, made sure to cover his sensitive spots, and even resorted to officialese when he was hurt: "Your last letter said that a picture was enclosed. It was not enclosed. This represents a hardship for me."[18]

Kafka probably realized only in retrospect that his new self-prescribed strategy was not gratis and did not always provide the relief he sought. Living in the trenches made the world seem like a system of trenches that he could observe in excruciating detail but no longer truly experience. And camouflage is strenuous work. Kafka had inflicted censorship on himself—grotesquely at the same time that state censorship also compelled him to exercise caution—and forced himself to perform an act of dissimulation and maintain a deliberate silence, and this wedge between desire and language, this constant vigilance about striking a safe tone, drained his psychic energy. It is impossible to determine what demanded the greatest sacrifice: worries about the war, the escalating pressure at the office, or the manic work on a psychological bulwark and the resultant isolation. The psychosomatic price was extremely high. Insomnia, heightened sensitivity to noise, and headaches became chronic; Kafka endured bouts of pain and migraines that went on for days and ate him up inside. Even the earplugs he ordered from Berlin did not help in the slightest. He had recurrent chest pains. Kafka's notes indicate that the phases of depressive emptiness he had previously experienced only as threatening episodes now recurred regularly and with an intensity that was hard to bear. "Incapable in every regard—completely"; "feeling of unhappiness that almost tears me apart"; "hollow as a shell on the beach"; "incapable of living with people, of speaking"; "complete indifference and apathy"; "bleakness, boredom, no, not boredom, just bleakness, senselessness, weakness." During a Sunday excursion with Ottla and the Weltsches, he even felt "as though on a rack"—feigning interest and making small talk were still unfamiliar customs.[19]

But where was the benefit? Wasn't the pain of the humiliation Kafka had suffered in the Askanischer Hof easier to bear than this apathy, this endless chafing at his own armor? That remained to be seen. At least on the outside, Kafka seemed more poised, and the distance boosted his resolve. He suggested to Felice Bauer that they meet again in Bodenbach; she could bring whomever she liked, but he would prefer that she come alone. And he even reminded her of an especially sensitive date, the celebration of their engagement a year earlier, while skirting the words "I" or "you"—as though he were talking about mutual friends of theirs and as though his own sensitivity was anesthetized on this very point: "Do tell me where he intended to carry her off to; it is inconceivable. He simply loved her and was insatiable. Today he loves her no less, though he may finally have come to learn that he cannot win her over so simply and easily, even if she consents."[20]

We do not know whether she commented on it; evidently Kafka could no longer faze her with his rhetoric. But after Bodenbach she did not want to travel alone; this time she would bring two girlfriends along, she answered after some hesitation, and one of them would be Grete Bloch. Kafka's heart was probably pounding when he read this message. A few months earlier he would have come right back with some suitable way of avoiding the meeting. But now . . . no objection, no show of emotion, either in his notes or in his extant letters. Kafka really was up to the challenge of traveling to Bohemian Switzerland at Whitsun in 1915, spending two and a half days in the company of the women who would function as his "judges," and visiting sights recommended in the Baedeker travel guide. He could be relatively certain that the past would not be dredged up—especially not the tribunal in Berlin, which now lay ten months in the past—the presence of Felice's other girlfriend, a Fräulein Steinitz, precluded intimacy and (Felice had tactics up her sleeve as well) was likely invited for *precisely that reason*. Instead there was a superficial reconciliation with Grete Bloch. And in the evening, back in the hotel, the world had moved on a bit anyway; the past was even a little further in the past: Italy had just declared war on Austria-Hungary. Perhaps it was all over anyway; what point was there in holding a grudge?

The price Kafka paid for retaining his composure remained his secret for the time being, and the fact that one was tense, exhausted, overworked, and irritable required no special explanation in a time of war. But Kafka had learned to use the back exit; he was *not present*. Having overstepped the mark between self-observation and dissociation, he stood beside himself, a position that made him distraught and down-to-earth at the same time. "If I were another person observing myself and the course of my life," he had noted in February, "I would have to say that everything must end in futility, consumed in never-ending doubt, creative only in self-torment. But as someone who is involved, I go on hoping."[21] Someone who is involved in his own life? The very notion sealed the split. But Kafka went a crucial step further: He left the burrow, hid nearby, kept watch on the entrance, embraced the entire entrenchment including the naked creature hiding inside, and enjoyed the view from an untouchable distance.

This radicalized form of self-observation—stepping outside himself—now sought expression, and Kafka quickly found a suitable linguistic form. He began to experiment with third-person discourse when describing himself. This discourse soon joined the arsenal of his literary stylistic devices. No sooner was Felice Bauer back from her trip than she received the first samples.

> Dear Felice, you recently asked me several fanciful questions about F.'s fiancé. I am now better able to answer them, for I observed him on the way home in the train. It was easy to do, because there was so much crowding that the two of us were sitting literally on one seat. Well, in my opinion, he is totally wrapped up in her. You should have seen how he spent the long journey seeking memories of F. and of her room among the lilacs (he never takes anything of the kind with him on his travels at any other time).... I believe the person in question has greater faith in me than in F.

> Dear Felice, listen, he says he is frightened. He says that he stayed there too long. That two days were too much. After one day it is easy to disengage oneself, but a stay of two days creates ties that are painful to detach. Sleeping under the same roof, eating at the same

table, experiencing the same daily routine twice over—this might almost be said to constitute a ceremony following a dictate.

Literally on one seat. The fiancé in question and I. It almost sounded like an echo from days gone by, when Kafka parodied his own sufferings and used them as a means of flirtation. But a few hours after he sent these postcards, he crept back into the secure burrow and wrote in his diary: "A great deal of unhappiness since the last entry. Going to pieces. To go to pieces so senselessly and unnecessarily."[22] He could not think of anything else to write, and closed the notebook. Two or three pages were still blank. They still are.

Had Felice Bauer gotten distracted or been misled? For a moment, perhaps. In July, she agreed to spend two days with Kafka, in Karlsbad, this time without chaperones. His ploy had worked.

But it did not turn out well. On Kafka's thirty-second birthday, she sang songs to him as he trudged along beside her, worn down by insomnia. The novels she brought him as presents—*The Brothers Karamazov*, Strindberg's *Inferno*—did not help either, nor did the promise she had jotted down on the end paper of Dostoevsky's novel: "Perhaps we'll read it together very soon." Finally, on the trip home, when they traveled in the same train until Aussig, she could no longer contain herself, and it became a "truly vile journey."[23]

But this time he brought a memory back to Prague that would offer some small solace. Felice Bauer had brought her camera along to Karlsbad, as she always did when traveling, and Kafka was allowed to snap a few shots. They took pictures of the sights and of each other. Since Kafka was so eager for photographs and never seemed to be satisfied with the samples she gave him, she had the good sense to suggest that he develop the film in Prague and choose the shots he wanted copies of. But when Kafka went to get the negatives a few days later, he was in for a surprise. Felice, a technical expert and amateur photographer, had inserted all the rolls of film backwards, the light-sensitive side to the back, the protective paper to the front. All the pictures were blank. The his-and-her Karlsbad smiles were lost to eternity.

CHAPTER TWO

No Literary Prize for Kafka

Any sacrifice should be made for art—apart from the sacrifice of art itself.

—Karl Kraus to Herwarth Walden

Reddish brown oilcloth notebook with light blue flyleaves, containing twenty sheets (not attached to the spine except for the last one), yellowish-white unlined paper with rounded edges; length 24.85 cm, width 19.8–20.0 cm; in two quires of 2 and 18 (both originally 20) sheets originally with sewn bindings (2 tacks); red pattern; watermark type 2 a and 3 a; sheets 19^v und 20^r blank. Sheets no longer sewn together.[1]

IT IS DOUBTFUL WHETHER KAFKA WOULD HAVE INSTANTLY RECOGnized the object being described here in minute detail. He knew manuscripts of other writers either as auratic relics behind glass—such as the immaculate copy of Goethe's "Mignon's Song," which he had marveled at in Weimar because he thought it was the original—or as handwritten pages and notebooks marked up with diagonal lines and corrections in the margins, the kind that lay around on the desks of Max Brod and Ernst Weiss (not to mention the scraps of paper in the pockets of Franz Werfel's trousers and vests). The former descended straight from Olympus, the latter was day-to-day business.

No author at the beginning of the twentieth century—least of all Kafka himself—could have imagined that his written legacy would soon be measured, photographed, and described as though it were a set of papyrus rolls from an Egyptian burial chamber, and abstract interest in the medium and the materiality of the sign was alien to that generation. Unlike beautifully printed book pages, notepads and notebooks were considered expendable items, and in keeping with the times, Kafka tore out pages to keep personal notes separate from literary ones, filled his notebooks from front to back and back to front at the same time, switched back and forth between pen and pencil, interspersed shorthand with longhand, and added pensive scribbles between the lines. Nowadays, laser printers make even rough drafts of literary texts look like polished works, but back then, drafts bore the marks of the creative process. Brod has no qualms about entering his own wording in red on his friend's posthumous pages, although he considered Kafka a literary genius and a leading figure of a new religiosity. Brod entrusted some of these irreplaceable pages to the postal service, and even made gifts of manuscript pages.[2] Of course, Brod knew that the "historical-critical edition," which archives and annotates every accessible syllable, is the crowning glory of the classic author, and he was absolutely certain—although the thought made him uneasy—that scholarly editing would pin down Kafka's work in an unalterable form. But it never would have crossed Brod's mind to focus on the *paper* Kafka used. What for? The ultimate version was what mattered. Brod went to great lengths to tidy up the scene of the crime before the philological investigators showed up.

Half a century later, Kafka's notebook pages were held up to the light, and the paper manufacturer's watermarks were revealed, along with four-leaf clovers arranged in specific patterns that varied slightly according to whether the page was "left" or "right," thus yielding crucial evidence that enabled scholars to reinsert pages where Kafka had haphazardly removed them, and thus to date texts. Was any more proof needed that literally *everything* was significant? Every single detail was noted: width, height, color, cut, rounded edges—an exhaustive description for all eternity. Meanwhile, the original, which is now known to scholars as "K Bod AI, 10" ("Bod" stands for the Bodleian Library in Oxford; "10" indicates that this is Kafka's tenth diary volume), is slowly but surely falling apart.

It seems highly unlikely that he was consciously aware of the watermarks his steel nib was gliding across, and he never would have dreamed that one day someone would actually *count* the words on each manuscript page, one by one. He would have been amused, and Brod would have been dumbfounded. The literary scholar Malcolm Pasley furnished proof that this odd process can be used to date individual passages in *The Trial*—a precious expansion of our knowledge of a novel that has been canonized throughout the world—although its author did not even clearly specify the order of the chapters.[3] Of course, there is no denying the comic aspect of crawling inside the author's material legacy, but in the end, we revel in the pleasure of the intriguing solution, the triumphant complex maneuver that triggers a shock of joy and recognition. At any rate, we cannot return to a pre-scholarly view, and we would only be fooling ourselves if we now sought the oft-cited "untainted" view of Kafka.

The result was an unmitigated disaster. *The Trial* and *The Man Who Disappeared*: incomplete and probably incompletable. "Memories of the Kalda Railway," "The Village Schoolmaster," "The Assistant Prosecutor," the Blumfeld story, and another two or three short pieces: nothing finished, all fallen apart, bits and pieces, fragments, and ruins every which way. Only the extremely bloody "In the Penal Colony" could be salvaged and perhaps published after some patching up. Such was the output of months of dogged effort, the unripe fruits for which Kafka had sacrificed his sleep, vacation time, any opportunity for rest and relaxation he had wrested from the headaches, the noise in the rented rooms, the mounting pressure at the office as a result of the war. Since Kafka was averse to saying anything about his works in progress, no one around him is likely to have had a clue about these struggles, and it was only when philologists trained their attention on preserving every little pencil mark that some indication of the extent of this existential debacle began to emerge.

Now that creative writing has to compete with harder-hitting and more rapid media, it is not writing itself but the compulsion to write that is considered an obsolete passion. Kafka's fame makes it difficult for us to empathize with his despair in writing. We know that in the end he did *not* fail, and we wonder what else he could have hoped for.

That "in the end," however, arises from a retrospective overview of his life as it unfolded against the backdrop of the era. For Kafka himself, who may have hoped or expected to have several decades ahead of him, this achievement could not have been a consolation, even if he had understood and accepted his own literary standing.

To gain a better sense of how his everyday life meshed with his posthumous significance, we need to fathom how close Kafka actually came to his self-imposed goal and what consequences literary success would have had. *The Trial* is relatively easy to assess in this regard because it is obvious that Kafka conceived of the structure of this novel as a clearly defined circular form. On the first and last pages, the protagonist is on his own, but between those points, the social radius of Josef K. is paced off chapter by chapter: the landlady, the fellow tenant, the colleagues, the bosses, the restaurant companions, the uncle, the mother, the lawyer, the lover—and, of course, the court itself. We do not know whether Kafka was planning to bring in additional courtroom scenes or shady advisers from the periphery of the court, but the social relationships of the accused are almost completely fleshed out; and although there are only hints about the chapter involving his mother, its overall scheme can be divined. We do not feel as though we are left with the vague contours of a fragment, and as inscrutable as the text is, the remaining gaps that Kafka would have had to fill in to complete the inherent, compelling logic of this work up to the end are clearly recognizable.

The extratextual barriers to publication had also fallen away; Max Brod had seen to that. Kafka never had to bow and scrape; he had an influential publisher. He had not heard from Kurt Wolff for quite some time, and Wolff was not in his Leipzig office at all for the time being, but he would have accepted a completed novel—including this one—without hesitation. Since production time was quite brief by today's standards, *The Trial* could have been published in the fall, or by the end of 1915 at the latest. And even if the immediate quantifiable success failed to materialize, the public's need to be entertained during the war was stronger than ever, so Kafka would have been assured of highly prominent backing by writers including Thomas Mann and Robert Musil, and there would have been no shortage of readings, tributes, and new acquaintances or even friendships. The images are enticing:

Kafka in conversation with his translators, at the coffeehouse table of the influential Karl Kraus, at a reception in Samuel Fischer's villa in Grunewald. No doubt, a publication of *The Trial* would have soon brought Kafka well beyond his exceedingly limited milieu and assured him a good number of contacts (both pleasant and annoying) that even Brod would have envied.

"[A]ll this fever, which heats my head day and night, comes from a lack of freedom," Kafka concluded the following year,[4] and it doesn't take many "would-haves" and "could-haves" to gauge the agonizing futility he must have felt as he assessed and reassessed the situation. The war had prevented him from jumping ship at the last minute, and his own ebbing energy now pushed any remaining options for freedom way into the distance. He still knew that failure was neither inevitable nor irreversible. But the disparity between all that had been within easy reach and the current reality of Prague, which was hopelessly dominated by his anxieties about the war and by overly long hours at the office, was nothing short of horrifying. Kafka began to notice unequivocal symptoms of exhaustion back in early January 1915, and soon thereafter he set aside the manuscript of *The Trial*, continued sporadic work on stories he had already begun, and tried out new things and rejected old ones. April 9 was the last time his diary mentioned "good work," and in May, Kafka even gave up the diary itself and refused to read aloud to friends. It was like a long final exhalation followed by a frightful silence. He could not know that this paralysis would last more than one and a half years. In September, he managed to start a new diary, but from the very first sentence, he was convinced that it was "not as necessary as it once was," and because he saw no sense in filling the pages with the repetition of old laments, he made entries only when special events, meetings, or ideas he got from reading compelled him to do so. Otherwise, there was silence for weeks on end. Toward the end of 1916, when the physiognomy of his city and the world around him had become distorted beyond recognition, Kafka finally undertook yet another attempt to justify life by "work."

It is no wonder that under these circumstances Kafka showed little initiative to push for publication of even his completed works. That had not always been the case. He knew that his years of effort must have seemed like a flash in the pan to his readers, and that the literary world regarded him as a minimalist who lacked the stamina for larger-scale projects. He had published only two books to date, and even they looked quite slight: the prose pieces in *Meditation* amounted to a mere ninety-nine pages, and *The Stoker* was only forty-seven pages long. Everything else was scattered among newspapers and magazines, and not even the major ones. Even "The Judgment," the only one of his stories Kafka did not find fault with and often enjoyed reading aloud, had been published in an anthology compiled by Brod that did not sell.

Kafka had certainly tried to improve this situation. He had proposed a volume of stories to Kurt Wolff and received an immediate acceptance. "The Sons" was the working title of a book project that would present a compilation of Kafka's creative phase from 1912—at least the texts he considered presentable: "The Judgment," "The Stoker," "The Metamorphosis." But he spent too much time dithering with the manuscript of "The Metamorphosis," and Wolff neither prodded him nor made any inquiries, and gave no indication—as Kafka is sure to have expected—that he had any recollection of his own "binding declaration" in April 1913. Although Brod never failed to bring up his friend's name with Wolff, Kafka received nothing but a few reviews and the publisher's almanac—a paltry show of interest. In August 1914, when Kafka heard that both Kurt Wolff and his editor Franz Werfel had gone off to war, and that an astonishing ten of Wolff's twelve staff members were now on the battlefield, he stopped counting on any kind of support from Leipzig. That was just fine with him. If the publisher—contrary to his usual habits—had now suddenly inquired into Kafka's plans and literary projects, the timing would not have been opportune, because he would have to explain why the novel was still not moving ahead. Kafka avoided conversations of that kind to whatever extent possible. And since he had tried in vain already twice to place "The Metamorphosis" at least in a journal—the manuscript had been lying on the desk of René Schickele, the editor of *Die weissen Blätter*, for half a year—he did not want to talk about publications at all. He was not about to beg and plead.

But suddenly, in mid-October 1915, Brod handed him a letter from Kurt Wolff Verlag, along with several copies of *Die weissen Blätter* hot off the presses. Evidently Kafka's address had been misplaced, and they had to have Brod forward the package to him. The matter was so pressing that there was no time to call in the publisher personally. Instead, someone named Meyer had signed this letter. When Kafka leafed through the magazine, he could hardly believe his eyes: "The Metamorphosis" had been printed in full, without his having seen the galleys.

Georg Heinrich Meyer, forty-seven years old, was a good-natured, somewhat longwinded, but wily businessman with a pleasant-looking mustache and an avuncular manner. He was considered incapable of dissimulation and had no trouble winning over people's confidence—although his constant display of optimism seemed a little suspect, in view of the fact that after training to be a bookseller, he had already failed with two of his own publishing companies and was up to his ears in debt, all of which was no secret in the publishing business.

Given these circumstances, it was quite surprising that Kurt Wolff had selected this man to be his managing director and appointed him his deputy when the war began, especially in light of the fact that Meyer was not even able to bring in his own contemporary authors from his failed enterprises. As meticulously produced as his books had been, his literary program was rather humdrum, and the regional literature he favored—he had even published a magazine on this subject—was a grotesque contrast to the avant-garde literature he now had to promote on behalf of Wolff. On top of that, Meyer's ex-authors were producing predominantly patriotic trash, while Wolff was the only major German publisher who consistently refused to publish pro-war literature. Apart from a few bibliophile gems on Meyer's backlist, there was little to interest Wolff, and the latter was well-advised to continue insisting on his own standards of literary quality and to reserve the right to make decisions about what to include on the list, even though communication, particularly in sending manuscripts back and forth, was now extraordinarily difficult and did not allow for quick decisions. Every now and then, Meyer traveled near the Belgian front to keep Wolff informed, but once the publisher was posted to the Galician war zone in April 1915, this option was also cut off, and from then on, Meyer had to attend to the day-to-day operations of the publishing company, including the "care and feeding" of the authors, virtually alone.

We can well imagine the looks Franz Werfel, Kurt Pinthus, and Walter Hasenclever gave one another when the casually dressed Meyer made his debut, yet Wolff's odd decision would turn out to be the right one. Meyer, who had spent several years traveling from bookstore to bookstore for Deutsche Verlags-Anstalt, had enormous experience on the business side, and countless conversations had given him a precise idea of what impressed retail booksellers and what actually appealed to a readership whose habits were increasingly shaped by cultural trends and publicity. Evidently this was the know-how that Wolff had been seeking. And it is doubtful whether his publishing company, which offered neither war poetry nor collected letters nor the ever-popular reports from the front, could have survived the first year of the war economically intact without Meyer's sound sales ideas. While he impressed the readers of daily newspapers with extensive advertising—advertising not only for the publishing company, mind you, but for individual new books, which was highly unusual at the time—he enticed booksellers with special discounts, which amounted to a violation of a sacred economic principle of the book publishing industry and promptly led to complaints about the "American distribution methods" of Kurt Wolff Verlag. If you ordered and paid for thirty copies of Gustav Meyrink's best seller *The Golem*, you were sent *forty* copies. Any novice could see that based on the cover price, this made for an incredible 55 percent discount. And Meyer's poster campaigns on advertising pillars gave offense because literature was being packaged for the first time as a pure media event and put on a par with the sensationalism of movies. The advertising copy, most of which Meyer wrote himself, even reinforced this sense of dubiousness, banking on rousing emotional reactions without the slightest connection to the books in question. The works of the Nobel Prize laureate Rabindranath Tagore were advertised as "real Christmas books," and in advertising Carl Sternheim's *Napoleon*, the analytical tale of a master chef, Meyer concocted the slogan "Reading this novella is like eating at the luxurious Sacher Hotel," whereupon the author threatened to shoot him dead.[5]

Anyone who knew the standard accounting in publishing was sure to realize that such elaborate promotions far exceeded traditional book budgeting. Who would fill the financial gaps Meyer was creating?

Why, the authors, of course, was Meyer's delightfully simple answer. Meyer was the first publishing director who dared to make the authors contribute to the advertising expenditures for their own books, a positively astonishing ploy at a time when advertising was not considered nearly as important to a book's sales success as it is today, and many publishers had no advertising budgets at all. Meyer devoted himself passionately to making this sound appealing to his authors. Evidently, he followed some irate authors right to the train station to convince them up to the very last second, with remarkable success. Even the penny-pinching Max Brod agreed to dedicate a quarter of his standard royalties to finance a series of advertisements for his novel *The Redemption of Tycho Brahe*.

There was no discussing literary content with Meyer, the notorious "sales whiz." He barely glanced at submitted manuscripts, and he even kept track of book titles according to how he viewed their marketability; years later he was still calling Kafka's "In the Penal Colony" "The Gangster Colony." He nagged authors to keep plugging away at their novels—and promised "sensational success" even to Kafka's novels, of which he did not know a line—but letters from authors that required immediate responses went unanswered by the dozens. Meyer could barely make heads or tails even of Werfel's poems, which he considered "the only meaty part of Kurt Wolff's skimpy meal" in the crisis-ridden years of 1914–1915, and said as much to the author, who was also his colleague.[6] By contrast, Meyer reacted to media events that swayed readers and thus sales potential with seismographic flair and an activism that was both inventive and naively reckless.

He acted the same way in the case of Kafka. The decision process can no longer be reconstructed today, but the fact that René Schickele, who felt that Kafka's "Metamorphosis" was too long for his journal *Die weissen Blätter* but decided to print it after all, was almost certainly reacting to Meyer's intervention.[7] And Meyer, in turn, now suggested that Kafka agree to have the story printed as a stand-alone volume in the series "Der jüngste Tag," as well, *without delay*, the very same month, followed by a new hardcover edition of *Meditation*. All this activity after years of silence on the part of the publisher was somewhat disconcerting. But Meyer offered a plausible explanation:

> The Fontane Prize for the best modern writer will soon be awarded. As we have learned in confidence, Sternheim will receive the prize for three of his stories: "Buskow," "Napoleon," and "Schuhlin." But because Sternheim is a millionaire, as you are surely aware, and it would not be appropriate to give a millionaire a monetary prize, Franz Blei, who is in charge of the Fontane Prize this year, told Sternheim to give the sum of, I believe, eight hundred marks, to you, the worthiest recipient. Sternheim has read your works and is, as you can see from the enclosed card, truly inspired by you.

Even though Kafka was somewhat indignant, he had to admit that this was not bad news. The idea that Meyer had just "learned in confidence" about such an important event was absurd: The prize money came from funding provided by Erik Schwabach, who was Wolff's chief investor; Sternheim and Kafka were Wolff's authors, and the critic Franz Blei, who would be presenting the prestigious prize on behalf of the Association of German Writers, was closely allied with the publishing company. During the previous year, Meyer himself was the editor of *Die weissen Blätter* and was also regarded as the "discoverer" of Sternheim. The whole thing seemed like a marketing ploy, perhaps even thought up by Meyer. Kafka had already learned that Meyer was capable of this kind of thing, while Meyer evidently did *not* know with whom he was dealing:

> Consequently, you can expect the following for "The Metamorphosis": 1) Payment from *Die weissen Blätter* (I don't know what arrangements you had with Schickele about that), 2) Payment for *Der jüngste Tag*, which may amount to a lump sum of 350 marks for a small print run—the highest amount ever paid for *Der jüngste Tag*—and also 800 marks for the Fontane Prize. So you are quite a lucky duck![8]

Unfortunately, this type of argument was lost on Kafka. Meyer's assurance that it was not his own fault, but Schickele's and the current way of the world, that Kafka had not ever seen page proofs for "The Metamorphosis" did nothing to obscure the fact that Kafka had been blindsided, and the situation reflected a blatant disregard for authors' rights. Meyer had no intention of letting up the pressure in his push to make Kafka successful. While the inquiry to Kafka was still en route, he sent off the manuscript for the book edition of *The Metamorphosis*, and a few days later—before the author had any time to think it over—the galleys were complete. This time, though, Kafka had the opportunity to make numerous minor revisions in the text, which he considered far more important than the amount of the payment. But the agreement with Wolff that his next book would contain *several* stories was, of course, rendered moot because Meyer had taken the matter into his own hands.

After pondering the situation briefly—and most likely talking it over with Brod—Kafka was prepared to live with the new situation. He himself had stated repeatedly that he was "quite eager" for publication of "The Metamorphosis."[9] A full three years after he had written the story, this wish was finally fulfilled, and no one would have understood Kafka's refusal. Kafka could not refrain from a few ironic barbs at Meyer's expense, but he also made suggestions for the book design and was even uncharacteristically assertive about the cover, on which he absolutely did not wish to see the hapless Gregor Samsa pictured: "Not that, please not that! . . . The insect itself cannot be drawn. It cannot even be shown from a distance."[10] Luckily this message did not get buried in Meyer's huge piles of papers and was passed on to the illustrator (Ottomar Starke, a close friend of Sternheim), who respected Kafka's wish.

But what about the peculiar way the Fontane Prize was awarded? The honor went to the famous Carl Sternheim, but the money to the unknown writer from Prague? Kafka had trouble accepting this.

> According to what you have written, and particularly from what you wrote to Max Brod, it seems that the prize is going to Sternheim, but that he would like to give the money to someone else, possibly to me. As kind as such a gesture certainly is, it does raise the question of need, not of need regarding the prize and the money, but need in regard to the money alone. The way I see it, it would not matter at all whether the recipient might need the money sometime in the future, rather the decisive factor should be only whether he needs it at the moment. As important as the prize or a share in the prize would be for me, I would not want to accept the money

alone without a share in the prize. My feeling is that I would have no right to do so, since I do not have that requisite immediate need for money at all.[11]

And that was that. Kafka could just imagine the quizzical looks on the faces of his colleagues and his boss, who had literary interests himself. They knew the precise monthly earnings of a civil servant in the "first salary bracket of the third rank," and would wonder why he would be accepting publicly offered monetary gifts.

Not that Kafka would have begrudged the privileged Sternheim the prize. Even a wealthy writer was not immune to the tribulations of the war. Sternheim, who was psychologically unstable as it was, had to give up his cozy home on the outskirts of Brussels for a period of time (because of his compatriots, the German occupiers; not because of his Belgian neighbors), and performances of his plays met with resistance from the Prussian censors. Once he was associated with the Berlin *Aktion* circle, Sternheim became a political object of hatred and was harassed relentlessly by the military authorities. All this was well known in Prague. Even so, Kafka was annoyed by the casual manner in which he was informed about his own, secondary share in the prize. Unhappy or not, why didn't the donor himself write a friendly note? Why not at least Franz Blei, who knew Kafka personally and might have been able to give reasons for this odd process? Was it really the case that Sternheim had merely been "told" by Blei?

Kafka got no further information from Meyer, who was indifferent in matters of style and tried only to dispel his doubts without paying serious heed to them. Meyer had never encountered an author who suddenly has the equivalent of half of a lower-level civil servant's annual salary fall into his lap, yet has to be talked into accepting it. And what author—apart from the rare writing millionaire—could afford eccentricity of that sort? Meyer was surely not a bit surprised that Kafka ultimately agreed to accept the gift and even to thank Sternheim in writing. Why wouldn't he? Kafka welcomed recognition but not a handout, and ever since the humiliations in Berlin, he was bent on defending his self-respect at almost any cost, so he had trouble bringing himself to write to Sternheim. "It is not very easy," he complained to Meyer, "to write to somebody from whom one has not received any direct word and to thank him without knowing exactly what for."[12] For all we know, his fear that his friends would reproach him may have ultimately tipped the scales. But when the busy Meyer, who was on the job almost around the clock in the empty offices of Kurt Wolff Verlag, broke down under the tremendous work pressure four weeks later, Kafka told himself that he was not at fault.

There was no known response from Carl Sternheim. Since Kafka had no immediate use for the eight hundred marks that Sternheim had given him, he invested them in war bonds. It was the only literary honor Kafka would ever receive, but he could not know that at the time.

Perhaps the major indication of how little Kafka's contemporaries understood him is that nearly all attempts to encourage him in his work, to motivate him, or to "praise" him went astray in some strange way. Certainly, being extolled as a "lucky duck" by the head of a publishing company, who ought to have had at least a vague idea about the intellectual status of his author, could be chalked up to the usual cruel irony that kept flaring up in the friction between life and literature, and Kafka still had enough of a sense of humor to report this special distinction to his friends. As far as misjudgments and misunderstandings were concerned, he had experienced far worse—for example, when the Viennese writer Otto Stoessl thought the volume *Meditation* was brimming with "light, yet heartfelt cheerfulness" and "the humor of a good solid constitution,"[13] which was of course intended as high praise but was so alien to the intention of the texts that Kafka must have entertained serious doubts about his own ability to express himself.

Max Brod, in turn, reached for superlatives. "He is the greatest writer of our time," he noted in his diary after Kafka had read him two chapters of *The Trial* in April 1915. He was absolutely overwhelmed, and his oral tributes were no less subdued.[14] But Kafka, who certainly knew how to enjoy the resonance of his texts, did not take pleasure in these kinds of attributions, which had nothing to do with his own experience and hence did not even flatter him. He had drawn occasional parallels between his own situation and that of authorities such as Grillparzer, Dostoevsky, Kleist, and Flaubert, and had even referred to them as his “true blood relations”[15]—but not on account of his literary output. After all, when in the entire history of literature had there been such a disparity between effort and yield? What great writer had not produced any novel, play, or classical verse, or come up with a single idea worth preserving for months on end? Who needed supernatural peace of mind to come up with one true sentence? The very comparison was absurd, and even Brod had to realize by now that it was not just a matter of character flaws, a lack of energy or discipline, or the anxious concerns of a neurotic perfectionist. No, the inner material, the powers of imagination themselves were what kept eluding Kafka, and *this* was the reason that Brod’s hymns of praise rang hollow.

But Franz Werfel took the cake. Kafka was quite irritated by the fact that Werfel had been praising “The Metamorphosis” to the skies for years although he knew it only by hearsay and had never bothered to look at the manuscript even as an editor at Kurt Wolff. Now that the story had appeared in print, he finally caught up on his reading, and was stunned at what he saw. He now knew that he had underestimated—indeed, utterly failed to appreciate—Kafka, this slender shadow behind Max Brod. And he just had to tell him as much to make up for everything. But how do you praise the creator of a text like *this* one? Werfel, who tended to indulge in pathos anyway, pulled out all the stops, and his reaction must have shaken Kafka to the core. It was amazing that this eternal youth, basking in his own fame and lacking any insight into human nature, with everything seeming to come his way, would manage to craft the most absurd, naive, raw, true letter of praise Kafka ever received in his life:

> I cannot begin to tell you how overwhelmed I am, and my sense of security has been given a beneficial jolt by you, and I feel (thank God!) quite small.
>
> Dear Kafka, you are so pure, new, independent, and perfect that one ought to treat you as if you were already dead and immortal. One doesn’t typically have these kinds of feelings for people who are still alive.
>
> What you have achieved in your last works has *truly* never existed in any literature, namely taking a well-crafted, concrete story that is almost real and making it into something all-encompassing

and symbolic that speaks to a tragic dimension of mankind. But I'm not expressing myself very well.

Everybody around you ought to know that and not treat you like a fellow human being.

I thank you profoundly for the reverence I am honored to have for you."[16]

Already dead. Not for *people who are still alive*. In any case, not *a fellow human being*. Kafka had always suspected and feared as much—now he had it in writing.

numb people of Prague. Was it a dream, a rumor, a mistake? Evidently not. By the next morning, Prague was bedecked with flags.

On that day, May 3, 1915, as Kafka was poring over the title page of the *Prager Tagblatt*, down at the bottom, in the shadow of the news of victory, he came across a second headline that was far less conspicuous but sure to grab his attention, as he was part of the group in question: "Repeat Medical Examinations for Militia Classes 1878–1894." The official explanation read that although men born in these years had already been examined at the onset of the war, it had since come to light that the medical "regulatory commissions" had not employed uniform criteria, and the resulting inequities now required rectification.

Even the most credulous patriot must have seen through that lie. Since when had the authorities—especially the military authorities—cared about equity? The simple truth was that of the more than five million men in Austria-Hungary alone who had been gathered together and quartered in barracks since August 1914, one quarter was already out of commission—killed, captured, missing in action, or wounded and thus no longer fit for the front lines. The state urgently needed reinforcements, especially with a new calamity on the horizon that the government tried in vain to conceal from newspaper readers. Neutral Italy, an ally on paper, had defected, and had been negotiating for quite some time with the enemies, who promised them an enormous payoff to enter the war.

The current scenario—a war on three fronts that was sure to devastate the Habsburg Empire—represented the worst possible threat to the Austro-Hungarian army. Top-ranking officers, including Franz Conrad von Hötzendorf, head of the general staff and one of the most aggressive supporters of the war, had declared that it was impossible to stand up to Russia, Serbia, and Italy all at once, and right from the start they called for political measures to avert this nightmare. No price would be too high. The Austrian government attempted almost desperately to stay on good terms with Rome, making offers that were so generous and acquiescent that they had to be concealed from their own population. But the price had gone up. The Italian government kept raising the stakes, no longer demanding just the Italian-speaking

South Tyrol but also the port city of Trieste, even casting an eye on Dalmatia and Albania. And while Vienna was still deliberating whether giving in to these demands would amount to capitulation, the counteroffers in Paris, London, and St. Petersburg were steadily rising: military rear cover on land and at sea, coal shipments, and reparations in cash. Italy just had to choose, and the enemy would pay.

News of these secret negotiations soon reached Vienna, as well, and by mid-April it was clear that it no longer made sense to try to keep Italy out of the war with additional concessions. The kaiser now decided to pass as well. It seemed more honorable to let the Italians invade than to continue haggling and doling out before the eyes of the world gifts that one would have to retrieve later by force.

Italy's declaration of war on Austria-Hungary was announced on the afternoon of May 23, 1915, which was Whitsunday. No one was surprised at this point; the only startling part was that the king of Italy went to the effort of signing a document that consisted of absolutely meaningless statements and did not name a single concrete reason for war—apart from declaring that the time was right to grab whatever there was to grab.

A few days later, at 8 A.M., Kafka reported to the Schützeninsel in Prague, whose spacious banquet halls were now frequently used for military purposes, mainly as a meeting place for prospective new enlisted men. It was a holiday. Bells were chiming, and very few people were out on the quays. On this island, which normally served as an entertainment spot, Kafka now found himself amidst an excited babble of voices, primarily in Czech.

We do not know how many hours he spent here, whether he ran into people he knew, or if he spent the time chatting or reading the newspaper. And it certainly seems possible that he thought about how he once, at this very spot, had awaited a sexual initiation. He had plenty of time to look around at the unreal scene. Hundreds of men sat and chatted around him; they were brought together not because they spoke the same language, observed the same religion, or belonged to the same social class, as was usual in their leisure time, but rather because of a single, utterly abstract criterion: their "infantry class," that is, their birth year. All were the same age. Today was the day for thirty-two-year-olds.

Kafka knew what was in store for him, although his previous encounters with the military had taken place more than ten years earlier. At that time, the army decided against bringing him in under the "One Year Volunteer" designation for enlistees with higher education who could later serve as officers. This decision did not come easily; three assessments and long deliberations were required to convince the examining officials that the thin, lanky student was unfit for physical stress. The procedure had been relatively peaceful and easygoing back at the beginning of the new century, when even stronger men than Kafka were able to escape military service with less effort. No one could have guessed that one day Austria-Hungary would resort to bringing in the unfit, the nervous, and the emaciated.

Up against the wall, please, get undressed, 5′11″, step forward, stand up straight, feet together. Any ailments? Family history of disease? Do you need glasses? Now open your mouth, palate normal, hearing ditto, take a deep breath, arms forward, out to the side, now crossed behind your back, make a fist, legs apart and bend forward . . . finally the dreaded grab under the testicles . . . and *the judgment*: fit for armed infantry service for the duration of the war, category A; next, *další, prosím*!

Did the number of men really matter? The politicians said it did, and the high-ranking officers believed this. They took it for granted that they needed a numeric mass of soldiers, a formation of bodies (as they had learned back in the cadet academy), and they considered it quite modern and up-to-date to tally up individual psychological traits as destructive potential. They particularly enjoyed carrying on about the "character material" of their subordinates. At the same time, they coyly skirted the issue of whether the sheer accumulation of weapons, vehicles, and raw materials was what truly counted, and whether twentieth-century wars might actually be decided not on front lines but on assembly lines. That kind of thinking went against the atavistic images of battle they took such pleasure in. Rudimentary codes of honor still applied right up to the technocratic top brass of the military hierarchy, who were often taken in by their own propaganda. Even at the beginning of the world war, there were generals who could not get used to the idea of killing the enemy from a great distance, that is, *without seeing him*.[2] Veteran officers were notoriously averse to experiments with weapons in breach of international law, especially with poison gas. *We are soldiers, not pest exterminators*.

Of course, there were good reasons to be wary of this warfare technology, which was troublesome, unreliable, and vulnerable to changes in the weather. Machinery did not replace manpower; in fact, it required intensive maintenance and incessant patching and tinkering. Four thousand trucks sent the Germans off to the west, but two-thirds of them broke down before reaching the Marne—an entire crew of mechanics could not prevent that from happening. "Big Bertha," a monster of a howitzer with shells that weighed nearly a ton, could be transported only on tracks that had to be laid expressly for this purpose, close to the front—dangerous heavy labor that everyone dreaded. Then there were the very latest inventions, still in their embryonic stages, which often occasioned more laughter than fear: sneezing powder shells in Flanders, tear gas at the eastern front, pilots who dropped pointed steel projectiles ("flechettes") and aimed down with shotguns, and finally the first "tanks," unwieldy, twenty-eight-ton dinosaurs that were easy to capture and even more easily sank into mud or sinkholes.

Still, there had been impressive displays with some new and clearly superior machinery that could function largely on its own and reduce the individual to an impotent disposable entity. The new well-cooled machine guns that could fire up to ten shots per second proved to be quite a fiendish invention; in the first weeks of the war, they caused vast numbers of casualties and required radical shifts in thinking. If a single machine gun nest could fight off hundreds of attackers, it obviously made no sense to count up the numbers of soldiers and officers mobilized throughout Europe to establish "superiority."

Even so, this hefty machine gun was a static defensive weapon, and soldiers were safe as long as they remained in a trench and did not spring into action. This was no longer the case with the advent of the second technological shock, the introduction of the "barrage" in December 1914. The barrage removed any last vestige of protection for the individual. There was no way to find refuge—or even to capitulate.

correspondence as rapidly as possible was in the best interest of the institute, otherwise the businesses in question would have grounds to suspend their payments. Hence, once the institute received word that Kafka had passed his medical examination, it felt perfectly justified in filing a petition to exempt Kafka, its extremely competent civil servant, from military service, along with the mathematician who did the preliminary work for Kafka, on the grounds that the two gentlemen were "indispensable . . . for this task." That made sense to the military command—to an extent. Alois Gütling, Kafka's colleague (who was also an amateur writer), was spared for an additional two months, but Dr. Kafka, who apparently was more the focus of public attention, was exempted "for an unspecified period"—that is, until such time as his case was reconsidered.[4]

Kafka must have expected this exemption, but he could not make anyone understand the reasons for his disappointment. Even Felice Bauer was evidently baffled, although she ought to have known him better than his parents, who were always worried about possible implications for the family. It is easy to imagine why that last meeting in Karlsbad, just a few days after the decision about Kafka's immediate future had been reached, culminated in ill feelings, probably even in a quarrel. He again brought up fundamental issues in vague terms, while Felice argued in practical terms, which made Kafka's most recent attempt to break away by joining the army appear irrational, socially irresponsible, and perhaps even suicidal. And did she think he could endure a life in uniform? She surely played this trump card, as well.

The counterstrike was not long in coming. Kafka had finally arranged with Felice to take the vacation together at the Baltic they had planned the previous year, *before* the confrontation in the Hotel Askanischer Hof: their first trip together, a first trial run at living together, three whole weeks—assuming, of course, that Kafka remained a civilian in spite of his fervent desire to become a soldier and was thus somewhat mobile. This condition was now fulfilled, and Kafka did leave Prague—but alone. In July 1915, just weeks after the medical examination, the institute's claim that Kafka was indispensable, and the meeting in Karlsbad, Felice Bauer unexpectedly received a postcard from Rumburg, in the northernmost part of Bohemia. Kafka wrote that he could no longer stand being in the city and barely cared where he went. His first idea had been Lake Wolfgang in Austria, but that would have meant seventeen hours in the train, so he was now at the Frankenstein sanatorium outside of Rumburg for just two weeks, which, he explained, meant that they could still have a week together in the fall, "in the worst case." That was scant consolation, but Felice Bauer quickly came to terms with the situation and told him she would send a letter with new, more modest travel plans. Kafka told her not to bother, because this final week now had to be canceled as well. Officials who were declared indispensable would not get any vacation time at all—effective immediately.[5]

And that was that for them in 1915. Another end, another parting. A full year would pass before they saw each other again, and it seemed unlikely that the couple would experience any other marvel.

Kafka wrote very little about his stay in Rumburg—calling it a vacation would be euphemistic—and he no longer anticipated a freer life closer to nature, as he had just three years earlier, when he arrived at the legendary "Jungborn." All he wanted was to be left alone. He had chosen the "Frankenstein Sanatorium for Physical and Dietetic Treatments," just thirty minutes outside of Rumburg in Frankenstein because he knew it was the best of the few remaining tolerable institutions in Bohemia and because the war made it difficult to impossible to get to any conceivable distant goal that was pretty, new to him, and reasonably comfortable. Rumburg became Kafka's temporary quarters and a veritable symbol of his bureaucratically controlled life because the town was situated in a part of Bohemia that jutted out toward Germany, and hence his official papers would not allow him to travel any more than a few hours to the west, north, or east.

He liked the hilly surroundings and the seemingly endless silent woods; the landscape was mild, soothing, and almost comforting. Even so, it took Kafka no more than a few days to realize that his escape had been too hasty and the destination was not especially well chosen. The administrative district of Rumburg was part of his professional jurisdiction, and when Kafka peered down at the industrial town from one of the many lookout points, he must have thought of the 303 companies here that had recently had to be reclassified and written to, or the sixty-two warnings and eight charges his department had fired off to Rumburg in the past year, or the mercifully few (seven) grievance procedures on his desk. He knew these numbers inside out, and they brought him right back to reality.[6]

Moreover, this was the least opportune moment to be at the mercy of his own body and seek out the regression that attracts people to sanatoriums. Rest cures, special diets, therapeutic baths, and medical supervision suddenly struck Kafka as an unreal world full of pseudo-activity that offered not relaxation but banal repetition, "almost another office, in the service of the body,"[7] and only people who were *truly* ill—that is, ill in the eyes of others—could submit to it. But Kafka wanted no part of it—not now. He was fit for active duty, so what was he doing in a sanatorium? He had not given up on his plan to enter the military, which did not recognize or accept invisible ailments. He knew after just a few days that "I will never go to a sanatorium again."[8] He stuck to his resolution as long as he could.

He first approached his boss, Eugen Pfohl, the head of the business department, on Christmas Eve, 1915. Kafka was well prepared; in the previous night he had not only worked out all the ifs, ands, and buts, but had also *sworn* to himself to speak frankly and not let himself get derailed.

Kafka laid out his argument with his typical exactitude, but quite atypical assertiveness, explaining that the state of his nerves would leave him only the choice between four options. The first was that everything remain as is, with insomnia, headaches, and heart palpitations, which would eventually "culminate in brain fever, insanity, or something of the sort" (this *something of the sort* was the most powerful threat). The second option—taking another vacation—would not be a real solution (Rumburg had proved that) and in wartime would be an impermissible privilege for a duty-bound official. The third option would be immediate *resignation* (by this point, Pfohl has to have realized that Kafka was being serious), but for family reasons, that option was out of the question for the time being. The fourth and final option was military service, which might prove liberating but would require the Workers' Accident Insurance Institute to release its top official, Kafka, by promptly withdrawing its "claim" with the military command.[9]

This was strong language. The following day, Kafka was still proud of having openly used the word "resignation" for the first time and thus "almost setting off an official shock wave in the institute"—which was no exaggeration, because an official truly was far more likely to go crazy from overwork or to take his own life than to forgo his pension voluntarily. Kafka had broken a taboo. But it did not help. No matter what tactic he tried, his boss stood firm because Pfohl was well acquainted with Kafka's nervous complaints and vacillations, and he knew that applying moral pressure would do the trick. He replied he, too, was seriously ill and in urgent need of a dreadfully expensive one-week course of treatment with "hematogen" to build up his blood. Perhaps they could undergo this treatment together? If Kafka left for an extended period—or did not return to his job at all—the department would be "deserted" and "collapse," Pfohl explained. So Kafka was being offered a stay at a sanatorium together with his boss—and there was not a word about military service. Kafka declined with thanks.

Several months later, he approached the higher-ups with a second proposal, which was well-conceived and more thoroughly prepared. According to official sources, "claimants" were not entitled to a vacation in 1916 unless there were extenuating circumstances, and even then a leave was granted for no more than a few days. Kafka took this bad news, which of course had been expected for quite some time by all concerned, as an occasion to write a letter to the director, and again cited his own frayed nerves, but wisely reduced the number of possible decisions to *two* in order to forestall additional excuses. Either, Kafka reasoned, the war would be over by the fall, in which case he would ask for a long—very long—unpaid vacation, since his ailment was not organically manifest and thus not subject to verification by the official medical personnel, or the war would go on, in which case he wanted to serve in the military and requested that the claim be withdrawn.

Three days later, on May 11, 1916, Director Marschner asked his employee to come to his office for a talk. Quite a while back, the two had developed a relationship that was not quite friendship but was trusting, and fostered by their mutual literary interests as well as by Kafka's professional sense of responsibility. It was a tacit assumption in both the letter and the conversation that the two of them could discuss personal matters frankly. Appealing to the institute *formally* to release one of its best staff members would have been pointless.

Marschner, like Kafka, relied on this license to intimacy. Although Kafka was fully aware that nothing short of his life was at stake—as he noted in his diary—he unexpectedly found himself in a situation that was objectively funny. Marschner was extremely well prepared. He had clearly consulted with Pfohl and adopted Pfohl's successful strategy of ignoring Kafka's ludicrous plans and instead appealing to his conscience. He offered him three weeks of vacation time and tried to persuade him to take a break *immediately*, fully aware that this offer was against the rules, and that Kafka knew as much. Marschner was thus willing to assume a personal risk to satisfy Kafka's need for a vacation, even though, Marschner argued, his own position, which carried far greater responsibility, was even more likely to make someone ill than Kafka's. Did Kafka ever have to work for eleven hours; did he ever have to worry about losing his job? Marschner had to prevail against "enemies" determined to cut off his "mainspring of life." *That's* what makes you ill.

Kafka wavered. Didn't this whole thing bear an awful resemblance to situations with his father, who, when confronted with justified complaints, just like Pfohl and now again Marschner, clutched at his weak heart and stifled any opposition with his own tale of woe? And why not a word about Kafka's writing? Was it possible that Marschner, who knew and appreciated Kafka's literary achievements, considered the pain of years of silence irrelevant?

Kafka held tight to his last shred of resolve. No, three weeks of vacation time were not enough, and not what he had been hoping for. He wanted to become a soldier. Escape the office, come what may, even without pay, for a half or a full year, even if the director found the idea laughable. Yes, dear colleague, let us continue this conversation some other time.[10]

For the first time I see you rising,
Hearsaid, remote, incredible War God.
How thickly our peaceful corn was intersown
with terrible action, suddenly grown mature!

Small even yesterday, needing nurture, and now
tall as a man: tomorrow
towering beyond man's reach. Before we know it, he's there,
the glowing god himself, tearing his crop out of the nation's roots,
and harvest begins.[11]

Admired, controversial, disparaged verses, composed during the first hours of the world war, yet mere particles of a vast, suffocating cloud of verbiage arising from the well-educated classes, pouring into the offices of newspapers, magazines, publishers, and finally the brains of readers. Thousands of poems *a day*, supplemented with letters, eyewitness accounts, exhortations to hold out, indignation about the treacherous enemy. A breathtaking, towering, explosive cloud over the land.

Rainer Maria Rilke, the author of the "Five Songs," had no need to fear that his verses would go unheard in the general cacophony. They were eagerly awaited. Who better than Rilke to give just the right lofty, ultimate form to the colossal moment in history? The first war almanac, which was published by Insel Verlag, was a worthy place to celebrate this event.

But by the time the almanac came out, the author was filled with remorse. "I have no 'war songs' to offer, by any stretch of the imagination," he bluntly informed the Berlin publisher Axel Juncker. Of course, he had to concede that he had already submitted "a couple of songs ... but they cannot be regarded as war songs, and I would not like to contemplate the idea of their being used elsewhere." That was in October 1914, not even three months after the rising of the glowing War God.[12]

Rilke's short-lived exaltation and the disillusionment that began to take hold of him after just a few days can be tracked in his correspondence, which conveys a shocking impression of a paradigm shift in Rilke's experience and reactions and makes the mood and pulse of those days almost physically tangible to us today. His lofty rhetoric, which plays with hollow myths, strikes us as positively delusional and is comprehensible only as an expression of his speechlessness when facing appalling new circumstances that demanded new literary forms and images that Rilke did not have at his disposal.

Still, he soon realized that the battle cries were not the real problem of this modern war, and not—as Freud lamented—an overall legitimation of the natural lust for murder, but a hitherto unknown, hoodwinked, suicidal, and yet coldly calculating and calculated collectivity: "the disturbing part is not the fact of the war, but rather that it is being used and exploited in a commercialized world that is nothing but profane." Rilke was even blunter in placing the blame: "throughout this war, rash lies spread by the newspapers came up with one new fact after another; you get the impression that since there has been this press coverage carried to an extreme, a war cannot stop once it has started. Those disgraceful papers are always one step ahead of the actual events." In other words, the war was anything but the primeval, intoxicating event Rilke wanted to accompany with his Five Songs. "Blessed am I, beholding the possessed . . . ," he had written there. Now he realized that it was a mere product of ordinary people.[13]

Rilke's notes provide important testimony, particularly because he not only endured but also reflected on the process of disillusionment, without leaving out anything. Rilke came out and said what others suppressed or flatly denied—such as Stefan Zweig, who adopted the propaganda from day one—but contended he was "secure [in] my world citizenship." He stuck to this claim for decades to come.[14] Hugo von Hofmannsthal derived "great pleasure" from buckling on "a polished saber," yet went to great lengths to avoid serving at the front, and, after the successful intervention of influential friends, complained about the "horridly agonizing feeling . . . of not being there with the others."[15]

Rilke knew almost from the start that he would not be there, and, more significantly, that the outcome did not hinge on him or any other individual. He was openly dismayed when he was suddenly declared fit for military service in November 1915 and had to report for training a few weeks later at the First Infantry Regiment in Vienna. But luck was on his side. The Austro-Hungarian monarchy went easy on him; in January 1916, Rilke was sent to the war archives, where he was kept busy filling out index cards and ruling lines on paper.

Kafka's insistence on joining the military is one of the most baffling decisions of his life; psychologically motivated empathy will not get us very far. We would have an easier time understanding an act of desperation or a fleeting indifference to his own fate—and Kafka would not have been the first to seek refuge in barracks. But that was not the case. His endeavors to serve in the military were well thought out, purposeful, and spirited, and they were repeated for years on end. He was determined to make it happen. Even gentle persuasion by Marschner—whom Kafka considered an indisputable authority, and who wanted to shield his deluded subordinate from injury and death, refused even to discuss Kafka's wish, and did not even file Kafka's written request—did not dissuade him from his plan.

> I will stick to the following: I want to join the army, to give in to a wish I've suppressed for two years; for a variety of reasons that have nothing to do with me personally, I should prefer to have a long leave. But this is probably impossible for concerns that pertain to both the office and the military.[16]

He noted this down just a few hours before that all-important talk. As on so many other occasions, Kafka made a show of weighing his boss's arguments carefully without budging an inch. But the counterforces were overpowering, and it did not help that he had won the battle with his own misgivings and given confident expression to his will. He would get his long vacation, several vacations, in fact—albeit for reasons he could not imagine at this time—but he would never get to wear a uniform. In August 1916, he would be assigned to "Austro-Hungarian IR No. 28" (the Prague infantry regiment that had been temporarily disbanded in the previous year because of mass desertions), but on the very same day he was deferred from military service, evidently on the basis of a new petition by the Workers' Accident Insurance Institute. Marschner, the managing director, was unyielding, and thus the game was repeated in the following years: On October 23, 1917, he was suspended from active duty until January 1, on January 2, 1918, an extension was granted until June 30, and then "Civilian Kavka" (which is how his name appeared on the recruiting sheet) was permanently relieved of duty.

He did not regard this outcome as good news, or even as a bit of freedom that had fallen into his lap. He must have known how sharply his situation contrasted with that of the Austrian literati, who, regardless of their patriotic proclivities, were so bent on working in the war archives, the war press office, the war welfare office, or on some other innocuous typing job that this desire soon became the butt of jokes. Of course, it is hard to picture Kafka engaging in collective *Heldenfrisieren* (hero adornment), embellishing glorious military achievements for the purpose of exploitation by the press. It would have been quite understandable for one of those numerous writers and journalists whose connections got them special treatment and now served their kaiser as copywriters for war documents to ask to be put back on active duty when moral revulsion got the better of them.[17] But Kafka did not know anyone who could have rescued him from the line of fire and transferred him to a desk job far from the front. He had shaken hands with a few influential politicians and military men but had no ongoing contact with them, and it is unlikely that he would have been able to talk his way out of several months of "basic training" at a barracks, followed by "transfer" to the Isonzo front. In all likelihood, he owed the fact that he reached his thirty-fourth birthday alive to Pfohl and Marschner. Didn't he know that?

Even though his diaries and letters reveal little about the reality of the war, he must have understood its nature right from the start, and by 1915 he had detailed knowledge about it. Like Rilke, he experienced disenchantment when he saw the riled-up masses, and he grasped the fact that the second raucous patriotic rally on Altstädter Ring just under his windows was an organized spectacle.[18] Then came the eyewitness reports, the agitated descriptions from his two brothers-in-law and institute colleagues. There were also reports from Hugo Bergmann, Otto Brod, and other Zionists in Prague, many of whom had enlisted; the horrifying and disillusioning experiences of the Jewish refugees from Galicia back in the fall of 1914; the experiences of the doctor and writer Ernst Weiss in military hospitals behind the front lines; and finally the notebooks kept by Egon Erwin Kisch and Werfel, excerpts of which were read aloud in semipublic circles. Kafka could also find out from Musil what to expect at the Italian front, especially in mountain warfare, the gruesomeness of which boggled the mind. Musil was treated at a hospital in Prague in April 1916, and the two got together at least once during that time.

Even the onlookers crowded around the "model trench" had trouble believing that they were getting a realistic impression of the war, and Kafka most certainly knew better. He was aware that the Austrian army was not just fighting but also spreading epidemics, hounding the public, and hanging people from lampposts and trees "as a deterrent to spies"—on mere suspicion. He knew about hunger, frostbite, sleep deprivation, overcrowded military hospitals, frontline brothels, and tear-gas grenades, and even if he had stopped up his ears so as not to hear more, there were far too many witnesses to this horror. They were in every café; not even the police informers lurking at the next table (whom the Czech satirist Jaroslav Hašek so enjoyed tricking) could stop them from talking. It was simply impossible to hear nothing and remain ignorant, and by 1915 even the censors gave up the attempt to keep the sensory reality of the war from newspaper readers.[19] Kafka's brief trip to the Hungarian base, where for the first and only time he saw a scene completely dominated by the military, was not terra incognita; just a few weeks earlier he had certainly read up in *Die weissen Blätter* on how things looked, in the area from Sátoralja-Ujhely to the Carpathian front.[20] In addition, there was now a hellish official channel to the war for Workers' Accident Insurance Institute staff members who had remained behind:

Chemical industry: People without an arm or foot can be office workers, gatekeepers, or weighers.

Roofers: Maimed or deformed legs disqualify.

Dyers: Those missing an arm or forearm are rendered unusable. (Prosthetic foot with stilt cannot be used.)

Hairdressers, barbers, and wig makers: People who are missing a little finger or an eye can still be used, provided that the second one is completely healthy. Facial disfigurement and the wearing of eyeglasses constitute an inability to work, because the sight of wounded or disfigured hairdressers' assistants drives away customers.

Laborers: Can be used if missing a foot, an eye, or jaw.

Cardboard cutters: One eye is sufficient. Missing left foot would need replacement with a prosthetic leg.

Mechanics: Both arms necessary. Precision mechanics can be one-armed.

Photographers: Retouchers or copyists can be missing the left arm or individual fingers as well as an eye.

Carpenters: Cannot be used if missing an arm, but they can if only a hand is missing. Missing an eye or the jaw is not an impediment.
Dental technicians: Must have both hands, but can have prosthetic legs.[21]

Up until the fall of 1914, it appears, a military deed was regarded as a game of life and death. Soldiers who killed others ran the constant risk of being killed themselves, and the very act of participating in this game held out the promise of honor and fame. The loser, the "fallen soldier," also scored a symbolic win in dying a "hero's death," even if his final maneuver was senseless and suicidal. The "heroes of Langemarck" were actually naive high school students who were restylized as German national heroes and accorded mythic status. A soldier blown to pieces by a grenade while in the latrine became a hero solely because he had risked his life in the service of the common cause and in doing so made the ultimate sacrifice. Every schoolbook stated this as fact, and official letters of condolence to despairing wives and mothers offered heroic status as the only effective consolation, a consolation of a grateful collective memory. People were still far from embracing the heroism of predatory self-preservation of the variety later found in Ernst Jünger's *Storm of Steel*.

One of the first lessons of the world war was that there were many ways to "be killed in action," but there was also the possibility of survival, a complication that stripped the term "heroism" of any last vestiges of an aura. Word got around that someone who laid his life on the line risked winding up with a stomach wound, an arm torn off, paraplegia, or a lacerated face, and this possibility was as sobering as it was obvious. Both the combatants and their families were essentially in agreement to mention these risks as little as possible, and the infantile idea that things of that kind could only happen to *others* was a pathologically widespread conviction in the trenches of Europe. And then there were the administrators and the ideologues of the war, who vastly preferred the "fallen" to the severely disabled, since the latter required material support and remained in the public view as living reminders.

The symbolic overloading of death and the hush-up surrounding the risks of injury by common consent meant that society was left dumbfounded by the extent of these consequences of war. People assumed they were well-equipped, with the medical battalions, field and military hospitals, ambulance service, and the work of the Red Cross, which was protected by international law, and the far less popular "aid to wounded war veterans," which saw to everything that went beyond medical issues. But none of these institutions was prepared to cope with a mass phenomenon, especially not the *social* consequences, which were acknowledged only reluctantly under the massive pressure of events.

In February 1915, the Austro-Hungarian ministry of the interior issued a decree that the branches of the Workers'Accident Insurance Institute add "aid to soldiers returning home" to their range of duties. This administrative idea was born of necessity—there was no time to install new social networks, so they fell back on the available ones—but it also had a subtle social policy logic. The workers' insurance was primarily responsible for the victims of modern technology, that is, for people who had suffered harm from technology in the workplace, including "cripples" in uniform who had suffered severe accidents on the front. The seriously wounded and blinded, the amputees, and the soldiers and officers who could not be rendered fit for military service again by any medical means were "returning" for good.

The task was daunting and required immense administrative effort. The first step was to establish "public crownland agencies" to coordinate care and handle registrations, therapy, retraining, and job placement for disabled veterans. All these functions were in turn subdivided into a series of committees, and, in typical style for Austria-Hungary, entailed cumbersome bureaucratic procedures and the imposition of rigid social distinctions. There were "primary individual hearings," "veteran record cards," and "disabled veterans taxation registers," and there was a sharp distinction between the aides who represented the state agencies and served in a merely advisory capacity (politicians, clinical physicians, Red Cross representatives, and military commanders) and those who actually carried out the tasks at hand.

The ministry of the interior was certainly pleased that this "agenda" was carried out almost exclusively on the premises of the Workers' Accident Insurance Institute, by its in-house staff. This arrangement was by no means a matter of course, and came about primarily because of

sive correspondence (most of which fell to Kafka), poring through professional publications, consulting physicians, and last but not least, making trips and inspections. Kafka's letters and diaries made little mention of these matters, but apparently these new duties took up several hours of each of his workdays up until the end of the war, and people soon sought him out privately for information on the subject of disability pensions.

We would not know much more if Kafka's boss had not decided to appoint him a special agent and entrust him with a delicate mission that would shed some light on what he was experiencing.

> Soon after the outbreak of war, a strange apparition, arousing fear and pity, appeared in the streets of our cities. He was a soldier returned from the front. He could move only on crutches or had to be pushed along in a wheelchair. His body shook without cease, as if he were overcome by a mighty chill, or he was standing stock-still in the middle of the tranquil street, in the thrall of his experiences at the front. We see others, too, men who could move ahead only by taking jerky steps; poor, pale, and gaunt, they leaped as though a merciless hand held them by the neck, tossing them back and forth in their tortured movements.
>
> People gazed at them with compassion but more or less thoughtlessly, especially as the number of such apparitions increased and became almost a part of life on the street. But there was no one to provide the necessary explanation and to say something like the following. . . .

Words from the pen of Vice Secretary Kafka, the opening sentences of a fund drive, printed in a local newspaper.[26] These suggestive words draw in the reader with a familiar image and a poignant feeling. He had done this sort of thing before, but in this new territory, he was stepping onto a minefield of collective emotions, and he needed to inform the public about the gravity of the situation.

It had been known for quite some time that injuries and other traumatic events could lead to grave and sometimes bizarre "hysterical" reactions in seeming disproportion to what had triggered them: crying fits and vomiting, apathy, paralysis, phantom pains, bedwetting, panic attacks. There had been isolated cases of this kind in the wars of

1866 and 1870–1871. Railway accidents and severe workplace injuries were also known to leave people physically "healed" (even when amputations were involved) but psychologically disturbed to the point that they could no longer perform their jobs. Science had not yet come up with a convincing explanation for cases of this kind. At times they were labeled "emotional inferiority," and some people were suspected of feigning psychological injuries in order to claim an accident pension.

With the beginning of the world war and the avalanche of "war neuroses," this picture changed so drastically that the medical profession at least officially called a temporary halt to its methodical hunting down of phonies and "pension neurotics." The psychological and psychomotor impairments that resulted from high-tech warfare and nerve-shattering barrage fire were too widespread and severe. These included facial tics, stuttering, muteness, deafness, blindness, and especially "hysterical tremors" accompanied by violent shivering and uncontrolled trembling that could go on for months and years undiminished, which Kafka described in powerful terms. By 1915, these *Kriegszitterer* (shell shock victims), as they were soon dubbed, had become a "part of street life." The sight of these victims made the processes of habituation and dissociation far more difficult than bloody bandages or empty sleeves. The sufferings of the *Kriegszitterer* were undisguised, as though forcing the public to stare into an open wound, and the state generally took it out on them by withholding badges honoring their service.

Where could these people go? As long as they remained in the clutches of military psychiatry, "traumatic neuroses" were often more fought off than treated with therapy, and patients were subjected to severe electric shocks, placebo operations, induced choking fits, and weeks of total isolation. The public was given only vague and euphemistic (mis)information about these cruel treatments, which in some cases resulted in death, and even the experts who rejected the extremely painful "faradization" with alternating currents (the notorious "Kaufmann cure") had no doubt that these were basically legitimate therapeutic approaches.

It was left to the initiative of individual physicians to test and refine these new methods. One of these physicians was a Dr. Wiener, who was on staff at a small medical unit in the Rudolfinum in Prague. The people of Prague were woefully uninformed about what was taking place here, just a few minutes away from Kafka's office, and what measures were preventing traumatized "soldiers returning home" from actually returning home (provided that the screams of pain did not penetrate through the walls), but Kafka, who was now responsible for therapies, knew a great deal. Although he was spared the ordeal of witnessing the progress of the psychiatric sciences—that was a matter for public health officials—he was in close contact with a whole different world, in which blood and shiny instruments, physical agony and quietly whirring machines, antiquated and cutting-edge technology interlaced. He knew that this world had once been his own imaginative creation, in the fall of 1914, even if he had relocated it to an exotic "penal colony." But this—two, three years later—was reality, and it was torture by today's standards and by his own. Back from the tropics, right there in the center of Prague.[27]

Thankfully, the huge Garrison Hospital on the Hradčany, the chief institution in Prague that treated these patients, steered clear of this kind of therapeutic furor. The few staff psychiatrists were dealing with far too many patients, so the highest priority was given to delegating and thus disposing of the rapidly mounting problem. It was considered especially troublesome to treat the injured and the shell-shocked in the same building because of possible "contagion." Eventually, the mentally ill patients were assigned to wooden barracks at the Belvedere in Prague. These barracks remained under military supervision, which was happy to leave the expansion and maintenance to the Public Crownland Agency. This was the beginning of the "Prague-Belvedere Temporary Psychiatric Hospital," where as many as eight hundred patients were given electrical massages, steam baths, quartz lamps, diathermy, and hydrotherapy—treatment options in contemporary sanatoriums that were familiar to quite a few men in the Workers' Accident Insurance Institute, who had been patients themselves at one time or another.

This was no solution for the Kingdom of Bohemia as a whole, and the paltry subsidies the ministry of the interior was willing to provide made it impossible to implement on a larger scale. Alexander Margulies, the director of the "temporary psychiatric hospital," recommended soliciting donations to acquire and renovate a large sanatorium. But who would entrust his savings to an anonymous office in these inflationary times, even if the people there were as friendly as those at the insurance institute? It was like bestowing gifts on a bank. Pfohl and Kafka quickly realized that their "Committee on Therapy" had to adopt a different, less bureaucratic profile to become accepted and thus attractive to donors, with fewer regulations and more philanthropy. It had to be a charitable organization. Two organizations, one for each of the two segments of the population, would make it easier to appeal to group solidarity. Accordingly, a "Bohemian Association for the Establishment of a Public Sanatorium for Nervous Disorders" was set up for Czech patients, and a "German Association for the Establishment and Maintenance of a Veterans' and Public Psychiatric Institute in German Bohemia" for returning German soldiers—subtle linguistic distinctions in which any educated person in Prague was well versed.

Naturally it fell to Kafka to tackle the issue of propaganda. He very nearly wound up on the "preliminary committee" of the German Association, where he would have served beside a Reichstag representative, a captain, a court counselor, and a business tycoon, but he was able to get out of this assignment in time. Marschner also sat in this select circle, and once the decision had been made to publish another impassioned appeal for funding with as many high-profile signatures as possible, there was little doubt as to who would write it. Yes, we have an official in the institute, linguistically quite adept, perfectly suited to write up a report. He also writes literary texts, and he even won a prize . . .

> Fellow Countrymen!
>
> The World War, in which all human misery is concentrated, is also a war of nerves, more so than any previous war. And in this war of nerves, all too many suffer defeat. Just as the intensive operation of machinery during the last few decades' peacetime jeopardized, far more than ever before, the nervous systems of those so employed, giving rise to nervous disturbances and disorders, the enormous increase in the mechanical aspect of contemporary warfare has caused the most serious risks and suffering for the nerves of our fighting men. And this in a manner that even the well-informed can hardly have imagined in full. As early as June 1916, there were

> over 4,000 disabled veterans with nervous disorders in German Bohemia alone, according to conservative statistical data. And what more is yet to come? How many of these men with nervous disorders are lying in hospitals outside of Bohemia? How many of them will return from being prisoners of war? Immense suffering is crying out for help.[28]

That was not especially original. Wilhelm II had prophesied a full two years before the catastrophe that the next war would be won by the nation with nerves of steel. This prophecy now seemed to be coming true; never before had a war "gotten on the nerves" of the civilian population to this extent, and the longer it went on, the more popular the "nerve-fortifying" elixirs whose omnipresent advertising conveyed the impression that the key battle was actually taking place in the pharmacy. Kafka's message did not offer that kind of optimism, but its rhetoric was just as ingenious. He employed platitudes to depict the new threat looming on the horizon, the *Kriegszitterer*, as a somewhat logical consequence of what everyone knew, or thought they knew: the draining and collapse of soldiers' nerves.

It is difficult and disconcerting to recognize the author Kafka in slogans like these. Of course, a manifesto designed to appeal to a gathering of local dignitaries loyal to the kaiser could not avoid catchphrases, and it is unlikely that the approximately 130 mayors, physicians, attorneys, landowners, bank directors, and district court councillors, who (in addition to Kafka himself) eventually signed the text would have agreed to dispense with patriotic padding. But Kafka was prepared to go even further and appeal to newspaper readers to recall "our victorious armies," "these times, which teach us love of fatherland country," and "the many fine proofs of the public's sense of patriotism." He even claimed that the state had already fulfilled its duty to the disabled veterans, which may be the most unabashed lie he ever committed to paper. But in the center of all his official appeals is the palpable and unbefitting suffering of the individual, whose dignity—here Kafka concurred with Marschner, a social policy expert—had to be preserved even when that individual was completely incapacitated, and who was *entitled* to aid: "No, this article is not a request to the charitable, it is an appeal to duty."[29] Kafka was not ashamed of this morally imperious tone. Evidently no one had to persuade him that the end really did justify the means, and his appeal to the German "fellow countrymen" was one of those very rare samples of his official writing that he chose to share with Felice Bauer.[30]

From a propagandistic point of view, it was clever not to focus the arguments solely on the issues of the war, which could end the very next month, so why donate money? Nervous disorders were also found among proletarian and petit bourgeois civilians who were unable to afford convalescence in a sanatorium, not to mention psychiatric treatment. There was simply no institution to care for patients of this kind (which could have dire outcomes, as Kafka had once experienced in the Dvorský Nursery). That, too, would now change. Once the "soldiers returning home" were taken care of and peace had been restored, the new sanatorium could be opened to the general public, and German Bohemia would have an exemplary "public psychiatric hospital."

Perspectives of this sort were persuasive, and the donations were so abundant that in a matter of months there was enough capital to buy a sanatorium. But *which* sanatorium? Kafka would have been just the man to come up with the perfect solution, but he wasn't asked, because very early on—probably long *before* the association was founded—a venue had been agreed on, one that every neurasthenic in Bohemia was familiar with. And it was no coincidence that the captain serving on the "preliminary committee" of the association and as a high-ranking expert for the care of the war disabled in the army was none other than Herr Direktor Eger from the Rumburg-Frankenstein sanatorium, where Kafka had spent his brief vacation the previous year. We do not know whether Eger recognized his former patient during the negotiations, but Marschner is sure to have pointed out the connection.[31]

Once again, as so often in the past, his job stood in the way of moving ahead with his life. Kafka had had quite enough of the enclosed illusory world of sanatoriums; he was longing for focus, not organized relaxation, and if there was any need for further evidence that true recuperation was not a question of amenities, Rumburg provided it. That was over and done with. And now this obsession with the idea of a sanatorium was coming back to haunt him through an altogether different channel, in the form of a mountain of time-consuming correspondence that conformed to the standard rhythm: Kafka dictated, Pfohl signed, and Marschner negotiated where six-figure sums of money required a certification by rank and title.

The well-coordinated trio came through successfully in this effort, as well. On May 15, 1917, a mere seven months after the establishment of the association, a small, semipublic party gathered in Rumburg to celebrate the transfer of ownership of the sanatorium and commemorate the departure of Eger, the previous director. There were instructive words to an undoubtedly wary staff now preparing for an entirely different clientele and being placed under military supervision. In charge of the proceedings was Dr. Marschner, whose humanitarian commitment was again bearing fruit. Chief Inspector Pfohl accompanied him. The third man remained in Prague to keep an eye on things at the central office, and he surely needed no persuasion to stay there.

The key promise with which the enormous sum of 600,000 kronen was eventually collected was kept.[32] A few months after the end of the world war, in February 1919, Rumburg became a German-Bohemian public psychiatric institute, with sharply reduced costs of treatment for the needy. The objective had been achieved, and that could have been the end of the story. But twenty years later, a new renaming followed, one that the initiators—Marschner, Pfohl, and Kafka—would never have predicted or endorsed: it was retooled as a Nazi "Sudeten German District Sanatorium Rumburg-Frankenstein." But none of them lived to see that day.

"Germany declared war on Russia—Swimming in the afternoon." The height of trivia juxtaposed with a worldwide catastrophe, the personal and the global separated only by a dash. Isn't that the very essence of the writer's alleged naïveté and obliviousness to his surroundings?

It is conceivable for a writer to take the pulse of his era and make it come alive in language and images, yet still be out of his depth when it comes to palpable engagement with the world, although this constellation is exceedingly rare. Far more often someone who is truly at home in two worlds is misunderstood as being "out of touch" in the public, social cosmos, which he shapes and endures in combination with others, and in an interior psychic space dominated by feelings, dreams, fantasies, associations, and ideas, which he inhabits alone. Anyone whose experience inside his head offers as vast and constant a stream of impressions as the world outside cannot stay focused on the here and now. But where is he then? In a different realm.

An individual who appears to be out of touch with reality is rarely in the privileged position of being able to open and close the subtle locks between inside and outside at will. The vortex pulling him inside his head is always palpable, but the reality principle demands that he remain perpetually alert; people expect him to limit himself to things that can be communicated. Anyone who starts talking about daydreams on the street, in a store, or at the workplace alienates people, no matter how intense and meaningful those daydreams are. He remains alien because he understands and acknowledges a second world, and for the most part, and to his detriment, he remains just as alien in that interior world for the same reason. He is present, but neither here nor there.

That condition can culminate in insanity, and Kafka justifiably feared winding up insane throughout his life. But it has little to do with the accomplishments society expects of the individual. Someone who is alienated from the world might function perfectly well as a craftsman, attorney, teacher, or politician, or as a vice secretary of an insurance institute, and his struggle to balance himself—poised like a man with one foot off the ground—can easily remain hidden from view, without a trace, as it probably has in thousands upon thousands of brains.

It appears likely that Kafka knew more details about the actual horrors of the war than the overwhelming majority of authors of his day; he certainly had no need of a "model trench" to gain a realistic idea of the situation on the battlefield, especially once the regulation of the damage done by war had become part of his job. He had seen, spoken to, and negotiated with the maimed and the shell-shocked, and was administratively involved in their lives. It is virtually certain that Kafka had to visit the two "schools for the disabled" in Prague, just a few stops away by streetcar, where instruction was given on how to function with artificial limbs—and here, too, the "Committee on Therapy" did not need to have extensive correspondence—and thus he entered into the zone of silence of the war, which to the population at large, including nearly all his friends and relatives, remained on the level of hearsay.

But the more light that is shed on Kafka's comprehensive overview, the more the naive image of a writer out of touch with reality and unaffected by the war fades away, and the darker it becomes in the psychological labyrinth where knowledge and experience consolidate into resolutions. Kafka knew what it meant to become a soldier, yet there is little doubt that he wished to do so anyway. "It would have been half a lie," he noted after the last unsuccessful talk with Marschner, "if I had asked for an immediate lengthy leave and for my dismissal if it were refused. It would have been the truth if I had given notice. I didn't dare to do either, so it was a total lie."[33] It was the old dream of leaving he had been dreaming on a nearly daily basis since his first encounter with Felice Bauer, and since that night of writing that had produced "The Judgment." But while he dreamed, the world outside was changing. Of course, he should have gone away back then; he had realized that quite some time ago. In 1912, giving notice would have brought him to Berlin, to the greatest possible independence of mind, into an erotic relationship, to the threshold of marriage and family and also to means of sidestepping the war more easily.[34] In 1916, by contrast, giving notice invariably led to the trenches, then possibly to a military hospital, captivity, disability, the void.

He knew it, yet he still did not address the subject, even in his private notebooks, which were safe from the prying eyes of the censors. It almost seems as though at this decisive moment Kafka lost all interest in strategic forecasting, as though his bureaucratic thirst to calculate what the future held and thus to withstand the fear of the unimaginable had been slaked. He knew it. He knew full well what was in store for a man at the front who blanched at the sight of a horse's bloody knee even in peacetime.[35] But there was a second scale on which the dead weights of years of a forced standstill were assembled. What was stopping him? He did not wish to *arrive* somewhere, as he had in 1912; he wanted to get *away from here*, at almost any cost.

Kafka cannot have failed to realize that his behavior seemed downright peculiar. A mid-level official insisting that his superiors send him either to war or on vacation—no wonder even Marschner, who was well aware of what was at stake here, could not suppress a smile, unaware that long ago, Kafka had resolutely added the military profession to the arsenal of his escape fantasies. Back in the spring of 1915, he had declared "war or vacation!" to Felice Bauer, as well, and in a somewhat different vein a few months later (in which he spoke of himself in the third person), he wrote: "At the moment there seem to be only two possible remedies for him—not remedies in the sense that they can undo the past, but they might be able to protect him from future occurrences. One would be F., the other, military service."[36] Felice Bauer (in contrast to the institute director) cannot have been amused to see herself placed in the ranks of *remedies*, and the distancing "he" made the matter even clearer, and thus worse.

Protect him from future occurrences: That brings to mind the nervous threats that Kafka made to Marschner. But his thoughts did not appear to be veering toward suicide; it is unlikely that Kafka could even summon up the energy to visualize a concrete end to his life by this point. He found himself careening down an inclined plane whose slope kept steepening, and *everything* was tugging him in the same direction. He was cooped up in the office for fifty-hour workweeks, his desire to write stifled by headaches, insomnia, and increasing isolation. Kafka welcomed any prospect at all of making a fundamental change and warding off the psychological decline he was experiencing with the agonizingly intensified sense of time of a drowning man. Vacation, marriage, military service ... it made almost no difference which one. Even the lack of personal responsibility on the part of ordinary soldiers, "men in uniform" who need not struggle to justify what they were commanded to do, must have seemed like a sweet temptation to Kafka at this time. "My headaches were no better in Karlsbad than in Prague," he wrote after another business trip. "Things would be better at the front."[37]

So was war a remedy? In the first year of the war, some suggested that the physical fight for survival was an appropriate cure for neurasthenia and hypochondria. It was a simple calculation of trading imaginary concerns for real ones. Moreover, "daily life in the fresh air," which the frontline soldiers enjoyed, was said to work wonders "for many who had been considered homebodies," and even for "chronically ailing pale consumptives."[38] It is unlikely that Kafka was impressed by this sort of nonsense, which even psychiatrists were spreading without any direct experience. He knew that "fresh air" was deadly in many places (namely mixed with diphenylarsenic chloride) and that the din of battle did not always have the desired bracing effect, as was clearly evident from the *Kriegszitterer*.

But Kafka was not immune to the moral pressures, both subliminal and manifest, experienced by every man deemed "fit for military service" who was still at home. This pressure could assume alarming proportions. Carl Sternheim, a supporter of Kafka's, carefully calculated when he could and could not show his face in public. At any time, a critic might wonder in print why this young, seemingly vital man was proving a success in the theater instead of at the front, and that could work to his detriment. In the denunciatory atmosphere of Prague, with finger-pointing every which way and claims that it was the Germans, or the Czechs, or the Jews who were most skillful at shirking military duty, one could wind up being cited as a "case study" by the other side. There goes another one called "indispensable" and granted an exemption—in Kafka's case, a Jew, of course.

Once Italy declared war, this pressure was stepped up markedly, because those who started to doubt that the punitive action against Serbia had really been worth a world war could now point out that the Habsburg monarchy had been deceived and betrayed. Even confirmed pacifists had to concede that the horrifying war in the high mountain regions and the senseless killing at the Isonzo indicated an enforced, defensive war. As a consequence, political and chauvinist reasoning receded into the background, and morality took center stage.

> All arguments now have to stop. Every man who is not an "intellectual" has to report for duty. The time is past for considerations of indispensability and irreplaceability. Everyone and no one is indispensable or irreplaceable. Even the most highly gifted artist or scientist cannot achieve anything higher in his life than to vouch for the moral law, which has been trampled upon.[39]

It is unlikely that Kafka would have wholeheartedly endorsed this appeal to call a halt to thinking, but the shackles of irreplaceability his bosses used to keep him away from the war had become a source of shame, and these lines from the *Schaubühne*, published in Berlin just days after Kafka's military exemption, must have hit a raw nerve (assuming that he read them, which is quite probable). But what was the logical basis of this feeling of shame? If Kafka did know so much more about the physical reality of the war than everyone who issued appeals to patriotism, why this vacillation, this nagging conscience? Why the resolution to act like lemmings *in spite of it all*? Didn't he have any "opinion" about the war?

One of Kafka's defining characteristics was that his decisions, although carefully deliberated, were rarely determined by overall considerations, convictions, or concepts. He never used deductive reasoning for the mere sake of consistency. It seems odd at first that he was adhering to a "pliant" pattern of behavior that was the norm for intimate personal relationships and morally proper within that domain. Even if someone's image of his parents is utterly realistic and free of illusions, and he sees right through the social and ideological dependencies in which they are ensnared, he will still rarely be guided *purely* by penetrating insight in decisions that pertain to his relationship to his parents. This deviation from logic comes as no surprise; it is an integral part of being human, and Kafka himself, who saw through his father, hardly ever used this knowledge as a weapon, nor did it bolster his own weak position in relation to his father. If people need to get along, being right is rarely the point.

Still, it was highly unusual, and disconcerting even to his closest friends, how his logic from the personal sphere spilled over into his job, politics, and the world as a whole, and thus into areas in which it seemed out of place and out of touch with reality. Of course, he had an opinion about the war, just as everyone did: he was a moderate patriot, he feared a military defeat of Austria, and by the third year he regarded the pointless killing as a derailment of world history, a social perversion. In this respect, Kafka did not stand out intellectually. He had neither the prescient political perceptiveness of Karl Kraus nor the elitist mind-set of Thomas Mann or Werner Sombart, both of whom tried to justify the ongoing carnage by invoking ideological constructs and notions of historical compensation.

But Kafka stood apart from the great majority of his male peers—including Max Brod, Felix Weltsch, and other friends in Prague—by virtue of his oddly "unenlightened" social behavior. Neither his general knowledge nor his particular views about world affairs had a noticeable effect on his behavior. It would not have crossed his mind to "rush to join the colors" to defend the Habsburg monarchy—or, as Sombart claimed, the community of "heroes" against a gang of "merchants"—nor did his insights into the most immediate and cruel consequences of the war make him steer clear of the war. Kafka seems to have paid just as little heed to all the political journalism that had swelled to cacophonous proportions under the pressures of events as to the political palaver at the office and at home, which has made some commentators conclude that he was cold and indifferent to the subject.

That view is incorrect. Kafka took the war *personally*, in the strictest sense of the word. Even though he remained impervious to abstract reproofs ("In these trying times, it is imperative . . . when our Kaiser calls upon us . . ."), he was receptive to prelinguistic, gestural, spontaneous outbursts, to which he had always granted a higher degree of truth and considered himself defenseless in the face of their moral implications. Arguments left no impression on him, but gazes penetrated right to his core: the gazes of his father daydreaming about his own time in the military when the two brothers-in-law told about their wartime experiences in Galicia; the gazes at the office when postcards from colleagues on the front, colleagues he was used to seeing in starched shirts, were passed around (Kafka also received these cards, one of which said "And what will tomorrow bring? Who even asks?")[40]; the gazes of young Zionists when the conversation turned to the heroic deeds and war decorations of Hugo Bergmann; the gazes of middle-aged women, the mothers of enlisted sons, to whom it would have been impossible to explain what right he had to stroll across Altstädter Ring; and finally, the gazes of the victims on the steps of the Workers' Accident Insurance Institute, whom Kafka could not avoid because of the nature of his job.

No, he had *not* changed. Had the arguments of the eastern European Jews, even of their most eloquent spokesmen, ever had a profound influence on him? There is barely a trace of evidence to that effect in his diary. Instead, he described their self-confident, skilled gestures and compared them with the awkward public appearance of Brod. That was enough. Had he ever asked Felice Bauer what she thought? He sought her eyes, her hand. "What a marriage requires," he explained, "is personal harmony, that is, a harmony that runs deep beneath any opinions, and thus a harmony that cannot be analyzed but only felt. . . ."[41] He might have added, "That's how I feel about everything, including the Jews and the war." He had to cope with the looks people gave him, and the irrefutable fact that he spent his life, which had lost its direction, sitting around in the office. This incongruity, untruth, and lack of harmony ran *deep beneath any opinions*.

Even his family and Felice Bauer were unlikely to have realized how uncompromisingly Kafka adhered to this logic of intimacy. Because he did not always show it, and as desperately as he sought signs in the gazes and gestures of others that were meant for him, he knew how to withstand reproofs that were aimed *explicitly* at him. He had been told by his father often enough that he had it too good. Now, with the war and shortages, this silly lament expanded into a constant, palpable social pressure, into a generalized indictment that was written all over everyone's face and to which Kafka did not want to yield without a fight:

> Don't laugh, F., don't look upon my suffering as despicable; of course, so many people are suffering now, and the cause of their suffering is something more than whispers in the next room; at best, however, they are fighting for their existence, or rather for the bonds between their existence and that of the community, and so am I, and so is everyone.[42]

Kafka also insisted on his rights. But he made no mention of his envy of those who were fighting for all the world to see. They were the ones he wanted to join up with. This is the only place he would find harmony and truth, and, if luck was on his side, a liberating way out.

> To Police Headquarters in Prague:
>
> In the matter of the petitions regarding merit distinctions in recognition of outstanding service in the area of wounded veterans' care, we nominate Dr. Franz Kafka, vice secretary of the Workers' Accident Insurance Institute for the Kingdom of Bohemia in Prague, for admission to the ranks of the group that has been so recognized.
>
> Dr. Franz Kafka's contributions include overseeing the institute's technical division and preparing and carrying out the agenda

> of the Committee on Therapy since 1915. He is in charge of the correspondence regarding the establishment and management of the clinics. Especially notable have been his contributions in matters pertaining to the veterans' psychiatric hospital in Frankenstein, run by the Public Crownland Agency.

This distinction for Kafka was proposed by the "Public Crownland Agency for Returning Veterans" on October 9, 1918. But since when was the Austro-Hungarian police in charge of awarding decorations? It always had been; the first thing that needed to be ascertained was whether complaints had been lodged against the candidate at any place and time, and to find that out, all Austrian police stations leafed through the relevant file boxes and communicated the results by telegram. Once this nationwide data comparison had produced a negative (which is to say, favorable) outcome, the police headquarters in Prague issued a categorical recommendation on October 20:

> There is nothing in our files to indicate anything negative in either the civic or the ethical regard concerning Dr. Franz Kafka, vice secretary of the Workers' Accident Insurance Institute.[43]

So he had not been "slandered" by anyone. A first-class acquittal and a certificate for a commendation from the highest authorities. Nevertheless, he was denied this prize, as well; just three weeks later, those highest authorities had quietly left, and the pending decorations were forgotten.

CHAPTER FOUR

The Marvel of Marienbad

Seeing as we'd come for pleasure, we had to hurry up and indulge in some.

—Louis-Ferdinand Céline, *Voyage au bout de la nuit*

"I'VE SEEN A GREAT DEAL RECENTLY; FEWER HEADACHES." A laconic note in his diary. What was he talking about? The crippled war veterans? The sights in Prague? The refugees who were leaving? The movies? "What a series of entanglements with girls in spite of all my headaches. . . . [T]here have been at least six since the summer." Girls? Where did Kafka have the opportunity to meet six girls? We do not learn anything on this subject, and biographers have nothing to go on but scattered hints in the extant documentation. There are contours, shadows, and mute gestures; the rest is reconstruction.[1]

Chance occurrences muddle the picture of a past productive life and even consign entire epochs of this life to oblivion: destroyed manuscripts, letters and photographs scattered in exile, ignorant or unapproachable heirs, the early death or anonymity of witnesses, and the greed of collectors. The biographer has little choice but to forge ahead stoically with what remains after this process of disintegration, disappearance, and disregard, yet unable to shake the nagging suspicion that the very point at which the documentation breaks off might represent the most interesting and even crucial episodes.

The darkness that descended on Kafka's life in the summer of 1915 was *not* one of those chance occurrences. He did not find his way out of this self-created and self-sustained darkness for a full year. Kafka was in a state of suspended animation imposed by the war, and his intermittent (though energetic) attempts to get away did not yield tangible results. Evidently he was going about it the wrong way.

He was determined to give notice as soon as the war was over, relocate to Berlin, take stock of his situation there in some garret, and gather new strength. He told Felice Bauer about this plan only when asked directly, as though it were the most natural thing in the world. But it is not enough to know what *would* be done, and the self-assurance that came with Kafka's determination began to erode under the pressure of a crippling uncertainty. When will the time come? What do I do *until* the time comes?

We know very little about what he did and experienced in the winter of 1915 to 1916. This lapse in the documentation stems from his loss of interest in recording the standstill; his rare and grumpy letters and scanty notes barely went beyond the minimum. "It is not as necessary as it once was," he concluded on the very first page of a new notebook, "I needn't get upset; I'm upset enough as it is, but to what purpose, when will it come. . . ."[2] In subsequent entries, we hear about the trench in Prague, the war bonds, the partial literary prize, the somewhat chance publication of "The Metamorphosis," the futile battle with his bosses. There is only a single glimpse into Kafka's everyday life, through which he seems to be flitting like a shadow:

> Utter uselessness. Sunday. More than the usual insomnia at night. In bed until a quarter past eleven, with the sun shining. Walk. Lunch. Read the paper, leafed through old catalogues. Walk, Hybernergasse, City Park, Wenceslas Square, Ferdinandstrasse, then in the direction of Poddol. Managed to stretch it out to two hours. Now and then severe headaches, once a positively burning headache. Had supper. Now at home. Who on high could look down upon all this with open eyes from beginning to end?
>
> Open the diary expressly to lull myself to sleep. But see what happens to be the last entry and could picture thousands of identical ones over the past three or four years. I wear myself out to no

> purpose, should be happy if I could write, but don't write. Can't get rid of the headaches anymore.[3]

Headaches and insomnia were the final remaining constants. Kafka mentioned them on nearly every page, and tried in vain to play up any sorts of "interests" to counter his exhaustion and often hazy consciousness. Even his readings now seemed utterly at the mercy of his moods and state of mind on a given day. He read memoirs from Napoleon's Russian campaign and even drew up a long list of Napoleon's military "errors," then he leafed through the Bible. There is not a single reference to contemporary literature. Kafka now seemed to fear even the pleasant surprises afforded by Flaubert, Dostoevsky, and Strindberg. He went to the theater for a Werfel premiere, but evidently stopped going to the movies altogether.

It is impossible to tell from a distance—and it is perhaps even objectively unclear—whether Kafka's increasing isolation, which is quite evident even in the scanty source material, deepened his depression or grew out of it. Of course, this insight into his own social and mental isolation, which he had formulated back in May 1915, remained as bitter as it was true: "there is no one here who understands me in my entirety." But Kafka was not giving anyone the chance to do so. He relied on a small circle of confidants, especially Ottla, who began to take on a maternal role; Max Brod, who had become more accessible again; and in all probability Felix Weltsch, as well. But Kafka was less and less visible beyond this very narrow circle, and on the rare occasions that he did appear in public—a document indicates that he met with Heinrich Mann in late December 1915[4]—he invariably brought friends along as a safeguard.

Relationships that demanded more from Kafka threatened to disintegrate. He no longer deigned to write to his own family—again, with the exception of Ottla—while the old conflicts continued to smolder, above all the inexorable decline of the Kafkas' asbestos factory because of the war, which still made for heated arguments at the dinner table. But even when decisions of existential import needed to be made, Kafka now consistently steered clear of opposition or disputes; even if he had been able to seek refuge in the trenches, his parents would surely have been caught unawares. He had always been terribly secretive, and Brod had taken him to task for that quite often. But he knew by now that his friendly scoldings were falling on deaf ears.

Ernst Weiss, who was working as a physician in various military hospitals but continued to correspond with Kafka on a regular basis, also became estranged from Kafka. Weiss had little tolerance for neurotic inhibitions and dubious behavior; he regarded Kafka's bond with Felice Bauer as pure folly, and he must have thought it delusional of Kafka to keep dreaming of Berlin through all the breakups and humiliations. Even so, the relationship between the men ripened from an initial position of respect as fellow writers into a friendship that even brought them to address each other with the informal *Du*[5]—an uncharacteristic departure from the distance that Kafka otherwise allowed only with friends with whom he shared deep-rooted and "indissoluble" bonds. The two men had few opportunities to see and speak to each other—on occasion Weiss visited his mother, who lived in Prague—but the distance and his friend's chaotic life made every get-together a festive occasion. This was an ideal state of affairs for Kafka, who craved human contact but feared additional, enduring demands that hit too close to home.

This balance was upset in the spring of 1916. It is certainly no coincidence that their friendship came to an end when Weiss moved to Prague, apparently hoping to spend longer periods of time there and perhaps get a comfortable position as a regimental doctor. It seems likely that Kafka was ambivalent about this move. Unlike Brod, who had long since learned to respect Kafka's need for peace and quiet and his occasional passivity, Weiss could simply not imagine a friendship that was worthy of the name without ongoing contact. He was one of the very few who could give Kafka a moral boost, instill new hope, and bring in new perspectives, but the intensive feedback he expected reflected his own needs and prospects, not those of his sensitive friend, who considered such demanding attention clingy and sometimes even draining. "He was forever trying to win people over, and was forever disappointed," Hans Sahl noted in his recollections of Weiss in his later years. "He both spoiled and tyrannized his friends."[6] It is amazing how fittingly this characterization also highlights the contrast to Kafka, who unexpectedly and forcefully shut the door, and soon thereafter, matter-of-factly and without any apparent sadness, reported the separation to Felice as a fait accompli:

> We shall have nothing more to do with each other as long as I am not feeling better. A very sensible solution.
>
> The rift between us, caused first by me and then by him, and finally prompted by me, was the right thing, and occurred on the basis of an absolutely unquestionable decision, which is certainly not often the case with me.[7]

What had happened? Kafka left the matter vague; letter censorship was likely one of the reasons he opted not to depict the concrete circumstances of the rift. Still, he intimated that Weiss had made "the same crude accusations"—accusations of dishonesty and irresponsible maneuvering—that had made the split in the Askanischer Hof inevitable. But if any resolve could make Kafka, who was feeling worn out psychologically, reach an "unquestionable decision," it was this: he would tolerate no repetition of the tribunal in Berlin.

Weiss's more explicit plaintive letters to his lover, Rahel Sanzara, shed light on what was really going on. Kafka, he explained, had surprised him by refusing to provide a public endorsement of Weiss's second novel, *The Battle*, which in his eyes made Kafka an "evil hypocrite." Hadn't Kafka always expressed the highest admiration; hadn't he even offered to lend a hand with the final revision of the book? Weiss had taken these gestures as signs of collegiality and friendship that seemed to run deep enough to make Kafka more than willing to write up a little review. But Kafka kept him hanging, gave him false hope, then turned him down.

It is certainly possible that Kafka gave him an explicit promise back in the summer of 1914, when the two of them spent a few days at the Baltic—because of sincere enthusiasm for *The Battle*, of which he even had a copy, and perhaps also out of gratitude for Weiss's eulogistic review of "The Stoker." It is even conceivable that Kafka—contrary to his professed inability to analyze literary texts—would have honored his promise if the novel had been published just after its completion. But S. Fischer Verlag dithered for a long time; the catastrophic slump the book trade had suffered since the outbreak of the war forced pro-

was stagnation, mental decay, hard to tolerate even in the mirror of the diary and absolutely unacceptable to any other person. And so Kafka came up with a coping mechanism to avoid all emotional utterances arising from his current state of mind by sending out general reports at increasingly long intervals. Because he had already pondered them over and over, they provided no insight into his own experience.

> [T]here are circumstances in which there is little difference between expressing and keeping mum. My suffering is roughly fourfold:
>
> I cannot live in Prague. I don't know if I can live elsewhere, but the most definite thing I know is that I cannot live here.
>
> Furthermore: This is why I cannot have F. now.
>
> Furthermore: I cannot help (it is even in print) admiring other people's children.
>
> Finally: Sometimes I feel I shall be ground up by these torments on every side. But my moments of suffering are not the worst part. The worst part is that time passes, that this suffering makes me more miserable and incapable, and prospects for the future grow increasingly more dismal.
>
> Isn't that enough? She has no idea what I have been through since the next to last time I was together with F. For weeks on end I've feared being alone in my room. For weeks on end my only sleep is feverish. I go to a sanatorium, and am convinced of the idiocy of doing so. What am I doing there? Is it a place where nights don't exist? What's even worse is that the days are the same as the nights there. I come back and spend the first week in a daze, thinking of nothing but my—or our—misfortune, and neither at the office nor in ordinary conversation am I able to take in more than mere superficialities, and even then only between the aches and tensions in my head. A kind of imbecility comes over me. Wasn't I rather like that in Karlsbad?[13]

Kafka must have been aware that something was amiss here. There were no *people* in this inventory of suffering. Felice, who came to life in social interactions, was surely baffled by how Kafka could speak of suffering without any concrete reference to family, friends, or colleagues, not to mention the perfectly presentable successes he had experienced as a writer, which seemed not to have the slightest bearing on his hermetically sealed unhappiness. She had had to read in the newspaper that he had been (indirectly) awarded a literary prize—which was a far less common and hence more significant event back then—and he mentioned the surprise publication of "The Metamorphosis" (as a magazine piece and a book) so offhandedly that it was almost insulting. Well, she had never asked about his writing . . .

After Kafka's treatise on the fourfold root of suffering, there seems to have been no other letter until December 1915—a full four months later, by which point the Christmas vacation was approaching and, with it, the inevitable question from Berlin he had been dreading. Felice urgently proposed that they meet, because she was "sad" about him. But Kafka turned her down, stating "You shouldn't see me like this," "even now, I could only bring you disappointment once again." Felice nonetheless toyed with the idea of traveling to Prague but eventually gave up and spent a few days skiing in Garmisch instead. "Very commendable," he told her. Then, in January, in response to her almost desperate inquiry, came an updated report that his health was unchanged; he continued to suffer from headaches, insomnia, and internal ailments. "I can't think of any solution, and I don't know where you could see a solution that hasn't been tried before. . . . Naturally the living man in me is hopeful, which is not surprising. But the judging man is not." By early March, his replies had become quite curt: "As long as I am not free, I don't wish to be seen, and don't wish to see you." Finally, another month after that, a farewell by telegram: "not getting a passport, fond regards= franz."[14]

* * *

> Only in an operetta can the happy man be someone who forgets what cannot be changed. This kind of viewpoint would be tantamount to suppressing the evidence, or should at least be regarded as such. In truth, the happy man is someone whose assessment of his own requirements sets the bar so far below a decree from on high that the pleasure of a substantial excess salary results.

If Kafka had been destined to live his life to the age we project nowadays, he would surely have come across this famous definition of happiness, which an Austrian senior administrative officer declares on the closing page of Heimito von Doderer's novel *The Strudlhof Steps* (1951). And he would have been thoroughly amused by it. The comic contrast of intimacy and studied officialese[15] was one of his own stylistic devices, put to especially brilliant use in *The Trial* and *The Castle*. Here, too, there are passages of a deliberately inadequate, dry, lifeless language, the subliminal effect of which readers would find hard to ignore: even before they understand, they *hear* the sound of a misguided mind rifling through paperwork where ultimately life itself is the decision maker—a proof *ex negativo*, a demonstration of what does *not* work.

Form belies content in Doderer, as well. His definition of happiness, obviously inspired by Schopenhauer and the diametrical opposite of the accessible *fun* of an unbridled achievement-oriented society, seems convincing at first, but the glib solution is unsettling. If the measure of happiness really can be *calculated*, is it conceivable that simple subtraction is all that is required to lead more than two millennia of metaphysics to its goal?

But that is not the only question; there are more trapdoors lurking. The inescapable conclusion from Doderer's definition is that it is sufficient to take back one's own hopes and dreams to enhance the likelihood of experiencing true happiness—a purely defensive strategy with limits each of us has to sound out for himself. It is therefore not the cleverest thing to abandon your life dreams altogether—or even to define them in negative terms, that is, to expect nothing but pain and unhappiness, which would make the absence of pain the signal of happiness. Is *that* what he meant?

It almost seems as though the marvel of Marienbad—the happiness that Kafka experienced in the summer of 1916 like a "decree from on high"—provided concrete evidence that Doderer's reflection was no mere mind game bound to culminate in gloomy quietism. But what else could be expected? Is it conceivable that what appears to be a primitive trick of self-restraint is only the reflection of a paradoxical psychological dynamic: resignation in the name of rescue, wallowing in unhappiness in order to ward it off? And how ought we to imagine this wondrous mechanism?

Kafka would have welcomed as happiness any kind of relief back in the spring, even a single pain-free, energetic day. He was in worse shape than ever, both emotionally and physically. He was still refusing to submit to conventional medical treatment, but now he was willing—probably at his family's insistence—to get at least a checkup by a neurologist. The diagnosis—"cardiac neurosis"—was perfectly vague and clarified absolutely nothing.[16] But Kafka was suffering, and it was quite evident to others, which is surely the only reason that his bosses virtually forced him to take an additional vacation. They must have been convinced that even the stern resident physician would not refuse his consent.

It would not have occurred to anyone around him that Kafka was *not in bad enough shape yet*—an idea that was not so outlandish in view of the extant documents, as fragmentary as they are. After all, toward what end was Kafka using whatever residual energy he was able to wrest from his ever more frequent bouts of exhaustion and pain? Essentially to avoid exposure and humiliations and to retain his composure, which explains his sudden rift with Ernst Weiss, his refusal to see his former fiancée, and his uncharacteristically imperious, downright obstinate scenes in the offices of Pfohl and Marschner. But all these tactics were socially defensive: escape from the critical gaze of the others, escape into solitude or anonymity. To keep his composure, Kafka was prepared to sever his remaining ties and even to risk death in the trenches. He gained a modicum of self-esteem, but his fleeting moments of pride came at a high price; he was in the process of destroying any prospect of a fundamental lasting change, a change that, whatever shape it might take, had to include the people closest to him—the very people he was now keeping at bay, whose empathy he was testing in the extreme and who would at some point turn away from him. An honorable resolution not to throw himself into anyone's arms—as long as there *were* still arms available to him.

But in May 1916, just in the nick of time, Kafka's personal facade fell away. Marschner refused to let his rebellious subordinate go off to war. Kafka's prompt refusal to accept special favors was no more than a symbolic gesture. Just a few days later, the temptations became overwhelming; Kafka took a trip to Marienbad for a business meeting, and despite the windy, rainy weather, he was delighted by the town, clean and untouched by war, with its many parks and surrounding woods. It was peaceful here because there were no guests from abroad, and it was "inconceivably beautiful." He had not realized that such places still existed within reach, just a few hours by train from the "pit" in Prague, and after his first look around the place, he knew he would come back soon.[17]

The tone of his messages changed. Kafka had felt a breath of fresh air; he was able to stretch his limbs and get down to writing. But settling into his situation was no easy matter; he had not had much practice in this. How could he convey that to Marschner without sacrificing his dignity? He needed to step up the pressure, and an attack of his body to surmount the final hurdle. From May 23rd to the 28th, a full five days and nights, he was tormented by incessant headaches that made it agonizing to pore over the files and precluded any kind of relaxation on the weekend. Now he had reached the crisis stage, the reserves depleted, further retreat impossible. It was do or die. He would accept the three weeks of vacation he had been offered, with humble gratitude, and travel to Marienbad. "I wanted to stick to my decision . . . but I can't stand it."[18]

Now his psychological defenses began to topple like dominoes. Felice Bauer, who noticed that something of vital importance was going on, used the moment to descend on Kafka with a startling suggestion: what if they were to spend their summer vacation together? It would be the first time they had seen each other in almost a year and the first intimate venture away from the prying eyes of their families. This step would have unforeseeable consequences. But Kafka was all for it, and "exceedingly in agreement, of course," without a trace of misgivings. He eagerly declared that the only possible destination was Marienbad; indeed he was already dreaming of harnessing his utterly wasted productive energies right there, in the distracting proximity of a woman, *this* woman.[19]

Kafka was losing his composure, and enjoying it. He knew that he was once again putting himself to the test, but he did not *want* to know it. He waited patiently for Felice's signal, and within a few weeks he was able to work his way through the outrageous mountains of files and put his office in perfect order—as though for good. Finally, on Saturday, July 1, the final dictations, handshakes with his colleagues, the pleasure of parting. Unfortunately his unsuspecting family demanded its share of him and made him sacrifice half a day of his vacation time to come to the synagogue to attend the wedding ceremony of a highly successful relative. Kafka sat through a long litany ("How goodly are thy tents, O Jacob, and thy tabernacles, O Israel . . .") while staring at his watch.[20] Finally, early on Sunday afternoon, he got away. He sat in a train compartment—third class, as usual—enveloped in the only sound that had never disturbed him: the thumping and rumbling of metal wheels on the tracks. Behind the windows, the city slowly receded.

He sought and found an image that united near and far, the mysterious distance of what appears closest to us and the provocative presence of the unattainable, yet *nearly* attainable, off in the distance: a dialectical image, a thought-image.

Kafka made intensive use of this image, an image of extreme simplicity and supposed innocuousness: it was *the door*, and its noble derivative, the gate. His works have doors that are not closed and nonetheless remain impassable (the gate in "Before the Law" and the door through the peephole of which the *Castle* official Klamm can be seen); doors that open out into impenetrable darkness (Kafka's vision of the cover image for "The Metamorphosis"); dilapidated doors that open by themselves ("A Country Doctor") or are on the verge of falling apart (access to the painter Titorelli's room in *The Trial*); doors that invite torture and death just by touching them ("The Knock at the Manor Gate"); and finally, doors that alter their degree of accessibility from one moment to the next for no apparent reason. In April 1916, Kafka invented a door of this last kind as an anticipatory symbol of what he would experience two months later.[21]

But on his very first day in Marienbad, he came across a new, aesthetically sophisticated variant: "with Felice. Door to door, keys on both sides."[22] Of course, hotel rooms have keys; doors with keys are too common for him to have made a special point of the fact. But this double door, which he inspected with his eyes and ears, was an almost indiscreet symbol, and today of all days, his thirty-third birthday, he was a bit more susceptible than usual to these kinds of references.

Evidently Felice's side of the door was open from the start. She also had obstacles to overcome: going on vacation with a man as an unmarried—not even engaged—couple, and with a person who two years ago was cursed to hell, was not easy to make plausible to the family. At least in a sanatorium, everyone is systematically focused on himself . . . but Kafka had rejected that idea, and conventional considerations or requirements of public morality now interested him so little that he had trouble recalling them. Why didn't she do it his way? Saying nothing at all at home was the safest option—at least not saying anything of any consequence.

No sooner was Felice out of her mother's sight, however, than she blossomed. At the train station in Marienbad, she greeted an anxious Kafka in the tender and natural way he had always hoped for in vain in Berlin. Even the stumbling blocks they had to deal with on their first days in Marienbad—switching hotels, constant rain, and of course Kafka's sensitivities and rigid habits—did nothing to change that. "Tribulations of living together," he noted on the third day, and although he was undoubtedly aware that Felice had far more reason to complain, he twisted the knife a little deeper: "Impossibility of living with F. Impossibility of living with anyone at all."

Above all, it was probably his hyperalert consciousness that kept him in suspense. Kafka knew—and he was unable to push aside this thought by day or by night—that *something* had to happen soon. Of course, the external circumstances were happy as never before, and he himself had brought them about. But that was exactly why the rendezvous in Marienbad was fraught with the stress resulting from the expectations of an experiment that would decide everything: If four years of preparation were not enough to attain something resembling fulfillment under circumstances like *these*, any further hope would be illusory. This would be good-bye forever, a good-bye the meaning and necessity of which would be proved beyond a doubt. What was actually driving him to submit to these "tribulations of living together"? Nothing but "strangeness, pity, lust, cowardice, vanity," he felt, "and only deep down, perhaps, a thin trickle worthy of being called love, inaccessible when sought out, flashing up once in the moment of a moment.—Poor Felice."[23]

A desire for intimacy does not appear on Kafka's list, although he knew that this impulse could mushroom into an almost irresistible craving that would cloud over all his inhibitions and logical counterarguments. No one knew that better than he, and he had already come up with correspondingly oppressive images in *The Trial*. But he had forgotten what it meant to savor fulfillment. He considered sexual desire more irksome than ever (prostitutes—even fictitious ones—had not appeared in his notes for quite some time), and he could not bring himself to fuse that desire conceptually with the bittersweet infatuation in Weimar, the moment of happiness in Riva, the awkward flirtations in Prague just a few weeks earlier, or his own surprising willingness to seek out Felice's company. As keenly as he observed himself, he failed to establish these connections, and the detachment of sex from tenderness, which had had a long tradition in Kafka's bourgeois milieu, certainly played a part in that—even though it was evident in his case only in internalized form, as a mental filter, a blind spot of self-perception. His psychological experience seems split apart by fundamentally incompatible longings: to escape from the hypervigilant cell of his own consciousness; to be understood by other people and accepted in peace; and to be transported by togetherness with a woman—skin to skin, mouth to mouth—in a way that would engage every fiber of his being. Kafka knew all that, yet he refused to accept that they were manifestations of one and the same desire, a desire deeply rooted in the somatic and therefore impossible to conceive of or fulfill.

In Marienbad he crossed this threshold, and Felice, who evidently herself felt longing for the first time, made it possible. And it was high time; it was the final chance, the crisis point had been reached. Kafka could hardly contain himself. "What kind of person am I!" he lamented on a hastily written postcard in pencil. "What kind of person am I! I am torturing her and myself to death." But just a few hours later, they enjoyed Marienbad in the full sunshine, "an afternoon wonderfully mild and lovely."[24] Soon after, the double door opened. They had five days remaining.

> It really seemed to me that the rat was now in its very last hole. But since things could not have become worse, they took a turn for the better. The ropes with which I was bound together were at least loosened; I got my bearings somewhat while she, who had always held out her hands into the utter void to help, helped again, and with her I arrived at a human relationship of a kind that I had never known before and that came very near in quality to the relationship

> we had achieved at our best periods as one letter writer to another. Basically I have never been intimate with a woman, apart from two instances—the one in Zuckmantel (but there she was a woman and I was a boy) and the one in Riva (but there she was half a child and I was totally confused and sick every which way). But now I saw the look of trust in a woman's eyes and could not close myself off. Much has been torn open that I wanted to preserve forever (not individual things, but on the whole); and I know that through this tear will come enough unhappiness for more than a lifetime—still, this unhappiness is not summoned up but rather imposed. I have no right to fend it off, especially since, if what is happening were not happening, I would make it happen on my own, simply to have her turn that look upon me. I did not really know her; aside from other doubts, I was hampered back then by actual fear of the reality behind this letter writer; when she came toward me in the big room to receive the engagement kiss, a shudder came over me; the engagement trip with my parents was sheer agony for me, every step of the way; I have never feared anything as much as being alone with F. before the wedding. Now all that has changed and is good. Our agreement is in brief: to get married soon after the end of the war, to rent a two- or three-room apartment in a Berlin suburb, each to assume economic responsibilities only for himself; F. will go on working as she has all along, and I—well, as for me, I cannot yet say. But if I try to paint a picture of the situation, the result looks like this: two rooms, perhaps in Karlshorst; in one of them, F. wakes up early, heads off, and falls exhausted into bed at night; in the other room there is a sofa on which I lie and feed on milk and honey.[25]

Brod must have been shocked by this lengthy and remarkably orderly report, not only because torment and desire appear so intertwined, but even more because he was learning for the first time about events whose psychological repercussions Kafka had not revealed for three whole years. No one had known about the "torture"; Kafka worked through his feelings privately. And there is no doubt that Brod, who had at least two erotic relationships besides his marriage, had to first translate Kafka's austere language, ricocheting between sharply contoured images, into his own experience. The sexual connotations were unequivocal but oddly focused on the female gaze, and hence on the most immaterial elements. An attempt to be discreet? Perhaps. But if Brod had been able to leaf through Kafka's diaries back then, he would have found this: "the very gaze from her soothed eyes; the opening up of womanlike gazes," Kafka wrote in describing Felice.[26] Right to the end of his life, this gaze remained the symbol of everything good, the assurance that redemption was not only conceivable but feasible, "once in the moment of a moment." For him, *this* was the marvel of Marienbad. And the extant note about Felice's "fine body" is found only on a slip of paper, written shortly before his death.[27]

He held fast to the memory of her gaze, and he took it astonishingly well that the "feminine mystique" was bound to close up once again at some point. Marienbad was no paradise; their daily routine was as mundane as anywhere else, even at their elegant hotel, Schloss Balmoral (Felice had evidently insisted on the amenities this hotel had to offer). They took walks, roamed through the woods, visited two tourist cafés—the Egerländer and the Dianahof—recommended in their Baedeker travel guide, struck up casual acquaintances with people at nearby tables, and read the newspapers together (the inferno of the Somme had just begun, but no one here could or would imagine that). Late in the evening, they sat facing each other, on Felice's balcony, at a little table with an electric lamp. He accepted the fact that she had yet to forgive him completely for the old suffering; he had nothing against writing to Anna Bauer and addressing her as "dear mother," the way a son-in-law would—after all, they had *de facto* renewed their engagement, even if Kafka strictly avoided using this word—and he even got through a visit with Felice to the nearby health resort in Franzensbad (where Julie Kafka and Valli were staying, and casting searching looks at him) with a feeling of ease that would have been unimaginable to him just a few days earlier. He wrote to Brod that it was "extraordinary, so extraordinary that it really terrifies me at the same time."[28]

This state of untouchable and anxiety-free floating on air did not end when Felice left. To his disappointment, his insomnia and headaches still plagued him even though everything was now going well. Moreover, because of an apparent mixup by the hotel management, Kafka had to spend the remaining week in the much noisier room Felice had occupied, with guests on both sides, behind (now firmly shut) double doors. But when he sat on "her" balcony in the evening, in "her" seat, he could again see her eyes trained on him, which gave him a sense of peace. Years later, Kafka still considered the six happy days they spent together and the eight happy days he spent alone the greatest unsolved mysteries of his life.[29] Fourteen days—nothing in comparison with the hundreds upon hundreds of nights from which they were wrested, but an astonishing, wonderful, and unique experience for a nervous self whose time did not fly by but entailed struggle every step of the way, and the only relaxation he experienced came as complete exhaustion.

We are similarly mystified. What had happened to those seemingly insurmountable *objective* hurdles that had beleaguered Kafka for years and made it impossible for him to move forward with marriage? The well-founded fear of a life at the office, of the burden of providing for his family, of a family trap sapping his creative energies, of the end of writing? Hadn't Kafka himself declared just a few months earlier, "desperately, like a caged rat," that the ongoing outward "lack of freedom" was the essence of his unhappiness?[30] And hadn't he stylized the process of deciding between marriage and literature as an essential self-mythologizing?

Max Brod, who not only knew this litany but also chimed in himself on occasion, must have been dismayed when he caught on to the meaning of the happy message. Had Kafka succumbed to a momentary temptation, or had he really forgotten? Not at all. He had burst out of his chains and found a way out that none of his friends could have imagined—a solution beyond any conventions. Better still, he had a woman at his side who supported this solution and, to all appearances, even wished for it. "[E]ach to assume economic responsibilities only for himself," was the pivotal sentence in Kafka's letter. "F. will go on working as she has all along. . . ."

That was a shocking option, of which Brod and Weltsch, both married men, could only *dream*, realizing it would entail scandal. Felice, who put off her mother's questions this time with remarks along the lines of *no, no details, we don't know yet, we shall see, when the war is over*, was aware of that as well. Of course, Kafka acted much the same way. Julie and Valli, who visited him on his last day of vacation, were given only the scanty information that they had reconciled and that there would likely be a wedding some day.

This casual attitude would have been unthinkable before the war, not to mention the secret financial arrangements through which Kafka and his fiancée were essentially turning their backs on their social background. A man's ability to provide for his wife and a woman's facility in maintaining a domestic haven and supervising the children's education in keeping with their station in life were still central elements of the bourgeois way of life and features that clearly set them apart from the proletarian milieu. Of course there were respectable families that lived exclusively off the wife's inheritance, but even in those cases the male function of securing the family's livelihood remained intact as the facade; and of course, bills and checks continued to be signed by the husband. It was out of the question for a wife and mother to enter the job market. That would arouse social or even moral suspicions and taint the man with a hint of pimping. The only exceptions were in metropolises, liberal academic milieus, artists' circles, and marginal subcultural networks under the sway of the *Lebensreform* movement, which promoted a back-to-nature lifestyle. But there were no models of that kind in the Prague bourgeoisie; the rights and duties of the provider still applied as much as they ever had. Even Max Brod made a point of stating that he was married while he was involved in royalty negotiations. This provincial gesture would have been near inconceivable in Vienna.

It must have been especially shocking for the older set to watch these conventions crumble and grow obsolete so quickly; this was one of the most immediate, perceptible consequences of the war. Suddenly women were needed on the labor force, even in areas that were previously off-limits to them: the countless number of female munitions workers working day and night were stylized as legendary heroines of the home front in all the countries at war. But above all, the sudden public presence of women resulted in social turmoil. Passengers were flummoxed the first time they took a streetcar conducted by a woman, not only because they were fearful (and their fear was fueled by physicians and psychologists), but because it was an anomaly, an alarming and irreversible break with tradition. Even though the conservative press did its best to assure them of the opposite, everyone understood that women who took on these jobs in place of the men on the front were not just "chipping in." They would not be vacating these newly conquered spots, not even after the expected victory that would restore peace. Things would never be the same.

The surprising public recognition now bestowed on domestic work also reinforced this suspicion. No one (apart from a few feminists) had thought of reading the term "housewife" as a job title. Shopping, cleaning, cooking, and taking care of the children was how married women typically spent their days; these were gender-specific services learned by imitation, even if they were delegated to household staff. By 1916, however, with the onset of the economy of scarcity, quite a few of these skills were classified as essential to the war effort. The entire "women's sphere" was abruptly upgraded in public discourse and became a political and thus *serious* subject, with predictable consequences. Housewives now had to read the business section of the daily newspaper to find out which groceries were being rationed, what market prices the authorities had set, on which days baking cakes was forbidden, and what penalties they would face if they spread a "defeatist attitude" in the longer and longer lines composed almost exclusively of women. Even the very core of domesticity, the realm of sexuality and reproduction, came under increasing scrutiny. For the first time, women with many children enjoyed official tributes; for births, and even for breast-feeding, there were government allowances. If an unwed father was a soldier, generous state subsidies were paid—while infidelity, which would weaken a married man's morale on the battlefront, was decried on both moral and political grounds.

The fact that the conditions of the war necessitated allowing—and imposing on—the "weaker sex" a multitude of new, important, and *visible* functions gave the emancipation of middle-class women a far more powerful boost than the organized women's movement, which was by and large stuck in traditional values rooted in love of country and loyalty to family, would ever have been able to achieve. The historical sources clearly show that this process was extremely significant in shaping social history. But the picture blurs once you examine concrete effects in everyday life and changing mentalities. How else can it be explained that a woman like Felice Bauer, who tided over her entire family from time to time and even *before* the war held a professionally responsible and unusually "advanced" position, waited until the war to even the score in her social and moral behavior, that is, to avail herself of the latitude to which she had been entitled economically for quite some time? After all, she had experienced a less formal, laxer, and somewhat more matter-of-fact interaction between the sexes for years in her urban professional milieu.

Most likely, the economic shift alone is not enough to explain such sweeping changes within a single generation. In fact, it is conceivable (and in the case of Felice Bauer, even likely) that the "egalitarian" drift of the job market was regarded not only as liberating, but also as threatening and deracinating, which would explain a woman's desire to cling to tradition at least on a personal level and play the role of the wife, the daughter, the lady, the fiancée. There had to be another major trigger to promote this change deep within individuals, namely in the arena of sexual identities and mentalities, a change that modernized society had been preparing to accept as a *possibility* for a long time.

This trigger was the war, and its brutal dissolution of ethical constraints. Why adhere to laws that might not even apply by tomorrow? Why remain faithful to a man who might be dead or in captivity? Why deny yourself a pleasure that will require a ration coupon the following month, or no longer be available at all? Why save if everything is becoming more and more expensive, why economize while others profit outrageously from the war? And finally, why all the long-drawn-out courtship rituals in a world that has fallen apart, in which people, institutions, and values disappear and where any planning that extends beyond a few months is built on a shaky foundation?

It won't make any difference now. This feeling first took root in the private sphere and, by 1916, typified a dramatic shift in social mentality that no counterpropaganda could stop. Questionable liaisons, hasty marriages, and a markedly increasing percentage of illegitimate births were only the outward, visible side of a far more wide-ranging social upheaval. People had become hedonistic, the conservative newspapers groused, and hedonism was the worst sin of all at a time in which hundreds of thousands were laying their lives on the line. Was this really hedonism? Surely not. People took whatever was still there, because they knew it wouldn't be around for long. And in the proximity of death and destruction, life becomes livelier. That was the sum of it.[31]

held everyone in its sway, the ability "to make history" and to move one's own vassals around like metal shavings in a magnetic field, the only exception being the immortal Goethe (from whose visits the memorable Hotel Weimar derived its name), who was granted this lofty status despite his lack of retinue. That underwent a fundamental change much later, after several additional decades of operating the health resort, and today's travel guides for the Czech town of Mariánské Lázně point out that Chopin, Gogol, Ibsen, Mark Twain, Johann Strauss, Nietzsche, Dvořák, Mahler, and Freud—all famous but without wielding power—also spent weeks or months living in Marienbad ("tarrying" had gone out of fashion). And at the end of this long list is a Jew from Prague, the least powerful of all. But he had a very idiosyncratic concept of prominence. He wrote to Felice, who had just left:

> Imagine, we were not even aware of the most distinguished spa guest in Marienbad, a man in whom so many place their trust: the rabbi of Belz, now the chief representative of Hasidism. He has been here three weeks. Last night for the first time I joined him and some ten of his entourage on his evening walk.[1]

They had really missed out on something—inexplicably, in light of the fact that the "Israelite" lodgings and restaurants were just a few minutes from the center of town. But that small, higgledy-piggledy grouping of houses was not a sightseeing attraction and it took a written request by Brod to get Kafka to visit it.

This was not his first opportunity to see Hasidic authorities and their followers up close. There were Hasidim in Prague, as well, who were washed ashore with the waves of war refugees and wound up in the cheap neighborhoods on the outskirts of the city, but they kept to themselves, steered clear of social spots, and were never even seen in the Reform synagogue, which they considered impure. There were certainly plenty of Jews, especially in the German-speaking historic city center, who knew about their presence only from newspapers.

Not Kafka. In 1915, the year before Marienbad, an intermediary named Jiří (Georg) Langer had offered to provide him and other interested parties in Zionist circles a glimpse into the lives of the sectarians. Langer was a Western Jewish renegade from Prague, who, to the horror of his middle-class Czech parents, had become a follower of a

Galician "wonder rabbi" at the young age of nineteen and, soon after, began to parade around his hometown in a caftan, with side curls and wide-brimmed fur hat, surrounded by the scent of onions. Langer was a phenomenon unto himself, albeit a maddening one: fanatical, self-sacrificing, demonizing of women, a fundamentalist par excellence. Not even the army could whip him into shape; no threat of punishment made an impression on him, especially not on the Sabbath, and after a few months he was labeled "mentally bewildered" and discharged. Of course Langer, who had an enviable knack for picking up Hebrew, had studied Hasidic scriptures and arcane kabbalistic writings, which surely piqued Kafka's curiosity, and Brod's even more, because those were the heart and soul of a Jewish tradition that remained largely inaccessible even to the cultural Zionists of Prague. The tendentious anthologies of Buber—romanticizing versions of Hasidic legends, with language Kafka found "unbearable"—still dominated the cultural Zionists' image of a specifically Jewish "spirituality."[2]

If Buber's folklore were taken at face value, the reality of eastern European Jewish life, such as the sight of a small group of followers rallying around the rabbi of Grodek in a dreary inn in Prague-Žižkov, could only be disillusioning. Langer, who assumed the role of tourist guide, steered his somewhat reluctant acquaintance to a circle of men who were dressed in black, praying loudly, then lowering their voices into a disconcerting whisper. They came just in time for the "Third Meal" of the Sabbath, a holy custom that was utterly incomprehensible to outsiders, in which the table of the *tzadik* ("righteous one") and the food he passed around took on the mystical quality of altar and sacrifice. But Kafka and Brod were nonplussed. Kafka in particular was much more preoccupied with the peculiar relationship between cleanliness and dirt that he observed here than with the rituals, which meant nothing to him. He was reluctant to help himself to the fish from the shared dish, in which the rabbi had just rummaged around with his bare fingers, and failed to realize that even this physical contact was not unplanned, but a sacred act. "When it comes right down to it," he remarked to Brod on the way back to town, "when it comes right down to it, it was like being among a wild African tribe. Blatant superstition."[3]

Kafka's eyes were trained on the rabbi himself: what really qualified this person above all others; what were the visible features, the perceptible characteristics that established his authority? "What makes a rabbi is a nature that is as strongly paternal as possible," he noted in his diary. It is unclear whether this was his own view or one of Langer's emphatic clarifications.[4] In either case, it was an idealization, because Kafka surely knew that in the centers of Hasidism, at least thirty in Galicia alone, the dynastic principle had applied for generations. Not only was the office of rabbi and his position of authority inheritable, but also the status of the miracle-working *tzadik*, who had direct access to the higher spheres. In these provincial yet relatively glamorous "courts," many different rulers had been venerated, rulers who were not always paternal and who also required financial contributions from their followers.[5]

Kafka's detailed report from Marienbad shows that after the disillusioning excursion to Žižkov he maintained a lively interest in the mystery of authority. The prominent spa guest Shalom Rokeach, the rabbi of Belz, was one of the most influential figures of Hasidism, and one of the most uncompromising. It is hardly a coincidence that the youthful convert Langer chose this man to be his teacher, because the "court" of Belz, north of Lemberg, near the Russian border, adhered rigidly to time-honored traditions, and its ritualistic Hasidic daily life was immune to any innovation (Hasids even rejected the use of silverware). Belz was Jewish territory in its own right, a place in which time had seemed to stand still for centuries, and attracted a steady stream of pilgrims even from abroad. But as early as the first weeks of the war, the village was overrun by Russian troops, the rabbi fled to Hungary, and his congregation was scattered.

His health was likely the sole reason that brought the rabbi to Marienbad; the awkward attempts of the Hasidim rushing to fetch him the healing waters he required takes up a remarkable amount of space in Kafka's thirteen-page report to Brod. He would abstain from any interpretation, he warned at the outset, and stick to what he could see with his own eyes; "but one sees only the tiniest details, which is certainly significant in my opinion. It speaks for truthfulness even to the most idiotic. Where there is truth, all that can be seen with the naked eyes is details."[6] That sounded convincing, and Kafka certainly appreciated the rare opportunity to observe such an exotic figure up close. Langer smoothed the way for this contact when he suddenly turned up in Marienbad, and access to the rabbi was also facilitated by the fact that the rabbi could not shield himself here as he normally did. Beyond any respect Kafka felt, his delight in the scenic presentation was also aroused: the sixty-one-year-old rabbi, stout, in a silk caftan, with a white flowing beard and a tall fur hat, striding through the woods in the pouring rain, accompanied by a small group of obsequious *gabbaim* who had to walk next to or behind him, one carrying a chair, another a dry cloth, a third a glass, and a fourth a bottle of water . . . that was certainly comic. But where did Kafka see any truth here?

> He inspects everything, but especially buildings; the most obscure details interest him. He asks questions, points out all sorts of things. His whole demeanor is marked by admiration and curiosity. All in all, what comes from him are the inconsequential comments and questions of itinerant royalty, perhaps somewhat more childlike and more joyous; at any rate they unquestioningly reduce all thinking on the part of his escort to the same level. L[anger] tries to find or thinks he finds a deeper meaning in everything; I think that the deeper meaning is that there is none and in my opinion this is quite enough. It is absolutely a case of divine right, without the absurdity that an inadequate basis would give to it.

Once again, this was Kafka's characteristic unerring gaze at work, a gaze that he could train on his own father, the high school teacher at the lectern, the idolized founder of anthroposophy, the eastern European Jewish spokesmen in Prague, or the affable president of the Workers' Accident Insurance Institute. It is the gaze directed at power, the gaze that captures the essence of the emptiness behind the scenes without settling into a state of smug complacency. Kafka felt deep empathy with the "serene, happy faith" directed so single-mindedly at a bare center. He was familiar with it, and people in Marienbad who kept their distance from the Judengasse would have admitted that they were as well: it was the childlike feeling with which they had paid tribute to *their* Kaiser and listened spellbound to the jovial catchphrases he had polished over the decades, while disdaining the subservience of the Hasidim.

But that was not the kind of information Brod was seeking. Of course, he valued Kafka's unerring powers of observation, and when he compared the report in the *Berliner Tageblatt* that came out at the same time, in which an obviously uninformed correspondent went on about the "wonder rabbi's mysterious eyes,"[7] he knew whom he could rely on. Kafka picked up on the fact that the *tzadik* was *squinting*: he was blind in one eye, and that was all there was to the mystery. But what interested Brod most of all—and what he had hoped to find at the Žižkov inn, as well—was the vision of an original, unadulterated, authentic Judaism. Kafka did not address this subject.

Did the Hasidim live at the source of the Jewish spirit, of Jewish folk culture? That was a point of contention even among cultural Zionists and advocates of a Jewish nation. People marveled at the radicality and self-assurance with which they turned everyday activities—song, dance, and prayer—into rituals of worship. An unending Sabbath, an unending celebration of fusion with God, without the sting of self-doubt, devoid of any feeling of tragedy, in childlike irresponsibility. The Hasidim interpreted the Torah and Kabbalah literally; they lived out what others only handed down. But Hasidism had also suffered the fate that inevitably corrupts any religious ecstasy that is rendered everlasting: it developed from a mystical revivalism into a rigid cult that kept its adherents in a blatant state of dependence and ignorance. Buber had tried to maintain a distinction between the despotic rule of the *tzadik* and an original, socially innocent Hasidism, but this argument sounded far too much like an honor-saving device and, on closer inspection, proved historically untenable.

The fact that the Hasidim roundly rejected any form of Zionism (which was then regarded as an impermissible anticipation of the work of the Messiah) also unsettled Brod, who clung to idealist thinking. The well-intentioned evening discussions at the Jewish People's Association, which were designed to mediate between East and West, had proved to be out-and-out failures, and Brod had to accept the fact that he was dismissed as a typical Western Jew by the Orthodox immigrants, no matter what he said. Even worse was that the Hasidic leaders began to take an active political role; they opposed Zionist-minded candidates whenever the opportunity arose. The "wonder rabbi" of Belz even formed alliances with Catholic government officials, which must have amused the liberal Jews of Prague but horrified the Zionists. Gradually this man became a formidable opponent—

long before he turned up in Marienbad—and Brod was now keen to see for himself what went on in his inner circle.[8]

On two occasions, Kafka joined the rabbi's evening walk with Langer (he was the only Jew in short garb), then he had seen quite enough. What he found here was not some sort of mysterious archetypal Judaism, but a spiritual disposition that to his mind ran deeper than all forms of limited sectarianism, *deeper than Judaism itself.* Brod would have been bewildered to learn that in the same week that Kafka was observing the *tzadik* and listening to the agitated Langer, he was reading a book he had chosen expressly to bring to Marienbad from the university library in Prague, a biography of Countess Erdmuthe von Zinzendorf, a Christian sectarian and co-founder of the pietistic community in Herrnhut. Brod regarded that as an utterly different, distant realm, but in Kafka's view, it represented the same frame of mind, the same totality of thinking, feeling, and living, and the same truthfulness. In a report to Brod, he had claimed in passing to be using the key concepts "truth" and "truthfulness" synonymously, and he meant it. Kafka had been convinced for quite some time that truth could not be the extract of philosophical or religious judgments but rather had a fundamentally moral and social dimension. Truth cannot be taught; it has to be lived. It is a force field whose source remains hidden, but its radius is the only conceivable place for a life befitting a human being—irrespective of all the oddities that may ensue in a life like that. Examples that touched on Kafka's own realm of experience included vegetarians, eastern Jewish actors, calisthenics devotees, and pietists and other mystics. A true life, *dans le vrai*. Now that Kafka and Felice Bauer had decided to marry, he tried to persuade his bride-to-be of this, as well.

Kafka turned preachy, and the small, often self-ironic admonitions he had interspersed in earlier writings as running gags suddenly took on a tone of urgency. Felice had known him long enough to realize that he loathed ordinary chit-chat, and that when he talked about aspirin, fresh air, and third-class train rides, there was invariably an underlying issue of totality. Now the issue of totality was becoming explicit, and the disparity between the plain everyday matters that were so important to Kafka and the ponderous arguments *why* they were important to him loomed larger than ever. He admitted that he had something against needlework. And a life without a proper lunch would not do either. He wrote her from Marienbad requesting that she stop crunching lumps of sugar with her teeth, even if that was just the beginning, because "the path to the top is unending."[9] He was being dead serious.

She promised to do better. She accepted the idea that pure sugar could not be beneficial for a set of teeth that was not in the best shape anyway (she was constantly running to dentists, although she did not like to admit it), but Kafka seemed to believe that these kinds of small, painless acts of self-discipline were merely the first rungs of an endless ladder that somewhere, up above the clouds, led to the realm of perfection. Felice Bauer began to get the uneasy feeling that his intentions were didactic, and her suspicions were quickly borne out. No sooner was his Marienbad freedom over, no sooner had Kafka returned to his desk in Prague in late July, than he began to come up with actual lessons.

He asked her to pay a visit to Friedrich Feigl, a painter in Berlin whom Kafka had known as a schoolboy and whose work he admired from afar, and to pick out a picture by Feigl that could serve as "a standard Jewish wedding gift" for a cousin, and he assured her somewhat ambiguously that she had "an unerring eye." It is odd that Kafka put less emphasis on the painting itself—which would cost a month's salary—than on Felice's visit to the painter's apartment and his wife, or rather on the impressions Felice would gather there. She should just go there, and she would "see a great many valuable things," he assured her. What sorts of things? She wanted to know. The pedant from Prague explained, "In my opinion, what's worth your while to see is the exemplary nature of the totality, the design of a household management based on a great deal of truth, little of which is tangible."[10]

Once again, Kafka was invoking the concept of truth, as he invariably did in connection with bestowing the highest praise, yet he was quite vague about his criteria for distinguishing the true from the untrue. He simply introduced the concept as though it were self-evident. And he had to admit that he did not even have a clear idea of the exemplary "household management" of the Feigls; he knew the wife only in passing, and the apartment in Berlin not at all. It was simply the *form* of life together that he had in mind, the seemingly successful blend of marriage and artistic work, the concrete utopia, the secret of which he had wanted to draw out of Feigl more than once.[11] But a utopian vision seeks enactment, and Felice Bauer, who faithfully did what Kafka had asked, found the painter in a mood that seemed anything but happy. These were certainly nice people, but she could not for the life of her discern any sort of "exemplary nature"—and she failed to see any guideposts for her own future marriage. Once again, as so often in the past, Kafka's didactic dodges made no impression on Felice's sober judgment. But he had one last trump card to play, and it would prove to be a true game changer, to their astonishment.

While they were together in Marienbad, he had told her about a Jewish Home that had been established in May 1916, on Dragonerstrasse 22 near Alexanderplatz (now called Max-Beer-Strasse), in Berlin's infamous Scheunenviertel, which had had to absorb an enormous number of eastern European Jews—both refugees and armaments workers hired in occupied Poland—since the beginning of the war, and was especially hard hit by the increasing scarcity of food. Siegfried Lehmann, a young physician, had become the director of the home, the main task of which was to take care of eastern European Jewish children and teenagers, which was an endless task because the comprehensive safety nets of the Jewish community had long since been unable to ameliorate the suffering resulting from the war, and even orphans could no longer count on finding shelter in a Jewish home, that is, in the home of *any* Jew who felt responsible. These children faced the prospect of utter neglect. The home would fill in by caring for them, educating them, guiding them in their search for practical work, and providing them clubs and companionship and mutual support from children their own age. The success of this project depended on donations, volunteer work, and the idealism that arose from the concept of a Jewish nation.

Kafka knew from personal experience how dedicated and motivated—and thus malleable—Eastern European Jewish children could be. More than once he had looked on as Brod tried to impart a sense of Western language and culture to a group of Galician girls stranded in Prague, some without their parents. Kafka even went on group excursions with the teenagers. The task delighted him, not only because it was socially useful and earned their gratitude—Kafka had experienced that in the "war relief effort," as well—but especially because he felt free here, and beyond the confines of his father's conventional world that allowed for no new ideas. In this lively encounter between western and eastern European Jews with an unsettled outcome, directions were mapped out, and the teacher was also the student. It was not some theoretical principle determining the outcome of the experiment but life itself, the living example that people were offering each other.

Kafka was heartened by Felice Bauer's initially positive, if wary, reaction to this project and hoped she would take an active role. In Marienbad, their trust and intimacy had blossomed; now they needed an intellectual bond, a unity of purpose that was deliberate, deep, and stable and would concretize the symbiosis they sought. He had long believed that a marriage could not be justified on any other basis, and so he had no reason to conceal his fervent hope: "on the whole, and beyond, I can think of absolutely no closer spiritual bond between us than the one created by this work."[12] *This work*: He was, of course, no longer referring to literature. That dream was over.

Kafka provided Felice's address to the Jewish Home, and no sooner was Felice back in Berlin than she received an invitation to visit it. He did not let up; nearly every day he pressed for news, gave her advice, and not even her repeated promise to write to Lehmann and to look into the matter "quite actively" was enough for Kafka. Why write? Just go there![13]

But much as she sympathized with the cause, there was no way that this efficient and alert worker could do so without making further inquiries. Kafka was so exuberant about the idea of the home that he failed to realize that he was sending her into a poverty-stricken neighborhood, an area she would normally not set foot in, with countless peddlers, Polish prayer rooms, kosher poultry stores, and backyard *mikvahs*. Unlike Kafka, Felice pondered the practical problems that lay ahead. Instructing children and discussing pedagogical issues with other helpers required a certain degree of theoretical education, which college students were more likely to have. Would she even be taken seriously in this circle? Then there was the question of Zionism. She had developed some interest in the Zionist movement years earlier, and had even seriously considered a trip to Palestine, to the astonishment and delight of her friends in Prague, but the ideological policy disputes left her cold. She was not well informed, and since this project in Berlin was squarely aimed at young Zionists—ideologically guided by Martin Buber and Gustav Landauer—she would face outsider status in this regard, as well. Last, but by no means least, this was a group of children raised in religious households, primarily Orthodox, who had been raised with Jewish prayers and rituals and were conversant with names and concepts from the Old Testament. These children were bound to ask her, a Western Jew, questions that might prove embarrassing and could not be answered without an open admission of skepticism and ignorance.

Felice Bauer's doubts—and presumably her blunt question about what he thought of Zionism—evidently prompted Kafka to take a stand. He tried to ease her fears by explaining that it was not a matter of Zionist conviction at all. "Through the Jewish Home, other forces, much nearer to my heart, are set in motion and take effect. Zionism, which is accessible to most Jews today in at least its outer fringes, is merely an entrance to something far more important."[14] With this nice thought, Kafka was once again conjuring up a bent of mind that went beyond any concrete convictions. But when Felice (accompanied by Grete Bloch) finally went to visit the home and to hear a lecture by Lehmann, she heard the cultural Zionist turns of phrase, all revolving around the concept of *Volk* as a source of strength, and had to admit that she had felt estranged from this type of rhetoric for quite some time.

Kafka disagreed. This newly discovered solidarity was buoying his spirits, and he declared that it was purely about humanity and thus something absolutely fundamental: "You will see people in need of help there, and opportunities to give help sensibly, and within yourself the strength to render this help—so help. That is quite simple, yet more profound than any basic ideas." And he appended this appeal to Felice's social soft spot—she was pliable here, as he knew—by summoning up all his eloquence and continuing with his own lecture, a lecture in which he pulled out entirely new stops. This was undoubtedly the first time that she was seeing *this* side of Kafka:

> As far as I can see, it is positively the only path, or threshold to it, that can lead to spiritual liberation. The helpers, moreover, will

attain that goal earlier than those who are being helped. Beware the arrogance of believing the opposite; this is most important. What form will the help in the Home take? Since people are sewn into their skins for life and cannot alter any of the seams, at least not with their own hands and not directly, one will try to imbue the young people—at best respecting their individual characters—with their helpers' spirit and more indirectly their way of life, that is, to raise them to the standard of the contemporary educated western European Jew, of the Berlin variety, which admittedly may be the best type of this kind. That would not achieve much. If, for instance, I had to choose between the Berlin Home and another where the young people were the Berlin helpers (dearest, even with you among them, and with me, no doubt, at the head), and the helpers simple eastern European Jews from Kolomyia or Stanislawow, I would give unconditional preference to the latter Home—with a great sigh of relief, and without blinking an eye. But I don't think this choice exists; no one has it; the quality corresponding to the value of the eastern European Jew is something that cannot be imparted in a Home; on this point even family education has recently been failing more and more; these are things that cannot be imparted, but perhaps, and this is the hope, they can be acquired, earned. And the helpers in the Home have, I imagine, a chance to acquire them. They will accomplish little, for they know little and are not very much of anything, yet once they grasp the meaning of it, they will accomplish all they can with all the power in their souls, which, then again, is a lot; this alone is a lot. The connection between all this and Zionism (this applies to me, but doesn't have to apply to you, of course) lies in the fact that the work in the Home derives from Zionism a youthful vigorous method, youthful vigor generally, that kindles national aspirations where other means might fail by invoking the ancient prodigious past—admittedly with the limitations without which Zionism could not exist. How you come to terms with Zionism is your affair; any coming to terms with it (indifference is out of the question) will give me pleasure. It is too soon to discuss it now, but should you one day feel yourself to be a Zionist (you flirted with it once, but these were mere flirtations, not a coming to terms), and subsequently realize that I am not

> a Zionist—which would probably emerge from an examination—it wouldn't worry me, nor need it worry you; Zionism is not something that separates well-meaning people.[15]

This was powerful and radical, and, if taken literally, would bring Felice Bauer's bourgeois existence to the breaking point. Kafka's insistence that the Zionist helpers would be serving their own interests was not a paradoxical exaggeration on Kafka's part. It was the very attitude with which the initiators of the Jewish Home set themselves apart from the organized Zionism of the previous generation. Mere charity was inadequate, in their view, and it diminished the consciousness of a common Jewish history and identity. "The Western Jew goes to the people," Lehmann wrote in retrospect, "not merely in order to help, but in order to become one with them by living and learning with them. . . ."[16] That was the language of Buber, spoken from the cultural Zionist lectern and far above many people's heads. The apolitical Kafka deliberately avoided invoking the word *Volk* and related language, and there is no known instance of his ever having used this word affirmatively—not to mention normatively—prior to 1920. Instead, he championed compassion, freedom from prejudice, and basic sincerity. Rhetoric had no place here; only devotion to the people mattered.

Of course Kafka's stance was not as unideologically pure and apolitical as he claimed: he idealized the eastern European Jews, and he would never walk away from this Zionist legacy. Nonetheless, he placed the responsibility of "spiritual liberation"—when would he ever have said something like that?—squarely on the shoulders of the individual, on his devotion not to a party, a movement, or an ethnicity but to real live people, and he did not want to focus on anything else. "The people are the main issue," he told Felice, "only the people,"[17] and he meant both western and eastern European Jews. Like many others of his day, Kafka was unable to break free of idealization and typification, but he always pictured collective concepts of this sort as though they were set off by quotation marks, without granting them a binding moral force. Collectives, he felt, were nebulous entities, multilayered and inconsistent. They rarely offered the homogeneity young Zionists were after, let alone proximity to the *Volk*—not in the melting pot of an urban ghetto. Lehmann himself left the Jewish Home in Berlin once he had realized this.[18] But what remained was the face of the individual, impossible to ignore.

Kafka's statements underscore the fundamental difference between his views and those of Max Brod, and quite a bit of friction must have resulted. Brod no longer defined himself as a writer or a critic but as a Zionist; he regarded himself as serving a movement with concrete political, organizational, and cultural aims, and even when he appealed to the conscience of the individual, his language was interwoven with the political phraseology of the day, and sometimes even contaminated by an offputting zealous, missionary undertone. Even Buber felt duty-bound to caution him to exercise restraint. Gustav Landauer thought he was hearing jarring elements of a Jewish chauvinism from Prague; Brod actually seemed to be asserting the superiority of the Jewish over the Christian religion.[19] But this was only a sideshow because for Brod, what mattered was active participation; mere verbal avowals of Judaism à la Schnitzler, Werfel, Wassermann, and Stefan Zweig exasperated him, even when these authors were simply stating their own convictions and feelings.

Kafka reacted quite differently, focusing his attention not on the avowal of an issue or its practical application but rather on a stance of absolute authenticity, which lent substance and weight to avowals of any sort. Authenticity was a seamless accord, free of outside interference and catchphrases, an accord of thinking, feeling, and acting: *harmony with oneself, and truthfulness.* Kafka found examples of this truthfulness in the oddest places, irrespective of his own convictions: in the Old Testament, in Napoleon, Grillparzer, and Dostoevsky, in Gerhart Hauptmann's *The Fool in Christ: Emanuel Quint*, in Rudolf Steiner and Moriz Schnitzer, in the pietist community in Herrnhut as well as at the "court" of the rabbi of Belz, in the married life of Feigl, the painter, and in the national Jewish idealism of a student whose physical existence Kafka went so far as to declare more valuable than his own. And Kafka recommended to Felice Bauer, as a future "teacher" at the Jewish Home in Berlin, not background reading on Jewish, political, or pedagogical subjects (as Brod certainly would have done), but—urgently and repeatedly—Lily Braun's *Memoirs of a Socialist*, which she had tried to read years earlier but found boring and put aside. He asked her to have another look at it because "even a trace of the frame of mind" of this book would be enough for the work that now needed to be done at the home, while he roundly rejected the attitude of the Prague Zionists who crowded into the synagogues in order to make a statement.[20]

There is no doubt that this criticism was also aimed at Max Brod, who after his conversion to Zionism and the Jewish nation also began gradually to immerse himself in the religious dimensions of Judaism. It appears unlikely that the two friends had explicit arguments on these issues. "What do I have in common with Jews?" Kafka had noted in his diary back in 1914—evidently without thinking about how, strictly speaking, he could have been able to ask this question only as a *meshumad*, someone who has left the faith. "What do I have in common with Jews? I barely have anything in common with myself."[21] Brod had surely heard these kinds of adamant disclaimers in the past. Kafka had acknowledged that in general it was the duty of a Jewish author to support his own people, yet he steered clear of doing so himself—apart from donating a couple of kronen to Palestine here and there. Brod had learned to hold back and avoid confronting Kafka on a factual level. Instead, he tried to draw him in indirectly, for example by arranging for publications.

The legend "Before the Law," the centerpiece of Kafka's *Trial*, was first published in the fall of 1915 in the Zionist *Selbstwehr*,[22] which no doubt pleased Kafka, even though the range of the paper, which had been fighting for survival since the beginning of the war, had been drastically reduced (people like to quip that "*selbst wer* [even someone who] has it in hand doesn't read it"). But did *Selbstwehr* have to go ahead and name the new author as a "contributor"? That was a bit premature, and as it turned out, there were no additional contributions by this "contributor."

Buber had much the same experience when in late 1915 he asked a series of authors whether they would be willing to contribute to *Der Jude*, a forthcoming new journal with a self-assured national Jewish orientation. Since the omnipresent Brod had been with this project right from the start, Kafka also received a publicity circular, which contained nothing but the usual slogans; there was no personal message. Buber wrote that it was now time "to proclaim, certify, and present [Jewish] totality as something alive." That was a requirement that Kafka neither could nor would fulfill: "Your friendly invitation comes as a great honor to me," he assured Buber, "but I cannot comply with it; I am—and with some hope in my mind I am saying 'for now,' of course—much too dejected and insecure to consider speaking in this community, even in the most minor role."[23] That sounded a bit feeble. When had a writer ever turned down publicity on the sole basis of *insecurity*? But Kafka could not conceive of making public avowals, let alone representing some kind of "totality," without being absolutely sure of his ground—that is, considering it part of his own identity. That was not the case "for now."

Buber was not surprised that Kafka had turned him down, and he did not see it as an essential loss for his journal. He probably had no more than a vague memory of the author in Prague—Kafka's visit to Buber's apartment in Berlin had taken place years earlier—and there were no pertinent essays, let alone full-fledged works that would fit his concept. For the time being, the idea that Kafka was in a position to contribute at all was nothing but an assertion on the part of his ambitious impresario. The latter, however, had ulterior motives for making his recommendation. In Brod's view, a journal that pushed for a Jewish nation with its own cultural foundation had to feature examples of recent Jewish literature, and only the best would do. But what was "Jewish" literature? Buber pointed out to him that it could only be literature in the Hebrew language, or at least in Yiddish, whereas German writing was not genuinely Jewish and thus had no place in *Der Jude*. Brod was dumbfounded. Since when had Buber, of all people, used these kinds of pedantic criteria? What mattered, he chided, was not a set of tangential characteristics like language, but the substance, the "spirit" of the literature, which was why the younger Western Jewish authors such as Werfel, Kafka, and Wolfenstein were not part of German literature but rather a "special group in Jewish literature."[24]

Brod wanted to supply a convincing example on the spot. He offered Buber a foundational essay called "Our Writers and the Community," which pitted the ethos of social action—in his view the distinguishing feature of Jewish literature—against the amoral narcissism of the Expressionist avant-garde. Brod argued that a crucial marker of an author's moral and thus aesthetic reorientation was the extent to which he broke out of the entanglements of a rootless individualism, or at least aspired to. By this yardstick, Brod continued, Kafka was the "most Jewish" writer of all, because his yearning for community ran deepest; indeed, Kafka regarded solitude as a sin and thus came close to adopting "the loftiest religious concept of Judaism": redemption of the world rather than the self. Brod suggested illustrating his idea by printing it alongside Kafka's short prose text "A Dream," which he had been able to "tear from the grasp" of the reluctant author.[25]

Jewish, more Jewish, most Jewish: a dubious progression, a hair-raising hypothesis, and an utterly unsuitable illustrative example. What was *Jewish* about the dream—or rather, the vision of a man who climbs into a grave alive because he is so attracted to the gold inscription on his own gravestone? Using Brod's own benchmark, Kafka's "A Dream" was more like an example of the exact opposite, namely a surreal spiraling of a narcissism that no community could save from blissful self-destruction. Buber would not be swayed from his resolve to exclude German-language literature with texts like that and had no choice but to turn it down, although he tried to blunt the force of this rejection by adding high praise for Kafka. Brod was undeterred. If *Der Jude* was out, he would try *Das jüdische Prag*, an anthology that was published in late 1916 as a subsidiary of *Selbstwehr*. A few days later, Kafka's "A Dream" was even published in the *Prager Tagblatt*, where his colleagues, sisters, and parents would see it.[26] And this was not the first time: if Brod "tore something from your grasp," it was sure to appear in the newspaper in a flash.

Kafka must have noticed that the dogmatic tone with which Brod drew sharp distinctions between Jewish and non-Jewish literature was undermined by his striking lack of cogent criteria, and that Brod's literary judgments could be swayed by personal relations and penchants. Brod had displayed this vociferous yet fallible adherence to his principles as far back as Kafka could remember. These were nothing but strategic and prescriptive labels for literature, and it was regrettable but unavoidable that nearly all Jewish journalists echoed this rhetoric. Wasn't the Aryan opposition doing the very same thing?

> Max's essay, "Our Writers and the Community," may appear in the next issue of *Der Jude*. By the way, won't you tell me what I really am? In the last issue of *Die neue Rundschau*, "The Metamorphosis" is mentioned and rejected on sensible grounds, and then it says

> something like "There is something fundamentally German about K's art of narration." Max's essay, by contrast, claims "K's stories are among the most Jewish documents of our time." A difficult case. Am I a circus rider on two horses? Unfortunately I am not a rider; instead, I am lying on the ground.[27]

He should have waited a few weeks. By November, an anonymous reviewer of "The Metamorphosis" declared in the *Deutsche Montags-Zeitung*: "The book is Jewish." This brought the score to 2-1, in favor of Brod, in favor of the Jewish spirit.[28]

Attributions and demarcations of this sort seem odd today, and the heated debates about worldviews and isms of every shade and hue at the turn of the twentieth century seem insipid in view of the paltry insights these debates ultimately yielded. In the ranks of the Zionists (not only in the cultural Zionist faction), impassioned avowals trumped incisive analysis right from the start, and the appearance of dissenters was constantly met with outrage, long before the arguments had even been weighed. The point was not insight but identity, and identity is not subject to compromise; it must strive to remain *immune* and divest itself of anything that does not belong to it.

Kafka was quite familiar with this logic; his notion of truthfulness was essentially purist and, to the chagrin of those around him, did not allow for compromises, whether the issue was eating a roast, buying furniture, or working on a journal. On the other hand, he conceded everything possible when it came to mere opinions or philosophical views. He did not proselytize, and he wanted to persuade only people who were close to him and whose lack of understanding upset him. Sometimes this attitude could come across as indifference, but authenticity does not work by consensus; you can be truthful and set the whole world against you, and if Kafka's social conscience was eating away at him, it was certainly not because he was unable to share the views of the majority.

The advocates of "movements" could not afford to take this broad-minded an attitude to those who held different beliefs. Save the world, yes, but on our terms. A position like that could be maintained only by ignoring the prevailing power structures and influences, and focusing instead on long-term objectives. Zionist spokesmen consistently suppressed the fact that the overwhelming majority of German-speaking Jews adamantly refused to be "saved" by any writers, Hebrew teachers, or Polish refugees, and that even of the less than 4 percent of Jews who were Zionists, only a very small fraction actually went to Palestine. "A Zionist is a Jew," Leopold Schwarzschild summed up, "who with the full force of his national conviction works toward resettling another Jew in Palestine by means of money from a third Jew."[29] The irony also hit a raw nerve among Prague Zionists: claim and reality were grotesquely at odds, and the result was a lack of truthfulness, but anyone who tried to address this lack openly instantly bumped up against ideological limitations. One could not declare the behavior of such a large majority *un-Jewish*.

Equally problematic was the degree to which this need to assert an identity and set boundaries spilled over into literature, an area in which the unique and inimitable occupies the highest rung and where no writer could settle for being a mere representative of a movement or a trend. The sheer amount of paper and effort squandered on the question of whether an author or an individual work could be classified as symbolist, expressionist, or activist, as "Jewish," "quintessentially German," or some other literature; the sheer number of relationships between colleagues, and even between friends, that fell apart over questions of this kind becomes comprehensible only as a symptom of a pervasive *horror vacui*. When nothing is self-evident anymore and suddenly anything goes, the waving flag of the collective, isms, and *Volk* ultimately remain the reliable identifying marks. The dogged attempts by Kafka's early reviewers to pigeonhole him typified the era.

Brod's increasing tendency to take collective labels of this kind more seriously than intellectual physiognomies could have easily spelled the end of his friendship with Kafka, as well. He was mistaken in interpreting Kafka's enthusiasm for Jewish cultural activities as a sign that the latter's views were steadily approaching those of his friend. The gap between Kafka's ethics of truthfulness and Brod's identity politics had widened to the point of forcing Brod into a balancing act: in order to remain on speaking terms with Kafka, he had to drop the role of the propagandist, which he could do *because* it was a role, and because Brod was not only an ambitious Zionist but also a vulnerable and somewhat mawkish man who was disillusioned by the war and struggling to find a direction. Brod needed to relax, come out from behind his shield, and cultivate friendships by putting aside factionalism. Moreover, Brod was still highly receptive to literary skill.

"I personally," Brod wrote to Buber, who remained obstinate about not wanting German-Jewish literature, "consider Kafka (along with Gerhart Hauptmann and Hamsun) the greatest living writer! If you only knew his substantial, though unfortunately incomplete novels, which he sometimes reads to me at odd hours. What I wouldn't do to make him more active!"[30] That was true conviction; he had more *personal* knowledge of the deep impact of Kafka's language than anyone. But as a Zionist, Brod held an altogether different view because there was a principle at stake: the principle of kinship, the logic of which dictated that it ought not to have been possible for there to be a linguistic potential of Kafka's quality, not among *German-speaking Jews*, because "the language is only entrusted to us," Brod asserted, "and hence we are uncreative in the purely linguistic sphere."[31] We, the Jewish authors, are the perpetual residents of foreign cultures. Brod was surely careful not to fuel Kafka's self-doubts with arguments like that, but if Jewish authors were patently uncreative in the German language, Brod was treading on fairly thin ice when he declared Kafka's work essentially Jewish. He risked this step in order to be able to admire it openly. Once again, apparently, it was a matter not of consistency but of identity.

Years later, in a long, somewhat baffling letter, Kafka even wrote about the "appropriation of others' property," about a German-Jewish "gypsy literature that stole the German child out of its cradle." He did not name names or include his own texts, but it is striking that Brod, who ought to have been able to infer a definitive conversion to cultural Zionism from these polemical statements, did not respond. Had he grasped the fact that this argument also undermined his own work?[32]

The eastern European Jewish neighbors looked askance at the Jewish Home in Berlin. What was going on there? When the windows were open, singing or reading could be heard, and sometimes hammering and sawing, as well. When the children came home, they told their parents, most of whom were workers and merchants, about the evils of haggling and the joys of solidarity, with each taking responsibility for the others. It was unfathomable: twelve-year-olds were sitting in judgment of their classmates' misbehavior, and even weighing in about their adult teachers. "A.K.," which stood for *anständiger Kerl* (decent fellow), was their highest honorary title. They memorized poems and brought home strange books that had nothing to do with real life. And on the weekends, they hiked through nature for hours on end, and even spent the night on straw, then regaled their parents with stories of how fabulous it looks when the sun goes down. This would give them the necessary survival skills for the menacing metropolis?

It took quite some time for many adult eastern European Jews to venture into the Home to take advantage of the counseling for expectant and new mothers or the legal or medical advice that was offered there free of charge. But the social and mental barriers between the counselors and their clients could not be eliminated with goodwill alone, and Siegfried Lehmann's stated goal of ensuring that the residents of the Scheunenviertel regarded "the Home as the centerpiece of all vital questions of daily life" proved elusive.[33] "Jewish *Volksarbeit*" (work on behalf of the Jewish people) focused more and more on children, whose impressionability and gratitude made up for all the setbacks.

Felice Bauer, who, like Kafka, valued people over principles, was impressed and even enthusiastic about the atmosphere of the Jewish Home from the moment she stepped foot inside. She found comfortable, sparkling-clean rooms; it was more like an apartment than an institution. There was a reading room, a bathing area, a little workshop, and even a piano. And she met interesting people: a nursery school teacher from Palestine, a young rabbi, a composer, several medical students. Well-known personalities, such as Buber and Landauer, even turned up from time to time. There were also young radicals, among them Zalman Rubashov (who later went by the name Zalman Shazar; no one would have imagined back then that one day this man would become president of the state of Israel) and Gerhard Scholem (who later went by Gershom, and wrote commentary on the texts of Felice's fiancé). There was not a trace of academic pretension; everyone who had been swept up in the prevailing spirit of optimism was welcome to contribute on a regular basis. The practical problems dominated, so reliability counted far more than Zionist avowals, which Felice Bauer neither could nor would furnish. No one appears to have held that against her. Even Lehmann (who was able to pitch in for only a few months before being drafted) was impressed by the energy with which this working woman took on myriad tasks. Twice a week, she arrived at the home at about 5 or 6 P.M. and stayed until late in the evening. She joined weekend excursions and did a great deal of typing. She wrote that the Jewish Home tended to absorb all the energy of its staff; coming from her, that was meant as praise. Kafka became a bit uneasy at hearing this—yet Felice was apparently still not stretched to her limit and went to lectures on Strindberg on other evenings.

Of course, it was not just a matter of getting a few children off the street and caring for them. The pedagogical approach focused squarely on Jewish themes, so the volunteers were expected to take part in regular group discussions about religious, cultural, and pedagogical issues and undergo supervised training. Felice Bauer's group wrote reports on a pedagogical standard work, Foerster's *Lessons for Young People*, and discussed it chapter by chapter, which of course was easier for the students there than for Felice, a technical executive officer who was not used to interpreting texts. Luckily she had a friend who had made that very thing his profession: In the midst of his office work, Kafka hastily skimmed the essential sections of the book and typed a report that Felice needed only to read aloud.[34] He also acted as a literary adviser and silent donor—for example, when he sent a dozen copies of Chamisso's *Peter Schlemihl* to give out to the children to read together.

Felice Bauer had feared that religious education would be given top priority, but this was not the case. The readings were by and large secular and Western, and in line with her own middle-class education, which gave her a feeling of security. It also made sense to her that the experience of beauty—whether in nature or in German prose—was an important pedagogical and moral medium. Evidently there was general agreement that they should *show* the children as much as possible, even if it went far beyond their intellectual grasp, and the reading list was an odd compilation of a conventional curriculum and a sprinkling of Zionist recommendations. Kafka was dumbfounded by their decision to impose Lessing's *Minna von Barnhelm* on the youngsters. Call a halt to that right away, he advised. But then he was dismayed to learn that in the Zionist Girls' Club, a gathering place for the older girls and young women, even Brod's "community" essay was being discussed, a text that required the knowledge of the latest Expressionist literature. But Felice assured him that everyone was enthusiastic about it; the term *community* had created a true feeling of collective retreat, and the girls were about to write a thank-you card to the author. But, it occurred to her, "have you ever really thought about this yourself? And what do you think about Max Brod's community idea?" Odd question. Did she still not know whom she was dealing with? He would have had to hand over his own diaries to her to reply honestly.[35]

Others criticized the random and scholastic nature of the Jewish Home readings. Young, ideologically trained Zionists in particular wondered whether the (re)socialization and Western education of eastern European Jewish children might not be heading them toward assimilation. Where did that leave Jewish tradition and the preparation for Palestine? The eighteen-year-old Scholem chided the head of the Jewish Home for "spending time on nonsense and literary prattle" and suggested instead "learning Hebrew and going to the sources." Scholem did not hold back on the subject of the counselors either, whose "fashionably draped skirts" displayed a lack of national fighting spirit. *Volksarbeit* in the diaspora (he used the Yiddish word *golus*) was meaningless, he claimed, a waste of Jewish resources if it did not serve the actual work that would really begin in Palestine. Buber's oft-cited pedagogical maxim, "Become a *mensch*, in the Jewish spirit," may have sounded elegant and touched a chord, but neither in the areas in the East from which the refugees came nor here in the German Reich would there ever be a solution to the Jewish question, not even with the best and most Jewish *menschen*. Moving to Eretz Israel was the only solution.[36]

This was surely a sobering thought for the volunteers, who had trouble countering Scholem's eloquent and erudite arguments, but not for Kafka:

> The debate you are describing is typical; in spirit I am always inclined to favor proposals such as those made by Herr Scholem, which demand the utmost, and thus nothing. Proposals such as these, and their value, should not be gauged by the actual effect that is displayed. I am speaking in general terms here. The fact is that Scholem's proposals are not unworkable per se.[37]

But what is the value of *unworkable* proposals? Their value lies in their truth, of course, their truthfulness. Scholem was delighted to discover later in life, when he was seventy, that Kafka's commentary about him had been quite positive.

A postcard every day, and sometimes a letter as well on special occasions. Even a presentation. And quite a few questions. Just as long as their contact was not broken off altogether. And he would keep his own complaints to a minimum.

The reader senses that the marvel of Marienbad made Kafka not only more compassionate but also more realistic. He now knew that it was not enough just to rely on wishful thinking or repeated assurances to keep them close. The relationship with a woman—especially where a great distance was involved—needed an interest in common, a project. And he was able to persuade Felice that work in the Jewish Home could be this project. "I feel quite comfortable among the children," she wrote, "and in fact much more at home than I do at the office."[38] Kafka was happy to read this. Of course, she was good at business and hardworking, and he admired her for that, but she also had the sensible voice of a woman with whom one could talk, and live; that was what he wanted to hear, word for word, and he could rightly claim that this happiness was his doing. He had given her the impetus, he had persevered, he had done everything just right. Mightn't he deserve applause? But life is not a homework assignment. Calculations that are *too simple* often fail to work out.

CHAPTER SIX

Kafka Encounters His Readers

The only place to eat your fill is at your own table.

—Eastern European Jewish proverb

Dear Sir,

You have made me unhappy.

I bought your "Metamorphosis" as a present for my cousin, but she doesn't know what to make of the story.

My cousin gave it to her mother, who doesn't know what to make of it either.

Her mother gave the book to my other cousin, and she doesn't know what to make of it either.

Now they've written to me. They want me to explain the story to them because I am the one with a doctorate in the family. But I am baffled.

Sir! I spent months fighting it out with the Russians in the trenches without flinching, but if my reputation among my cousins went to hell, I would not be able to bear it.

Only you can help me. You have to, because you are the one who landed me in this situation. So please tell me what my cousin ought to make of "The Metamorphosis."

Yours sincerely,
Dr. Siegfried Wolff

THIS WAS ONE OF THE DROLL REACTIONS KAFKA'S TEXTS ELICITED from his early readers—a harmless harbinger of the enormous discursive surge that would descend upon his posthumous writings a generation later. And this Siegfried Wolff really did exist; he lived in Berlin-Charlottenburg, and his doctoral degree was genuine (in political science), as was his military service in the trenches (wounded in 1915). He earned his living as a bank manager. It is unlikely that Kafka passed up the chance to have fun with a pointed little reply.[1]

His diaries barely broach the subject, but by the time *Meditation* was published—the book that turned him from a writer into an author—Kafka also came to know the strange experience that accompanies the emergence of *readers*, and of literary texts that took on lives of their own and pulled away once and for all from the author's control and will to perfection. "Reception history" is the technical term; from the perspective of readers, this is the natural reference point of literature because they generally do not know any other. For the author, by contrast, the text is the result of an effort in which events, ideas, associations, rejected variants, random thoughts, writer's blocks, and narcissistic flights of fancy fall into place to form an entirely different story. Even for the most successful author, the beginning of this reception also signals an end: the product is taken out of the author's hands, and unknown people have a go at it. Kafka was not spared this experience. It was astonishing—and at times absurd—what could be read into his brief texts. But in contrast to Brod, he resisted the temptation to pontificate or to wield the authority of the creator. He kept his own interpretation to himself and left readers to theirs.

It was due in large part to the tradition of reading aloud to his close friends that Kafka grew accustomed early on to the sight of autonomous readers with autonomous judgments and avoided indulging in overly private linguistic frippery. He greatly enjoyed reading aloud, which enabled him to test out his successes and share—and thus enhance—the pleasure of success. Of course, this was best achieved in front of a small, handpicked audience to which there was some personal connection: his own sisters; Brod, Baum, and Weltsch; the Bauer family; or at least a semipublic group such as the guests of Frau Direktor Marschner, who maintained a "salon."

It was far more difficult to get Kafka to agree to read before an anonymous crowd, where he was sure to resist any form of self-promotion, and his pleasure in reading aloud was marred by interference from his superego, by nagging doubts as to why *he*, of all people, was here making himself the center of attention. Kafka was not afraid of his audiences, but he bristled when their curiosity went beyond the texts and focused on himself, and he felt positively ill when a high school student who was an avid reader addressed him as "Your very faithful disciple."[2] On one occasion, he had read to a crowd of strangers in Prague, his confidence buoyed by the success of his story "The Judgment"—but that was four years earlier, and since then no occasion had presented itself, nor had he sought any out. Even in his circle of friends, Kafka had long restricted himself to the role of listener. What would he have read aloud? Everyone was waiting for him to finish *The Trial* and *The Man Who Disappeared*, but Kafka had had enough of well-intentioned encouragements; he *knew* that a novel was out of the question as long as this war went on. And thus he had taken to reading other writers' texts aloud, to keep his voice in practice, with Ottla as his only listener, on hot summer Sundays, lying in the grass in a quiet valley, far outside the city.

This peace was interrupted by an unexpected invitation: The Galerie Neue Kunst Hans Goltz in Munich invited Kafka to organize a literary evening with his own texts. That was startling. What did he have to do with this city; who knew about him there? He had once wanted to study in Munich and had spent two weeks looking around the city, but all he had to show for it was a dim memory. On the way back from Riva, in 1913, he had spent a few hours strolling through Munich—that was virtually all. He had no knowledge of the lively scene in Schwabing, apart from the anecdotes he heard from Franz Blei, but that was long since eclipsed by the beacon-like presence of the literary metropolis of Berlin. *That* is where he would have liked to give a reading. Some of his acquaintances in Prague had made a name for themselves in Berlin years earlier. Even Oskar Baum had sponsors there, but before Kafka's name had a chance to reach the people in charge, the world war severed his tenuous connections.

Even so, Kafka's decision to travel to Munich was made in a matter of hours. No sooner did he have the invitation in hand than he was dictating his application for the obligatory passport. He quickly realized that this was no mere local event. Hans Goltz, a bookseller, publisher, and art dealer, was putting together a momentous series oriented to the Berlin avant-garde, called "Evenings for New Literature." Salomo Friedländer was first in line, and Else Lasker-Schüler, Alfred Wolfenstein, and Theodor Däubler had accepted invitations to appear there. This series looked quite respectable, although Kafka was not comfortable with the fact that the organizer used the trendy phrase "German Expressionists" to advertise the series.

But how had they come upon him? There was no apparent reason—except perhaps the insightful and admiring essay that had been published that summer in the *Berliner Tageblatt* and named Kafka in the same breath as Kleist.[3] Or did they already know that at long last, *The Judgment*, a slender volume he had talked his publisher into printing, was forthcoming as a book? That was not it either. The simple truth was disheartening. Just as in the previous year, when he was awarded the Fontane Prize money, he was merely an also-ran. The actual invitation went to Max Brod, who was far better known, and Brod had suggested having Kafka read sometime, as well—together with another author if the talented writer from Prague was not enough of an attraction on his own. "My desire to go has diminished accordingly," Kafka sighed.[4] Just a single appearance on stage in all those years, and once again he owed it to Brod.

Still, he did not want to turn it down. The trip to Munich offered him the opportunity to meet up with Felice—which was no small matter in view of newly restrictive passport regulations that made pleasure trips to the German Reich next to impossible. A traveler now had to prove that the trip was necessary; have in hand an Austrian passport, a "border crossing certificate," and an official stamp from the German consulate; and register with the German police when entering and leaving the country. Since readings were considered a component of a writer's profession, they were generally recognized as a legitimate reason for a journey upon presentation of an invitation (provided that the individual in question was "dependable and unobjectionable," as can be read in Kafka's police file). But a weekend trip to Berlin would require a recent engagement announcement, and that was now out of the question.

Felice immediately declared herself willing to sacrifice two precious vacation days, and to spend a Friday and a Sunday in the train, just to see Kafka again for a few hours. She was unhesitating in matters of this sort, and she even wondered why he did not seize the opportunity to make an illegal detour via Berlin, where he could have also visited the much-discussed Jewish Home. But Kafka was not interested in skirting the law, although letter censorship prevented him from saying this in so many words. Still, he did find out that the trains from Prague and Berlin combined on their way to Munich and that they would be able to celebrate their reunion in the dining car around noon. He, too, was counting the hours.

There were more serious complications, as well. What did Kafka have to offer an audience in Munich? He would not consider reading from uncompleted works. Kafka had no desire to feign the self-assurance of a Thomas Mann, who was at this very same time on a reading tour with his *Felix Krull* fragment. On the other hand, he wanted to convey to his readers an idea of how he had developed since his debut and where he was at present. The only suitable unpublished text was "In the Penal Colony." But this story would put even the most obliging listeners to a hard test, and he already held the proof in his hands. Kurt Wolff, who had been discharged from military service a few weeks earlier and was finally back at his publishing house in Leipzig, had expressed misgivings about publishing "In the Penal Colony" as a separate volume. His letter has not been preserved, but Kafka's reply makes it evident that this was not a matter of tactical fine points but something fundamental:

> I am very pleased to have your kind words about my manuscript. Your criticism of the painful element accords completely with my opinion, but then I feel the same way about almost everything I

> have written so far. Take a look at how few things are free of this painful element in one form or another! To shed light on this last story, I need only add that the painfulness is not peculiar to it alone but rather that our times in general and my own time in particular have also been and still are painful, and my own for an even longer time than the times in general. God knows how much farther I would have gone along this road if I had kept on writing, or even better, if my circumstances and my condition had permitted me to write as I longed to, teeth biting lips. But they did not. The way I feel now, all I can do is wait for quiet, which means that I am representing myself, at least to all appearances, as a true man of our times. I also agree entirely that the story should not appear in *Der jüngste Tag*.[5]

Kafka rejected Wolff's alternative suggestion, which was more polite than enthusiastic, to group the story with others. And he informed Wolff defiantly that he would soon be reading "In the Penal Colony" in public.

Kafka's standard panoply of self-accusations surely revealed an undertone of annoyance to his perceptive publisher. The unusual twist this time around was that Kafka did not justify his work solely on the basis of inner necessity but as a symptom of the era. Evidently it took him aback that Lieutenant Wolff could look back on two years in combat in France and in the Balkans and still regard the atrocities and physical crassness in the "Penal Colony" as "painful." Of course, the one was monstrous reality and the other *mere* literature. But what writer who took his own work seriously could accept this order of priority? Did he really have to explain to Kurt Wolff that literature, *truthful literature*, is measured by only how far it can penetrate to the core of reality? Kafka's story had originated at a time when an orgy of violence had been unleashed in the world, a hyperreal violence that seemed to veer off into the realm of fantasy. It would have been a simple matter for him to make this connection plain as day to the publisher, but then the letter censor would have understood it as well.

As alien as thinking in political terms was to Kafka, he was well aware that "In the Penal Colony," which ends with the death of a technocratic tormentor, could certainly be read as commentary on current events and was therefore anything but an appropriate text. Plenty of reasons could be found to call a halt to the reading. The decision would be made in the press office of the Munich police headquarters, to which any public recitation had to be submitted in advance, and it was difficult to predict what the textual exegesis there would yield, particularly in view of the fact that the name of Goltz, the art dealer, was anathema to the Munich police. On several occasions, Goltz, who promoted the work of Franz Marc and Wassily Kandinsky, had provoked passersby with avant-garde art, and next to the artists' haunt Café Luitpold, the police had been called in to disperse an angry crowd gathered in front of the display windows on Briennerstrasse.

Thus, Kafka's reunion with his beloved Felice depended upon the goodwill of an anonymous and inaccessible police officer in Munich. Even for Kafka, who confronted the power of official certifications on human lives on a daily basis, this was a remarkable experience. "It is still making me nervous," he confessed a few days before his planned trip, "no matter how harmless it is by its nature, I cannot imagine that it will be authorized."[6] Harmless? Of course, there was no specific regulation compelling the state and society to shield the public from Kafka's story. But Hans Goltz was given to understand that it would be best to avoid using the term "penal colony" in the public announcement because penal colonies were under the purview of the Bavarian War Ministry, and it would be unwise to provoke that ministry's censor. Goltz therefore came up with a group of titles and selected a truly innocuous one: "Franz Kafka: Tropical Fantasy."[7]

Could things get any worse? They could indeed. Now came the news that Brod was unable to get vacation time and that Kafka would have to represent Prague "Expressionism" all alone, on his own behalf, on November 10, 1916. The only eyewitness account appears to be a cock-and-bull story:

> As he spoke his first words, a stale smell of blood seemed to fill the room, and a strangely stale and pallid taste crept over my lips. His voice may have sounded apologetic, but his images cut into me like a razor. . . .
>
> A thud, confusion in the hall, a lady was carried out unconscious. Kafka continued reciting his text. Twice more, his words

> made people swoon. The ranks of the listeners began to thin out. Some fled at the last moment before the vision of the author overwhelmed them. Never have I observed an effect of spoken words like this. I stayed to the very end. . . .[8]

We would love to know more. Who were the three unhappy people, and how had they happened upon a reading by Kafka? And what exactly had knocked them out: those unspeakable poems by Brod (which included a long "Cosmic Cantata") that Kafka read as an introduction and to excuse his friend's absence, or the "smell of blood" that arose from the podium, or was it mere boredom that put them to sleep? And what did they do when they awoke? Did they press charges for bodily harm? Against the owner of the gallery? Against Kafka?

A marvelous slapstick fantasy, of course, with a writer who keeps right on reading while his listeners are being carried out or taking to their heels. Still, it is exasperating that the only detailed description of Kafka's reading in Munich, written by the Swiss author Max Pulver, is itself nothing but a fantasy; literally every detail is invented, and it draws on the most simple-minded Kafka legends.[9] Even decades later, the visionary, amateur astrologer, and future graphologist Pulver had yet to understand what an opportunity he had let slip by. He had witnessed the only reading Kafka ever gave outside of Prague, and had evidently also observed Kafka's only encounter with Rilke—an extraordinary event for Kafka himself, whose life, otherwise low-profile and seemingly remote from the world of literature, rarely presented an occasion for meetings of this kind. Everything about that night remains oddly hazy: the well-known local gallery on the second floor of Goltz's bookstore, decorated with New Secession artwork; in it, several dozen audience members, most in overcoats (Munich had also suffered from a lack of coal for quite some time), among them Rilke and several other authors and critics, and of course Felice Bauer, surely at a place of honor in the first row. Afterwards, there was the usual little gathering in the restaurant, unfortunately without Rilke but with a group of local literarati, including Eugen Mondt, Gottfried Kölwel, and Max Pulver. "I shouldn't have read my dirty little story." That is the only credible statement we have from this evening.[10] After a long time, he had again tried to revel in his own success—to no avail.

The newspapers picked up on this as well. The next day, when Kafka was still in Munich, the *Münchener Neueste Nachrichten* reported that he had been "quite an inadequate presenter." On Sunday, when Kafka was heading home on the train, the *Münchener Zeitung* reported that he was "a lecher of horror." And on Monday, the *München-Augsburger Zeitung* criticized him for having been "too long, and not captivating enough." He stopped trying to get hold of any more reviews. And of course he agreed with all the criticism, and even corroborated "the truly huge failure of the whole thing":

> I misused my writing as a means of getting to Munich, where I have no other intellectual ties whatever, and after two years of not writing I had the incredible nerve to read in public, despite the fact that I hadn't read a word even to my best friends in Prague for a year and a half. Incidentally, I also recalled Rilke's words once I was back in Prague. After some extremely kind remarks about "The Stoker," he went on to say that neither "The Metamorphosis" nor "In the Penal Colony" had achieved the same effect. This observation may not be easy to understand, but it is perceptive.[11]

Rilke had evidently read *everything*—this in itself allowed Kafka to return to Prague full of determination, despite everything that had gone wrong. What did he care about a few audience members who thought the reading had dragged on for too long, or the journalists who did not regard his subdued manner as the slightest bit Expressionist? It was far more important to him that in this alien milieu, no one was interested in Kafka's roles as brother, friend, lover, colleague, lodger, factory owner, or Zionist. He had been invited and received *exclusively* as a writer. They talked about his work and asked him about the literary scene in Prague; some even asked him to evaluate their poetry, as though his critical judgment mattered. He did not consider this justified, particularly in light of his dismal performance in Munich, but it was useful as a sober reminder that he was juggling too many roles in Prague. And that he had a task still to be tackled.

After letting just a few days pass by, he entered a realtor's office, stating that he needed an apartment right now. That was the first essential step: a large, quiet apartment that was his alone.

Felice Bauer was the first to take in his sudden change. And she knew the part she had played in it. Hidden behind Kafka's hasty determination was a disappointment that dug deeper than the outward fiasco of the reading. They had not been able to maintain the intimacy of Marienbad in such a narrowly defined situation dictated by strangers and schedules. What could they do with the few hours they had available to them? The closeness they longed for failed to materialize, tensions arose, and they wound up quarreling in a café—perhaps about the Rosh Hashanah greetings that Felice's strict mother was expecting and that Kafka had refused to send, or about the flowers he was supposed to give his parents on Felice's behalf, which he had also refused to do. When it came to family obligations, he was as stubborn as ever. She accused him of "selfishness"—just when Kafka, in his view, had immersed himself in her life to the point of surrounding his own identity, identified with her work in the Jewish Home, and hammered home their common interest for weeks and months on end.

She wrote him a letter from Berlin in which she tried to assuage his fears by assuring him that it would not happen again. He replied that it certainly would (and he turned out to be right), but that she of all people should know better than to accuse him of selfishness. This accusation, he explained, was warranted, but—with a suddenly self-confident tone that was new to Felice—selfishness itself was just as warranted, when it was directed "less, incomparably less, at the person than at the thing." "At the thing" meant "at writing." And as though he had to banish the last remaining shadow of the Askanischer Hof (the cold breath of which he surely felt in the café in Munich), he added, "my sense of guilt is strong enough as it is; it doesn't need to be fed from the outside—but my constitution is not strong enough to choke down this kind of food very often." *I'm* the judge here; no one else. That was the old strategy in a nutshell.[12]

Kafka pulled back. His longing for symbiosis had failed to materialize; in the days after Munich, he began to understand that there was no way around it, no hope of fulfillment as long as he insisted on bringing literature into the mix. But Felice had read "The Metamorphosis," and in Munich—most likely unaware of its content in advance—she had endured the shock of "In the Penal Colony." It was unfathomable to her that unleashing these kinds of fantasies, toying with terror, even openly crossing into revolting territory could ever become a foundation upon which two people could build an intimate life together. With all the goodwill in the world, she could not extend her empathy quite this far. She made vague reference to a "solution," some pragmatic approach that would reconcile literature and marriage after all, but she did not get any more concrete, and Kafka, in turn, did not believe in pragmatic approaches of this kind.

The Jewish Home abruptly vanished from their correspondence. Kafka continued to send books; he provided a list of recommended literature for adolescents and even had his author's royalties sent to Berlin. But he no longer asked questions or gave advice or upheld their common interest. Felice, in turn, did not grasp the profoundly imaginative nature of his interest. Talking over issues pertaining to eastern European Jewish children mattered more to him than the children themselves, and hence their written reports, in which he could pit his ideas against reality, were more significant than their concrete appearance. The mighty, identity-building utopia of truth and the true life was the core around which all his imaginings revolved, and the Jewish Home, he had hoped, was an example that would teach her what these terms meant to him. But he found her unchanged and unmoved, and the compass needle that was always pointing to truth was turning, no longer facing Berlin, but instead to a couple of empty notebooks Kafka had bought.

"Christmas? I won't be able to travel."[13] This time he was not referring to the passport regulations. Felice appealed to Kafka with suggestions, but Kafka pointedly ignored them. He needed the holidays, the few free days, for himself, more urgently than ever. He would tell her why later.

The curtain fell in late 1916, and once again, the documentation dwindled. Only a single letter to Felice Bauer has been preserved from the first half of 1917, and only a few lines from Kafka's diary. The two of them had not seen each other for four, five, or even six months—a gentle, tacit, and predictable erosion of their bond.[14] As soon as Kafka's seductive voice fell silent, it became obvious that something crucial was lacking and that the absence of any caressing gesture or any erotic element indicated a blank space that could not be filled for any length of time, either by working together on the eastern European Jewish project or by exploring the problems of their western Jewish identity, or even on the strength of Kafka's extraordinary empathy. Symbiosis is possible only in a state of obliviousness that gives free rein to one's own longings, such as dreams and delusions. But it is impossible to bring about symbiosis deliberately and systematically. Efforts to force the issue, even those that bring short-lasting success, are sure to culminate in disappointment.

CHAPTER SEVEN

The Alchemist

I bent my head over my sheet of paper and looked at the shadow of my pen.

—S. J. Agnon, *The Letter*

ALONGSIDE THE NORTHERN ENCLOSING WALL OF THE HRADČANY, on the interior side, within the confines of the castle, there is one of the countless relics of Old Prague: Alchimistengasse (Alchemists'Alley), also known as Goldenes Gässchen (Golden Alley), a unique architectural specimen accessible only from the side because it dead ends in both directions. A row of tiny houses, consisting of only one or two rooms, hugs the wall, and the houses are recessed into it. Legend has it that the alchemists of the crazy Holy Roman Emperor Rudolf II lived here in about 1600. These dwellings are lined up like painted boxes, their low doors made for people from a bygone era. It is a touching sight.

In the fall of 1916, one of these houses added a new tenant: twenty-four-year-old Ottla Kafka. A room with an open hearth in the tiny basement, grimy and dilapidated, for a mere twenty kronen. Just the right thing to furnish as a cozy hideaway and to relax a little during her rare free hours, away from the prying eyes of her father, or to have a frank chat with Irma, her cousin and best friend. And if Ottla's lover,

Gässchen. The purported prior residents, the legendary alchemists, had been in the same boat three centuries earlier.

That the state, the world, or time gets "out of joint" every now and then is one of those euphemistic sayings with a dark subtext that is suddenly and devastatingly revealed after decades of sounding trivial and clichéd. Of course, that happens rarely, and not every generation has to experience it. Traditions come to an end, wealth is squandered, and people laugh about yesterday's morality: something is always getting thrown out of joint, but the earth continues to revolve and life goes on.

The idea that *everything* had been thrown out of joint, and that if life went on at all, it would be totally different or unimaginable, began to creep up on people in the Habsburg monarchy in the winter of 1916–1917. They had gotten used to the war and regarded it as a scourge of fate, the end of which they would have to await patiently. The abrupt loosening of moral strictures and the shift in social roles necessitated by the war made young people revel in a feeling of liberation. Those further along in years clung to the belief that when the crisis was over, the women who were working as conductors and in munitions factories would return to their roles as housewives. And death? Everyone knew someone who was in mourning for someone, and even the most naive people now understood that after such massive adversity, which touched every social class, there would be no sudden return to normality. But could an entire populace stay numb with pain? Everyone knew from past experience that this was impossible. Any war, even a lost one, was relegated to memory by some point. People figured that even this wound would heal.

But now the assault came from an utterly unexpected direction, and took aim at the very core of society, namely its food supply. People began to starve. It was bad enough that for the past two years people had been counting their needs crumb by crumb: they could have a daily ration of forty grams of sugar, one-quarter liter of milk, twenty grams of fat, and ten grams of coffee substitute; even bread was weighed out by the gram, and it took good connections to get more than a loaf per week. This was a subtle reminder of the allocation of feed rations for animals, an impression that was only reinforced by harsh reminders to chew the reduced rations longer (which health buffs in the back-to-nature movement had been advocating for some time). Humiliations of this sort from government officials were now the order of the day, and the positive side of these precise specifications was the resultant fair distribution. But taking the paternalistic language of the authorities at face value once again proved unwise because the consumption granted to the individual was not the assured minimum to which people were entitled. Municipal bakeries and inexpensive soup kitchens were quickly set up to prevent hunger revolts, but the authorities were no longer able to guarantee anything. They were not functional in either the military or the civilian domains. And neither the newly founded nutrition agency nor the countless state-controlled centers designed to monitor all redistribution centers during the war (there was even a center for rags) nor the draconian penalties for "illicit trade" and illegal supplies made a dent in this situation.

Exerting moral pressure was an effective means of masking this unforeseen governmental failure and shifting the responsibility to the people. Anyone who complained that municipal bread consisted increasingly of potato flour, acorns, and wood shavings, anyone who disliked the taste of nettles or had something against cigarettes that were half-filled with beech leaves had to endure strict reminders that "our men in uniform out in the battlefield" had very different issues on their minds (which was not even true, to hear the men on leave from the front describe things). Personalization of the problem was a favorite stopgap measure to rechannel people's growing rage: since it could not be admitted openly that the widespread adversity was in part an outcome of the enemy naval blockade, and since the newspapers were equally unable to report about the catastrophic failure of the administration, they launched a fierce campaign to fight unscrupulous "hoarders" and (preferably Jewish) "middlemen" who created shortages in order to drive the prices up.

But the more people who were now themselves forced to ignore the law, to get what they needed on the black market, or even to steal field crops from farmers like thieves in the night, the less anyone cared about spectacular trial reports or bothered to grouse about the few beneficiaries of the war. In the long run, hunger won out, and people's bodies were longing for something other than propaganda. The hitherto unfathomable reality was now plain as day: a prosperous and powerful state in the center of Europe, a state with a brilliant history and imperial ambitions, was no longer in a position to feed its people. Barring a miracle, it would have to let them freeze, as well, in the coming winter. People began to feel like homeless beggars.

The shock and psychological upheaval unleashed by this failure extended far beyond any direct physical privations. People felt as though they had been cast into a dog-eat-dog society in which hard work, frugality, and loyalty were no longer rewarded, but instead social shrewdness and brazen self-assertiveness, flexibility, and first-rate connections prevailed, which signaled the dissolution and even inversion of the middle-class value system—a moral catastrophe that aroused fear and despair.

Despite this, or for this very reason, hardly anyone believed that this was an irreversible derailment of the *system*. Instead, there was a great deal of finger-pointing. People railed against the indolence of petty bureaucrats, then against the authorities who had failed to make provisions, then against the army leaders who helped themselves to the dwindling resources without regard for others, and, last but not least, against the ministerial lineup in Vienna, which was evidently incapable of putting its foot down. The hungry Viennese, in turn, railed against the eastern European Jews, who crowded into the lines with their many children; then against the Hungarians, who no longer supplied grain because feeding their cattle and pigs was more important to them; and finally against the Czechs, who set aside more and more of the arranged coal shipments for themselves. Increasingly, a lament was giving voice to the rampant social regression: "If the kaiser only knew!"

The immediate vicinity of the monarch remained an oasis of tranquility amidst the cacophony of hatred and the aimless despair, a haven from legal and political wrangling into which anybody could project what made him happy, where everyone could revel in an utterly illusory feeling of closeness. Everybody knew everything there was to know about the personal disasters Franz Joseph I had had to cope with in his infinitely long reign. By contrast, no one had the least idea of the actual responsibility the kaiser bore for the death, mutilation, and emaciation of his subjects. Every schoolchild was aware that the dutiful ruler set to work at 5 A.M. each day. Few had any idea of what this work actually consisted of. Everyone considered him a giving and stabilizing figure: the contents of the daily reports from the palace essentially revolved around whom the kaiser had allowed to appear before him and whom he had promoted or honored; apart from that, there were paternal admonitions, expressions of thanks, and exhortations to hold out. People rarely gleaned what the kaiser actually wanted, the decrees he was preparing, and what he himself had decided. Even the people of Prague did not know that he had spared them the prospect of martial law. In March 1915, he had given orders for all royal gardens to be turned into vegetable beds. That was what people remembered.

The idea of keeping the peak of the power pyramid under a veil of fog and presenting the kaiser as an apolitical, nonpartisan figure was in line with Austrian tradition and part of a clever political, social, and psychological calculation. But in a state perched at the edge of the abyss, whose public discourse was dominated almost completely by struggles over distribution and nationalistic squabbling, there was no choice but to keep the monarch out of these issues systematically. He was the Great Mediator, the ultimate common reference point behind which chaos loomed and whose grandeur no one dared question. Inconceivable that one of the parties would have been able to attack him, let alone in the form of a physical assault, as had just happened to Austrian Prime Minister Karl Graf Stürgkh in October 1916.[4] But it was equally unthinkable that this super-patriarch could turn away, that his dynasty could be extinguished. Even the most aggressive nationalists would have had trouble imagining a postwar world without the House of Habsburg.

But this question suddenly shot to the surface. Franz Joseph I died on November 21, 1916, just one day after the fifth war bond was launched, one month after the violent death of his prime minister, an unfathomable sixty-eight years after his coronation as kaiser of Austria. The well-known witticism that the Habsburg subjects were born and died under one and the same kaiser portrait was not so far from the truth: many had lived in the feeling that the kaiser had *always* been present, and it would be difficult to track down anybody with a vivid memory of the legendary period *before* Franz Joseph.

The shock wave that coursed through the populace far surpassed the mourning that the death of a frail ruler would have occasioned at other times. This was a symbolic end of the world for every individual, and an unmistakable sign that after this loss there could no longer be a return to the smug world of the turn of the century, which was increasingly idealized in memory, even if this war somehow ended relatively well (as only the generals believed by this point). Of course, a legitimate successor was on hand, and in a matter of hours after the terrible news, the twenty-nine-year-old Archduke Karl, a grandnephew of Franz Joseph, was designated kaiser. The dynasty stayed alive. But the visible efforts of Karl I to gain authority right away and take forceful measures to deal with the supply crisis made it clear that the new kaiser had to *prove* something and was acting like a politician, entangled in the pragmatic demands of the day. There was no symbolic representation. The final anchor had broken loose; no office could now prevent the world from getting "thrown out of joint" once and for all.

There is no doubt that the fierce social tremors in the final months of 1916 sent shock waves through Kafka, as well. The degree to which he consciously reflected on them can be gauged only indirectly from the extant sources, but it is certain that they affected him psychologically. Even the well-to-do Kafkas suffered shortages, despite the many helpful connections they had in the area around Prague as wholesalers. A letter from Julie Kafka to Felice Bauer—written at the very beginning of that catastrophic winter—reveals unequivocally that even at this time, neither money nor connections could make for full stomachs:

> We observed the Jewish holidays like proper Jews. We closed up shop on both days of Rosh Hashanah, and yesterday on Yom Kippur we fasted and prayed diligently. It was not difficult for us to fast, because we've been practicing for that the whole year. Incidentally, here in Prague the hunger problem has not grown too severe yet, and we would be delighted to have you over very soon.[5]

The meaning of this message was quite plain, as even the censor (whom Julie evidently feared less than her son did) must have realized. The hunger "here in Prague [was] not too severe yet" in comparison even to Vienna, where there was already looting and disorder, and certainly not as bad as in Berlin. Although no one could have predicted then that the following months would go down in German history as the *Kohlrübenwinter* (turnip winter) and that thousands would die of malnutrition in the cities, word had gotten around that life in the German capital (in contrast to Prague) had begun to assume the contorted features of an unrelenting fight for survival. It was hard to come by food there, and even those with an executive salary had to make do with the "standard-issue sausage" now available (which tasted the way it sounded) and the authorized 0.7 eggs per week. Julie Kafka could not understand why her son did not invite his long-time girlfriend to join the family for dinner in Prague over the Christmas vacation, where she could have been served something better than cattle feed. And Felice wasn't offering to visit either. Was this really a reconciliation?[6]

Kafka, who ate very little anyway, had an easier time than most with the dwindling daily rations. He did not care for meat or cake, and the now-pathetic menus in restaurants and coffeehouses made no difference to him. He told his concerned sister Ottla that at Alchimistengasse he had more every evening than he could eat,[7] and even the looming absence of coal (heating at night was already forbidden) could not stop him from staying in his new sanctuary for as long as possible. When Brod visited him there and Kafka read a text to him—there was now something to read aloud again—Brod was amazed at this "monastic cell of a real writer," and had the impression that Kafka was suffering less than he from the horrors of the third winter of the war.[8] He was probably right. Kafka might have replied that this was the age of the ascetics. A dark time, an icy time, time to write.

Four unlined octavo volumes, each about eighty pages in length—a compact size suitable for carrying around town in his breast pocket—have been preserved from the winter of 1916 to 1917. Two additional notebooks that Kafka must have used are missing.

These nondescript pads, which are filled with writing down to the last page (Kafka scholars refer to them as the Octavo Notebooks A through D), offer a startling and confusing sight: long, short, and very brief entries, prose and dialogue, a couple of lines of poetry, dated and undated texts, normal handwriting randomly alternating with shorthand, a scattering of headings, entire pages crossed out, word-for-word repetitions, disjointed statements, fluid transitions and long dividing lines punctuated by doodles, mysterious names, an address, drafts of letters, a checklist of errands, torn out and mixed-up pages, a random slip of paper . . . everything looking as though he had spread his papers out all over the floor while writing. The disorganized notebooks of the manuscript for *The Trial* were the first ordeal Kafka left to his future editors; this was the second. Max Brod may have failed in this endeavor, but his work proved to be instructive for his successors.[9]

A second look does not make this textual jungle seem any more familiar. A contemporaneous reader, even someone who had read the few published works by Kafka, would not have recognized *anything* here: no sign of "Kleistian diction," realistic narration, smatterings of fantasy, or humorous slapstick and carefully calculated slips that Kafka had developed with such gusto in the abandoned "Blumfeld" story. Although Kafka retained a carefully controlled presentation, he allowed his imagination to roam far more freely and radically, and the result is an unparalleled zigzag between the real world and the world of language. "I was stiff and cold, I was a bridge" are the first words in Notebook B; "Every person carries a room within him," it says a few pages later. An undead phantasm prophesies: "No one will read what I am writing here." "We had set up camp in the oasis. My companions were asleep," a traveler reports, and "Yesterday a swoon came to me. She lives in the house next door. . . ."

The experimental context in Kafka's notebooks (or in the Kafka critical edition) will bemuse even readers who are acquainted with some of these texts: there are countless variants, interruptions, shifts of perspective, and cross connections. This manuscript is like molten lava, creating the illusion of potential fluidity even where Kafka himself had decided on a definitive version "ready for publication." A lengthy passage in Notebook D begins: "We all know Red Peter, just as half the world does. But when he came to our town for a guest performance, I decided to get to know him better, personally." Red Peter? Of course—that is the chimpanzee in "A Report to an Academy" who recounts the tale of his captivity and how he became a human. Half the world knows this canonical Kafka text, which has become popular primarily in solo acts staged by countless actors. In Kafka's notebook, the ape first appears in an interview with a journalist; two additional entries follow, both of which veer off into unrelated topics, and only then does the reader come to the well-known introductory words: "Honored Members of the Academy! You have done me the honor of inviting me to submit to the Academy a report about my previous life as an ape." But in the free monologue that follows, the naive and meddlesome journalist is not forgotten. Kafka/Red Peter describes him gruffly as one of "the ten thousand writing windbags who give vent to their views about me in the newspapers."[10]

But these kinds of echoes and reflections are mere spin-offs in his sweeping presentation of literary forms. It is as though he were determined to try out *everything* that narrative traditions have to offer—parables, fables, fairy tales, reports, lists, monologues and dialogues, flashbacks and background stories, first-person and third-person perspectives—and swirl them together. He blended all that tradition had yielded and emerged with an extraordinary new synthesis, turning lead into gold.

This should not be mistaken for Expressionism, and most certainly not for *écriture automatique*, "automatic writing" that was designed to outwit censorship from the writer's own psyche and was launched by the Surrealists a few years later. In Kafka's writings, everything remains within bounds, and the very multitude of attempts is the strongest evidence that he was still subjecting his ideas to a rigorous selection process: Anything that was not viable or vivid enough, or lacked organic coherence, or seemed like a mere "construction" was eliminated. Moreover, Kafka never got carried away into manipulating the foundations of language itself; there were no word coinings, no pointless alliteration, imitation of oral speech, misuse of grammar, or accumulations of dashes and exclamation points. Standard German remained the only medium Kafka respected, and he never deliberately went beyond its limits, and certainly not for mere effect—yet the journey *within* this medium took him into uncharted territories.

That was certainly not Kafka's intention at the beginning of these productive five months, and his first steps seemed quite innocuous. It was his third intensive writing phase since the fall of 1912, and he wanted to try something new, something that no one would expect of him but would not shock anyone either. His first choice was drama, which was generally acknowledged to be part and parcel of the writer's craft. Prominent authors such as Gerhart Hauptmann and Arthur Schnitzler went back and forth between prose and drama, according to the requirements of the material, without being singled out as multifaceted talents. Even authors with clear preferences sometimes dabbled in different genres—Thomas Mann wrote a play, and Carl Sternheim several stories. The poet Rilke published an extraordinary novel, and Werfel enjoyed box-office success with his *Trojan Women*. And of course there was Kafka's impresario, Max Brod, who covered every possible genre, from ghost stories to Zionist poetry. So why not write a drama?

His attempt fell apart. No matter how much Kafka wrestled with the text—the unparalleled number of corrections and deletions suggests that he spent weeks slaving over it—and as carefully as he kept separating the wheaf from the chaff and piecing his text back together, "The Warden of the Tomb" remained a fragment, and he considered only a few scenes developed enough to be recited. Kafka even typed up a clean copy on his own for potential recitation, but it is unclear whether anyone actually got to hear the dialogues.[11]

"The Warden of the Tomb" is not one of Kafka's significant achievements; later readers did not know quite what to make of it, and attempts to revive it on smaller stages have remained episodic. Kafka too obviously leaned on literary models (Strindberg in particular); the construction was too awkward, and the work too piecemeal. It opens with a long-winded report to set up the actual sensation, namely, the apparitions of royal ancestors. Shakespeare was better able to accomplish this in the first act of *Hamlet*. Kafka was well advised to lay aside the "impossibilities" with which he had filled most of the first notebook and to return to the type of writing at which he excelled.

He now cleared the decks for a pyrotechnic display of his imagination. "A Country Doctor," "The Bridge," "Up in the Gallery," "The Next Village," "The Bucket Rider," and "A Fratricide" were written in December and January; "Jackals and Arabs" and "The New Attorney" in February; "An Old Page" and "Eleven Sons" in March; "The Cares of a Family Man," "A Visit to a Mine," "A Crossbreed," and "A Report to an Academy" in April. And of course the "Hunter Gracchus" project, which dated back to Riva, on which Kafka worked from January to April, as well as several other important fragments, including "My Neighbor," "The Knock at the Manor Gate," and "The Great Wall of China" (including "An Imperial Message"), which were all written in February or March. This collection of gems might not have been enough to establish his worldwide fame, but it certainly ensured a worldwide *exegesis* of Kafka, a humble approach to his writing, groping its way with eye and index finger and taking the text as revelation, snatching it away from the realm of mere mortal criticism once and for all. In particular, the mystifying texts from Kafka's octavo notebooks lured critics, and then general readers, into picking them apart letter by letter in the quest for meaning—an approach that would eventually extend to Kafka's entire oeuvre.

Now that the creative process has been illuminated by scholarly editing, this tendency toward fetishizing the text strikes readers today as unenlightened and naive. No admirer of "The Metamorphosis" or "The Stoker" can doubt that these works, despite their linguistic precision, elasticity, formal unity, and apparent timelessness, share a genetic connection. These stories themselves have a history and reveal highly personal experiences, penchants, and obsessions of their creator. They are the result of a craft learned and practiced over the course of years. Even Kafka's claim that he could have done all of this even better under more favorable conditions cannot be brushed aside, and no study of the revisions in the manuscripts is required to be able to take these kinds of self-doubts on the part of the author seriously.

Of course, with the prose pieces in the octavo notebooks—one hesitates to call them "stories"—Kafka drew his readers into treating his works with unparalleled reverence. The sheer multitude of motifs, images, and themes convinces us that the author is circling around himself. Where variations and affinities are found, they are clearly *deliberate*, and even the private obsessions and little games testify to a freedom that differs from the monochromatic punishment fantasies in the earlier works. These are texts of a sometimes unreal fullness and perfection, texts that on the surface yield no trace of their genesis. It seems inconceivable that the two long, flawless sentences that have found their place in countless textbooks under the title "Up in the Gallery" could have been subject to revision or even have had preliminary stages (although it is impossible to verify in the absence of manuscripts[12]).

Anyone who looks at the octavo notebooks themselves, hoping to find evidence that even these revelations did not just pop into his head but were the result of hard work, is likely to be let down. The context is chaotic, of course; the traces of pen and pencil attest to the fact that here, too, everything was precisely what he had intended from the outset. Precisely where the perfection is beyond any doubt, the creator of these texts seems quite sure of himself. The manuscript of "An Imperial Message," for example, has next to no substantive corrections—although Kafka perused it critically with an eye to publication. It truly seems as though everything was in place right from the start. The author as creator *ex nihilo*.

Supposing it were possible to show an experienced reader Kafka's octavo notebooks as part of a blind study, with place, time, and author unspecified. In all likelihood, the reader would be quick to classify these notebooks as a product of literary modernity, and note a profound orientation crisis going well beyond the individual, but would be hard pressed to pick up on the fact that these texts were written during a terrible winter in a wretched cottage, by fingers stiff with cold, just minutes away from lines of starving people, in a dilapidated, freezing, dimly lit city under military rule, by a mid-level civil servant whose professional concerns included amputations and nervous shocks.

But the reader might figure out that this author had lost an emperor, which is the explicit point of "An Imperial Message," a brief legend-like story in which even the emphatic order of the dying monarch is not enough to get a message to its recipient. In "An Old Page," the emperor stands similarly helpless at the window and watches his seat of royal power go to ruin, and "The Great Wall of China" states explicitly: "The empire is immortal, but the individual emperor falls and plummets." The brief drama "The Warden of the Tomb" plays shortly after a changeover of power. The new prince has been in office for only a year, his authority is shaky, and even his own wife is on the side of his enemies.[13] And the short prose piece "The New Attorney" recalls a legendary monarch and conjures up a world devoid of leadership: "Nowadays—as no one can deny—there is no one like Alexander the Great . . . no one, no one can lead the way to India . . . no one points the way."

One of the primary reasons that Kafka has come to be regarded as oblivious to reality and politically remote is that he focused less on great losses themselves—even when they were catastrophic—than on the larger *significance* of these losses, and the way they laid bare the essence of the era as a whole. The decline of a great symbol, the end of a tradition, the tip of the pyramid chopped off—like most of his contemporaries, he experienced these events as signs of an irreversible dissolution. In everyday life, it was less the privations and increasing limitations that impressed and preoccupied him—he endured all that uncomplainingly and with astonishing patience—than the symbolic nature of these events. Of course, it was bad when Ottla came back from the coal merchant with an empty bucket.[14] That had never happened before, and it was a threat that even Kafka could not ignore altogether when the temperatures in February 1917 sank below minus 20 Celsius. Theaters, movie theaters, and schools were closed on occasion, the gas supply was stopped during the day, the streetcars by the early evening, and during the night, Kafka groped his way through the frozen and deserted historic town center in complete darkness. But "The Bucket Rider," a story Kafka wrote during the worst days, in which a freezing first-person narrator begs for coal, would not have been written if Kafka had not regarded this deathly atmosphere as a symbol of his day. We read right near the beginning: "behind me, the pitiless stove, before me, the sky, every bit as pitiless," and this "every bit as" is unmistakable: the stove is not the only thing that is empty. The first-person narrator does not go back into his own cold room but instead disappears into unspecified "regions of the icebergs," like the country doctor in the story of that name, the closing sentence of which supplies the hermeneutic key: "Naked, exposed to the frost of this most wretched of ages, with an earthly carriage, unearthly horses, I, old man that I am, drift about."

Kafka was painfully aware that these daily nuisances were harbingers of epochal catastrophes to come. At the very time that the state began leaving its subjects to their own devices and suffered the loss of its highest representative, Kafka started reorganizing his life and writing. He tried out new avenues in both arenas. The close chronological connection is astounding,[15] the coincidence obvious, mere chance out of the question. Kafka was reacting *productively* to a crisis that compelled him to overcome inhibitions, break with old habits, and seek means of survival. Like many others, Kafka regarded real-life events—all kinds of shortages, the death of the kaiser (from whom Kafka got his first name)—as definitive confirmations that life would no longer be as it once was; the conclusion he drew for himself was that it could no longer go on the way it had been. The loss forced him to muster new strength; at the same time he *unleashed* this new strength and, with it, a stream of images and ideas. Two years earlier, he had gotten past the debacle in the Askanischer Hof in much the same way. Once again, the dynamic that was so extraordinarily characteristic of Kafka, a dynamic that shaped and energized him, was set in motion. It was the dynamic of catastrophe. A letter that arrived late or a slight cough in the room next door made him falter, yet a world that was falling apart appeared to offer him boundless new resources.

On November 24, 1916, two days after he learned of the death of Franz Josef, he tried to make it clear to Felice why having his own apartment was more important to him than ever, even more important than the prospect of seeing her again: "This apartment might not restore my inner peace, but it would at least give me a chance to work; the gates of paradise would not fly open again, but I might find two slits for my eyes in the wall."[16] *Paradise*: It was the most powerful image he could present, a colossal sign of redemption that no one had ever claimed for literature. But he sensed that it was no longer a wall separating him from the imaginative freedom he was yearning for. On the very same day, he hurried over to Alchimistengasse and opened his first, still-blank octavo notebook, surrounded by the smell of fresh paint.

He did not know that he would be spending half a year here. And he could not have realized—or shall we say that he could not have realized "as far as is humanly possible"—that with virtually the first words he committed to paper (a stage direction of "The Warden of the Tomb"), he had already found a staggeringly precise image of his own life and, at the same time, the motto of his future work: "cramped stage, open at the top."

CHAPTER EIGHT

Ottla and Felice

We live at the edge of outer space here. An attempt is being made to live here.

—Halldór Laxness, *Kristnihald undir Jökli*

On one of the first days that Ottla Kafka entered her renovated cottage on Alchimistengasse, she discovered a slender volume on the table: *The Judgment*, published by Kurt Wolff Verlag, twenty-nine pages in length. She knew about it; after all, she had been there four years earlier when her brother, keyed up after not getting any sleep all night, had charged into his sisters' room with his story, the ink still wet on the pages. That is how long it had taken for the work to be published as a book, and now it was there in *her* house as a gift. She opened it up. The flyleaf bore the cryptic dedication "For F." (of course—for whom else?), but underneath was a handwritten dedication by the author: "To my landlady." She was charmed and flattered, and hastened to write to her future husband, Josef David, about it. But there was a second line, a strange signature that muted her pleasure: "The Rat of Palais Schönborn." This would have been difficult to explain to Josef David, so she kept it to herself.

It was one of his typical jests at his own expense: Kafka put himself down, and everyone laughed. He truly did feel utterly out of place in that huge apartment advertised for rent in Palais Schönborn; just looking up at the high ceiling sent a shudder down his spine. But the property manager told him that there were other, more down-to-earth accommodations and brought him to a wing up on the third floor, where Kafka could hardly believe his eyes: "an apartment consisting of two room without a kitchen, that seems altogether to live up to my wildest dreams."[1] It was not immediately available, of course, but might be at some point.

Kafka was set on *this* apartment and refused to look at any others. But could he justify the effect that a change from the status quo would have on his work? Ottla's cottage on Alchimistengasse, which he was reluctant to occupy as a short-term arrangement at first, had proved to be an ideal writing nook, and once Ottla's girlfriend, a petite girl named Růžena, had been hired to clean, heat the cottage, and carry coal, Kafka could even spend his evenings up at the castle with a clear conscience. He even toyed with the idea of moving there with all his meager possessions and thus putting his asceticism to an enormous new test, which would have sealed his position as the family fool, as his father had been predicting for years.

But the family was spared this further embarrassment because suddenly—about two months after seeing the simple apartment in Schönborn—Kafka received the news that it was now up for rent, and that no more than an oral agreement was needed. And this time he followed his first impulse. He wanted to embrace this dream, even though he was soon assailed with the usual debilitating doubts, which threatened to derail his firm resolve. He thought of six arguments against taking the apartment and six for it. He presented every last detail to Felice Bauer, taut with the stress surrounding this existential decision. But at this point he was seeking not her encouragement, or her cool hand on his forehead, but her *approval*:

> [A]fter the war I want to try to get a year's leave of absence to start with; this may not be possible right away, or even at all. Well, if it worked out, the two of us would have the most wonderful apartment I could imagine in Prague, all ready for you, though only for a comparatively short time, during which you would have to do without a kitchen of your own, and even without a bathroom. Never-

> theless, it would be to my liking and you could have a thorough rest for two or three months.[2]

There was astonishing information here. No kitchen, no bath? So this was a proletarian apartment, by Berlin standards.[3] But there was a bigger consideration at issue: If Kafka truly wanted to move to Berlin after the war, as had so often been discussed and agreed on explicitly in Marienbad, he could not simply take an extended leave from the Insurance Institute; he would have to give notice. If, on the other hand, he seriously believed he could manage to combine writing and office work over the long term and continue living in Prague as a civil servant, *she* was the one who would have to give notice, in which case she could rest as long as she liked. There was a degree of logic to the circuitous, oddly legalistic language Kafka used in his letter regarding the measures to be taken—their own apartment, yes or no, no or yes—yet it was oddly hazy on the *intention* underlying this decision.

This peculiar form of rhetoric, which obscures the situation with analytical precision, is an essential component of what is now called Kafkaesque. In Kafka's letters and diaries, it always appears as a protective response to a situation crying out for immediate action but with overly complex and imponderable consequences. Kafka's style of argumentation, contaminated by legalese and abruptly turning convoluted, was a sure sign that the issue at hand was vital to him, that the pending decision was highly charged. He described the "saga of my apartment" as "a vast subject" in the very first sentence, and claimed that he could convey only a tiny fraction to Felice; as his epistolary treatise as a whole shows, this was not intended as a joke. But what on earth was so unnerving about a little relocation within one and the same city, from one very familiar street corner to the next?

Of course Kafka's pragmatic doubts could not be brushed aside. More by accident than design, he had found his way to a new, psychologically balanced and extremely productive rhythm, so what would be the point of jeopardizing it with more experiments? He knew from experience that time was limited, and that even a prolific winter could be followed by a new standstill.

But the source of Kafka's agitation lay elsewhere, and all this talk of pros and cons could not disguise the fact that a symbolic act was at stake. A rented furnished room like the one on Lange Gasse could still be regarded as an exclave of the home territory; it was no more real a residence than a student dorm, even if one was well over the age of thirty, whereas the key to one's own apartment was the visible and unmistakable symbol of emancipation and striking out on one's own. He was well aware that even on Alchimistenstrasse, opening and closing the door of his "own" house was a new, pleasurable experience, and Ottla, too, savored the surreptitious delight of the key in her pocket and the thrill of home ownership, and it gave her deeper satisfaction than the actual use of the little house, which was limited to a matter of hours anyway.

The result was a powerful emotional bond between the siblings in that dark and icy winter of 1916 to 1917, a mutual reinforcement of impulses that yearned for independence. It cannot be determined from the existing documents whether Kafka was a role model or merely an adviser—either way, Ottla could rely on his support in taking a stand against their parents, even if he was unable to follow through on his sister's emancipatory leap. But she noticed that he, too, now sought to put an end to the standstill that had gone on for years. He complained less often, wrote in a more disciplined manner than he had in a long time, sought an apartment, and even tried to safeguard his plan financially by applying for the position of secretary of the Workers' Accident Insurance Institute, which would raise his pay by two salary brackets.[4]

Kafka must have become aware during his summer outings with his sister that Ottla's growing need for independence would not be satisfied merely by "peaceful" means; that is, means that would be acceptable to his whole family. And he understood quite well—seeing as he felt much the same way—why she initially projected this need onto nature, in which at least the *appearance* of freedom was so easily attainable. She was enchanted by paths along the outskirts of Prague that she had known for ages, even Chotek Park, which she had been going to since childhood; in the Bohemian Forest, where she spent several days alone, the warm summer rain sent her into ecstasy, and on Alchimistengasse, she kept urging her brother to look up at the starry night sky. "There is something very wrong," she wrote to Josef David, "in spending life in the city, in the shop. I'm not making any plans now, but a person can dream. I wouldn't hesitate for a second to decide to spend my whole life in the country, here or elsewhere, and never to see the city again. . . ."[5]

Of course she *did* make plans, and she knew quite well that the battles that lay ahead would not revolve around her love of nature. In November 1916, while she was secretly furnishing her little house, she first told her parents that she no longer wished to work in the family business and would rather pursue agriculture or horticulture, and she would find a way to acquire the necessary knowledge. This was a lot for the family to swallow, a revolt of the kind the family had never seen. Her father's harsh and unwavering reaction was to pronounce her crazy. He regarded the social topography from the center—that is, from the box seat on Altstädter Ring he had fought so hard for—and associated flat land with humiliation, helplessness, and lack of education. That was where he had come from, and the Kafkas no longer had any business being there. His wife agreed. Ottla, who was perennially defiant and clearly derived pleasure from tormenting her parents, would have shocked and scandalized her parents just as much as if she had kept company with the staff (with whom she had always been on very good terms). But she was serious about this, and when it turned out three months later that Ottla had made inquiries into agricultural schools and vegetable gardening and that Franz—a real "scoundrel," as his father called him—even supported her in these efforts, a good deal of shouting ensued in the family's living room once again.[6]

Ottla was now twenty-four years old, and well into marriageable age. Of course, they had to expect that one day in the not-too-distant future, they would have to make do without her in the shop—and she would certainly be missed. Just a few months earlier, her father had made a point of praising her diligence (to a third party, of course). But Ottla was not going after a fiancé; instead, she had been captivated by the Zionist Club of Jewish Women and Girls' disdain of the world of business and reverence of sweaty work in the fields as the pinnacle of human happiness. Yes, the daughter of another wealthy merchant in Prague had taken the idealistic talk of this "club" at face value and had gone to Palestine as a farm worker, against the vehement protests of her family. These were nice role models.

But it was also a warning to her parents. Now that Ottla was taking her first determined steps and looking for a place in an agricultural college in February 1917, one of the Zionist papers published a long article about "agricultural training for girls" in Palestine[7]—a powerful description that was just the thing to spur on Ottla's will to self-sacrifice. If the conflict with her was driven too far and she was forced into a corner, she would be gone for good, or if they ever saw her again, it would be years later, with Ottla as a tanned colonist. A nightmare for the Kafkas.

The fact that it did not get to that point was not the doing of her father, who was always hollering and insisting on maintaining the status quo, but owed to the subtle strategies of compromise and integration, expertly handled by her mother, that were handed down within Jewish families. If there was a threat of a serious rift, she would need to cut her daughter some slack, but not more than the radius of their own extended family allowed. Anyone who wanted to go and could not be dissuaded from his or her chosen path either through accusations or moral pressure was let go—but not granted freedom.

It had been seven years since Karl Hermann, Elli's fiancé, had been introduced to his future brother-in-law Franz as a paragon of energy and business sense. Times had certainly changed. After marrying into the family, Karl had proposed the idea of an asbestos factory. That factory had long since ceased production; the dreams of a second Kafka economic miracle, or even a career as an entrepreneur for their son Franz, faded away in the enormous wave of bankruptcy that came with the war and the closing of the international markets. The money invested by Hermann Kafka and the uncle in Madrid was lost, as was the involvement of Franz, who had been exasperatingly indifferent from the very start and longed for the day when that depressing workshop in Žižkov would finally close down. And that is precisely what happened in 1917: the last hope of getting the business up and running again was dashed. At the end of the year, the files were closed and the liquidation began—at the same moment that asbestos, which was vital to the war effort, was being subjected to rigid government control. The difference between fancy goods and industrial raw materials proved to be yet another painful wartime lesson for the Kafkas.[8]

To the family's astonishment, the inventor and (according to the district court) "sole liquidator" of the asbestos factory, namely Karl Hermann, had come up with a new idea for making a profitable investment of his money (and presumably also his wife's). In his German-speaking hometown of Zürau (Siřem) in northwestern Bohemia, he had acquired a farm about fifty acres in size that was deep in debt and had been poorly run by a relative. It is unclear how Karl Hermann pictured this new, high-risk operation, whether he was speculating on his family's assistance or the dramatically rising prices for field crops, or even envisioning a leisurely life as an estate owner. But evidently he did not find anyone who wanted to take the reins, and as an officer on active duty, he had scant opportunity to manage it himself. If the war did not come to an end soon, this project could be written off as well.

Then a clever idea came up at the Kafkas' dinner table. It was as astonishing as it was obvious. If Ottla could not be talked out of leaving the city, why not have *her* run this farm? There was little to lose: Ottla would do everything in her power to bring her knowledge up to speed as quickly as possible because she wanted to prove herself. Her finances would remain under the supervision of the family because she would have to work out the income, expenditures, and overheads with the people who had supplied the start-up capital: Karl Hermann if he was on home leave in Prague, as was now the case, or Elli if he was not. And if the project was successful, they could even count on Ottla's gratitude—gratitude for offering her the physical basis for the very rural life she had lately been promoting so forcefully as the only life suitable for human beings. But Karl and Elli owed a moral debt as well: after all, it was the Kafkas who were taking their now-worthless property off their hands and sparing them yet another financial debacle—so it was only fair for Elli to take Ottla's place in their parents' store for at least a few hours a day. It was *perfect*. And no matter how the father might rail, he had to acknowledge that this plan was more ingenious than anything he could have thought up himself.

Ottla grabbed at the offer. Zürau was her chance to get away without breaking off contact with her parents, which she feared far more than her defiant pronouncements would suggest. The prospect of managing her finances on her own for the first time was also enticing; that alone was worth the effort. Once the venture was in full swing—most likely by the coming winter—she would acquire the theoretical foundations needed to qualify for the vocational school she was hoping to attend. Until then, all she needed was a basic set of agricultural literature, which her brother would send her. In mid-April 1917, she bade farewell to Alchimistengasse, Franz, and her beloved cousin Irma, and set off for the country. Did she have any idea what she was getting herself into?

Kafka must have regarded his sister's coup as a miracle. No matter how involved he was in the practical preparations, and no matter how clearly he saw through his parents' gambits, he was still flabbergasted by her ability to pull it off: a city girl as the leaseholder of a farm, in unfamiliar surroundings, fending for herself. Ottla was obviously determined to accomplish the impossible. Her very first written report proved what she was capable of: it was a sensible, pragmatic letter (which was, like all subsequent reports, pored over in Prague before being forwarded to the farm owner serving in the military). Even her father—who surely was privately mourning the loss of his most diligent worker—took the news from the village so calmly that the family was astonished. Of course, Ottla was homesick. Even more than her desire to see Josef David, she longed for the familiar streets of Prague. But she did *not* write that in this letter, and she was ashamed to admit it even to Irma.

Ottla's absence also hit Kafka harder than he had anticipated. During the previous summer, it had begun to dawn on him (and he stated as much to Felice) that he was no longer Ottla's mentor, that she was actually the person he wished to have as his *mother*. This mother image became part of the siblings' banter. In the first letter he sent to her in Zürau, he claimed that it was only logical that the very day she left, the room on Alchimistengasse turned ice cold. A storm had blown out the fire in the stove "perhaps by chance, perhaps intentionally."[9] And when she finally brought up the issue of the emotional price of her departure, he replied:

> I was already feeling utterly abandoned by you and, thinking of an eventual future (always thinking of the future), I told myself: So she will let me go to rack and ruin, after all. But that is completely

> wrong, even aside from your letter, for with the house up there you've ushered in a better time for me, which is still going on now, even though I unfortunately have stopped working up there (because of the lovely days and the difficulty sleeping that comes with them) and what is more, you are away. Of course, there is plenty to complain about, but it is still incomparably better than the last few years.[10]

Better, on the whole, more or less—but "incomparably better"? He could scarcely convince Ottla that his work (which he had "unfortunately ... stopped") depended on the weather in Prague. That was precisely the kind of explanation typically employed to handle existential questions within the family. She had left that behind. Her brother underestimated her.

On Tuesday, July 10, 1917, Kafka was crawling around on all fours in his sister Valli's apartment, looking for a small purse, the handbag belonging to his fiancée, Felice Bauer, and he was in a state of near panic because there were nine hundred kronen in this bag. On the day before, they had been at the Brods', both embarrassed, Kafka in oddly formal clothing, with a high stand-up collar, as though making his first visit as a fiancé; then they had gone to the Weltsches, and afterwards ... Felice was certain—but not *absolutely* certain—that she still had the purse with her. They searched the closets and drawers, and threw the whole family into a dither. *Such a large sum of money*. And time was running out. On Wednesday the couple was supposed to leave for a trip to Hungary, Felice to see her sister Else in Arad, and Kafka as her escort at least as far as Budapest. There was no choice but to go through every possibility systematically, so Kafka started by hurrying over to the Weltsches. No, Irma Weltsch informed him rather curtly (without noticing that Kafka was feeling desperate about the looming loss), the purse was certainly not there; if it had been, they would have let him know right away.[11] So back he went to Valli's apartment, where Felice had been staying for the few days of her visit to Prague. Everything had already been turned upside down, but Kafka began once again to make a systematic search of the floor, looking under the chairs, closets, and beds. Then he grabbed hold of Felice's suitcase, and underneath it was the purse.

Felice Bauer's sudden appearance in Prague—she had not seen the city for more than three years—seems odd. There is no letter or even a note by Kafka indicating how this reconciliation had come about after their correspondence had ground to a halt. But this cannot have been a spontaneous visit or an attempt to catch him unawares.[12] If Kafka was prepared to accompany Felice on her trip to Hungary, he would have had to apply for a passport weeks in advance (as he had for his trip to Hungary with Elli) and overcome Director Marschner's resistance to granting time off to his remaining staff, especially to those eligible for military service, and vacations were restricted to an absolute minimum. But above all, Felice's appearance in Prague meant there would be the inevitable get-together with Kafka's parents, with all the ceremonial trappings. His parents knew about the engagement in Marienbad, and Kafka and Felice needed to get their stories straight when facing an inevitable barrage of indiscreet and intrusive questions ("When are you finally going to get married?"). A formal celebration of a *re*-engagement had no place in the inventory of bourgeois family rituals, but they could at least celebrate their reunion and the fact that they had ironed out misunderstandings that had stood in the way of their marriage for so long, a marriage that had been decided on years earlier and been blessed by their parents. It appears likely that Kafka had resumed more frequent contact with Felice by May 1917 and made elaborate preparations for her arrival, and the odd visits he and his fiancée made to his closest friends also indicate that the couple had in some way gone ahead with the idea of regarding the agreements they had made in Marienbad as binding.

Even so, these were not happy days; that flash of relief he felt when recovering the purse was the only hint of elation. The pressure of convention, the skeptical glances of his parents, the show that Kafka put on, arm in arm with his fiancée, and that she really could have spared him, as Brod rightly pointed out,[13] surely dredged up memories he would have preferred to keep buried forever, memories of Whitsun in 1914, of that ill-fated "engagement expedition" to Berlin, which had given his most intimate longing a pragmatic twist and left him with awful visions for a long time to come. Of course, Kafka's self-confidence had grown, and when he thought back to the unsuccessful furniture shopping with which things had ended three years earlier . . . he would know how to avert a situation like that in Prague. But what about that bundle of cash that Felice had in her purse? Was it for her sister in Hungary? Or funds to go toward her future life together with Franz? He did not like people who thought of everything, but *she* certainly thought of everything.

Kafka's practical measures, by contrast, proved utterly unrealistic yet again. The supposedly "most wonderful apartment I could imagine in Prague," the apartment in Palais Schönborn, which he had described to her so enthusiastically as a future sanctuary for the two of them, turned out to be a dank, pathetic bachelor pad that smelled musty even in the summer, no matter how much time and effort Růženka, who was now taking care of both of Kafka's homes, devoted to scrubbing and heating. Even if Felice, who set great store by a cozy home, could have brought herself to invest some of her savings to settle in here for some time in comfort—but still without a bathroom, kitchen, or (and this was the most incredible part) even a front-door key—this misguided decision on his part hardly seemed to be a sign of his serious desire for them to share their lives. And the dark green writing cottage on Alchimistengasse, built in 1600, which he probably had to show her as well, only confirmed this impression. It would have been interesting to watch her poke her head in warily, clutching her hat.

Both of them were surely pleased to get out of Prague at long last, but they were happy for different reasons, and the few days they spent together in Budapest did not bode well. Kafka must have been struck by the stark contrast between the affectionate and relaxed close relationship he had recently enjoyed with Ottla and his growing estrangement from the woman he still wanted to marry but with whom every get-together—especially in the presence of family members—became a strenuous exercise. "I did tolerably well on the trip," he wrote to his sister, "but it was certainly not a trip for relaxation and reconciliation."[14] Not much more could be revealed on a postcard, but the couple was at the brink of breaking up for good, and when they finally boarded their trains in opposite directions, with Kafka heading to Vienna and Felice Bauer southeast to Arad, it was unclear when and if they would ever see each other again. He wrote her two long letters after his return, and both went unanswered. Neither has been located.[15]

Kafka's best known and most frequently reproduced portrait shows him with his fiancée Felice Bauer. It is the only photograph of the two of them together. This conventional posed photograph had Kafka standing, and Felice sitting on a chair, which, in order to even out the difference in their heights is either the height of a bar stool or is perched on a pedestal. Kafka is wearing a light summer suit with a handkerchief in the breast pocket, a dark patterned tie over a white shirt; Felice has on a long skirt and white blouse, with a locket that presumably contains a picture of Kafka, and a black purse on her lap—probably the one containing the nine hundred kronen. They are barely touching; only Kafka's oddly bent hand is resting on a fold of her skirt. Both are looking straight at the camera, and two studio lamps are reflected in their pupils. Felice, her full lips parted slightly, looks expectantly at the camera, while Kafka's expression is indeterminate. Is he smiling? It seems so at first, but something about these facial features is off, like one of those optical illusions that seem to keep shifting. This mysterious, almost eerie impression starts to make sense only when you try to read these uneven features one side at a time, at which point you realize that it *is* an optical illusion. If you cover up the right side of Kafka's face, you see a definite smile around his mouth and eyes; covering the left half reveals a serious, attentive neutral expression. The epiphany of a secretive truth, which is often seen on posed photographs.

But why did they choose to visit a professional photographer in 1917? That did not usually happen unless there was a formal occasion, and in this case, the occasion has to have been their decision to renew their engagement. It is an engagement picture, and on Felice's left hand we see the engagement ring (presumably the same one that she had cast off in fury in the fall of 1914). There had been no time for a visit to a photographer's studio in Prague; the prints would not have been finished in time for the trip, and no one likes to be photographed while entertaining panicked thoughts about a lost bundle of cash. But the sister in Hungary was expecting a picture, and thus the final opportunity presented itself in Budapest. And it truly was the final one. Both of them may have sensed that it would be a farewell picture, a photograph that would record them as still together in principle but devoid of any erotic connection. A photograph that gave those who looked carefully enough a glimpse into the future.

Nothing is known about Felice Bauer's trip back to Berlin. Evidently she did not pass through Prague.

CHAPTER NINE

The Country Doctor Ventures Out

When I opened up the book, when I read your name in print, I looked at it as if I were seeing you.

—Bettina von Arnim, *Goethes Briefwechsel mit einem Kinde*

> My life is just monotonous and proceeds within the prison of my innate, threefold misfortune, in a manner of speaking. When I can't do anything, I am unhappy; when I can do something, there isn't enough time; and when I look to the future for hope, the next thing I know is that the fear is there, the wide-ranging fear, and then I am even less able to work. An exquisitely calculated hell. Yet—and this is the main point—it is not without its good moments.[1]

As Kafka had known for quite some time, these were more than mere moments. Back in February 1917 he had taken stock for the first time and wrote a list of eleven titles, full of dashes and question marks: the usable extract from three octavo notebooks. One month later, another list, this one more self-confident, with twelve titles in a well-defined sequence. This was a table of contents, without a doubt, and unequivocal proof that Kafka was again thinking of the publication of a *book*.

His publisher's expectations were surely not the reason; Kafka had not heard any words of encouragement or support from the head office in Leipzig for a long time. His skepticism about Kurt Wolff had been reinforced over the past three years. No one seemed to recall the explicit promise of combining "The Judgment," "The Stoker," and "The Metamorphosis" in a nicely designed edition—Kafka was still in mourning for this unrealized book that would bear the title *The Sons*—and Meyer, the good-natured but perennially flustered managing director who could rarely be persuaded to read a book but always got a thrill from churning out good publicity and turning handsome profits, only warmed up to "propaganda ideas" and big sums of money. In the end, Wolff had rejected the idea of including "In the Penal Colony" in his prominent series, *Der jüngste Tag*, and he had left Kafka uncertain as to whether he would ever want to publish this story at all.

There are reasons to doubt that he did, and Kafka could no longer hope for preferential treatment. Over the course of a few short years, this small, manageable publishing company, in which editorial meetings could be conducted over a bottle of wine, had grown into an enterprise that made the established competitors appear outdated, even though it was not an economic threat at this point. Wolff was expanding, taking series and collected works from other publishing companies, and he no longer needed to send out publicity circulars. Instead, *he* was the one being courted by a growing number of authors, including well-established writers. Even "house authors" at publishers such as S. Fischer and Cassirer were known to cast envious glances over to Leipzig, with its highly attractive combination of publishing intuition and imaginative advertising.

The 1916 catalogue listed more than four hundred titles in print, and Wolff had to limit the additional influx of new publications. How could they keep the sheer mass of paper under control? Qualified editors were no longer available, and as long as the war went on, there was little hope of being able to delegate the evaluation of manuscripts and work with authors on a larger scale. Werfel was a soldier, Albert Ehrenstein had fallen out with Meyer, Johannes R. Becher, who was addicted to morphine, put in no more than a brief appearance, and Brod, as an outside consultant, was too far away to take an active role in the day-to-day operations.

Moreover, there were hints that the publication list was stretched too thin, which threatened in time to dilute the publisher's identity. Wolff sought to counteract that impression by classifying his books into series and themes. The first and most successful of these series, "The New Novel," did not reinforce Kafka's faith in his own future role. While all of Brod's novels were published in new editions, side by side with works by Anatole France, Knut Hamsun, and Heinrich Mann, Kafka realized that his own writing would have no chance in this series. If his publisher was really planning to offer a platform to the European novel in the middle of a world war—and there was some evidence that both his emphasis on novels and the internationalization of his publishing list could be understood as political and cultural gestures—Kafka could not count on preferential treatment with inconsequential little gems, the "impossibilities" of his octavo notebooks. Sure enough, in late 1916, when Kurt Wolff asked his authors to send him texts for the new annual almanac, he simply assumed that they would be excerpts from *novels*. Any writer would want to be included in this high-profile almanac (*The New Novel*) with a print run of thirty thousand copies. But Kafka had nothing to submit, and the short prose piece "A Murder," which Brod suggested on his behalf, was rejected on the spot. There would be no exception for Kafka.

It was cold comfort to see his name in the *Prager Tagblatt* again for the first time in years.[2] Kafka was able to get a good view of its subscribers gathered together on his evening stroll down from Hradčany Castle. But publishing in periodicals, Brod kept explaining to him, was not a bad way of keeping himself visible. Small literary forms offered excellent opportunities to achieve a scatter effect to which publishers and critics would eventually have to react. That made sense to Kafka, and he now replied to invitations more frequently; even his strict reservations about the world of publishing gradually began to dissolve. The relevant bibliographies for 1917 list nine texts of his in newspapers, magazines, almanacs, and anthologies—most of them arranged by Brod—and a great deal more was planned. Kafka promised *Die schöne Rarität* (The beautiful rarity), an exclusive literary and art journal, that he would contribute on a regular basis, and he even managed to elicit a hasty commitment from Josef Körner, a literary scholar who was condemned by the war archives to edit *Donauland*, a patriotic magazine.[3] There is no doubt that he would have been delighted to accept an offer from *Die neue Rundschau*, which was still the most prestigious literary magazine in the German language. But since Musil had gone off to war, Kafka no longer had an advocate at S. Fischer Verlag, and this was not the least of the many consequences of the widespread catastrophe that had already befallen Kafka.

While enjoying his heightened productivity, Kafka began to change his attitude not only with regard to magazines but also in his interaction with other authors. Although he was still unable to bring himself to offer unsolicited texts for publication, he sometimes interceded on behalf of others. The poet Gottfried Kölwel, for example, who had attended the reading in the Galerie Goltz in Munich, considered Kafka influential enough to put in a good word for him with Wolff (but Brod wound up doing it for him behind the scenes). Rudolf Fuchs, a Prague writer and translator with whom Kafka got together on occasion, also asked for his sponsorship—successfully, because Kafka was able to get Martin Buber interested in some of Fuchs's poems. Kafka even played the intermediary on his own accord, for example when he also showed Buber poems by Ernst Feigl, a Prague poet, without the latter's knowledge.[4]

Anyone who could convey a feeling of unaffected sincerity and a true personal interest could persuade Kafka to do just about anything, and he was not thrown by social, cultural, or ideological differences. He had proved as much in 1911 when he roamed the streets of Prague with the ragged and peculiar-looking Yitzhak Löwy, to the horror of his parents and the astonishment of his friends. Moriz Schnitzer, the artless health fanatic whom Kafka admired while seeing him for what he was, was similarly far from presentable: in the literary coffeehouses (which he would never have entered), Schnitzer would not even have been appreciated as an entertaining character, and he was utterly hopeless as a speaker—which Kafka readily admitted, without considering it an ad hominem argument.[5]

But Kafka would even have been willing to form an alliance with his own antipodes, as he demonstrated in July 1917 in the night train from Vienna to Prague, where he came across two boisterous men with whom he had a passing acquaintance: Anton Kuh, the journalist and elocutionist who spent a good deal of time in Café Arco in Prague, and

Otto Gross, a psychiatrist and psychoanalyst who was also a writer. These two made an odd couple. Kuh played the clever fool (and sometimes the homosexual, which guaranteed him even more attention), and the forty-year-old Gross was a notorious figure, mired in vicious rumors, who came straight from what the bourgeoisie would define as hell. Gross was a drug-addicted physician, anarchist, and inmate at various psychiatric clinics. He was wanted by the police for years as an alleged murderer. He had also had four children by four different women; he was the lover of three sisters at the same time; and then, at the instigation of his own father, the prominent criminal law professor Hans Gross, he was arrested in Berlin, committed to an institution, and declared mentally incompetent in a sensational trial. The case of Gross had been widely publicized in many magazines, including *Aktion* in Berlin, and Kafka must have had a pretty good idea of who he was. Gross was only six years older than Kafka, yet he had already lived out an enormous range of what life has to offer, from intellectual mountain hikes with Freud, whose favorite student and patient he had been, to the misery of the delivery rooms and hospitals at the battlefield, where he attended to the suffering of *others*. And there was also the war he waged in public with his own father, which kept the courts busy even after the latter's death and which Expressionist circles followed with great interest, as though Gross, who struck sparks of social revolt from psychoanalysis and was thus fighting not just his father but the whole notion of patriarchy, had taken on the sufferings of an entire generation.[6]

The train was crowded, like every long-distance train during the war, which left the travelers Kafka, Kuh, Gross, Gross's girlfriend Marianne ("Mizzi") Kuh, and Sophie Kuh, who was eight months old, no choice but to ride out the night in the corridor. No one heard a peep from the baby, while Anton Kuh sang and blathered, the way he often did onstage, and Gross held forth in a commanding, endless monologue, paying no heed to Kafka, who was nodding mechanically and wearily with a frozen smile (and Gross probably had no idea that he was speaking to a former student of his father, Hans Gross). Evidently Gross was pontificating on one of his latest ideas, a matriarchal interpretation of Genesis, in particular of the Fall. When Kafka described the scene several years later, he no longer recalled any details of what he had heard, but he retained a vivid visual impression of the encounter—and the conviction that there was "something vital" in him.[7]

But Kafka did not have much of a chance to appreciate this vital something. Just a few days later, they had their second and final encounter. Brod had invited him to a little social gathering that included Otto Gross, Werfel (who had also traveled in from Vienna), and Brod's childhood friend, the musician Adolf Schreiber. We have no information about how this distinguished gathering went, apart from the fact that here, too, Gross's charismatic manner led to a startling outcome. Kafka, who had always enjoyed the panoply of magazines more as an onlooker than as a participant, who now too agonized over even the most innocuous publishing opportunity before reaching a decision—this same Kafka was talked into helping *found* a magazine, which would be called *Papers on Combating the Will to Power*—a provocatively antipatriarchal title that would not have occurred to Freud in a million years but would surely meet with approval in Gross's milieu, the Bohemian circles in Vienna, Berlin, Munich, and Ascona and that moreover recalled parodistically the *Papers on Combating Alcoholism* that was published in Vienna.

Brod was not amused, and Werfel was similarly wary; it would certainly not have been opportune for him, as a prominent conscript, to be associated with a disabled morphinist and declared enemy of militarized society. Kafka, by contrast, was raring to go; and although he was surely told that no matter how brilliant Gross might be, he was unreliable (no one would entrust him with money, let alone ideas), Kafka wrote two letters asking what had become of the planned magazine. "If ever a magazine seemed tempting to me over an extended period of time (they all seem tempting for brief moments, of course)," he wrote to Brod, "it was Dr. Gross's, the reason being that on this evening at least, it seemed to me that it emanated from the blaze of a certain personal bond. Can a magazine ever be more than a sign of people moving toward a greater personal connection?"[8]

Nothing came of it. Three years later, Gross, who had become increasingly unpredictable and mentally debilitated as a result of his drug addiction, came to a wretched end on the streets of Berlin. Nevertheless, there was later a fierce sequel to that evening in Prague; Franz Werfel would see to that.

Kafka's sustained interest in Gross must have felt like a thorn in Max Brod's side, and it is no coincidence that he made no mention of it. "Sign of people moving toward a greater personal connection" sounded particularly awkward coming from him, but it was the ideal basis for a magazine in Brod's view, as well. But how did Kafka picture establishing a common interest with a man whose vocabulary did not include the term "Jew," and for whom all questions regarding the politics of Jewish identity—including Zionism—were, at best, peripheral to a far more encompassing cultural crisis? And when Kafka talked about "tempting" magazines whose stance he supported, why didn't he focus on *Der Jude*, the leading journal of central European Jewry, the way to which Brod had personally paved for him?

Brod's insistent inquiries to Buber about why no exemplary German-language literature was published in *Der Jude* did eventually have some effect, even though the basic dissent continued. According to Brod, the crucial criterion of whether a literary work was or was not part of the corpus of Jewish writings was "Jewish spirit," but for Buber it was language. Buber conceded to Brod "that naturally there are elements of a specifically Jewish spirit in German literature in an odd synthesis with a German one." But, he argued, that did not make it Jewish literature: "It goes against what I think and feel for a work to belong to two literatures; and you would presumably not disconnect Werfel (or yourself) from German literature."[9]

But that was precisely what Brod was thinking. And by naming Werfel, Buber had provided a persuasive example that gave rise to passing doubts on his own part about not including literature in his magazine. Werfel was no longer an egotistical "literary figure"; he had matured during the war, and devoted himself to religious issues, particularly the question of religious identity. He hesitantly began to look into his own Jewish roots, while his sympathies grew for the contemplative, unworldly introspection of an idealized Christianity (for which Brod censured him[10]). The world, his experience seemed to have shown him, could be aided only by a miracle, not by ideologically based activity and certainly not by a blend of literature and party politics as practiced by some Zionists in Prague, because ultimately—and this was the very point of Werfel's agreement with Otto Gross—this led only to another form of organized power, no matter how honorable the motives. The Zionists claimed that being radical meant ceasing idle chatter and getting down to work. It would be truly radical, Werfel countered, to make the individual the absolute centerpiece. The self, and even more the writing self, is responsible to itself, and at most responsible to God, as well, but to no other being.

This was certainly not Buber's position, and pure contemplation was the last thing he wanted to prescribe to "national Judaism," which was on the rise throughout the world. But the intensity with which Werfel struggled to find an approach of his own impressed Buber far more than Brod's loyalty to Zionist principles: this almost desperate earnestness, this struggle for authenticity had to shake up even those who had believed that the only things that mattered were the proper ideology and the concrete successes of the "movement." Buber printed sixteen new poems by Werfel, with a preface that claimed that this poet's innermost aspiration was a Jewish one.[11]

That was what Brod had been waiting for: there would be German literature in *Der Jude* after all. But if Werfel was featured here, why not Kafka as well? No sooner had Brod received the April issue than he sent another request to Buber to look into manuscripts from Kafka, who had written "many beautiful little prose pieces, legends, and fairy tales recently."[12] Brod knew, of course, that he was stretching the truth here, but his pitch was enticing and was sure to have the desired effect on Buber.

The moment was quite opportune because Kafka, who was still in his nervous and euphoric phase of production and had just begun to fill an additional octavo notebook, was eager to go ahead with publication of the fruits of the previous winter. When he actually received an invitation from Buber in mid-April 1917, he did not hesitate for a second to submit clean copies of virtually all his recent works so that the editor could choose for himself. Buber was clearly impressed but was concerned about how he would justify to his readership publishing texts that offered so many interpretive possibilities. Nothing remotely like them had ever appeared in *Der Jude*. He selected two prose pieces to which a Jewish subject matter *could* be attributed—"Jackals and Arabs" and "A Report to an Academy"—and in order to maintain at least *some* connection to the ethical and religious slant of his magazine, he suggested using "Two Parables" as a main heading. Kafka promptly rejected that idea, arguing that these were not parables, but merely "two animal stories," and readers should not be misled into expecting more from them.

And that is how it was done. "Jackals and Arabs" was published in October 1917, and "A Report to an Academy" in November. For Kafka, these publications were cause for both celebration and jitters, his first appearances in print for an influential Jewish readership. "So I shall be published in *Der Jude* after all," he wrote to Buber, "and always thought that impossible."[13] Surely no other author has disclosed the intellectual thrill he experienced while reading his own printed work this starkly:

> Always take a deep breath first after outbursts of vanity and smugness. The orgy while reading the story in *Der Jude*. Like a squirrel in a cage. Bliss of movement. Desperation about confinement, the mad persistence, feeling of misery despite the calm exterior outside. All this both simultaneously and alternatingly, a sunray of bliss still lingering in the excrement of the end."[14]

Buber's insistence that every single published text remain within the parameters of Judaica—a self-imposed limitation that had come under criticism[15]—had very problematic consequences in the case of Kafka's "Jackals and Arabs," which featured a group of animals that had been waiting for its savior from time immemorial and could easily strike readers as downright anti-Semitic. These animals are pushy and servile, insisting on their own "purity," yet they greedily devour the carrion thrown down before them. They stand in stark contrast to the ironically superior Arabs, imperious masters who reinforce the natural hierarchy with a flick of their whips. This was clearly about acculturated Jews who were incapable of shaping their own destinies, and whose occasional rebellions against the hand that fed them were not to be taken very seriously.

So Kafka had portrayed Jews as jackals (and, to enhance his image, even maligned *actual* jackals, which do not just lie in wait for carrion). That was harsh but did not necessarily fall outside the ideological parameters of Buber's magazine.[16] And people were used to the many disparaging animal metaphors (Jewish wolves, swine, goats, snakes, and spiders) that had coursed through German literature for centuries.[17] The highly educated readers of *Der Jude* were far more likely to be shocked by the extremely positive depiction of the Arabs, whom the Zionists promised participation in the economy, education, and hygiene "according to European standards" (while they were often regarded merely as a reservoir of cheap labor by the Jewish immigrants in Palestine). Kafka's text depicts the Arabs as the far superior race, as the traditional majority that tolerates the presence of jackals, of Jews, only as garbage pickers and clowns.

Equally possible, though less compelling, was a Jewish interpretation of the "Report to an Academy," or, as Kafka's friends called it, the "ape story," the memoirs of an ape driven by force to deny his own nature and to adopt human habits. This story could be read as a parable of how civilization works or as a searing indictment of the unnaturalness of middle-class constraints, but also as the history of Jewish assimilation and self-alienation. Buber knew and welcomed the fact that the readership of *Der Jude* was sure to peer into *this* mirror; for Brod, the Jewish interpretation was the only conceivable one, and in *Selbstwehr* he praised Kafka's story as the "most brilliant satire on assimilation that has ever been written." Elsa Brod read the story to the members of the Club of Jewish Women and Men in Prague—in the auditorium of the *chevra kadisha* (burial society).[18] But if Red Peter, the captured, trained, and hence psychologically subservient ape really is a metaphor for the assimilated Jew, what does the original world of the *non*-assimilated Jew look like? Red Peter himself cannot (or chooses not to) communicate anything about his origins, although the nameless academy explicitly asks him to do so. The remaining traces of his "previous life as an ape" suggest that while it was a free, even paradisiacal form of existence, it was not preferable to "civilized" life in every respect. Here, too, Kafka had chosen an *inferior* species with negative connotations as the symbol of the Jewish people, and it is not surprising that most of his Zionist-minded readers blocked out the logic of this image to keep the text enjoyable.

For Buber it was an experiment without a sequel; the next few volumes of *Der Jude* contained no literary texts. But for Kafka it was a confirmation of his work, a successful test run, and of the numerous smaller publications in 1917, those in *Der Jude* were certainly the most important and gratifying ones. Even so, Kafka had been aiming at a longer form and a far wider literary readership, and his plan to compile the new prose texts in a volume of their own was so fully developed even before the correspondence with Buber that he already knew its title. His next book would be called *Responsibility*.[19]

But why didn't the publisher know any of this; why didn't he have this book under contract? Kafka was sure that Wolff had heard about the new texts and still hadn't made any overtures. Kafka was not the only one struck by Kurt Wolff's increasingly erratic, even mysterious behavior. When Wolff did write, he was charming, almost affectionate, but he never did so without a concrete reason. And even if there was a reason, Wolff was not necessarily the one to write. Kafka was wary, and as much as he feared rejection, he would have preferred a discussion that was more consistent and candid. Brod had little leverage with this issue; he had even more problems of his own with the publisher's negligence.

Still, Brod's tenacity, which had already made Buber relent, now had an impact in Leipzig, as well. On July 3, 1917, Kafka's thirty-fourth birthday, Wolff gave the long-awaited signal that he was ready to try a new gambit and asked Kafka to submit the manuscripts from the previous winter "in a typewritten copy," now that "to my great delight, I recently learned in a letter from Max Brod . . ." and so forth.[20]

Wolff's enthusiastic response suggests that he must have been quite impressed by what he saw. Although the prose that Kafka was now writing, which was without literary precedent, and re-created from vivid dreams, destroyed any hope for a forthcoming novel in the near future, and although the new pieces must have reminded him of the failure of *Meditation*, Wolff again suggested using a bibliophile design, even for "In the Penal Colony." Wolff assured Kafka that although he still considered this story unsuited for the inexpensive series *Der jüngste Tag*, "it goes without saying that I never thought of forgoing the publication of this work, which I greatly admire and esteem."[21] This assurance bore little resemblance to what Wolff had said the previous year.

Kafka, who was elated by these offers, came to regret not having had the reserve necessary to hold off a bit; these were promises, and he knew full well not to take everything that was promised in Leipzig literally. But in the summer of 1917, Wolff went a big step further and offered his author a colossal enticement. Kafka, encouraged by Wolff's quick assurance, cautiously inquired whether he could now count on support from his publisher as a full-time writer who would marry, leave his civil servant post, and move to Berlin. Wolff neither hesitated nor equivocated: "As far as your plans for the future are concerned, I wish you all the best, from the bottom of my heart. It is my sincerest pleasure to assure you that both now and after the war is over you will receive continuous material support; we will certainly have no trouble working out the details."[22]

He could not have hoped for a more definite affirmation. For the first time ever, Kafka was getting a message from his publisher that focused not on a text, a forthcoming book, or a strategic publishing decision but on his status as an author. This was one of the most significant letters he had ever received. And Wolff had to be aware (since he knew Kafka's situation far better than he let on) that an offer like this meant that he was guiding not only Kafka's writing but also his existential decisions, that he was assuming responsibility for him. This was what persuaded Kafka, so much so that he was moved to promise something he never would have agreed to in the past, namely to step up his productivity: "If my strength should hold out to some reasonable degree, you will get better work from me than 'In the Penal Colony.'"[23]

Things would turn out differently. As though everything essential had been said, Wolff abruptly stopped corresponding with Kafka, informing him neither when the first proofs would be coming nor that the war had made it difficult for him to get the quality of paper and go ahead with the uncommon print design he had promised. The project went through a seemingly endless, grotesque series of mishaps before Kafka's short prose works could finally be published.

These mishaps began on the very first page of the new book. Kafka had now settled on a more neutral title, and decided that the volume should not be called *Responsibility*, but instead *A Country Doctor: Short Narratives*. Evidently he was using the same line of reasoning that led him to reject Buber's suggestion: both "responsibility" and "parables" steered the reader's attention squarely to a layer of meaning behind the text, and both terms not only invited interpretation but even hinted at the *correct* interpretation, or at least suggested that the interpretation the author hoped for could be found. But—and here lies the origin of

Kafka's lifelong refusal to interpret his own works—the literary text has to accomplish this on its own and effectively banish any notion that "Jackals and Arabs" is no more than an "animal story" or that the title story "A Country Doctor" is simply a novella about doctors.

For Kafka, then, the choice of a title had far-reaching implications. Although it took several reminders to the publisher, he insisted on examining the title page, as well—and it was a good thing that he did. When he finally received the proofs, he discovered that the book's subtitle had been changed, without his authorization, to *New Meditations*. This decision was not only inconsiderate to the author but also made no sense. What did the merciless logic of the "ape story" or the unfathomable dreamlike events of "A Country Doctor" have to do with the fleeting impressions of *Meditation*, which Kafka had long since consigned to his literary past?

And the question of the order in which the prose pieces Kafka had selected would be printed was handled quite carelessly by the publisher, although back in August 1917, just after Wolff's generous offer, the author had submitted a precise table of contents.[24] The galleys, which Kafka could use to restore the original order, were incomplete. Their arrival was delayed for months, and they were sent only after Brod intervened repeatedly. In September 1918—by which point the manuscripts had been in Kurt Wolff's hands for more than a year—Kafka received a confused letter from Meyer, the business manager, which again misstated the order of the pieces, and Meyer had not even noticed that two titles on his list, "A Homicide" and "A Fratricide," were in fact one and the same story. No one at this publishing company seemed to be finding the time for a careful reading. "A Homicide" was the very text that Wolff did *not* wish to include in his almanac, and "A Fratricide" was the improved, authorized version of this story, which had already been published. Kafka must have been amazed to discover that Wolff published the first, long-outdated version in a future almanac under the old title—without consulting him, and without even sending him an author's copy.[25]

Naturally even established literary publishers were forced to improvise as the war went on. The entire course of production, from editing to printing, suffered from a lack of qualified staff, and the shortage of all raw materials, which were no longer freely available but had to be applied for at central government bureaus, made reliable planning nearly impossible. Kafka knew the meaning of "war economy" from his own personal experience, and he was surely not surprised by the fact that Wolff was reluctant to keep apologizing to his authors or sending them memos full of empty promises. Wolff was finding it difficult to cope, but he also failed to appreciate the gravity of the situation. In 1917 he was still planning to relocate the publishing company to a costly palace in Darmstadt. He founded the Neuer Geist Verlag to publish nonfiction, and while people feared that the coming winter would bring the chaos of hunger revolts, he was promising an author like Kafka, who still lacked widespread name recognition, very costly deckle-edged paper and half-leather covers produced by the leather glove manufacturer Rudolf Werfel.[26] A year later, just a few weeks before the end of the war, in the midst of a severe crisis in the book trade, Wolff was pressing for the publication of "In the Penal Colony" (which Kafka had deemed deficient) as a bibliophile Drugulin edition, which had become wildly expensive to produce. The delighted author understandably hoped it could be accomplished, but the publisher's optimism was downright reckless.

Wolff appears not to have developed a better sense of how to deal with his author in Prague even as the years went on. Although he would have had no trouble getting a visa to Bohemia after his military service, which would have enabled him to meet Kafka in person, he let this rare opportunity slip by, when Kafka was interested in a long-term close relationship with a publisher. On top of that, he undermined Kafka's budding trust in him by inexplicably running hot and cold, sending charming letters followed by months and even years of silence. As hard as Kafka tried to understand the publisher's point of view ("you really have to scream," he wrote to the editor of *Donauland*, "to be heard by a publisher drowning in authors"[27]), he could not shake the feeling that a truly interested publisher would not act like this. And if Kafka had been able to carry out his plan to relocate to Berlin in 1919, it is unlikely that he would have prodded Wolff to make good on his promise of "continuous material support."

The issue of self-esteem moved to the forefront in the spring of 1918, when Kafka was surprised and flattered to receive invitations from *two* other German publishers, Erich Reiss and Paul Cassirer, who both focused on the literary avant-garde and had published the leading magazines *Pan* and *Die Schaubühne*. Opportunities like these—and this time without any intervention from Brod—had never come Kafka's way, and since he had the distinct impression that *A Country Doctor* was no longer desired or had been forgotten altogether in Leipzig, he demanded an explanation from his publisher. The reply came not in the form of a personal letter, but as a new batch of proofs with no cover note. It was exasperating in the extreme. Brod assured him that all publishers were that way at this time, and he might as well stay with Wolff.[28]

One Wednesday night, Rabbi Baal Shem Tov, the founder of the Hasidic movement, came to an inn on one of his journeys. "I am a famous cleric," he explained to the innkeeper. "I heard that a very wealthy man is celebrating his wedding in Berlin, and want to get there in time for the Sabbath; perhaps I will be able to earn some money there." The innkeeper replied, "What are you saying? It is fifty miles from here to Berlin. How are you going to get there by the beginning of the Sabbath?" Rabbi Baal Shem Tov said, "I have a very good horse and will be in Berlin before the Sabbath begins." The innkeeper laughed and said, "That is impossible, unless you fly through the air." The rabbi was in no more of a hurry the following day, and delayed his departure until Thursday night, but in this one night he covered the entire distance.

Another rabbi, whose name was Lejb Sores, was spending some time in a Russian town near Mogilev at the Dnieper River. One day, he asked for the horses to be harnessed and for a servant to give him a ride. "And once they had ridden out of town, the servant suddenly felt as though they were flying through the air, and he saw cities and villages down below. They rode for two hours. Finally they came into a big city," which was, astonishingly, the metropolis of Vienna, 1,200 kilometers from Mogilev as the crow flies.

The eponymous country doctor in Kafka's story is summoned in the midst of an icy winter by a critically ill patient, who lives ten miles away, but the doctor's horse died the previous night and he cannot get hold of another. Suddenly two powerful horses push their way out of a ramshackle pigsty, with a groom in tow who harnesses up the carriage as if it were the most natural thing in the world, and, without waiting for any orders, claps his hands. "[T]he carriage is swept away like a log into a current; I still hear the door of my house bursting and splintering from the groom's assault, then my eyes and ears fill with a rushing that steadily penetrates all my senses. But that, too, for only a minute because, as if my patient's yard were opening up right in front of my own courtyard gate, I have already arrived." Ten miles in the blink of an eye. The country doctor's dream horses accomplish what the Hasidic horses failed to do: they break the sound barrier.

Kafka discovered the motif of inexplicably fast, driverless horses in a collection called *Legends of Polish Jews*, which he acquired in 1916, shortly before he began writing on Alchimistengasse.[29] He not only elevated the naively described miracle into an utterly unreal domain that could not be depicted in images but also posed a question that surely would have seemed irrelevant to the Hasidic storytellers: What about the journey back? We learn nothing about how Rabbi Baal Shem Tov left Berlin. Rabbi Lejb Sores's journey home turns out to be a simple repetition: two hours from Vienna to Mogilev. This is the part that struck Kafka as implausible, and in a deeper sense untrue, because going away and coming home are not symmetrical events any more than descent and ascent. While I am away, something happens *back there*, and never again will I find *exactly* what I left. I am also changed in the process; the experience of distance is a sobering one. The folk tradition supplied the image, but Kafka transformed it into a symbol; for him, there was no doubt that the horses *cannot* fly back: "[A]s slowly as old men we dragged through the desert of snow. . . . I will never get home at this rate. . . . Naked, exposed to the frost of this unhappiest of ages, with an earthly carriage, unearthly horses, I—an old man—wander about."

Kafka wrote the brief stories in *A Country Doctor* in the space of a few short months, and he sent the typescripts to Kurt Wolff Verlag on July 7, 1917. Proofreading, production, printing, and distribution of this slender volume took almost three years, until May 1920—during which time the world as they knew it had come to an end—for *A Country Doctor* to be published at last, in a print run of about a thousand. His return to Prague was passed over in near silence; it was noted by a single reviewer.[30]

CHAPTER TEN

Mycobacterium tuberculosis

The wisest of us breathe involuntarily.

—Herman Melville, *Mardi and a Voyage Thither*

SATURDAY, AUGUST 11, 1917, 4 A.M. KAFKA WAKES UP. HE SENSES that something is wrong with his throat. Spittle collects in his mouth, and his attempts to get rid of it do no good. He gets out of bed and lights a lamp. He sees that it is not just spittle, but blood, clotted blood. That is odd, but not a calamity requiring immediate clarification while he is half-asleep.

Kafka wants to go back to bed, but he cannot because suddenly he feels something welling up in his throat. Blood fills his mouth; he rushes over to the washstand, and it pours, bright red, into the white bowl; he takes a handkerchief, walks a few steps in the oversized, empty room, goes up to the window, opens it, sees the Hradčany nearby bathed in the early twilight, he leans forward, looks out aimlessly at the quiet, deserted street. But more and more blood gushes out of his mouth over long, helpless minutes. Finally it appears to slow down and then stop. He splashes water on his bloody hands, then lies down carefully, neither unhappy nor happy, just a bit relieved, and the sleep he has been hoping for comes quickly.

Three hours later, the dedicated housekeeper, Růženka, comes in to wake Kafka, heat the room, and make some breakfast. The first thing she sees is the blood-spattered washstand. "*Pane doktore*," she says in Czech, and looks way up to Kafka, who is two heads taller than she, "*s Vámi to dlouho nepotrvá*" (Doctor, you don't have long to go).

The most astonishing part of Kafka's written accounts of the events of that morning is his uncomplaining acceptance of the surprising emergence of the deadly threat, and his relief at the way this illness enabled him to get a good night's sleep. The salutary effect of Marienbad had long since worn off, as had the comforting delight of literary success, and for months he had been plagued by anxiety, insomnia, and headaches the way he was during the worst periods of the engagement battle, so it was understandable that when the pains suddenly stopped and his weakened body gave itself over to sleep, he almost took the danger in stride—defying all logic.

But of course, a visit to the doctor is in order when blood gushes out of one's mouth—even if he considers conventional medicine nothing more than harmless superstition. Kafka knew an internist, a Jew, who seemed reasonably trustworthy: a corpulent fifty-year-old doctor named Gustav Mühlstein, whom he had seen a year earlier when he was suffering from persistent bouts of pain. He liked Doctor Mühlstein because he was refreshingly free of the professional posturing designed to cow the patient, which Kafka had always hated—above all, the standard combination of feigned sympathy and ostensible omniscience. The amiable Mühlstein, by contrast, had no trouble admitting that he could not find anything wrong with Kafka apart from pronounced anxiety. And the headaches, the insomnia? The only way to address those issues was to lead a healthy lifestyle. Kafka should cut down on smoking and alcohol, eat more vegetables than meat—no meat in the evenings!—and go swimming every once in a while.

The unintentionally humorous Mühlstein clearly lacked insight into human nature, but perhaps he was able to make an accurate diagnosis. After Kafka had finished his office work for the day with a slight cough, he went over to Obstgasse to have his chest examined. The doctor found that he had a severe case of bronchial catarrh, and prescribed some sort of tonic. Kafka was told to drink three bottles of it and return for another examination in a month. But what if the hemorrhage should recur tonight? Then don't wander around in your room; stay in bed and come again tomorrow.

This was not what Kafka wanted to hear, and the next day, when he returned to Mühlstein's office—sure enough, the bleeding had recurred—he was so sure of his own diagnosis that this doctor's circumlocutions made no impression on him. Soon after, he had to report back to Ottla, and he did not mince words:

> 3 possibilities: *first*, acute cold, as the doctor contends, and I deny; would I catch cold in August? Especially in view of the fact that I am not prone to colds at all. If anything could have caused it, it would have to be the apartment, that cold, musty, ill-smelling place. *Second*, consumption. The Dr. rules that out for now. Anyhow, he claims, we'll see that everyone in big cities is tubercular; a catarrh of the apex of the lung (that's the phrase, the way people say piglet when they mean swine) isn't so bad; you inject tuberculin and all's well. *Third*: this last possibility I barely hinted to him; naturally he promptly rejected it. And yet it is the only right one and is also quite compatible with the second. Recently I've been suffering dreadfully from the old delusion again; incidentally, last winter was only the longest hiatus to date in these five years of suffering. It is the greatest struggle that has been inflicted on me, or rather entrusted to me, and a victory (which might be manifested in the form of a marriage, for example; perhaps F. is only representative of the presumably good principle in this struggle), I mean, for my personal world history, a victory with a somewhat bearable loss of blood, would have had something Napoleonic about it. Now it appears that I am going to lose the struggle this way. And sure enough, as if everything had been called off, I have been sleeping better since that episode at four o'clock in the morning, although not much better; but above all the headache, which I thought couldn't be treated back then, has stopped altogether. I picture my participation in the hemorrhage somewhat as though the incessant insomnia, headaches, feverish conditions, tensions so weakened me that I became susceptible to something consumptive. . . .
>
> So that is the status of this mental disease, tuberculosis. Incidentally, I went to see the doctor again yesterday. He found the

> lung noises (I have been coughing since that time) better, rejects the idea that this is consumption in even stronger terms, says I'm too old for that, but since I want some certainty (though even that does not afford complete certainty) he will have me X-rayed this week and my sputum will be examined.[1]

Even Kafka, who was partial to naturopathic medicine, had evidently hung on every word of this conventional practitioner, as any other patient in his situation might have done, and his description of the doctor's findings appears to be accurate. The problem was that Kafka had withheld important, perhaps even crucial, information, which did not give the doctor a proper chance to evaluate his condition. Weeks before the hemorrhage, he had noticed that his saliva had a reddish tinge, and although this alarming symptom never quite disappeared, he had ignored it at first, then it slipped his mind. Had Mühlstein been aware of this case history, he surely would have taken the matter more seriously and would not have brought up the option of a common cold. But Kafka was in no mood for recriminations after the fact. He was the only one who *knew* that in all probability it was tuberculosis, but he did not reveal how he got to this astonishing certainty, or why he was more inclined to trust the maid's spontaneous judgment than the expert's optimistic view.[2]

Kafka was not a "cooperative" patient, and most certainly not an "easy" one—which, however, did not alter the fact that he had come into the wrong hands. Mühlstein's soothing words lacked any medical foundation. Kafka was not too old to contract tuberculosis of the lungs, and it had been known for some time that the reactivation of an earlier, latent tuberculosis is possible into old age—particularly under the conditions of malnutrition, poorly heated apartments, and chronically dirty streets that sent up an incessant cloud of dust during the war years. The statistics to which Mühlstein could have referred had been compiled in the prewar years, but after 1915, the picture in the big cities had changed drastically, and, primarily in the lower classes (including hundreds of thousands of refugees), tuberculosis had gradually assumed the character of a national epidemic, accounting for a quarter of all deaths. Of course, this was not Kafka's social milieu; his living conditions were privileged, but if Mühlstein had taken a careful medical history, he would have known that his patient's office was open to the public, that he often came in contact with people who were ill, and that there was a great deal of coughing at his workplace.

There was no cause for alarm, Mühlstein reassured him, because tuberculin would do the trick. But Mühlstein's stated faith in this miracle drug was not necessarily sincere, let alone a sign of medical competence. New variants of tuberculin derived from dead tuberculosis pathogens kept coming onto the market without any successful clinical testing; even the infamous "old tuberculin" with which Robert Koch had suffered an international disgrace almost three decades earlier was still being used by internists and military doctors for active immunization. But patients were right to fear it because an incorrect dose could induce severe reactions ranging from high fever to an attack of tuberculosis. There were no reliable guidelines for the "correct" dosage, which varied significantly from one individual to the next. Even before the war, people were justifiably wary of seeking tuberculosis treatment in sanatoriums. Kafka had no intention of exposing himself to risky treatments; when Mühlstein had to admit that the "bad cold" hypothesis was wrong and announced he might inject tuberculin after all "so that I will have done everything possible," Kafka would not hear of it, and thought it preferable to head to a health resort. But he was told that there was no need to leave town; it could be cured right there in Prague.[3]

Kafka was far from the layman his doctor considered him, and if Mühlstein had paid a bit more attention to his patient's professional background, he would have learned that Kafka had served on Eugen Pfohl's committee overseeing therapeutic treatments for more than two years, a committee that had become increasingly involved in the treatment of soldiers suffering from tuberculosis. Kafka did not volunteer this information, but he must have been aware that Mühlstein's attempt to play down the danger—"everyone in big cities is tubercular"—was downright irresponsible. Anyone who read the newspapers knew that just about everybody who lived in any city in central Europe had been infected with tuberculosis; it was equally well known, however, that in 95 percent of all cases, the immune system isolated the pathogens and rendered them harmless, at least in peacetime. Kafka did not want to know whether he was "tubercular"; he wanted to know whether he had an acute case, and he demanded certainty about whether it had advanced to "open tuberculosis," which only an analysis of the sputum could establish. It is hard to imagine that it required the initiative of the patient to request this procedure. Evidently the outcome of this test was negative (otherwise he would have been admitted to a sanatorium), but the X-rays showed a bilateral "apical catarrh of the lungs" and thus confirmed Mühlstein's diagnosis.

Kafka wanted certainty in large part because he would not be able to conceal such a serious problem for long, but he also did not want to worry anyone needlessly. He was determined not to inform his parents. Three weeks went by before he told Ottla about his condition, and a full month before he filled in Felice. It seems that Felix Weltsch was the first person Kafka took into his confidence, but Weltsch was preoccupied with his ongoing marital crisis and with preparations for an upcoming move. Brod, by contrast, who came home from his vacation on August 21, ten days after the hemorrhage, was aghast at the apparent carelessness with which Kafka put himself at the mercy of a clearly indifferent family doctor. Brod insisted that Kafka see a specialist, a doctor of the caliber of Professor Gottfried Pick, director of the Laryngological Institute of the German University, and to make sure that his frugal friend Kafka did not back out at the last minute, he accompanied him to the waiting room.

Pick did not need X-rays to determine that the apexes of Kafka's lungs were infected. He warned Kafka that this could be the beginning of tuberculosis, and strongly urged him to spend several months in the country. *This* was what Kafka wanted to hear. The only question was whether a private home in a small village in northwestern Bohemia would be suitable, far away from any medical supervision and with his own sister as a caretaker. Of course it would, the professor told him, but Kafka would have to eat quite a lot, and in order to promote the formation of blood and weight gain, he would need to take arsenic compounds and report in regularly. These were the contents of the medical report Kafka carried home like a precious gift.

Brod was taken aback. Go to Zürau to convalesce? In the winter, to that rainy dump, without any decent doctors in the area? What would happen if he started hemorrhaging again? Evidently Professor Pick thought he was destitute, otherwise he would have sent him to

Merano or to one of the famous Swiss sanatoriums. Brod insisted that this misunderstanding be cleared up as soon as possible, and on September 10, Brod accompanied his friend to the appointment. But as always, when it came to existential decisions, Kafka prevailed; he had had enough of sanatoriums of any kind, and he shuddered at the thought of an anonymous spa facility full of ailing patients. He could try the famous "hypercaloric diet"—eating as much as the body could absorb—anywhere; in fact, he had already begun to do so, albeit reluctantly and only to follow doctor's orders, which ran counter to any naturopathic advice. But he wanted to go to Ottla, and he would surely throw the arsenic away.

Kafka's friends could not be blamed for being utterly baffled at his reaction to his illness, and his family felt the same way later. This was tuberculosis, a matter of life and death. But Kafka seemed unperturbed; he was doing what he thought was right, he laughed, and he made shockingly fatalistic, almost cynical statements. "I think," he wrote sheepishly to Brod, "that I must have seemed like a terrible person to you yesterday."[4] That was certainly the case. Kafka *did* apologize for his flippant behavior, but it remained inexplicable. Even if he initially shrugged off the issue of physical survival—which was as alien to him as suddenly finding himself in a trench—he did have to acknowledge that this was a turning point that called all his plans and hopes into question, including his ability to get married and to write literature. Just a few short weeks earlier, he had received the letter he had long awaited from Kurt Wolff, the promise of "continuous material support" if he embarked on the life of a freelance writer. Didn't he grasp the fact that he would have to regain his health for this letter and offer to retain their inestimable value?

He did. There is no doubt that for all his seeming nonchalance, Kafka was profoundly affected by the emergence of tuberculosis. The clearest evidence is the sudden halt to his diary entries, the remaining pages of which remained blank. Instead, he started a new octavo notebook, dedicated exclusively to literary notes. But here, too, the shock of his illness intruded: "If I should die or become utterly incapable of living in the near future—the likelihood of which is great, since I have coughed up a good deal of blood in the past two nights—I may well say that I was the one to tear myself to shreds."[5]

Over the following months, Kafka was repeatedly obliged to deal in writing with complaints and anxious questions about his illness. His replies were uncharacteristically candid and detailed. Apparently he was shifting a portion of the now-essential task of reflection from his diary to his correspondence. His new situation had forced him out of isolation and had aroused a desire for communication and understanding. Never before had Kafka's logic of the imagination, his characteristic mode of thought, come to the surface as clearly as in his tuberculosis letters, beginning with the first report to Ottla, which contained an obvious contradiction: If he thought he already knew the "only correct" explanation for his illness, why seek out medical advice?

At first, Kafka did exactly what would be expected of a person in his situation: he adopted the standpoint of the medical profession and pondered causes and possible remedies. He had no doubt that the damp apartment and the unhealthy cottage on Alchimistengasse were partly responsible for the outbreak of his illness. As chance would have it, the cottage rental had been terminated recently and was not available for the following winter of writing anyway. As for the apartment in Palais Schönborn, which Kafka had once longed for and savored as a manifestation of his independence, Kafka himself gave up on it without much thought and without even having other lodgings in mind, which meant that for the time being he had to return to his parents' warm but noisy apartment. He also thought about whether tuberculosis, or the susceptibility to tuberculosis, might be hereditary—a central medical topos of his era[6]—and he was later intrigued to learn that two of his mother's relatives suffered from chronic lung disease. Ultimately he showed more initiative than his physician in attempting to identify the hidden pathogen. He did not believe in either tuberculin or arsenic, but his refusal to subject his own body to those kinds of experiments was not irrational and had a solid medical foundation.[7] Kafka was wrong about the bronchial catarrh: as if by accident, he fell back on an old self-image he had long ago tossed aside. It was untrue that he was "not prone to colds," and there were other indications that this was no mere cold.

Kafka's ideas about psychosomatic correlations were also sound. If the efficiency of the immune system is crucial in warding off the all-pervasive *Mycobacterium tuberculosis*, and if, secondly, the immune system can be weakened not only by malnutrition but also by psychological stress (which no doctor would have contested even at that time), then the more than five years of "incessant insomnia, headaches, feverish conditions, tensions"[8] really could have prepared the ground for the tuberculosis. And if he hoped to recover, it was crucial to reduce this stress, which would mean not succumbing to panic and jumping at the chance to find specialized medical care in the best possible climate but rather going to a pleasant environment. And that was certainly not the factory-like health resort in Davos. David Epstein, a physician in Kiev, wrote in his well-received guide to tuberculosis, "Some of my patients elect to stay with relatives in the country over convalescing in a sanatorium, and return home with very nice outcomes."[9] That would have been a doctor to Kafka's liking.

Meanwhile, he was not making it easy for his friends and family to see him as a sensible and responsible patient, and it was no wonder that Brod thought he had to take Kafka by the hand like a schoolboy. When anyone spoke to him about tuberculosis, the conversation invariably developed along the same lines: Kafka quickly brushed aside anything stemming from a conventional medical and psychological perspective, as though it was hardly worth mentioning; by contrast, he tried doggedly, loquaciously, with sprawling images, as it were in a different dimension of his mind, to wrest some meaning from his illness, read it as a sign, and even assign it moral dignity. In writing to Ottla, he called it a "mental illness," and in conversations with Brod, he characterized tuberculosis as a "final defeat" and as "punishment" for wishing so often during his long struggles with Felice that a violent solution would liberate him from the pressure to make decisions. At the same time, the bleeding infection was a "symbol." This was his point of departure in beginning his new diary volume in early September.

But this was territory into which none of his Prague friends was able to follow him. Brod had no sympathy for a perspective of this kind, nor was he willing even to try to adopt it. After all this time, Kafka could still not bring himself to seek a compromise between marriage and literature, the way every acceptable role model did, and he regarded this conflict as a "battle" on the stage of his own self, a battle that had to culminate in a life-threatening illness. Brod wrote to Kafka that if he were in Kafka's shoes, he would know what to do. "When I see Fräulein F[elice] and bring to mind the nice things you always say about her, I cannot understand your resistance."[10]

Felix Weltsch elaborated on Kafka's illness theory—just as naively—only to inform him that what mattered was not theories and images but rather living "as long as possible, as peacefully as possible, and as well-nourished as possible, in good air":

> Where the path to recovery is so clear and so in line with your views and wishes, there is no reason to fear complications, unless your theory of health and natural reason leads you astray with false special theories concerning your ailments. I would like to add this to your overall therapy: Don't go looking for any *chochmeh* of an anthropomorphically distorted nature as the reason for your illness; it is only the result of a bad apartment, poor nutrition, a hundred twists of fate, and most likely psychological depression, as well. However, the latter alone is *not* sufficient to bring it on, and the best remedy for that would be letting out your breath, living in the country, and changing your lifestyle completely. In my own view, a firm resolve to get healthy also helps, and will have an effect on your psychological contours.
>
> Of course, it is more difficult to speak this plainly about other things weighing on your mind. (I repeat: There may be a connection between what depresses you and your physical condition, but I categorically deny that the connection is compelling, or even at all powerful.) But I guess none of us is in a better situation, neither Max nor I.[11]

His annoyance is palpable. Kafka's friends found it neither comprehensible nor acceptable for him to devote more attention to the proper explanation for his illness than to "conquering" it. They seemed to be saying that if his theory were valid, *everybody* would be ill: Max Brod, wearing himself out from running back and forth between his wife and lover, and Felix Weltsch, who endured his wife's hysterical symptoms with gritted teeth. Didn't that prove how futile it was to dwell on hypotheses of that kind?

They had a difficult time with Kafka. His statements about the dangerous illness seem oddly self-assured, sensory, and at times downright theatrical, even to modern readers who have internalized the paradoxical forms of expression of literary modernity. But when we look over the correspondence of that little circle, it seems equally odd that Brod, Weltsch, and Baum had not developed any real feeling for Kafka's psychological volatility after more than a decade of close personal contact, or understood his vulnerable, literally exposed life and his sense of reality, maintained in spite of it all. This sense of reality was what told him what to do and what not to do for his illness. But it was a far more basic need, over which he had little control, that compelled him to derive meaning from what had happened.

Max Brod feared for the life of his friend, and he recorded his fears in his diary. Kafka himself did not fear the end in the slightest, and for years he was able to suppress the thought that his own death might be preceded by a long, painful, and wretched process of dying. His fears centered instead on psychological breakdown, disintegration of his identity, the opening up of his personal boundaries, the proximity of insanity, and the existence, or at least hint, of an ongoing arbitrary, senseless chain of events. Felix Weltsch himself had provided the fateful catchphrase with his claim that "a hundred twists of fate" had a role in this ailment, which was obviously meant as consolation. But for Kafka, the concept of twists of fate stood for the absolutely unendurable, and robbed him of the only psychological weapon he could summon up—namely, to identify with the misfortune, make it part of his own identity, and subject it to the logic of his own life. But twists of fate undermined this integration and made it impossible to come to terms with it or take cover in the psychological shelter of understanding what was happening. But Kafka had reached the breaking point: There was no such thing as meaningless twists of fate; there *mustn't* be.

This position was nonnegotiable, and as it turned out, his penchant for theorizing, which his friends gently mocked and regarded as bizarre, was vitally important for Kafka and essential to his psychological survival. He welcomed any and all psychosomatic interpretations because they clarified the catastrophe and thus enhanced his psychological integration. He rejected anything that called the existential significance of his illness into question. His manner was friendly, but any opposition fell on deaf ears, as evidenced in his reply to Weltsch:

> With regard to the causes of my illness, I am not obstinate, but hold to my opinion, since I am to some extent in possession of the original documents about my "case," and can even hear the first lung in question literally rattling its approval.
>
> Of course you're right that the essential thing needed for recovery is the will to recover. I have that, but, to the extent that this can be said without affectation, I also have the opposite will. This is a special illness—you might say an illness bestowed upon me—quite different from the others I have had to deal with previously. Just as a happy lover might say, "Everything in the past was just an illusion; only now do I truly love."[12]

An illness bestowed upon me? Kafka was talking as though he were standing at an open grave where no one wanted to hear about terrible twists of fate, no matter how justified by the facts, but rather about tragedy or destiny or suffering inflicted upon him. The language is of a distraught piety, which buttresses the unfathomable with grand pronouncements to provide some sort of focus to eyes darting about in the dark.

But Kafka was not aiming merely at illuminating his misfortune. He always spoke of his illness in positive images. He did not utter a single cry of anguish, and when he did complain on one occasion, it was about the disparity between the uniqueness of his "case" and the somewhat routine "tackling" of a common national epidemic, rather than a failure of his tormented heart, which would have been more consistent metaphorically and therefore made more sense. He wrote to Ottla, "There is undoubtedly justice in this illness; it is a just blow, which, incidentally, I do not feel at all as a blow, but as something quite sweet in comparison with the average course of the past years, so it is just, but so coarse, so earthly, so simple, so well aimed at the most convenient slot. I really think there has got to be some other way out."[13]

Kafka grumbled as though God had punished him with a mere head cold, but basically he was content. He sounded facetious, but he was utterly sincere because the new burden of tuberculosis was far easier to bear than the oppressive moral and social pressure from which it would have freed him on the spot. If he was really as ill as he suspected, and the blood that oozed for weeks on end left no doubt about it, no one—neither his parents nor his fiancée nor his bosses nor his Zionist friends—could prevent him from focusing on himself from now on. Indeed, the tuberculosis supplied a justification for social retreat and thus a secondary benefit from his illness that far exceeded the usual leeway he sought. Never again would he have to justify not taking part in any family ventures, or his lack of business sense or interest in pursuing a bourgeois career. Felice would finally understand that his physical constitution, to which he had made such repeated and cryptic reference, really was a crucial impediment to his starting a family. And the best part was that the Workers' Accident Insurance Institute had to relax its grip on him and grant him freedom. These may well have been some of the first thoughts to cross Kafka's mind when he awoke from his tranquil sleep the morning after the hemorrhage. He felt a sense of relaxation, and his mood was brighter than it had been in months. He was so high-spirited that he even confided to his publisher off in the distance that his illness, which had been "lurking" for years, had now finally broken out. "It is almost a relief."[14]

The only strange thing was that no one seemed prepared to accept this. For Brod, the acknowledgment of a conclusive defeat would be devastating; for Kafka it meant first and foremost that the battle was over. But if he felt relief and even talked in terms of relief, how could the tuberculosis be a punishment at the same time—weren't his colossal pronouncements full of holes? The punishment *was* the relief because it meant that his trial was at an end. The only thing remaining was the shame that he had not achieved this end on his own.

Kafka wrote to his mother on September 5 that he was nervous, so nervous that he would not be moving to another apartment for the time being but instead would try to get as long a vacation time as he could and spend it with Ottla in the country.

Did she realize that anything was amiss? No one who had a clue about what was going on in Prague administrative offices would fall for this story. Take a vacation because he felt nervous—in the middle of a world war? Julie Kafka evidently did not have a clue and believed her son. She was pleased that he was taking care of his health, and shared the news with her husband.

Matters turned serious the following day, when Kafka made an official statement of his illness at the Workers' Accident Insurance Institute. He sat in Eugen Pfohl's office and placed Professor Pick's medical report on the table, his "passport" to a new life. He had resolved to press for retirement, a permanent exit from his office and "career," but he was uneasy about doing so, because if tuberculosis was actually a mental illness bursting its own banks—and he did not have the slightest doubt about this—the office was in no way responsible for it. On the contrary: the regular hours, the dispassionate paperwork, and the equally dispassionate conversations with his colleagues offered stability and helped blunt the fear of looming insanity. What would have become of him *without* the office? As difficult as it was to admit, the tuberculosis, or another equally consequential catastrophe, might have befallen him much earlier.[15] But with qualms of this kind, he was in no position to be adamant to his kindly boss, who was putting in as many hours of overtime as everyone else. No, Kafka assured him, of course he had no intention of exploiting the institute; a vacation would also be a possible solution.

The crucial exchange with Director Marschner took place a day later, on September 7. Kafka, who had not given up hope of retiring, found himself on the defensive yet again, especially once Marschner tried to console him, telling him not to take the illness too hard, and that it would be much harder on the insurance institute to have to do without such a valuable employee. An early retirement (with a correspondingly smaller pension) would of course be out of the question, Marschner explained, since it could not possibly work to Kafka's advantage, but Marschner would be able to approve a three-month vacation on the basis of the doctor's note without the need for a formal application.[16]

This was not a triumph, but it did mean three months in Zürau, three months of freedom. Ottla's consent came as expected, and once Kafka had left his workplace in exemplary shape, he began to pack. He was in a hurry and could not even get together with his friends one last time.

On Wednesday, September 12, 1917, the day of Kafka's departure, Max Brod rushed over to the Kafkas' apartment on Altstädter Ring from the post office during his lunch hour. He was upset that Kafka was leaving; it would be their longest separation in many years, and at this time he was plagued by worries that he could not imagine confiding to anyone else. Kafka had also suffered a blow at the last moment, when he received an uncharacteristically sad card from Felice, who did not even know about Kafka's illness and the toll it was taking on him. Kafka gave Brod this letter to read, and they discussed it. Kafka said that he could not get married while stricken with tuberculosis. Then they said goodbye in the hallway; Brod had to get back to the office.

At 2 P.M., the train would head west. Unfortunately, it was a slow train that took three and a half hours to go less than a hundred kilometers. Since Kafka was unable to carry his luggage to the train station by himself (which likely included food for Ottla), two young men from his father's fancy goods store used wheelbarrows and the elevator to bring the luggage down to the ground floor from the apartment. Then Kafka pointed to a suitcase and said, "Take the coffin."[17]

CHAPTER ELEVEN

Zürau's Ark

A stone is heavy only at the place where it belongs.

—Albanian proverb

Zürau is as lovely as ever, though it is getting wintry. The goose pond outside my window is already freezing over from time to time, the children are skating, and my hat, which the evening gale blew into the pond, almost had to be pried loose from the ice in the morning. Mice have been appearing in awfully big numbers, which cannot have escaped your attention. I have driven them off a bit with the cat I carry home from across the square every evening, holding her "warm in my arms." But yesterday a crude bakery rat, who probably had never been in a bedroom before, broke in here with an incredible banging and I had to call in the cat from the next room, where I had confined her, due to my incompetence at teaching her sanitation and my fear of her leaping onto the bed. How readily the good animal sprang out of a box of unknown contents, which was certainly never meant for sleeping in, and belongs to my landlady; then all was still. Other news: One of the geese died of excessive stuffing, the fox has mange, the goats have been to the buck (who is evidently a particularly handsome fellow; one of the goats, who had already been taken there, had a flash of remembrance and ran back to him again all the way from our house), and soon the pig is going to be butchered just like that.[1]

Geese, mice, rats, cats, foxes, goats, pigs, moles, rabbits, chickens, dogs, cows, and horses. Kafka found himself on a small, teeming planet, unfathomably far from the urban hustle and bustle on the Wenceslas Square, which housed only a single species, apart from horses pulling carriages, and just as far from the dimly lit sterile world of the Workers' Accident Insurance Institute, in which nothing moved spontaneously. But the village was populated by an extensive family of all kinds of living creatures that got up at the crack of dawn, each drowning out the others, the three hundred fifty human residents among them.[2] When the sun went down, it quieted down just as uniformly because no one felt like willfully extending the God-given day. There was no electric light in Zürau. Anyone who did not want to sleep needed petroleum for a lamp, and petroleum was expensive. Finally, in the dark, only the mice were left as the last heralds of an infinitely procreating life.

No electricity, no running water, no paved streets. No coffeehouses, no movie theater, no bookstore, no newsstand. No post office, no telephone in the village. The Michelob (Měcholupy) railway station could be reached only by horse cart. And above all: no friends. Who was there for Kafka to talk to? The grumpy old foreman who did not want to take orders from Ottla but was happy to accept a bottle of rum; Mařenka and Toni, the two maids; the neighbors, all farming families whose hub was the village green; and occasional peddlers, who were invited to come in by Ottla and with whom Franz then divided his meal. He often had difficulty understanding the local German dialect.

Still, he had known what he would find here. He had visited his sister in Zürau two or three times during the summer and had described everything in glowing terms. His parents, by contrast, shook their heads in dismay; Hermann Kafka could not help but picture Wossek, the village of his childhood, a village marked by poverty and hard labor. The only contact Max Brod and Felix Weltsch had with nature was as flaneurs seeking an aesthetic contrast to the city: the panorama, the river, the silent woods, the mild air. Zürau had little to offer in that regard. Its landscape was moderately hilly, with farmland, hop gardens, and small wooded areas, and it lacked a nice country inn. Rugged nature, flat land, a whiff of manure permeated with the reek of three village bars in which the seasonal workers swilled watery war beer, and nearby (much too near for someone with tuberculosis) a dusty clay pit.[3] Brod did not come here a single time, and Weltsch tried to figure out whether the food he might be able to bring back from Zürau justified the effort involved in making the trip. It was inconceivable for anyone from Kafka's intellectual milieu to want to share this rural life for more than a few days—not to mention all the contemporary urbane figures who today are grouped with Kafka, such as Thomas Mann, Arthur Schnitzler, and Karl Kraus, none of whom would have voluntarily gone to this wasteland.

> On the whole I am not reading much; life in the village suits me so well. Once you get over the disagreeable feeling of living in a zoo set up according to the most modern principles, in which the animals are given complete freedom, there is no more comfortable and above all no freer life than life in a village; free in the intellectual sense, and minimally oppressed by the world around you and before you. This life cannot be equated with that of a small town, which is probably frightful. I would always want to live here. . . ."[4]

Kafka was ill, of course, and specific criteria were important to him. His friends picked up on the fact that he was idealizing a way of life that he was forced to lead anyway. He was also in luck with the weather. Several weeks after his arrival, it was still so warm and clear that he was not confined to his dark room, which faced north. Nearly every day, in the late morning, after drinking a glass of milk in bed, Kafka carried an upholstered chair and two easy chairs out to a little hill and spent the day lying stripped to the waist, like a tourist in the countryside. Whenever the mood struck, he took the time for a short walk over the adjacent hills or to the neighboring town of Soběchleby along the footpath. "[T]he freedom, the freedom above all," he wrote to Brod after the very first walk, which was understandable because he was away from his office, writing under the sun of a long late summer.[5] Only later did it dawn on him that this unceasing sun in Zürau meant there would be a prolonged dry spell that would culminate in a catastrophically poor harvest in 1917, and it would take multiple requests and good connections to get grain for the coming year. The "lovely weather" brought Ottla's farm to the brink of destruction.

Kafka had no choice but to adapt to a profoundly alien social fabric. He had to forgo conveniences and—what is worse—alter his habits. It was no longer within his power to be alone at will. Zürau was not a sanatorium where you could have your meal brought to your room if you did not like the person sitting next to you at the table. It would have been absolutely unthinkable to stride across the Ringplatz to the house with "the only piano in northwest Bohemia" to complain about the noise, or about two inexhaustible "hammerers" pounding on wood and metal on the dot of six in the morning.[6] Kafka's favorite place at the dinner table was also taken on occasion when the grumpy foreman brought along some of his buddies, which meant that there would be no peace and quiet in Ottla's room either, which was directly adjacent to the kitchen, separated only by a glass door. When this happened, he had no choice but to go back to his own room in a different building. But the mice were waiting there—a nuisance that increased dramatically when the nights turned cold and made Kafka shudder in positively phobic horror. He had to accept the situation, and there was no place to register complaints in Zürau.

Thanks to Ottla, Kafka was able to unwind and to focus his remaining energy on adjusting to the new situation in spite of all these adversities. Ottla continued to offer her brother a sanctuary and provide him everything he needed, just as she had on Alchimistengasse, and although she had her hands full cultivating fifty acres of land with only a few helpers, she was able to ease his initial feelings of unfamiliarity and his fear of being a nuisance to all these hardworking people. "Ottla is truly bearing me up on her wings through the difficult world," Kafka wrote just after he arrived, and just a few days later, this feeling had grown so much stronger that he ramped up his imagery: "I live with Ottla in a good little marriage," he reported to Brod, "marriage not on the basis of the usual violent high currents but of the straight influx by way of small coils."[7] A utopian condition, it seemed. But Brod had long since ceased to be surprised by moods of this kind; he knew that Kafka longed for the "usual" just as much as everyone else, and that the sight of a baby carriage was enough to swing the pendulum in the opposite direction.

Kafka had reason to defend and underscore his own desexualized version of happiness. Far more quickly than he had expected, the day of reckoning was approaching. Felice Bauer was horrified by the apparent resignation with which Kafka accepted the tuberculosis, and she was stirred by a combination of sympathy and an uneasy conscience, and perhaps also the memory of Marienbad. She wanted to see him, ascertain that he was being well cared for, and find out what would happen next. She felt that the matter was extremely urgent in light of the catastrophe that had befallen the two of them. She sent a telegram announcing that she would be coming to Zürau, and without waiting to hear back from Kafka, she boarded one of those awful replacement trains that took a full day and night to get from Berlin to Prague, unaware that Kafka had the farewell letter complete in his head and almost down on paper.

Kafka dreaded this confrontation because it would inevitably put him in the wrong. The first insight he took away from his days lying in the lounge chair was that an era of his life was inexorably heading to an end, an era in which he had pursued the clash between literature and marriage as an anguished spectator whose only choice was to wait for the last act of the performance. After all that had happened to him, he resolved not to let this passivity, this ongoing entanglement in unholy compromises, go on any longer. He had received a sign. The tuberculosis bore a clear message that it was time to take stock, focus on the essentials, and accept his assigned task once and for all, with all that that implied. Kafka had fewer doubts than ever regarding the nature of the task.

Felice Bauer found him a changed man. She had probably expected him to be dejected and in need of affection and a little support in facing up to his illness, and she surely had arrived firmly resolved to avoid everything that stood between them and to defer to his needs for a few hours, in accordance with her usual pragmatic way of expressing her sympathy. But Kafka was not dejected at all, and nothing was further from his mind than seeking comfort in discussions of convalescent care. It annoyed him to hear her lecture him about boiling milk, the unsuitability of his dark room (in which she spent two nights alone), and the necessity of frequent meals, warm blankets, and medical supervision—essentially a heightened form of Brod's commonsense approach. But Kafka was now interested in fundamental questions of identity and meaning, life and death. And he felt neither the inclination nor the capability to build a bridge to his fiancée, to let her share in the mental radicalization that the hemorrhage a few weeks earlier had forced on him. He no longer reached out, and he maintained his silence. He felt bored with the woman who was once his lover, and made no attempt to conceal his boredom.

These were bleak and miserable hours, as Felice Bauer had expected, but in a very different, and far worse, sense. Five years after their first meeting, all subjects they had in common were exhausted, Kafka's interest in her work at the Jewish Home appeared to have faded,[8] and there were only vague pronouncements about his own plans. She had intended to offer consolation, but she kept running up against a "barrier" (as she called it a few days later), and instead of being emotionally generous, she had to battle with a feeling of humiliation. She had softened since the confrontation in the Askanischer Hof, but it seemed as though Kafka was once again deliberately forcing her into the role of the accuser. She had spent thirty hours in the train for this? Eventually she traveled back to Prague, together with Ottla, who had some errands to run in the city. The two women sat across from each other for several hours, but it is unlikely that they were able to talk out their vital shared concern.

At the end of her stay, Felice Bauer had to pay a couple of farewell visits, seeing Max and Elsa Brod and Kafka's parents, who were overcome with curiosity, but still uninformed about the situation. Julie Kafka asked whether Franz's bad mood had lifted in Zürau. Felice replied that she did not notice any improvement.

> As you know, there are two combatants at war within me. During the past few days I have had fewer doubts than ever that the better of the two belongs to you. You have been kept informed about the progress of the war for five years by word and silence, and the two in combination, and most of that time it has caused you suffering. If you were to ask if it was always truthful, I can only say that with

no one else have I suppressed deliberate lies as strenuously, or—to be more precise—more strenuously than I have with you. There have been some deceptions, very few lies, assuming that there is such a thing as "very few" lies. I am a person who lies; for me it is the only way to maintain an even keel, my boat is quite fragile. When I examine myself in regard to my ultimate aim, I find that I do not actually strive to be good, to comply with the highest court, but rather quite the opposite. I strive to survey the entire human and animal community, to recognize their fundamental preferences, desires, and moral ideals, to reduce them to simple rules, and as quickly as possible to develop in conformity with these rules so as to be agreeable to everyone, indeed (here comes the leap) to become so agreeable that in the end I might openly act out my inherent baseness before the eyes of the world without forfeiting its love, as the only sinner not to be roasted. In short, my only concern is the human tribunal, and I would like to deceive even this, though without actual deception.

Apply this to our own case, which is not just an arbitrary one, but actually the one most truly representative of me. You are my human tribunal.

These two, who are at war within me, or, more accurately, whose war I consist of, apart from one small agonized residue—the one is good, the other evil; from time to time they switch roles, which confuses the confused war even more; but until very recently, however, I could still believe, despite any setbacks, that the most improbable would happen (the most probable would be eternal war), which always seemed like the radiant ultimate goal, and I, grown pathetic, wretched over the years, would at last be allowed to have you.

Suddenly it appears that the loss of blood was too great. The blood shed by the good one (we will now call him the good one) in order to win you serves the evil one. Where the evil one of his own accord would probably or possibly not have found a decisive new weapon for his defense, the good one offers him one. Secretly I don't believe this illness is tuberculosis at all, at least not tuberculosis right now, but rather a sign of my general bankruptcy. I had thought it would go on and it didn't. The blood is not coming from the lung, but from a decisive stab delivered by one of the combatants. . . .

> And now I am going to tell you a secret that I don't even believe myself at the moment (although the darkness that falls about me in the distance at each attempt to work, or think, might possibly convince me), but really must be true: I will never be well again precisely because it is not the kind of tuberculosis that can be laid in a lounge chair and nursed back to health, but a weapon that continues to be of supreme necessity as long as I remain alive. And both cannot remain alive.[9]

Elias Canetti called this letter the most distressing one Kafka ever wrote, so distressing that Canetti found it a struggle to quote from it.[10] He was put off in particular by the blending of the real and the metaphoric blood, which he judged to be "an unworthy myth and a false one" and saddled with a blatant lie because, Canetti explained, it was untrue that "the better" of the two combatants belonged to Felice. In fact, nothing at all belonged to her at this point, since Kafka had long since decided to break things off with her.

We understand Canetti's antipathy: after hundreds of letters, after a desperate courtship, after the fulfilled days in Marienbad, at the end of a sad—but shared—five-year history, Kafka did not come up with words of consolation or gratitude. His letter is a self-analysis awash in sparkling images, aimed at an imaginary audience and paying no heed to the woman it is addressed to, whose has just as much of a stake in this matter as he. "When I examine myself in regard to my ultimate aim . . .": that is not the intimate language of a letter, it is a confession that might have spared the accused Josef K. the maximum sentence; it is *literature*. Proud of his precise, vivid, and paradoxical summation, Kafka copied this passage twice, word by word, in his diary and in a letter to Brod. And Felice Bauer must have shuddered as she read, "You are my human tribunal," no matter how tentative, wavering, or uncomprehending her feelings for Kafka might have been. This astoundingly forceful and destructive statement left no room for hope. You don't live with, or touch, your own judge; you *face* your judge.

But what did Canetti mean when he declared Kafka's myth *false*? Kafka's self-portrait and his interpretation of his illness and his relationship with Felice were disconcerting, even shocking, because they did not adhere to emotional or factual logic, and skillfully avoided bringing in statements one might expect in this situation ("We don't have anything in common any more," or "You don't understand me," or "We're not in love"). Instead, Kafka availed himself of an arsenal of mythical imagery and loaded but inexplicable terms: battle, blood, weapon, sin, court, good and evil, darkness, death. Kafka tossed off even a term like "general bankruptcy" as though that said it all, as though it were not a metaphor they could use to ponder the practical meaning together. He did not "communicate" but instead presented a myth: *That is how it was, that is how it is, that is how it will be*. But this faith in the imaginative power of associative fields, this literalness of timeless images and metaphors is a characteristic of all myths, and in this sense *every* myth is false because a myth, unlike psychology, has no awareness of its own scope. Like a work of art, it aims at intrinsic persuasiveness and coherence, and the element of truth it contains is intended as the *whole* truth.

Kafka was evidently unaware that the complexity of his somatic and psychological realm of experience could not be explained, let alone tackled, with such archaic means, no matter how attractive they were from a literary point of view. His discovery of metaphors that wrested meaning from the absence of happiness boosted his confidence, lifted his spirits, and even swelled his pride. The price he paid was that he lagged behind his own level of insight and had to cut off too many loose threads. He suppressed or withheld anything that was incompatible with the myth, fully aware of how this was stretching the truth. Kafka knew that there were other possible variants, and he had already confided some of them to his friends or his own diary, but he made sure to conceal them from Felice.

What would she have said, for instance, about the "good little marriage" her fiancé claimed to have with his own sister? Felice Bauer was not small-minded on the subject of eroticism. Three years earlier, she had accepted Kafka's bittersweet affair in Riva uncomplainingly, and she had had some experience of her own with incestuous feelings. Although she had always considered Ottla immature and rather dull, she could only approve of Ottla's obvious affectionate closeness with Franz, to the degree that it benefited him as a patient. But how could the obvious comfort he was enjoying be reconciled with the status of the "general bankruptcy" Kafka was claiming? It was not all that general, and it appeared that the great happiness in Marienbad, which Kafka had tossed aside, had some secret connection to the little happiness in Zürau: The former was hard-fought, the latter came gratis. Had he simply opted for the easier path? There was not a word about this in Kafka's mythical letter, nor was there a word about Ottla.

There were other, more mysterious ideas that Kafka would hardly have been able to reconcile with the self-portrait meant for Felice. "I haven't yet written down the essential thing," he noted after two months in Zürau, "I am still going in two directions. The work awaiting me is enormous."[11] This, too, did not sound like defeat and the end—far from it. Kafka had interpreted tuberculosis and the forced upheaval of his routines as a cathartic crisis right from the start, as a chance to dispense with inessentials and to focus his remaining strength. To mark the occasion, he had opened his new diary volume in Zürau with a reminder to himself:

> You have the opportunity, as far as this opportunity is at all possible, to make a new beginning. Don't throw it away. If you insist on digging deep, you won't be able to avoid the muck that will well up. But don't wallow in it. If the infection in your lungs is only a symbol, as you say, a symbol of the infection whose inflammation is called Felice and whose depth is called justification; if this is so then the medical advice (light air sun rest) is also a symbol. Take hold of this symbol.[12]

This, too, is the voice of self-mythologizing, but this myth is unequivocally directed at the future, and its view is clear-eyed. Max Brod quickly realized that Kafka's letters from Zürau had far fewer complaints than Brod was used to seeing from him. They were astoundingly calm letters, especially when they touched on the essence of his own unhappiness, and calmest of all when they spoke of his irrevocable failure. This performative contradiction baffled him all the more because his own fits of despair—mostly an outgrowth of his conflict between two women, which was worse than ever in the fall of 1917—made it impossible for him to think clearly. This calm in Zürau was not reassuring at all; it was eerie. Felice Bauer must have felt the same way about it.

Kafka tried to vindicate himself one last time, in his final documented letter to his fiancée, written as though from afar, in a voice no longer meant for her. He wrote that their encounter in Zürau had tormented him as well, but did not make him unhappy. The difference was a matter of perspective: To be unhappy, you need to *feel* the misery in your own body, but someone who is tormented merely *observes* it. Never had Kafka stated so candidly that he was no longer involved, and the only reason Felice Bauer could continue to hold out hope after these avowals was Kafka's earlier pattern of "exaggerations." She knew his penchant for extreme fluctuations, and she knew that he could be soothed and even seduced, although the tuberculosis was now making everything far more difficult.

Felice Bauer stepped up the pace of her letters to Zürau, in spite of her suspicions that their relationship was over. Breaking things off with someone ill with tuberculosis and in such bad shape went against the grain of her social disposition. In Berlin, she discussed the matter with her girlfriend Grete Bloch, who was surely horrified to learn about Kafka's apparent indifference. Eventually Grete, who was evidently none the wiser for having interfered some years back to disastrous effect, contacted Kafka and declared that she would be writing a detailed letter. This threat robbed Kafka of his sleep. Since Felice's last visit, a shadow had come over Zürau. Suddenly he felt incapable of receiving visitors or enduring even the slightest encroachment. When a letter from Felice arrived, he would let it lie unopened for hours, and his fear of more complaints—all of which sounded like indictments to Kafka's ears—made him feel so ill that he was unable to eat.

Brod (and, later, Canetti) failed to appreciate the extent to which Kafka was struggling for psychological survival. Kafka's dissociations seemed too serene and self-assured, his interpretations too well thought out, his descriptions of rural life too literary, and his notorious "mouse letters," which were passed around in Prague, too humorous. He had shed his ritual laments of earlier years and seemed on his way to a mature, compelling eloquence. But wouldn't desperation take a different form? Kafka, wide awake in his lounge chair in Zürau, posed this question:

> Have never understood how it is possible for nearly everyone who can write to objectify pain while suffering it; I, for example, in the midst of my unhappiness, perhaps with my head still burning with unhappiness, can sit down and write to someone: I am unhappy.

> Yes, I can even go beyond that and with as many flourishes as I have the talent for, all of which seem to have nothing to do with my unhappiness, revel simply, or contrapuntally, or with whole orchestras of associations. And it is not a lie, and it does not still my pain; it is simply a merciful surplus of strength at a moment when suffering has raked me to the bottom of my being and plainly exhausted all my strength. But then what kind of surplus is it?[13]

In describing the writer, Kafka came up with a tautology: We cannot know whether (nearly) everybody who can write is also capable of articulating his or her most profound personal unhappiness, because we have no relevant evidence from those who *cannot* write. But Kafka was focusing on an experience that was extraordinarily characteristic *for him*, a truth that continued to prove wonderfully unfailing: "You never know what you have on hand in your own house," a character in "A Country Doctor" declares. Hitting rock bottom freed up new reserves that would protect right him to the end. But this is precisely why he was convinced that from now on, his only security lay within himself. Life—in the most emphatic sense of the word—had shut itself off from him. As much as he feverishly awaited the intensely demanding "task that lay before him," it came from a wholly indeterminate, remote darkness.

Was it the "good" or the "bad" combatant tugging at him? Canetti contended that Kafka's insistent claim that the woman he once loved represented the good, or at least the better, principle was a lie, or at best an act of false chivalry. Hadn't he decided long ago to go a very different route? Hadn't Kafka called himself a "person who lies" in the very same letter? But it was clearly Canetti who could no longer stand the tension and who—after an exhaustive study of the *Trial* files—was pressing for a judgment *post festum*, a resolute commitment to literature that would close the case once and for all. For Kafka himself, by contrast, the ambivalence persisted, even after the decision, as evidenced in a poignant postscript to that letter (which Canetti was not aware of), a single sentence on a separate sheet of paper, a sentence that briefly silenced the din of the rhetorical struggle and allowed him to grieve over what he had lost:

> One more thing I want to say: there were and continue to be moments when in reality or from my recollection, mostly from my

> recollection of your way of looking at me, you are even more to me than usual, and, in essence, something higher seems to break forth; but I am, as usual, too feeble to hold on to it or to hold on to myself in face of it.[14]

Those were the closing words. Felice, of course, insisted on her right to hear the judgment face to face. She would turn thirty in just a few weeks and was no longer a girl.

Professor Pick had advised Kafka to come to Prague once every four weeks for a checkup; and because Brod was with Kafka when he was given this advice, Brod began put pressure on him a few days before the month was over. Kafka hesitated. What good would an examination do? There were no hemorrhages, nor was there fever, and only a nagging cough and slightly rapid breathing reminded him that he was not in Zürau as a vacationer. In only four weeks, he had gained seven pounds, and from the waist up he was as suntanned as a farmer. Kafka claimed—although this was an exaggeration—that his mother had not even recognized him when he picked her up at the train station. He looked better than he had in years. Wouldn't the professor run him out of the place once he saw him? Kafka had received sympathetic letters from the Workers' Accident Insurance Institute, and there were inquiries about his health. When he was in Prague he had to endure looks from his distressed co-workers, who probably considered him a lucky devil. Kafka felt ashamed.

Brod finally had to come and get his reluctant friend. The occasion presented itself in late October, when Brod and his wife were invited to a literary event organized by Zionists in the northwest Bohemian town of Chomutov. Kafka boarded the Brods' train, attended the reading, and spent one night in Chomutov. The next day, they all traveled to Prague together. There is no doubt that Brod sized up the situation more clearly than the unsuspecting Julie. Neither Kafka's suntan nor his weight gain made any impression on him, and the Prague professor's predictably reassuring opinion did nothing to dissuade him from his conviction that something would happen before the onset of winter. He threatened Kafka, more in earnest than in jest, that he would go to Kafka's parents "as a last resort," if Kafka remained so stubborn and did not find a more suitable environment and a milder climate. Only the south could cure him, Brod maintained, adding with charming naïveté that even a "generally accepted resource" could turn out to be the right one. But Kafka was unimpressed by what others thought, and he reminded Brod that "not even the professor said anything about the south."[15]

Kafka felt healthy enough to suppress most thoughts of any real danger. He was far more concerned about the image he projected than about his physical condition itself. Here he was, a civil servant spending several months lying on a meadow without the least outwardly visible sign of illness and being fattened up by his sister, in the middle of a war and surrounded by people who were working hard. Even if no one dared to attack "Herr Doktor" outright, they would look at him disapprovingly and ask unpleasant questions. Kafka was probably projecting this social pressure for the most part, but that was all it took for him to ignore the doctor's orders and throw himself into farm work, which he was drawn to anyway. He picked rose hips, set up a vegetable garden, got down on all fours and dug potatoes from the ground, fed the cattle, drove the horse and cart, and even chopped wood and tried his hand—rather clumsily—at the plow. All this relaxed him, improved his sleep, and soothed his sore conscience. No sooner did he return from his first visit to the doctor in Prague than he confided to his sister that he wanted to stay on, this time for real. All he would need, he told her, was his own little cottage in town, a garden, and farmland. Kafka dreamed of becoming a farmer, and no one understood that better than Ottla: "I myself believe," she wrote, "that God sent him this illness; without it he would never have gotten away from Prague."[16]

Of course, Kafka was still far from leaving Prague. Director Marschner continued to reject an early retirement for him, although he did hint that the three-month vacation could be extended with an appropriate medical certificate. Ottla was no more successful when she went to see Marschner in November, although she was presumably more candid than her defensive brother. Still, Marschner agreed to come to Zürau himself for a few hours; perhaps once they were away from the office, he could make his deputy department head understand what was and was not in his own interest. And while he was at it, he could explain the current limits of directorial authority. Needless to say,

Marschner would make every effort to keep Kafka out of military service for the coming year, as well.

The negotiations with their own parents, who still exerted moral pressure on Ottla, proved to be far tougher and more painful. For a while, they had consoled themselves with the expectation that having their daughter out in the country would help get good square meals on their table in Prague, at long last. For quite some time, it had not been possible to maintain a food supply fit for human beings without the black market, and the Kafkas, like everyone else who still had cash on hand, had a trustworthy supplier who came on a regular basis—Kafka even recommended him to his friends—but who could not guarantee delivery on time and had already attracted the attention of the police. It soon turned out that Ottla would not be able to fill the gap, because the economic and bureaucratic trickery she had to contend with in Zürau was just the same as in Prague. "Horrible price inflation," the pastor of Soběchleby (who had come to the area just a month after Kafka) noted in dismay. "Major food shortage not only in the cities, but also here. Profiteering and mean tricks are predominant."[17]

Ottla would have said the same; her farm was far too small and poorly equipped. Not even the potato supply went according to plan; the distribution of field crops was strictly regulated, and the two tons per year her parents hoped to get for the entire extended family remained a pipe dream. Still, Ottla did send a big container of milk or a couple of eggs to Prague from time to time (although she did not have any cows or chickens herself), as well as flour, a loaf of bread she had baked herself, a couple of partridges, and some venison. Kafka attempted to share these precious items with his friends and even with his bosses, but that was possible only on occasion, and in small quantities, because the "first pick" was always reserved for his family in Prague, as he regretfully reported, though it was only right and proper, because Ottla was in far greater need of regular support. Soap, beef tallow, petroleum, and paper were nearly impossible to come by in the country, and it soon became apparent that even apples and pears, vegetables, fruit juices, and nuts were most welcome gifts for the vegetarians in Zürau. Julie prepared at least one package a month for Kafka to bring to the train, sometimes throwing in a little chocolate, some baked goods, and old newspapers.

It is easy to imagine her husband's reaction to this increasingly lopsided exchange of goods. His frame of mind was now at a low point, anyway, because the sales at the fancy goods store kept decreasing; the fourth winter of the war was approaching and new hardships lay ahead. Irma Kafka wrote that the "proprietor" was often right, objectively speaking, but his shouting and scolding at the shop was almost unbearable, and Julie's constant warnings ("Don't get so upset! Think about your heart!") had little effect. And this state of affairs was now on record: one of the employees had recently flown into a rage and sued Hermann Kafka for slander.[18]

It was now difficult to face Hermann Kafka, who must have grasped instinctively that no matter how intransigent Ottla and Franz appeared to be, they bore the brunt of any disagreements. Ottla in particular was desperate for a kind word from her father (whose endlessly repeated stream of complaints about his difficult childhood she now understood far better), and with a sense of guilt of an ongoing dependence she tried to avoid any further quarreling about her lifestyle when she came to Prague for visits.[19] Hermann, in turn, had qualms about withdrawing his support from his hard-working daughter, whose toughness he had underestimated, and any attempt to end her experiment in Zürau by cutting her off would have met with vehement opposition from Julie, so he usually made do with reminding her that he had been right once again, and on the rare occasions that he sent a brief letter to Ottla, he gave the address as "*currently* Zürau."

It proved to be difficult to include her brother in this volatile state of peace. How Franz could manage to spend weeks and months on a lounge chair watching Ottla slave away was incomprehensible to his parents—quite apart from the fact that his hole-in-the-wall in Zürau required expenditures for rent and food. He remained vague about where he would be living after his return, and when Julie or Irma went to visit an apartment on his behalf, he saw nothing but the faults and found nothing to his liking. An explanation was needed quite soon.

By now, more than a dozen people knew about Kafka's tuberculosis: Felice, Ottla, Irma, Růženka, the Brods, Weltsch, and Baum, as well as an undetermined number of executives and colleagues at the Workers' Accident Insurance Institute. He had impressed on all of them the importance of keeping the bad news from his parents, but how long could this facade be maintained? A single leak was enough to cause a blowup. Max Brod could easily be the source of the leak, since he had explicitly threatened to tell all and had already spread the news to others.[20]

In mid-November, Kafka decided that the time had come to stop subjecting his sister to the constant pressure to explain the situation, and he asked her to let their father—but not their mother—in on the true reason for his time off from work the next time she visited them. The result was startling: Hermann was shocked and abashed, and he kept asking whether Zürau was the right place for someone with tuberculosis, whether Franz had everything he needed there, and whether it was true that he was not in danger. For a moment, the patriarch stepped out of character. He was used to leaving all the family's emotional issues to Julie and expected that problems, apart from the financial, were taken care of by the women without involving him. But now—probably for the first time in decades—*he* was the one with a secret, which required him to exercise a degree of diplomacy and even pretense toward his own wife. The Kafkas' customary silent treatment, from which he had reaped the greatest benefit in the past, suddenly became an oppressive burden, and no one who knew him would have bet on his ability to endure the unaccustomed self-discipline. Nevertheless, Kafka was angry when he found out that his father had not held out even three weeks before spilling the truth to a horrified Julie. Kafka considered that "thoughtless."[21]

Can a tuberculosis patient marry? Even start a family? Kafka had no medical literature available to him in Zürau, but he fixated on the question and noted with great interest that Flaubert's father, a physician, was tubercular, yet he still had a genius for a son: "There may have been a tacit question for a few years as to whether the child's lungs would go down the drain (I suggest this expression for 'rattle') or he would instead become Flaubert." Examples like these were just what Brod was after. Brod sought to brighten Kafka's fatalistic frame of mind and kept adding new names of people they both knew who had recovered from infections of the apexes of the lung none the worse for wear, and without needing to modify their aims in life: "If you take a closer look, everyone has already had tuberculosis."[22]

Then again, the mainstream medical view was significantly more guarded. Single men with acute infections were told by their doctors not to enter into any close relationships, and female patients were generally treated even more strictly. "Marriage ought to be restricted to patients in the so-called 1st stage," wrote Gustav Weiss, a physician in Prague, "and if a so-called healed tuberculosis has not reemerged for at least two years." Other authors recommended a waiting period of at least three years,[23] and Kafka's internist, Dr. Mühlstein, was relieved to hear that his patient had postponed his wedding plans of his own accord, for an unspecified period.

The fact that even "closed," noncontagious tuberculosis was feared enough to be accepted as grounds for separation came as a considerable psychological relief to Kafka because otherwise he would have had to explain why he no longer wanted to agree to any waiting periods and why he considered his illness incurable. The scare word "tuberculosis" gave his parents a plausible explanation for their son's bizarre behavior to offer to their own extended family. Getting engaged twice to the very same woman without a marriage resulting sounded devious and dubious, and it touched on the same questions of moral reputation that had been eating away at the stern mother of the bride for quite some time. But *tuberculosis*—that was something else again; that was *tragic*. Kafka made extensive use of this social rule without having to exploit his illness as a mere excuse. He did see it less as a medical obstacle to marriage than as a sign, an imperative to steer clear of marriage. This conviction was so deep-seated that it gave him the strength to put an end to the love affair, which had clearly fallen apart.

When Felice Bauer boarded the passenger train again at Christmastime of 1917, she must have sensed that a decision was imminent. She seems to have planned another visit to Zürau, far away from any interference from and obligations to the family, which is what Kafka had always had in mind in the past. But the ground had shifted. Zürau now represented Kafka's actual and thus highly vulnerable life, while Prague was more neutral territory. Kafka needed three days to think itover, then opted for a final meeting in Prague.[24]

> December 25. Kafka and Felice came in the evening. Both unhappy, neither spoke. December 26. Kafka came at seven-thirty in the morning, tells me I should give him my morning. Café Paris. Turns out he doesn't want me to give him advice; his firmness of purpose is admirable. Just spend time together.—Yesterday he told F[elice] everything quite clearly.—We spoke about everything but that.—In the afternoon, Schipkapass [a pub in Prague-Dejwitz] with Baum, Weltsch, the 3 women.—Kafka unhappy. He is not sparing himself the pain of inflicting pain on her. I'm different. He said to me, "What I have to do, I can do only alone. Become clear about the ultimate things. The Western Jew is not clear about them, and therefore has no right to marry. There are no marriages for them."

Even Max Brod's terse diary notes, only excerpts of which have been preserved, provide ample evidence of the drama springing from Kafka's stress, as revealed in his harshly impersonal and judgmental generalizations of his friends, whose marriages he implicitly declared nonmarriages. He braced himself for the final act and moved ahead without any evident hesitation. No sooner was he alone with Felice than he got down to the decisive conversation, unfazed by the look of pity on her face. Then he expected her to chat with his friends and their wives in a clamorous café, which was probably the last thing she wanted to do. Kafka's conduct was downright cruel.

The following day, December 27, he brought Felice Bauer to the train station. She had given up and, with great composure and self-restraint, accepted the decision of the man she had probably come to love only the previous year. She did not wish to argue with a man who was ill, and she was evidently even able to come up with words of comfort, all the while retaining a glimmer of hope once they agreed to stay in touch by mail. Kafka, by contrast, was absolutely sure that he would never again see this anguished woman he was helping into the train one last time—and he would be right.[25]

Kafka was now unable to get together with any member of his family. He unexpectedly showed up at Brod's inhospitable office, although he knew that it was impossible to have a private conversation within earshot of one of Brod's colleagues. Kafka looked pale and severe, and he claimed that he just wanted to rest for a moment. He sat down on a small chair positioned next to Brod's desk for meetings with bearers of petitions and other clients, but after a short time Kafka lost his composure and an utterly unexpected, heartrending scene ensued of the kind Brod had never witnessed: Kafka broke out into sobs, and tears streamed down his cheeks. All he could say was, "Isn't it terrible that such a thing has to happen?"

Kafka would later claim—with a hint of pride—that he had never cried so hard in all the years since his childhood as he did on that morning. He now knew that he could still, on occasion, be like everyone else.[26]

Kafka's parents had been hoping for a cozy Christmas, with the family gathered around the table once again, but this was not to be. Franz was not the only one trying to steer clear of a pleasant family get-together; Ottla announced that she would not be there. Even though she had postponed her plan to use the winter break to further her agricultural training, she informed her indignant parents that she would be remaining in Zürau anyway. What was there to do on bare fields at this time of year? What plausible reason was there to spend the holiday with two (equally idle) farmgirls instead of with her own family—and to burn precious coal in the process?

There *was* a reason, but it required secrecy: Ottla's boyfriend Josef David had a few days' leave from active duty, and the couple had never found such an opportune occasion to spend time alone. Of course, that would mean leaving poor Franz in Prague to bear the brunt of the new round of tirades that soon rose back to their customary volume. The fact that his son had just gone through the most painful parting of his life did not make the family patriarch see any need to hold back, nor did the tuberculosis that Franz had contracted in Palais Schönborn (willfully, it seemed to Hermann), in an apartment that he had been told was useless in no uncertain terms.

But the object of Hermann Kafka's greatest resentment was once again the absent Ottla, who, he feared, would soon turn into a farmer and thus be out of the running to be matched up with a respectable suitor. That girl ought to experience actual hunger, Hermann Kafka hollered (just after eating fried sausages and a Christmas goose from

Zürau, while Franz choked down a pig's tail), then she would know what real problems were. It was easy, he argued, to walk away from your poor parents if you then got packages from them. Ottla was ungrateful, crazy; the whole situation was abnormal, and Franz was complicit in and even to blame for this nonsense.

This was nothing new at the Kafkas, and yet, it seemed, this scene did not go quite according to plan. Even days later, Hermann was still furious about his son's waywardness. This time, Kafka refused to stay silent. Aloof and downright condescending, he fired back quick-witted retorts. This was obviously a conspiracy, and it would not help for Hermann to vent his own fury on the store employees, as he usually did. It was a clear defeat; he had accomplished nothing.[27]

Kafka had quickly settled down since Felice's departure, now that he was liberated from the decision-making pressure that was obstructing everything, and he was able to distinguish idle chatter from battles truly worth picking without being thrown by his father's booming voice. "As long as we cannot do without his help in keeping hunger and money worries at bay," he explained to Ottla, "our behavior toward him will continue to be constrained and we will have to yield to him in some way, even if we do not do it outwardly. Something more than just our father is coming out of what he says to us, more than our merely unloving father." He was almost serene, but not forgiving. He would not stand for this man calling him ungrateful, crazy, or abnormal any more. "*Abnormal behavior is not the worst thing*," he retorted coldly, reveling in his parents' stupefaction, "*because normality is, for instance, the World War*."[28] That struck a chord.

CHAPTER TWELVE

Meditations

I am always wrong, except, sometimes, where to be wrong is to be right.

—Samuel Beckett to Barney Rosset, 1956

ARMISTICE WITH RUSSIA. IN CAPITAL LETTERS, POUNDED ONTO A thin paper strip in the little post office in Flöhau. Sender: someone named Max Brod; recipient: that friendly Dr. Kafka in the nearby village of Zürau, the man who received mail nearly every day. It arrived early in the morning on December 4, 1917, at an hour when Kafka was typically still in bed. By the time he held the envelope in his hand, wondering at its contents, the rumor had already spread through the village.[1]

Several times over the previous year, people had been startled by reports that sounded quite unlike the standard announcements of victory and inconsequential write-ups of people in the news. These reports leaped off the page, hinting at the contours of a changed world that lay ahead. In March 1917, the Russian tsar had been forced to abdicate by the military and by politicians. This colossal event spread fear throughout Europe, above all in Austria, that a precedent might be established. If the ruler of a world power was so easy to bring down, it seemed unreasonable to expect that the tottering regime of Kaiser

Karl would fare much better once the numerous internal enemies of the Austro-Hungarian monarchy took action. People were shocked to see what an abrupt turn of events could result in November, when the Bolsheviks came to power by means of a coup and immediately began to liquidate the old system and banish its beneficiaries—with a brutality that made even confirmed democrats shudder. But what if this was the only feasible route to world peace? Lenin announced on the very day of his victory that he would "immediately sign peace terms to put an end to this war." Four weeks later, the weapons on the eastern front fell silent, and he was forgiven for almost everything.

These events were followed with great excitement by the people Kafka knew in Prague, as well, and there were debates about possible consequences for the fate of the "Jewish nation." Jews in Russia were hopeful that the era of forced displacements and state-tolerated pogroms was finally over, and that daily life would return to normal, even if it took years for the directives of the new leadership to get to every last Siberian village. For the more than 300,000 Jewish refugees who were driven out of Galicia and Poland by the war and who had been waiting in hovels and camps since the winter of 1914–1915, there was also a bright spot on the horizon: if the peace in the East was a lasting one, they could return to their villages, and those who considered that too risky might find that when the world war ended, they could make their way to America, the paradise many had dreamed of.

On the other hand, the Russian Revolution and the communist claim to international validity gave fresh momentum to anti-Semitic conspiracy theories. The term "Jewish Bolshevism" came into fashion, and people started calculating how many of the men and women elected to the Council of People's Commissars in Petrograd were of Jewish descent. They had shown the will and the ability to seize power, and the Jews in Germany and Austria were now also thought capable of this—the more obvious their own political and military failure became, the more people were willing to buy into this notion. The governments were now far more tolerant of open anti-Semitism in the press than at the beginning of the war, and when the ire of the starving population was aimed at nameless Jewish usurers and war profiteers instead of its own government, there was little effort to set people straight. Quite the contrary: at the end of 1916, the government began a so-called *Judenzählung* (Jewish census) in the German field forces in an effort to confirm one of the most persistent anti-Jewish prejudices, namely that Jews were underrepresented in the military and thus lacked patriotism and shirked their duties. The census did not bear out this notion, but the Jews regarded the census itself as a humiliating process and as a revocation of civic equality. "We are used to being counted," Buber wrote with a mixture of perplexity and irony, "so the Germans are the ones who ought to be protesting."[2]

Even half a century after their "emancipation," Jews were continually confronted with hatred. Disparaging glances, leering remarks, and pointed exclusions were everyday occurrences. Through the years, many had grown accustomed to these incidents and learned not to take them "personally," so they rarely made the effort to recall or record them. Kafka's and Brod's notes contain no more than occasional traces of these kinds of experiences, although they were ubiquitous in Prague, particularly since the influx of Jewish refugees from the East. One evening, when Kafka attended the salon of his director's wife, Emilie Marschner, another guest acknowledged his presence with this remark: "So, you've invited a Jew, as well."[3] We do not know whether Kafka heard this comment, but he might have been more amused than offended by its extreme narrow-mindedness and not have bothered to record the incident.

Acculturated Jews typically presented a stoic facade to maintain their self-respect, which was feasible only because they felt safe in principle. In most cases, Jews were equal before the law, and Jewish allegiance to the state (which strikes us in the post-Nazi era as baffling, with the wisdom of hindsight) originated in the protection and justice that was promised by the state while being denied by the social community. It became truly threatening for the Jews—far more threatening than for any other comparable group—when the highest authorities themselves reverted to shows of force that were common before the era of liberalization and made it clear that this protection could be revoked at any time.

These signals were in evidence in Prague, as well. Eastern European Jews had a hard time of it here: they came in cattle trucks, many lived in camps, infant mortality was high, and people froze and starved. At first they were divided as to whether the state itself—the great guarantor—registered this misery with anti-Semitic malice while everyone was suffering from the coldheartedness, depravity, and shortages that resulted from the war. But in February 1917, the city council announced that from then on, "Israelite refugees"—and no others—were barred from using the streetcars in order to contain a typhus epidemic. The city had been hit by severe frost, and it was nearly impossible for those living on the outskirts to get to the central markets on foot. This measure clearly showed that a line had been crossed; this was no longer a question of benign neglect, but of overt administrative exclusion of an entire demographic group. The issue became a scandal, and although the censors went to great lengths to stifle criticism,[4] the situation in Prague was being scrutinized publicly in the Reichstag in Vienna.

But tests of Jewish identity came from a totally different direction, as well, and forced people to reassess their own role completely. In November 1917, there was a solemn declaration by the British foreign secretary, Arthur Balfour, to support a "national home" for the Jewish people in Palestine. It was the first time a world power had ever taken such an explicit and affirmative stand on the goals of political Zionism, which consequently moved up from a marginal ideology to a power factor, as Herzl had dreamed from the very start. A roar swept through the Jewish press; all publications reprinted the Balfour Declaration for weeks on end, and in Prague, *Selbstwehr* even put out a special supplement.

And yet, no one was jumping for joy about this unexpected breakthrough. Although actions were sure to follow from such a concrete statement issued by the British cabinet, the British were talking as though they had long since won the war, and announced in a patriarchal manner that they would be taking care of the Palestine people as a whole, without saying a single word about the *current* rulers of Palestine, the Turks.[5] This could mean only one thing: the offer to the Jews was predicated on the tacit assumption that the Central Powers would suffer a total defeat, and even the most radical Zionists in Germany and Austria did not look forward to this outcome, let alone the majority of Jews who remained steadfastly loyal to the kaiser.

The Balfour Declaration implicitly posed a question of conscience, with the fate of millions at stake, namely, the question of identity.

Anyone unable to put aside loyalty to his own state and the life strategy of assimilation—and most German and Austrian Jews *were* unable—felt obliged to reject the British offer as loudly and unequivocally as possible. "Germany is our only homeland, and should remain so," announced the *Allgemeine Zeitung des Judentums.* But how ought all the others to act, those who were finding it harder to say "homeland" since the last census? What was left for those who took the concept of a Jewish nation seriously? To avoid the decision for the time being, they could discount the declaration as British propaganda, as did *Dr. Bloch's Österreichische Wochenschrift*, the official publication of the large Jewish community in Vienna. They could hope for ongoing good collaboration with the Turks—which Max Brod had recently sought to justify in *Die neue Rundschau*—and thus declare the declaration superfluous.[6] Or they could tear down the psychological barriers, give up identification with the traditional majority, and bank on the military defeat and downfall of their own state. As painful as that was, for everyone who no longer believed in assimilation, there was in truth and in the long run only this path, as political events soon made clear to those who were still on the fence. On December 7, 1917, the United States declared war on the Habsburg monarchy. Two days later, exactly one month after publication of the Balfour Declaration, the British entered Jerusalem, and the defeated Turkish troops fled in panic. It was obvious whose side the Jews would have to take from then on. The ARMISTICE WITH RUSSIA, while letting up the pressure, came far too late and did nothing to change that.

"The doctor is a goodly man / God will forgive him all He can." A ditty about Doctor Kafka by a dialect poet in Zürau. It is unlikely that he would have mentioned this homage to his friends when he was still healthy, so why now?[7]

Even though it took months to dawn on him, the magnetic pole to which his life was oriented had transformed his situation. This transformation had set in back on Alchimistengasse, imperceptibly at first, and it led to an unexpected result that he did not appear to become fully aware of until he was in Zürau, and certainly by the beginning of 1918: Kafka no longer felt like and defined himself as a writer. He wrote, but writing had become a means to an end; he had another goal in mind.

There are indications of this change in the prose pieces of *A Country Doctor* and in the notes he wrote parallel to them. These are austere texts, with prose that kept tipping into the analytical sphere, with Kafka's pleasure in scenic development peeking through only in spots. Kafka even considered a title that would have been equally suited to a work of nonfiction: *Responsibility*. Of course, the imaginative density of the texts in *A Country Doctor*, the wealth of remarkable ideas, and the oneiric overlapping of present and past were all *poetic* achievements that brought Kafka's writing into a new dimension, but he now laid claim to a broad validity that extended beyond the realm of literature. He wrote in "The New Attorney":

> Nowadays—as no one can deny—there is no one like Alexander the Great. Although many know how to commit murder . . . no one, no one can lead the way to India. Even in those days[,] India's gates were beyond reach, but their direction was indicated by the royal sword. Today the gates have been brought to another place entirely, farther and higher; no one points the way; many carry swords but only to wave them around, and the gaze that tries to follow them grows confused.

While this is dramatic, it is also tendentious and sounds more like cultural criticism than literature. After months of waiting for the galley proofs, when Kafka had long since forgotten the table of contents he had assembled on his own, he was still sure that this piece, with its programmatic pronouncements, belonged at the beginning of *A Country Doctor*. Of course, he could not foresee that the contemplative mode etched into almost every page of this thin book and with which Kafka played his literary games[8] would become the predominant direction of his writerly life. The hemorrhage saw to that.

"Are you writing something?" Brod could not help but pose this question. Just three years earlier, Kafka had been fighting for every free hour to devote to literature; even for the stories in *A Country Doctor*, he had endured discomfort that demonstrated his utter devotion to his work. But now? Kafka was in shaky health, yet well provided for in Zürau. He had escaped the office for months on end; he was free. Still, there was no indication that he intended to use this freedom to produce literary texts. "I'm not writing," he replied curtly. "My will is not aimed squarely at writing either."[9] Not *squarely*.

It was not a good idea to pressure him, and no one back home seems to have urged him to put the months on a lounge chair to more effective use. Brod and Weltsch had learned that even Kafka had little control over the ups and downs of his productivity, and he could certainly not be prodded by others. When they thought back to how often he had disregarded the needs of his own body to push ahead with his writing, they were somewhat relieved to find that now that he was stricken with tuberculosis, he was not jumping in to tackle a new demanding project.

It turned out, however, that Kafka was not nearly as idle as he was letting on. Shortly after his arrival in the village, he had recognized the rare and wonderful opportunity to "make a beginning," and his writing was still part of that plan, though not narrative texts. His friends in Prague would have been astonished to learn what was happening over the following months in the blue notebooks (now known as Octavo Notebooks G and H) that Kafka had stocked up on. There are intermittent echoes of the past winter here, as well, echoes of the dream-studded prose he had invented on Alchimistengasse—the ironic dismantling of cultural myths, as in his "The Silence of the Sirens" and "The Truth about Sancho Panza," would have been particularly well suited to the *Country Doctor* volume, as well.[10] But even these pieces are no longer really narrative; they are experimental setups, trains of thought derived from and shaped into images. And they represent Kafka's approach to a task he was formulating in a radical new way. In conversations with Brod at the end of 1917, he insisted that his task would no longer be *absolutely* literary, but instead moral. "What I have to do, I can do only alone. Become clear about the ultimate things." That sounded uncharacteristically melodramatic, but he was dead serious, and it ultimately signaled his departure from literary life. Almost in passing, Kafka reminded his friend three months later that *A Country Doctor* was likely to be his "last book."[11]

This is not how it turned out. But Kafka's conviction that the contents of the Zürau octavo notebooks were purely for his own edification and unsuited for publication—and certainly not in the self-contained form of a book—was borne out in an ironic sense. The notebooks consist mainly of compactly formulated notes that focus on religious and philosophical questions, on good and evil, truth and falsehood, and alienation and redemption. Unsurprisingly for an author who was still suffering from the shock of a bloody awakening, they are ultimately notes that keep reaching to the edge of an abyss, where thinking comes up against its own destruction. Much of it remains fragmentary: time after time, there are scattered sentences that trail off into the void, interspersed with aphorisms and penetrating imagery, punctuated by an array of exploratory comments that Kafka set off with slashes. There are few comparable examples of this form in world literature: Valéry's notebooks (a motherlode of this type of writing, which, however, became accessible only after 1945) and, of course, Pascal's *Pensées*. It is no mere coincidence that in the very days before Kafka fell ill, he leafed through Pascal's chaotic notes: Shortly thereafter, *following* the catastrophic event, he seems to have taken up this form of writing right away, as a form that was open enough to penetrate into virtually untrodden territory.

> I am going astray. The true path is along a rope—not a rope that is suspended way on high, but only barely above the ground. It seems intended more to trip you up than to let you walk across it.
>
> A cage went off to catch a bird.
>
> His exhaustion is that of the gladiators after the combat; his labor was the whitewashing of a corner in a civil servant's office.
>
> The fact that there is nothing but a world of the mind takes away our hope and gives us certainty.
>
> He runs after the facts like a novice skater who also practices someplace where it is forbidden.
>
> This feeling: "I am not dropping anchor here" and in no time feeling the swelling, buoyant tide all around.
>
> If we had not been expelled from paradise, paradise would have had to be destroyed.

> Ready at all times, his house is portable, he lives in his home at all times.
>
> Lamentation at the deathbed is actually lamentation over the fact that dying in the true sense did not occur here; we must still content ourselves with this dying, we are still playing the game.[12]

What tide? What house? What game? Hope of what, certainty about what? And a rope, a handbreadth suspended over the ground ... certainly a vivid image, but what path is said to lead above the ground, and how is that the *true* path?

Kafka's Zürau meditations (it is doubtful that he would have accepted the term "aphorisms") are far less familiar to most readers than the narrative works. The texts are unsettling; their contents and aesthetics are difficult to assess, and they seem more like a collection of enigmas than works of literature. They attest to an act of reflection that tackles the hardest of tasks, and here and there, Kafka is able to come up with formulations that appear to operate at the outer limits of human cognition and several steps beyond, in the clear, rarefied zone between knowledge and wisdom. And yet he never comes to an end; every sentence, every image provokes further interpretation, and in lieu of thetic statements, Kafka's short critical reflections and paradoxes are not only ambiguous but also parts of a larger unit. The cage that catches the bird remains utterly puzzling out of context, although it is clearly set off in the manuscript. Kafka seems to have been experimenting, and to have broken off his experiments at various stages of their development, at times prematurely. Scholars continued to ponder where and how to integrate the Zürau notes into Kafka's literary legacy. Most readers are not inclined to consider them an integral part of his oeuvre.

But astonishingly, there are strong indications that Kafka himself saw this quite differently. In February 1918, he began to check over his notes to see what could be regarded as useful and valid. He took a pile of stationery (which was a precious item during the final year of the war), folded and cut the sheets horizontally and vertically, and created more than a hundred slips of paper; then he began to number the slips and fill them with selected notes—one "aphorism" per slip of paper, in order of its date of composition—and make occasional revisions, which were sometimes quite sweeping. In other words, Kafka took this seriously; he distilled ideas and short critical reflections, of which he had the impression that they were developed as far as human insight could go and were formulated precisely enough to be preserved. We can only surmise *why* Kafka went to the effort of making this set of slips of paper; months later, he was still complaining to Brod about his supposed "loafing" in Zürau, and it is therefore highly unlikely that he was showing the slips of paper to others,[13] let alone considering publication. But it is certain that he would not have made clean copies of and numbered mere sketches, preliminary stages, or drafts. Also, Kafka must have gone through the set of papers again at some later date because two dozen of the selected notes are crossed out in pencil. And almost three years later, in the latter part of 1920, he supplemented his collection with eight new aphoristic texts. He evidently attempted to update this repository of knowledge to reflect his own intellectual development by means of supplementing and trimming.

The question of whether this was still *literary* writing did not weigh on Kafka's mind; it was *writing*, albeit on a different level. "I can still have passing satisfaction from works like *A Country Doctor*, provided I can still write such things at all (very improbable). But happiness only if I can still raise the world into the pure, the true, and the immutable."[14] One of Kafka's best known and most pointed commentaries on the meaning and aim of his literary work. Kafka was outlining the enormous work that he felt was awaiting him after giving up on marriage, and he indicated that he would certainly try his hand at new *narrative* texts to live up to this task. But he was setting himself a colossal challenge here—even artistic perfection seemed too little to him. Still more colossal was the self-confidence he mustered to consider the possibility that he could actually grasp a transcendent truth, pure and simple. He now wanted *everything*: success, insight, vindication, happiness.

Max Brod published the Zürau reflections from Kafka's literary estate in 1931, and because Kafka himself had made a selection and thus had already taken what might be considered a first step toward publication, it seemed justified to disegard the context of the notebooks for the time being. Of course, Brod figured he would need to enhance the

stepped up his missionary zeal at this time. Kafka sometimes came to him with vocabulary questions, and was the picture of wide-eyed innocence when asking Brod how to pronounce the Hebrew numbers, so Brod was flabbergasted to learn, shortly before Kafka's departure for Zürau, that Kafka had pushed his way through forty-five lessons within half a year without letting on to anyone. "This solitary furtiveness!" he groused in his diary, only to concede that there was something "very good" as well as "bad" about Kafka's bewildering reserve.

Even Brod must have sensed that for Kafka, the solitary nature of the decision, the freedom from any need for self-justification, which the Zionists generated to excess, was "good." He wanted to learn Hebrew primarily for himself, not for Palestine, and as clearly as he was aware that without the influence of friends he would not have come up with this idea at all, it was vital to him to make the decision all on his own and not as part of a political or cultural program of renewal. Perhaps Brod now understood for the first time—and his ambivalent commentary in his diary indicates as much—that the astonishing (and much-touted) independence of Kafka's judgments and decisions could be had only at the cost of well-developed social reserve, an immunity to well-meant insinuations of all sorts, and that only truly free decisions could help Kafka to shape and stabilize his fragile self-image—which of course did not stop him from measuring himself against the less autonomous achievements of others, at times with a sense of satisfaction: the Zionists in Prague, Kafka remarked ironically, were condemned to keep going back to the opening lesson in Rath's textbook because they used the summer vacation to forget what they learned.[19]

His own decision to learn Hebrew proved far more lasting; even after the hemorrhage, Kafka continued his vocabulary practice, and by the end of 1918 he was able to carry on a simple conversation in Hebrew. He took a course in Prague, and both Friedrich Thieberger (a high school teacher and former Bar Kokhba activist) and Georg Langer (who was well-versed, albeit narrow-minded, on the subject of religion) gave him private instruction. Weltsch and Brod sometimes joined in as well. They learned in a small group, but even during their first tentative efforts at corresponding in Hebrew, Kafka made the most of his head start, such as in this remark to Brod: "Your Hebrew is not bad;

there are a few flaws at the beginning, but once you get into it, it becomes flawless."[20]

Of course, no matter how much energy Kafka invested in the new project, and despite the great pride with which he later considered it one of the few positive facets of his life in Prague (as Brod recorded in his diary), for a long time it remained an experiment, a means of self-definition that did not require exclusivity and neither restricted his other interests nor had much discernible influence on them. "We are all fighting just one battle," he noted a few days after arriving in Zürau. "If I reach out for weapons behind me when attacked by the last question, I cannot choose among the weapons, and even if I could choose, I would have to grab hold of 'unknown' ones because we all have only one arsenal of weapons."[21] In other words, the way we wind up coping with a life-threatening crisis is not entirely of our own choosing. He confirmed this idea impressively with his apparently random selection of books in Zürau. Felix Weltsch, who was a librarian, was astonished to hear that Kafka was requesting not Jewish or literary biographies and autobiographies, but any kind at all, as long as they were written in either French or Czech. Magazines were ordered, packaged, and sent to Zürau: *Die neue Rundschau*, *Die Aktion*, *Der Jude*, *Jüdische Rundschau*, *Selbstwehr*, *Proszenium* (a theater journal), *les tablettes* (a pacifist journal) . . . Kafka devoured them all. He also read Dickens, Herzen, the diaries of Tolstoy, most likely Schopenhauer, the correspondence of J.M.R. Lenz, and analyses of current issues by R. M. Holzapfel, Max Scheler, Hans Blüher, and Theodor Tagger. It almost seemed as though Kafka, freed from the responsibility of choosing, wanted a display of the entire "arsenal of weapons."

In view of the wide range of intellectual influences Kafka opted to consider in the winter of 19171918, a narrowly Jewish interpretation of his meditations cannot be justified under any circumstances, and his reading list gives no indication of an explicitly *religious* interest either. The sole exception was the writing of Kierkegaard, which he started studying somewhat more systematically in November. He read *The Moment*, *Fear and Trembling*, and *Repetition*; he also reread Kierkegaard's diary entries and wrote detailed letters about them to Brod. Even in these letters it is abundantly clear, however, that Kafka—as always—was not especially curious about the finer points of theological and intellectual history. The *case* of Kierkegaard is what caught his attention, in particular the issue of Kierkegaard's fraught engagement, which seemed strikingly similar to his own, and the philosopher's consistent refusal to take life "as it was," for which he paid dearly. Kafka was impressed by Kierkegaard's existential gravity and his radical privileging of individual experience. Kierkegaard was able to frame his own issues as highly abstract philosophical discourse. He acknowledged and articulated his highly personal conflicts paradigmatically, even at moments of the profoundest torment, and shone a spotlight on the question of *legitimacy*.

Kafka was hearing echoes of his own questions in Kierkegaard. Can there be any justification for merely observing and describing life in lieu of living it ourselves? Is there any authority conceivable beyond social obligations, an authority that may not only permit, but even demand that we challenge our own group? These are questions that gnaw at the foundations of any social community, that can never be resolved once and for all, and that perpetually recur in myriad guises. Jurists and censors know the problem all too well; it affects the degree of artistic "moral impropriety" that a society can tolerate. For the writer, in turn, it is a question of survival; he knows that his powers of imagination are anything but socially acceptable and that they begin to bleed dry when they succumb to the pressure of outward conformity. And theologians regard it as the biblical snare par excellence, the divine test of obedience: the command to Abraham to kill his only son and thus to violate a fundamental rule of the social community—in favor of a "higher" rule. In *Fear and Trembling*, Kierkegaard picked this very episode to demonstrate that faith in a higher order (whether it be God, art, or morality) guaranteed neither well-being nor security, and in fact goes hand in hand with fear: fear of the leap that cannot be undone, the absurd, and the void.

Kafka was well acquainted with this fear, and a letter he later wrote to Robert Klopstock shows that the story of Abraham continued to weigh on his mind for years and must have captivated him to the point of total identification. Kafka thought up contemporary variants that could have come straight from his literary cosmos. There is, for example, someone

> who would be as ready to carry out the order for the sacrifice on the spot, like a waiter filling his orders, but who would still never perform the sacrifice because he cannot get away from home, he is indispensable, the household needs him, there is always something that has to be attended to, the house isn't finished, but until the house is finished, until he has this security, he cannot get away. The Bible recognizes this too, for it says: "He put his house in order."

That is a humorous, subversive, and playful approach to the myth, but in the background is the spirit of a different Abraham, one who fails to amuse:

> One who certainly wants to carry out the sacrifice properly and in general correctly senses what the whole thing is about but cannot believe that he is the one who was meant, he, the repulsive old man, and his child, the dirty boy. He does not lack the true faith—he has this faith—he would sacrifice in the proper manner, if he could only believe he was the one who was meant. He is afraid that he will ride out as Abraham and his son, but on the way will turn into Don Quixote. . . . An Abraham who comes unsummoned! It is as if the top student were solemnly to receive a prize at the end of the year and in the expectant silence, the worst student, because he has misheard, comes forward from his dirty back bench and the whole class falls apart. And it is perhaps not that he has heard wrong, for his name was actually spoken, because it is the teacher's intention that the reward for the top student is at the same time the punishment of the worst.
>
> Terrible things—enough.[22]

Terrible, certainly, not because there was an unfathomable theological or ideological problem being negotiated here but because it is first and foremost a life experience, an affront that the Abraham myth calls back painfully into consciousness. For Kafka, questions of whether one is "meant" (to receive good fortune, talent, a task, an obligation, . . .), how to recognize that one is meant, and whether one can ever be sure of being meant are not issues of religious conviction, and even when he brought in religious images, myths, or schools of thought, it is far from certain that he was speaking about religion.

Hence, the palpable resistance with which both Kafka's diaries and the Zürau meditations meet every attempt to distill a positive religious content. Never did Kafka establish a direct connection to God.[23] He thought of God almost exclusively as a protagonist in biblical myths, especially in the story of paradise lost. But even here, God remains a role, a conceptualization, and not even a consummate one.[24] Kafka did not take any of these exegetic considerations into account in his set of slips of papers. But wherever he dropped the literary perspective, wherever he bypassed imagery and metaphorical language and spoke directly about the issue of religion, he immediately built up an intellectual distance:

> Man cannot live without a steady faith in something indestructible within him, even if both the indestructible element and the faith may always remain concealed from him. One of the ways this concealment can be expressed is the belief in a personal god.[25]

A wonderfully profound idea, formulated with utter simplicity. But no one who believes in a personal God would speak this way. And Kafka later eliminated even this aphorism (this is one of the few meditations that truly *is* an aphorism). If we were to regard Kafka's slips of paper, in the final version endorsed by the author, as the printer's copy of a work, we would be left with a text that never mentions God.

But this is equally true of Kafka's more prominent works, and Brod's claim that the "aphorisms" built on something long in the making is not entirely incorrect. The deeper we delve into the Zürau reflections, the clearer it becomes that Kafka was not nearly as far removed from his narrative universe as it might first appear. He used all the rhetorical means at his disposal to conjure an all-encompassing transcendence that caught up everything in its spell (the law, truth, the indestructible, . . .), and in the same breath he shifted this transcendence into a hopeless distance. It is as though he were compelling all his readers to stare in the same direction, only to tell them, "the direction is correct; *there it is*, but your eyes don't reach far enough to see it, and they never will." A devastating reply, but nothing new. This gesture into the void already predominated in *The Trial*.

But it is not a religious gesture. Kafka blocked off every exit and plugged up every gap. He showed the shadows but never the accompanying light. At times, a ray happened to shine through and cast warmth ever so briefly—then he hurried to correct the oversight. He initially wrote "something indestructible," but in the final copy in the files, he altered it to "something indestructible *within him*." In Octavo Notebook H, he wrote that we develop "no less profoundly bound up with mankind than we are with ourselves—through all the sufferings of the world until we are all redeemed together." This, too, sounded like a religious promise, an absolutely positive expectation amidst all the uncertainty, and Kafka hastened to rectify this misunderstanding by crossing out the words "until we are all redeemed together" and writing over them: "together with all our fellow men." With a stroke of the pen, he wiped out any hope, brought us back to the history of mankind, and severed the final transcendental connection. All that remained was the now doubly invoked *secular* togetherness, and death was eliminated as a medium of redemption. His rationale is stunningly simple: "Life on earth cannot be followed by a life beyond because life beyond is eternal and therefore cannot have a temporal connection to life on earth." And with that, the very last door slammed shut.[26]

In conversations as well as in his writings, Kafka appears to have spent years under the spell of these thought patterns, which reveal the enduring influence of Plato more than of Jewish literature, which disappointed Brod, who had thought that his friend was well on his way to embracing religiousness. It was, of course, impressive how seriously Kafka took notions of truth, goodness, and permanence; he also made frequent use of religious or religious-sounding terms to apply the highest possible tension to the ideas he considered vital. "Writing as a form of prayer"—that sounded impressive, and at least seemed far removed from bloodless metaphysics.[27]

But when Brod now tried to pin down his friend as to the actual religious meaning of these terms, he met with resistance. Kafka had no interest in religious catchphrases, and on the matter of the supposed guarantors of that spiritual world, which he considered the only real one, he was capable of downright blasphemous statements. He readily and repeatedly countered the idea that his tubercular illness could be a kind of trial by ordeal with a paraphrase from Wagner's *Meistersinger*: "I would have thought him more refined."[28] In a conversation with Brod, Kafka described people as "nihilistic thoughts that came into

God's head," but he hastened to assure Brod that this did not point to the existence of an evil creator of the world, as some gnostics claimed, but merely to "one of his bad moods." Taken aback, Brod asked him when there would be any hope outside our world. Kafka replied with a smile, "Plenty of hope—for God—an infinite amount of hope—only not for us."[29]

It seems strange that at a time when everything was falling to pieces, when the course of world history had sped up, millions of individuals were in disarray and at the mercy of mere chance, and history was devolving into an unimaginable number of exciting stories, a storyteller would pull away from telling stories and turn instead to the seemingly ahistorical, the "last things": good and evil, truth and lie, life and death. This was likely Kafka's way of seeking a foothold under vastly changed circumstances. At times, he himself no longer knew how to distinguish between a last insight and a last attempt at rescue. He was experiencing a universal crisis that went beyond the powers of imagination: a world war, the disintegration of a society and its values, and the demise of his own state. On top of that, he was observing this crisis from an exposed vantage point—the Jewish one—which remained shaky when everyone else felt they were on firm ground. And to add insult to injury, he had to cope with the invasion of a second, equally threatening, but utterly *personal* crisis, an attack on his now-bleeding body.

Both Kafka's meditations and his letters from Zürau reveal that he was keenly aware of this double impact. He understood that under conditions like these, it would no longer suffice to vindicate himself in front of his own internal court, in front of his fiancée or a couple of well-meaning friends. Even the most powerful and persuasive metaphors—such as the bellicose wording in his final letters to Felice—rang hollow when they stayed within the confines of a merely personal mythology of pure introspection. He found that when he grappled seriously with the work of reflection, it inevitably carried him beyond the frame of reference of his individual fate. He needed to entrust himself to these centrifugal forces to discover his place in the vortex of disintegration.

Max Brod was the first to be confronted with this new and surprising dimension of Kafka's thought, in the seemingly harmless context of the odd serenity, even cheerfulness, with which Kafka appeared to accept his illness, behavior that no one in Prague could make any sense of. Brod wrote to him in Zürau, "If I weren't afraid of upsetting you, I would tell you that your letters are evidence of great calm. Well, now I've said it—which goes to prove that I'm not really afraid that this or anything else could upset you. You are happy in your unhappiness."[30]

Kafka was not hearing, or inferring, this reprimand for the first time, and just a few months earlier he might well have replied by rattling off a set of self-incriminations and employing a well-rehearsed defensive strategy of assuming the stance of the most merciless judge and meting out self-justice. This time, however, he responded not with complaints, but with a powerful counterattack:

> Dear Max, It has always surprised me that you apply the expression "happy in unhappiness" to me and to others, and that you mean it not as an assertion or statement of regret, or possibly as an admonition, but as a reproach. Don't you realize what that means? The mark may have been set upon Cain with the agenda buried in this phrase, which of course carries with it the implication "unhappy in happiness" at the same time. When someone is "happy in unhappiness," it follows that he has fallen out of step with the world and, moreover, that everything has fallen apart for him, or is falling apart, that no voice can reach out to him clearly any longer and so he cannot follow it straightforwardly. Things are not quite so bad with me, at least so far. I have met with both happiness and unhappiness in full measure, although you are quite right as to my average experience, and you are also largely right about my present state, but you must say so in a different tone.[31]

Brod was too startled to reply. Never before had Kafka undertaken such a forceful attempt to explain his own behavior as typical of his era, as symptomatic, and with a serene air of superiority that banished any thought that he was fishing for excuses. No, he was serious about this; he now had a real aversion to anything resembling psychological cunning,[32] and since he had long suspected that Felice was laboring under the same misapprehension, he attempted to clear it up with her preemptively. He quoted Brod's "crude" reproach, asked whether it was what she might be thinking as well, and provided a detailed paraphrase of his reply, intensifying its imagery in the process. A person who is happy in unhappiness, he wrote, is someone "who has destroyed the world and, incapable of resurrecting it, is hunted through its ruins."[33]

These were not rash impulses. The laconic tone of Kafka's notes dated August 1917, and stemming from the days immediately preceding and following the hemorrhage, mark the exact point at which laments about his own disorientation widen out into a far more extensive analysis. These notes begin vaguely: "Do you think so? I don't know," then assume a sharper focus: "Whatever I touch falls apart," and end with a poetic twist: "The woods and the river—they swam past me while I swam in the water."[34]

Numerous other fragments in the Zürau meditations make it clear that Kafka was not propelled by an abstract, impersonal will to knowledge. He sought instead to link highly personal events with the larger societal picture, to situate himself in his era. He hoped to find a place where it was possible to stay alive intellectually. Kafka acted like an underdressed man who is loath to cover his nakedness with awkward movements and decides he would rather take the stage unclothed: that is, where nakedness no longer carries a stigma but conveys a *meaning*. It was the tuberculosis, he explained, that had offered him this "new way out, which in its completeness had so far seemed impossible." This "way out"

> would entail my confessing not only in private, not only as an aside, but openly, by my behavior, that I cannot acquit myself here. To this end, I need do nothing but follow the lines of my previous life with full determination. As a result I would hold myself together, not squander myself in meaninglessness, and keep a clear-eyed view.[35]

Kafka was recharting his course. The notion he was not "acquitting" himself was, of course, an old refrain. But now he had to think through the practical and intellectual consequences of the change he was contemplating. And it was just a small step to the decision not to acquit himself at any cost, but instead, as Kierkegaard's diaries had recently taught him, to insist on his own standards: "As soon as a man comes along . . . who says: However the world is, I shall stay with my original nature, which I am not about to change to suit what the world regards as good. The moment this word is spoken, a metamorphosis takes place in the whole of existence."[36]

In Zürau, Kafka took this step. What had begun as a way out led to a new, radically altered interpretation of his own life. The resultant stream of self-confidence was tremendous, and the unexpectedly clear view gave him the prospect of an autonomy that seemed miraculous after all the years of neurotic self-imposed captivity. He had opened a window and let in air that was ice cold—too cold, perhaps, to endure it for long and to live in it, but he was not thinking about that now. It was the hour of insight.

> It is not inertia, ill will, awkwardness . . . that cause me to fail or even get me near failure: family life, friendship, marriage, profession, literature. It is, rather, the lack of ground, of air, of imperatives. It is my task to create these, not in order to catch up with what I have missed, but instead so that I have not missed anything, for the task is as good as any other. It is even the most primal task of all, or at least the pale reflection of that task, just as one may, on climbing to heights where the air is thin, suddenly step into the light of the far-distant sun. And this is no exceptional task, either; it is sure to have been faced often before, although I don't know whether to such a degree. I have brought nothing with me of what life requires, so far as I know, but only the universal human weakness. With this—in this respect it is gigantic strength—I have powerfully absorbed the negative element of the age in which I live, an age that is, of course, very close to me, which I have no right ever to fight against, but to an extent a right to represent. The slight amount of the positive, and also of the extreme negative, which tips into the positive, is something in which I have had no hereditary share. I have not been guided into life by the deeply sinking hand of Christianity, as Kierkegaard was, and have not caught the last corner of the Jewish prayer shawl flying by, as the Zionists have. I am an end or a beginning."[37]

CHAPTER THIRTEEN

Spanish Influenza, Czech Revolt, Jewish Angst

I fear that some creator has overreached.

—Hans Henny Jahnn, *Fluss ohne Ufer*

"Franz Kafka, who was awarded the Fontane prize for his stories 'The Stoker' and 'The Metamorphosis,' withdrew from the public eye and bought a garden somewhere in German Bohemia, where he is seeking a return to nature in his vegetarian diet and interests." This statement appeared in the *Prager Tagblatt* in the summer of 1918.[1] The legendary Radio Yerevan quips about life in eastern Europe came later, but this type of reporting existed back in Kafka's day, as well. The gist of the announcement was correct, although Kafka had not been awarded the Fontane prize—just the money that came along with it. He had not bought the garden in which he was working; it was part of his sister's property, and even she had not bought the land, but rather leased it from her brother-in-law. Kafka had not "withdrawn" from the public eye—he was attempting to cure his tuberculosis. And he had been back at his desk at the Workers' Accident Insurance Institute for the past six weeks. All this nonsense had been concocted at Café Arco—and there is no doubt that Max Brod contributed his insider's perspective. It was highly unlikely that the record would be set straight there.

By early April, Kafka had decided not to request any more leaves of absence from Director Marschner. The three months that had been approved at the outset stretched into nearly eight, and at no point did the institute exert the least bit of pressure on him. That was the best policy it could have adopted, Kafka noted admiringly: "[T]hey hold their peace, are patient, pay, and wait. It isn't easy to hold out."[2] On April 27, he tidied up his vegetable garden for the last time, and three days later, Ottla brought him to the Michelob train station with a horse and cart. On the morning of May 2, Kafka showed up at the office of his immediate superior, Pfohl, with a slight cough but looking healthier and better nourished than he had in years.

Kafka soon realized that the institute's clever "policy" of leaving him alone for a good three quarters of a year stemmed not from tactical or humanitarian considerations but rather from the organizational chaos that had inevitably ensued with the increasing tensions between Czechs and Germans. Two days before Kafka's departure to Zürau, the honorary president of the institute, Otto Přibram (who, despite his name, was of German nationality) had died unexpectedly, and the Czech members of the board, who were suddenly in the majority, insisted that only a Czech member could succeed him. When the Germans rejected this and were unable to prevail with paper ballots, they opted not to attend any future board meetings. As a result, the insurance institute was now essentially operating with no one at the helm, and fruitless attempts at arbitration dragged on for months until the newly founded "ministry for social aid" intervened by sending the board home and appointing a provisional administrator. Still, now that the administration was preoccupied only with itself, Director Marschner could (and had to) decide pending vacation requests as he saw fit—a lucky coincidence for Kafka, and one of the rare opportunities in his life when luck and external circumstances worked in his favor.

But what was taking place at Kafka's office was just a relatively innocuous offshoot of the atmospheric changes that had come over Prague by this time. Since the city was in no postion to continue to ensure provisions for its residents—not even one quarter of the official bread rations (which were meager as it was) could actually be had—the mentality of ruthless "wangling" had taken over, procuring the essentials without giving any thought to the law or social responsibility. The only thing that still functioned reliably was illicit trade, and the few who could afford it lacked for nothing. But where did all the goods traded "under the counter" come from, and where did they go—and who was reaping the benefits of the shockingly exorbitant prices? These were questions that took on increasingly partisan casts. One side claimed that the Czech farmers were the ones lining their pockets; the other countered that the food was being smuggled to Vienna, or even into the German Reich. The remainder supposedly disappeared into the cellars of Jewish black marketeers, and they, in turn, brazenly denounced unwelcome competition, especially Czech, to the authorities on a regular basis, as any child knew.[3]

It was only a matter of time before rumors of this kind spilled over into street politics. Strikes and hunger demonstrations had been everyday occurrences for quite a while in Bohemia, but in 1917 the number of incidents mounted. The targets of the attacks were not "the authorities" or "the wealthy," but anyone at all who declared allegiance to a rival nationality. This undercurrent barely made a ripple during the mass demonstrations in Prague, in which as many as 150,000 people took part in January 1918, but a mere two months later, "hunger riots" that the authorities could barely contain were clearly targeting Germans and Jews. And it now appeared that it did not take Jewish refugees from the East to incite more anti-Semitic wrath. Although their number steadily decreased, and although more and more refugees were deported to their hometowns in Galicia and Poland by force—with eager assistance from the Jewish community, which wanted to be rid of these "pests" once and for all[4]—anti-Semitic rage was more and more openly and menacingly manifest. *Selbstwehr* magazine reported in August 1918 that the situation in Prague had grown unbearable and that it was literally impossible to walk through the city on any street "without encountering this revolting expression of national venom."[5]

Under these circumstances, the Kafkas could not be blamed for securing what they had acquired over the course of more than three decades of hard work while there was still time. They kept their anxiety about their possessions in a perpetual subliminal tension; they would sooner forgo rest and relaxation, which they desperately needed, than expose their shop to the danger of mismanagement or embezzlement for even a single day. But now that even their own staff was joining the big strikes[6] and a growing crowd gathered under their windows on Altstädter Ring again and again, this state of anxiety reached a new pitch. Who could possibly guarantee that the looting, which had so far been restricted to food and coal, would not spill over into other areas? It was such an obvious expectation that Jewish merchants would be the first to be hit, as history had shown time and again, that there was no point in spelling out the reasons for their fear.

Hermann and Julie Kafka decided to call a halt to their entrepreneurial career, to give up their fancy goods store as soon as possible, and to invest their accumulated business capital in a more stable and less conspicuous manner. In January 1918, they purchased a large modern apartment house at Bílekgasse 4, where most of the residents were Czech. The purchase price was a half million kronen. The new landlords, bursting with pride, spent weeks speaking of nothing else and devoted themselves zealously to the task of honing an extensive set of house rules. The building was paid for with the enormous sum of money they received from selling the business to one of Julie's relatives, Bedřich Löwy, who evidently believed his Czech first name would enable him to blend into the crowd and was thus somewhat less pessimistic. The previous owners had several months to close the door on their life's work, and on July 15, the responsibility was passed on to Löwy.

Even though Kafka was well informed about the events in Prague, he must have been surprised upon his return from Zürau how profoundly everyday life had already been eroded: daily brawls between Czech and German high school students, furious demonstrations by innkeepers who had nothing left to offer their guests, evacuations of malnourished children, streetcar and passenger train cancellations lasting for days on end, loud arguments in front of kiosks that handed out cigarette ration cards; in the outskirts of the city, stones were sometimes hurled at helpless officials. This was a social travesty of the Prague he had left eight months earlier. But as long as he remained fit for work, there was no escaping this predatory society. The only option appeared to be coming to terms with the situation and stoically awaiting the end of the war; even the rapid publication of the *Country Doctor* story collection, even an unlikely literary success would not have made a difference. Kafka also had to give up his plan to look for a new apartment and thus to maintain a modicum of independence; the fear of spending another winter in unheated rooms during the war was too great—where would he get the coal? And he could not risk being helpless in the face of another hemorrhage. The only remaining choice was to return to his parents' apartment, as difficult as this decision was after their recent conflicts. Kafka decided to write a letter to his father to prepare for this move (unfortunately, the letter has not been preserved), but bringing things out in the open had always been the worst strategy for lifting the family's mood. Once again, the patriarch ranted and raved in the shop for days on end; not daring to vent his anger on his son, he took it out on the staff instead.[7]

Kafka missed the easy closeness with Ottla in Prague, and the way they could revert to childhood behavior without repercussions. She had no part in his meditations' analytical astuteness or preoccupation with death, but he often found that her very presence lifted his spirits and filled him with boyish cheer; and he teased her and made a point of intruding on her rare free moments.[8] He was unable to act this way even in the company of his closest friends in Prague, where he struck a very different tone. Max Brod took it hard when Kafka informed him that friendships were not part of the indispensable substance of his life and that he was therefore determined to become even more reclusive and sever his remaining ties. Brod feared that this new escalation of his purism was starting to assume hostile dimensions.

Kafka did not ultimately follow through on this decision to wipe his social slate clean—presumably it would have taken some concrete hope and an encouraging perspective to justify such a rigid step. So he stayed with his usual walks, occasional group outings, and swimming with others in the Moldau River. Still, Kafka was able to keep up a new "rustic" outlook, which had come to seem more of an expression of authentic life, for his life in Prague. He began to spend his free afternoons at the Institute for Pomology, Viniculture, and Horticulture, which was located in the northern part of Prague, right next to the baroque Troja Palace, and offered a broad view over the city. Lessons in horticulture had been introduced here recently. It did seem a baffling form of continuing education for a thirty-five-year-old senior civil servant, but there was nothing wrong with wanting to apply expert touches to one's own garden plot—many who were suffering from hunger longed to do so—and this pretext had served Kafka well some years earlier at the Dvorský Nursery.

Back then, of course, he had regarded garden work as therapeutic. The label "nervousness" could be used to justify the oddest habits, and he had been following naturopathic recommendations, which advocated just about any kind of exercise as long as it took place outdoors. But in the meantime, clearly under the influence of his Zionist readings, physical activity had become a moral aim for him, a question of existential style. The slow and deliberate attention required for work with plants was one of the achievements he wanted to keep as pure as possible, whatever the social consequences. He did not even use the regular two-week vacation to which he was entitled for the stay at a health resort he had been urgently advised to take, opting instead for additional training in gardening. In September 1918, Kafka worked in the nurseries of a large market garden in Turnov in northern Bohemia, and he did not feel as though he lacked for anything.

It is easy to see why this odd decision gave his parents and friends pause. Still, they must have been relieved that his thoughts had not turned to Zürau again. That outpost had become unsustainable, and when Ottla was in Prague for a few hours—which happened less and less often—she seemed like the symbol of a hopeless battle to her family, and now even to her brother. Ottla was gaunt, overworked, and disillusioned. Seeds and fodder could no longer be obtained legally, and the villagers had given up hope of getting administrative assistance once the terrible food crisis in the nearby Bohemian industrial areas had exhausted the last government reserves. The German Reich had to be appealed to to head off mass starvation. And the Germans stepped in to help: flour for military aid was now the motto. But these supplies did not make it as far as Zürau, because the people there were still managing to scrape by.

The Zürau mission had proved futile, and even Irma, an admiring sympathizer since Ottla first went there, now advised her to break off this doomed experiment. There was nothing more to earn there; even Karl Hermann eventually had to admit this. He visited his farm in August and quickly reached an agreement with Ottla to dissolve it altogether within one or two months. The elder Kafkas were relieved. This was the decision they had been urging for months, and it provided a good opportunity, they figured, to get Ottla's life back on track, which for them meant her return to Prague, immediate enrollment in a school of home economics, and bringing back the marriage broker. But they were mistaken. What made Ottla give up was neither the laboriousness of the farm work nor the insufficient supply of food, which could not go on indefinitely, but rather the wretched drudgery, day in and day out, without any hope of a bright future, the impossibility of making headway, learning something, creating professional opportunities for herself under these circumstances. Still, her path was not leading her to Prague; she refused even to discuss that option. The long-planned and repeatedly postponed agricultural training was now on her agenda, and that would finally get her the professional status she had been seeking. This was exactly what her brother envisioned for her as well, and he immediately began to make inquiries at the insurance institute and to send out letters to the directors of agricultural schools. Budweis was one possibility, or Děčín, or the large horticultural school in Klosterneuburg, just north of Vienna. The choice was not simple, in some instances because high school diplomas or evidence of extensive prior knowledge were required, which Ottla could not produce, and in others because women were admitted only as auditors and would not be permitted to take the examinations. Finally Kafka advised her to apply to the Agricultural Winter School in Friedland. She would be the first woman ever to study there. To alleviate his sister's fear of further financial dependence, he offered to pay her tuition for the time being, which took at least one argument off the table as far as their parents were concerned. However, the quarreling about Ottla's stubbornness and Franz's irresponsible support continued to heat up and could have easily resulted in a long-lasting rift if another event of a very different dimension had not intervened, an event that united the family, albeit in fear and only on the surface, for several weeks.

Previously strong, healthy people are suddenly complaining about crippling headaches, pain throughout the body, stuffed noses, bad colds, lack of appetite, sensations of heat followed by mild shivering fits, and, above all, overwhelming fatigue. A feeling of dryness, a scratchy throat with slight difficulty swallowing, and some

> degree of hoarseness soon follow; at the same time a debilitating urge to cough that tires out patients and can thoroughly exhaust them. . . .[9]

This was not the common flu. These were the symptoms of an illness that would develop into a devastating pandemic extending throughout the world, with a momentum that made the massive infection attack like a natural disaster and instantly overwhelm social and hygienic protection systems. The first cases were identified at the end of September, and within the first week in October, about two hundred people died in each of the two metropolises of Vienna and Berlin. By mid-October, up to two hundred were dying *per day*. Schools, theaters, and movie houses were closed; the beginning of the fall semester was postponed at all universities; and the authorities appealed to people to avoid crowds. But it was too late. More than 15 percent of the population had been infected with so-called Spanish influenza,[10] and while the municipal mortuaries were overcrowded, whole departments in hospitals had to close down because there was no longer a single healthy doctor or other medical professional available.

But the uncontrollable risk of infection (with an incubation period of only one to two days) coupled with the breakneck speed with which the epidemic spread from one part of town to the next, from one region to another, were not the only horrific aspects of this epidemic—even more distressing was the swift force with which people were stricken. The pains in their arms and legs intensified rapidly, their tongues turned gray, their temperatures often soared within just one or two hours. And stories were told of people who were in the best of spirits one evening and by the following noon lay dead in one of the hastily built coffins.

Nevertheless, the Spanish flu was not lethal *per se*. Those who were able to take to bed at the first sign of symptoms and rest until these subsided had about a 97 percent chance of survival—assuming there were no complications such as pneumonia. But no known flu epidemic had ever resulted in so many and such severe cases of pneumonia, most of them as early as the third or fourth day of contracting the flu. The mortality rates that were reported from the individual clinics were dreadful, with patients bleeding to death and suffocating. And it struck those who seemed healthiest and most active. People between the ages of twenty and forty had to fear the worst.[11]

Kafka was stricken with the flu at the height of the epidemic, on Monday, October 14. The doctor who was sent for, Dr. Heinrich Kral, noted that by noon, Kafka's fever had risen to 105. He listened to Kafka's lungs but was unable to discover anything alarming, and because his patient initially failed to tell him about his barely cured apical catarrh of the lungs, this was a doubly fortunate finding. It is quite conceivable that Kafka was putting the doctor to a little test, but it is just as possible that he was already beginning to downplay the danger because the symptoms of tuberculosis—shortness of breath, constant coughing, and night sweats—had ebbed during the summer, and Professor Pick had been speaking in terms of a "very good" state of his lungs. The garden work in Turnov had been good for him, and he seemed to have gotten over the worst.

But in view of the acute crisis, this finding did little to reassure anyone, especially his mother, who was consumed with fear on the first day and kept bursting into tears. It was a lucky coincidence that Ottla—who had already left Zürau—was spending a few weeks in Prague until her agricultural classes started up. She was evidently the only one who could keep a cool head and take charge of her brother's affairs. During the next few weeks, she kept his office apprised of the situation, and also his closest friends, since Kafka was not allowed to have visitors. He soon had to put down his pen, as well. He had written to Brod shortly after his illness began that he had "some fever" and was confined to bed, and would have to cancel their next Hebrew lessons together.[12] This was his last known message for nearly a month.

Now came what everyone feared the most: pneumonia. We have little information about its course—no one in the family had any cause or opportunity to put the details of this catastrophe on record—but it is likely that Kafka, like nearly all patients in his situation, spent weeks coughing up blood this time. His fever apparently rose to about 106, a number that must have astonished even a doctor who was racing from one flu patient to the next.[13] Kafka had entered the zone of delirium, and at any moment, organ failure could set in. Brod was horrified to learn that his friend's doctors were close to the point of considering his case hopeless. Evidently the crisis had gotten to the point where the doctor's calculated optimism in dealing with the family could no longer be justified.

The medical establishment stood by helplessly while the Spanish flu wreaked havoc (it took eighty more years for the virus—H1N1—to be identified); it could do virtually nothing for the mass outbreak of pneumonia either. Patients were given medications to bring their fever down (aspirin, Pyramidon, and quinine); for shortness of breath, they were injected with camphor. In addition, every clinic was experimenting with its own in-house remedies (adrenaline, electrocollargol, neosalvarsan, mercurous chloride, etc.) without achieving any significant results, so Dr. Kral's prescriptions cannot have been very helpful for his patient. But it is clear that the least additional strain—such as transporting him to a hospital—would have meant certain death for Kafka and that the only effective way of nursing him back to health would be intensive care at home. Soon he was moved into his parents' much more comfortable bedroom. Black marketeers brought the special food he required, fearless maids kept the place spotless, and there was a daily medical update. The family's comfortable social status ultimately enabled him to escape his brush with death—and Kafka must have soon realized that his debt to his parents had mushroomed during this awful autumn of 1918. The only real consolation was that he had not infected anyone else. And that was in itself a minor miracle.

The Spanish flu, which resurfaced in a second and far more powerful wave in the spring of 1919, then died down as suddenly as it had appeared, is now considered an event of global historical significance because of the enormous number of victims it claimed. More than twenty million people succumbed to the pandemic. Although Asia and Africa were hit the hardest proportionally, the viral infection spiraled into a social and demographic catastrophe in the United States and Europe, as well.

The flu also appeared at a time of major political upheaval, and unbeknownst to the general public, the flu and politics went hand in hand in many ways that few could analyze because there was no reliable information to go on. Today it sounds odd that coverage of the epidemic that claimed so many lives slipped to the third page of many daily newspapers, and incomprehensible that there was no requirement to report cases of the flu without delay; unfathomable that an Austrian minister of public health believed that he could reassure the people by promising three tons of aspirin.[14] But what else could he have said? The flu was terrible, of course, but by the next week everything might be over and done with. The collapse of the military fronts, the depletion of economic resources, hunger riots, and the threat of civil war were incomparably worse because their long-term consequences were unforeseeable. Moreover, the implementation of comprehensive hygienic measures required an undisputed government monopoly of power or at least the intact authority of the administration. But just when there were finally good reasons to prohibit large gatherings, the public space had slipped out of government control. Demonstrations and national rallies had become hot spots where history was being made—and people were not covering their mouths with handkerchiefs.

The Spanish flu was perceived as a limited catastrophe against the backdrop of a far more comprehensive one and was consequently brushed aside at the first signs of improvement. It became a matter of course to accept the deaths of others without being able to prevent or even fully grasp what was happening. Weren't many more people dying of hunger than of the flu? Politicians flatly denied it, and censors suppressed any mention of concrete numbers, but it was the truth. And it no longer mattered whether the soldiers' stamina and willpower were undermined by hunger or by influenza or by both; people stopped caring whether the military hospitals were merely full or terribly overcrowded. The armies of the Central Powers were not just weakened—they were finished: no more replacements of serviceable weapons, no vehicles, no fuel, no rations. Starting in April, there were open mutinies among returning war prisoners who did not want to go back to the trenches, and the soldiers on the western front could barely be induced to advance. The German navy refused to carry out orders. Austrian, Hungarian, Czech soldiers, who one year earlier, in the twelfth and last Battle of the Isonzo, had broken through the Italian front lines, made their way home on their own.

The juxtaposition of influenza epidemic and political crisis assumed the oddest forms under these circumstances. The flu acted as the great equalizer, acting to hold up the flow of history and thereby assuming historic dimensions. Martin Buber, for example, suffered from pneumonia just as the attention of the entire Zionist movement was focused on him, because many supporters expected him to tackle the practical problems of liberated Palestine right after the conclusion of a peace treaty. Buber, however, followed his doctor's advice to take it easy and to retreat from the public eye for the time being. His longtime friend Gustav Landauer came down with the flu as well. Landauer, a pacifist and socialist who had eagerly awaited the end of the Wilhelmine Empire virtually since the day the war began, was confined to bed in the first, crucial days of the coup, and in Munich, the strategically pivotal capital of the newly established Bavarian Soviet Republic. Plagued by pains in his arms and legs, he could barely get around.

Many who yearned to experience the great moment in history were now condemned to watch the end of a four-year inferno, the downfall of a regime tainted with blood, and the dawn of a new era from the sidelines. But in Kafka's life, this conflict between body and history escalated to a colossal paradox because in the fall of 1918, right on Altstädter Ring—this very familiar square, bordered by urban architecture, in which he knew every paving stone and nearly every face on the street—became a stage of world politics, and Kafka had a box seat. Perhaps he was reminded of August 1914, when he had watched the truculent, demagogically staged rallies with an "angry look." But this time, everything was different. There were no roars of triumph, no blustering speeches. Directly under his window, decisions were being made.

On the very first morning of Kafka's influenza, the family was awakened by unusual sounds, the clank of weapons, and shouted orders. When they opened the curtains, they saw something alarming: entire platoons were appearing from the dark side streets in full marching order and beginning systematically to cordon off Altstädter Ring. There were also unusual numbers of policemen. The view from the windows that faced toward a dimly lit Niklasstrasse revealed shadowy images of soldiers entrenched behind machine guns and cases of ammunition. The muzzles of their weapons were facing outward, toward anyone approaching the Ring. What had happened?

It was the fear of revolution that had set the military chain of command in motion, and this fear was warranted. The *Národní výbor*, the national committee in which all Czech parties were united, had decided to organize mass demonstrations throughout Bohemia on October 14 to protest the catastrophic supply situation, the causes of which were thought to be in Vienna and in the notorious preferential treatment given to territories with an ethnic German majority. But the two leftist parties represented in the *Národní výbor* did not want to stop at verbal protests; they envisioned a general strike and called upon the workers on the outskirts of Prague to gather in the center on this day. A source at military headquarters reported, "According to leaflets we have found, there is an intent to proclaim an independent Czech state from the balcony of city hall in Prague and the community centers in the suburbs."[15] This was high treason. Even if people knew that it was not (yet!) the official line of the national committee, it was the concrete threat of a coup, and once it got under way, it would sweep along more moderate middle-class Czechs. Replacement troops were brought in immediately, and while the red flags were being rolled out expectantly in the outlying areas, the massive military force effortlessly dispersed the groups of demonstrators and bystanders who had ventured onto Wenceslas Square and Altstädter Ring. The situation in the provincial towns was brought under control just as quickly. Only in Strakonice, in southern Bohemia, a special officer named Karl Kraus had proclaimed the Czech Republic—mistakenly, as he declared in court the next day.

There is no doubt that on this morning, Kafka followed these developments on Altstädter Ring intently as long as he could stay on his feet. He saw that all the shops remained closed, and the familiar sounds of the streetcars could not be heard. This silence was not like the quiet of a Sunday morning; it was threatening. People were waiting for shots to be fired, and wild rumors were circulating. But in the evening, the cordons were suddenly taken down, and behind the withdrawing soldiers, people laughed in relief. The Czechs knew that these Austro-Hungarian shows of force would not go on for long, and even the *Prager Tagblatt* reported the following day about the "liquidation of the old state" with an ironic note that it should "proceed in an orderly and calm manner" without interference from the censors.[16]

A mere two weeks later, the time had come, and now there was no need for leaflets or political directives. All that was required to set things off was a rhetorical spark. Even a mere misunderstanding could put an end once and for all to nearly four centuries of Habsburg rule over Prague and Bohemia. The final attempt by Kaiser Karl to avert the fall of Austria-Hungary had now failed: his pitiful manifesto of October 16, which promised "All My Peoples" that he would establish a federal union with substantial autonomy for all nationalities, sounded far too much like the belated confession of an accused man in the hope that extenuating circumstances would save him from a hopeless situation. Karl's offer had already been superseded by the political reality, and U.S. President Woodrow Wilson, the actual addressee of this announcement, no longer had any interest in entering into discussions with a regime that was clearly doomed. In the meantime, entire Austro-Hungarian divisions were refusing to obey orders, and even soldiers stationed in the capital were already declaring their allegiance to their "own" national states, so Karl had no choice but to offer the Allies unconditional negotiations in the matter of an armistice—unconditional meant regardless of whether the German "brothers in arms" still wanted to carry on the war.

On October 28, 1918, at about 10:30 A.M., a rapidly growing cluster of people formed in front of the editorial offices of the *Národní politika* (National politics), Prague's most important Czech daily newspaper. The reason was a message board with a single word in big red letters: *Příměří*—armistice. It was the word millions were awaiting with bated breath. *Armistice*. The nightmare was over. But was the message reliable? Passersby gathered here and spent twenty minutes staring at the poster and excitedly discussing the matter. Then an employee of the newspaper came out and covered up the handwriting with a longer text that was read aloud by the people standing up front. It was the official notification by the Austrian foreign ministry and the wording of the "Andrássy Note" that had been sent the previous evening to President Wilson by way of neutral Sweden. Sure enough, it was about an armistice, and even, in a roundabout way, about the right of the Czechs to autonomy. That was all people needed to hear. There was an enormous racket, songs were sung, people came running from every little street, and red-and-white flags, which had been laid out in readiness quite some time ago, were finally unfurled from the windows of the editorial offices. Of course, some of the more level-headed among them sensed that this enthusiasm was a bit premature and based on a misunderstanding because the war was still raging, and the subtle difference between an armistice that had merely been offered and one that was already signed still marked the difference between death and life for many who were at the front. But no one in Prague cared about this subtle distinction anymore. *Kde domov můj?* Where is my home? That was the question, in a Czech song (which would later become the national hymn), that would resound countless times on this momentous day. It seemed as though the answer was finally evident.

In the Kafkas' apartment—where someone was fighting for his life in a different way—the events of the day were first announced by some sort of noise from far away, the crowd now heading to Wenceslas Square as if on cue. Some groups ran across Altstädter Ring. Calls of "Long live Masaryk!" "Long live Wilson!" and "Down with Habsburg" could be heard, and people could not believe their eyes when they saw soldiers, and even officers, running along with this rising mass, throwing their combat daggers onto the ground and tearing their military decorations from their caps. The floodgates had opened up, and the Czech military was defecting. For German Jews, this could only spell danger, and it was best to wait out the situation behind locked doors. At most, the Czech staff could be sent to Wenceslas Square to find out whether a pogrom was developing, and they reported that everything was going along almost peacefully. Laughter and song accompanied the dismantling of double-headed eagles and their replacement with Czech and American flags. German company signs were torn down or painted over, reluctant officers were challenged to prove themselves or they were simply pulled into the fray, and no one was afraid of the machine guns that had been hurriedly set up at the Café Rokoko. Within one or two hours, thousands had gathered on Wenceslas Square, and they would not be removed by force. There was no one to stand in the way of the Czech national committee, which, though nearly as surprised by the events as the cheering crowds, quickly proclaimed an autonomous Czechoslovakian state.

Later that evening, for the first time in months, every gas lantern was lit, and the city was illuminated the way it had been in peacetime. Processions of Chinese lanterns paraded across the squares as it started to drizzle, and the Kafkas—who surely spent several more hours waiting behind their windows—witnessed the fall of a now-helpless great power on Altstädter Ring in a kind of historical fast motion. In the afternoon, there were still-lowered bayonets, military trumpet calls, and furious people shouting at the Hungarian and Romanian soldiers who had been summoned but were standing there shrugging their shoulders. Shortly thereafter came the heavy tripods, the huge reels of film, and Czech cameramen to capture the images of the day, illustrations of a future Czech foundational myth. Finally, there was the familiar early morning call that had made people wince for four long years but now promised something altogether different, unimaginable: *Extra, extra, read all about it!*

It was a miracle virtually without historical precedent that the events of October 28 and the declaration of the Czechoslovakian state unfolded without any bloodshed, and the city of Prague had to give credit to the leading members of the Czech national committee, or rather to the members who were there, because the actual architects of the new state, who had already achieved official recognition for the Czech nation on the stage of global politics, were still in exile—Beneš in Switzerland, Masaryk in the United States—and the means of communication then available were simply not quick enough to consult with them in drawing up a list of the most urgent administrative steps or obtaining concrete instructions. Prague lacked a major role model to take the place of the Kaiser, an authority to urge the victors of the day to practice restraint and inspire new confidence in all others—particularly the Germans and Jews.

Of course, the people of Prague were also lucky; a reckless attack by the energized crowd could have easily resulted in a massacre.[17] But above all it was the effective and extremely speedy measures of the Czech politicians, who were left to their own devices, that resulted in a largely peaceful route to success. Within a few hours, they took over the police station, post office, telegraph office, and governance, and in personal negotiations they succeeded in inducing the commanders of the Habsburg army to retreat from all public squares (including Altstädter Ring). To maintain order, members of the national Czech Sokol were put in place—they could be identified by their red shirts—and when things really escalated, bands were brought in to play music to encourage celebration and head off thoughts of revenge. It took a mere twenty-four hours to put together Czech volunteer troops and have them swear an oath to the new state, and by the very next day, the military command on the Kleinseite had nothing left with which to counter this threat. It was stripped of power, and the last stubborn generals to maintain their loyalty to their Kaiser were taken into custody.

Czech politicians were well aware that the severest threat to civil peace came from within their own ranks. What would happen when the music stopped? What could they do if the sudden surge of national sentiment were vented unchecked on the Germans and Jews? They were asked this question quite bluntly by politically minded Jews, who in turn did whatever they could to mobilize all available forces. Just six days before the change of power, they succeeded in establishing their own "Jewish national council" in keeping with the model of the other nationalities. Presumably it was the sheer anxiety about a potential pogrom that ultimately made an alliance between the feuding assimilationist, religious, and Zionist groups possible,[18] and the international reputation of the Zionist minority, which had grown substantially since the Balfour Declaration, gave it the leading role—at least in the public perception. Max Brod was elected co–vice chairman of the national council, and thus the task fell to him of signing on additional still-hesitant Jewish organizations in Bohemia to negotiate with the unreceptive local dignitaries of the Jewish communities and eventually to speak in front of the most powerful Jewish conventions in Prague that the city had ever seen. A Jewish memorandum was designed with requests to the future Republic of Czechoslovakia, and almost simultaneously with the beginning of the formation of the republic, the head of the Jewish national council handed the paper to the new rulers in person. It asked for the recognition of Jewish nationality, for civil, administrative, and legal equality, and for cultural autonomy.[19] And all this was not presented in the usual tone of subservience, but rather with the unequivocal hint that the Czechs were under international observation. The goodwill Wilson granted the Czechs rested in large part on the condition that they treated national minorities in their own country differently from the way the Habsburgers had, and this point would have an important role in the future determination of the state borders. This was now the only trump card that the Germans and Jews could play in their politically subordinate position—but it was an extremely effective one.

For the first time in his life, Max Brod was dealing not merely with the innocuous and inconsequential "intellectual battles" he enjoyed waging in coffeehouses or with journalistic advocacy of various ideologies, but instead with decisions upon which the welfare of a vast number of people depended. He had been made into a politician, a representative, which presented a logical constancy he could not ignore. Precisely because of his frequent mediation between the two cultures, Brod was a figure who commanded respect from the Czechs. He had promoted Czech authors, he had translated, and initiated translations, and he had begun to help a Czech composer, the sixty-four-year-old Leoš Janáček, to achieve international esteem later on—over the opposition of Czech professional critics.[20] All this repeatedly provoked the annoyance of German chauvinists, while it qualified him in the eyes of the Czech national council, even among notorious anti-Semites, as a serious conversational partner.[21]

With prominent contacts like these, Brod was of course now much in demand as a source of information. People could obtain far more reliable details about the situation of the Jews from him than from any daily newspaper. Although there is no specific documentation to this effect, Brod must have provided the Kafkas a relatively unvarnished image of the situation—and the way things looked, they could consider themselves lucky to have given up the family business in time. People kept hearing that Jews were being boycotted, that Germans—and German Jews in particular—were being let go from their jobs under the flimsiest of pretexts, and there were even cases of Jewish business owners firing their own Jewish employees as a precautionary measure so as not to get on the bad side of their Czech customers. The former fancy goods shopkeeper must have been relieved to have been spared ordeals of that kind. Owning an apartment building was a social bed of roses by comparison; looking at an apartment building did not tell you who owned it.

Kafka, who was quite enervated by his illness, needed time to take in the changes in Prague, but what he saw from his own window was enough to convince him that the world he had known had begun to slip away forever. Contracting a fever as a subject in the Habsburg monarchy and reemerging from it as a citizen of a Czech democracy was certainly eerie, though a bit comical, as well. But there were more immediately pressing, even shocking events, such as the appearance of Czech demonstrators who, in an excess of revolutionary fervor, pulled down the centuries-old, more-than-fifty-foot-high Marian column right in front of his eyes and thus painfully encroached on the topography of his childhood. Perhaps if he had been healthy, he would have joined the crowd to find out *why* this happened. But it took him another two weeks to regain enough strength to leave the house.

When he was ready to go out, he entered a world that was ending the war formally but had yet to regain peace. The streets were full of people who had just been enemies: French, Italians, Russian prisoners of war. The German street signs had been removed, and there were new flags on every corner. There was no longer a Franz Joseph train station; it was now called Nádraži Wilsonovo (Wilson Train Station); the national railway station had become Nádraži Masarykovo, and Franzenskai was now Masarykova nábřeží. There was already an October 28th Street. The war kitsch that had defaced shop windows for years was gone. In its place, postcards with anti-German and anti-Semitic caricatures were now being offered for sale.

A different world, one that he could not have imagined. He had written so many letters, so many notes on the subject of a glorious future "after the war" in which he had wanted to leave his job, move, marry, and become a writer full-time. Now that the decisive hour had arrived, he did none of these things. He was ill. The tuberculosis, which had appeared to be cured, reemerged with the onslaught of the fever. Kafka lost weight, coughed, and sometimes gasped for breath. And even though he did not yet know that he had been dealt a severe blow with the Spanish flu, he clearly felt the symptoms of a physical decline, which relegated all his life projects into other, future, better times.[22]

Some decisions seemed to be falling into place by themselves. According to what people were saying, he would be thrown out of the Workers' Accident Insurance Institute anyway, now that it was under Czech management and had done away with the German official language, assuming that this institute, which was on the brink of ruin with worthless war loans in the amount of 82 million kronen, had any future whatsoever. Berlin, which was half-starved and suffering severely under the ongoing trade blockade, was liberated politically, but pent-up social conflicts were being battled out with a horrifying relentlessness. That city was no longer a place for Kafka to pin his hopes on. A life as a professional author seemed utterly illusory anyway since Kurt Wolff had forgotten his own promises for so long. On top of that, Kafka had invested the majority of the money he had saved up for so long to enable him to make the leap into an independent life—18,000 kronen in all—in war loans and thus gambled it away.

"Without realizing it, I have secretly evolved over the years from a city dweller into a countryman, or something very like it."[23] He had made this tentative statement two years earlier, but now that he had experienced life in Zürau, he was firmly convinced that he had to return to the country. Once he had resolved to take action, he was capable of decidedly unbureaucratic maneuvers. When Kafka showed up for work faithfully on Monday, November 19—after an absence of five weeks and in visibly bad shape, his path did not lead straight to Director Marschner's office and a discussion about his future tasks and a possible convalescent leave, but to the waiting room of Dr. Kral, who kindly provided a doctor's note Kafka could use to grant *himself* this leave. He explained to Pfohl, his astonished department head, that he would like nothing better than to continue carrying out his duties, but the doctor was against it, and anyway, "the current period of transition [would make] an absence from work relatively excusable"—in other words, with all the bickering over who was responsible for what in this office, his absence wouldn't be noticed anyway. Pfohl, who had been receiving partridges and venison from Zürau for months, had no choice but to swallow this bitter pill and, as requested by Kafka, to make it palatable to the director, as well.[24]

But where should he go now? Ottla had already left for Friedland, the northernmost tip of Bohemia, an area that Kafka knew well from his business trips: "a remarkably beautiful, sad town, as I recall."[25] As much as he would have liked to spend a few weeks with her there, it was impossible. Even his sister had her breaking point. She was taking two agriculture courses simultaneously to finish her training as quickly as possible, and taking care of Franz would have been far too much for her to handle. Besides, Friedland was in German Bohemia, a zone experiencing great political unrest. The residents wished to belong either to Germany or to the new "German-Austrian" state and vehemently refused to cooperate with the government in Prague. Because the Czechs did not want to give up the "historical borders" of Bohemia, clashes were sure to follow. This would not be a tranquil or secure spot for a Jewish convalescent.[26]

It was evidently Kafka's mother who brought up the idea of the village of Schelesen (Želízy), about twenty miles north of Prague, near the confluence of the Elbe and Moldau Rivers and, thus, in the Czech sphere of influence. Only a stone's throw away in times of peace; many people in Prague knew the thickly wooded area as a countryside summer resort, and the Kafkas had also spent their vacation there once.[27] Now, of course, it was difficult to get to Schelesen; there were not that many trains back in service, and the few that did run were quite overcrowded. On the other hand, there was a trustworthy establishment that belonged to a Fräulein Stüdl from Prague. She was in her mid-forties, and personally acquainted with the Kafkas. She ran a small boardinghouse in Schelesen that accommodated almost exclusively guests with lung diseases. This was a tolerable compromise and an opportunity to get out of Prague without requiring lengthy correspondence and passport formalities. Kafka agreed to the idea, and Julie, still worried about the life of her son, insisted on accompanying him on the trip there to instruct Fräulein Stüdl in the care of her son. Julie Kafka's ulterior motive was clear: she would be able to arrange for regular confidential reports.

Shortly before their departure, however, he suffered a relapse, and once again his fever persisted for days. Kafka was unable to run his final errands, and even had to send his mother to the insurance institute to explain the new situation to Pfohl. Eventually the date of departure was set for Sunday, November 30, and by the day before, Kafka was back on his feet. He had survived and was happy to be getting away. There was not enough time for a last visit to his friends, but he wanted at least to shake hands with Brod. Brod was as energetic as ever, racing from one meeting to the next, pumping hundreds of hands, writing, speaking, and writing some more. Kafka had been noticing for weeks that Brod seemed like a "warranty of life."[28] But they missed each other.

A few hours after Kafka's departure, Max Brod got home and found a brief note from his revitalized friend to the effect that their Hebrew practice could finally continue, maybe even by letter.[29] That was heartening to read. But for now, Brod needed to lie down. He was running a fever. Brod had the Spanish flu.

CHAPTER FOURTEEN

The Pariah Girl

Just when you least expect it
Just when you feel at ease
That's when you get selected

—Devo, "Pink Jazz Trancers"

KAFKA LAUGHED. HE COULD NOT STOP LAUGHING. AFTER A FEW weeks, the laughter began to hurt. It was disconcerting, almost humiliating—not because he didn't enjoy tomfoolery but because it was laughter with ulterior motives, laughter with a woman about whom he knew next to nothing, a laughter that was not born of intimacy but stood in for it in some odd way. There was simply no good reason for this laughter.

This was Kafka's second stay in Schelesen. The first had lasted only three weeks, and he had returned to Prague before Christmas, but his constant coughing, coupled with fever that tended to rise in the evening, worried even the public health officer at the Workers' Accident Insurance Institute, and he certified that his patient's convalescent leave had to be extended, this time for at least three months.[1] Since the institute (which now bore the name Úrazová pojišťovna dělnická pro Čechy v Praze) evidently had to demonstrate that the reins were being tightened, Kafka was kept on tenterhooks for a while; his leave was granted only in installments and was always subject to revision. But it gradually became clear that he was not being edged out of his job. Kafka had a good command of Czech officialese, even in dictation.[2] He had always steered clear of national disputes, and his position was not exposed enough to be worth attacking in any sustained way by Czech chauvinists—quite in contrast to the area of responsibility of his German bosses, who were now accused of years of mismanagement and German "chumminess." They were publicly discredited and even in danger of losing their pension funds. As was the case in all other offices in Prague in which similar dramas were now unfolding, changes were speedily implemented in the insurance institute: Eugen Pfohl was fired and replaced by Kafka's older coworker, Jindřich Valenta (which spelled the end of a career for the fifty-one-year-old Pfohl, who died a few months later). Director Marschner was demoted and in March 1919 had to accept mandatory retirement.[3] Kafka barely escaped the onslaught, and the fact that he was on friendly terms with Valenta and with the new director, Bedřich Odstrčil, apparently saved him from anti-German harassment during this critical phase.[4]

On January 22, 1919, Kafka moved into Stüdl Inn once again, without knowing how long he would be able to stay. The only thing he was sure of was that this time he would not be as alone and undisturbed as on the first visit. A nineteen-year-old girl from Prague suffering from a catarrh of her lung apexes had also rented a room here. She was a shy girl named Hermine, and even though Kafka was having his meals brought to his room, simple courtesy required him to make at least some effort at conversation when they were on "rest cure" together—on a covered balcony, snugly wrapped in blankets, with a view over forests and fields. Since the few suitable topics were used up in no time, Kafka took the opportunity to have Hermine quiz him on the Hebrew vocabulary he was boning up on every day. In any case, she knew the Hebrew characters. But Kafka did not let on to her why this matter was so important to him.[5]

About ten days later, another guest arrived, again a young woman from Prague. She was petite, charming, and suffering from lung disease, but despite her illness, she had a lively, unassuming personality. Her name was Julie—just like Kafka's mother—and her family name

Wohryzek, a name that was fairly common in Prague, is one he must have encountered quite often. She did not have a trace of the inscrutable, coquettish mannerisms of other girls. She was no longer a teenager, but not quite a lady either, as Kafka soon discovered. He watched her with a smile. They fell into conversation, first on the balcony, in earshot of Hermine, who was now somewhat miffed, then in the somewhat cramped dining room, where Kafka now deigned to sit, so that he could stay next to her a little while longer. It was hard for him to take his eyes off her, and whenever he looked at her, she laughed. When she laughed, he also began to laugh. They trudged together along short paths in the snow, launched into stories, switching back and forth between German and Czech, punctuated by laughter. And when they ran into each other, they burst into laughter even before they spoke.

> A common and astounding phenomenon. Not Jewish and yet not not-Jewish, not German and yet not not-German, crazy about the movies, about operettas and comedies, wears face powder and a veil, possesses an inexhaustible and unstoppable collection of the brashest Yiddish expressions, overall quite ignorant, more cheerful than sad—that is roughly what she is like. If one wanted to classify her ethnically, one would have to say that she belonged to the group of shopgirls. And at the same time she is brave of heart, honest, unassuming—such great qualities in a creature who is certainly not lacking in beauty, but is as wispy as the gnat flying against my lamplight.[6]

It was not the first time Kafka was succumbing to this kind of appeal. Felice Bauer, he had once noted in a state of great excitement when he first met her, looked like a maid.[7] Julie Wohryzek, it now occurred to him as he was describing her, was essentially a "wispy creature" relative to the characteristics that lay dormant within her. These characteristics were not run of the mill; they made Julie stand out as the inimitable, unique person she was, yet as a woman, he found her commonplace. She represented what everyone wanted: a temptation.

Max Brod was quite familiar with this defensive magic; for him, too, women were "representatives," and he would have been no more inclined than Kafka ever to call a man a "creature." Brod idealized sexuality, and Kafka feared it, but they shared a discursive vocabulary and imagery. Maybe this was why Brod kept deceiving himself about the extent to which he "knew" Kafka: he confused understanding with agreement, and that appears to have been the case this time, as well. "Pretty girls don't interest him the way they do me," he had noted a year earlier after a conversation with friends. Did he really believe that?

Not much is known about Julie Wohryzek, even regarding her relationship with Kafka; any biographical data derive from police files and the later recollections of a few family members.[8] Kafka must have noticed at their first conversation that she did not come from a well-to-do bourgeois family; despite her powder and veils, anyone who used "brashest Yiddish expressions" so uninhibitedly was certainly not part of the Jewish establishment, which placed great store by deliberate and complete *forgetting* of Yiddish as a sign of successful acculturation. Julie was more likely to have grown up in a petit bourgeois household. Her father Eduard, who started out as a grocer in Zájezdec (east of Prague, in the vicinity of Pardubitz) had moved in 1888 with his wife Mina to the rundown Josefstadt (Josefov), the former Prague ghetto, surely in the hope of social advancement. But unlike Hermann Kafka, he was unable to achieve entrepreneurial independence. He worked as a cobbler, then became a *shammes* (synagogue caretaker) in the suburb of Královské Vinohrady (now called Vinohrady), a poorly paid position, which likely forced his four children—three daughters and a son—to contribute to the family livelihood at an early age.

Julie did her part. She completed commercial training, then did clerical work in a series of offices, including five law firms. She finished her last job in May 1918, then helped out in her younger sister Růžena's fashion store, but she was no longer physically capable of working a full fifty hours a week. A chronic bilateral apical catarrh of the lungs had been diagnosed, the situation was grave, and she was told she would have to convalesce at a health resort. The family evidently collected some money for her, and Julie, who had now lost a great deal of weight, applied for a passport for Switzerland in August 1918 to visit a sanatorium in Davos. It was wartime, the Austro-Hungarian police department was still functional, and her application was denied. Like Kafka, she was left with no choice but to look for alternatives in the vicinity of Prague, and she ultimately opted for Schelesen.

She had a whole host of surprises to offer her new acquaintance. He considered her very young, but just a few weeks later she celebrated her twenty-eighth birthday. Kafka made some guarded inquiries into her Jewish identity, and slipped in the word "Zionism"—and found out that not long ago, she had intended to marry a confirmed Zionist, but he was killed in the war. Her older, married sister Käthe attended Jewish functions, and her best friend was even in the Jewish youth group Blau-Weiss (Blue-White) and had heard a number of lectures by Max Brod. No wonder that Julie read a Zionist work that Kafka had Brod get for her more thoroughly and with more insight than her apparent lack of knowledge and her feminine interests would have led him to believe. Kafka was taken aback, and he had trouble explaining to Brod that this clerical worker was turning out to be more interesting than she had appeared at first glance.

Brod did not learn the full truth, and the little hints Kafka dropped were not much to go on. Kafka and Julie laughed a lot in Schelesen, one of his letters said, "but it is also a difficult time. Well, for the moment I am bearing up, but it is no coincidence that my health is suffering. Besides, this time is coming to an end in its present form within a few days."[9] In other words, Julie had begun to pack her suitcases, and Kafka would be left behind all alone. He did not mention the fact that he had spent sleepless nights thinking about her—for the first time in a year—and Brod would certainly not have thought him capable of being kept awake in the throes of erotic self-denial.

Kafka was in love, and he noticed that his affections were amply requited. The snowballing sexual tension and the combination of fear and excitement surrounding the direction their relationship would take scared off both Franz and Julie. They steered clear of each other on occasion, and eventually they even stopped eating together. Instead, they sent innocuous little notes from one room to another. Kafka was tormented with longing; he felt as though a barely healed wound had been torn open again. Moreover, he had to wonder whether what he was experiencing was indeed authentic: a woman and a man at an isolated boardinghouse, far from family and friends, in a quiet snowy setting, relying only on each other, dangerously ill and hence full of lust for life—this was an old familiar scenario, somewhat literary in nature, but still giving rise to real pain. The ending was predictable: in ninety-nine out of a hundred cases, it would all be over when one of the two departed. And Kafka was firmly convinced that there was no other possible outcome, that this encounter would have to end the same way as that sweet flirtation back in Riva. Was it worth all this? The desire, the secrecy, the farewells, the sorrow, the painful memories—not to mention the intrusive questions from his parents, who would find out about it right away. Better to keep fighting his feelings. And Kafka held out to the last day. When the young woman said good-bye, they were still using addressing each other as Herr Doktor and Fräulein Wohryzek. He stayed in Schelesen for three more weeks on his own, until the end of March. He resisted the urge to write her, and he waited in vain for her to write from the city. But little by little, the pain of the sudden quiet yielded the certainty that this could not possibly be the end. And he would be right.

> [B]ut when I returned to Prague, we flew to each other as if driven. There was no other option for either of us. Still, it was up to me to guide the whole thing.
>
> And now there came a relatively happy and peaceful time. Since it was beyond our strength to stay away from each other, we abandoned those efforts. . . . We could be seen together in the deep woods, in the streets late in the evening, swimming in Černošice, and if at any time anyone had asked us whether we were going to be married, we would both have said no. . . .

Words from a long letter, a letter of justification, from Kafka to Julie's sister Käthe in November 1919—the only document, which came to the public's attention after some twists and turns, that provides insight into Kafka's new passion.[10] Apart from this letter, Kafka maintained his silence and explained no more than the bare minimum to his parents and evidently even to his friends. He kept Julie away from any social ties that had shaped his life up to this point—with the exception of Ottla.[11]

Kafka now wore a social disguise that was difficult to read: obliging, cooperative, never dodging a communicative challenge, yet full of icy reserve when his personal problems or his writings were mentioned.

He pointedly avoided settings in which these might come up, and instead showed a clear preference for situations in which he could lead, teach, and help—not in order to make others dependent on him or to control them, but in the instinctive expectation that as a benefactor he would remain above the fray. As long as he was sacrificing his precious time, or dispensing advice, money, or books, he did not need to give more of himself. This behavior was that much harder to fathom in light of the fact that Kafka's devotion was typically *less* superficial and more reliable than required by social convention. Not only was his advice helpful; he was also extraordinarily empathetic. Kafka always assumed the perspective on life and the needs of the other, needs that he was then able to visualize clearly even when they pertained to a woman, a youngster, or a person from an altogether different social and religious background. This earned him trust, and people enjoyed confiding in him. This made it all the more surprising when Kafka himself did not let his guard down for anyone.

The Klaus brothers from Prague experienced Kafka's reserve firsthand. Kafka had met Victor Klaus, a chemist afflicted with lung disease and a cousin of Felix Weltsch—at a Hebrew course, and ran into him again in Schelesen. They lived in adjacent rooms for a while, and together they sifted through the extensive library at Stüdl Inn. They also read Dickens together. But when Victor's seventeen-year-old well-read and ambitious brother Hans came to visit on the weekends, he was made to understand that questions about Kafka's illness, and even about his literature, were better left unasked. This restriction was hard to fathom for a high school boy and budding writer who was used to interacting with like-minded people. A few short months later, his first texts were published; for him, literature was an inexhaustible wellspring of excitement. Of course, even the silent Kafka remained an authority for the novice; starting at the end of 1919, he visited Kafka about a dozen times in his office at the insurance institute, told him about the literary group "Protest," which he had cofounded, and occasionally handed him one of his attempts at literature to find out what he thought of them. Kafka listened to him patiently, gave him helpful tips and books, and provided several media contacts that might help Hans Klaus get established. However, the psychological divide between mentor and pupil remained intact, and as soon as the conversation touched on Kafka's own life, he "clammed up."[12]

Kafka's relationship with Gustav Janouch, who was even younger but just as excited about literature, followed the same pattern. His father, who was Kafka's colleague, brought the two of them together—evidently hoping that the writer would have a stabilizing educational influence on the sixteen-year-old daydreamer. The Janouch family was dysfunctional, and Gustav escaped from his parents' constant arguing by indulging in fantasies of boundless literary power and harmless posturing; and instead of going to school, he hung out in coffeehouses and libraries, dressed as an "artist" in a floppy hat and a colorful scarf.

Janouch, who went by the name "Axel" at this time, impressed everyone with his knowledge of literature. Thackeray, Whitman, Laforgue, Strindberg—he knew them all. He was also a good pianist, and tried his hand at linocuts. But his obvious craving for recognition, which he tried to achieve by churning out an endless stream of poetry, represented a comic contrast to his immature appearance and his adolescent antics, which tried even Kafka's patience at times. "He came to my office," Kafka later wrote, "crying, laughing, shouting, brought me a pile of books to read, then apples, and finally his sweetheart, a little friendly daughter of a forester; he lives out there with her parents. He considers himself lucky, but sometimes conveys the impression of being frightfully confused, and doesn't look well. He wants to get his diploma and then study medicine ('because it is quiet, modest work') or law ('because it leads to politics'). What kind of devil is stoking this fire?" Janouch was already eighteen by this point; it is easy to imagine the disturbance he had been creating at Kafka's office for two years now.[13]

But even the notorious *Conversations with Kafka*—that conglomeration of authentic, half-true, stylized, and clearly invented conversational fragments that Janouch published several decades later in two different versions, with the assistance of Max Brod[14]—even that impenetrable thicket of lies and truth reveals distinct traces of Kafka's defensive maneuvers to seal off his personal life from these young friends. Particularly the supposedly "recorded" statements by Kafka that show hints of self-characterization or can even be read as confessions—that is, sentences that begin with "I"—are among the least credible and get his diction wrong in an often grotesque manner. The name Ottla never appears in these *Conversations*, nor does Julie Wohryzek's, and even Milena Jesenská seems to have been known to Janouch only as a translator—evidently all access to these connections was closed off to Janouch. Kafka also refused to engage in discussions of his published works, and the most Janouch could get out of him were inconsequential remarks about the connection between life and literature, and when Janouch kept insisting, Kafka broke off the conversation.[15]

Even so, Kafka retained his sympathy for the confused young man and clearly adhered to a pattern of behavior that had characterized his (equally perplexing) friendship with Yitzhak Löwy a few years earlier. The naïveté with which Janouch turned his psychological problems inside out and made himself vulnerable triggered Kafka's protective instinct, presumably because he could identify with this behavior: *That's how I would be if I were not so calculating*. It almost seems as though Kafka was trying to wipe his moral slate clean by lending a hand to this fragile man. He helped Janouch line up his first small publication, excused his boasting, and even asked the literary group led by Hans Klaus to show him some consideration and accept Janouch so that he would have social and intellectual support. It was all in vain. Janouch never got past mere attempts at literature; he went off and was soon forgotten.[16]

Kafka's personal notes exhibit few traces of contentment, success, or self-confidence, not only because he—like almost everyone who keeps a journal—sought relief in the written lament and thus dedicated a disproportionate amount of ink and time to unhappiness, but also because he felt a pronounced atavistic aversion to admitting to feelings of happiness. He did not want to jinx them. He fretted that the written admission of success, or even a clear hint in that direction, would inevitably trigger a setback. Kafka acted as though he were facing a malevolent demiurge and needed to darken the windows of his own home to keep away its prying eyes. And since he now felt like a survivor, he became even more cautious. More and more frequently, Kafka did not put down in writing the essence of his experience; he adopted the habit of allusive discourse, as though fearing that a higher authority would be eavesdropping. He eventually even introduced a personal shorthand, which readers today are at pains to decipher.

> a new diary, really only because I have been reading the old ones. A number of reasons and intentions, now, at a quarter to twelve, impossible to ascertain.
>
> Was in Rieger Park. Walked up and down with J. along the jasmine bushes. False and sincere, false in my sighs, sincere in closeness, trustfulness, feeling of security. Uneasy heart.
>
> Constantly the same thought, longing, anxiety. Yet calmer than usual, as if some great development were going forward the distant tremor of which I feel. Too much said.[17]

That is all: the only extant personal notes from the beginning of 1919—when he met Julie Wohryzek—and December of that year, no more than a trickle in comparison with the cascades of words that had inundated his relationship with Felice from the start. Still, the phrase "feeling of security" stands out. As far as we know, Kafka had never used it before, and did not bring himself to do so in the future either, and even the minor details he reveals here are "too much said."

And yet he was not even identifying his own longing, that relentlessly throbbing and frightening thought. What thought was that? The seduction of the girlish Julie? That is unlikely because this was not a disembodied love from the start; the later letter to Julie's sister revealed the intensity of the passion quite clearly. The fact that Kafka was having a sexual relationship that extended beyond a one-night stand for the first time in a good many years—we don't know how many—may have contributed substantially to dispelling his tormenting psychological tensions and giving him a more serene vision of what lay ahead, with the exception of one single question: the question of marriage and family. *This* was the thought that was perturbing Kafka incessantly, because it aroused an old longing and an even older fear.

Kafka and Fräulein Wohryzek had already come to an agreement on the subject of marriage while they were in Schelesen. Both felt that there was good reason to discuss it, and both spoke as frankly as the circumstances of people who met while convalescing from their illnesses would allow. Julie, who had dressed in black, like a widow, after the violent death of her fiancé, assured him that she would *not* marry, and her desire for children was not strong enough to shake this conviction. He, in turn, declared that he was *unable* to marry, as he had proven amply by having kept a woman hanging for five years and pressuring her to marry, even becoming engaged to her twice, only to shatter her hopes. Even so—and this is where the surprising agreement between the two came to an end—he regarded "marriage and children as the most highly desirable things on earth in a certain sense."[18] His view had not changed, he explained, even though over the years he had not come one step closer to realizing this goal.

They could have left it at that. Kafka himself called the summer of 1919 a "relatively happy and peaceful time," filled with a "relatively peaceful happiness." That is, happy in comparison to anything that he had ever experienced with women, including the few marvelous days in Marienbad. But the idea of making this situation everlasting, of setting up camp in front of the gates of marriage when everyone else appeared to enter them effortlessly, was something that Kafka had more and more trouble coping with. "I could not make do with this life ... what was good about it was only a halfway thing, and not even that; what was bad about it was thoroughly bad." So it was a provisional arrangement, not only in the spiritual sense, for the social and familial constraints under which Kafka's new happiness was being realized were much like those of the controlled environment of a high school romance. Both he and Julie were living with their parents, who watched their every move. They had no place to meet without other people around and had to rely on trysts in nature and (presumably) country inns far outside the city. He could not introduce Julie to the wives of his friends or to his colleagues, and when he ran into a relative while walking arm in arm with her, there was great embarrassment. Even if he had been able to get past all the moral qualms that every man of his class and generation had internalized and subject his parents and the rest of the world to the spectacle of a couple living out of wedlock in a shared apartment, Julie's relatives would surely not have stood for it. It is hard to imagine them handing over their "girl"—even if she was already "experienced"—to a civil servant who refused to make any commitments.

1 The only photograph of Franz Kafka and Felice Bauer together, Budapest, July 1917

2 Entrance to the "model trench," Prague, 1915

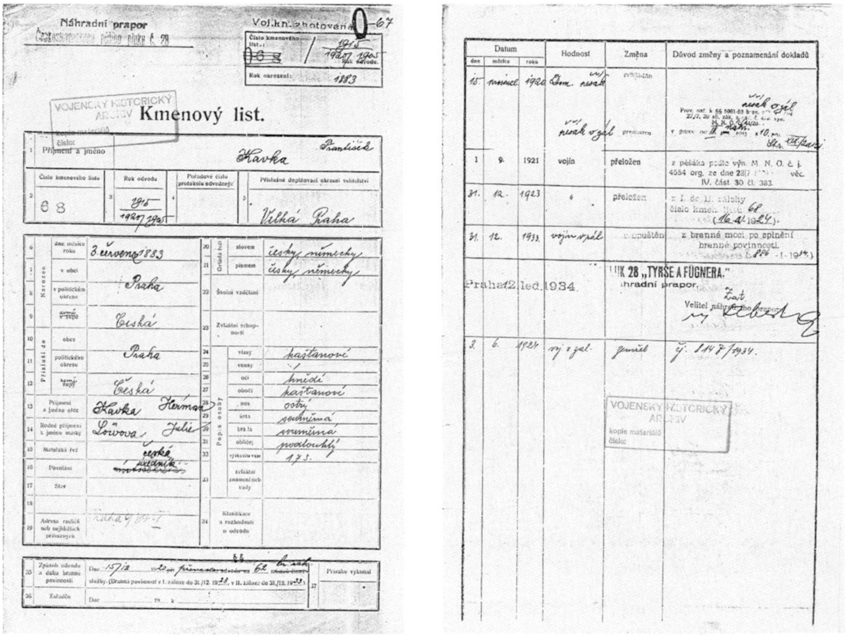

Náhradní prapor

Voj.kn. zhotovená 0-67

Číslo kmenového listu: 68 / 1915 1920 / 1905

Rok narození: 1883

Kmenový list.

Příjmení a jméno: Kavka František

Číslo kmenového listu: 68

Rok odvodu: 1915 1920 / 1905

Příslušné doplňovací okresní velitelství: Velká Praha

Narozen: den, měsíc, roku: 3 července 1883; v obci: Praha; Česká

Příslušný do: obce: Praha; politického okresu: Praha; Česká

Příjmení a jméno otce: Kavka Herman

Rodné příjmení a jméno matky: Löwova Julie

Mateřská řeč: česká

Ovládá řeč: slovem: česky, německy; písmem: česky, německy

Popis osoby: vlasy: kaštanové; oči: hnědé; obočí: kaštanové; nos: ostrý; ústa: souměrná; brada: souměrná; obličej: podlouhlý; výška: 173.

Datum	Hodnost	Změna	Důvod změny a poznamenání dokladů
1. 9. 1921	vojín	přeložen	z pěšáka podle výn. M. N. O. č. j. 4554 org. ze dne 23/7 … věc. IV. část. 30 čl. 383.
31. 12. 1923		přeložen	z I. do II. zálohy
31. 12. 1933		propuštěn	z branné moci po splnění branné povinnosti.

Praha 12. led. 1934.

PĚŠÍ PLUK 28 „TYRŠE A FÜGNERA." Náhradní prapor.

3\. 6. 1924

VOJENSKÝ HISTORICKÝ ARCHIV

3 Kafka's military card (with his name spelled "Kavka")

4 Franz Kafka, late 1917

5 Felice Bauer, 1921

6 Berlin-Charlottenburg, Wilmersdorfer Strasse 73 (the corner building on the left). The Bauer family moved here in April 1913.

7 Julie Kafka, 1920s

8 Josef David and Ottla Kafka

9 Frankenstein sanatorium near Rumburg (northern Bohemia)

10 Georg Heinrich Meyer

11 The rabbi of Belz, Marienbad, 1916

12 Georg Langer

13 Marienbad. Schloss Balmoral, the hotel at which Kafka and Felice Bauer stayed in 1916, is on the far left.

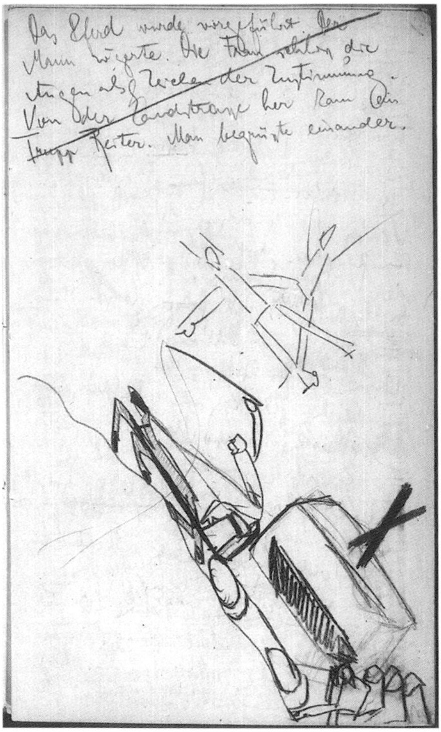

14 From "Octavo Notebook A," late 1916

15 Alchimistengasse in the Hradčany in Prague. Kafka used the second cottage from the left for his literary work in 1916–1917.

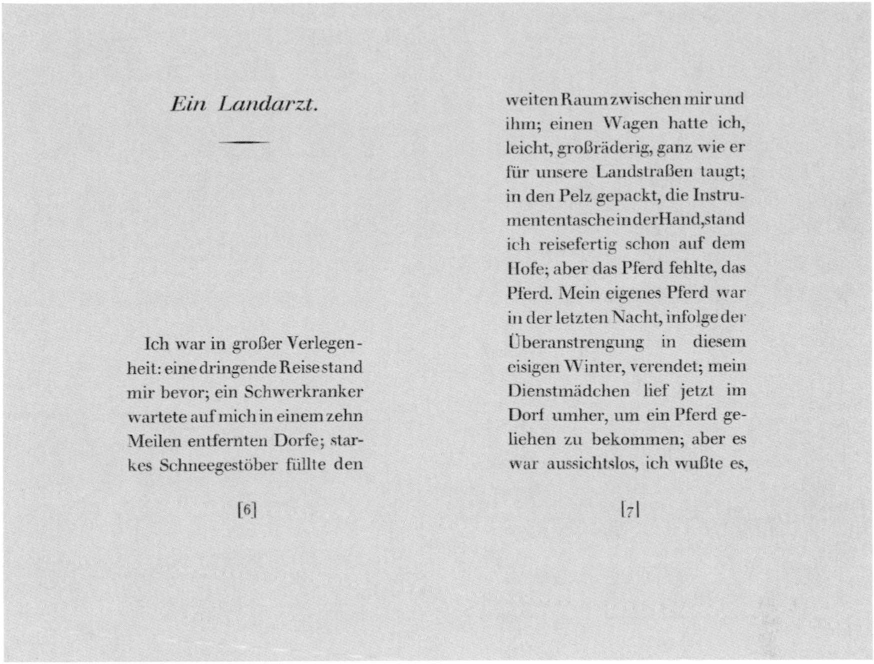

Ein Landarzt.

Ich war in großer Verlegenheit: eine dringende Reise stand mir bevor; ein Schwerkranker wartete auf mich in einem zehn Meilen entfernten Dorfe; starkes Schneegestöber füllte den

[6]

weiten Raum zwischen mir und ihm; einen Wagen hatte ich, leicht, großräderig, ganz wie er für unsere Landstraßen taugt; in den Pelz gepackt, die Instrumententasche in der Hand, stand ich reisefertig schon auf dem Hofe; aber das Pferd fehlte, das Pferd. Mein eigenes Pferd war in der letzten Nacht, infolge der Überanstrengung in diesem eisigen Winter, verendet; mein Dienstmädchen lief jetzt im Dorf umher, um ein Pferd geliehen zu bekommen; aber es war aussichtslos, ich wußte es,

[7]

16 From the volume *A Country Doctor*, Kurt Wolff Verlag, 1920

17 Otto Gross, 1919

18 Ludwig Hardt

19 Advertisements in the *Prager Tagblatt*, 1917–1918

20 Zürau

21 On a field near Zürau, 1917. From right: Kafka; his secretary, Julie Kaiser; Ottla; their cousin Irma; the maid Mařenka.

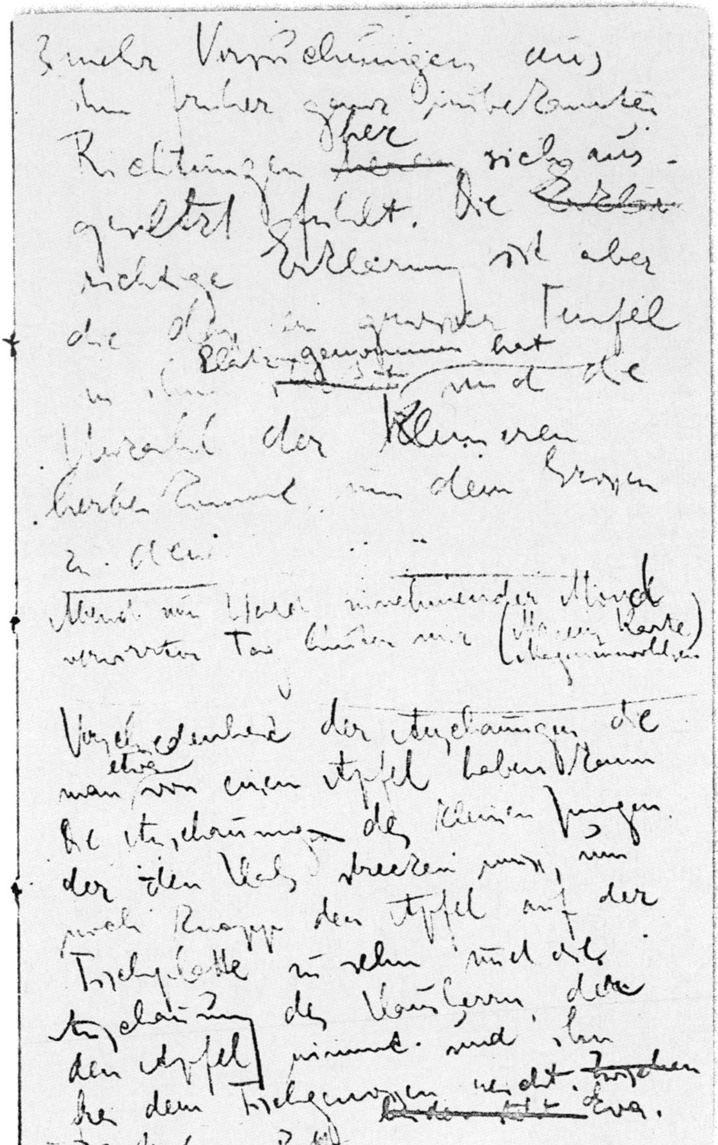

22 From "Octavo Notebook G," October 1917

23/24 Prague, October 28, 1918: founding of the Republic of Czechoslovakia

25/26 Prague, December 21, 1918: Masaryk's return from exile

27 Stüdl Inn, Schelesen

28 Julie Wohryzek

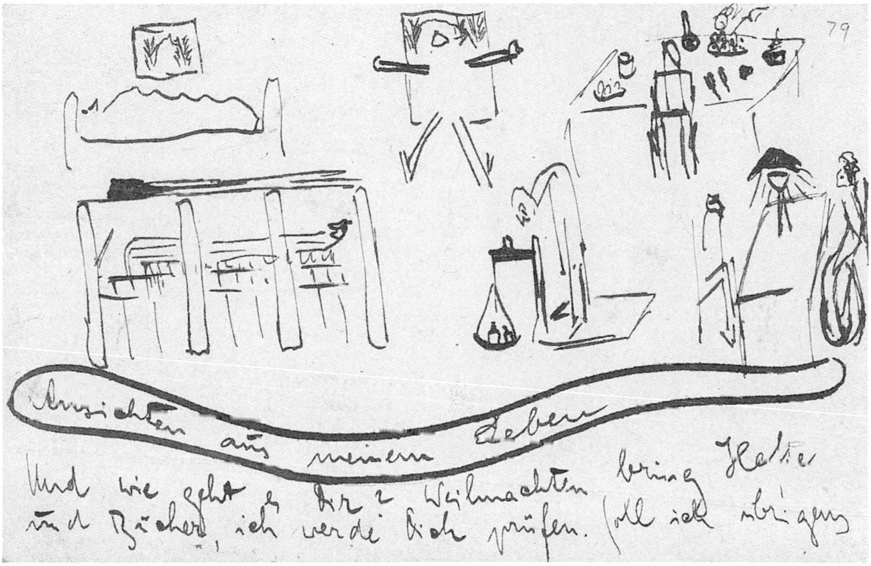

29 Postcard to Ottla Kafka, December 1918

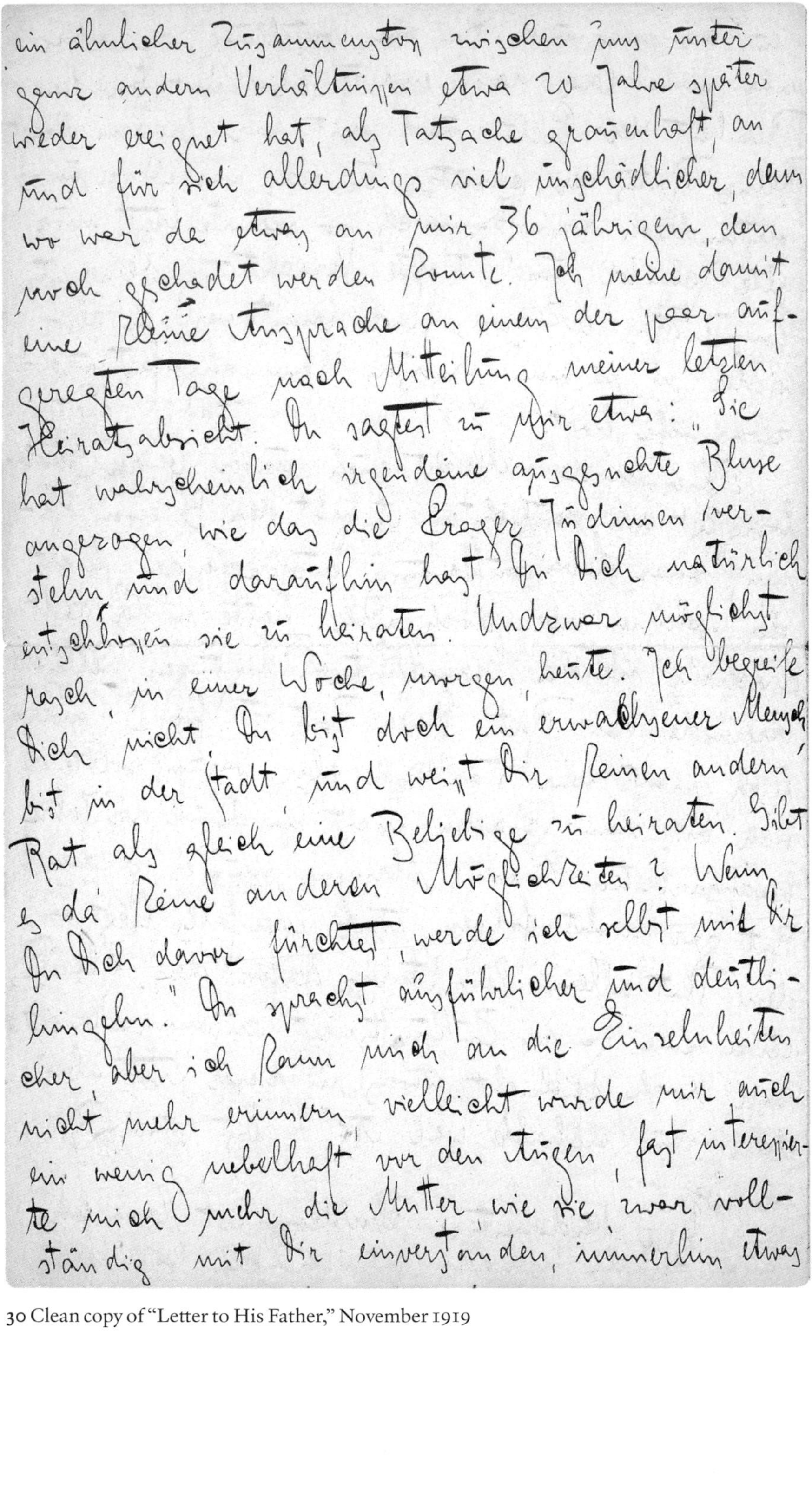
ein ähnlicher Zusammenstoß zwischen uns unter
ganz andern Verhältnissen etwa 20 Jahre später
wieder ereignet hat, als Tatsache grauenhaft, an
und für sich allerdings viel unschädlicher, denn
wo war da etwas an mir 36 jährigem, dem
noch geschadet werden konnte. Ich meine damit
eine kleine Aussprache an einem der paar auf-
geregten Tage nach Mitteilung meiner letzten
Heiratsabsicht. Du sagtest zu mir etwa: „Sie
hat wahrscheinlich irgendeine ausgesuchte Bluse
angezogen, wie das die Prager Jüdinnen ver-
stehn, und daraufhin hast Du Dich natürlich
entschlossen sie zu heiraten. Undzwar möglichst
rasch, in einer Woche, morgen, heute. Ich begreife
Dich nicht, Du bist doch ein erwachsener Mensch,
bist in der Stadt und weißt Dir keinen andern
Rat als gleich eine Beliebige zu heiraten. Gibt
es da keine anderen Möglichkeiten? Wenn
Du Dich davor fürchtest, werde ich selbst mit Dir
hingehn." Du sprachst ausführlicher und deutlicher, aber ich kann mich an die Einzelheiten
nicht mehr erinnern, vielleicht wurde mir auch
ein wenig nebelhaft vor den Augen, fast interessier-
te mich mehr die Mutter wie sie zwar voll-
ständig mit Dir einverstanden, immerhin etwas

30 Clean copy of "Letter to His Father," November 1919

vom Tisch nahm und damit aus dem Zimmer gieng. 23

Tiefer gedemütigt hast Du mich mit Worten wohl kaum und deutlicher mir Deine Verachtung nie gezeigt. Als Du vor 20 Jahren ähnlich zu mir gesprochen hast, hätte man darin mit Deinen Augen sogar etwas Respekt für den frühreifen Stadtjungen sehen können, der Deiner Meinung nach schon so ohne Umwege ins Leben eingeführt werden konnte. Heute könnte diese Rücksicht die Verachtung nur noch steigern, denn der Junge, der damals einen Anlauf nahm, ist in ihm stecken geblieben und scheint Dir heute um keine Erfahrung reicher, sondern nur um 20 Jahre jämmerlicher. Meine Entscheidung für ein Mädchen bedeutete Dir gar nichts. Du hattest meine Entscheidungskraft (unbewußt) immer niedergehalten und glaubtest jetzt (unbewußt) zu wissen, was sie wert war. Von meinen Rettungsversuchen in andern Richtungen wußtest Du nichts, daher konntest Du auch von den Gedankengängen, die mich zu diesem Heiratsversuch geführt hatten, nichts wissen, mußtest sie zu erraten suchen und rietst entsprechend

31 Hellerau experimental school, early 1920s

32 Gustav Janouch

33 Director Bedřich Odstrčil, Kafka's superior

34 Ottoburg Inn, Merano-Untermais

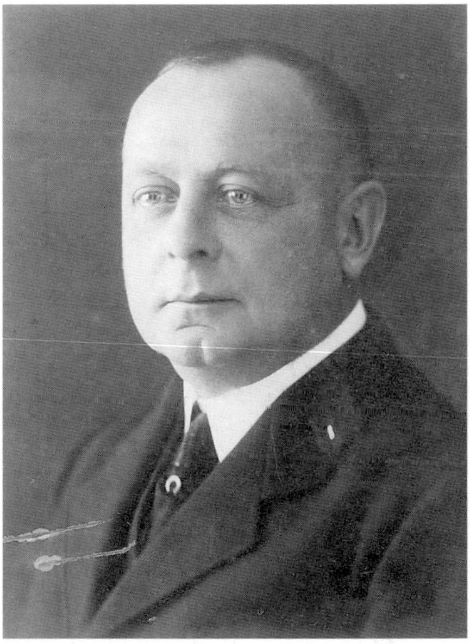

35 Jan Jesenský

36 Milena Jesenská, 1915

37 Milena Jesenská, ca. 1920

38 Franz Kafka, ca. 1920

39 Café Herrenhof, Vienna

40 Ernst Pollak, 1913

KMEN

LITERÁRNÍ TÝDENNÍK

ROČNÍK IV. V Praze, dne 22. dubna 1920. ČISLO 6.

Franz Kafka: Topič

Fragment

Se svolením autorovým přeložila Milena Jesenská

Když 16letý Karel Rosman, který byl svými chudými rodiči poslán do Ameriky, poněvadž ho svedla služka a měla s ním dítě, vjel již v zpomaleném parníku do newyorského přístavu, spatřil sochu Svobody, kterou již dávno pozoroval, jakoby ve světle náhle prudším. Její paže s mečem trčela jaksi nově vstříc a kolem její postavy vanul volný vzduch.

»Tak vysoko,« řekl si, a v tom, vůbec nemysle na odchod, byl stále rostoucím množstvím nosičů pomalu posunut až k zábradlí.

Jakýsi mladý muž, s nímž se byl při jízdě povrchně seznámil, řekl, předcházeje ho: »Nu, což pak nemáte pražádné chuti, abyste vystoupil?« »Jsem přece již hotov,« řekl Karel usmívaje se, a zdvihl z dobré nálady a poněvadž byl silný chlapec, kufr na ramena. Když však pohlédl za svým známým, který se již vzdaloval s ostatními a mával při tom hůlkou, s úlekem zpozoroval, že zapomněl dole v lodi svůj deštník. Rychle poprosil známého, aby mu laskavě u jeho zavazadla okamžik posečkal, čímž muž nebyl příliš obšťastněn, přehlédl ještě situaci, aby se při návratu vyznal, a pospíchal pryč.

S lítostí nalezl dole zavřenu chodbu, která by jeho cestu byla velice zkrátila, což patrně souviselo s vyloďováním cestujících, a bylo mu namáhavě si hledati cestu nespočetnými malými místnostmi, po krátkých schodech, které stále za sebou následovaly, korridory, neustále se zahýbajícími, prázdným pokojem s opuštěným psacím stolem, až skutečně, poněvadž touto cestou šel teprve jednou nebo dvakrát a vždy ve větší společnosti, úplně zabloudil. Ve své bezradnosti, poněvadž nepotkával lidí a slyšel jen nad sebou šoupání tisíce lidských nohou a pozoroval z dálky jakoby dech, poslední pracování již zastavovaných strojů, počal bez přemýšlení tlouci na první malá dvířka, na která při svém bloudění narazil.

»Vždyť je otevřeno,« ozvalo se uvnitř a Karel otevřel dvéře s poctivým oddechnutím. »Proč tlučete tak zběsile do dveří?« řekl ohromný člověk a skoro se po Karlovi ani neohlédl. Jakýmsi malým, svrchním oknem padalo ponuré, nahoře na lodi již dávno opotřebované světlo v žalostnou kabinu a v ní stáli těsně vedle sebe postel, skříň, židle a muž, jakoby složeni ve skladišti. »Zabloudil jsem,« řekl Karel, »ani jsem toho tak za jízdy nepozoroval, ale to je strašně veliká loď.« »To je pravda,« řekl muž s jistou pýchou, nepřestav se při tom nimrati se zámkem malého kufru, který oběma rukama vždy znovu přitlačil a čekal při tom na sklapnutí závory. »Ale pojďte přece dovnitř,« pokračoval muž, »nebudete přece státi venku.« »Nevyrušuji?« ptal se Karel. »Ale jak pak byste rušil?« »Jste Němec?« pokusil se Karel zabezpečili, poněvadž mnoho slyšel o nebezpečí, které hrozí v Americe nově příchozím, obzvláště od Irů. »I jsem, jsem,« řekl muž. Karel ještě váhal. Tu muž náhle uchopil kliku a přisunul dveřmi, které rychle zavřel, Karla k sobě dovnitř. »Nemohu vystát, dívá-li se sem

61.

41 Milena Jesenská's translation of Kafka's "The Stoker," April 1920

42 Jarmila Ambrožová

43 Robert Klopstock

44 The main building of the sanatorium in Matliary

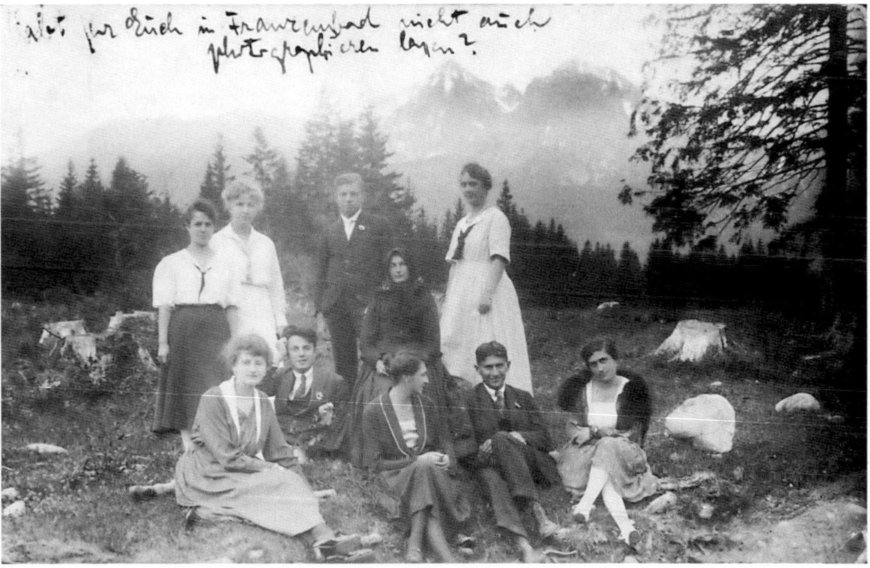

45 Kafka and other guests at the sanatorium; standing, Robert Klopstock

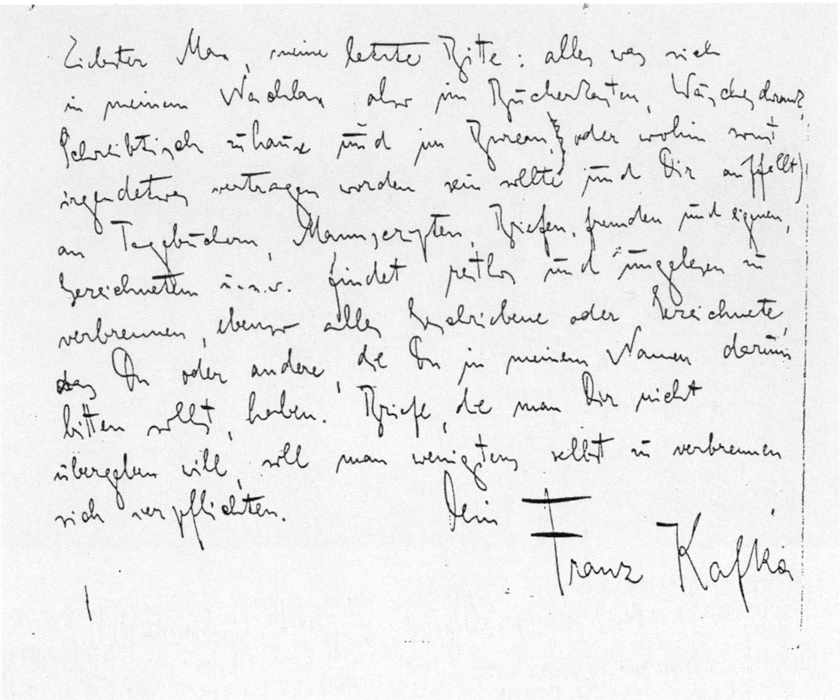

Liebster Max, meine letzte Bitte: alles, was sich in meinem Nachlass (also im Bücherkasten, Wäscheschrank, Schreibtisch zuhause und im Bureau, oder wohin immer irgendetwas vertragen worden sein sollte und Dir auffällt) an Tagebüchern, Manuskripten, Briefen, fremden und eigenen, Gezeichnetem u.s.w. findet restlos und ungelesen zu verbrennen, ebenso alles Geschriebene oder Gezeichnete, das Du oder andere, die Du in meinem Namen darum bitten sollst, haben. Briefe, die man Dir nicht übergeben will, soll man wenigstens selbst zu verbrennen sich verpflichten.

Dein Franz Kafka

46 Kafka's provisions for his will, fall/winter 1921

47 Max Brod, 1918

48 Kafka near Spindelmühle, January/February 1922

49 Spindelmühle, Friedensthal district; on the right, Hotel Krone

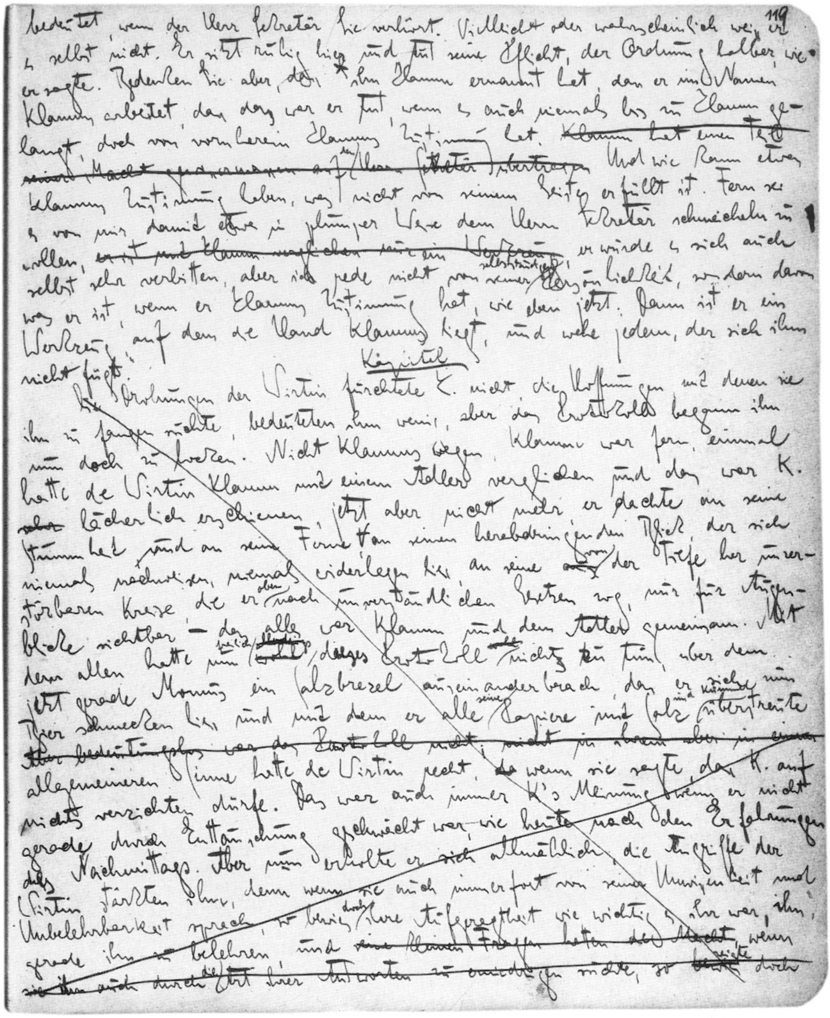

50 From the manuscript of *The Castle*

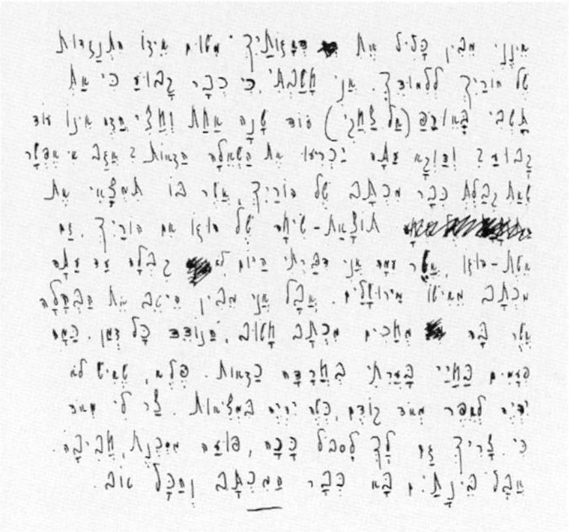

52 Draft of a letter from Kafka to Puah Ben-Tovim in Hebrew

51 Puah Ben-Tovim and her husband, Josef S. Menczel

53 Exclusive residential area of Planá nad Lužnicí

54 Ottla David and her daughter Věra, 1921

55 Kafka's nieces Gerti, Hanna, and Marianne, 1922

56 Vacationers in front of the guesthouse in Glückauf, Müritz 1923. On the right, with the striped skirt, Kafka's sister Elli, on the right next to her, Marie Werner, the "Fräulein" of the Kafka family. The child on the far right is Elli's daughter Gerti, and the fifth child from the right is her daughter Hanna.

57 Franz Kafka, 1921

58 Dora Diamant, ca. 1924

59 Glückauf guesthouse in Müritz, Baltic Sea

60 Berlin-Steglitz, Grunewaldstrasse 13

61 German banknote, 1923

62 Berlin store on Leipziger Strasse, 1922; the sign reads: "No sales to foreigners"

63 First edition of the volume *A Hunger Artist*, with four of Kafka's stories, November 1924

64 Sanatorium Dr. Hoffmann, Kierling

65 Professor Markus Hajek, Laryngological Clinic, Vienna; presumably 1922

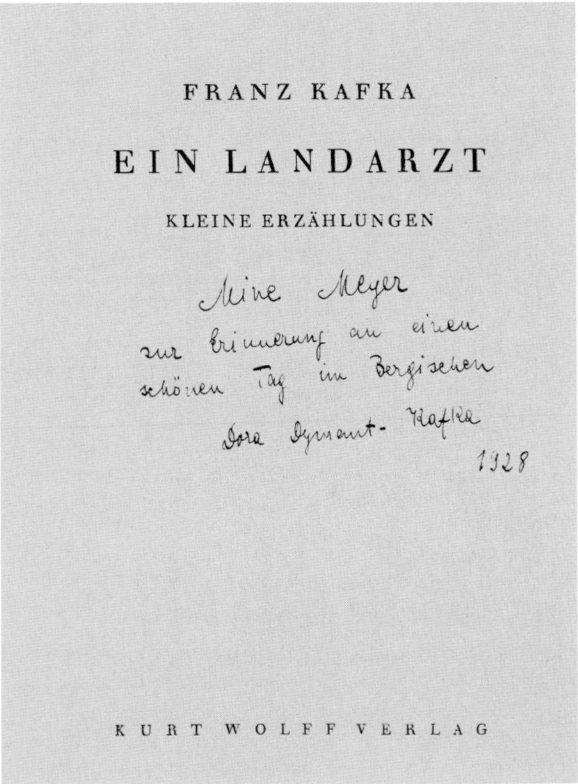

FRANZ KAFKA

EIN LANDARZT

KLEINE ERZÄHLUNGEN

Mine Meyer
zur Erinnerung an einen
schönen Tag im Bergischen
Dora Dymant-Kafka
1928

KURT WOLFF VERLAG

66 Dedication by Dora Diamant, who signed her name as "Dymant-Kafka"

67 Kafka's grave at the New Jewish Cemetery, Prague-Žižkov

68 Hermann and Julie Kafka, late 1920s

In tiefstem Schmerz geben wir bekannt, daß unser Sohn

JUDr. Franz Kafka

am 3. Juni im Sanatorium Kierling bei Wien, 41 Jahre alt, gestorben ist. Das Begräbnis findet am Mittwoch, den 11. Juni um ¾4 Uhr auf dem jüdischen Friedhof in Straschnitz statt.

PRAG, am 10. Juni 1924.

Hermann und **Julie Kafka,**
Eltern,
im Namen der trauernden Hinterbliebenen.

3392

Von Kondolenzbesuchen bitten wir abzusehen.

Hluboce zarmouceni podáváme zprávu, že náš syn

JUDr. František Kafka,

zemřel dne 3. června t. r. v sanatoriu Kierling u Vídně, jsa stár 41 roků. Pohřben bude ve středu, dne 11. června t. r. o ¾4 hod. odpol. na israel. hřbitově ve Strašnicích.

V PRAZE, dne 10. června 1924.

Heřman a **Julie Kafkovi,**
jménem veškerého příbuzenstva.

24229

Kondolenční návštěvy se s díky odmítají.

69

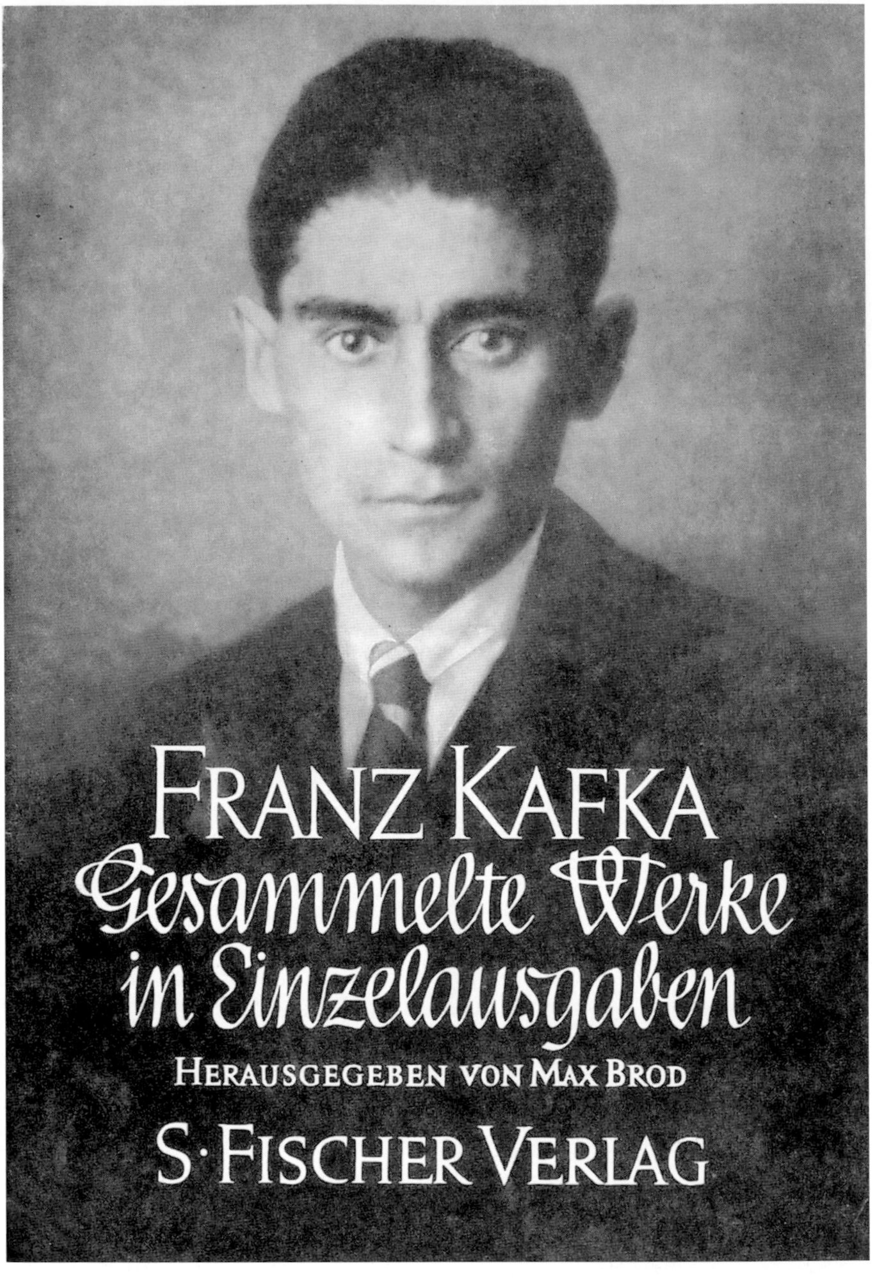

70 Publisher's catalogue, 1950. This last extant portrait photograph of Kafka was probably taken in September 1923 at Wertheim Department Store in Berlin.

Kafka considered this situation ignoble. He began to speak about marriage again, but now for real. He begged and pleaded. This time, he reasoned, all the conditions seemed "so much more favorable than in the past; so much so that it would be impossible to imagine them any more favorable." Julie was also in love. She was not pressuring Kafka in any way, and evidently she seems to have shown understanding for his complex nature, his oddly strict morality, his insistence on following through, and the foibles that made his daily experience both richer and more difficult. Kafka, in turn, had discovered her "almost magical nature." He felt a deep closeness to and accord with Julie, and enjoyed an erotic dimension that had been closed off to him in the past, namely dependable intimacy. This would be a "marriage of love," he declared, "but even more a marriage of reason in the higher sense." Julie was taken aback. In particular, Kafka's repeated references to having children some day met with slight resistance on her part, and the very idea that this notorious bachelor whose hair was beginning to turn gray was dreaming of a big thriving family was a bit disconcerting. But she did not want to lose him, and eventually she gave in and warmed to the new idea. They got engaged very quietly and presumably without witnesses.

> She probably put on a blouse that she had picked out carefully—something those Jewish women in Prague are good at—and right away, of course, you decided to marry her, as fast as possible, in a week, tomorrow, today. I can't understand you: after all, you're a grown man, you live in the city, and you don't know what to do but marry the first girl who comes along. Aren't there any other choices? If you're frightened, I'll go with you myself.[19]

The voice of his master. Kafka noted down what he recalled of this conversation, in an enhanced literary form, in better German, and reduced to the factual essence. It was not possible to do more; while Hermann's sonorous insults were ringing in his ears, he felt as though he was experiencing one of those awful dreams in which even before the climax, you become certain that this cannot be true. He was no longer really listening. His father had talked about a brothel, about prostitution, and the two of them were not alone, speaking in confidence, man to man or father to son—no, he had done this right out loud, in the middle of the peaceful living room at the Kafkas', in the presence of his wife. Kafka glanced her way, and for a moment he felt shame on his mother's behalf more than on his own. Julie Kafka got up without saying a word, took something from the table, and left the room with it.

Kafka realized on the spot that this was an archetypal scene. A déjà-vu stirred within him; he had experienced this humiliation once before, when he was a teenager and had taken his parents to task for keeping him in a state of sexual ignorance and thus exposing him to great risks, whereupon his father offered him some conventional advice about how to "go about such things without danger." Well, that is how he was, and if we look at it from the comic perspective, the young whippersnapper back then may have justifiably turned red when he heard this reply. But twenty years later, the head of the family was still acting as though he were talking to a child, as though his son had problems that could be solved by wearing condoms. Kafka reprimanded him for this "ghastly" echo. "You could hardly have humiliated me more deeply with words and shown me your contempt more obviously."[20]

It was the culmination of loud quarrels that had been going on for days. Hermann Kafka could not calm down after learning about his son's new engagement, and even though his wife took a more conciliatory tone and was intent on maintaining at least some semblance of peace, she had to agree with everything he was saying. A fiancée from a penniless family, the daughter of a *shammes*.... If this disgraceful marriage were to happen, Hermann ranted, he would leave the country. Not to mention that the extended family would regard him as a liar. Less than two years earlier, they had told everyone why Franz had broken up with his elegant fiancée from Berlin, whose praises he had sung for so long. The official explanation was "tuberculosis." And now that Franz was in markedly worse shape, he had new plans for marriage—to a sick woman? He would be a laughingstock.

This confrontation cannot have come as a complete surprise to Kafka. He had had to endure blame about the erratic way he had planned out his life a good hundred times already. Since, as his father believed, he was incapable of deciding on a wife on a social par with himself intentionally and responsibly, it would be a woman who would have to do the deciding for him. Kafka was so familiar with this disdainful prediction that he had long since internalized it and even made it part of his father imago.

Here, readers of Kafka encounter one of the eeriest anticipations known to the history of literature, and at the same time find a clear indication that this father's ruthlessness could not be explained merely as a personal character flaw. It was more like the kind of standard patriarchal maneuver seen in many families: if it is no longer possible to prevent adult sons and daughters from making their own decisions, the parents can deal a crushing blow by denying that these were their own decisions in the first place. Kafka had described this exact scenario with astonishing accuracy seven years earlier, in his story "The Judgment." Here, too, an old businessman claims that sexual lust was the motive behind his son's engagement and thus tries to humiliate him:

> "Because she lifted up her skirts," his father began to trill, "because she lifted up her skirts like this, that revolting ninny," and to illustrate that, he lifted his nightshirt up so high that the scar from his army days could be seen on his upper thigh, "because she lifted up her skirts like this and like this and like this, you went after her. . . ."

Kafka must have been struck by the awful coincidence that these venomous sentences were now appearing in print once again.[21] Of course, the real Hermann Kafka would not have made those kinds of obscene gestures or lifted up his nightshirt in front of his son. But the fictitious and the real father shared, to an eerie degree, a will to moral subjugation. What comes across as utterly convincing in the scene thought up by Kafka, as the gestural expression of a deadly logic of relationships, seemed like an almost implausible, theatrical attack in the reality of 1919.

Kafka surely noticed that something was amiss here, that his parents' indignation seemed out of proportion to what were essentially feeble objections. Leave the country because your son is marrying a penniless woman? Hermann could not mean that seriously—at a time when everyone was happy just to have survived, when every family considered itself lucky if the sons were neither killed nor wounded nor taken captive. The war years had wreaked havoc with the optimism of generations of Jewish bourgeois family planning; even Kafka's parents cannot have failed to register that. And now such a ruckus on such trivial grounds?

Kafka would soon get the key to this mystery, and happenstance—along with renewed intervention by Max Brod—preserved it for posterity. The doggedness with which Kafka was keeping the woman he loved away from the rest of his friends had also aroused Brod's concern and curiosity, and it seemed equally odd to Brod that Kafka was again contemplating and arranging for an upcoming marriage—in mid-September—without ever having sought his advice. A few days later, Brod ran into one of his former girlfriends, who, as luck would have it, knew all about the Wohryzeks. Her report was deeply distressing: "St. disparaging of W.," Brod noted, "all strumpets. . . . How do I tell him?—Maybe his parents know."[22]

It is safe to assume that we can delete this "maybe." The Kafkas treated marriage candidates about whose background they were uninformed just like new business partners, and having one of the numerous private investigators gather information was a matter of routine. Years earlier, when the Bauer family was involved, the Kafkas had still asked their son for his consent, and weeks of discussions had ensued. This time, they did not repeat that mistake, and their inquiries into the Wohryzeks went on without his knowledge. But they did not dare to present him with at least the results—perhaps out of cowardice, but perhaps also recognizing that it might give rise to an act of defiance on his part.

Kafka learned only later that the humiliating argument with his parents had centered not on his fiancée's poverty but on her purported sexual permissiveness. It is no wonder that his father immediately hit upon the idea that his weak-willed son had been calculatingly seduced. There is additional evidence to support this idea. When Kafka was still in Schelesen and needed to make up his mind as to whether he was up for a visit from Oskar Baum that would last several days, his key counterargument was: "finally, he would be bringing me an abominable 'report' that Max has already told me something about." And even if all his other reservations proved unnecessary, "he would be bringing the report no matter what."[23]

The background story is not entirely clear, but two conclusions are inescapable. The first is that Brod had already read this report but Kafka had not, so it was a relatively new document, and the second is that Oskar Baum, who had never interfered in Kafka's family affairs in the past, would not be deterred from presenting this unpleasant news to him in writing, which can only mean that the dossier was *intended* for Kafka. There are no further details available about this affair, nor do we know the actual contents of this "abominable report," but only two scenarios seem plausible: either Julie Kafka visited the Baums and asked them to present the information to Franz and to dissuade him from his plans to marry with friendly advice—an action that she was entirely capable of—or Max Brod had informed his friend about the bad reputation of the Wohryzeks ("how do I tell him?") and was now pressuring him to seek information—or to have information gathered by a third party—to catch up with Kafka's parents' state of knowledge. This was now evidently happening by way of Baum and with Kafka's tacit agreement. Some paid snoop was declaring the Wohryzek sisters—and hence their family—pariahs.

Of course, Kafka was loath to read the assembled rumors about Julie's wanton life. He knew better and trusted his own experiences; his long letter to his prospective sister-in-law Käthe, who was of course also implicated in this calumny, was respectful, without a trace of condescension. He had seen Julie herself in Schelesen as erotically reserved, and she now showed him a tender devotion that ruled out the very idea of lies and infidelity. And even if he had had his doubts, he was saved from the torments of jealousy—and most certainly the jealousy of an alleged "past" of the woman he loved—in large part by the overwhelming certainty of not being worthy of his current happiness for long, and he was encouraged to make the most of it "in spite of it all." Others might want to "possess" a woman, but not he: Kafka used this phrase like everyone else at that time, but he did not experience the feeling associated with it.

Once again, Hermann Kafka was confronted with the fact that he had a lawyer for a son who was perfectly capable of striking back rhetorically at the crucial moment. *So go ahead and forbid me to get married*, Franz retorted coolly to his scolding. That hit the mark. The elder Kafka was certain to stop short of pronouncing an explicit curse. He shied away from this drastic act, and the risk of breaking apart the family once and for all, especially before the eyes and ears of his wife, the highest authority when it came to matters of the heart. "Do whatever you like," he would typically retort. "As far as I'm concerned, you have a free hand. You're of age; I have no advice to give you." These old, oft-repeated sayings had no purpose other than to mask his own helplessness.[24] And sure enough, Hermann backed off this time, as well, and gave up his offensive resistance, and soon this topic was avoided by the family. All further decisions were now made outside the confines of the Kafkas' home.

There are indications that the Wohryzeks also had certain misgivings but handled them quite discreetly in their dealings with Kafka. They were surely happy to see Julie as the future wife of a Jewish civil servant with a good income, who also had the advantage of being a writer with cultural interests to add color to life—an extremely considerate man who was good-looking and could laugh. On the other hand, this civil servant was ill; he was constantly coughing, he had to stay home from work again and again with a slight fever, and most likely he would require long and expensive stays at health resorts to show any improvement. These were not good conditions for starting a family.

Kafka had known for quite some time that the doctor would have a big say in the matter. In September, he went to Professor Pick for a thorough checkup, with mixed results: the lung specialist told him that he was physically capable of marrying only if he finally put on some weight. The very idea of being ordered on a "fattening diet" made his stomach turn, and he confided to Brod that he would be utterly incapable of choking down the quantities required of him. Even so, he did not want to give up the plan he had fought through at home, and for a while the practical difficulties distracted him from his doubts and anxieties.

The housing shortage in Prague was a major obstacle. During the war, construction had come to a near halt, many apartments were in wretched condition, and as a result, the price of acceptable housing soared. Kafka had witnessed the truly tragic example of a colleague, the father of Gustav Janouch, who shared not only an apartment but even a bedroom with his ex-wife. The two of them simply had nowhere else to go, and even the presence of their son failed to brighten their mood in this confined space: he, too, just got in the way. Kafka also came to the painful realization that a desirable living space remained out of reach; even the salary of a mid-level civil servant was not enough to maintain a reasonably comfortable apartment in the downtown area. The shares of a German cooperative building association he had acquired before the war were now worthless, and asking his parents for one of their rental apartments on Bilekgasse was out of the question after his latest confrontation with them. After weeks of effort, Julie was able to wangle an offer in the new section of Wrschowitz (Vršovice), near her family but many streetcar stops away from the center of Prague. This apartment—a single furnished room with thin walls, which would eat up almost half of his annual income and would thus be a makeshift arrangement yet again—was certainly not what they had been hoping for, but even so, it was a stroke of luck under the circumstances. Kafka agreed to take it, and announced that their wedding would take place on one of the following Sundays, in late October 1919, at a civil registry office in Prague.

He was now just a tiny step away from marriage; a few short days stood between him and his long-imagined fantasy of waking up together with a woman, a life companion. Strange, giddy days—Kafka would later say that he spent them in a state of utter "delusion,"[25]—and the many errands and formalities he now had to attend to also sped up the passage of time and drowned out the chorus of inner voices. Finally there were only forty-eight hours to go. Then they learned that although the apartment had been firmly promised to them, it had gone to another applicant.

> The essential obstacle, however, which is, unfortunately, independent of the individual case, is that I am obviously mentally incapable of marrying. This comes out in the fact that the moment I make up my mind to marry, I can no longer sleep, my head burns day and night, it is no longer a life that I lead, I reel about in despair. It is not actually worries that cause this—not that I don't carry around countless worries, in keeping with my sluggishness and pedantry . . . but I'm hit hardest by something else. It is the general pressure that comes from anxiety, weakness, self-contempt.[26]

The wedding was called off, postponed, adjourned until some indefinite time in the future. Kafka, who had pressured Julie into making

The few notes by Max Brod that have been preserved from these months contain an additional little secret. They reveal that Kafka, the writer who was not writing at this time, truly *was* exposed to certain "perils of literature," but in a sense that was very different from what he was trying to convey to the Wohryzeks, namely in his capacity as a reader. He was devouring, and was deeply impressed by, Knut Hamsun's recently published major work, *Growth of the Soil*, a saga of peasant life of breathtaking intensity, in which, it seemed to him, he himself appeared, as Eleseus, the eldest son of the titanic landowner Isak. A skeptic who is both physically and mentally incapable of accepting his father's inheritance, Eleseus would rather live in town at the expense of his family and later even emigrates to America. This character is alienated from his own heritage and is deemed a failure by the accepted value systems of his community—and ultimately even by his own values. This was fuel for Kafka's private myth; he used the name Eleseus in his diary as a self-explanatory shorthand. But why do all the people in this novel stray; why can't they be content with the simple things in life? Kafka had a clear vision of the reason. "Women spoil everything," he explained drily to his friend.

CHAPTER FIFTEEN

The Unposted Letter to Hermann Kafka

We are tormented by possibilities we have lost. Being certain of an impossibility is a benefit.

—Karl Kraus, *Sprüche und Widersprüche*

FRÄULEIN OLGA STÜDL WAS TICKLED PINK WHEN A FAMILIAR GUEST arrived. She knew his family from Prague. He was a modest, polite, humorous man, a few years younger than she, who had already spent several months in her boardinghouse in Schelesen the previous year. They had developed some degree of familiarity back then; she told him that she had remained alone after a failed engagement, and her guest, in turn, read aloud to her on occasion, and once even handed her a pile of galley proofs for a little book of his that would soon be published and wanted to know what she thought of it. He had spent a good deal of time with another guest, a young woman who was also ill, and she had noticed that the two of them had grown closer. But he had obviously not been cured. He was complaining about headaches and insomnia, and he was now coughing more than a year earlier. But that was nothing unusual; there was quite a lot of coughing at the Stüdl Inn.[1]

Kafka had now signed up for two weeks—far too little time to convalesce. He was here for different reasons, as Fräulein Stüdl would soon find out. And he had come in the company of a prominent writer. Max Brod wanted to relax for a few days and finally have a good long talk with Kafka, who had been out of sight for a long time and had shared his summer holidays with a woman this time. Brod was exhausted; the Zionist day-to-day politics, the disputes with Czech politicians, the fruitless discussions, the many trips, lectures, campaign speeches—past and future—made him enjoy Kafka's calm, intense presence and the walks in the snow-dusted woods as a kind of spiritual revival. Brod had come quite close to becoming a professional politician: he was fifth on the list of the predominantly Zionist "slate of candidates of the party of committed Jews" that took part in the Prague Jewish community elections on June 15, 1919, but only the first three were elected. It is unlikely that this made him unhappy. The privilege of being able to sit in the office of the classically educated President Masaryk from time to time and even to receive foreign envoys in his own apartment was not enough to make up for the public insults to which Jewish politicians were regularly subjected.[2]

Brod was able to stay for only a few days, then he left Kafka behind alone in Schelesen. "It was so wonderful (for me) to be together with you," he wrote to him. The parentheses reveal that Brod was well aware of his friend's different perspective on the situation. "I am feeling tolerably well, since no demands are being made upon me," Kafka reported to Ottla, "though Max was here up to now."[3] And a visit from Oskar Baum was imminent. This amounted to too many demands; Kafka was occupied with a project that required his complete concentration during the brief undisturbed time that remained to him here.

He had already tried several times to reach some kind of understanding with his father by means of letters. When they conversed, his father gave short shrift to any criticism, no matter how cautiously worded. It is not clear how often Kafka attempted to appeal to his father in writing, but we do know he wrote at least two such letters from Zürau, and days of utter bedlam were the result. There was even a third letter that his mother did not pass on to her husband. Also, a fragment of an undated letter has been preserved, addressed to Hermann Kafka at his health resort in Franzensbad. This letter was prompted by renewed accusations that Franz was utterly indifferent to family matters, in particular to financial ones—a sensitive point for Kafka since the debacle with the asbestos factory. He accordingly adopted a defensive stance: "So I am beginning this letter without self-confidence, and only in the hope that you, Father, still love me in spite of it all and will be a better reader than I am a writer."[4] But Kafka soon lost any interest in these kinds of submissive gestures—a superficial reconciliation was the best one could hope to achieve in this way, and that was not worth the effort. After everything that had happened in this family in the previous year, and certainly after his father's scornful attacks on the planned wedding, a letter of that kind had to be quite different. Above all, it had to create clarity, clarity as the foundation of a more humane way of living together. Kafka was also in agreement on that point with Ottla, the only person to whom he confided his new plan. Now that she was living with her parents again, she too had ample reason to await the imminent duel between her brother and father with a pounding heart, but also with an element of hope.

Ottla's situation had deteriorated again since the end of the previous year; her boyfriend Josef David was responsible for that. Without any announcement, and evidently against Ottla's will, he had introduced himself to the flabbergasted Kafkas as their future son-in-law. He was invited and scrutinized by the family—including Franz, who had been filled in on the situation—while Ottla, who was in Friedland at the time, helplessly awaited the outcome of the confrontation. She had made it clear to her parents that she would not agree to do what her sisters had done, namely to offer herself up to the dubious market of the marriage bureau. She wanted to make her own choice. Of course, no one would have imagined that she would wind up with *this* candidate.

Twenty-seven-year-old Josef David came from a Catholic family. His father was a sexton in St. Vitus Cathedral, he had no material inheritance to expect, and he defined himself as a national democratically minded Czech. All three characteristics would certainly have denied him access to the Kafka family a few years earlier, but now, with the euphoria surrounding the establishment of the Czech state just weeks ago, the social balance had shifted. Ambitious young Czechs who, like David, had returned from the war unscathed could now feel like victors, while the German Jewish bourgeoisie, whose prosperity was now regarded as a stigma, was forced into a defensive mental stance.

Ottla was fully aware that the meeting between her lover and her parents entailed sources of conflict that were not just individual in nature but also tacitly societal. Josef David was not immune to the recent growing wave of anti-Semitism, and Ottla had found it necessary to caution him quite bluntly not to rail against the Jews in general and to make an exception only for her.[5]

Kafka assured his distraught sister that David's debut was "splendidly easy and natural; no one seemed heavyhearted."[6] He was exaggerating here, as he so often did. The fact that the Kafkas went to great lengths to treat the self-assured suitor (who was not formally seeking their approval) without social condescension had reasons that he knew as well as Ottla. Even weeks later, Kafka's parents found it extremely unpleasant if David caught them in the act of enjoying a roast goose, which, during this period of constant shortages, they could only have gotten from the Jewish black marketeer. They breathed a sigh of relief when David accepted an invitation to join them for dinner.

Of course, once they got past the initial embarrassment, it turned out that there was not much to be said against this young Czech man. He was ambitious and culturally minded, worked in a savings bank while studying law (for which he paid the tuition himself), and would soon be receiving his doctorate. He also played the piano, spoke some French and even more English—he had encouraged Ottla to learn this language years ago, as well—and when he was not talking about his career prospects or the time he had spent in England, he enjoyed discussing his stamp collection and soccer. Even Hermann Kafka had to concede that this was a man who knew what he wanted, and with whom one could have a good conversation. Only in Czech, of course. David refused to switch back and forth between the two languages as nonchalantly as the Kafkas did;[7] indeed, he refused to speak German at all, although he was fluent in the language. When they asked him something in German, he replied in flawless Czech, as was a matter of course for any nationally minded citizen of the new republic. The Kafkas did not dare to object to his face, but they did ask Ottla whether Josef David could be less obstinate on this point, because it was really quite exhausting and made their get-togethers uncomfortable. But once David told them he was a reader of the patriotic newspaper *Národní Listy*—while the Kafkas continued to display the German-language

Prager Tagblatt on their coffee table—they realized that they would either have to get along with him or throw him out.

> He has made a fine impression on us, but I can't deny that he also seemed quite foreign to us and takes some getting used to. He is surely a very decent & intelligent person, but Father has some misgivings: first, his small salary, then his religion; well, let's hope everything turns out for the best.[8]

Ottla could not oblige her parents; the man she loved simply lacked the right pedigree, and all the ambition and charm in the world would never fully make up for that. Still, she had expected furious accusations from Prague, and these were more like the routine reservations that were inevitable with such a clash of cultures and did not need to be taken very seriously. If her father had misgivings about someone but her mother took a liking to him, her mother generally prevailed. The Kafkas visited the Davids, Josef David's parents and siblings were introduced to the Kafkas, they got better acquainted over a nice game of cards, and finally the prospective son-in-law had to undergo a test that would seal the new bond once and for all. He was introduced to two responsible relatives who ranked high in the family on account of their diverse cultural and political contacts: the attorney Robert Kafka, who came from the town of Kolin, and his wife, Elsa. Their vote was unequivocal: they assured Hermann and Julie that David was talented and would go far in life—and it had been a long time since they had liked anyone else as much.[9] That sufficed. A few days later, the family suddenly started calling the suitor, Dr. Josef David, "Pepa," or even "Pepíček." On his name day, the Kafkas gave him six pairs of monogrammed socks, and Julie invited him to call her *maminka* (mother) instead of *milostivá paní* (ma'am). The die had been cast.[10]

We can only speculate why more than a year went by before there was finally a wedding, but we do know that in 1919 there were additional serious quarrels between Ottla and her parents, who evidently took "Pepa's" side against their own daughter. They were pleased to see their rebellious daughter on a tight leash. But Ottla had no intention of doing what all her relatives were now expecting of her, namely to do nothing but prepare for marriage to David, who was domineering, overambitious, and at times hot-tempered. He had so little respect for her interests, so often stayed at the office until late at night (which seemed "unnatural" to her), and spent so much time with his Czech cronies at the Sokol gymnastics club that she felt he didn't need her at all and might be better off without his Jewish lover.[11]

Once Ottla had passed her examinations at the agricultural school in March, she returned to her parents' apartment in Prague, but only to look for suitable employment, as the manager of a farm or a nursery, or something along those lines. But the months of effort she devoted to this pursuit were wasted, and, in her disappointment, her thoughts again turned to Palestine, where women with her qualifications were urgently needed. Several of her Zionist girlfriends from the Club of Jewish Women and Men in Prague were now determinedly preparing for emigration. The increasingly hostile atmosphere in Prague made it easier for them to leave, and for Ottla, the idea of bidding them farewell forever and remaining behind in Prague with the status of a bride must have been hard to take. But whom could she go to for advice now? Who could offer her the understanding and support needed to make decisions with such far-reaching implications? Her fiancé did not share her longing for the countryside at all, and, needless to say, he had no interest in Zionist ideas; they were none of his concern. She could not discuss plans that entailed separation from her parents in front of them. Her cousin Irma—the only friend to whom Ottla could confide absolutely everything—had died suddenly in May 1919 (probably from the Spanish flu). And Ottla's brother was spending this summer with another woman and tormenting himself with decisions that were just as momentous. Nevertheless, Ottla carried on with her efforts; in the spring of 1920, she sent out an application to Opladen, Germany (near Cologne) for an agricultural training course for Palestine. She even asked Max Brod to put in a good word for her to help her get one of the few free spots in the course—but these efforts were all in vain.[12]

Because Ottla and Josef David were now living in the same city, and Kafka and his sister were even under the same roof, no correspondence is available from this critical phase. We cannot gauge the extent to which Ottla had to fend for herself, or why she was unable to make her dream of independence come true despite her experience in Zürau and her completion of her agricultural examinations. Kafka's last messages to Friedland demarcated the rift within the family. He implored Ottla to stand on her own two feet, and he became downright gruff when she was plagued by a bad conscience and contemplated a trip to Prague to discuss the future of her career with her mother, who constantly declared that she wanted only the best for her children without having a clue as to what this "best" might be. She sent generous quantities of food and demanded obedience in return.[13] Kafka was not as upset by the fact that Ottla's obligingness and willingness to take advice and to admit her mistakes was barely acknowledged by her mother—and by her father not at all—as by his parents' crude interference in his own life. These maddening quarrels, which he observed resentfully from the sidelines, with little room for input on his part, were a major factor in his decision to push ahead with a comprehensive and blunt reckoning in the fall of 1919, and they help clarify why Ottla became a central theme and why his sister was his natural ally in this undertaking. Ottla was the co-plaintiff, the procedure was set up in consultation with her, and she examined the records.

Dearest Father,

You asked me recently why I claim to be afraid of you. As usual, I was unable to think of any answer to your question, in part for the very reason that I am afraid of you, and in part because accounting for this fear would involve too many details for me to keep in mind adequately while talking. And if I try to give you an answer in writing here, it will still be very incomplete because even in writing, this fear and its consequences hamper me in dealing with you and because the magnitude of the subject goes far beyond the scope of my memory and reasoning. . . .

Oddly enough, you have some idea of what I mean. For instance, you recently said to me, "I have always been fond of you, even though outwardly I didn't treat you the way other fathers generally do, precisely because I can't pretend the way other people can." Now, Father, on the whole I have never doubted your goodness toward me, but I consider this remark incorrect. You can't pretend, that is true, but to use that reason to maintain that other fathers pretend is either just an opinionated attitude, and as such not open

> to discussion, or—and this in my view is what it really is—a veiled expression of the fact that something is wrong in our relationship and that you have helped bring about this situation, without it being your fault. If you really mean that, then we are in agreement.[14]

An inauspicious start. He cannot explain his fear of his father because he is afraid of his father—who would believe that? And his father is said to have admitted long ago that he was partly responsible, albeit in a veiled manner and without being fully aware of it. It takes his son to tell him what he *actually* wanted to say. This was condescension at the very least.

Kafka's "Letter to His Father" has enjoyed enduring fame, but Kafka scholars have not quite known what to make of it. It is a core text of literary modernity, yet its manipulative element demands analysis of and commentary on its moral stance. It is an indisputably powerful analysis of bourgeois psychogenesis, in particular of the psychological roots of power and dependence. Kafka's letter is on a par with Freud's case studies in its vividness, clarity, and intuitive grasp of the exemplary, the perceptual value of which extends far beyond the individual. It is obvious that psychoanalytical literature influenced the letter, but Kafka never relies on general hypotheses or gives in to the temptation to curtail strenuous arguments with psychological constructs and terminology. He was at the height of his intellectual and linguistic powers, and his letter, read as autobiographical testimony, is one of the most impressive that has ever been published.

Even so, the letter has thrown quite a few posthumous readers for a loop, and nearly every commentator has expressed misgivings about it. Max Brod felt he had to steel readers against its exaggerations and "constructions" even before publishing the letter in its entirety; Klaus Wagenbach decried its value as a primary source; Heinz Politzer analyzed it as highly refined prose and grouped it with the literary work; psychoanalytically oriented biographies have regarded it as "symbolic parricide."[15] Suspicions that Kafka was aiming less at an objective depiction of their life together than at the rhetorical defeat of the letter's recipient have undermined the credibility of the letter. Its unusual length—in the original, more than a hundred handwritten pages—

raises a red flag. Stories can run this length, but not letters. Hadn't Kafka even accused himself of having employed argumentative tricks and denounced the letter as a "legal brief"?[16] In particular, the baffling shift in perspective at the end of the letter, which startles every reader, seems to substantiate this view. Suddenly Kafka begins to speak in the voice of his sixty-seven-year-old father, anticipating Hermann's objections to his son's concerted indictment in direct speech. He waxes artistic and grows playful, and appears to lose sight altogether of the letter's intended recipient; he knows what his father will say anyway, and he can formulate it more elegantly and astutely, and therefore has no need of an actual reply, which raises the question of whether the letter was conceived in the *hope* of getting a reply.

Kafka's heroic undertaking to make an intolerable relationship less so in one fell expository swoop is an outgrowth of a self-clarification project that appears to have started in his youth. He had compiled a large number of observations and memories in his diaries that used the family dynamics to explain his extraterritorial status and seemingly unparalleled alienation, and we can assume that he looked through this material (and perhaps even brought it with him to Schelesen) before he tackled the letter project: there are word-for-word correspondences to notes he had taken much earlier.[17]

Kafka had once dreamed of writing an autobiography; later, after suffering painful defeats in his life , he focused his energy on compensating for the weaknesses he had disclosed and finding his way to a socially acceptable normality. It took his illness to convince him that such attempts were pointless; the only way out, he now thought, "would entail my confessing not only in private, not only as an aside, but openly, by my behavior, that I cannot acquit myself here. To this end, I need do nothing but follow the lines of my previous life with full determination. As a result I would hold myself together, not squander myself in meaninglessness, and keep a clear-eyed view."[18]

He initially conceived of this "following the lines" in concrete terms. Kafka wanted to return to himself, to make a point of embracing the diminishment of his social life that he had formerly decried—isolation, bachelorhood, observer status—as fate, and thus find his way to some sense of peace. Sartre called this strategy "making something out of what you've been made into," which should not be mistaken for mere resignation or retreating into the comfort of what is easily attainable. To identify deliberately with characteristics that the community regards as strange, insane, or antisocial requires a high degree of reflectiveness, which Kafka sought to achieve by linguistic and literary means, as a reader and a writer. This explains his extensive reading while in Zürau and his meditative style in the Zürau notes.

But following the lines also meant sticking to the facts. The notion that Kafka distorted the actual events to suit his purpose and that the "Letter to His Father" cannot be used as a biographical source is utterly misguided. His father was there, after all; he was the closest witness to all the events that the plaintiff was laying out before him as evidence, and any factual error or false quotation would have shown up Kafka and robbed the letter of its impact. Hermann Kafka's contemptuous remarks about his own employees ("That sick dog should hurry up and die!"), his son's friends (he compared Yitzhak Löwy to vermin), and even a relative who had served him devotedly almost to her death at an early age ("The dearly departed left me with quite a mess," he said about Irma) were uttered—or rather, spat out—exactly as Kafka stated.

It is clear after even the first few pages that Kafka had selected these recollections according to a set of strategic and didactic criteria and had arranged them in a manner that might be called literary—and the letter writer was well aware that even his father, who had no regard for literature, would not fail to notice its artistic element. But why would the longest letter that Kafka ever wrote differ fundamentally from any of his other letters in this regard? The question of how literally to take Kafka's messages can be answered either for the correspondence as a whole or not at all, because he was never content simply with conveying information; every observation he communicated, every event went through a process of linguistic and visual distillation, became a miniature, a metaphor, a minor tragedy, or, more frequently, an anecdote. Kafka played with language, delighting in his command of it. On the other hand, his eye was trained to single out the essential, distinctive, or instructive elements. He would need to steer his reader's attention quite deftly to convey his message, and literature gave him the tools he needed to prune inessential elements, highlight or embellish significant passages, play with his reader's expectations, develop a narrative dynamic, and use bon mots to draw in the letter's intended reader.

These propaganda-like narrative techniques—which were certainly also familiar to him from the cinema—must have been the most natural thing in the world for Kafka when he wrote the "Letter to His Father." He was not after a complete chronology of the events or an autobiographical record with a balanced picture of his father; he wanted to show that it didn't matter whether a father's behavior toward his child is objectively and invariably cruel and that even relatively harmless interventions, such as incessant irony, inconsistent orders, scornful gestures, or loud threats of punishment can have a devastating effect if they aggravate existing complexes in the "victim," such as a profound feeling of inadequacy or even nothingness. Kafka freely admitted that something of this kind had to have been present in him already, but he sought to understand—and communicate—how the encounter of two such fundamentally different people, of *this* father and *this* son could have led to such an enduring devastation, apparently impossible to undo after the fact, and to an unparalleled emotional handicap, complete with unrelenting alienation, hurt feelings, misunderstandings, and mutual misapprehensions.

Accordingly, Kafka's theme was the imaginary: the echo of the paternal being in the consciousness of the child, and the multilayering of reality by means of images infused with fear. Over the course of long passages, the letter draws a careful distinction between the "true" character of the father—"basically a kindhearted and tender man"—and the overpowering father imago: "as a father you were too strong for me." This distinction was important to Kafka primarily because he sought to free himself from the tormenting and futile question of guilt at long last. No one can help being what he is. No one can help the fact that another person wields an influence on him in this and no other way. Kafka implored his father to leave aside the recriminations once and for all: "The effect you had on me was the effect you had to have, but you should stop considering it a particular malice on my part that I succumbed to that effect." It was the *effect* that Kafka sought to explain, but the realm of the imaginary cannot be described in the language of facts, which his father knew better than anyone, so Kafka invented vibrant images, like those in his literary texts:

cursed everything and everyone. He brushed aside his children's accomplishments with a sneer. When he ran out of ideas, he raised his voice or wallowed in self-pity, but even harder to bear was his social opportunism, his witless admiration for anyone who had more than a million in the bank or could boast some sort of imperial title. And the hatred with which he persecuted his own youngest daughter revealed what his much-heralded sense of family really amounted to. These were not mere impressions or emotional reactions; they were facts. It was the portrait of a domestic tyrant.

This time, Kafka did not hold back in the slightest; he leaped at the opportunity with obvious glee. The need to let off steam had become overwhelming after the humiliations of the previous weeks, and the bitter quarrels about Ottla set his own conscience to rest, now that he could see that his father tormented people who clearly did *not* deserve it. Moreover, the days he devoted to concentrating exclusively on his own biography laid open deeper and deeper layers of memory, the intensity of which Kafka could not detach himself from. They reached way down to the roots of a forbidden hatred that he had great difficulty admitting even to himself.

There was just a single time that he had not only made explicit reference to this nearly uncontrollable aggression but also acknowledged that it was an inescapable psychological reality: "I have been . . . deceived by them, and yet I cannot rebel against the laws of nature without going mad. So again there is hatred, and almost nothing but hatred." With this admission to Felice Bauer, he had tried to make her see that although he was weary of living with the "the herd at home," he was still unable to take a firm stand against his own parents. This letter ultimately assumed the look and the range of a manifesto and was so important to Kafka that he first formulated it in his diary.[20] It was the attempt to get to the bottom of a clearly irreconcilable rift, an entanglement. But back then, the letter was addressed to his fiancée, an outsider who bore no responsibility for what had happened in the past, and by adopting her perspective, Kafka was able to retreat to the position of the observer, to stay "on topic," and to refrain from using invectives that could have degraded his parents. The "Letter to His Father," by contrast, was in-house communication. The recipient—the adversary, the responsible party—sat at the same table, and that made it impossible for Kafka to remain a dispassionate adviser on his own behalf. His letter is tainted with hatred, and it is nowhere near as controlled and tightly constructed to achieve his goal as Kafka might have later believed. The past is overwhelmingly present, the wounds keep on bleeding, and the imaginary is timeless. To make this point, Kafka is prepared to sacrifice even literature: "My writing was about you; in it, I merely lamented what I was unable to lament at your breast. It was a deliberately drawn out farewell from you." That may have been true once, or at least a substantial facet of the truth, twenty years earlier or perhaps even just fifteen, but it was certainly untrue for the present of the war and postwar periods. Max Brod, who first saw this letter in the literary estate, felt quite uneasy about this passage because he found that Kafka was diminishing his own pleasure in creative achievement.[21]

Once again, Kafka was adhering to the logic of the imaginary, the logic of a private myth, and subordinating actual events to this logic. He was aiming at a constellation that was hidden behind this reality, a constellation he considered as unshakable as the foundation of a house—no matter what changes take place in the upper floors as the years go by. Hence the overwhelming impression that even when Kafka talked about experiences that dated back to his childhood, it was a matter not just of harking back to decades past but of describing a perpetual state that eludes chronological classification. It is as though a tiny step was connecting the most remote periods. Or "marching in place," as Kafka later sought to grasp the law of his life.[22]

But if there is no real development, only shifting forms of a fundamental unhappiness, there is also no possibility of ending the pending procedure with a fairly negotiated settlement that would bring a sense of relief, much less with an acquittal. Contrary to the intention of his letter, Kafka denied that there were any attempts at true communication; he depicted a family in which only the adult children reflect on what is unfolding and the parents act blindly, a family in which anything that does not foster material and social self-preservation is met with either silence or dismissive phrases, yesterday and today. And yet the father, we learn in passing, asked about his son's fear and professed to like him; Hermann read a book about education and family that

Franz recommended.[23] There were conversations that at least touched on the tormenting conflict. These are contradictions, and it does not appear as though Kafka was fully aware of them.

We do not know the extent to which he was thus also questioning the inner truth, the persuasiveness, and the desired effect of the "legal brief"—we would need additional independent testimony to assess how selective Kafka's memories and thus the family portrait he drew actually were. It also remains unclear what he actually hoped to gain from such a stylized and wide-ranging lecture, apart from momentary relief. The sober, somewhat preachy closing words are these: "that it might reassure us both a little and make our living and our dying easier." No talk of reconciliation. Kafka knew quite well that reconciliation could not be achieved by explanations alone, and indeed was not even desirable as long as the adversaries did not negotiate on an equal footing. Reconciliation with an oppressor whose rules continue to dominate would be subjugation. Reconciliation with someone alien to oneself, whose presence and influence one grudgingly tolerates, would be an empty gesture. As long as Kafka remained under this yoke, his letter would be caught up in a performative contradiction that would render it unresponsive. He drew out the farewell, thus forestalling any resolution. He named his adversary with incredible candor but could not let go of this adversary.

People who were close to Kafka were perennially baffled by his odd ambivalence, and Kafka was often asked why the approval—or, for that matter, praise—of his benighted father really mattered to him, particularly when he chose to adorn his next book, the *Country Doctor* stories, with a dedication to this overpowering adversary. "Not that I could appease my father this way," he declared to Brod, "the roots of this antagonism run too deep, but I would have done something; if I haven't emigrated to Palestine, I would at any rate have traced the way there on the map."[24] That did not sound very convincing and certainly did not account for the urgency with which he pursued the matter of the dedication.[25] It is far more likely—as Brod probably figured out—that Kafka secretly reveled in the image of his father finishing up one of his usual evenings of card games, then settling into bed with his son's latest literary project at long last, and coming across a page with just three words: "To My Father." A hilarious idea, and a very clever gambit because his father would have no choice but to feel something like pride, and maybe even force himself to express some words of gratitude, and then the book would casually lie on the table the next time a relative came to visit. We do not know whether this fantasy was ever realized. Kafka later claimed that this dedication to his father had been meant ironically, but he was evidently dead serious when he said this.[26]

> We cannot overstate the importance of the impression that the seemingly towering giant of a father makes on the small, needy creature. . . . [E]verything the child gets and needs belongs to him; he is the ultimate authority to whom the child turns, and the child's stubborn and self-centered defiance falls apart in the face of his will. Punishment and reward come from him. The child has to smooth things over when the father is angry, and obeying him is a matter of upbringing and of budding intelligence.[27]

This text, by Paul Federn, a follower of Freud, was published about nine months before Kafka tried his hand at a phenomenology of patriarchy. The similarities between his interpretation and Federn's are astonishing, right down to the nomenclature, although there is no evidence that he had even heard of Federn's treatise about the fatherless society. But the topic was on everyone's mind: the breakdown of major power systems, the expulsion or murder of political father figures, and people's desperate attempts to create substitute authorities as quickly as possible—a principle deeply ingrained in the individual psyche seemed to be taking hold in each of these catastrophic manifestations. Psychoanalytic theory had already provided a plausible explanation for why, in the microcosm of the family, the power of the father consolidated into an encumbrance, a handicap that had lifelong implications and far outlasted the actual presence of the father. In Freud's view, people could become aware of this mechanism but could not slough it off.

Otto Gross disagreed vehemently even before the war years, arguing that fixation on paternal authority had a disastrous effect on social interaction. To get to the root of this fixation, he claimed, the analyst's couch should be bypassed in favor of a look at the social sphere. Any attempt at social and political emancipation, he emphasized, needed to take into account powerful individual psychological factors that drive man back into bondage. Gross wrote in *Die Aktion* that "the revolutionary of yesterday" was bound to fail because that revolutionary "bore the authority within himself. But now we can recognize that the heart of all authority lies in the family." Hence, he argued, "the revolutionary of today" should not aim merely to combat the father; he has to take a stand against the principle of power itself, the *patriarchal right*.[28]

Kafka, who was a keen observer of intellectual life in Berlin, undoubtedly recalled Gross's early publications. In the summer of 1917, Gross proposed the creation of a new magazine that would be devoted to the problem of authority: "Papers to Combat the Will to Power" (it is noteworthy that he did not opt for the briefer "Papers to Combat Power"). Kafka was intrigued. It was not about raising your hand against your own father—even though Expressionist literature was developing a momentary fondness for this archaic gesture, as evidenced in Hasenclever's stage classic, *The Son* (1915); Werfel's novella "Not the Murderer, but the Murdered Is Guilty" (1920); and Arnold Bronnen's *Patricide* (1920)—but rather about the insight that the enemy lay within, that the victim was no less fixated on power than the perpetrator. The odd paralysis that prevents Kafka's protagonists from going away and starting anew comes from this very insight: wherever they turn, they carry the poison within themselves; they are stuck in the force field of an overpowering authority, even if they protest, as the accused man in *The Trial* attempts to do for a while. The father imago remains powerful, even when the actual father is frail or absent altogether. And Kafka was the one who found the suitable literary expression for this image of the father by having it act as a physical presence. It is quite conceivable that this was the very reason that Gross found Kafka the perfect collaborator: because he had understood the psychological realism of "The Judgment" and "The Metamorphosis."

Kafka was of course less interested in theoretical models and sociopolitical utopias than in practical remedies. What ought to happen concretely; how could one imagine an upbringing that puts an end to the vicious circle of oppression and self-oppression? There were middle-class liberal pedagogues who operated far more naively than Gross, whose training was in psychoanalysis, and who nonetheless hit upon suggestions that amounted to a revolution in child rearing. One prominent example was Friedrich Wilhelm Foerster, whose writings on popular science were widely read. Foerster advocated bringing up children without corporal punishment or any exercise of parental force. When Foerster's *Lessons for Young People* (1904) became required reading for all teachers—including for Felice Bauer—in the Berlin Jewish Home, Kafka began to look into it more carefully. Kafka must have been instantly drawn to Foerster's inductive, positively anti-abstractionist thinking, which was always oriented to "real life." He was particularly impressed that Foerster's pedagogy focused on the development of existing abilities and emphasized that the child already had a personality to be treated with respect. According to Foerster, the amoral and destructive tendencies dormant in every child should be suppressed not by using force but by rewarding and thus reinforcing the equally inherent positive counterforces.

That sounded reasonable and humane, but Kafka noted the dark underside of this philanthropic ingenuousness. Children and teenagers, Foerster had stated, should be guided in their desire to do good not by a need to obey but by their own free will. They should be inspired to do what their parents and teachers approve of from within, and they should learn to gain control over their human weaknesses and egotistical impulses and even to derive pleasure from this self-control. But this would mean that Foerster's pedagogy would be part and parcel of the psychological dynamics governing the bourgeois family: the will of the teacher becomes the will of the pupil; the child becomes the executor of an authority that was instilled in him—consciously or unconsciously, forcibly or by the more subtle means of character formation. The child can love or hate this authority but cannot free himself from it. "Bringing up children as a conspiracy by adults. We lure them from their free-spirited romping into our narrow dwelling by deceptions in which we perhaps believe, but not in the sense we pretend. (Who wouldn't want to be a nobleman? Shut the door.)" And a few days later, he added ironically, "We are permitted to crack that whip, the will, over us with our own hand."[29]

After the meditations in Zürau and intense autobiographical probings in the letter to his father, Kafka came up with far more radical ideas about a suitable upbringing for human beings. He had fundamental questions about the pedagogical competence of the family, and he wrote several detailed letters to his sister Elli, urging her not to keep her own son—Kafka's nephew Felix, who would soon turn ten—alone in his room but rather to have him join a group of children the same age and learn to interact within a community.[30] Before the war, the "garden city" of Hellerau, which had a temperate climate, had been a center of the *Lebensreform* (back-to-nature) movement. Kafka had never completely lost interest in this movement, and Hellerau now struck him as the most suitable community for Felix. In 1920, the Neue Schule Hellerau was founded there, a boarding school in the countryside on the model of the progressive Odenwaldschule, with big, bright classrooms in the legendary festival theater. Girls and boys were instructed together, and the "comrades" had a substantial say in all decisions that affected them. But most of all, the school project followed the model of the *Arbeitsschule* (holistic activity school) with kitchen, garden, metal and wood workshops, air bath, and its own playing field. Physical and mental capabilities were to be fostered here on a par until individual talents emerged clearly; a specialization in a technical or academic track came later, in the higher grades, beginning at age fourteen, with ongoing, highly personal advising by the teachers. The school brochure, which Kafka had sent to him, explained that all education and training took place within the confines of a tightly knit community: "At their own discretion, the children bond with teachers, who live together with them, and thus form close communal groups, which we call 'pedagogical families,' and which are called upon to tackle the human and didactic tasks of working and living together."[31]

Pedagogical family: in Kafka's mind, this term must have resonated like a religious promise, a utopia that was the diametric opposite of the petit bourgeois, oedipally charged, and hermetically sealed family hell that his "Letter to His Father" illuminated so pitilessly. The school brochure, which he lost no time in passing along to Elli, featured a statement of purpose that surely reminded Kafka of the beginnings of the Jewish Home, which could not come close to fulfilling all that it promised and had to make countless compromises. But it was the unmistakable taste of freedom that Kafka was taking in here, and he was rarely mistaken on that score. "Along the way, I learned what freedom is," Peter de Mendelssohn, a pupil at the Neue Schule, recalled half a century later, "and I will never forget it." Kafka, who had not experienced this freedom, noted in reference to himself, "If he is asked what he actually wants, he cannot reply, for . . . he has no concept of freedom."[32]

The idea of a boarding school in the countryside was quite appealing to Elli and Karl Hermann. They had been thinking that their son ought to leave the confines of Prague, and they were likely also hoping to spare him from the constant anti-Semitic hostilities in the city. Elli worried that Felix was too young for experiments like that, but Kafka did not accept that argument:

> One can be too young to be put to work, to marry, to die—but too young for a gentle, unconstrained education that brings out the best? Ten years are not many, but in some circumstances ten can be an advanced age: ten years without physical exercise, without hygiene, in a life of luxury, above all in a life of luxury without exercising the eyes and ears and hands (except for sorting out his spending money), caged with the grown-ups, who basically—it can hardly be otherwise in ordinary life—let off steam at the expense of the children. Ten years of this sort are many.

Elli was impressed by this argument, but she had lingering doubts about the long period of separation from her son if she sent him to Hellerau, and she wondered whether the school offered adequate preparation for the practical professional life of a man. But maybe it was the right place to educate a girl? When Gerti, her second child, turned ten, Elli and Karl Hermann went to see Hellerau for themselves. They met a teacher named Lilian Neustätter, the lover and future wife of the new headmaster, Alexander S. Neill. Lilian Neustätter advised them not to enroll their daughter, and thus the "pedagogical family" never got beyond a dream for Kafka and his sister.[33]

Kafka's colleagues at the Workers' Accident Insurance Institute would have been astonished to learn that Dr. Kafka, who devoted the majority of his office hours to writing letters, had taken two weeks of vacation time in order to *write a letter* to someone who lived in his own apartment. Even the department head, Jindřich Valenta, knew nothing of this plan when he received a brief message that Kafka would like to stay on in Schelesen for three additional days, assuming that the nice weather continued.

Kafka had devoted the first week almost exclusively to developing a workable design to sort out in his head the memories that were bombarding him and to note down phrases that would come in handy (the surviving handwritten version is clearly a final copy). The inn was quiet once Brod had left, and apart from Fräulein Stüdl and an eighteen-year-old girl with an interest in agriculture, whom Kafka knew as "Minze," there was hardly anyone to talk to. Even so, the time frame proved too limited to undertake a task of this scope. Besides, the letter could not be sent without showing it to Ottla first. Kafka had once asked his father whether he honestly believed that Ottla always aggravated him on purpose. The reply was an unqualified yes. That was certainly debatable—Hermann Kafka did not even think his son was capable of such malice. But the question of how to approach this issue kept him awake at night. "I can barely bring myself to write about Ottla," he finally admitted. "I know that I am jeopardizing the whole effect I hope for from this letter."[34]

Ottla came to Schelesen that weekend. When she read the letter, she must have been as stunned by its overall tone as by the passages that pertained to her. As far back as she could remember, no one had ever spoken to their father so bluntly, and neither Kafka's constant assertion that no one was to blame nor the fact that he did not let himself off the hook could obscure the fact that this was a merciless reckoning. Their father was not being forgiven for a single thing he had done; it was a reckoning with interest and compound interest and was surely unique among letters fathers have received from their sons over the ages. Ottla's reaction is not documented, but in contrast to her brother, who had immersed himself in distressing memories for weeks on end, she could certainly picture its devastating effect on her father. Life in a family that was held together in large part by habitual repressions would be virtually unbearable after an attack of this kind, and the case of Ottla had certainly demonstrated that their father was incapable of distinguishing between protest, criticism, and insults. On top of that, the timing could not have been worse. A few hours before Kafka left for Schelesen, Elli had given birth to her third child—a girl—and the prospect that Hermann and Julie would be willing to subject the rules of family life to such exhaustive inquiry at the very moment of getting to know their new grandchild was extremely unlikely. Ottla would have had no trouble picturing the predictable uproar, and Kafka had to give more thought to his plans.

Even so, he did complete the letter, though it is unclear what became of it. Max Brod reported that Kafka had every intention of having his father read it, but he did not hand it to him directly but instead gave it to his mother to pass along. However, she gave the letter back to him (Brod does not mention whether she had the opportunity to read it) and the issue was never broached again.[35] If this version is correct, Kafka himself made sure that his family was spared the showdown he had gone to such great lengths to prepare, because even if the envelope was sealed, its very heft made the looming disaster apparent. He knew full well that his mother was quite capable of taking decisive action when she wanted to keep her husband from getting upset.

On the other hand, his later statements about the letter sounded as though he himself was the one dragging his feet about handing it over. He made reference to a "gigantic letter I wrote my father about half a year ago but have yet to give him," and he followed up by saying, "I might want to give it to my father someday after all."[36] This suggests a possible error on Brod's part. Kafka appears to have hesitated at first, then spent a long time pondering how to get past the practical obstacles and his moral qualms so that he could employ this weapon after all.

Presumably it was the cathartic effect of this major autobiographical project that kept him from readily pronouncing it a failure, and the satisfaction of having illuminated such an inaccessible psychological region and tackled such a complex and painful problem intellectually. Regardless of whether the letter made its case, Kafka was still unwilling to put the letter away in his drawer in November 1919. And he was far less able to imagine declaring the matter over and done with after this act of self-enlightenment. He was all fired up for more. No sooner had he completed the "Letter to His Father" than he got to work on another detailed defensive letter, this one meant for Julie Wohryzek's sister. A short time later, he pulled out his diary, which had lain untouched for months, and began once again to compile small self-reflexive notes, comparable in their imagery to the Zürau meditations.

But Kafka was no longer writing about ethics and religion, or about evil and truth; he now focused on his own life, and the more accurately he tried to trace the contours of his life, the more alien they appeared. He went around them the way one might observe a house. He eliminated the pronoun "I," and spoke of himself in the third person. He had already done so in earlier letters, as a playful distancing device, but now it struck him as the only correct perspective, and he kept it up for about two months. These notes are known as the "He" aphorisms, some of which have become famous and the object of numerous interpretations. But most impressive of all—and there is no doubt that that this is a derivative of the letter to his father, a product of weeks of self-analysis—was Kafka's realization that the *capability* for freedom is established in childhood, but the desired liberation itself does not comes from outside the self. Freedom requires mental anticipation: "he" has to know how to proceed when the doors finally open, otherwise he would just go *away*, away from himself, from being trapped within himself to floating freely in the void—and this would not be a promise, but a threat. Kafka understood that he was keeping watch over himself, that he had the key in his own pocket.

> He could have resigned himself to a prison. To end as a prisoner—that could be a life's ambition. But it was a barred cage. Casually and imperiously, as if at home, the racket of the world streamed out and in through the bars, the prisoner was really free, he could take part in everything, nothing that went on outside escaped him, he could simply have left the cage, the bars were yards apart, he was not even imprisoned.[37]

A beautiful image—and a formidable one. He would return to it.

CHAPTER SIXTEEN

Merano, Second Class

The only proper solitude is the kind where you are preoccupied with yourself.

—Karl Kraus, *Sprüche und Widersprüche*

Director Bedřich Odstrčil was aghast. A medical certificate on his desk, issued by Dr. Kodym, the public health officer, stated that one of his immediate subordinates, Dr. Kafka, soon to be promoted to "secretary," was not only in a poor overall state of health, despite several convalescences at health resorts, but also displayed "symptoms of an advanced pulmonary infiltration." Inflamed tissue could indicate a variety of conditions; after all, Dr. Kafka had already survived a severe case of pneumonia. But the word "advanced" indicated that disaster lay ahead.

Odstrčil, Director Marschner's successor and a confidant of Masaryk, had thought highly of Kafka for a long time and thought it impossible for the Workers' Accident Insurance Institute to do without such a competent official—regardless of whether he was a German or a Jew—even after the political changeover. When the institute was restructured in early 1920 and legal matters were delegated to a central place, the experienced legal expert Kafka was the clear choice for this function. Of course, everyone knew that the institute would be taking a risk; in 1919, Kafka had been able to work for only seven months, and it did not look as though he would ever be restored to good health. On the other hand, the new position would ease his burden. He was no longer deputy head of an outsized department in which he had to deal with accident prevention, rehabilitation measures, and official publications in addition to the dreaded classification of thousands of businesses into risk categories; instead, as the head of the Joint Drafts Department, he could now focus squarely on the significant legal correspondence that came up in the other departments. And because 1919 was a "classification" year, which always brought a storm avalanche of protests and trials, the decision was made to postpone it for several years (by which point Kafka was no longer on staff), so it was relatively calm on the legal front for the time being. Still, the somewhat peculiar organizational status of his position must have made people wonder what was going on. There were still dozens of officials in the newly created scaled-down departments for which Kafka now did the groundwork, but the Joint Drafts Department consisted of a single job. Kafka was the manager of a one-man department, and thus the boss of *no one*.

Odstrčil was obliging, but he could become prickly when he felt snubbed. He was just forty-one years old, and his authority was not yet firmly established, so he insisted that the chain of command be respected. He had made that crystal clear to his company lawyer when Kafka had—for the second time—treated himself to a few extra vacation days. But that was all forgotten when Kafka, who had once again spent several feverish days in bed, sat in the director's office in late February 1920 to discuss the consequences of this devastating doctor's report. Dr. Kodym had recommended a lengthy convalescence in a sanatorium; Odstrčil could authorize two months for the time being, and he added, "If you are doing well there, write to the institute and you may stay on longer."[1] The next day, Kafka received a written confirmation of his sick leave, and on the following day the details of his salary raise. Anyone with good connections was in good stead at this institute—remarkably little had changed in that regard.

Kafka had decided months earlier—presumably shortly after the wedding had been called off and after the conversation with Brod in Schelesen—that he would not be spending the spring in Prague. "In

February I will be going to Munich, with certain hopes, for about three months," he had declared, and he had even asked Julie Wohryzek to go with him.[2] This decision was astonishing in several regards. If he got through December and January without fever, he could use the regular five-week vacation for Munich and apply for unpaid leave thereafter, but if his health took a turn for the worse, the medical health official would surely not send him to a "health resort" with a population of 630,000.

But why Munich of all places? What "hopes" were aroused by this city that had been shaken by political murders and violently suppressed revolts? Since his reading there three years earlier, Kafka had no more ties there to speak of. He must have had Kurt Wolff Verlag in mind, which had just moved to Munich from Leipzig in October 1919 with the majority of its employees, who now numbered sixty. Wolff, who had spent years commuting between Darmstadt and Leipzig, finally wanted to have his publishing house and residence in the same place, and to combine the merits of artistically inclined Munich (which contrasted sharply with the commercial focus of Leipzig) with an environment that was pleasant in both climate and culture. This time he did *not* heed the advice of his managing director, Meyer, who was of course drawn to the media city of Berlin. But the move brought the publishing house to a halt for several months. Heated apartments were hard to come by, the supply situation was catastrophic, and a bookstore strike made for additional delays. Kafka must have known that under these circumstances it was pointless to inquire about the status of his *Country Doctor* stories. Even so, he contacted Wolff—evidently at Brod's insistence—and stayed with his plans to go to Munich until new bouts of fever convinced him that he was in need not of a vacation but of genuine recuperation.

Wolff was clearly interested in meeting his shy author in person for the first time as well. For no apparent reason, he asked about Kafka's plans—which he had never done before—and offered him practical assistance. Only afterwards did Brod tell him the true nature of Kafka's illness, and he had to advise Kafka in all honesty not to come to Munich. Kafka now tried to find accommodations in the Bavarian Alps, in Partenkirchen, only two hours from Munich by train, in a place that was highly recommended for "the early stages of tuberculosis."[3] But no sooner had he reserved a room than the news arrived that owing to the shortages in all Bavarian health resorts, a ban on foreigners had been imposed and no entry permits were being issued. Without a permit, he would not be able to get a visa for Germany. And with that, Kafka's patience ran out. He decided to do something highly unusual: heed the advice of his friends and his doctor.

He was still awaiting his official appointment as secretary of the institute. On April 1, 1920, he sat down at his desk to dash off a quick reply to a letter from "Minze," the young agriculturally inclined woman he had met in Schelesen and to whom he now imparted occasional advice in an avuncular tone. "Tomorrow I leave for Merano. The fact that I am going alone is . . . the best part, although even the best part is far from good."[4] The following evening, Ottla brought him to the night train. It is possible, but unlikely, that Julie Wohryzek was also at the train station.

Merano, which enjoyed the finest landscape and climate of any health resort in the eastern Alps, had seen better days. Since the railroad line had opened over the Brenner Pass (1868), and particularly since the turn of the century, this small town in Austria had experienced a positively explosive development in tourism. In the last year before the outbreak of war, there had always been more guests than residents, and the majority of these guests—which included many well-to-do patients and convalescents from eastern Europe—stayed longer than a month. Merano, situated in an alpine bowl opening out to the south, and protected by mile-high walls of rock to the north, enjoyed the reputation of a luxurious subtropical outpost and was served by coaches from Paris, Berlin, and Vienna. In the lobbies, the little parks, and the immaculate, dust-free promenades, English, French, and Russian conversations could be heard; expensive rented automobiles and cabs dominated on the roads, and daily life in Merano was presented to guests as a well-organized "season," offering a nonstop series of tennis lessons, excursions, picnics, spa and military concerts, evening entertainments, garden parties, and horse races.

Under these circumstances, it was quite easy to ignore the fact that the up-and-coming town of Merano was located in a political hot spot.

Even after Italy entered the war, and after virtually all the spa guests beat a hasty retreat, no one seriously believed that the long arm of world history would reach down into the charming valleys of South Tyrol. But in November 1918, Merano was permanently occupied by Italian troops. These minor victors of the war insisted that from then on, the Italian state had to be secured by a "strategic" northern border, and that could only be the watershed far north of Merano, a line that led over the Brenner Pass. The populace, which was predominantly German, had no say in the matter, and only after the Treaty of Saint-Germain-en-Laye did the South Tyroleans grasp the fact that they were stranded on the wrong side. Italian irredentism had seized its historic opportunity; Merano remained under Italian sovereignty as part of the Alto Adige region.

It is unclear how Kafka was able to get an entry permit to this unstable zone, occupied by former adversaries; presumably his experience in dealing with official procedures and formalities worked to his advantage. He must have noticed from the very moment he arrived after a twenty-four-hour trip, including two thorough luggage checks, and finally set foot on the plaza of the Merano train station, that the shadow of the war still lay over the spa resort. He found a gathering of Tyroleans brimming with patriotic sentiments, tensely observed by *alpini* and *carabinieri*, who were busy with the formal dedication of an imposing monument in memory of the local hero and "freedom fighter" Andreas Hofer, with an emphasis on the current political situation. "For God, Emperor, and Fatherland" had been chiseled onto the pedestal. A provocation.

Kafka had certainly found out back in Prague that at this time Merano had only a single place with elegant accommodations, namely a hotel called Frau Emma, which was also at the train station. The more surprising part was that Merano was still plagued by shortages nearly a year and a half after the end of the war, so conspicuously that it was like being transported back to the awful year of 1918. There were long lines outside the bakeries, food ration cards, "meatless days," dirty streets, and untended parks; ransacked churches were missing their bells; the municipal theater, the spa treatment center, and all the public toilets were locked up. Merano was mired in debt, and the municipal authorities were sitting on a pile of worthless war bonds, at the mercy of the occupying forces and delighted to greet any guest who spent a few lire here, even a guest as frugal as the man from Prague, whose entry in the guest book at Frau Emma read simply "official." But although Kafka was taken with the protective anonymity of the big hotel, and although he knew that he could expect top-notch accommodations, he could not ignore the room prices and mingle with the rich Italian guests for at least a week or two. After the very first breakfast—it was Easter Sunday—he began to wander through town, in the rain and unusually cold temperature, to look for a quiet and reasonably priced place to stay. He was determined to avoid a sanatorium, but there were plenty of rooms available, and he would be welcome anywhere. Kafka eventually discovered an inn encircled by closely planted trees in the residential area of Merano Maia Bassa (which was still an independent community at the time). He was shown around the grounds, then he inspected the bedrooms and the dining room, and decided to stay there once he was assured that the friendly, corpulent owner was not put off by his vegetarian and other preferences. Fifteen lire a day—four and a half Czech kronen—were not too much for an institute secretary.

He was in a room that was nearly at the ground level, and the doors opened out onto a garden with huge blooming bushes. It was still cold, and Ottoburg Inn was heated at night. But during the day, every ray of sun found its way onto the comfortable balcony, and when Kafka kept still, birds and lizards came up to him.

He enjoyed being alone away from home, and after the excruciating family power struggles of the previous year, he was more determined than ever to disallow anything that reminded him of home and enforced intimacy, so he had some regrets about not having remained at the hotel. He wrote to Ottla that staying in this inn was like living in a "family crypt," or even a "mass grave," although Merano was of course "incomparably freer, more expansive, more varied, grander, with purer air and stronger sunlight than Schelesen."[5] At first he tried to avoid running into the other guests—there were sixteen rooms at the inn—and when they sat together in the dining hall in the evening, he disappeared into his room, which was adjacent to it. During the first few days, he insisted on eating his vegetarian meals at a small separate table, explaining to the proprietor that he wanted to "Fletcherize" in peace. She accepted his request; she had presumably accommodated far gruffer hypochondriacs in her time. The other guests were not as comfortable with the idea of a man sitting alone in a corner and endlessly and methodically chewing each and every bite. A former colonel in the German Reich, who was whiling away his time between two elderly ladies at the common table, waved him over and asked him to join the group.

Kafka gave in. He knew that he would be the only Jew at this table. There were many Jews in Merano; he had seen and even spoken to several at Frau Emma, and a few minutes down the road from Ottoburg Inn, there was a Convalescent Home for Indigent Israelites. But here he was the only one, and he likely feared that this would make for a painful experience.

But the fact that he would soon make his quiet garden room a place of incomparable exhilaration went beyond his powers of imagination. He also could not know that he was breathing in the mild southern air for the final time, that the palms, cypresses, and pine trees that all flourished here would be the last he saw in his life. He was glad to be away, and surely also glad not to be in Munich. He sat and watched the world go by, as he typically did while traveling, he read newspapers, and he drank fruit sodas for the first time in a long time. Occasionally he reported to Ottla and Brod by mail; he obediently let his parents know what there was to eat in the inn. He felt under no obligation to pursue his actual work; he did not write—and had not written anything for a long time apart from his secret meditations—and the fact that he had once invented exciting stories seemed more important to others than to himself, for example to a young Czech woman, a Mrs. Milena Jesenská-Pollak. He had received an inquiry from her from Vienna the previous year, a request to be granted permission to translate something into Czech. He had nothing against that, and was even a bit proud. He showed the letter to his fiancée Julie, a few days before the planned wedding. In the winter he had a brief meeting in a coffeehouse with Mrs. Pollak, who was originally from Prague. He had only a vague memory of her face, but then another letter arrived in which she complained that she could no longer breathe in Vienna. That interested him. She did not appear to be a reliable correspondent, however, and failed to reply to Kafka's inquiry. But he was quite eager to see her translation; in Merano he had time, even for letters that fell on deaf ears. There was no reason not to approach her once again. "I'm living quite well here," he assured her, "the mortal body could hardly stand more care. . . . I would so like to share Merano with you. . . ."[6]

She did not reply this time either. Was this tone too personal? Or had something happened in Vienna? He knew that the young woman had a difficult life there, although she was married. He felt obliged to ask once again, this time a little more urgently. If she was having a difficult time in Vienna, why not leave the city for a while?

That is easy to answer. She had to work, she finally replied, because she did not get a penny from her husband. She wrote for newspapers, mostly for mediocre features sections, and at night she translated, most recently Kafka's "The Stoker."

And she had a lung disease.

CHAPTER SEVENTEEN

Milena

I am one of those machines that can explode.

—Friedrich Nietzsche to Peter Gast, 1881

> The world order was not made for her the way it was for the rest of us. She broke the rules every minute of every day. She took her due, even if regular people would call her actions theft or robbery, and was also very generous. For her, nothing was impossible; anyone she loved and was protected by her could feel free to carry on without having to watch his back—whatever he needed, she would supply: money, the enchantment of love, seduction, elegance, intrigues. Milena snatched down the blessings of heaven with clenched fists. She would have been capable of murder if motivated by pure friendship.[1]

JUST LIKE FELICE BAUER, MILENA JESENSKÁ WAS LITTLE MORE than a name attached to a rumor for several decades, one of those incorporeal shadows that turn up in the light beam of genius only to vanish once again. She was enveloped in an aura of literary fiction, in an echo chamber of letters—stirring, passionate letters, with her name on their envelopes. Milena was an address.

After World War II, a thin trickle of cultural memory was kept alive only in Prague, by personal encounters, legends, and the few extant texts she wrote, namely the memory of Milena as an amazing woman and an even more amazing journalist. Now that her writings and other documents of her life have become accessible in languages other than her native Czech, we have a better understanding of the woman whose path intersected with Kafka's. Unlike Felice Bauer or Julie Wohryzek, her personality was stronger than Kafka's. It is conceivable that he could have molded himself to Milena, but it is not conceivable that she would have followed him into *his* world. She knew that, and she gave reasons for it.

Kafka must have heard of Milena Jesenská long before they exchanged their first letters. Soon after the war began, when she was in her final year of high school, she and two girlfriends went to Café Arco on a regular basis. They were young, flamboyant Czech girls in flowing gowns with neither corset nor hosiery, full of life, sassy, and bold, surrounded by German writers. Kafka is sure to have noticed these stylish groupies from time to time, but it seems unlikely that he thought there was more to them than an adolescent desire to flaunt themselves. The three girls added a welcome erotic element; no one pictured them as future journalists and translators, despite their solid literary education. The wild stories that were soon circulating about Milena, Jarmila, and Staša were titillating—though it was hard to say how much was true.

Toward the end of the war, the girls came by less and less often, and Kafka no longer went there at all. Jarmila and Staša married Czech men, but Milena married one of the ringleaders of the Arco, the writer Ernst Pollak, and the two of them moved to Vienna. When she wrote to Kafka, she was twenty-four years old. Her experiences went well beyond the risqué rumors in Prague and could not be reconciled even with thc vague idea of Bohemian libertinism. Two abortions. Two suicide attempts. Shoplifting and document forgery. A lesbian relationship. Drug abuse. Work as a baggage handler. Cohabitation with her husband's mistress. It was as though she was turning the world order on its head, both economically and morally. Her actions were reckless and profligate; she took and gave, knowing full well that in the end she would come up short. *Já jsem ten který platí* was how she later summed up the law governing her life: I am the one who pays.[2]

Milena Jesenská was born on August 10, 1896 in Prague-Žižkov. She learned early on that money and love, social success and personal unhappiness could be excruciatingly entwined. Her father, Jan Jesenský, who came from a respected but impoverished Prague family, used the dowry of his wife, Milena Hejzlarová, to launch his dental career, but demanded all for himself the degree of freedom that came with his growing prosperity. Jesenský was still a student when his daughter was born, but by 1902, the family could afford to move to a modern new building on Obstgasse, just a few steps away from Wenceslas Square, and Jesenský opened his well-appointed dental practice in the same building. A year later, he was awarded his postdoctoral degree, and from then on he went back and forth on a nearly daily basis between lecture hall, dental clinic at Charles University, and his own crowd of patients, who were probably all Czech.

Doctor Jesenský was energetic and ambitious, a skilled physician specializing in stomatology and a fiercely dedicated nationalist, one of the numerous Czech academics who were in constant competition with German colleagues and institutions. At home, he played the role of the loving despot. The daily routine had to follow his needs to the letter, or there would be angry outbursts. Jesenský spent his evenings with his friends from the Sokol, indulged in a number of love affairs (evidently also with his patients), or gambled his earnings on card games at the men's club. On the weekend, he still had energy for excursions to the outskirts of Prague and for long walks that were never long enough for his liking. This was a person whose ostentatiously jovial mood could be just as depressing as his rancor.

It is hard to imagine that this marriage fulfilled Milena's mother's dreams. As the daughter of a teacher, she had enjoyed a wide-ranging education, and although she was certainly capable of playing a good hostess and making pleasant conversation, her interests went in a different direction.[3] She loved beautiful fabrics and furniture, and she dabbled in woodturning and pokerwork. She took full charge of her daughter's education. Dr. Jesenský's involvement in this distaff domestic sphere was minimal to start with, and he bowed out of it even more once their second child, a son (who was of course named Jan), died when he was only a few months old.

The fact that Milena remained an only child, and that there was no younger brother in the picture, was apparently of crucial significance in shaping her path in life. If Jesenský wanted the family *name* carried on in science and hoped to maintain the social status achieved by means of education, his only choice was to provide his only child the best possible schooling. He decided that Milena would enter the field of medicine after completing a college preparatory program. In 1907, the eleven-year-old was sent to Minerva, a Czech girls' high school.

This was certainly an auspicious choice. Minerva was far more than a school; it was one of the few institutions with which the Czechs of Prague had achieved an impressive head start in creating a pioneering girls' school after years of disputes with the authorities in Vienna. This educational institution provided girls a full-fledged classical education, including modern languages,[4] and qualified them to enter any academic profession. The culturally minded Germans had nothing of this kind. Both teachers and students had a powerful awareness of belonging to an elite and standing at the forefront of a movement. Minerva was founded in 1890, and now the first graduates were teaching there and bolstering their students' ambition to demonstrate to the female German establishment what Czech women were capable of. Gradually, Minerva became a matter of identity, even a form of life that blurred the distinctions between the generations. Together with the highly dedicated teachers, they went to art exhibits, concerts, and theater performances. The "Minervists" were also encouraged to participate in sports, and they were granted privileged access to swimming pools and tennis courts. They took organized hikes, and in the winter they practiced ice skating. Dr. Jesenský was suitably impressed. Like most nationalistic Czechs, he had internalized the view that physical exercise was crucial to the rise of a young nation.

The Jesenskýs' pride in their gifted daughter was presumably their only remaining bond. But this fragile triangle was not destined to last. Milena's mother contracted a chronic illness—probably pernicious anemia—and died in 1913 after years of infirmity. At her father's insistence, Milena became her mother's primary caretaker. She spent every afternoon in her mother's room, and in the final months she made sure that her mother, who was barely able to move by this point, took her medications at the prescribed times during the night. This experience was radically disillusioning because for the teenager that she was, it signified a kind of imprisonment, which inevitably fueled her fury and hatred toward her inconsiderate father, who avoided responsibility and did not modify his lifestyle in the least, and toward her innocent mother, whose death she ultimately awaited like a liberation.

Subsequent events must have struck Dr. Jesenský, whose grief was far from overwhelming, like an unfathomable punishment. His lovely, docile daughter, whom he regarded as a reserved young lady prone to losing herself in reveries at the piano, buried in novels, and engrossed in art books, turned into a devil within the space of a few months. Evidently she was making up for lost time and was desperate to escape the smell and the queasy conscience emanating from the sickroom. Of course, the seventeen-year-old could not be blamed for losing her perspective and running riot after a tragic blow like this, but the way Milena acted out her new freedom and drew attention to herself was tantamount to a declaration of war against her father. She plundered his bank account, forged his signature, piled up debts, stole his clothing to give away to needy friends, and even stole the morphine vials Jesenský kept at his dental practice, for which he was held accountable. She developed an obsession for flowers, buying bouquets and having them charged to her father; she was also caught plucking flowers in public parks at five in the morning. She had love affairs, got pregnant, and her father again footed the bill. But worst of all—and she knew quite well that this was the most painful provocation for the nationalistic Jesenský—Milena got involved with Germans, spent time on the German boulevards with her girlfriends, and scandalized both Germans and Czechs whenever she could. It was as though she was on a feverish quest to test her own boundaries, orientation, and authority; it was as though she was punching at her father's chest but not getting beyond his wallet.

Jesenský's hope that the disciplining effect of medical studies would calm her down and bring her together with more serious-minded people was also dashed. The pointless experiment lasted only two semesters. Milena greatly preferred hanging out with people to studying. She could neither organize nor structure her learning, let alone dissect corpses. But above all, it seems to have been the inevitable specialization that put her off not only from medicine but from every academic discipline. Her intellectual and aesthetic interests were sprawling and playful, and she was drawn only to topics she found relevant to herself. She soaked up whatever struck her fancy—literature, music, art. She went to concerts even when there was standing room only, and if seating was available, she brought along a musical score. But music as a discipline or a science, not to mention as a means of earning a living, were options that were every bit as ill-suited to her as the field of medicine. And hence the courses she took at the Prague Conservatory after breaking off her study of medicine were only markers on a path to an education, but they did not prepare her to enter a profession.

Jesenský appeared to play along for a while; he held back from applying any direct force, and merely asked family friends to look after Milena on occasion, but he was unable to prevent public scandals. One day he heard that his daughter had gotten together with a writer and planned to marry him. A German, of course, and to make matters worse, a Jew notorious for his womanizing. Dr. Jesenský had had quite enough. Milena was just twenty and still a minor. He invoked his legal right and said no.

Ernst Pollak, born in 1886 and hence ten years older than Milena, was an unknown in German-language literature, but in literary *circles* he was one of the Prague bigwigs—the notable case of a "writer without a body of work."[5] Like Brod, Kafka, and Pick, he had chosen a run-of-the-mill profession—he was a foreign-language correspondent for the Austrian Central Bank—but his impressive erudition, eloquence, and refined literary sensibility made him the adviser of an entire generation of Prague authors. Pollak's closest friend was Werfel, and Pollak had known Willy Haas since Haas was a schoolboy. His contact with Brod, by contrast, was sporadic (Zionism was not a topic that interested Pollak), but they had known each other for years from literary coffeehouses.

Pollak did not cut an impressive figure, and his attempts to augment his slight frame with conspicuously elegant clothing often appeared comic. A 1913 photograph shows the twenty-seven-year-old looking like a sad salesclerk. Even so, people who knew Pollak were struck by his riveting personal magnetism; he often eclipsed even prominent writers when literary issues were under discussion. Pollak milked his charismatic gifts for all they were worth, adding a touch of arrogance for good measure and hoping to cover for his painful inability to write—a virtually overpowering neurotic writer's block—by playing up his conversational skills. His compulsive promiscuity was also clearly compensatory in nature, although this behavior was common practice in literary circles and evoked no reaction beyond psychoanalytically tinged jokes, but by and large it only served to enhance his aura.

This was the man that the daughter of the distinguished Dr. Jesenský had chosen as a husband. There is no indication that Dr. Jesenský went to the effort of hiring a detective to gather information about her intended, but he had no need to do so; his aversion was rooted in ideological reservations. He abhorred the very idea of having to introduce this Jewish freewheeler and man-about-town as his son-in-law. After standing by Milena with great sensitivity when she had an abortion (which nearly cost her her life), he had hoped that the bloody shock would finally bring her to reason. But Milena declared that from now on she would live with Pollak, with or without a marriage certificate.

Once he realized that his reproaches were getting him nowhere, Jesenský resorted to drastic measures. With the help of a friend who worked as a medical officer—Dr. Procházka, the father of Milena's best friend Staša—he had his daughter committed to a psychiatric institution in Veleslavín, a suburb of Prague, in June 1917. A diagnosis of "pathological deficiency of moral concepts and feelings" was all it took to lock up a young single woman for nine months. Pollak tried to put pressure on Jesenský by challenging him to a duel—of course, word got out about this immediately in the Czech and German coffeehouses—but this helpless and somewhat quaint gesture was lost on Jesenský, who knew a thing or two about duels, and about who was and was not a worthy opponent.

Of course, time was on Milena's side. Once she had gotten over the shock of her new surroundings, she began to find ways and means of making contact with the outside world, and she was even able to see Pollak on a regular basis. Jesenský gradually realized that once his daughter was no longer a minor she might go into free fall if they had not reached an understanding. She steadfastly refused to enroll in a course of study, and her semi-public scandals were incompatible with what he considered behavior befitting the daughter of a prominent doctor, especially one who was caught up in a wave of nationalism, so he concluded that there was only one possible solution: Milena had to get out of town. If she left Prague, the gossip would grind to a halt. Jesenský was now prepared to buy her off by paying her debts, getting her a trousseau in keeping with their social status, and providing a dowry and a monthly allowance—whatever it took. On March 14, 1918, Milena married her two-timing writer, the king of "Café Pollak."[6] A few days later, they set off for Vienna.

> There is no fuel, no coal, no wood, no coke. The trains are not running anywhere in this country, the factories stop every minute, the shops close at five o'clock, a little carbide lamp flickers in restaurants and coffeehouses after eight o'clock. Soon, electricity will be cut off for private use and we will have to light candles—which are unavailable! There is nothing to heat the place, nothing to eat.... The amount of food you get for a week is enough if you're extremely modest—in quantity and quality—for a single meager dinner. There is one loaf of bread (which they refer to as a *Laberl*) per person, and although I have gone through a two-year school of hard knocks here, I have not been able to choke down this yellow, hard, old, moldy "godsend."[7]

This is not how Milena had pictured Vienna. Long before the end of the war, it became evident that the catastrophe of defeat would affect the political center far more severely than the periphery. Bohemia and Hungary curtailed their deliveries of food and coal to the capital and, after the proclamation of the new nation, states even discontinued them altogether at times. Vienna, a city with more than a million inhabitants, became a helpless colossus whose lifelines had been severed. The centuries-old hierarchy of power had been turned on its head. Up to now, the Czechs, Slovaks, and Hungarians were the ones who had to keep fighting to hold on to a fair share of their own resources, but it was now the government of the rump state of "German Austria" that was begging for grain in Prague and Budapest, and because it had nothing to offer in exchange, it appealed on the basis of "humanitarian considerations."

At first, Milena Pollak was unable to adapt to the new and unexpectedly grim situation. Her husband did have a steady income—he had himself transferred to the Vienna branch of his bank and now held the title of foreign exchange trader—but it did not come close to financing the lifestyle to which they were accustomed. In a matter of months, the dowry had been squandered and Milena's trousseau sold or pawned. At that point, Pollak stubbornly refused to hand over any money to his wife, since it would just slip through her fingers—for dresses, jewelry, flowers, cocaine. He decided it was high time for her to provide for herself. She figured he was probably right on that score, especially in view of her new debts in Vienna, which did nothing to endear her to the few people who were able to help her out. (Pollak's personal debts evidently did no harm to his own reputation.)

Milena's later hint that she had come close to opting for prostitution in the dire postwar situation in Vienna certainly seems credible.[8] By this point, she had overstepped virtually all boundaries that defined a bourgeois girl's social and moral universe, and she may have had an easier time coping with an anonymous degradation than appealing to her father for help again. She was more comfortable accepting tips from railway travelers, whose luggage she sometimes carried into their hotels, or from freezing locals who had to make it through the winter and needed her to bring chopped wood to their apartments.[9] Teaching in Czech schools, where she was probably most welcome as a graduate of Minerva, offered her a short-term respite from her predicament. About 5 percent of the populace in Vienna used Czech as a colloquial language, and there was a need for private tutoring in the language. But then she was caught stealing again and had to appear before a German-Austrian district judge. Her now-legendary excuse was "I was having an erotic crisis."[10]

Milena Pollak lacked any social standing in Vienna. The prominent family name, the network of emanicipated Czech women, her local fame, which she had relished when she promenaded down the German and Czech boulevards—none of that counted here. She had to observe from afar the long-awaited national liberation, the founding of the Czechoslovakian state, which she welcomed every bit as enthusiastically as her father. In everyday life, this event brought nothing

to a close, she began to write down what she had seen. The result was a series of reports from Vienna, which so impressed the deputy editor-in-chief of the liberal Prague daily *Tribuna* that from then on, he paid for everything that flowed from Milena's pen. At the age of twenty-three, she was earning her first money with intellectual work. Pollak laughed when he saw the Czech articles, but Milena lost no time in reporting her triumph to her father: signed "M.P."

At about the same time, she first experienced Prague under Czech rule. This may well have been the same visit that enabled her to have a brief talk with Kafka and what was then the more important meeting with Arne Laurin from the *Tribuna* (who had himself gone hungry in Vienna during the war). The fact that she had the confidence to speak in German to Kafka, who had become a local celebrity, was a sign not only of her growing self-assurance but also of an expanding knowledge of current German-language literature and her unusually rapid progress in learning the language. She still made plenty of mistakes, of course, and she missed punchlines and subtleties, but Kafka had the distinct feeling that his texts were in the proper hands. And because he was as yet unaware of the true nature of the Pollaks' marriage, he thought he could rest assured that Milena's translations would at least be looked over by a bilingual connoisseur of literature—although he kept this thought to himself.

In early May 1920, Kafka received the latest issue of *Kmen* (The stem), a literary weekly published in Prague. The very first page bore his name and the title of his piece: *Franz Kafka: Topič. Fragment. Se svolení autorovým přeložila Milena Jesenská* (The Stoker. A fragment. Translated by Milena Jesenská with the permission of the author). He was "almost disappointed," he wrote to Milena, not to find any personal message from her in the envelope that was delivered to him at Ottoburg Inn but only his own story, "the voice I know all too well from the old grave." But he was just being coy. She had no idea that Kafka had already made his sister Ottla race out to order twenty copies of this issue. Milena knew that this was the first translation of one of his literary works, and she could be proud to have persuaded the Communist editor of *Kmen*, Stanislav K. Neumann, to print "The Stoker" as a stand-alone volume on twelve double-columned pages.

In yet another indication of how seldom she had spoken with Kafka, Milena waited until now to ask him whether he was able to read this translation. She learned that he did indeed understand Czech quite well, and he encouraged her to use her mother tongue when writing to him, because only then does "the entire Milena" emerge, as her translation confirmed: "it [is] inconceivable to me that you would go to all this effort, and deeply moving to see your faithfulness toward every little sentence, a faithfulness I would not have thought possible to achieve in Czech, let alone with the beautiful authority you attain. German and Czech so close to each other?"[14] And again, a few days later, "even though the truth of your translation is obvious it still continues to amaze me—hardly a single misunderstanding, which wouldn't mean so much in itself, but I find there is constant powerful and decisive understanding, as well."[15] She knew that this was very high praise indeed. Even so, she must have been relieved to be encouraged to write to him in her own language from then on, while he stayed with his.

The days of lugging suitcases were over. In spite of the ongoing privations—on some days she had nothing to eat but apples and tea—Milena Pollak kept up a steady work pace and delivered her manuscripts on time. She essentially stopped seeing her husband's circle of friends and stayed at her desk instead. In 1920, she published an average of three feature articles a month in the *Tribuna*, and in addition she had numerous translations in *Kmen*, including texts by Franz Werfel, Alfred Döblin, Gustav Meyrink, Gustav Landauer, Rosa Luxemburg, and Upton Sinclair. She had read everything by Kafka she could get her hands on in the bookstore, and her evident favorites were the pieces in *Meditation*; she translated all of them and published a selection. In the fall, she was even able to get the complete text of "A Report to an Academy" accepted for publication in the *Tribuna*.[16] "Whatever you want to do with the books and translations will be fine," Kafka wrote after she proved her mettle as a translator, and he had no cause to regret this full power of attorney. Milena Jesenská—it was only here that she still used her maiden name for her publications—became *Kafka's* translator, and he quickly grew accustomed to this. When another woman tried her hand at translating one of his texts without consulting him, he grew angry and resented her "meddling in our affairs."[17] *Our* affairs.

CHAPTER EIGHTEEN

Living Fires

The prior pain, the pursuant pleasure: Who would resist it?

—Goethe, *West-Östlicher Divan*

"ARE YOU A JEW?" FOR A MOMENT HE THOUGHT SHE WAS JOKING. After all, she already knew so much about him, even the long and excruciating story of his engagements, which she evidently heard from Pollak. And she didn't know he was Jewish?

Readers today are certainly surprised. Had Kafka ever been confronted with such blunt questions? Eight years earlier, in his correspondence with Felice Bauer, it had taken months of fumbling attempts to get beyond the ritual phase of flirtation and superficial chats about how they were feeling. Their financial circumstances and family quarrels remained shrouded in mystery right to the end. The painful subject of what it meant to be a Jew was touched on here and there but was never discussed outright. The term "anti-Semitism" did not come up a single time in the hundreds of pages of their letters.

By comparison, his relationship with Milena developed at a positively explosive pace. Both protagonists appear to have been determined to dispense with social niceties. This time it was the young woman who first coerced, then encouraged Kafka to open up more than he ever had before. His first letters adhered to the established pattern of generating warmth in order to enjoy warmth, but after just a few weeks he was confronted with unexpected confessions and equally candid questions that went to the very core of his existence. She did not shy away from talking about Pollak—she loved him and felt ill-treated by him—but she also wanted to know whether Kafka had a lover. It was not a "confession" to tell him that she lived from hand to mouth, and sometimes on food sent from Prague, and she was not being coquettish when she spoke about her body (which was tubercular) after just a few letters. Perhaps she assumed that a writer in Prague who had spent several evenings at Café Arco would recall the rumors about Minerva students anyway, and she was quite used to dealing with people who knew about her, whether she liked it or not. But that was not the whole story. Her refusal to stick to the rules of bourgeois discretion posed an utterly new challenge for Kafka. She dispensed with social diplomacy and rhetorical doubletalk. If he was overly cautious or vague, she asked for specifics or even expressed her disapproval.

Milena was not indifferent to the tenderness he conveyed even in the very first letters. She appreciated the fact that a man was concerned about her without expressing an overt sexual interest. "And what are you going to do now?" Kafka asked when he found out about her lung disease. "The fact that you're being looked after a little is probably insignificant. Anyone who cares about you has to realize that you need a little looking after; nothing else really matters."[1] Nice sentiments, strikingly different from Milena's daily grind. Of course, these sentiments sounded noncommittal. Kafka saw the matter differently.

> If we look at the whole thing as a school assignment, you had three possible ways of dealing with me. For instance, you could have told me nothing at all about yourself, but then you would have deprived me of the happiness of knowing you and the even greater happiness of being able to put myself to the test. And so you really weren't allowed to keep yourself locked away from me. Then you might have kept certain things from me or glossed them over and you could still do so, but in my current state I would sense this even if I didn't say so, and it would hurt me twice as much. So you aren't

> allowed to do that either. There remains only the third choice: to try to save yourself a little. . . .
>
> What you say about your health (my own is good, just that I don't sleep well in the mountain air) does not satisfy me.[2]

That was going a bit far even for her. Kafka was not only writing letters, he was talking *about* letters, as though there had been substantial correspondence between them. And the "happiness of knowing you"? "In my current state"? She did not understand that; after just a half dozen letters, you can't "sense" much of anything, and surely this was no way to get to "know" someone. Statements like these made her wonder which of his comments ought to be taken at face value. She also suspected that his letters were tactical and self-censored: "Not a single word that was not carefully considered" did she find in Kafka's letters. This man was certainly not spontaneous; it seemed to her that there was an unmistakable reserve. Of course, she could not know how much he prided himself on his unflagging moral vigilance and his determination not to allow himself even a hint of an ulterior motive, which was why he was mortified when she demanded that he be honest.[3]

Still and all, she sensed an infusion of warmth from Merano, which she needed and began to grow accustomed to. At the end of May, messages began to pour in on a nearly daily basis, and she replied to them just as regularly and in great detail. Milena Pollak's letters have not been preserved,[4] but they were evidently full of erratic mood swings that Kafka had trouble following. She mentioned feelings of nothingness and even of self-hatred, and occasionally she indicated that major revelations would soon follow, only to launch into complaints about the ridiculousness of the people with whom her husband surrounded himself. She was quite sensitive, and feared that Kafka would not take her seriously. She failed to get some of his odd jokes, and she refused to show him her own journalistic writings. But she did not want to lose him—*jen strach o Vás*, Kafka quoted, "only fear for you" if their contact should break off.[5] If too much harshness crept into her letters, she followed up with a telegram, and in mid-May—a few days after he urged her to use the familiar *Du* form of address—she sent him flowers.

Kafka was overwhelmed by the temptation to revel in letters that took the place of sensory experience and created a parallel world and an unbounded realm of the imagination in a manner that is normally limited to literature, surpassing the intensity of the physical experience of life. Kafka knew full well that this temptation would exact a high price, and in the aftermath of the lonely Zürau meditations and the last mute encounters with Felice, he understood that unhappiness was a likely outcome, yet he succumbed anyway. For a few weeks, he did not feel as though he was simply repeating a lesson learned; the utterly unexpected but clear opportunity he now had, for the first time in his life, to ally himself with a woman who was his physical, emotional, and intellectual equal made him forget that he was toying with the same long-familiar drug. He began once again to "drink" letters, reading them over and over again, listening to the sounds of the sentences and their overtones and undertones. He spread out the pages and touched his face to them, knowing full well that this pleasure, which was robbing him of sleep at night, was "preposterous."[6]

Milena did not appreciate these imaginative excesses. She was not leading the outwardly carefree life of a convalescent at a health resort who could steer clear of virtually any disruption and revel in daydreaming, and she had a different vision of the purpose of letters. Kafka's yearning for pure, symbiotic intensity was something she had experienced in the past—indeed, Milena had once spent years pestering a beloved teacher with letters—but adolescence had set her straight. What mattered to her now was the content. She took letters literally, and expected more than dreams, metaphors, and nice words; she wanted questions and answers that were suffused with life. "You complain about some letters," Kafka, who sensed the difference right away, wrote to her, "you turn them every which way and nothing falls out, but if I'm not mistaken, those are the ones in which I was so close to you, my blood so controlled, so controlling yours, so deep in the forest, so resting in rest."[7] That was not enough for her. In her experience, loneliness would not go away by listening to a disembodied voice far away. Letters might serve as a prelude to reality and help preserve memories, but reality took precedence over the imaginary, and this precedence was absolute and independent of circumstances, which is why even the most intense, loving correspondence falls short of a painfully imperfect, but physically fulfilled love affair. Two hours of life, she summed up almost coldly, are more than two pages of writing. "Writing is poorer," Kafka replied, "but clearer."[8] And there it was, plain as day: each was longing for a different type of peace.

It is easy to rouse a dreamer playing with letters; sometimes it takes just a few innocuous words. "Are you a Jew?" or "When are you coming to Vienna?" were questions that went well beyond writing on stationery; these questions demanded not gestures but concrete information. She had no idea of the abyss she was leading him to.

> Something strange has happened, which I "report" to you at least by way of hints. Reiner, the young editor of the *Tribuna* (they say a very fine and really exorbitantly young man—perhaps 20 years old) has poisoned himself. This was while you were still in Prague—I think. Now the reason comes to light: Willy Haas had an affair with his wife (whose maiden name was Ambrožová; a Christian, a friend of Milena Jesenská and similar to her, I'm told), though it ostensibly remained within platonic bounds. No one was caught or anything like that; only the woman so tormented the man (whom she had known for years prior to getting married), mainly with her words and her behavior, that he killed himself in the editorial office. Early in the morning she went with Haas to the editorial office to find out why he hadn't come home after the night shift. He was already in the hospital and had died before they arrived. Haas, who was just about to take his last exam, broke off his studies, fell out with his father, and is running a film magazine in Berlin. Apparently he's not doing very well. The woman is also living in Berlin and it is expected he will marry her. I don't know why I'm telling you this gruesome story. Perhaps only because the same demon is causing us to suffer and so the story belongs to us just as we belong to it.

Kafka received this message from Max Brod on June 12, 1920. The same day, he copied it out for Milena, almost verbatim, discreetly omitting only that the woman who had driven her young husband, Josef Reiner, to his death was a "Christian" and a "friend of Milena Jesenská." But why go to all this trouble? This disaster had occurred months earlier, back on February 19, when Kafka was still in Prague, so he must have known that Milena had been informed firsthand about the fate of her friend Jarmila quite some time ago, and in far greater detail. Why indulge in this rumormongering?[9]

And Kafka went one baffling step further. He framed the quoted episode with an introduction and a conclusion that were nearly as shocking. "*You belong to me*," he assured her as a lead-in to the story, underlining this phrase, "even if I should never see you again.... How will we go on living? If you say 'yes' to my letters, you cannot go on living in Vienna." He then appended: "I repeat: you cannot remain in Vienna. What a terrible story." Presumably even a woman like Milena Pollak, who was accustomed to theatrical surprises and had a penchant for staging some of her own, must have gasped when she read this. If she understood it correctly—and how else could it be taken?—this was nothing short of a call for her to leave her husband and begin a new life with a man she had met once—just briefly—and actually knew only from his literary texts and a handful of personal letters. His double insistence was punctuated by a suicide story with no apparent connection to the decision he was asking her to make. There is no documentation of whether she questioned his sanity after this shock, but she would have been justified in doing so. She began by telling him details she had learned from Jarmila herself, but of course she asked Kafka to explain why *this* unfortunate incident had affected him so deeply that he tied it in with his highly personal affairs, particularly since he did not appear to know Jarmila at all, and "Herr Haas" was not a close friend.

Milena might have gleaned the explanation she was anxiously awaiting if Kafka had not withheld the key to this mystery. The very words he had kept to himself when copying out this passage were the crucial ones. Brod's report from Prague had arrived at a critical moment, almost the same hour in which he had decided to get serious and put Milena on the spot. This was a moment of great excitement, and it was simply impossible for him not to read the disastrous news—in which the name Jesenská unfortunately appeared—as a commentary on his own fate. His attention wandered from the foolish Jarmila to Willy Haas, who had obviously acted in full awareness of his responsibility: he was a Jew, and he had destroyed the marriage of a Christian woman. This story—Kafka was now convinced it was a divine inspiration—was meant for him. And this certainty led him to display his Jewish fear, however briefly, in a way that probably made a bewildered Milena shudder:

> The thing I find most appalling about the story from the start is the conviction that the Jews are bound to fall upon you Christians, just as predatory animals are bound to murder, although the Jews will be horrified since they are not animals, but rather hyperalert. It is impossible for you to imagine this in its full scope and power, even if you understand everything else in the story better than I do. I can't figure out how entire nations could ever have thought of ritual murder before these recent events (at most they may have felt general fear and jealousy, but here there is no question, we see "Hilsner" committing the crime step by step; what difference does it make that the virgin embraces him at the same time?). Still, I also don't understand how nations could believe that the Jew might murder without stabbing himself in the process, for that is what he does—but of course the nations don't need to worry about that.
>
> Once again I am exaggerating, these are all exaggerations. They are exaggerations because people seeking salvation always throw themselves at women, and these women can be either Christian or Jewish.[10]

So this was the reason that Brod mentioned that this story affected all of them, and why Kafka "read it ten times and trembled at it ten times."[11] Both identified with the Jewish "perpetrator"; both saw an example in Haas. But only Kafka felt a compulsion to elaborate on this story. Just at the moment of the decision, these images were gaining an even greater hold over him. He trailed after them like a sleepwalker, and he missed the moment because they derailed his thoughts. He talked about murder and even brought into play the unfortunate Leopold Hilsner, the alleged "ritual murderer" of an innocent Christian girl that the media had made a symbol of a hated race.

Kafka could hardly have hit upon a concept that was more charged with collective angst, and Milena was more baffled than ever about what he was after with these harsh words, which escalated her girlfriend's story into a political issue. These were not "exaggerations"; these were morally devastating judgments, and only confirmed anti-Semites would be likely to concur. Did he actually suspect her of having anti-Semitic feelings? After all, he had given her a sarcastic explanation of why her question in Czech as to whether he was Jewish

(*Jste žid?*) sounded like a slap in the face, and of course she had tried to put his mind at ease. Kafka claimed that it was just a "stupid joke" and that he had just wanted to make her laugh with some phonetic games. To dispel any lingering doubts, he took this supposed joking a little further, went ahead full steam, and once again forgot whom he was addressing.

> I could sooner reproach you for having much too high an opinion of the Jews you do know (me included)—there are others!—at times I'd like to stuff them all, as Jews (me included) into, say, the drawer of the laundry chest, wait, open the drawer a little to see if they've all suffocated, and if not, shut the drawer again, and keep doing this to the end.[12]

Milena Pollak was the lover and the wife of a Jew. Her union with a Jew was what had made her leave her hometown. It is unlikely that reading these jocose messages would have brought a smile to her lips.

One year later, however, her letters to Max Brod proved that if provoked, she could conjure up the same ideological phantoms that Kafka was parading here. When Brod steered the discussion to one of her rivals, Milena fired back that all Jewish women were "wretched, bringing doom and gloom." She knew full well that she was talking to the Jewish husband of a Jewish woman.[13]

Some of Kafka's statements, especially in his Zürau notes, are powerful, but nearly indecipherable and downright dark. His remarks about Judaism fall under a different caliber of difficulty. Readers today, who look back on a bloody history, a distortion of language, and a demolition of discursive traditions find it extraordinarily difficult to grasp, let alone empathize with, this content. After the anti-Semitically motivated crimes of the 1930s and '40s, it is no longer possible to make the killing of the sum total of the Jewish population the punchline of a joke, to project ourselves into the consciousness of a man for whom crimes of this dimension not only lie in a murky future but are simply inconceivable, in which the idea of suffocating Jews is not inescapably linked to the concept of gas. Neither in the imaginative play with death—which is rare in his letters—nor in reflections on the anti-Semitic atmosphere in which he lived would it have dawned on Kafka that a fate of that kind could actually befall the Jewish population someday, and the notion that his own sisters would someday lose their right to life and be systematically exterminated like vermin went well beyond even an imagination infiltrated with chemical warfare. Kafka could be playful with the realm of the no-longer-human because it seemed just as implausible and fairytale-like as the sadistic fantasies in the children's book *Struwwelpeter*. We shudder at the thought of this naïveté. But that overstepping of the bounds of civilization, which Kafka could not have imagined, has *remained* unimaginable even after the fact, so the path to historical empathy may still be fairly intact.

To understand Kafka's comments about Judaism in the years following World War I, it is important to bear in mind that among Western Jews, an accusation of anti-Semitism did not carry the taint of blood it does today, and not even necessarily negative connotations. That is the only way to explain the fact that Kafka called one of Milena Pollak's feature articles "sharp and angry and anti-Semitic" but, in the same breath, pronounced it "magnificent."[14] On the other hand, he now started to mention experiences of exclusion and anti-Semitic hatred far more frequently. He felt compelled to go beyond issues of Jewish identity and pay closer attention to politics. He grasped the fact that the era of broad legal security for Jews was drawing to a close, and he reacted like anyone deprived of security: he grew more sensitive and wary.

This was particularly striking during the time Kafka spent in Merano. It was not the first time he had been surrounded for weeks on end by people who spurned Jews or at least had problems interacting with them. He had surely had similar experiences eight years earlier at Jungborn, the spa for natural healing according to Christian principles, without having thought it worth commenting on in letters or in his diary. The situation was quite different at Ottoburg Inn.

> Well, everyone in the group is German Christian. A couple of old ladies stand out; one general (former or present—it is all the same) and a colonel of the same sort, both bright, pleasant people.... But today, when I went into the dining room, the colonel (the general was not there yet) invited me so cordially to the common table that I had to give in. So now the thing took its course. After the first few words it came out that I was from Prague. Both of them; the gen-

> eral, who sat opposite me, and the colonel were acquainted with Prague. Was I Czech? No. So now explain to those true German military eyes what you really are. Someone else suggested "German-Bohemian," someone else, the "Kleinseite" district. Then the subject was dropped and people went on eating, but the general, with his sharp ears linguistically schooled in the Austrian army, was not satisfied. After we had eaten, he once more began to wonder about the sound of my German; perhaps it was his eye more than his ear that prompted his inquiry. I now tried to explain this by the fact that I am Jewish, which satisfied his scholarly curiosity, but not his human feelings. At the same moment, probably by sheer chance, for all the others could not have heard our conversation, but perhaps there was some connection after all, the whole group rose to leave (though yesterday they stayed on together for a long while; I heard that, since my door is adjacent to the dining room). The general, too, was very restless, though from politeness he brought our little chat to a sort of end before he hurried out with long strides. That hardly satisfied my human feelings either; why must I be a torment to them? But otherwise it is a good solution; I shall be alone again without ridiculously sitting off by myself, provided that they do not come up with some disciplinary action.[15]

His unruffled tone is deceptive; his pain was very much in evidence and dulled only on the surface. Kafka knew it was pure chance that everyone got up to leave at the same moment he announced that he was a Jew, but his gut feeling and deep-seated expectation, was so strong that he still sensed "some connection." It also seemed to him that the polite general was suddenly in a big hurry to leave, and Kafka even invoked the vision of a secret deliberation to banish the unwelcome Jewish dinner companion.

It took weeks for the immediate shock to die down and for Kafka to regain some degree of objectivity. He now conceded that things were not too bad, and that he had probably exaggerated. The general considered him a good listener and was friendlier to him than to anyone else. The colonel even called anti-Semitism "stupid," and if the conversation turned to "Jewish dirty tricks" and "brazenness," people would laugh and even apologize to him. In sum, "the anti-Semitism at the table shows all its typical innocence"; restrained and assimilated-looking people with whom one got along were let off the hook, while people were pleased to see the Jewish leaders of the Munich Soviet Republic—the nightmare of the German bourgeoisie—face the drumhead court martial.[16] Sitting at this table, Kafka must have soon realized how naive his original travel plans to Bavaria would have been, and he later remarked that they receive Jews there only to kill them.[17]

Brod knew all too well what Kafka was talking about. "Jewish brazenness!" He had been subjected to the same kind of language just a few days earlier, under far more threatening circumstances and in public, in a box seat at the Kammerspiele in Munich. Brod was there with Kurt Wolff and his business manager Meyer to enjoy the usual applause for Brod's apolitical, innocuous one-act play, *The Height of Feeling*. Audiences in other cities had invariably had a powerful, positive emotional reaction to it. This time, however, there was laughter and hissing, with a hail of jeers and heckling. Since the violent end of the soviet republic in Munich, any Jew who spoke in public had to brace for the possibility of a pogrom, and the majority of those laughing and yelling here had undoubtedly been pleased that Gustav Landauer, a minor figure in power politics, had been killed unceremoniously without so much as a trial or a ruling. Perhaps one or another of these audience members had been there when two months earlier, in February, a newly surfaced agitator named Hitler had proposed a simple administrative solution to the problem, namely revoking the citizenship of all German Jews and on this occasion—the founding of the National Socialist Party at the Hofbräuhaus in Munich, cheered on by a crowd of two thousand—also promised to work toward this goal "relentlessly" and "if necessary, put his own life on the line."[18]

Kafka felt vindicated when he read the dreadful news from Munich, albeit in a somewhat different sense from what Brod had expected. If the Jews were truly, as cultural Zionism maintained, a historically, culturally, and racially independent people that needed only to raise their awareness of their independence, then it was unacceptable for Jews to get overly involved in the political history of another people, no matter how idealistic the motives. This conclusion was fateful but compelling, and just a few weeks earlier, Martin Buber—in a solemn commemorative address about Landauer—made a point of affirming it, and counseled restraint. "He totally failed to recognize," Buber said about his murdered friend, "that the bloodstream of this alien ethnic organism differs in every respect from his and ours. He sought to impose the tempo of his blood, the rhythm of his blood, on this alien ethnic organism, he and a few other Jewish people along with him."[19] Anti-Semites employed these same arguments. But Buber's attitude—the ideological blindness of which is quite apparent today—made perfect sense to Kafka, and he adopted it for himself. And the reaction of the audience in Munich, he wrote to Brod, was certainly understandable:

> Perhaps the Jews are not spoiling Germany's future, but it is possible to conceive of them as having spoiled Germany's present. From early on they have forced upon Germany things that might have come to it slowly and in its own way, but which it was opposed to because they came from strangers. What a terribly unproductive preoccupation anti-Semitism is, and everything that goes with it, and Germany owes that to its Jews.[20]

Why wasn't Kafka furious? Why did he show such remarkable sympathy, even placing the blame for anti-Semitism on the Jews themselves? This attitude seems even more puzzling in light of the fact that the postwar period in Prague offered plenty of examples of confirmed anti-Semites *always* finding reasons and motives. Kafka was kept well informed by the newspapers and especially by Brod regarding how often physical attacks on German-speaking Jews occurred and how helpless the new government was in the face of this problem. There is little doubt that he had observed these kinds of incidents himself and that the threat of a large-scale pogrom, which was only narrowly avoided in late 1920, was not an essentially new experience:

> I've been spending every afternoon outside on the streets, wallowing in anti-Semitism. The other day I heard the Jews called *Prašivé plemeno* [mangy brood]. Isn't it natural to leave a place where one is so hated? (Zionism or national feeling isn't needed for this at all.) The heroism of staying on nevertheless is the heroism of cockroaches that cannot be exterminated even from the bathroom.

> I just looked out the window: mounted police, gendarmes with fixed bayonets, a screaming mob dispersing, and up here in the window the unsavory shame of living under constant protection.[21]

In Munich: Germans against Jews. In Prague: Czechs against Germans *and* Jews. It amounted to the same thing. But Kafka's summary makes it clear that his attention was focused not on the unquestionable right of the victims but on their moral position, which seemed objectionable to him because it was shameful to spend one's life behind a protective wall of bayonets. It was not a sign of strength to want to live where you were not welcome; it was offensive obtrusiveness. Kafka was infuriated by the fanatical desire of many Jews in Prague to assimilate, and he made uncharacteristically snide remarks about the ways in which German family names were altered into Czech ones, German-speaking children were suddenly sent to Czech schools, and people no longer wanted to be seen in the "German casino."[22] But above all it was Kafka's extreme sensitivity in matters of personal dignity that made him unable to muster up unadulterated hatred for the perpetrators and pure sympathy for the persecuted. The Czech anti-Semites knew what they wanted, while the German Jews just called for the police. A moral dilemma ensued: while the victims had right on their side, the social *role* of the Jewish victim could not be reconciled with self-respect. And this dilemma was contagious; it was picked up by the Jewish observer, who dreaded being lumped together with the other Jews.

Milena Pollak, who did not have a very clear sense of the changed atmosphere in Prague, had a hard time understanding why the issue of his Jewishness suddenly became so pressing. Why did he take this so personally? He had taken up with a woman of a different language and religion, and nothing indicated that he needed to overcome any misgivings. No one had pigeonholed her as a Christian for quite some time; she was as indifferent to questions of religion as Pollak was, and the contrast of religions was not a source of friction *within* her marriage. Kafka was evidently imagining things, and grappling with problems that were easy to solve by means of a heart-to-heart discussion. After just a few letters, in late May, she invited him to come to Vienna. Now that she knew the bizarre scenarios he was struggling with, she was more eager than ever. It was up to him to find a little peace. So why didn't he come?

Director Odstrčil had kept his word, and Dr. Kafka had made it easy for him to do so. No one at the insurance company had actually expected the newly appointed secretary and department head to return to his desk promptly at the end of May. Surprisingly, Kafka did not request an extension of his sick leave but asked only to follow it up with his regular five-week vacation so that he could stay on in Merano. He even had his sister Ottla go to the institute to state the reasons for this request. It would be impossible to turn him down in light of the most recent medical results.

Kafka could not promise a full recovery, of course, although the self-therapy he had decided to pursue nearly equaled the treatment he would receive in a sanatorium specializing in lung disease. The key element was to spend hours every day lying quietly in the fresh air, a routine well-suited to daydreamers like himself and requiring no guidance from others. The second element was his diet, which Ottoburg Inn largely adapted to his wishes despite the ongoing food shortages. Kafka was able to report a respectable weight gain—seven pounds. "I won't find such good lodgings and treatment again," he wrote to his sister, who must have been quite astonished by the complete absence of complaints.[23] Kafka had also met a suitable companion, an engineer and manufacturer from Bavaria with whom he took walks and little excursions, and Merano even offered him the opportunity to spend a few hours doing some light gardening.

But Kafka's increasing inability to get a good night's sleep kept him in a state of aimless agitation. His Baedeker travel guide claimed that insomnia was not unusual, and could be a reaction to the mountain air. But he could hardly count on sympathy with excuses like that in Prague, where he would be examined from head to toe upon his return. The ongoing lack of sleep threatened to undo the success of his convalescence; if he wanted to remain in Merano, he needed an effective remedy. Kafka drank beer and was talked into trying valerian tea. He even resorted to the hated bromides people used as sedatives, which did indeed sedate him but did not make him sleep. Of course, this failed

running leap into nearly impossible territory. If he did not want to cancel out all those letters—his and hers—he would now have to travel to Vienna, the metropolis he had once hated. He had prophesied the decline of this city years earlier, but now a very different, more auspicious light was suddenly extending over it from the West.[26]

On Monday, June 28, Kafka wearily packed his suitcase, took one last searching look at his reflection in the closet door mirror, said goodbye to the people who had taken such solicitous care of him for nearly a quarter of a year, and gave out tips to the staff. His dining companions bade him farewell—some in formal terms, and others in a heartfelt manner. Kafka mailed off a card to Ottla, and toward noon he boarded the coach headed for Vienna. He probably looked back for a while at the slopes of the deep valley he had explored on countless walks. They must have seemed quite far away to him, the frozen image of a past life. In the late afternoon, he had to endure long-drawn-out luggage checks at the Brenner Pass. He produced a visa for Austria that had expired quite a while back, but this lapse was graciously overlooked. Nightfall came after they passed through Innsbruck, and it was late when he got to the train stations in Salzburg and Linz. Kafka stayed awake.

> When he felt this fear, he looked into my eyes, and we waited a while, as though we couldn't catch our breath, or as though our feet hurt, and after a while it passed. Not the slightest exertion was necessary; everything was simple and clear; I dragged him over the hills on the outskirts of Vienna; I ran ahead, since he walked slowly; he tramped along behind me, and when I close my eyes, I can still see his white shirt and burned throat, and the effort he was making. He strode all day, up and down, walked in the sun, and not once did he cough; he ate a fearful amount and slept like a log; he was simply healthy, and during those days his illness seemed to us something like a minor cold.[27]

She called him "Frank." It was probably the first time anyone had addressed him with anything other than his real name, but this odd, intimate form of address originated in the way he signed his early letters to her as "FranzK," first with a period, then without one. A closer look revealed that his name was actually Franz, but Milena read it as

"Frank." Later he took to signing his letters to her as "Yours, F" or simply "F," but Milena stayed with "Frank" as long as he lived.

Her description of the four days they spent together in Vienna is the only one we have on record. Kafka's own letters provide only hints of what went on, invocations of happy moments of a level of relaxation that he had probably never experienced before. The fear of giving himself over to another person and thus to the chaotic fullness of life had turned out to be conquerable, and he spent months in solitary dreams savoring the memory that he had been able to cross the threshold of the forbidden zone of symbiotic happiness for a few hours. Of course, even Vienna had its disenchanting moments. On Tuesday morning, Kafka had taken a room in a shabby hotel at the South Station, but he was so exhausted that he put off meeting with Milena to the following day. They got together on the sidewalk in front of the hotel, surrounded by noisy traffic, and when they explored the places that his fantasy had been circling in on for weeks—the gloomy Lerchenfelder Strasse, where she lived; the post office on Bennogasse, where she picked up his letters—they glanced around furtively, fearing unwelcome witnesses. Up in the hills of the Vienna woods, however, where they were alone, his self-consciousness soon eased. The first day, Kafka wrote, was "unsure"; the fourth and final day was "the good one."[28]

But the quick decision that Kafka had secretly hoped for was not forthcoming. Milena was far from clear in her own mind what *she* was hoping for, let alone what it would be like to settle down together in Prague with a man whose mental presence was overwhelming, but whose sensuality proved to be shy, defensive, and rather naive. That final day in the forest—which was Kafka's thirty-seventh birthday—was the day they grew closest physically; it was almost a seduction. But if *fear* was his actual and most pressing issue, how was it possible that he recalled this day as the good one?

The question could not be answered without giving a voice to the otherwise mute domain of sex. It is difficult to appreciate today what a heart-pounding challenge this must have meant, the discursive obstacles, misgivings, and role constraints that had to be surmounted in 1920 before a man defined his own sexuality to a woman, especially if she was quite a bit younger, without flirtatious double entendres and the playful language of erotic courtship. There was something utopian about that; it held the promise of an unknown, unimagined happiness. Felice had always dodged Kafka's timid attempts to move from matters of the heart to those of the body. Milena, by contrast, posed these questions herself; she was experienced, and she knew that moments of mute happiness require an *articulated* trust. And Kafka now had this trust. He no longer drew a distinction between girls, women, and human beings who were feminine. He began to speak to all three.

> The most beautiful letters you have written (and that's saying a lot, since in their entirety, in almost every line, they are the most beautiful thing that ever happened in my life) are the ones where you endorse my "fear" and at the same time attempt to explain that I needn't have it. Although I may sometimes resemble a defense lawyer who has been bribed by my "fear," deep down I, too, probably endorse it; indeed, I am composed of it, and it may be my best part. And since it is my best part, it may be the only part you love. What else about me could be so lovable? But this is worthy of love.
>
> And when you once asked how I could have called that Saturday "good" with this fear inside my heart, it isn't difficult to explain. Because I love you (*and I do love you, you numskull, the way the sea loves a tiny pebble on its bed, that is how my loving engulfs you*—and may I be the pebble again with you, if the heavens allow), I love the whole world and that includes your left shoulder—no, the right one was first and so I'll kiss it whenever I like (and whenever you're kind enough to pull down your blouse in that spot) and that also includes your left shoulder and your face above me in the forest and your face below me in the forest and my resting on your almost bare breast. And that's why you're right in saying we were already one and I'm not afraid of this; on the contrary, it is my only happiness and my only pride and I don't at all restrict it to the forest.
>
> But between this daytime world and that "half-hour in bed" you once wrote of scornfully, as if it were men's business, there is an abyss I cannot get over, probably because I don't want to. Over there lies an affair of the night, absolutely an affair of the night in every regard; here there is the world and I possess it, and now I'm supposed to leap across into the night in order to take possession of it once again. But can anything be repossessed? Doesn't that mean it's been lost? . . .

> To resort to sorcery at night—hastily, panting, helpless, possessed—in order to capture what every day yields to open eyes! ("Maybe" there isn't any other way to have children[;] "maybe" children, too, are sorcery. Let's leave that question alone for now.) This is why I'm so grateful (to you and to everything), *and so it's samozřejmé* [natural] that I am extremely calm and extremely uncalm, extremely constrained and extremely free whenever I'm next to you, which is also why, in following this realization, I have, [*sic*] renounced all other life.[29]

It is unlikely that Milena Pollak grasped the full significance of this final sentence, particularly since he placed the comma in the wrong spot just when he was coming to the key phrase. It indicated that Kafka was taking leave of his own sexuality, not because he considered it a personal flaw but because he could not integrate it, because it had nothing to do with his striving for happiness, because it remained something alien that confronted his own psyche as an unfathomable, intractable force. *Good lures us into evil, and woman lures us into bed*, Kafka had noted tersely in Zürau. He had not been able to implement this ethical rigorism on a practical level. Julie Wohryzek had become his lover, the sexual longing was present, even in Merano, where he had spent weeks thinking about the chambermaid, and he would have seduced her had she given him any clear sign of interest. But, as he confessed to Milena, this was all "against my own clear will." For him, sex was like a detour, a way of being led astray. Even if he would not be lured into evil, he would wind up in a dark place where man and woman surrender themselves to a storm that eventually tears out of their grasp what they thought they had. Kafka could picture happiness only in images of peace, serenity, and total relaxation. Being able to forget that you're a "person seeking salvation"; no longer having to remain on your guard, leaving the doors open. Putting your head on her breast or her lap. Feeling the cool hand on your forehead. "[N]othing more, silence, deep forest."[30]

Kafka found the big apartment on Altstädter Ring almost empty; his parents would not be returning from their annual summer vacation in Franzensbad for another few days. Only Ottla was here, busily preparing for her wedding. She was the first person Kafka told what had happened. In turn, he learned from her how things had been with his girlfriend Julie and the state he would find her in. Both knew that he would now have a difficult time of it.

Kafka had another surprise in store. He had already told Brod that his life had changed, and that Merano had proved to be a turning point not in his health but in quite another sense. For the second time, he was in a romantic relationship that flourished not by means of physical contact but in letters, for the second time he was attempting to capture and hold on to an overwhelming erotic imagination. "She is a living fire, of a kind I have never seen before," he had revealed to Brod excitedly, "a fire, incidentally, that in spite of everything burns only for him."[31] *For him*: That was Ernst Pollak. Although he did not come out and say his name—out of concern for unintended readers—Kafka believed that he had dropped enough hints to make it clear what prominent couple he was talking about.

But now it turned out that his friend did not have a clue. He had racked his brain to try to figure out who the mysterious woman in Vienna might be, and it had not occurred to him that she would be a "Christian woman." This was a positively shocking discovery for Kafka because it meant that Brod had told him the tragic episode about Jarmila and her German-Jewish lover (and future husband) Willy Haas without any particular point in mind, let alone as didactic advice; it meant that he had slipped the name Milena Jesenská into his letter *coincidentally*.

Milena had asked him point blank in Vienna whether this story had any connection to them, and whether this was some kind of warning. No, Kafka had assured her, knowing full well how easily he got carried away by generalizations—no, no connection, no warning. And that turned out to be the truth. The official channels of the inner court remained unfathomable. But Max Brod, who had never found his friend in such an effusive state before, was equally dismayed. "He is very happy," he noted the night after the first time they got together. "But will he be able to cope with these tempests?" At the same hour, Kafka was sitting at his desk as well: [I]f it is possible to die of happiness then I will certainly do so. And if someone destined to die can be kept alive by happiness, then I will stay alive."[32]

CHAPTER NINETEEN

The Big *Nevertheless*

Streams move onward, but not the sea.

—Henri Michaux, *Je vous écris d'un pays lointain*

THEY HAD LAUGHED A GREAT DEAL WHEN THEY WERE TOGETHER, especially in the first weeks, in the little guesthouse in Schelesen. Later, they quieted down and dreamed of starting a family. They looked for a little apartment in Prague and chose their wedding day. But all that ultimately came to nothing. The laughter came to an end on the late afternoon of July 5, 1920, on Karlsplatz, the big, parklike grounds in the newer section of Prague. Kafka rushed over from his office after he finished work for the day, and Julie Wohryzek from her sister's nearby boutique.

The young woman was shaking from head to toe. She had known for weeks that she had a rival and had been waiting in vain for Kafka to return in late May, hoping in vain for their planned get-together in Karlsbad. She learned that there was a Czech woman with whom he'd been carrying on a correspondence—not a very persuasive reason for him to back out. How could the jottings of a stranger hold more meaning than the caresses of a flesh-and-blood companion? But now Julie found out that Franz had actually visited this woman, for several days, and there was no denying that he was a changed man, even though he kept insisting that nothing between them had changed and that he was simply so overwhelmed by this new experience in Vienna that everything else had lost its meaning and disappeared in comparison, which made a separation unavoidable. He repeated it several times; it was hard to understand. Now that it was no longer a matter of worries about money or a place to live, but of their lives as a whole, he was displaying an unaccustomed decisiveness, even callousness, and he turned a deaf ear to her pleas. Finally she replied that she could not go away of her own accord. "If you send me away, however, I will go. Are you sending me away?" "Yes," replied Kafka, who was likely bracing for an outburst at this moment without being able to leave the path he had chosen. "But I can't really go," said Julie.[1]

The pathetic little scene on Karlsplatz—and the only words of Julie Wohrzek on record—show Kafka in a very new and surprisingly matter-of-fact role: the lover who leaves one woman for the sake of another. No doubt he was well aware of the conventional nature of this scene. Defending this "girl" against his parents' opposition and against defamations of her moral character had been extraordinary, whereas his decision to drop her was downright ordinary. But in neither instance did Kafka have the feeling that he was making a truly *free* decision; instead he was capitulating to an overwhelming desire to do the right thing.

Of course this did nothing to allay his moral qualms. "You have done the greatest favor to this girl, beyond the momentary pain," he wrote to Milena weeks before their encounter in Vienna. She must have been astonished to read this. "I can't think of any way apart from this one that she might have freed herself from me." That sounded as though this problem was already solved, an obvious dodge that did not even convince Kafka himself. "I may have done the worst possible thing to her, and it is probably over," he confessed to his sister just a few hours later. "That is the way I play with a living human being."[2] That came quite a bit closer to the truth. But this time, Kafka's self-recriminations did not come close to the panicked intensity that had accompanied his break-up with Felice Bauer. Back then, three years earlier, he had firmly believed that he had destroyed the life of an innocent girl, derailing her for all time from her path as a woman, and when Brod told him in April 1919 that Felice had married, Kafka regarded the news as a belated reprieve. The definitive acquittal reached him in the spring of 1920, before he left for Merano: Felice had had a son, and although Kafka prudently refrained from congratulating her personally, he mentioned it to Ottla several times. But when he talked to Milena, who knew about Felice but not about the recent updates, he struck a tone that gave his former torment a gentle twist of irony: "for nearly five years, I kept battering away at her (or, if you will, at myself); luckily she was unbreakable, a Prussian-Jewish mixture, a strong triumphant mixture."[3]

Kafka's new realization that women were strong, that they could weather suffering and abandonment unscathed, undoubtedly now influenced Kafka's behavior toward Julie. He no longer had any doubt that objectively speaking, a separation would be the best thing for her. Nowhere did he express any concern about the future of this selfless woman who had put up with so many of his puzzling vacillations uncomplainingly. Still, she was thin-skinned when she felt insulted. Felice had kept her composure when they parted and had given free rein to her feelings only later, in a letter, but Julie displayed her desperation for all to see. There was cause for concern, at least for now, and although Kafka, arm in arm with her, felt less sympathy than an overall sense of unease, he did not dare rob her of all hope. She declared that she did not understand why this Czech woman in Vienna, who supposedly loved her husband, needed a secret relationship with another man—and that she intended to say as much in a letter to this Milena.

Kafka was taken aback, but he figured that this would secure him a couple of days in which nothing unfortunate would be likely to happen. And that was enough to make him agree to this senseless suggestion. But no sooner did he bring Julie, who was depressed, though somewhat calmer now, back to her house than he went to the post office and sent a telegram to Vienna: "girl is writing you answer kindly and firmly and don't leave me."[4]

The wave had crested. Kafka was floating on air. For several days, it seemed to him as though imagination and reality had merged, as though he had finally passed and surpassed that incessant test of endurance

This criss-cross of letters seemed just as convoluted as his most complex legal correspondence.

It had started with Max Brod. Milena wanted to see his letter that described the tragic story of Jarmila and Josef Reiner, and Kafka sent it to Vienna for her perusal. In return, he received a wild, belligerent, and distraught letter from Jarmila to her friend Milena; when Kafka read it, he felt as though he were gazing into hell. Shortly thereafter, Milena began to turn to Brod, whom she barely knew, to find out the real story about Kafka's tuberculosis once and for all. To ensure that Brod's wife did not read these letters, they were passed along by Kafka—in sealed envelopes. But Kafka soon realized what was going on, and because he found it undignified to be discussed like a medical case by the people closest to him, he asked Milena to stop.

Then came the complications surrounding Julie Wohryzek. Kafka had "allowed" her to write to Milena, but by the very next morning he was overcome with remorse. He sent Julie a letter by pneumatic post asking her not to do anything for the time being and to talk the matter over with him again. But it was too late. Julie had already written the letter to Milena as if in a daze, and dropped it in a mailbox. In order not to upset Kafka, she hurried to the main post office, where she was able to intercept the letter in time, but she could not be persuaded to destroy it; instead, she entrusted it to Kafka to pass along to Milena. Kafka resisted the temptation to open it. As a reward, he was soon handed Milena's marked-up reply. Julie also told him she would need the Pollaks' postal address in Vienna so that she could write to Milena's husband, as well . . .

A similar scenario, reminiscent of a house of mirrors, was developing at the same time with Staša Jílovská, who was once Milena's schoolmate, constant companion at the Café Arco, and later her most steadfast visitor at the psychiatric clinic. Milena longed to see her; she was the confidante who knew everything about her life and who might be best suited to find her a way through this stressful situation involving two men. And once again, Kafka became a reader and indirect participant. He visited the Jílovskýs, conveyed Milena's request for her friend to come to Vienna at her earliest convenience (which filled him with jealous tension), he sent off a long letter from Staša in which she provided critical commentary on Milena's situation, and he received this very letter back from Vienna so he could look it over.

Now the only thing missing was a word from the final protagonist, a letter from Ernst Pollak to his rival in Prague. Sure enough, Kafka, who had been living in a whirlwind of letters that he had himself stirred up and that took quite a while to settle back down, found out that Pollak planned to write to him, which came as no surprise. Milena was not interested in playing erotic hide-and-seek. Just a few days after Kafka left, she realized that the time had come for a frank discussion with Pollak, and it would need to include a possible return to Prague. "Ernst knows everything," Kafka read on the afternoon of July 8, which was a significant moment in his life, as he sensed right away, a moment that he happened to be spending with Brod, who was now sitting across from him on the visitors' chair in his office. They went to Café Imperial to talk this out, then Kafka hurried off to the post office to send Milena an express telegram: "[I]t was the only right thing to do, be calm, you are at home here. . . ." And in the same breath he offered to send her money.[7]

Kafka's reaction was generous and caring, but Milena had to admit to herself that Kafka failed to grasp the profoundly paradoxical nature of the situation. Ernst Pollak had been the one to introduce her to Kafka's stories, and he had been the one who never stopped praising Kafka as the greatest living writer in the German language.[8] It must have been a shock for this narcissistic bon vivant, who was perpetually tormented by his own creative sterility and whose self-confidence was far shakier than he let on, that this genius had turned to *his* wife. Moreover, he now got to read several passages from Kafka's letters—another of Milena's maneuvers that Kafka probably never learned about—and the linguistic intensity of his wooing must have made Pollak realize that this was no passing dalliance.[9] His marriage was in deep trouble; he barely knew how Milena was spending her days and nights. There had been outbursts of hatred and they had even come to blows. Now Pollak suddenly showed new interest. He was afraid of losing her, and perhaps he even began to see his wife through Kafka's eyes.

Of course he had no idea about the image he was himself projecting to Kafka. Kafka did not start out with any clear memories of Pollak:

"In the café circle he struck me as the most reliable, understanding person, quite calm and almost exaggeratedly paternal, although also inscrutable."[10] This was a very rare misjudgment on his part. But even the shocking details he came to learn about the life of the couple did not lead him to think less of Pollak or to take sides against him. On the contrary, a man who was able to have a bond with such a lively and self-assured woman had to have powers that Kafka could never hope to attain. All of a sudden he began to idealize and even attach mythical qualities to Pollak. Before his trip to Vienna, he had feared Pollak only as his rival; now that Milena was so tormented by her decision, he elevated him into a sphere in which a face-to-face confrontation was no longer possible and in which even jealousy was no longer legitimate. "You love him, whatever you may say," he remarked, "and if and when we unite (I thank you, you shoulders!), it will be on a different level, not in his domain."[11] That was quite easy to misunderstand, and it *was* misunderstood. It seemed as though Kafka was withdrawing physically and conceding to Pollak without a fight what the latter was entitled to sexually anyway. But Kafka had something more general in mind: the fearless dance over the abysses of life that this golden couple celebrated, the ability simply to live that was conferred by some powers or other, was something that Kafka could only marvel at from afar.

> I am not fighting your husband for you, this fight exists only within yourself; if the decision depended on a battle between your husband and me everything would have been decided long ago. I'm not overestimating your husband at all—it's even very likely that I'm underestimating him—but this much I know: if he does love me then it is a rich man's love of poverty (which to some extent is also present in your relationship with me). In the atmosphere of your life with him I really am just the mouse in the "big house," allowed to run freely across the carpet once a year at the most.[12]

Clearly Kafka was already beginning to come to terms with his imminent defeat. Once more he demonstrated the imaginative strategies he had honed over the years. He knew that the images he invoked were "exaggerated" and not intended to be taken literally. Kafka knew that Milena had read "The Metamorphosis," that she might misperceive as literary this image of the animal creeping over the carpet, gazing upward into the eyes of infinitely superior human beings. But this image was zeroing in on a disparity in vitality that Kafka—in both literature and reality—regarded as a decisive aspect that there was no getting around. The Pollaks' household was full of life, love, and suffering, whereas in the bachelor's household, everything was carefully considered, with no more than a bit of daydreaming in the mix, and a happy moment could occur only when "allowed." This had nothing to do with the human qualities that Kafka granted to his rival, not even with the pros and cons of Milena's decision. Kafka felt he knew that the marriage to Pollak was a dead end *for her* simply because she was burdened with terrible memories that only a radical fresh start could change. But the forces at work here were not amenable to considerations of that sort, let alone to practical suggestions. Milena remained dependent on Pollak, whatever Kafka would offer, and he grew gradually more convinced that he was facing an "indestructible unity," an "inexhaustible mystery."[13]

He had not felt that way in Vienna. Even now that Milena's daily letters made it increasingly clear how the decision was tormenting her, how ever new obstacles were piling up even in her, the most spontaneous, unproblematic person he had ever met, Kafka had faith that everything would turn out for the best. If she did not move to Prague on the spot, as he secretly hoped, she would simply come later—very soon, in fact. Any other outcome seemed incompatible with his experience in Vienna, which enveloped him not as a memory, but as a timeless present, as a continuous stream of energy that bore him through the days and nights. And Milena validated this feeling; she wrote that no matter what happened, it would be impossible for him to lose her. Was it conceivable that they were both deluding themselves? That the mouse scurrying across the carpet embodied the truth? Kafka was well aware that this would be decided not in letters, but in reality.

He faced the practical test sooner than he had expected. He had arranged with Milena that in case of dire emergency, each would stand by the other and board the next possible train without hesitation. A dire emergency was a very real possibility for Kafka: He spent several days expecting an act of desperation on Julie Wohryzek's part. To be on the safe side, he had asked Milena not to leave him alone in a catastrophe like that. But things calmed down within a few weeks. Julie gave up, and by the end of July she had disappeared from Kafka's life, his correspondence, and his thoughts without incident. "I don't believe," he remarked soon afterwards, "a transgression against another person could disturb my sleep, if it concerns only the other person."[14] He may have come to this realization because of his experience with Julie, his fiancée, whom he had defended so vehemently the previous year but was now abandoning. He had not given her a chance, and that mouse on the carpet, which for Kafka was a figure of the imaginary, had become her role.

He now seemed more preoccupied with Vienna train schedules than with the people around him. When and where would he see the beloved woman again? Kafka was hurt when Milena told him that they could not plan for a continuation of those innocent days in the forest for the time being, now that three people were involved. But he soon understood that the symbiotic intimacy into which he was nestled really could be destroyed by an encounter under radically different conditions. This was even true of Prague, far from Ernst Pollak's consuming influence. And thus he was more rattled than pleased when Milena began to speak in terms not of a move to Prague but of a visit. "I almost feel like asking you not to come," he replied. "Leave me the hope that you'll come *immediately* if I should ever ask you to when I'm in urgent need—but right now it would be better for you not to come, since you'd only have to leave again."[15]

Kafka was shocked when, just a few days later, Milena asked him to come to Vienna, not because she was "in urgent need," but for a talk that was urgent in its own right. She had received a letter from her father—the first in three years—which further complicated the dichotomy between the two kinds of lives she now had to choose between, because Dr. Jesenský contended that Milena had married solely to defy her father, and this marriage had failed. He offered her his help ("obviously," he wrote), but only if "certain specific conditions" were met. These conditions included separating from Pollak and returning to Prague. Jesenský was displaying the double bind that was apparently a standard tactic he had practiced for years, luring her in and then driving her away. On the one hand, he admitted feeling sorry for his daughter and being "terribly sad" about the longstanding rift between them; on the other, his letter was filled with gestures of dominance, and he signed off in a positively insulting manner: *Jesenský*.

What was she to do? There were now *two* men calling her back to Prague. Both loved her in their way; both enticed with selfless support, and both demanded the utmost from her, but one was a Jew, and the other an anti-Semite. "The way your father sees it, there's no difference between your husband and me," Kafka correctly noted, "to the European we both have the same Negro face."[16] But for Milena, this meant that a return was possible only on the basis of a lie or with the certainty of a scandal: telling her father that she was leaving a Jew in Vienna only to live with another Jew in Prague would have been tantamount to a declaration of war and might have hit Jesenský even harder than if she clung to the marriage. It is quite likely that Milena asked Kafka to come not only out of desperation about the letter and about the newly escalating, nearly unbearable pressure to decide, but because she wanted to see, face to face, how he would deal with a situation like this. It might be necessary to play hide-and-seek. There would be unpleasant encounters and situations, possibly a confrontation between Kafka and her father. Was he reliable enough to take that upon himself?

The answer to this question came more quickly than she had expected. Kafka turned her down, claiming that he would not be able to get vacation time authorized without a plausible reason. And with that, he had unwittingly placed his hand on the shaky scale, and suddenly Milena felt able to see the situation more clearly. Her reservations about Kafka's remoteness from reality had been confirmed, and she was furious.

> I . . . telegraphed him, phoned him, wrote him, pleaded with him in God's name to come see me for a day. I really needed it at the time. I cursed him to the death. He didn't sleep for nights, tormented himself, wrote letters full of self-destruction, but didn't come. Why? He couldn't ask for a leave. He was unable to ask the director, the same director he admires from the depths of his soul (seriously!) for being able to type so quickly—he wasn't able to tell the director he was going to see me. And as for saying something else—another

horrified letter—what was he supposed to do, lie? Lie to the director? Impossible.

That is the pointed version that Milena later sent to Max Brod.[17] Kafka really did feel incapable of lying to Odstrčil's face, the man who had supported him so patiently when he needed to convalesce and who had left it to Kafka to determine the date of his return. But Milena did not understand that. She argued that it couldn't be that difficult to come up with something that sounded plausible; he could just invent an Uncle Oskar or an Aunt Klara who has come down with a serious illness, and he could present a fake telegram and get a few days off—that is how *she* would have done it, and she wouldn't have agonized over it for a second. Absolutely impossible, Kafka replied, he would not be able to tell a story like that to his director with a straight face—but he had a much better idea.

Kafka, who could not stop thinking about Milena's cries for help, had once again pored over the train schedules of the Czech and Austrian railways, and he had discovered that a meeting in Vienna was indeed possible even without a formal application: departure from Prague on Saturday afternoon, after 11 o'clock, return early Sunday morning. That would give them seven hours together during the night. "But it gets even better," he added blithely. Why meet in Vienna, if they could meet halfway at the border, in Gmünd? There it would even be possible—by taking a local train—to spend a full twenty-one hours together. Kafka underlined the number for emphasis, and added "which we could (just think!) have every week, at least in theory."[18] That was the solution. Finally he was able to offer a well-considered, complete, feasible solution for one of her countless worries.

But this was a kind of gratification that Milena did not share. She was facing an existential decision, she was ill, she was hungry, and she was torn between the wish for immediate rescue and a loathing for male rescuers who made stipulations. The fervor with which Kafka sought the most risk-free compromises that did not upset the course of the world, his naive pleasure in discovering this sort of loophole, and the tedious quoting of train schedules, the enumeration of hours that were alloted to them must have struck her as pedantic, stifling, and downright obsessive. Most likely Kafka's fears and trepidations, along with the ingenious alternative solutions he proposed, made her suspect that he was capable of true self-confidence only in literature. He had called Milena his "teacher," and even "Mother Milena," even though she was all of twenty-four years old.[19] In the sphere of the imaginary, he was unhesitating, but she had to wonder whether he was willing or able to come through in reality.

Milena was prepared to let it come down to this test, as well; she calmed down, accepted his suggestion, and agreed to meet him in Gmünd. And she gave Kafka time. On some pretext—she *was* able to lie—she managed to disappear from Vienna for an entire weekend without arousing Pollak's suspicions. When she arrived in Gmünd in the late afternoon, Kafka was waiting for her. They took a walk, discussed the circumstances of their lives at great length, lay together in the grass, and spent the night in the same hotel. That is about all we know about their time together, which had been filled with hope. But the marvel of Marienbad would not be repeated here. Kafka failed to experience the closeness he had invoked on an almost daily basis since their first encounter; Milena found a lack of clarity and passion. He sensed immediately that the decision had been made in Gmünd. It was their second clandestine meeting, and it would be their last.

It could have worked, as they both knew, and readers of the *Letters to Milena*, which has been translated into many languages, find themselves in an impatient, expectant state of suspense even though they know the outcome of the drama. We ache for the protagonists to seize the precious opportunity that has been presented to them. It could have been a marriage of writers, in an apartment with two desks, each writer peering over the other's shoulder, commenting, teaching, and learning; an intellectual community of the kind that no one in Kafka's circles had been able to create and with which he would have been able to outdo all his friends who seemed so full of vitality. Milena admired his prose, and Kafka was intoxicated by her sensual, moving feature articles, which skillfully played with readers' expectations. He had never experienced this high a regard for linguistic expression when communicating with women; he had once learned from the legendary letters of the Brownings that something like this existed, that one could establish an erotic relationship on this basis and make it last, but that was too much like a fairy tale.

Milena's notorious frankness, which exasperated many people, did not in the slightest bother Kafka, who so often got carried away in allusions and images. On the contrary, it was the very undiplomatic nature of the way she spoke her mind that seemed to leave no room for ulterior motives; her remarks came across as authentic and reinforced his trust to see that Milena was certainly capable of revising even harsh judgments. He had typically reacted to slights with almost reflexive self-accusations, but he now responded just as candidly, and sometimes even asked her to take back unfair accusations in writing. Confronting a woman who was experienced far beyond her years, yet not fully mature and testing out her options, seemed to heighten Kafka's awareness of his own unexploited capabilities. And her perpetually blunt questions made him reveal precise information about calamities in his own emotional underworld. Never had Kafka spoken about his fear of life and sexuality in such concrete terms—he did not even shy away from telling her about painful experiences—and when she openly confessed that she still did not understand him and even accused him of not having any real notion of eroticism, he did not lapse into silence but had another go at explaining himself. But she assured him again and again that they would try it *nevertheless*. And then everything humanly possible seemed to merge into a single word because he had proved worthy of this "nevertheless."

But gradually he found himself entangled in a distressing constellation of other people's problems. The Pollaks' marriage was far from the dynamic alliance that could take on the whole world that it had once appeared to be; its masochistic dependencies had spiraled out of control. Kafka had sensed this but misconstrued it at first. "At the moment the only thing to be afraid of—I think—is your love for your husband," he wrote to her a few days after they got together in Vienna.[20] But that was the issue he was actually least worried about. He believed that for Milena it was a matter of a clear-cut decision between two men, a decision that could perhaps be swayed by awakening another love in her. Even the shocking certainty that she had gone right ahead and told Pollak what was going on disheartened Kafka for just a few hours, and his letters remained upbeat, tender, and humorous and self-mocking in spots. These were the letters of a man in love who was living for the moment.

It took several weeks for Kafka to figure out that this game was being played with different rules. He did find it irritating that she implored him repeatedly not to undertake anything on his own initiative, especially not to contact her husband, even to steer clear of him if he came to Prague for a few days. But what did this intrepid woman have to fear from the rivals meeting up? And that was not the only incongruity. She wrote that she could not leave Pollak now because he was ill—but what about her own health? After all, *she* had coughed up blood and her body kept growing weaker—she even lost consciousness at one point. Wasn't she herself in need of care, and had Pollak ever bothered to lend a hand? Nevertheless, she did not take Kafka up on his offer to finance a stay at a sanatorium (evidently because she would be at a loss to explain this sudden affluence), but she did accept the cash he included with a number of his letters. Eventually she spent several weeks in St. Gilgen on Lake Wolfgang with her ailing husband, although she knew that he had chosen this spot because his longtime lover had a villa there. But even now, Milena did not dare to carry on her correspondence with Kafka in her husband's presence. They agreed to use an alias, as they had in Vienna, and she received most of her letters by general delivery.

Kafka assured her that whatever she did would be right, and that the past was past. He would have considered it quite bizarre to try to intrude on the mysteries of her relationship with her husband, let alone to impose moral judgments on it. Still, he was struck by how strenuously she avoided anything that could endanger her attachment to Pollak, and because this anxious concern contrasted so markedly with her usual self-assurance, Kafka understood that this attachment was far from unproblematic, and that Milena was struggling with the torments of an addiction. When she was out of town, the question of who was polishing Pollak's shoes could prey on her mind even more than Pollak's *own* absences did, and that tried the patience of even the most obliging observer: "If you were to leave him," Kafka agonized, "he'll either live with another woman or move into a boardinghouse, and his boots will be polished better than they are now."[21]

The problem was that she did not allow Kafka to bring up these kinds of weaknesses, let alone make them *his* issues, yet she did everything in her power to integrate him into her social world. While shying away from the all-important closeness he sought, she fostered a growing intimacy on another level by linking up Kafka with her contacts in Prague—and thus also with her past in Prague. By asking him to carry out little assignments, she was gradually acquainting him with the key players in her Czech milieu: Arne Laurin, the *Tribuna* editor; her best friend, Staša, and Staša's husband; and finally even—rather to Kafka's horror—Jarmila Reinerová, the protagonist of that fateful Czech-Jewish tragedy that had rattled him while he was exiled in Merano. Kafka would have greatly preferred to avoid these encounters, and his harsh comments about the two women, who seemed like true "angels of death" to him, reveal strong resistance on his part.[22] But new reasons kept emerging to keep up these acquaintances. Moreover, Jarmila, who looked stony-faced and was clearly under the influence of drugs, would turn up at Kafka's office, or even his apartment, for no apparent reason, whereupon he needed to report all the details to Milena.

Kafka did not like being monopolized this way, not because Milena's assignments were bothersome—indeed, he went out of his way to ask for assignments, looked after her brother's grave in the worst summer heat, sent her books and magazines, and even ran around the city for hours to find a shirt for her—but because the introduction of a third, fourth, and fifth person confused matters and distracted him from the issue at hand. He would have been more than happy to minister to the needs of these people, whose extraordinary stories moved him, *together* with Milena, but he lost interest in playing the Prague outpost who was little more than a messenger, and he could not imagine what role he might have in this new milieu. It became clearer to him with each passing day that her old friends could easily take him for a ridiculous contender for Milena's love.

We may assume that Kafka's isolated but reasonably self-sufficient position during the war might have tempted him to give himself over to his epistolary romance for months on end—or rather, to transform the correspondence *back* into an epistolary romance little by little, but he considered it a social ordeal to be part of an ongoing entanglement in a woman's life. In the end, it was not the waiting, the jealousy, or the physical distance that utterly drained his last bit of emotional energy but rather another task she assigned him—the most onerous of all.

During that inauspicious meeting in Gmünd, Milena spoke about her wish to come to an understanding with her father. If the separation from his daughter really did hurt him, why had he lapsed into silence once again? What was he waiting for? Was he demanding guarantees, or did he even want to force his twenty-four-year-old daughter to move back in with her parents? Maybe, Milena began to think, it would be useful if he had a more objective picture of her situation beyond the Prague rumor mill (in which the word "cocaine" had an unsettling role), if he grasped the fact that she was struggling and working. Jesenský had an assistant on his staff in his dental practice who knew about his family problems. Perhaps it would be worth a try to bring her in as a liaison. But it would have to be made clear to this woman first that things in Vienna were a bit different from what they were imagining in Prague. Hence, there would need to be a comprehensive briefing with a reputable and eloquent mediator—and who would be better suited than Kafka? Milena asked him not to write long-winded letters but simply to call up this Frau Knappová and arrange for a private meeting.

It took two weeks for Kafka to bring himself to follow up. To his relief, Jesenský's assistant proved to be a pragmatic and open-minded woman who quickly understood that Milena's precarious situation, whether or not it was of her own making, could not be ignored by her father indefinitely. Knappová reported that Milena's escapades were no longer a taboo topic at the Jesenskýs', particularly because they considered the marriage over and done with and her return to Prague a certainty. But the professor was roundly rejecting an increase in the monthly allowance, and he was still wavering on the issue of whether to finance her stay at a health resort (which would of course take place on *Czech* soil). It did not help that Kafka came well prepared and produced evidence, namely the two most recent, highly graphic letters from Vienna, which talked explicitly about hunger and illness. The news that Milena was carrying suitcases at the train station in Vienna and sometimes even paid her husband's debts seemed to make no impression on him either. "Sending money doesn't make any sense. Milena and money. . . ." But Kafka kept at it. Surely, he suggested, she could at least be helped with something along the lines of "a gift certificate for a good lunch and dinner midday at the Weisser Hahn, Josefstädterstrasse."[23]

He had done what he could. His diplomatic skill was known to both his bosses and his own family, and he had not done a bad job here either. Knappová would speak to Professor Jesenský, and Milena would hear back soon—that was a promise. But Kafka's relief in passing this test was short-lived. Just a few days after sending off his detailed report, he got a furious telegram from Milena to the effect that she was not coming to her father as a supplicant and that Kafka should go to see Frau Knappová a second time "at once" to clear up the misunderstanding he had so recklessly caused.

Kafka carried out this assignment, as well, and tore up the telegram. He felt as though he had been beaten, but at the same time he sensed the cold certainty that this blow would have to be the final one. "You're absolutely right," he replied tersely, "the way I dealt with it was hopelessly stupid and clumsy, but nothing else was possible, for we are living in misunderstandings; our questions are rendered worthless by our replies. Now we have to stop writing one another and leave the future to the future."[24]

* * *

> "The great swimmer! The great swimmer!" the people shouted. I was coming from the Olympic Games in X, where I had just set a world record in swimming. I stood on the stairs at the train station in my hometown—where is it?—and looked out at the indistinct crowd in the dusk. A girl, whose cheek I stroked briefly, hung a sash around me, on which was written in a foreign language: To the Olympic champion.

A hallucination? A dream? The great swimmer has returned, but he has not arrived back home. The people are indiscernible to him at the banquet in his honor. He "cannot clearly recognize" the guests, nor can he make out what they are saying. The women are sitting with their backs to the table, and a sad man is delivering a speech while wiping the tears from his eyes. Finally the great swimmer feels compelled to clarify the situation. He rises and addresses the crowd with these words:

> Honored guests! I have, admittedly, set a world record, but if you were to ask me how I did it, I could not give a satisfactory answer.

> The fact is that I cannot even swim. I have always wanted to learn, but never had the opportunity. So how did I happen to be sent by my country to the Olympic Games? This is the question I've been pondering.

Readers of Kafka continue to ponder this even today because the fragment breaks off soon after without revealing how a nonswimmer could possibly achieve a world record. This text was written in late August 1920, presumably on the day that Kafka learned about the Olympic swimming competitions that had just been held in Antwerp. The top champions were athletes from the United States: Norman Ross with three gold medals, the Hawaiian Duke Kahanamoku with two gold medals and a world record. Kafka later blurred these blatantly obvious references. He had originally written "I was coming from the Olympic Games in Antwerp" but then replaced the name of the city with a big X. He also deleted the number "1500"—rightly so, because there was no record of this freestyle distance in Antwerp.[25]

The swimmer fragment is one of a highly compact series of literary pieces on a total of 51 loose pages, which are now collectively referred to as "Konvolut 1920." They display Kafka's typical pattern of multiple starts: narrative endeavors, separated by slashes, interwoven with recurring motifs, in various stages of development, generally untitled, often enhanced with supplementary material—textual variants, ideas to add on—that he hoped to integrate at some future time. But toward the end of the year, Kafka evidently placed these pages into a drawer without ever tackling them again. There are no signs of any later reworking, and there is no evidence that he ever read them aloud, let alone that he considered publication.

The fact that these texts nonetheless became some of Kafka's best-known challenging pieces, and even found their way into textbooks, stems from Max Brod's editorial approach. In the early 1930s, when Brod began to publish shorter texts from Kafka's literary estate, he at first favored complete texts, or at least those that offered a semblance of completion. He supplied titles of his own devising and thus canonized Kafka's notes from Zürau (from which he extracted "The Truth about Sancho Panza," "An Everyday Confusion," "The Silence of the Sirens," and others) as well as sheets of papers from 1920, which he muddled up terribly, and added his own scribblings, much to the chagrin of future editors. Of these, his first choices were "The City Coat of Arms," "A Little Fable," and "The Problem of Our Laws." Five additional pieces were included in the first multivolume edition: "Poseidon," "The Vulture," "The Top," "The Test," and "Fellowship."[26]

The second generation of Kafka readers thus had quite a comprehensive array to discover, and those who had known Kafka only as an author of Expressionist-style stories and failed novel projects were presented with an entirely different picture. It seemed as though this author had lost pleasure in opulent narration and instead—as the *Country Doctor* stories had already indicated—developed a penchant for more abstract forms, for the art of parable, the metaphorical escalation of philosophical problems, and above all, the form of the paradox, which he used to new effect. Up to this point, critics had been impressed in particular by Kafka's linguistic perfection—which riveted even those who objected to his far-fetched premises—but the prose pieces that now came to light were thought-provoking because they explicitly and irresistibly *challenged* readers to think.

One example is the piece in which a nameless philosopher stares at children playing with a top. It is immediately apparent that he is a literary foil, an abstract representative of an idea. The author does not even bother to provide a fictional setting, and the entire story unfolds on a single printed page. The top spins when hit with a whip, but as soon as the philosopher catches the toy to examine it, it turns into a "silly piece of wood." We understand what is meant. The formal appeal, however, is that *after* this epistemological revelation, which is not in itself particularly novel, Kafka fires off two additional points: "The screaming of the children, which he had not heard earlier, and which now suddenly pierced his ears, chased him away; he staggered like a top under a clumsy whip." The screaming of the children, who do not understand the top, but *possess* it, becomes a vital affliction, the impenetrable noise of life itself. And the final image, which suddenly bursts open the little scene, steers the reader's thought to the imperceptible hand that wields the *big* whip. But whose hand is this?

Even Brod's compilation reveals that Kafka kept circling around the same issues—alienation, the unbridgeable distance between consciousness and the world—with a limited set of motifs. Playing with the top and understanding the top are two different things, but Kafka conveys the impression that it is the player who gains the true insight, not the one who relies on observation and reflection. The short prose piece "Poseidon" rests on the same concept, this time with a comic touch: the Greek god of the sea administers his empire from his desk and has no time for extended trips. But how can he understand what he has never experienced? The same situation applies in "The City Coat of Arms," which reports about planning for the Tower of Babel, a perfect structure envisioned to reach up to heaven. But perfection turns out to require an infinitely long time. The plan gradually takes the place of the construction, and the inevitable frictions that arise from planning stand in for practical experience. Reflection brings everything to a halt. No one steps up to take the first bricks in hand, and the people who were bent on perfection ultimately build neither a perfect nor an imperfect edifice but rather nothing at all.

Many readers and critics who were introduced to Kafka by way of these early editions prepared by Brod were misled into believing that he was actually a philosophical author. They surmised that metaphysical truths lay under the hard shell of his didactic texts and parables, and Brod himself promoted this view by repeatedly pointing out the key role of the Zürau "aphorisms," as though their function was to come out and state what his narrative texts merely alluded to and at times deliberately obscured.

The inadequacy of this notion was proved when the strict division between biographical and literary documents and between works and fragments was abandoned. Now that Kafka's "writing" has been documented comprehensively and can be appreciated in its original context, we know that we are looking at an unparalleled continuum of linguistic expression. Athough he was quite rigid in the selection of texts he deemed worthy of publication, everything that Kafka created adhered to the dynamics of a cycle of imagination. Every question and reply arose from a network of highly personal experience. Even the most abstract problem throbs with the pain of creaturely existence and the torment of neurosis. And the more we explore this language, the less substantial the difference between "personal" and "literary" expression appears. "I, too, am very much against thinking through the options," he wrote to Milena shortly after they got together in Vienna, "I am against this because I have you; if I were alone, nothing could hold me back from this kind of thinking, since doing so transforms one in the present into a battleground of the future—and how can such devastated ground support the house of the future?" If we cut out the remarks intended solely for the recipient of this letter, we are left with a statement that could just as easily appear in Kafka's story about the Tower of Babel and could even serve as its conclusion.[27]

It is the image, the metaphor, that keeps the cycle going. Kafka's writings are never mere illustrations of "messages," let alone metaphysical propositions. Readers who misunderstand this underpinning of the creative process are more easily led astray with Kafka than with any other author. Kafka does not *seek out* an image; he *follows* it, and would rather lose sight of his subject matter than the logic of his image, as even some of his early readers noted. "Don't ask what it's supposed to mean," Kurt Tucholsky urged readers in the first review of "In the Penal Colony." "It's not supposed to mean anything at all. It means nothing at all." But these sorts of appeals to readers' aesthetic sensibilities fell on deaf ears; again and again, they failed to grasp the provocative enigmatic nature of Kafka's texts themselves, which did not leave Tucholsky cold either. He later even admitted that he was less fond of Kafka's *Castle* because this was "a book in which an 'interpretation' of the events appears almost unavoidable," while in *The Trial* the symbol had stood on its own. "[I]t lives its own life. And what a life. . . ."[28]

Tucholsky could not know at this point that the autonomous life of imagery took Kafka well beyond the boundaries of the individual work, the genre, and even the literary craft of writing. Kafka pursued his images into the vast thicket of associations, differentiating them and making the most of their dynamism, even when he was no longer aware that literature was being created in this manner and, indeed, even when he himself had not yet grasped the core meaning, the metaphor. The fragment about the great swimmer offers one of the most impressive examples. Brod initially opted not to include this fragment in his posthumous edition because it was barely more than a draft, and it was utterly unclear how Kafka intended to explain or clear up the bizarre situation. The manuscripts and biographical documents that were published later offer a very different perspective, showing that

Kafka had not exhausted the image of the swimmer who cannot swim. Because he often went swimming in the Moldau River in the hot late summer in 1920, it is even conceivable that the act of swimming itself kept that image alive and caused Kafka to expand on its inner logic. About two months after writing this fragment, he had a new idea:

> I can swim like the others, only I have a better memory than the others, I have not forgotten my former not-being-able-to-swim. But because I have not forgotten it, the being-able-to-swim does me no good, and I still cannot swim.[29]

This is undoubtedly the Olympic champion from Antwerp speaking, and the fact that this explanation is at odds with other statements in his speech ("I have always wanted to learn") did not disturb Kafka in the least. He had enhanced the coherence of his plot; readers now get a sense of why the man was practicing swimming. And the idea that one can master a task, yet fail at it in practice, is no longer an intellectual game but a vital paradox, a comprehensible experience. It is an experience of the kind that occurs mainly when people are put to the test. They cannot believe that they can do it, and consequently they cannot. With fear like that, no one keeps his head above water for long.

Milena Pollak quickly realized that a deep-seated fear was beleaguering Kafka and sapping his will to make practical decisions. He tried to explain it, to give reasons for it, and did not appear to be fully aware of the significance of the concept of fear, which he now frequently even placed in quotation marks, until battling it through with Milena. "I do not know its inner laws," he first allowed, "only its hand on my throat—and that is truly *the most terrible thing I have ever experienced or could experience*." Yet he felt that this fear had to have some sort of basis; it was something essential, a form of alertness, awareness that could not simply be conquered and was not treatable with therapy. Would Milena have been able to find anything endearing about him were it not for this fear? "It really is part of me and perhaps the best part."[30] But Kafka was unable to make it clear to her *how it felt* when that inner force welled up.

In early 1921, he continued this discussion with Max Brod, who was even less able than Milena to grasp how the happiness of a promising love could trigger fear. Fear of what? he kept asking. There was quite a long list, but suddenly Kafka realized that he had discovered, and even noted down, the fundamental image that could render the *experience* of fear as something literally groundless. He had failed to see that the image was right in front of his eyes. Milena would certainly have understood it, but he had not told her about it. It was a mortal fear, he wrote to Brod:

> Like a person who cannot resist the temptation to swim out into the sea, and is blissful to be carried away—"now you are a man, you are a great swimmer"—and suddenly, with little reason, he raises himself up and sees only the sky and the sea, and on the waves is only his own little head and he is seized by a horrible fear and nothing else matters, he must get back to the shore, even if his lungs burst. That is how it is.

The great swimmer, the Olympic champion. His secret is revealed. Of course he learned how to swim quite well, but he cannot put out of his mind that swimming is monstrous. And so he wins the world record by scrambling to get out of the water before anyone else.

> For a few days now I've been performing my "military service"—or more correctly "maneuvers," which is sometimes the best thing for me, as I discovered years ago. Sleep in bed as long as I can in the afternoon, then walk around for two hours, then stay awake as long as possible. But the catch is in this "as long as possible." "It doesn't work for long"—not in the afternoon, not at night, and yet I'm practically wilted in the morning when I come into the office. The real treasure lies hidden in the deep of the night, in the second, third, fourth hour; but these days if I don't go to bed before midnight at the latest I am lost, and so are night and day. Still, none of that matters, this being-in-service is good even when there are no results. Nor will there be any; it takes me half a year to "loosen the tongue," and then I realize it's over, that my permission to be-in-service has run out.[31]

She did not know him yet and could not be aware that this message contained a threat. Milena was young, but Kafka was old enough to recall the usual patterns. After the tribunal in Berlin, in late July 1914, he had settled into his nighttime work of writing *The Trial* in the fulfilling, even redemptive feeling of meeting an obligation. The situation in Zürau was similar, although there he filled notebooks instead of stationery. Now, in August 1920, it was the meeting in Gmünd that reminded him of unfinished business. "It was the first cut of the spade," were the first words he wrote shortly thereafter, and he repeated them to savor the moment. Of course he turned out to be right; he would not be able to make his way down to the abundant mines in which he had been digging in earlier nights. He would put off the task and leave behind only one batch of papers. But once again, his literary writing had created a distance, a fallback position that would ensure his survival. A few days later, the meeting with Jesenský, and Milena's tongue-lashing. Now he knew that he would have to bow out and stop spending his nights writing for her. From then on, every letter declared that it was time to stop writing letters.

Milena Pollak may not have understood her own part in the failure of this love. The letters she later sent to Brod, in which she attempted to provide a summary and sought his candid opinion, are highly ambivalent; they were a powerfully eloquent expression of despair that this opportunity was slipping away, yet also a questionable idealization of Kafka that shut him out of the community of those capable of life and love.

> The thing that you all call Frank's non-normality is actually his plus point. The women who got together with him were ordinary women and did not know how to live except as women. I think instead that all of us, the entire world and all people, are sick, and that he is the only healthy person, the only one who sees correctly and feels correctly, the only pure person. I know that he is not resisting *life*, but only *this kind of life*. If I could have brought myself to go with him, he could have been happy with me. But only now do I know all that. At the time I was an ordinary woman, like all women on the face of the earth, a little instinct-driven female. And his fear arose from that—rightly so. Is it possible for this man to feel anything that isn't right? He knows ten thousand times more about the world than all other people in the world. That fear of his was right. . . . He always thinks that he himself is the guilty and weak one. And yet there is not another person in the whole world who has his colossal

> strength: that absolute, unalterable necessity for perfection, purity, and truth.[32]

No woman, "ordinary" or not, can live with an incarnation of purity. The point of this tribute was that any other woman would have been just as doomed to fail. But when did she figure this out? Milena invoked a time before she had developed into a fully aware woman. But the moment of decision lay just a few months back, and at this time she had a clearer, far more multifaceted image of Kafka than the later icon of "Frank" she developed under the obvious influence of Kafka's self-stylization. She got to know not only his fear but also his humor, his charm, his practical and diplomatic abilities, and his longing for intimacy.

Even "at the time," in the fall of 1920, her conscience was eating away at her, not because she had fallen short of perfection but for the more mundane reason that she had let Kafka wait far too long, and even after months of correspondence she still did not dare to admit to herself that she would not get away from Vienna on her own. She nonetheless enmeshed Kafka in her life, as though a happy solution were just around the corner; a simulation of their potential life together that he saw through and that began to make his encounters with her Czech friends a torment. One day she would live with him, Milena wrote to him even in mid-October, and that would happen sooner than he thought possible. But Kafka replied that he considered it quite impossible, "and 'sooner' than 'never' is still just never."[33]

Although Milena was unclear about her own role and had great trouble keeping her disastrous dependencies and emotional highs and lows under control, she was exquisitely sensitive to Kafka's beginning retreat. She must have been pleased that he was writing again, but she soon realized that he was now returning to a well-established repertoire in his life, a self-protective strategy. This impression was more fitting than she could have imagined, and the repetitions were downright oppressive. Kafka read her letters only in bits and pieces or after days of delay. He wallowed in self-recriminations and self-destructive fantasies (one letter even contained a drawing of a man being torn apart), and he stylized himself as a dirty, nonhuman creature who had better crawl off in the dark. Ultimately he put up barriers and hid behind the irrefutable lament that he could not endure any more contact. Contact with *her*? Contact with *any* woman? "You're also right," he conceded, "to place what I've now done in the same category as the old things; after all, I can only go on being the same person and go on living the same life." But he had not been alert enough for a moment, because if he admitted that the radically new experiences this woman had enabled him to enjoy—an erotic, human, intellectual exchange that went beyond gender, age, language, and mentalities—would not alter his deeply ingrained behavior patterns or protect him from relapses, there was no point in reassuring himself yet again of his own autonomy. Hence the disclaimer: "But it was wrong and I regretted very much making comparisons to older events in my last letter. Let's erase this together."[34]

He still could feel that he was right; his feelings had not cooled off. This time, his longing was strong, almost uncontrollable, and Kafka was unable to find a dignified end. He could not bring himself to write a "last" letter for months; he did not discount the possibility of additional meetings, and it took him until the end of the year for the psychologically definite decision to lead to practical consequences and to a true separation. Even then, the story of Milena and Frank was not over. She would see him again, and she would mourn for him. But in accordance with his wishes, there would be no more talk of the future.

Kafka had found a closing statement of a sort by October 1, 1920, when he answered Milena's question, the context and wording of which we can infer. A rare example of an answer that does not even require a question because it contains everything we need to know. "Did I know it would go by? I knew it would not."

CHAPTER TWENTY

Escape to the Mountains

But now I lacked a more exact directive as to how I should structure my repentence.

—Christian Friedrich Daniel Schubart, *Leben und Gesinnungen*

"Would you like to go for a ride?" Kafka thought he had heard wrong. As usual, he was one of the last visitors of the day at the "swimming school" at the Sophieninsel. It would soon be evening, and he strolled along the big pool lost in thought. Then one of the lifeguards walked up and spoke to him.

A ride? He could only be referring to the rowboats moored nearby. But of course, Kafka was not being offered a free outing. A distinguished gentleman, a Czech property developer, wanted to be ferried to the Judeninsel, on the other side of the Moldau, and the lifeguard was looking for a rower who was young and strong enough to enjoy the pleasure of the ride, but old and reliable enough to bring back the boat. Before Kafka had fully registered what was going on, Herr Trnka, who was in charge of the swimming facility, came up to him. Could this boy actually swim? The lifeguard assured him that all was well. Then the Czech passenger came. They got into the boat, and Kafka leaned into the oars and rowed across the current. Yes, of course he could swim.

It's a nice evening, said the man. *Ano*, said Kafka. But a bit on the cool side. *Ano*, Kafka replied. He was straining his lungs to speak. You row quickly, said the Czech man. Kafka barely managed a smile. He pulled up to the Judeninsel with an elegant flourish. The gentleman thanked him courteously and stepped out of the boat but forgot to tip him. It would never have occurred to the man that he might have been rowed by a thirty-seven-year-old with a doctorate in law, who served as head of his department and suffered from tuberculosis. But Kafka proudly noted everyone's amazement when he moored the boat back at the Sophieninsel in such a short time. This had been his "greatest day of glory," he wrote to Milena.[1] It was a summer's day in early August 1920.

Four months later, the streets of Prague were covered in grayish slush, and Kafka was feeling drained. He had been running a low-grade fever almost all the time, and he alternated between chills and sweating. He was short of breath, and if he fell into conversation with someone outdoors and breathed in too much cold air, a coughing fit was sure to follow. His coughing did not let up even at night, and it sometimes went on for hours on end. Everyone—his friends and family, and especially his youngest sister, Ottla—agreed that something had to be done.

Ottla was now married, and had taken the last name Davidová. Kafka was virtually oblivious to the significance of her big day, which her parents considered long overdue. His thoughts were fixated on another woman. Still, when he looked at the members of the David family—some of whom he was meeting for the first time—he became aware that on this day, something was ending *for him*. Ottla scoffed at the idea, and even during her honeymoon she continued to assure him that he had not lost a thing, but Kafka felt that this was such cold comfort, so at odds with reality, that he dismissed it with a lame joke.[2]

He had misjudged her. Although it was certainly not easy for Ottla to adapt to the role of the housewife (a role she had resisted for years), and although she was now sure that she was pregnant (just a few weeks after the wedding), her brother's problems weighed on her mind as heavily as ever. She apparently knew every detail of what had hap-

opportunity that could arise at any moment to grab the rudder with a single firm resolution? Hadn't she patiently listened to, encouraged, and consoled him? It is certainly conceivable that memories of the Askanischer Hof were flashing through Kafka's mind at this time; there, too, they had had every right to demand explanations, but he could not provide them, and these explanations applied not to the open horizon of life but solely to the past. A tribunal that assessed the guilt and that could not, even in the unlikely event that he was acquitted, bring back a spark of lost hope. The difference was that this time Kafka saw the tribunal coming, which gave him the opportunity to claim the place of the judge and to adjourn the confrontation on his own authority. On the morning of December 2, the decision had been reached. After another virtually sleepless night, he abruptly changed direction and fled.

> I don't have the strength to leave; I can't bear the thought in advance of standing before you—I can't bear the pressure in my brain. Your letter is one unstoppable, boundless disappointment in me, and now this as well. You write that you have no hope, but you do have the hope of being able to leave me completely.
>
> I can't explain to you or to anybody what it's like inside me. How could I begin to explain why this is so; I can't even explain it to myself. But even this is not the main thing; the main thing is obvious: it is impossible to live like a human being around me; you see this and yet don't want to believe it?[7]

Two weeks later, Kafka sat in a train heading *east*. It was high time, and the constant questions about what he was still doing in Prague, with his depressing medical prognosis, in the dead of winter, were wearing at his nerves. Those who were pressuring him the most (including, most likely, Ottla) brought him to the train station. Ottla had wanted to travel there with him for a few days, but because of her pregnancy (and perhaps also because she was afraid of contagion), she decided to stay home in a safer environment. He rode second class, as he had when he went to Merano in the spring. But this time he would not be greeted by fragrant blossoms or palm trees.

He arrived late at night. An open carriage drawn by two horses was waiting at the train station, and took him for a thirty-minute ride through dark woods and over fields of snow that glistened in the moonlight. Then the sanatorium appeared. It looked like a single large building, brightly lit all around, like a hotel. But the coachman did not turn yet, and in a few seconds, Kafka was again enveloped in darkness. Eventually the vehicle came to a stop in front of a smaller, unlit building off to the side. There was no one around, and help had to be summoned. It took quite a while for the maid to come and take Kafka to his room through an ice-cold corridor. When the electric light was switched on, he was appalled at what he saw. Did they really expect him to live here? An old, broken closet, a simple door to the balcony with the wind whistling through the cracks, and instead of the central heating he was anticipating, a smoke-filled wood-burning stove. But the worst part was the iron bed; the mattress did not even have linens. He had no intention of lying down in that bed; he would rather spend the night in the easy chair with a blanket and foot muff.

Frau Forberger, the plump owner, came in to welcome Kafka. She had replied to his last-minute inquiry immediately and described her sanatorium in the best possible light, which gave Kafka the right to point out clearly that he had expected something quite different. And while she tried to calm down her guest with friendly but vague promises, Kafka was already thinking about where he could find a carriage for the following day to get him out of there as quickly as possible.

Eventually the maid came up with a brilliant idea. Kafka had come alone, but a room had been prepared for his sister, and Kafka had not been able to cancel it in time because the telephone system was out of order. It was a much better, larger, and warmer room, with a wooden bed and a new closet, although lacking the all-important balcony. Kafka could stay there and use the balcony of the (worse) adjacent room for the prescribed rest cure. And that is how it was worked out. When he woke up the next morning, he found that luck was with him. Ottla had brought him luck, even here.

Kafka was in a small hamlet in the High Tatras, with lodgings for out-of-towners spread out across a wide area: the former Matlarenau, situated in the Carpathian German settlement area—then Hungarian Matlárháza, now Slovakian Tatranské Matliary—nine hundred meters high, surrounded by coniferous forests, with a view of snow-covered ridges and the high-alpine Lomnický štít. Kafka was delighted to find that his "Villa Tatra" was sheltered from the wind on a big forest glade, and the sun had free access to his balcony and room, which faced south. And it was quiet all around; the place seemed nearly empty. He decided to try it out here, and told Frau Forberger that he would be staying for the time being. He figured he could find something better in a few weeks, but he kept that thought to himself.

He went over to the main building, to the breakfast room. He was curious to see the other guests, yet afraid of demanding encounters: the old familiar ambivalence. He would stay long enough to see the vast majority of them leave. But he could not know that quite yet.

CHAPTER TWENTY-ONE

Fever and Snow: Tatranské Matliary

I don't understand the demise of the hero—deep down in my heart, that is.

—Wittgenstein, *Tagebücher*, 1931

"THE GENTLEMAN WHO LIVES DOWNSTAIRS FROM YOU IS ASKING whether you would like to visit him sometime." Kafka had no real interest in doing so. He knew the man in passing, but they had exchanged only a few words. He was a friendly Czech man, about fifty years old. Apart from coughing and the ringing the bell in his room from time to time, he barely made a sound even during the day, and he evidently had no one here to talk to. The two other Czech patients, both women, had no interest in him, and certainly not the Czech officers from the military hospital even higher up the mountain, who used the sanatorium only as lodgings and for romantic trysts. It would be difficult to turn down a straightforward request. To make it clear that he was stopping by for only a brief courtesy call, Kafka went down to see him shortly before dinner, but the Czech man insisted he return afterwards.

The man was lying in bed, as he did most of the time, because he was suffering from an advanced stage of tuberculosis that had spread to his larynx. A long-winded recitation of the details of his illness was sure to follow. Kafka had listened to enough dinner table conversations the populated hills. Moreover, there was a group of health resorts for more discriminating guests; both the comfort and the hygienic conditions were well above the standard of the rest of Slovakia. Before the war, the High Tatras had been a popular summer resort for people from Budapest. Little by little, electric railways and paved roads had made the major health spas accessible, and after the war, this infrastructure was maintained for use by the emerging winter sports tourism.

But of course Dr. Kral had in mind a sanatorium that specialized in lung disease, with strict medical supervision and customized diets. Matliary did not begin to fit this description. Evidently Kafka had selected this place because of the low price, the prospect of vegetarian food, and an explicit promise that he would have the opportunity to garden. But Matliary catered to everyone, including skiers and hunters; food was served to order (lodgers were charged only for what they ate), and those in need of medical and nursing care—about thirty long-term guests in the winter—had to make private arrangements with the staff on call. The only physician was a Dr. Leopold Strelinger, a married, middle-aged, affable Jewish man who also lived in the Villa Tatra, just three doors down from Kafka. Kafka arranged to meet with this supposed lung specialist every morning but reserved the right to decide for himself which advice he would follow. Naturally, he refused the arsenic injections that Strelinger recommended (and always carried with him), and he cut the amount of milk and fresh cream he was told to use in half. Kafka noticed that Strelinger proved to be attentive even to severely ill patients, but he was an eternal optimist, which seemed unwarranted in view of his rather limited medical range and the fact that he did not keep up with the latest scientific advances.

The detailed reports Kafka sent to Prague show that the concerns about his medical care were well founded. A whole chorus of voices begged him to find a more suitable place as soon as possible. His mother contacted her brother Siegfried, the country doctor from Moravia, and Hermann Kafka even thought of going to Matliary himself and taking matters into his own hands. There was a real, well-known sanatorium specializing in lung disease just an hour's drive in Nový Smokovec, at one thousand meters above sea level. Kafka had brochures of this place, as well, but although he kept thinking of transferring there, it took him three full months to have a look.

As usual, he had trouble bringing himself to make changes in his daily life and habits, but this time, the obstacles proved insurmountable. In January 1921, Kafka was mired in a crisis that manifested itself in a nerve-racking sensitivity to noise. He decided not to move into the main building, which was far more comfortable and had central heating—but the newly installed "music room" posed a major threat—yet although the rooms adjacent to and above him were almost always vacant, he writhed in his reclining chair with heart problems, "almost in convulsions." All it took was for someone to hum a song beneath his balcony or for the sound of a soft but penetrating voice of some "foreign devil" to come from the floor above, several windows away, or the whistling of a handyman. At times, the psychological stress escalated to the point that Kafka considered fleeing to a better sanatorium, but a moment of reflection was all he needed to realize how he would fare in the far livelier Nový Smokovec, which was full of coughing, and the thoroughfare with the electric railway could be heard from every balcony. What good would the best chief physician be under those circumstances? Kafka was happy to forgo that experience. Of course, he had to wonder what part of the world he *would* find habitable if his nerves did not calm down soon. "At the moment everything gets on my nerves," he complained to Brod, "sometimes it almost seems to me that life itself is what gets on my nerves; how otherwise could everything be so nerve-racking?"[3]

Especially the people. From the start, Kafka was determined to avoid the typical health resort chumminess that grew out of boredom and force of habit. He was nursing his wounds. The act of grieving had drained him, and his fear of painful interactions, particularly with women, now far outweighed his social needs. Whenever he had to, he put on his usual engaging smile. He got along quite well with Frau Forberger, the owner, and he stayed on good terms with the staff with generous tips—especially in the kitchen, where he had numerous special requests. Only the dining room, with its assigned seats, remained a danger zone where things could easily take a disastrous turn, as they had in Merano.

The dining room was a likely spot to hear "innocuous" anti-Semitism, which had seemed omnipresent since the war. At Kafka's table, it was represented by a perfumed, powdered, nervous, and chatty

Czech "elderly lady" who was seated next to him one evening. His exasperation rose to the point of almost physical revulsion, and he had trouble calming down in his room after his first encounter with her. Kafka devised a devilishly underhanded scheme to set things straight: He would reveal that he was a Jew at the most embarrassing possible moment for her, and then she would surely steer clear of him. But he was wrong. The woman, who seemed to despise anything that was not Czech, proceeded to shower affection on her Jewish tablemate. And when Kafka learned that she was quite ill and had been bedridden with fever for days at a time, the tension melted away. In Matliary, Kafka felt the first stirrings of solidarity with the ailing, and it wiped out any feeling of wanting to differentiate himself from them; he even thought of trying to make up for his previous attitude. What did this frail woman have to do with the rabid hatred of Jews he had "bathed in" in Prague just a few weeks earlier? Kafka knew the true source of his sensitivity.

Arthur Szinay, an emissary from an altogether different world, sat right across from the two of them. Szinay was a twenty-five-year-old Jewish man from Košice in eastern Slovakia who was suffering from dyspepsia and would soon learn that his lungs were also infected. The elderly lady was surely dismissive of Szinay, but Kafka considered him "a young man to fall in love with."

> Charming in the eastern European Jewish sense. Full of irony, restlessness, moodiness, confidence, but also neediness. Everything is "interesting, interesting" to him, but not in the usual sense; it means something like, "It's burning, it's burning." He is a Socialist, but produces a great deal of Hebrew from his childhood memories, has studied the Talmud and the Shulchan Aruch. "Interesting, interesting."[4]

So this was a "hot Jew" of the kind Kafka had encountered among eastern European Jewish actors, especially in the unforgettable Yitzhak Löwy. As it turned out, Szinay attended every possible public lecture and gathering, and he reverently recalled seeing Max Brod in his hometown. He had even met Georg Langer in Langer's ultra-Orthodox phase. And now he had the good fortune to sit at a dinner table with a good friend of these celebrities. Szinay was overjoyed; Kafka almost had trouble steering clear of him.

Communication was quite difficult because Szinay's native language was Hungarian, and he had just started learning German in Matliary. He spoke neither Czech nor Slovak. He found everything Kafka told him "wonderful" but had to admit that he understood "less than half of it." Even so, Kafka felt that no one had ever listened to him with this degree of concentration and understanding, even if Kafka was merely rattling off the history of his stomach ailments.

Hungarian was the major language of communication in the small international group that had come together in the sanatorium in Matliary. The staff also spoke Hungarian, so the extremely sociable Szinay was in no danger of growing lonely. If Kafka disappeared into his room or made it clear that he wanted to be alone, he kept company with a young medical student from Budapest, who was almost as "interesting" and well-educated. Szinay kept insisting that the two of them ought to get to know each other. Why? Kafka asked. Why? The medical student echoed warily, since he was not fond of idle chatter. "Because I don't understand him and don't understand you. I am sure that you will understand each other." Despite this persuasive argument, it took some time for the meeting that Szinay was pushing so hard to take place.

It happened when Kafka was walking down the country road, because the forest paths were still piled up with snow, and a vaguely familiar-looking man from Budapest came strolling toward him with a book in German under his arm. Kafka peeked over at the book, said hello, and could not help commenting on it. "Are you Herr Kafka from Prague?" the young man asked. "Herr Szinay talks about you almost every day." And he told Kafka his name and profession: Robert Klopstock, medical student.[5]

It is not easy to conceive of a profession that would have done full justice to Kafka's peculiar combination of social skills and inhibitions. His bosses had never expressed any doubts that Kafka was cut out for work at the institute. Kafka's conscientiousness, linguistic precision, and negotiating skills made him the paragon of a civil servant. But Kafka himself doubted the legitimacy of his job at the insurance institute. No one outside this building—indeed, not even his colleagues in the rooms next door—would have been able to explain exactly what his duties were. Everything was too abstract and too detached from clients, who were reduced to case studies of insurance law or statistics.

Kafka's desire to observe the lives and struggles of people up close was rarely fulfilled in this profession; he was usually stuck behind piles of documents. But this desire grew as the years went by. Earlier in his life, he had satisfied it by reading a great range of biographies and autobiographical documents—not only of writers with whose lives he could identify—but now he focused increasingly on people in his vicinity. As he grew older, he was drawn to the lives of younger people who enjoyed varied and incomparably more attractive options than were available to Kafka himself. When and by whom were the courses set for these lives? Could these young people be guided, or even actively led? This was one of the few social questions—like his interest in progressive education—that fascinated him on a theoretical as well as a practical level. Particularly in his social actions, however, an unmistakable pedagogical inclination began to prevail.

The pattern came from his relationships with his sisters, especially with Ottla. At first, he had limited himself to widening her intellectual horizons by reading aloud to her and improvising little lectures, but he soon realized that the satisfaction that both derived went beyond the mere dissemination of knowledge. Kafka was certainly proud when Ottla could come up with an apt quotation from Plato, but far more meaningful was her pleasure in fresh insights, her heightened capacity for reflective perception, and her growing awareness of her own abilities and her own position in the world. But this maturation process could not be steered, only activated, and the results were unpredictable. The best that could be done was to respect the interests, the capabilities, and the limits of the other, and then let things take their course. Kafka began to accept the paradox that the teacher even had to subordinate himself to his pupil because a willingness to absorb and embrace something previously unknown is a quality that one cannot spark in others without having it oneself. Every teacher still has something to learn, and Kafka even acknowledged that in working with Jewish children from the east—in the refugee school in Prague or at the Home in Berlin—the teachers were the ones who derived the greater benefit.

Kafka's pedagogical skill in ferreting out, reflecting, and developing potential drew young people to him. Gustav Janouch and Hans Klaus virtually worshiped Kafka's unpedantic yet subtly compelling authority. Minze Eisner, whom Kafka met in Schelesen, was just shy of twenty and interested in agriculture. She found the sporadic correspondence with Kafka so meaningful that she kept it up for years and continually sought his advice (knowing full well that he always advised work and never relaxation). Similar relationships developed in Matliary, which in turn led to flurries of correspondence. The educational gap between Kafka and Julie Wohryzek must have tempted him more than once to spice up summer boat trips with a little tutoring, and even his correspondence with Felice and Milena had traces of a teacher-pupil rhetoric, although Kafka never explicitly pointed out his edge in knowledge and experience.

But his pedagogical pièce de résistance was his friendship with Robert Klopstock, who became Kafka's unwitting apprentice within the space of a few days. "Kafka's nature," he recalled decades later, "was so all-encompassing and overwhelming, yet devoid of any authority or power, that [I] asked no questions regarding his credentials or confirming his nature."[6] Oddly, for the first few weeks, he did not even seem to know who Kafka was. Dr. Kafka had introduced himself to everyone as an ordinary insurance official, so his new friends were intrigued to learn that the prominent Max Brod was planning to visit him in Matliary. Neither the solicitous Szinay nor the erudite Klopstock had any idea at first that Kafka was a writer. But of course, this could not be concealed indefinitely. Legend has it that when Kafka was asked whether he was the author of *A Country Doctor*, he replied in a whisper: "Oh no, not that."[7]

Klopstock was an anxious, melancholy man subject to severe mood swings, and his self-contradictory nature was a source of annoyance to others throughout his life. He was born in 1899 in Dombóvár, a small town in Hungary south of Lake Balaton, where his Jewish father held the post of "imperial Hungarian state railway chief engineer." After Adolf Klopstock's early death, his wife Gizella (née Spitz) moved to

Budapest with their two sons, Robert ("Robi") and Hugo Georg. Little is known about the time Robert spent at the Humanistisches Gymnasium, the high school he entered in 1912, but by the age of seventeen, he was proficient enough in German to read classical poetry and read it aloud to his friends. He evidently associated with Hungarian writers even at that time, but—as his outstanding grades on his transcript show—he was just as talented in the natural sciences. He apparently chose to study medicine for ethical reasons. Although he received his religious instruction from rabbis, Klopstock developed a strong affinity for Christian values, and he told Kafka, who recognized Klopstock's "need for people, the way a born doctor needs people," that Jesus was his personal guide.[8]

Evidently his wartime experiences reinforced his resolve. During his first semester in medical school, he was drafted into the army. He served in a medical corps, and was sent to the eastern front and to Italy. This chapter of Klopstock's life remains an odd lacuna in his biography; there are no extant recollections of the horrors he must have experienced here as an eighteen-year-old. It was apparently only after the war that he learned that he had been infected with tuberculosis in the medical barracks. In the fall of 1920, he interrupted his study of medicine and spent years in and out of sanatoriums, returning to the High Tatras several times before he was pronounced healthy.

While in Matliary, Kafka repeated a tried-and-true pattern of behavior: he turned the person closest to him at the time into a mediator and messenger to blunt the impact of the rest of the social world. Klopstock was ready and willing to assume this position. "Actually, I associate only with the medical student," Kafka wrote back home to Prague, "everything else is incidental. If someone wants something from me, he tells it to the medical student. If I want something of anyone, I do the same."[9] This assertion appears to be gainsaid by group photos showing Kafka relaxed and almost youthful in an obviously close group of fellow patients, but he used his relationship with Klopstock to pool his social contacts. He now had his meals brought to his room without fearing isolation, and "the medical student" also lent him a helping hand with his medical care. In return, Klopstock gained an adviser who knew how to listen carefully and was not thrown by social ineptitude and inexplicable moods. Now he understood why the dyspeptic Szinay had been so enthusiastic. For quite some time, Klopstock had been agonizing over a doomed love affair, and evidently his emotional ups and downs were written all over his face. He often seemed morose (as photographs show), which did not always win over friends, but Kafka was captivated by him. "I haven't ever seen such a diabolical spectacle from close up," he wrote to Ottla. "Hard to say whether good or evil powers are at work there; in any case, they are incredibly strong. In the Middle Ages, he would have been regarded as possessed. Yet he is a young man of twenty-one, tall, broad, hearty, red-cheeked—extremely intelligent, truly unselfish, considerate." Klopstock's boyish absent-mindedness seems to have aroused first Kafka's sympathy and then his feelings of friendship. He found Klopstock "positively handsome" when Klopstock, with a serious face, half-alert yet absorbed in daydreams, lay in bed in his nightshirt "with tousled hair." After only about two weeks, Kafka asked Ottla to send a package of books for Klopstock from his private collection—a rare honor.[10]

Klopstock must have been deeply impressed to find that one could have long and serious discussions about Zionism, Christianity, Dostoevsky, and love and clown around and think up practical jokes with one and the same person. They made fun of a Czech guest, a high-ranking officer who sat in his room playing the flute at regular intervals and could also be spotted sketching and painting outdoors. One day, this loner, whose name was Holub, decided to exhibit his artwork in Matliary. It was rather amateurish, and although it was sure to be a big hit at a sanatorium in the High Tatras, *healthy* art connoisseurs would ignore it. Kafka and Klopstock wondered how this man might react if he were to see his name in print, and they sprang into action. Kafka wrote a brief, anonymous review that heaped accolades on Holub's work for the German-language *Karpathen-Post*, and Klopstock came up with something similar for a Hungarian newspaper. And this prank caught fire in a most unexpected manner, when Holub, who could not read the Hungarian review, approached a waiter who was originally from Budapest, who in turn led him unsuspectingly to Klopstock, who, the waiter explained, was an educated man and would surely be the best person to translate it. As it happened, Klopstock was in bed that day with a slight fever, and Kafka was sitting with him when Captain Holub came into the room with the Hungarian newspaper. We can picture the scene that followed because Kafka wrote to his sister that he had spent half the afternoon laughing. Once this little farce had worked out so well, he lost no time in concocting the next one. He sent Ottla an article from the Brno daily newspaper *Lidové Noviny* in which German authorities were cited who claimed that Einstein's theory of relativity provided the basis for new tuberculosis therapy. But although he pointed out that he himself had fallen for this joke, which was printed in the April 1 edition of the newspaper, the whole family's hopes soared, and Kafka finally had to pull the plug: "You are really quite stubborn once you fall for an April Fool's joke."[11]

This was just a bit of delightful childishness, the joy of simple freedom from responsibility, which Kafka had long found an excellent way to recuperate. Nearly a decade earlier, at the Jungborn sanatorium, he had stayed on the sidelines, and in Schelesen he had been unselfconscious and even a little silly from time to time, but in Matliary he indulged in memories, daydreams, and sometimes the innocuous activities of the spa guests, who all considered him nice. Kafka was doing next to nothing here. He did not have the strength to take long walks, and he didn't read much beyond *Selbstwehr* and *Die Fackel*. It often took him days to finish writing a letter, he had ceased any work on literary texts, and when he was not out and about with Klopstock, he lay in the lounge chair on his balcony, a bottle of milk always within reach. He spent hours staring at the clouds or dozing on a quiet, secluded forest glade, letting the time pass by almost contentedly. And he defended this refuge and guarded against disturbances even from far away. "Don't write anymore," he wrote to Milena Pollak in early January, "don't write anymore and make sure we never meet again." This was no longer a mere request. Kafka was determined to lock away the past (even if it was not really in the past) in some inaccessible spot and throw away the key. He wrote to Brod that if Milena turned up in Prague or gave in to her father's pressure and traveled to the Tatra Mountains to convalesce, he wanted to be informed without delay in order to nip any surprises in the bud.[12]

He had turned his back on reality. Since creeping half-conscious out of his severely ill neighbor's room, he knew that there were good reasons to flee. Kafka's regression was apparently more than mere recuperation from the psychological stress of 1920, which had swirled around Milena like a huge vortex; he was also trying to dodge the new concrete shape his illness had taken, and he retreated into a fog for days on end. He admitted to Brod that he felt as though he were living outside the world, and implied that he was not eager to return. He avoided providing concrete details about his illness, no matter what anyone said.

Brod seems to have been the only one to frown on this strategy of denial during these months; his parents and others were duly impressed by his recuperative progress. As long as Kafka reported that he was gaining weight nicely—eight pounds in the first month—he had little fear of skeptical inquiries. He did his best to keep coming up with impressive numbers. Despite his distressing lack of appetite, and although the cooking in Matliary soon grew monotonous, he cleaned off his plate at every meal and even forced himself to eat meat. Not until March, when the end of his sick leave was fast approaching, did he have to admit that the symptoms of tuberculosis were not letting up, and that he had even experienced a desperate shortness of breath during a stretch of stormy weather. Dr. Strelinger noted a slight improvement in Kafka's condition—although he merely listened to Kafka's lungs and failed to order a sputum test—but he strongly urged an extension of his sick leave and warned that there would be a severe relapse if Kafka were to return to the office in March. That ultimately persuaded his headstrong patient, who seemed to fear reproaches from the Workers' Accident Insurance Institute more than the illness itself and was getting a bad feeling. At the eleventh hour, Kafka sent a call for help to Prague, which made Ottla head straight to the director. And Kafka was in luck once again: although he could not even produce a doctor's note from Matliary at first, and although he "forgot" to get an official medical examination in Prague, Odstrčil authorized an extension of his leave by two months, and later even by an additional quarter of a year, until August, at full pay. There had to be more to it than Ottla's diplomatic skill. Kafka could not help but suspect that in the longer and longer periods of absence he had proved to be expendable, even though the director was incredibly kindly, like a guardian angel.

Kafka breathed his first big sigh of relief when the winter storms died down and spring finally came to the High Tatras. In April, he was happy to report that he was nearly fever-free and that his coughing and shortness of breath had improved. Of course, this success was overshadowed by a whole series of ailments that kept him in bed for days at a time: colds, painful abscesses, and a severe intestinal catarrh with spikes in his fever that made him think that the end was near. He felt as though he was coming apart at the seams, and when he looked back at the times in Zürau and Merano, he had to admit that his health was going downhill, and that physical disorders had never dominated his life to this extent. Even the "objective findings" about his lungs, with which Brod kept trying to console him and which he considered the only essential factor, paled beside the evidence that his condition was deteriorating. Kafka's messages to Prague became more sporadic, and it took a medical "questionnaire" from Brod to elicit the information that Kafka had brought his weight up to sixty-five kilograms (which represented a gain of eight kilos) after months of dedicated effort. "You keep on writing about getting well," he wrote wearily. "That is out of the question for me."[13]

What could help him at this point? Everyone, evidently including Klopstock, recommended a change of scenery. Max Brod even suggested that they take a three-week vacation together at the Baltic Sea, accompanied by his new mistress. Impossible, Kafka replied; the doctor had strictly ruled out a maritime climate. Then maybe a summer resort with Ottla and her husband? He had reservations about that, as well. Kafka was ashamed of his constant coughing and bringing up phlegm, and even though he did not really believe that a person in the pink of health could be infected with tuberculosis, it still seemed irresponsible to expose Ottla's first child—Věra, who was born in March—to weeks of "filth." Moreover, the Davids had chosen Taus (Domažlice) in western Bohemia, at the north slope of the Bohemian Forest, as their vacation spot, and only about twenty miles from there, easy to reach by train, was the sanatorium where Milena was convalescing at this very moment. That was out of the question.[14]

Kafka remained so firmly fixed in place that he seemed to take root. Even the summer onslaught of tourists made no impression on him, and at some points he felt as though he would never get away from the High Tatras again unless he was brought home or carried off along with his lounge chair. There was no doubt that in this state of lethargy, he would have offered little resistance to any visitor from Prague who forced him to leave, but no one had the time to travel to Matliary. Ottla's baby's insatiable appetite weakened her and brought her to the brink of despair. And now that Brod had given up on his misguided attempt to live on royalties from the theater and had accepted a government post in the press department, which required minimal hours at the office but frequent attendance at Czech music and theater performances, he was unavailable as well. There was no chance that Baum or Weltsch would show up. They had not heard from Kafka for quite a long time, and they figured he was out of circulation. Not a single person came to visit him for three quarters of a year. His only company came from Szinay and Klopstock, Dr. Strelinger and Frau Forberger, the kitchen help and the Jewish waiter, and a few ailing women and a cheerful dental technician with whom he went on two or three excursions. Although there was plenty of friendliness, courtesy, and even admiration, did anyone really get to know him in all these months?

His return to Prague was delayed yet again. On August 14, 1921, about a week before he was to resume his duties at the office, Kafka awoke with a fever. His cough became deeper and kept him awake at night. Nothing serious, Dr. Strelinger told him; relapses of this kind were known to happen, and his lungs were looking good. Nevertheless, Kafka had to write a note excusing his absence to his director for the umpteenth time. Finally, on August 26, he boarded the train. He had written to Prague a few days earlier that he would not need to be picked up in the Tatras and would manage the trip alone. Now he regretted this decision. All the cars in the train were overcrowded. Weak with fever, he tried to sit on a suitcase, but later he even had to stand. His penny-pinching had compromised his health once again. He would have had an easier time with a first-class ticket. That was not something he could tell people at home.

Then a minor miracle came to pass. A first-class compartment had been occupied by four passengers who did not have any claim to it but were tired of standing for hours. These travelers, among them two railway employees and a woman whom Kafka knew slightly, had convinced the conductor to reclassify the compartment in view of the difficult situation, that is, to downgrade it to second class. The conductor did not want to turn them down, and started to post a big "2" on the door, but he had failed to take the other passengers' touchiness into consideration. There were two more people in the train compartment who had actually paid for first class, and they demanded to be reseated in a different compartment so as not to have to sit side by side with holders of second-class tickets. This freed up additional seats, and Kafka, who was feeling desperate by this point, was told he could occupy of one of them—a belated benefit of the Austro-Hungarian monarchy's caste consciousness.

We do not know how Kafka was welcomed back. He looked suntanned and well-nourished, in good enough shape to head for the Moldau swimming pool, yet people could not help but notice all his coughing. The "imminent recovery" that Dr. Strelinger kept promising if Kafka would only stay in the mountains long enough seemed highly unlikely. Maybe it was better for him not to hold his five-month-old niece Věra, whom he soon saw for the first time. But when he told everyone how well he had been taken care of in Matliary, they were willing to believe that perhaps it had been the right place after all and that he was actually returning from a long, long vacation.

He knew better, and had for some time. When he returned to the familiar world, with the need to recall and recount, everything he had suppressed came back to the surface. "It was a mistake," he had admitted to Brod back in the winter, "that I did not previously live with consumptives and as yet have not looked the disease straight in the eye. I have done that here for the first time."[15] This experience had been awful, and although he had to keep it from his parents, he could not forget it. And at some point in the coming weeks and months, he could not help feeling that the time had come to act on what he had learned. So he picked up a piece of paper and wrote down the following lines:

> Dearest Max, my final request: Everything I leave behind (that is, in my bookcase, linen closet, desk at home and in the office, or anywhere else has wound up that you notice) in the way of diaries, manuscripts, letters (from others and my own), sketches, and so

forth, to be burned completely and unread, as well as all writings and sketches you or others may have, and ask for them in my name. If people choose not to give you letters, they should at least pledge to burn them themselves.

Yours,
Franz Kafka[16]

CHAPTER TWENTY-TWO

The Internal and the External Clock

They that are with me have not understood me.

—*The Vercelli Acts*

THE ELOCUTIONIST LUDWIG HARDT WAS A BUSY MAN. IN HIS ADopted hometown of Berlin alone, he appeared onstage in dozens of well-attended events every year after the war, in addition to lecture tours that brought him to German-speaking areas throughout Europe. In April 1920, he performed in Munich. Thomas Mann wanted to see this virtuoso of the art of recitation up close. He invited Hardt to his villa, asked him to read aloud Mann's own story, "The Wardrobe," and on the following evening saw him at the lectern, thereby gaining an impression that went beyond the scope of a typical reading because Hardt was able to highlight the interplay of voice modulation, mime, and gestures like a complex musical score. His poise and versatility were compelling, and made every text he recited—poem, fairy tale, story, drama—dazzling from the very first line. At the same time, Hardt largely dispensed with the usual declamatory grandeur, and even went so far as to shrink the distance between the podium and the audience for a short time. When he imitated a famous actor to perfection—a popular variety act—Hardt himself burst out laughing.

Thomas Mann immediately agreed to support Hardt, who was none too successful in Munich, by writing a short review. For the final sentence, he chose the well-known closing line of Heinrich Kleist's "Anecdote from the Last Prussian War": "'In all my life,' said the innkeeper, 'I have never seen a fellow like that.'"[1]

Hardt, who was born in 1886 and trained as an actor in Berlin, had a slight build that contrasted oddly with his prominent nose and markedly receding forehead; he was once called "a goblin with a Caesar mask."[2] No one would have ever believed that this mercurial man was the pupil of Emil Milan, who worshiped the classics, and he had nothing whatsoever in common with the pseudo-sacred demeanor that the dramatist Gerhart Hauptmann adopted when stepping up to the podium. Hardt relied exclusively on the impact of his words, which he tried to tap to their full potential, and he often exploited the sparks that were sure to ignite when texts of different genres, different quality, and different eras were juxtaposed. The range of his repertoire was enormous. He recited almost everything by heart, and because he brought together classic texts with the most recent German literature in a very natural manner, his recitations always retained a playful character and appeared to be entertaining experiments with uncertain outcomes. Hardt achieved an eerie intensity when astounding the public with the current relevance of long-familiar plays. The poems of Heinrich Heine were particularly well suited to his presentations. Thomas Mann wrote that anyone who had not heard Ludwig Hardt recite Heine's "The Migratory Rats" could not begin to know the poem.

At some point during the winter of 1920–1921, Hardt came across the *Country Doctor* stories, which were barely known in Germany at that time—presumably on the recommendation of Tucholsky—and he decided to rehearse and perform some of them. The effect on audiences must have been extraordinary: according to the *Vossische Zeitung* critic who reviewed a performance by Hardt, Kafka's prose piece "Eleven Sons" made "the most powerful impression of the evening." The other writers whose works he recited that evening were Robert Walser, Georg Heym, Christian Morgenstern, Liliencron, Maupassant, Scheerbart, Börne, and Heine.[3] It must have impressed even Kafka (to whom Brod sent the good news to Matliary right away) that Hardt, in addition to two other pieces by him, had selected "Eleven

Sons," an enigmatic rhetorical text without any plot to speak of or message, a text in which everything depended on language and thus on a precise delivery. Kafka must have been aware of the strategic implications of this event for publicizing his name: if Hardt, whose name was far better known to audiences interested in literature than his own, took to the road with such a brilliant performance, it amounted to an advertising campaign. "In many cities," Soma Morgenstern, a friend of Hardt, recalled decades later, "people were hearing the name Franz Kafka for the first time at a Ludwig Hardt performance. In many newspapers, Franz Kafka's name was appearing for the first time, as an author whose prose Ludwig Hardt had recited."[4]

Of course, Hardt's name had been known in Prague for quite some time, even before 1914. Max Brod had briefly introduced him to Kafka,[5] but the war had prevented them from meeting again. In January 1921, Hardt returned to Prague with new material. His audiences were as enthusiastic as ever, and a third performance had to be arranged at short notice, but at this point Kafka was bedridden with fever during a snowstorm in Matliary and was probably unable even to follow the newspaper reports. Finally, that fall, there was news that Hardt was returning to the Mozarteum in Prague with a sensational act, and this time everyone involved was in attendance.

Hardt recited Kafka. Once again, he had selected three pieces from the *Country Doctor*, including "Eleven Sons," which he had used on several other occasions. Right before him, in the auditorium, was the friendly-looking creator of this diamond, surrounded by his closest friends, which was surely no everyday occurrence even for the elocutionist who was used to being invited to the homes of famous writers. He presented portions of his Berlin act, again placing Kafka side by side with Robert Walser, but afterwards took on the challenge of presenting scenes from *The Last Days of Mankind*, with which Karl Kraus, the author, had already personally curdled the blood of the people of Prague in this same hall.[6] Hardt did not shy away from comparisons with this other demon of literary recitation. And his success proved him right. The audience applauded and cheered until Hardt returned to the podium to recite some Gottfried Keller poems as a soothing finale. He knew everything and could do everything.[7]

This was the first time Kafka was hearing his own texts through the medium of a professional elocutionist, and it was one of his now-rare moments of happy excitement. "Please accept my thanks for the hours my heart was pounding with joy and awe," he wrote to Hardt, without exaggeration.[8] Hardt had made it evident—and for Kafka, this was like coming home after years astray—that he could feel comfortable and at ease in the enormous echo chamber of literary tradition. Hardt did not appear to draw a distinction between life and art; his emphasis was genuine, and Kafka was especially impressed by the fact that this Jewish performer could put on a brilliant show in a coffeehouse with eastern European Jewish jokes just as easily as in an auditorum with Heine's poems.

The evening after Hardt's performance, the two of them had an opportunity to talk at length, in part about the finer points of literary recitation. Over the following days, they met at the Hotel Blauer Stern and even at the Workers' Accident Insurance Institute, where a lucky set of circumstances put Hardt's sense of humor to mimetic advantage. Hardt was sitting on the visitor's chair at Kafka's office at the time they had arranged, waiting for Kafka, whose hat was displayed prominently on his desk. When Kafka came in a few minutes later, and—politely as ever—began to excuse himself for making Hardt wait, the latter replied drily, "The hat stood in for you perfectly."[9] This quintessential Kafka statement perfectly captured his position at the Workers' Accident Insurance Institute, or even in the world at large. Kafka laughed in relief. This was certainly different from the pompous nonsense that the *Prager Tagblatt* had been spreading about him lately, to the effect that Kafka was "an individual who needs a mediator like Hardt to emerge from his isolation." Did all of Prague need to know that? But Kafka had to admit that the hack writer was right.

Kafka worried that he would not see Hardt for months. He was not able to attend the second evening performance because his fever had returned, which was even more unfortunate because Hardt—in response to Kafka's request—had included a prose piece they both loved: Kleist's "Anecdote from the Last Prussian War." Luckily, Hardt spent a few more days in Prague than he had planned. Two additional performances were arranged, and Kafka used this unexpected opportunity to give him a book with a dedication (Hebel's *Treasure Chest*, "to give pleasure to Hebel"). After that, the elocutionist left Prague, and they stayed in contact only on occasion. But these encounters in Prague had left a lasting impression on Hardt. Even before he returned to Berlin, he urged Kurt Wolff to pay more attention to Kafka, who might well be Wolff's most important author. He continued to recite "Eleven Sons" often, and soon—as Tucholsky reported enthusiastically in the *Weltbühne*—he also included the spectacular "Report to an Academy" in his program.

Max Brod was certainly pleased to see Kafka return to the world of people so quickly, but he had only a vague, and far too innocuous, notion of the psychological isolation into which his friend had slipped during the long months in Matliary. It simply seemed to him as though Kafka had pampered himself far too much there and thus opened the floodgates to the ghosts of hypochondria. Now he was back in the city, which would surely be good for him.

The change in Kafka was truly remarkable. Although he was suffering from coughing fits and constant fever with the onset of the fall season, and he rarely ventured out onto the street when it rained, he struck up new social relationships, got together with old friends, such as Werfel and Langer, and received quite a few visitors: Ernst Weiss, Albert Ehrenstein, his "pupil" Minze Eisner, and at least two acquaintances from Matliary, including the very lively Szinay. And then there were the draining conversations with Janouch, who now lived outside of Prague but continued to come by the institute.

Kafka also went to great lengths to ease the way for Klopstock. He made (ultimately unsuccessful) inroads with Jakob Hegner in Hellerau to get Klopstock a temporary job as a printer and thus a place to stay in that town, which was known as "the garden city" (of course, Kafka had a medical idea in mind), and he sought out opportunities for the nearly penniless Klopstock to get journalistic assignments and continue his studies in Prague. Together with Weltsch, he even went to see the internist Egmont Münzer, who was a distant relative (though not someone he knew personally), to find out whether Münzer could use a

Hungarian "hospital aide."[10] Kafka tried to extend Klopstock's Czech residence permit and get him exempted from any fees, which entailed hours of waiting at administrative offices; he gathered information about possible internment because of political tensions with Hungary; and he helped restore his contact with Klopstock's older brother, Hugo Georg, who had ended up in Siberia.[11]

But far more astonishing things lay ahead. In early October, Kafka learned that Milena Pollak had completed her course of treatment in the Bohemian Forest and was spending a few days with her father in Prague on her way home. It is likely that she did not want to pass up this chance to see Kafka and deliver a message personally. She could hardly expect him to be willing to see her, after all his adamant defensive gestures, or even to receive her on his own turf. So for the first time, Milena entered the Kafkas' apartment on Altstädter Ring and saw his parents and probably also Ottla. Their reception cannot have been especially cordial ("I never got on well with his relatives," she later remarked),[12] but her conversation with Kafka himself went so well that they continued to see each other in the days that followed. In the end he opted for a single, decisive gesture, which represented a complete about-face from the silence of the previous months. He turned over all his diaries, the intimate documents of a whole decade, right down to the last page, and even tore out the pages he had written on from the most recent one—the twelfth—to complete the huge bundle.

Why? The fact that Kafka had marshalled the strength to surmount his fear of more sleepless nights and to risk another confrontation surely resulted from the inner liberation that his temporary return to "real life" and the variety of new encounters brought about. In Matliary, he had inhabited just a single psychological space, which every action on Milena's part immediately filled out to near bursting, but now he tried in essence to relocate their meeting in Prague—the first in more than a year—to an adjoining space and lock it away there both linguistically and emotionally. "I cannot say much about the main thing," he wrote to Klopstock, "for it is, even for myself, locked within the darkness of the breast, I imagine it lies there beside the disease on the same bed." He avoided putting a name to the "main thing"; he did not announce that a woman would be visiting but merely hinted at an event with the greatest possible distance, "It was extended for a day, now it is past."[13] It was the day he placed his notes in someone else's hands, forever.

There is no documentation as to what Kafka and Milena Pollak discussed in the fall of 1921, but her unexpected reconciliation with her father, the obstinate Professor Jesenský, which Kafka found incomprehensible and downright disappointing, must have been a major topic. But he was surely also tormented by Milena's implicit or explicit expectation of hearing a logical explanation of his own behavior, an explanation he had been able to provide only in bits and pieces, after dozens of attempts. After their days together in Vienna, he had toyed with the idea of unburdening himself morally and entrusting her with his case file. On several occasions, he told her he would give her the "Letter to His Father" to read, but he ultimately balked at the idea of confiding such a private matter to her.[14] Now that there was nothing left to lose, and because another fundamental revision would have been more than he could have handled, he came back to this idea, but the diary notebooks were much better than that letter. He had no other evidence on hand, and nothing more could be demanded of him. "Did you find some crucial thing against me in the diaries?" he asked her later on, emphasizing yet again that the closeness she would be sure to feel while reading them should serve not to revive the issue that was in abeyance but instead to "decide" it, that is, end it.[15]

When Milena next visited him in Prague—first in late November, then in January—Kafka had the distinct feeling that these were actually sick calls. Or had she already studied his notebooks in detail? If so, perhaps these were more like visits to a condemned man. "It is a long way," he noted, "to come from a position where I did not feel sorrowful at her departure—not truly sorrowful—to the point where I am endlessly sorrowful that she left. Of course sorrow is not the worst thing."[16]

The documentation from the second half of the year 1921 is too scanty to offer a vivid picture of Kafka's daily life, but he was clearly taxed by the effort of taking his friends' advice to work his way out of his social and intellectual lows. The first signals came from Matliary, where Kafka read Karl Kraus's latest attack on the German-Jewish literary scene, the "magic operetta" *Literature, or We'll See about That*, addressed first and foremost to Werfel, and he was inspired, during his long hours in the lounge chair, to write a broadly conceived essayistic letter to Max Brod. In early September, just after he returned, he worked his way through Flaubert's diaries, and in mid-October he decided to resume writing his own diary entries after a hiatus of nearly twenty months. He went to the New German Theater twice to see the comedian Max Pallenberg again, watched a film about Palestine, and attended a private reading, and it is quite probable that in late December he once again saw Karl Kraus in person when the latter gave another four readings in the overcrowded Mozarteum.

Without quite realizing it, Kafka had chosen a path that would lead him back to literature. There was no lack of encouragement for him to do so. In 1921, several of his shorter pieces had been reprinted in newspapers and magazines, including three in the semi-official *Prager Presse*, which had been launched at Easter. *Die neue Rundschau* published a lengthy essay by Brod bearing the title "Franz Kafka the Writer," which finally offered the prospect of nationwide attention; Milena was planning a volume with Czech translations of his works;[17] and Ludwig Hardt's recitations reminded Kafka that he was writing for more than a small group of friends. He was a writer. And never since that ill-fated reading in Munich had he realized so clearly that as a writer, he was a figure of public interest. It was actually conceivable that the much-admired Thomas Mann—to whom Hardt had read from *A Country Doctor*—would soon write something about him, and even Brockhaus Encyclopedia was showing an interest in him.[18] Until about the end of the war, Kafka was considered a local talent in German-speaking Prague; he had become a local literary celebrity, and he was dismayed to realize that the public was now able to identify him. When he showed up at an event, he drew whispered commentary, and when he was talked into dropping by Café Edison, as he did several times that winter, people stared at him so unabashedly that he took to his heels "with jangled nerves." "Nowadays I can no longer endure even people's glances," he wrote to Klopstock after an evening of this kind.[19]

He had always detested being the center of "general," feigned interest, but it was not merely a fear of people that made him stay out of the public eye. Those questioning and demanding glances in the coffeehouse were sizing him up, and they reminded Kafka of how long he had been idle. Three years, four years? Alchimistengasse had been the last time that he had not only devoted himself to long frenzied nights of literary production but looked forward to publication with happiness and pride. It was the winter of 1916 to 1917, infinitely far in the past, a time of health and hazy visions of life after the war. What followed were only his scribblings in Zürau, and they were not literature. When he opened the *Prager Presse* at Christmastime in 1921 and saw his "Bucket Rider" for the first time in print, it must have been hard for Kafka to picture the person who had written this and other texts in a cold little room on the Hradčany.

The disparity between his own unproductivity and the public's expectations after his earlier works became painfully clear when Kafka was astonished to receive a personal message from his publisher. Kurt Wolff made no attempt to disguise the fact that it had taken the initiative of a third party, as usual, to get him to write a letter. This time, the admonisher had been Ludwig Hardt. But Wolff had no intention of limiting his letter to polite inquiries about Kafka's health. He was well aware that after the endless delays in publishing the *Country Doctor* stories, he had to do right by Kafka before the author turned his back on him altogether, and so he went all out to woo Kafka.

> Our correspondence is infrequent and paltry. None of the authors with whom we are associated approaches us with requests or questions as infrequently as you do, and none gives us the same impression that what happens on the market to the books we publish is such a matter of indifference. It seems appropriate here for the publisher to state, from time to time, that thc author's indifference to how his books are faring does not shake the publisher's belief and confidence in their outstanding quality. I can assure you in all sincerity that among the writers we represent and publish, there are two or three at most whose work affects me as passionately and intensely as yours.
>
> Please do not take the visible success we achieve with your books as any indication of the effort that goes into selling them. We both know that it is usually the best and most estimable works that take

> time to find their response, and it does not happen instantaneously; we remain confident that the German reading public will one day be capable of giving these books the reception they deserve.
>
> It would give me great pleasure if you gave us the chance to demonstrate the unwavering confidence that ties us to you and your writing by submitting more books of yours for us to publish. Every manuscript you decide to send us will be welcomed and published in book form with loving care. If over the course of time you could give us, in addition to collections of short prose pieces, a longer, extended story or a novel—since I know from you and from Max Brod how many manuscripts of this kind are nearly finished or even completed—we would be especially grateful. Naturally, the public's receptivity for a single extended prose work is greater than it is for collections of shorter pieces. This is a tiresome and senseless attitude on the part of readers, but it is a fact. The interest aroused by a larger prose work of this kind would allow vastly wider distribution than we have aimed for up to now, and at the same time such success would help us to publicize your earlier works more vigorously.[20]

Few contemporary authors would have resisted the temptation of this letter, but Kafka was now shrewd enough not to take Wolff's charming overtures too seriously. The publisher did not say a word about how remiss his company had been with Kafka's manuscripts, and Wolff gave no indication that he was able to appreciate Kafka's situation. Kafka had now had to give up the dream of a free—that is, reasonably secure on a financial level—life of a writer. Wolff wanted access to the novels lying in Kafka's drawer; that was what mattered to him, and why he suddenly recalled the existence of these manuscripts after all these years was obvious. Max Brod had just publicly announced and talked them up in *Die neue Rundschau*. He called *The Man Who Disappeared* a "voluminous novel that is virtually finished, and plays tenderly and delightfully in a fantastic America," and described *The Trial* as "complete, in my view, although incomplete, incompletable, and unpublishable in the view of the author." Brod went well beyond revealing the title of this work to his readers; he recounted its contents and hailed *The Trial* as a model of literary perfection in a manner that strongly suggested that the novel was indeed essentially complete.[21] These were strong words, even in view of Brod's usual superlatives, so strong that Wolff feared other publishers would be intrigued. Time was of the essence: He let just one day go by—or two at the most—after the publication of Brod's essay before dictating his big pitch.

Kafka had no trouble figuring out that this new surge of attention was owed above all to Brod's well-intentioned but thoughtless indiscretions. At his next visit to Café Edison he would have to count on being asked how Josef K. was faring. And it was impossible to reply to the publisher's offers in all honesty without violating the dictates of politeness or self-respect. Since he could not bring himself to do so, he put off replying week after week. Eventually Wolff learned from Ludwig Hardt that nothing could be expected from Kafka, who was both "depressed" and "jittery." Nevertheless, the publisher had one more go at it shortly afterward, when word got around that Kafka's health had improved: "While you are recovering, if you manage to work on your manuscripts and texts, in accordance with your friends' wishes, please bear in mind the urgent request that my last letters to you contained."[22] Wolff got no reply to this letter either. But his admonition was now beside the point.

Nobody in Kafka's small circle of acquaintances would have expected Kafka to start reading to the public again, receiving visitors, making plans, or engaging with other people and the cultural life of Prague. Of course his standard repertoire of reactions was repeating itself; after long absences, he was temporarily more visible than previously, as he had been after Zürau and certainly after Merano. And his new friendships, especially with Klopstock and Hardt, were clearly stimulating for him. But his conditions for a return to the social sphere had changed radically, within and without, and not for the better. Back then, in Zürau, he had once again been able to seize the initiative. He had made decisions, had decided on a separation that was necessary and reasonable and enabled him to start anew. He had noted, with a hint of pride, "The work awaiting me is enormous."

Four years later, in the fall of 1921, this statement was no less true. However, the grief he had faced in Matliary resulted not in decisions but in thoughts of escape. This time, he had the feeling that he had missed out not on women or community but on life itself. All that had happened to him could no longer be explained away as a weakness of will, a lack of truthfulness, or the quagmire of bureaucracy; this chasm ran deeper, and a fundamental alienation would persist whether or not he made a point of adapting to it. His self-characterization as an "extraterrestrial" while he was in Matliary was no joke and, in his view, not even an exaggeration. A short time later, he noted, "You don't belong to the same species."[23]

Kafka was suffering through an existential paradox that had to stay hidden from his friends. No matter how intense and sophisticated the conversations he had in this winter in Prague, no matter how diverse the relationships he cultivated, his feeling of an unbridgeable gap grew more pronounced, regardless of how many lives he touched or how many coffeehouses, readings, and theater performances he was dragged to. Just as loneliness is most painfully obvious in a crowd, all these social contacts—even the new friendships with Klopstock and Hardt—only affirmed his unavoidable and incurable alienation. You have to be in the social whirl to sense that you do not belong to it. Never had Kafka experienced this as radically and fully as during these months of his apparent return to society. It was nothing special to feel somewhat apart from the world while at a health resort in the mountains; who wouldn't feel that way? But he had to prove himself in Prague, and Kafka was horrified to realize that in his familiar milieu, surrounded by people, his alienation not only persisted but grew to an unprecedented degree. It had been a decade since his "Metamorphosis" had depicted the fate of an outcast, a pariah in his own family. Now Kafka felt ostracized from the world as a whole.

The tuberculosis was in large part responsible for this radicalization, and Kafka was now finally beginning to understand and to accept its social dimension. He had to tell himself that his physical condition no longer gave him any latitude for "life planning" that extended beyond a few months. His illness offered him many opportunities to mask his own "otherness" and to provide plausible explanations for every retreat, every ill-mannered display of indifference. On the other hand, as his symptoms of tuberculosis became more visible, he became a presence who objectively no longer belonged. The community removed people like that to protect itself by siphoning them off to waiting rooms and sanatoriums. Thus the illness lent reality to the fears Kafka had expressed in literary form, hence his growing aversion to convalescent care and his repeated wish to return to the "village," and a "trade," that is, to any recognized form of social life outside of marriage.

By the spring, Kafka had become aware that the High Tatras would not bring about any substantial improvement in his condition, and his fears were confirmed within the first days of autumn in Prague. A drop in temperature three days after he returned to the office, along with damp, almost icy air, was all it took to send him to bed for hours in the afternoon. He began to cough and bring up pflegm more frequently, and he felt so weak that a broken elevator kept him from going outside. Afflicted by a constant shortness of breath, he now moved down the street at an unusually cautious pace. "Walking in the inner city on a warm afternoon, no matter how slowly," he wrote to Klopstock, "affects me as though I were in a room that had not been ventilated for quite some time, and did not even have the strength to open the window to get some air."[24] As much as he would like to have taken his occasional visitors around Prague, he found it impossible to do so.

In early September, Kafka realized that he would not last the following winter in the office, no matter how encouraging the "objective" results of his lung examination. He again began to make inquiries about sanatoriums, supported by Dr. Kodym, the public medical official who recommended an immediate continuation of his convalescence. He visited one sanatorium in Bohemia, wrote to another near Hamburg (most likely Geesthacht), and almost let himself be talked into signing up for the well-regarded Silesian health resort for people with lung diseases in Görbersdorf (Sokołowsko in Polish), where there were more tuberculosis patients than residents. But the decision-making process dragged on, as it had the previous year. Kafka no longer wanted to while away the months in some lounge chair far away from everything that kept him alive intellectually. Several nights with fever and coughing, which even robbed his family of any remaining illusions, did nothing to change this. His parents would not have found it very difficult to finance a brief stay at Davos or the Mediterranean, even though Czech kronen were not worth much abroad at that time. But Kafka turned them down. "I cannot go to the seashore; where would I get the money?" he explained to Klopstock. "Even if I wanted to 'take' it, I wouldn't be able to. Also it is too far for me: for reasons of health I am willing to go to the ends of the earth, for reasons of sickness at most ten hours."[25] The medical student, who kept asking about Kafka's health—he even sent telegrams from Matliary—could only shake his head at arguments of this kind. But Kafka's parents decided to step up the pressure.

On the morning of October 17, they told Franz that he needed to sit down and write a letter explaining his absence to the director of his institute so that he could see another specialist, Dr. Otto Hermann, right around the corner on Niklasstrasse. They had made an appointment for Kafka without his knowledge, which put Kafka in the embarrassing spot of offering his bosses a glimpse of his home life. But this visit bore unexpected fruit. Dr. Hermann, who gave him a much more thorough examination than the doctor in Matliary, explained to Kafka that even without traveling, there was plenty he could do to improve his health. A systematic health regimen that included massages, UV radiation, and a strict diet was also possible in Prague, even during the winter. His report indicated that this regimen was urgently needed: Bilateral lung catarrh, concluded on the left side (stage I–II, according to Turban), persisting on the right (stage II–III). Bilateral damping, on the left up to the crista scapulae, on the right to the hilum; murky on the upper left side at the back; bronchial breathing on the right side with rumbling, egophony, and increased fremitus. The X-rays reveal opacity over both apices and the hilar gland on the right. Granules in the sputum.[26] That said it all.

Even though this doctor again refused to call it what it obviously was—tuberculosis—Kafka quickly realized that the new finding was the direst to date. He still rejected the invasive methods of conventional medicine, but he now seemed willing to tolerate injections if his condition continued to deteriorate.[27] Dr. Kodym's reaction to Dr. Hermann's report must have alarmed Kafka, even though Dr. Kodym sugar-coated his diagnosis in explaining it to his patient before submitting a blunter version to the insurance institute, which stated that because the lung disease was advancing in the right lobe, Dr. Kafka needed another leave to convalesce, and the outcome was impossible to predict. "However," he wrote, "a complete cure is unlikely, so perhaps retirement would be more beneficial for both the patient and the institute."[28]

This was the first time the word "retirement" had been used in official communications, and from now on Kafka would no longer need to display the results of his medical examinations to the management. First and foremost, however, it meant that the days of petitioning for leave were over. On October 29, the Workers' Accident Insurance Institute granted him three additional months of leave. A few days later (probably on November 4), Kafka cleared his desk and said his goodbyes, somewhat less formally this time; since he had decided to take the doctor's advice and continue his medical treatment in Prague, he would occasionally run into his healthy colleagues and superiors on the street. "To me the institute is a featherbed, as heavy as it is warm. If I were to crawl out from under it, I would immediately risk catching cold; the world is not heated." A few months later, he seemed to hold a different view: "The institute is farther from me (apart for its money) than the moon."[29] It turned out that he was right on both counts. It was his final day of work at the office, which had tormented, challenged, and stabilized him, kept him from going to war, sustained him, and ultimately liberated him. What he had once dreamed about and longed for with every fiber of his being had now finally been realized: he would not be returning. It was over. But the fulfillment of his dream carried a stale taste of blood.

> Last week I suffered something like a breakdown, as total a breakdown as I had only that one night two years ago; at no other time have I experienced that. Everything seemed over with, even today there seems to be no great improvement. There are two ways of interpreting it, and it probably should be interpreted both ways. First: breakdown, impossible to sleep, impossible to stay awake, life impossible, or, more precisely, the succession of life. The clocks are not synchronized; the internal one races at a devilish or demoniac or in any case inhuman pace, the external one limps along at its usual speed. What else can happen but that the two worlds split

> apart, and they do split apart, or at least tear away at each other in a fearful manner. There may be various reasons for the wild pace of the internal process: the most obvious one is introspection, which does not allow any idea to rest, but chases up each one, only to become a notion of an idea that in turn is the object of renewed introspection.
>
> Second: this chase leads a person away from mankind. Solitude, which has been inflicted upon me for the most part, and in part sought by me—but what was this if not compulsion, too?—is now losing all its ambiguity and is going toward an extreme. Where is it leading? The strongest likelihood is that it may lead to madness; there is nothing more to say about that, the chase goes right through me and rips me apart. Or I can—can I?—even if just to the tiniest extent, stay on my feet and be carried along by the chase. Where, then, shall I be brought? "Chase" is only a metaphor. I can also say "assault on the last earthly boundary"—an assault from below, from people, and since this too is only a metaphor, I can replace it by the metaphor of an assault from above, aimed down at me.[30]

The voice of Kafka in January 1922 was serious and clear, operating with precise images, and almost analytical. He was reacting to a nervous breakdown with "first" and "second." He knew that he was in a situation in which complaining no longer did any good. He had been aware of that back in Zürau, as well, but then it was a matter of dignity and self-esteem and, above all, the question whether one can sidestep life forever, whether one did not have to ward off life's challenges that could not be reconciled with one's own essence, no matter how justified they were from a moral point of view. Now, in the fourth year of his illness, Kafka was forced to take another step back because the lack of synchronism between the internal and external clocks was no mere shortcoming or character flaw; this split extended all the way down to the foundations, and neither a vigorous will to normality nor the gesture of defiant self-affirmation could seal up or bridge the gap. But it could not be displayed either. None of the many visitors that winter—with the possible exception of Milena—could guess that Kafka was acting as his own social proxy, with abysses yawning open behind his mask with its impenetrable smile. He wrote in his diary that earlier in his life he had wanted to be different, and that it was a silly game, but now he had seriously attained this goal. And thus began a new era in his life, in which the question of guilt—deviating from laws that apply to everyone else—took a backseat to the far more pressing question of which law was relevant for him and on which side of the world he could go on living. In Kafka's late works, guilt and punishment would no longer have a prominent role. He now seemed to realize that ethical dilemmas were like exotic plants that flourish only on very fertile soil, where a coddled life results in an excess of strength. The danger of coming apart at the seams and of psychological implosion is, however, not a moral danger but the threat of insanity and death.

Kafka was taking stock. On an almost daily basis, he now took his diary in hand to help him visualize the precise contours of his changed situation. This direction "away from mankind" would be the loneliest of all possible paths, and there is no returning from it. But how did he get there in the first place? Was it a product of his upbringing, or pressure from his father, that pushed him over the edge of his own world? Or did it stem from his inexplicable "otherness," which kept him apart from the human community? Kafka wavered on this question and returned to it repeatedly over the course of the following weeks. He was no longer content to define himself as the victim of abuse that had occurred decades earlier. His "Letter to His Father" had allowed him to vent his psychological issues and list all his shortcomings. *Otherness*, by contrast, still preserves the notion of an identity that is unique and thus perhaps also worth defending. "No one's task was as difficult, so far as I know," he noted. "One might say that it is not a task, not even an impossible one.... But it is the air I breathe, as long as I go on breathing."[31]

Kafka's quest for suitable images now skirted metaphysical and biblical allusions. There was no more talk of paradise and original sin, of predestination and the law; he was now returning to sensory and literary images once and for all: the unheated world, the hunt, the thin air on high, the food that other people ate but he did not, the ingenious burrow that keeps pursuers away, and repeated exclusion, the two worlds separated by a trap door. Haltingly, then more and more compellingly, Kafka's powers of imagination returned, and he found images that were both simple and unfathomable, images to be engraved in cultural memory. Of course that was part of the "task." But this task, as he had known for a long time, could not entail inventing images for their own sake, no matter how lovely, penetrating, or astounding. They needed to express something that can be said only by poetic means. But when they succeed, they dazzle and thus bewilder. An image can be moving and still be false. It can be painfully beautiful and distract us from a horrifying truth. He would not be spared this lesson.

Kafka strung together a network of metaphors that gradually consolidated into the radical notion of two worlds: one, a world of people that he left and longed to return to in vain; and another, nonhuman world he had been part of all along, and in which he had to hold his own with dignity. A "tragic" image that had the power and persuasiveness of myth and that, as Kafka would soon demonstrate, was also extremely rich aesthetically. But was it true? He had not yet internalized it fully, and he was still playing with other models.

> There was not the least bit of enduring resolve in the way I conducted my life. It was as if I, like everyone else, had been given a point from which to extend the radius of a circle, and had then, like everyone else, to describe my beautiful circle round this point. Instead, I was forever starting my radius, only to keep having to break it off on the spot. (Examples: piano, violin, languages, German studies, anti-Zionism, Zionism, Hebrew, gardening, carpentry, literature, attempts at marriage, my own apartment.) The center of my imaginary circle bristles with the beginnings of radii; there is no room left for a new attempt, no room for old age, weak nerves, and no further attempt means the end. If I sometimes extended the radius a little farther than usual, in the case of my law studies, say, or engagements, everything was made worse rather than better by this little extra distance.[32]

The image of the circle and radius is convincing, but it implies and necessitates an intolerable conclusion, namely utter failure in his life. Was he really facing the same task as every other person? A law for all, without any prospect of anything else? That could not be the whole truth, either. Kafka knew that at least in the arena of literature, he had extended the radius not just "a little farther" but a good deal farther, far beyond all demands of an "enduring resolve" in leading his life. Kafka kept up his quest for images, and it seems as though he was aware that beneath all these little myths and big metaphors was an even deeper, hotter stratum of experience, a stratum in which even the pleasure in truth has to evaporate. Only one time in this winter did he succeed in shedding light on this innermost essence, for the duration of a thought, a single fearsome sentence:

> All is imaginary—family, office, friends, the street—all imaginary, far away or close at hand, the woman closest of all, but the truth is only that you are pressing your head against the wall of a windowless and doorless cell.[33]

Kafka was standing at the threshold of the world of Samuel Beckett, unprepared to endure it. He would eschew this image from then on, as though it had scorched him. He turned back and charted another course of his own.

CHAPTER TWENTY-THREE

The Personal Myth: *The Castle*

People need to be able to write if they don't speak.

—Gert Jonke, *Der ferne Klang*

A STRANGER ENTERS A COUNTRY INN. HE COMES UNANNOUNCED, but to his astonishment, a huge room—the "Princes' Room"—has been prepared for him. His suspicions aroused, he confronts the innkeeper and the chambermaid rather rudely, and they both admit that his arrival in the village has been expected for weeks, supposedly on the basis of a rumor that has leaked in from the castle. But the stranger is not satisfied with this information; he believes that the chambermaid herself has been charged by the castle to observe him. He has come to fight a "battle," and this might already be his opponent's opening gambit. Nevertheless, he wants to remain and wage this battle, even though a dizzy spell forces him to rest up for a while. The chambermaid, whom he was just scolding, is washing his face. "You want something from us and we don't know what," she says. "Speak to me candidly and I will answer you candidly."[1]

On January 27, 1922, Kafka arrived at the health resort in Spindelmühle, a snowy village in the Riesengebirge, 750 meters above the upper Elbe, just a few miles from the Polish border. He was joining his physician, Dr. Otto Hermann, who was spending a two-week vacation there with his wife and daughter; they drove up together in a sleigh drawn by two horses. Kafka had already corresponded with Hotel Krone, so he was of course expected. Nevertheless, he was not pleased at the outset: His suitcase was damaged during the trip, the lobby directory listed him as "Dr. Josef Kafka," the table in his room was rickety, the lighting was dim, and the hotel was noisy. But he was determined not to be thrown by these annoyances. He had made a decision to get something done, and here, in Spindelmühle, he would make it happen. Thrifty as always, he had brought a stack of blank paper with him, taken from a half dozen notebooks, to use as manuscript pages. Just a few hours after he arrived, he took them out of his suitcase and put them on the table. Ink and fountain pen were not quick to come by, so he made do with his pencil. He began to write: The story of a stranger who arrives in a village, where, he sensed, he has been expected for some time . . .

Kafka's third novel, *The Castle*, was impelled by a moment of intense concentration, a powerful interplay of reality and imagination. An ordinary event—the arrival of a man in a remote village—was transformed into literature almost in real time, before the moment was even past and its consequences could be assessed.

Kafka had expected this liberating moment and had made every effort to prepare for it in his diary. For several weeks it had seemed to him that only literary work could keep him from suffering the next, and perhaps definitive, psychological breakdown; he wrote to Klopstock that he had been "lashed" through "periods of insanity" that winter. Never had Kafka begun a literary work with such a conscious intention to engage in self-therapy, with such hopes that a salutary creative effect would stem his nerve-racking idle self-observation. And this hope seemed to be fulfilled: no sooner had he written down the first few sentences than he felt a new sense of strength, a new ground under his feet:

> The strange, mysterious, possibly dangerous, possibly redemptive comfort of writing: it is a leap out of murderers' row—observation,

> deed—observation in which a higher type of observation is created—a higher, not a keener type—and the higher it is and the less within reach of the "row," the more independent it becomes, the more obedient to its own laws of motion, the more incalculable, joyful, ascendant its path.[2]

Strong words when contrasted with the caution Kafka now used to qualify any glimmer of hope. But he was quite familiar with the way a successful literary invention veered away from outside events and intentions, and there was no doubt in his mind that he was experiencing it again. He had originally intended to write "redemptive *purpose* of writing" but quickly revised it to read "redemptive *comfort*." Writing is inward observation, but not the kind that revolves in useless spirals. This observation led into another dimension, like climbing mountains. The outward purpose of writing, by contrast, was achieved almost in passing: four or five nights of restorative sleep, the most significant gift he had had in a long time.

The manuscript provides a whole series of indications that when Kafka arrived in Spindelmühle, he had no more than a vague notion of the plot of his *Castle* novel; it is even likely that he initially interpreted the awkward welcome as "Josef K." in the Hotel Krone as a decisive hint. "Shall I enlighten them," he remarked in reference to this incident, "or shall I be enlightened by them?"[3] Presumably Kafka protested politely, as any other guest would have done, but in his new novel, which he began writing the same day, the protagonist is greeted by a knowing adversary who is perfectly capable of putting him in his place—just as in *The Trial*.

The first pages of the *Castle* manuscript do not give any indication of an epic scope; their jumpy, erratic diction would seem far more appropriate for the opening of a brief story. But Kafka broke off this first, "expressionist" endeavor either the very next day or the following one, and reversed course once again. He dispensed with clipped dialogues and instead crafted several carefully considered introductory sentences that—without alarming the reader at the outset—framed the goal of the novel in an emblematic image with a far more lasting impact:

> It was late evening when I arrived. The village lay under deep snow. Nothing could be seen of the castle hill; fog and darkness sur-

> rounded it, and not even the faintest glimmer of light gave any indication of where the great castle was. For a long time I stood on the wooden bridge leading from the road to the village and gazed upward into the seeming void.

The mute dialogue with a *seeming* void: It is as though Kafka was striking the basic chord that he would continue to develop, vary, and interpret in the months to come, on hundreds of pages. These sentences radiate ease and assurance. Kafka suddenly knew what he was after. In the first version, he had merely been tuning the instruments, but the comfort he had derived even from those few written pages flowed back into the writing and enabled him to craft passages of crystalline clarity. Now that we have been able to peer inside the manuscripts, we can see an astonishing display of how Kafka found his way back almost seamlessly to his own literary language and instantly assumed full control after years of narrative abstinence. It even seems as though this long fallow period inched him closer to his ascetic narrative ideal. In both language and plot framework, he now avoided anything that could be perceived as mere grandstanding. There is no farfetched catastrophe as in "The Metamorphosis," no criminological tension as in *The Trial*, no physical horror as in "In the Penal Colony." There is only a man who is inexplicably tenacious about gaining a foothold in a village, a man who lies and masquerades as a land surveyor to better his chances, who gets involved with women in order to make them help him, who picks up whatever information he can get his hands on and lies in wait for hints and innuendos, who puts himself in a position to be thrown out of houses and taverns, and who even performs menial labor without coming a single step closer to his goal, which is the "castle," an extraordinarily complex, unapproachable, and impenetrable authority that gives the "land surveyor" free rein and observes his actions from afar but refuses to grant him any unequivocal information about his status. All of this is told from the limited point of view of the protagonist, in an unhurried rhythm, with long dialogues and episodes from the lives of the villagers painted with a broad brush, and keeps leading into reflections that are both meticulous and fruitless and require patience on the part of the reader. The enormous shadow of the castle is all that holds this together.

Once again, there is a hierarchical demimonde that so strongly resembles the paper-strewn hell of *The Trial*, right down to specific details, that it seems like an extension or broadening out of the earlier novel: the same avalanches of files overwhelming the people, the same blend of power and sexuality, the same pointless yet fateful parsing of words, the same interplay of light and darkness, the interspersed slapstick scenes, the beds with weighty figures rolling around, and of course the compulsive control, the ubiquitous looks that break up any intimacy and subtly but, for modern readers, insistently evoke the world of the concentration camps.

Kafka provided ironic confirmation of this connection between his novels by once again choosing "K." as his protagonist's last name and having him introduce himself in a telephone call with the castle adminstration as "Josef"—it is the only time that his first name is specified. Also, Kafka subsequently decided to abandon first-person narration and to continue in the third person, as he had in *The Trial*. By this point, however, *The Castle* was already at the third chapter; if he wanted to maintain order in his manuscript, he would have to cross out words like "I," "my," and "me," in hundreds of spots and replace them with "K.," "he," "his," etc. It was tedious, mechanical work, but the manuscript reveals that this belated decision to alter the text throughout was not just spontaneous but essential because Kafka was about to take a literary gamble: the description of a sexual union. He had avoided doing so up to this point; in *The Trial* he had even introduced a brief interruption of his narrative flow to allow for a conventional silence. This time, he wanted to dispense with these kinds of devices. But was it possible to portray the ineffable directly in the first person? Linguistically, yes, but not psychologically, he discovered. His resistance remained insuperable, and at the last possible moment—in the middle of a sentence—Kafka took refuge in the distance that comes with third-person narration.[4]

A remarkable process, which is of great significance in determining the extent to which the land surveyor K. is really a stand-in for Kafka, as his name suggests, a kind of Kafka marionette its inventor used to parry the blows that fate dealt him. The wary stranger Kafka introduced in the first sketch was certainly not a self-portrait, but in his second go at the text, Kafka toned down the features that were least like his own. Shortly after the land surveyor's arrival, he chose to defend himself against the villagers with a cudgel, but Kafka immediately crossed out this sentence because by now he had a different, gentler, and less aggressive protagonist in mind.[5] He sought to make his individual motives more understandable and appealing so as to cast light on the profound darkness of his struggles. But the longer the land surveyor stays in the village, the more closely he comes to resemble his creator; his strength of purpose and optimism dwindle with each new experience, while his ability to cast a critical eye on his own behavior is enhanced. It seems as though Kafka fared just like his future readers: the protagonist came ever closer to him, and the disappointments that K. experiences led to identification and compassion, no matter how incomprehensible the forces that bind him to the village and the castle from the first to the last hour—which raises the question of whether *The Castle* may have been an autobiographical project from the start.

Years earlier, Kafka had made a habit of addressing his own mirror image in the second or even the third person whenever he wanted to frame general statements about himself as independently as possible from any mood swings he might be experiencing. The use of the second person—and even more so of the third—allowed for freer, franker reflection, and the language he unleashed in literary form even in his diary struck him as far more productive than the usual psychologizing turns of phrase that often came up in self-descriptions. Even so, he allowed for reflections of that kind only as a preliminary literary stage, and one of the few notes we have on record from the months he spent in Matliary is utterly unequivocal in this regard. "Writing refuses to yield to me," he noted here. "Hence a plan for autobiographical explorations. Not biography, but rather exploration and detection of the smallest possible components. I then want to construct myself out of them, like someone whose house is unsafe and wants to build a safe one next to it, if possible out of the material of the old one."[6] So he was thinking in terms of a literal reconstruction. But Kafka held that this act of self-dismantling right down to his own foundations was an act of sublimation. The writer to whom writing refuses to yield is condemned to playing autobiographical solitaire.

Kafka did not follow through on this resolution in Matliary, where he would have had the necessary time and tranquility, but he did so once he had returned to Prague. Here he was abruptly pulled out of the social lethargy of spa patients and compelled to restabilize his own position and review the state of his "own house" from the outside. Starting in mid-October 1921—shortly after he had given all his diary volumes to Milena—Kafka filled dozens of pages with self-analytical observations but carefully avoided lapsing into his earlier laments. He was no longer seeking quick relief but rather was laying out the pluses and minuses in an act of autobiographical revision.

> No matter how wretched a constitution I may have ... I must do the best I can with it, even in my sense, and it is hollow sophistry to argue that there is only one thing to be done with it, and this one thing is thus the best, and is despair.

Kafka was commanding himself to stop toying with his own demise and his "otherness." There would be no more self-imposed observer status in his relationships, not even with his family or with women. Once he had put battling behind him—with all the dependencies Kafka was now facing as a result of his illness, further battles were no longer possible—the remaining task was simply to make a detailed record of those battles and find ways to go on living with the unalterable result. Kafka was now using the calm pathos of insight to offset undignified desperation, and he struck a tone that sounds almost serene in comparison with the many laments with which he had always accompanied the most easily foreseeable disturbances and disappointments. Kafka wrote on the very first page, "I no longer need to make myself as painstakingly conscious of such things as I once did; I am not as forgetful as I once was in this respect. I am a memory come alive, hence my insomnia.[7]

Sure enough, the notes that Kafka regularly continued writing into the spring of 1922 showed a penchant not only for abstraction but also for a visual concentrate, a shorthand, even a private code. Nothing was "painstakingly" narrated, and there was no more quoting. Kafka was also no longer tracing the outlines of his life, as he had planned to do back in Zürau, but was instead just feeling his way along them, pooling years of experience into a series of short, tight statements that are utterly incomprehensible without knowing their biographical genesis. One example is this: "Longing for the country? It isn't certain.

The country strikes up the longing, the infinite longing."[8] That, in a nutshell, is what he took away from outings with his friends and with Ottla, from countless conversations about *Lebensreform*, from their own attempts at gardening, from the months in Zürau, Schelesen, and Matliary. He had learned that country life is not an end in itself, and does not guarantee happiness, but is itself just a sign.

Kafka so thoroughly studded other passages with private allusions and ciphers that the reader stands as if in front of a locked door—and can only hope that some coincidence will place the key in his hand. On January 18, shortly before his day of despondency and the "breakdown": "It is somewhat quieter, but then s[ex] comes as redemption or as aggravation, if you like." Two paragraphs later: "S. keeps working away at me, torments me day and night; I would have to get over my fear and shame and likely my sorrow as well to satisfy it." The following day: "Nothing evil; once you have crossed the threshold, all is good. Another world, and you needn't speak." And one day after that: "Seized by the collar, dragged through the streets, pushed through the door. That is how it is from a schematic view; in reality, there are counterforces, only a trifle—the trifle that maintains life and torment—less violent than the others. I the victim of both." These words were obviously not intended for readers, and their meaning and connection would be difficult to establish were it not for the lucky coincidence that a brief note by Max Brod has been preserved, who came away from a visit to his friend feeling "deeply shocked" because Kafka had told him he had been in a brothel but had failed to find even a hint of the easing of tension he was longing for. "Torment of the sexual organs" Brod noted meaningfully. So "s" did stand for "sex." Kafka, who feared his family's curiosity, could not write that down without resorting to an abbreviation.[9] But the coldness he had experienced spilled over into the world of *The Castle*: just eight days after what appears to have been the final time he slept with a prostitute, Kafka took a room in Spindelmühle and got down to work. In his novel, sexuality would symbolize the most profound human alienation and the futile hope of being rescued by others. And it was a highly personal, shameful memory that forced Kafka to retreat from his fictional I and to leave this experience to a He, a land surveyor.

The awareness that he simply had to come to grips with something was surely a prime motivation for Kafka to try his hand at a novel for a third time; this would be evident even if we knew nothing at all about the specific impetuses that drove him to write this book. But the most important entry in this long-overdue balance sheet was Milena, because his love of this woman had offered him an opportunity that might be his final, crucial one; his friends, who kept trying to keep him from making definitive judgments, thought so, and Albert Ehrenstein even claimed that with Milena, life itself was reaching out its hand to him, and Kafka would be deciding "between life and death." If that were taken literally—and Kafka considered this statement "essentially true"[10]—he had opted *against* life, with his eyes wide open. But why? Where was he hoping to wind up instead? This was one of the burning issues that preyed on his mind that winter. Only now did he become clearly aware that there had been such abstruse, seemingly senseless refusals again and again, and that it was not a lack of "offers" or "opportunities" that had kept him away from life. But what had? Had he distrusted the offers; had they seemed inadequate or too costly? Wasn't the right offer available, or had he waited for some nameless thing that would be revealed to him one day beyond all these opportunities? Kafka spelled out these pointed questions in his diary, while in *The Castle* he tried to translate the logic of what had happened, the logic of his own existence, into a language replete with images and thus bring it to light.

So this was an autobiographical novel, of course, but in an indirect, far more intricate sense than the seemingly straightforward correspondences between the novel and reality suggest. The seemingly infinite number of these kinds of detailed correspondences—both overt and veiled—surpasses even *The Trial*. Back in the mid-1970s, Hartmut Binder took nearly a hundred printed pages to explain the demonstrable biographical context of individual passages in *The Castle*.[11] A commentary of this kind on the basis of what we know today would likely be substantially more extensive and would encompass things he had experienced, read, and heard; word plays and evocative names; memories that lay decades in the past and impressions that were mere hours old—not to mention his many self-referential remarks and tacit connections to other works.

These correspondences are never easy, however, and the notion that Kafka wandered through a kind of psychological storeroom and plucked out the most interesting and useful pieces to furnish the parallel universe of his novel misses the essence of literary invention completely. The bridge on which the land surveyor pauses right at the beginning is clearly the bridge that Kafka himself crossed over a day or two before he wrote this passage, the bridge over the Elbe that was used to get from Spindelmühle to the Friedrichsthal section of town and Hotel Krone, which was located there. But that little bridge was made out of stone, and the bridge in *The Castle* is wooden. Why? Perhaps Kafka was recalling another little bridge, namely the one at the way into the town of Zürau, and that bridge really was made of wood. It is possible that this new situation brought back memories of 1917, but it is equally possible that Kafka had already read the little bridge in Zürau as a sign—a sign that he was now stepping onto a different shore—and that the bridge in Spindelmühle was remarkable only for that reason. And it is also conceivable that this symbolic nature was revealed only by the repetition, and that memory was actually "vitalizing" reality and making it decipherable.

The connection to the village itself is equally complex. Kafka was surely unprepared for the mass of snow and the biting cold he encountered in Spindelmühle; he feared pneumonia right away, and it is difficult to fathom why Dr. Hermann had brought him here of all places after forbidding him to go to Semmering (suggested by Werfel), which was supposedly too severe a climate for him. The running joke was "nine months of winter and three months of cold"—which was barely an exaggeration. Kafka was impressed by the landscape and found it more beautiful and manifold than the High Tatras. But shortly after he arrived, he found out how difficult it was to get around. He was unable to reach the Weisswassergrund, which was less than two miles away; he kept slipping in the snow, and when it turned dark, he had to turn around on the deserted path. "A senseless path, without an earthly destination," he noted in his diary; clearly he was wasting no time in establishing a link between this experience and the novel. Shortly thereafter, the land surveyor K. would also get stuck in the snow, during his first and only attempt to get as far as the gates of the castle on his own, and the forbidding snow becomes one of the central ciphers of the novel. Kafka got hold of fitting reading matter—a report about an arctic expedition—and he even put an ironic tourist bon mot about the weather to good use in the novel manuscript: winter in the village was very long and monotonous, the land surveyor was told, while the spring and summer did not last "much more than two days"; at least it seemed that way in memory, and it sometimes snowed even in the summer . . .[12]

There is no doubt that the world of *The Castle* can hardly be imagined without the physical experience of the Riesengebirge in winter, which Kafka immediately put to literary use, but the village in which the land surveyor winds up is *not* Spindelmühle, which was in a region that had been developed for tourists for decades. Spindelmühle (which was known as Spindlermühle/Špindlerův Mlýn beginning in 1923) was a health resort that advertised in many daily newspapers, and here, as in the High Tatras, there was a quick boom in winter sports. There were groomed cross-country ski trails (Kafka once tried out skis, which were called "snowshoes" back then, but quickly abandoned his attempt to ski); there were several ski jumps (where Kafka was a fascinated spectator), and an important attraction was an electric "toboggan run," which allowed even less agile guests to enjoy sleigh rides for hours, which Kafka greatly appreciated. Every sixth building here was a hotel or an inn, and most families had rooms to rent. The dominant political group in town was the Party to Increase Tourism, founded by Dr. Wilhelm Pick, who was the Jewish district physician, hotel owner, and community leader.

The nameless village at the foot of the castle hill was altogether different. Sports were unknown here, sleighs were no more than a means of transportation, and no one used skis. Two inns are mentioned: the Bridge Inn, which does not have a single usable room to offer, and the supposedly more elegant Gentry Inn, which, however, is just as unclean and is restricted to castle officials. There does not seem to be any other public space, which is also unneeded because strangers rarely come to this town, and no one thinks of doing business with travelers. It is made perfectly clear to K., after he is thrown out of one of the cottages, that people feel no need to offer hospitality because—and this statement would have sounded like blasphemy in the real Spindelmühle—"we do not need guests." An outside world does not seem to exist for the villagers, not even as a point of contrast, and letters and telephone calls serve only to maintain contact with the castle. The stifling, nightmarish feeling of a self-contained universe gradually becomes so compelling for the reader that the rare references to the outside world seem like jarring elements forgotten by the author.[13] And the castle itself? It exists only in the novel, not in Spindelmühle, so Kafka had brought in this idea as one of his formative experiences. The castle in Prague had stood in his field of vision for nearly four decades; he looked up to it, and, like everyone else, he was overshadowed by it, and on occasion the long forbidding rows of windows way up high glittered in the sun. "There was something crazed about it," Kafka wrote in the novel.[14]

Kafka's characters originated in an equally complex interplay between experience, memory, and invention. When Milena Pollak read *The Castle* in the late 1920s—and it is certain that she read it—she must have realized from the start that she herself appeared in this novel. Kafka's mischievous choice of name for the village annex of the castle (Gentry Inn, which in German is "Herrenhof"), and thus the key locus of the plot, was an invitation to seek out biographical allusions in the text of the novel, secret messages intended for her. The Herrenhof, a café in Vienna, had once been her stage, and even more that of her husband. In the novel's rustic Gentry Inn, it is the barmaid Frieda who at first is under the control of the powerful castle official Klamm and then becomes the land surveyor's fiancée for a few days. Frieda/Milena: the similarity in sound arouses our suspicions. But why is Frieda portrayed as physically nondescript, even downright homely? And her master, Klamm, who is mute and slumped over his beer when K. is able to observe him through a keyhole at one point, has little in common with the active, eloquent Ernst Pollak.

An even more obscure biographical puzzle is the family of Barnabas, whose real name is never mentioned but whose lot in life is developed into a sprawling tale in *The Castle*. There are three siblings: Barnabas, Olga, and Amalia, and the land surveyor's hopes are pinned on each of them in turn. Barnabas is young, strong, carefree; he brings the messages from the castle chambers, which is why K. is always exhilarated to see him. It is likely that Kafka had Klopstock in mind. Olga is also big and strong, yet gentle and fond of the land surveyor; it is striking that any sexual signal is avoided. Olga/Ottla: this is Kafka's youngest sister, hardworking, yet solicitous—just as he saw her in Zürau. But Olga serves the most menial castle workers as a freely available prostitute, and even though her willingness to suffer indignities stems from social and even moral concerns, Kafka has blurred the portrait of his sister beyond recognition. And finally there is Amalia, the only character in the novel who takes a clear stand against the castle, a woman who rebuffs the officials' brazen advances, knowing full well that her obstinacy will result in ostracism from the village community for herself and her siblings and parents. We cannot tell whether Kafka had an actual person in mind; no one with even a faint resemblance to the severe, taciturn, and impenetrable Amalia has been discovered anywhere in his circles.[15] Perhaps—as unusual as this was for Kafka—she was truly a mere invention; perhaps he encountered her in a dream—she must have been vague to him, as well, because in the second chapter she has blonde hair, but later it is black.

Kafka was zigzagging between word and world. It is unlikely that he set out to write an autobiographical novel, and it did not develop into a roman à clef. But particularly with regard to the female characters in *The Castle*, Kafka was displaying the high art of fleshing out each individual figure like a portrait of a living human being and nonetheless holding each figure strictly to her respective tasks and functions. Once again, there are compelling reasons to steer our attention back to his life.

In December 1920, Max Brod had once again reported a thrilling experience, this time with a chambermaid named Emilie, and known as Emmy, a twenty-seven-year-old Brod had met while staying at a hotel in Berlin and had almost "possessed." Listening to these kinds of adventure stories was nothing new for Kafka; they recurred at regular intervals, and only a few months back, when Brod was on a lecture tour, he had begun an affair in Brno with a lady (who was obviously married) and had gushed about her in the very same language. For Brod, these kinds of relationships were always the highest priority, no matter how hopeless they were. They overshadowed all other interests; even business appointments were timed to fit in with possible

> seriousness). But what more can there be? A love beyond national borders? Letter writing? Hoping for a fabulous February? You're demanding this much self-abnegation?

It seemed as though Kafka was summoning up more empathy for the situation of the young woman than for his friend's male distress. And he was not deterred by Brod's vehement protestions that these were not mere castles in the air, and he had been far more than just any guest in Berlin. Emmy was quite musical, he explained; she played the violin and spent her free time at concerts, and her greatest wish was to take voice lessons and work at the theater. He would support her in this endeavor to the best of his ability, both technically and financially. He had already received two (general delivery) letters from her, and they had arranged to meet again in Berlin. Well, if that's the situation, Kafka replied, seemingly relenting, he could only be ashamed of his objections. "Even so, my basic feeling on this issue hasn't changed; it is just not as foolishly easy to lay bare."[17]

Kafka's feeling would prove correct, but that gave him no sense of victory. When it came to women, Brod had attained all that was humanly possible; he was fearless, he had a conventional marriage, and now he was dabbling in the impossible. Kafka kept assuring Brod that this was not meant as criticism; who was he to criticize others when he had been such a pathetic failure in the realm of the possible? Brod could not accept such ambivalent admiration, and later Kafka even claimed to have "overestimated" his friend;[18] it seemed to him as though Kafka was so taken in by his own pessimistic ideology that he projected it onto the lives of others.

He was wrong on this score. Of course, Kafka's judgments about women had become increasingly clouded by fear over the years and had grown harsher and more "ideological." To the extent that women appeared in his own life, he viewed them above all as representatives: woman as disruption, temptation, emissary of life, or angel of redemption. But typologies of these kinds did not stop Kafka in the least from empathizing with a concrete feminine life and judging its social and psychological scope realistically. Women appreciated that. He did not dole out adulation or patronizing lectures—and even Milena, who was quite sensitive to critical judgments, felt that Kafka understood her better than her own husband did. The erotically charged pedagogical streak that Kafka displayed in dealing with younger women was often reciprocated with warmth and friendship, even gushing praise. Oddly, Emmy Salveter included Kafka (whom she had never met) in her evening Catholic prayers after receiving a few kind lines from him.

Kafka saw right from the first moment what she and Max would be facing. He had had his own experience with a long-distance relationship that went back and forth between Prague and Berlin, dependent upon post offices and train connections. In his relationship with Felice, there was the justifiable hope that one day this difficult state of affairs would be resolved. But Brod was asking Emmy to wait for him faithfully for months on end, without any prospect of a life together. Brod was not considering a divorce; he concealed this love affair from his wife for years, and there were grotesque scenes that seemed to him like fateful calamities, although they were ultimately inevitable. In the fall of 1921, he persuaded Emmy to visit him at the Zionist Congress in Karlsbad (where he had to fill in briefly as a delegate from Prague), but he was unable to talk Elsa out of traveling there too. Brod, who was completely overwhelmed by the situation, wound up thinking less about "work in Palestine" and "Jewish rebirth" than about how to prevent the two women from meeting. Of course, the attractive Emmy had other admirers, among them a twenty-one-year-old student. To make matters worse, this student was a "swastika wielder." The six-year age difference between Emmy and the student was probably the only reason he did not pressure her to marry him. Again Brod appeared surprised and embittered. All these sufferings, Kafka reiterated in the fall of 1922, were an expression of Brod wanting the impossible and risking "self-destruction" in pursuit of it. Kafka came up with a suggestion that he himself called "monstrous" while proposing it in all seriousness—namely, that Brod, Elsa, and Emmy live as a threesome, preferably in Berlin, far from the inevitable gossip in Prague. If this were to happen, however, Kafka and Brod would be forced to part ways for the duration. "But if there is room for two women around you, why wouldn't there be some sort of room for me, as well?"[19]

Readers in the twenty-first century are invariably baffled (and sometimes amused) by how strongly the literature of "classical modernity" was still marked by traditional, extremely crude notions of difference between the sexes. The idea that women were creatures of nature and that men stood for mind and action had little basis in psychosocial reality even before 1914, and it became obsolete altogether in World War I when women were given male responsibility and thus also male liberty, whether they liked it or not, while men—especially in their roles as fathers—proved to be fairly helpless in dealing with the fate that had been imposed on them.

Generalizations like these had always been morally hazy and could be employed to justify both contempt and worship of women—even at one and the same time. It depended on the ethical status accorded to the term "nature." Nature lacked consciousness or history; it was a chaotic and amoral domain in which there was neither knowledge nor logic but at best intuition, yet nature could also represent a utopia of non-disaffected life, and "redeem" the deteriorated self, as evidenced in the *Lebensreform* (back-to-nature) movement. The prospect of happiness that women held out was therefore profoundly ambiguous, and literature developed unending variations on this paradoxical theme: women as victims of social conventions (as in Ibsen and Schnitzler), as victims of their own nature (as in Wedekind), or as corrupters (as in Hamsun and Strindberg). Women could be childlike playthings, seductresses, ethereal sisters, or feisty mothers. The list may appear long, but the typological pattern was unvarying: where female characters appear, feminity unfailingly became the theme, whereas "human" tragedies that were not gender-specific tended to feature masculine heroes.

There was also an accompaniment of sexological literature, most notably Otto Weininger's *Sex and Character* (1903), in which "The Feminine" (abbreviated as "F.") is defined as a corrosive substance and women are simply denied any ability for reflection and for intellectual productivity: "The absolute female has no ego." The fact that this tautological 600-page tome, which was marked by hostility and largely undeterred by the facts, was published and republished in the 1920s—at a time when psychoanalysis was long since established—is proof positive of how deeply rooted these kinds of notions were in the collective consciousness. Weininger was taken seriously, and because he was radical, and anti-Semitic to boot, he was often considered modern, especially in rural areas. On February 14, 1921, when Oskar Baum gave a lecture about Weininger and the "Decline of Eroticism and the Jewish Character," the Urania Hall in Prague was completely sold out, and *Selbstwehr* published a detailed account of the evening. And the numerous lively and unpredictable feminine creatures in Brod's works—most notably in his novel *Franzi, or a Second-Class Love* (1922), which he wrote with Emmy Salveter in mind[20]—are unmistakably of the F. variety.

Kafka was unable to break free of the culturally overpowering myths of femininity: his lifelong fear of having to stand the test with "the woman" was just as ingrained in his personal neurosis as in the notion that women were agents of life. While they are temptresses, they are also nimble authorities who have a direct and inherent relationship with life-controlling forces. One can succumb to them, yet also appeal to them. In *The Trial*, Kafka had hit upon the momentous literary idea of taking this dual nature literally and lending it a visual, dreamlike form: Women move freely through the closed door of the court; they are sexually pursued and in turn they sexualize and feminize the court. Kafka developed this model much further in *The Castle*. Here, too, there are "forces" in command of the women that demand—and attain—their surrender. But in the reflection of power, the women acquire their own secret dignity, which makes them irresistible to the land surveyor. Their dignity is revealed less in words than in gestures and gazes: "When this gaze fell upon K., it seemed to him that it had already decided on matters pertaining to him about which he himself still knew nothing, but that gaze convinced him of their existence." It is the knowing gaze that will draw him to the nondescript barmaid Frieda, but this gaze dims as soon as her privileged access to the castle official Klamm breaks off. Equally inexplicable is the dignity of the innkeeper at the Bridge Inn; she, too, is an ex-mistress of Klamm, conservative to the point of willful ignorance, yet she is an authority in K.'s eyes. It is from her that K. learns that instead of pursuing the mayor, he would have been better off pursuing the mayor's nondescript wife, a woman "who runs everything" but who had not said a word in K.'s presence. Finally, K. dreams of the gaze of a "girl from the castle," a gaze from weary blue eyes that he saw only a single time and would do *anything* for.[21]

These are certainly not portraits of women, even though the blue eyes were likely based on Milena's. Are these paradigmatic women's lives, or case studies in social psychology—or is this a secret matriarchy of the village community? None of the above. Kafka's female characters utterly conform to their assigned functions in the novel. They are representatives of power and of a knowledge that is not acquired by social status but conferred on every female person; these are prototypes of a myth of femininity. And yet, these women never act like embodiments of male fantasies of fear and redemption but rather like creatures of flesh and blood. This is one of the most baffling mysteries in Kafka's magnum opus—and an absolutely unique achievement in the art of the novel, which here again surpasses *The Man Who Disappeared* and even *The Trial*—that Kafka was able to fuse societal and personal myths of the feminine and at the same time to maintain the individuality and credibility of his characters in an utterly fictional world. This linguistic and aesthetic achievement rests on a foundation of abilities that are rarely available in tandem and the same level of intensity, combining symbolic imagination with psychological empathy. Kafka was capable of idealizing Milena without forgetting her very real weaknesses, untruths, and limitations. He saw her girlfriend Jarmila, whose husband had taken his life, as a weak-willed player in a timeless tragedy; he wrote that it was as though she was carrying out "an assignment, not a human one."[22] Still, he was able to react to her situation so empathetically that she tried to get better acquainted with him. In a matter that was less spectacular but equally characteristic, he mounted a pragmatic defense of the Berlin chambermaid Emmy's interests even before getting to know her, yet interpreted her as a challenge and an essentially unmanageable complication posed by life.

Kafka's world was mythical in nature, with Old Testament and Jewish legends providing the templates, and it was only logical (even if Kafka did not state it openly) that he would try his hand at the canon of antiquity, reinterpreting it and incorporating it into his own imagination in the form of travesties, as in "The Silence of the Sirens," "Prometheus," and "Poseidon." However, *The Castle* sits at the pinnacle of this mythical landscape, and the characters in *this* game are not allegorical heroes but living people; they invite identification and pull the reader deep into the myth. Moreover, these texts adhere to a logic of the unconscious of the kind we know from dreams, which ensures that Kafka's language grabs us unawares; we succumb to it even before beginning to understand, and it lures us into the search for meaning. Kafka reinforces this provocation with a whole arsenal of literary sleights of hand that are difficult to make out at first. But if he should happen to leave the curtain open a crack and we catch a glimpse inside, he hastens to dim the light once again.[23] And yet he cannot leave his own mythical creation.

Kafka never wanted to interpret his works. The question is whether he *could* have done so. What, for example, do the unending, impenetrable hierarchies of the officials in *The Trial* and *The Castle* mean; what do they stand for? They are feared as powers, but they don't act. They reflect what goes on without taking part in or governing life; at most, they archive it. If they are attacked, or their demands are ignored, they back away. They allow strangers to move in on their women, are incapable of enforcing their own directives, and do not react when they are rebuffed aggressively, as by Amalia.[24] What kind of strange powers are these; where in the world would this be found? Even Kafka would not have been able to come up with answers in the sense of a definition or a one-to-one correspondence: perhaps our own inner self, the powers of the unconscious or the forces of life, the world behind the reality of the senses, the locus at which destinies are made . . . any attempt of that kind would obliterate the mystery of the metaphor and decapitate the symbol. At best, Kafka might have argued that our thoughts are always accompanied by mythical quicksand, and we cope with those kinds of ciphers every day. "It will be decided tomorrow," we say, for instance, or "It will come back to haunt us." Who is "it"? *They* are.

The world of *The Castle* is arcane and sealed up tight. It is only since the manuscript of the novel with all its textual variants has been accessible to the public that we know that Kafka was increasingly undecided about the further development of the plot, but that he understood the archaic laws governing this underworld right from the first line. There are of course even more hidden doors; Kafka's diary notes, and letters that were written before and during his work on *The Castle*, often function as commentaries. They show that Kafka was working with building blocks of the myth outside the novel, as well. These set pieces existed even *before* the literary endeavor, often as images and metaphors or as stage settings, all sharing an unmistakable imaginative and logical connection. These images are reproduced in a great many intertwined variations, and even before Kafka thought of giving them literary form, a closely meshed, proliferating tissue bringing in ever new ideas sprouted from them: a personal myth.

At the center of this web of connections lies the certainty that there are forces from which any happiness has to be wrested. Early on, Kafka had introduced the concept of ghosts in what was initially a conventional image, but the image evolved into an autonomous idea that slipped further and further out of his control. "To each his own: you get the guests, and I the ghosts," he had once written to Felice in jest. Shortly thereafter, however, he reported in detail how he had lured the ghosts to him over the years and that they kept growing in number and size: "[T]hey came in through every door, pushing in all that were closed; they were large, bony ghosts, nameless in the multitude; it was possible to fight with one of them, but not with all the ones surrounding. If one were writing, they were all benevolent ghosts, but if one were not writing, they were devils." By early February 1922, in Spindelmühle, Kafka had internalized this idea so fully that he did not even need to put a name to it; all he had to do was to summon it up: "Escaped them," he wrote after a few nights of astonishingly good sleep. "Reckless to say that. It calls them out of the woods as if the light had been lit to help them find the way." Finally, in the spring of that year, the ghosts became the subject of a brief mythological lecture prepared for Milena Pollak. Kafka held them up as forces of destiny that undermine life and bring disaster on all of mankind.

> The easy possibility of writing letters—from a purely theoretical point of view—must have brought ruination to the souls of the world. Writing letters is actually communication with ghosts, not only with the ghost of the recipient, but also with one's own ghost, which secretly evolves inside the letter one is writing or even in a whole series of letters where one letter corroborates another and can cite it as a witness. How did people ever get the idea they could communicate with one another by letter! One can think about someone far away and one can hold on to someone nearby; everything else is beyond human power. But writing letters means bar-

> ing oneself to the ghosts, who are greedily awaiting that. Written kisses never arrive at their destination; the ghosts drink them up along the way. This ample nourishment enables them to multiply so enormously. Mankind senses this and struggles against it; in order to attain a natural communication and a tranquility of soul, and to switch off the ghostly dimension as far as possible, man invented trains, cars, airplanes, but nothing helps anymore. These are evidently inventions devised at the moment of crashing. The opposing side is so much calmer and stronger; after the postal system, the ghosts invented the telegraph, the telephone, the wireless. The ghosts will not starve, but we will perish.[25]

The opposing side. The phrase reveals that his mythopoeic imagination had reached the next level. Although the recipient of this letter could not know it, Kafka had just written a novel about this opposing side. But in *The Castle*, the fiends (who work mainly at night) are no longer a chaotic mob but emissaries of a system, officials who are not free and are themselves subjugated to an unfathomable will. Somewhere inside the castle a highest authority lives; it is the castle of Count Westwest, without whose tacit approval not a creature can stir. This creature with the unearthly name is mentioned on page 20, only to disappear behind a smoke screen of endless chatter. And no one penetrates these walls by waiting patiently for them to become porous—as in Kafka's "Before the Law" legend—or by the land surveyor's challenge to a "fight." The highest authority exists, but it remains unrelentingly remote, and thus the crucial question of whether it is hostile or even evil remains a matter of conjecture. Kafka himself was not clear on this. A few months before beginning the novel, he wrote:

> The systematic destruction of myself over the years is astonishing, it was like a slowly widening breach in a dam, a purposeful action. The spirit that brought it about must now be celebrating triumphs; why doesn't it let me take part in them? But perhaps it hasn't yet completed its work and can therefore think of nothing else.

A few days later, however, Kafka found another interpretation: "The wonder, the indecipherability of my not having perished already, of the silent power guiding me."[26] A law, an authority, a spiritual power

sense of pride flashes up in Kafka's writing, the dignity of a creative power that needs no justification and blazes its own trails:

> I am elsewhere; it is only that the attraction of the human world is enormous, in an instant it can make one forget everything. Yet the attraction of my world is strong as well; those who love me love me because I am "forsaken" . . . because they sense that I have the freedom of movement that I utterly lack here on another plane in times of happiness.[30]

Never before had Kafka provoked his "ghosts" this directly. He felt he could now articulate this because he had begun work on a major novel, his magnum opus, in which his writing momentum merged fully with the form and content. The writer has moved to a desert and describes his arrival in a desert that is *white*. What happens in his novel is an onslaught against the "earthly boundary," as is his work on the novel itself, for which Kafka was now prepared to put everything on the line once again. The other people—in reality and in the novel—are gawking witnesses to his presumption, but deep inside they feel a respect that they themselves do not understand. The land surveyor arouses hope, especially in women. It is as though they had always awaited him, as though only he, a stranger, could succeed in breaking the spell. Of course he never will, but the author who invented him just might.

The Trial and *The Castle*, the world of officials and of peasants, and yet the same mythical universe in which neither professional status nor social standing, neither education nor experience, nor even intellect and social perspicacity actually matter. It is the same process, guided by the same opaque rules—although not in the same phase. "The worlds of *The Trial* and *The Castle*," Roberto Calasso tells us, "run parallel to all other worlds but not to each other. Each is, rather, the extension of the other."[31] Kafka demonstrates this in large part by making only *The Castle* include a past. The trial against Josef K. began out of the blue, ex nihilo; it was as though the stage lights suddenly went up, and there was no mention of a formal decision-making process prior to the arrest. By contrast, the complications involving K., the land surveyor, have a past history that can be probed and is stored in the memory of the villagers. It goes like this:

One day, long ago, the village mayor received a surprising message: A land surveyor was being appointed, and they were to ready all plans and sketches needed for his work. A land surveyor? The mayor wrote back that the village sent its thanks, but it had no need of a land surveyor. But this reply went not to the original department—which shall be called A—but to another department, B, and even there it was incomplete; an empty file folder indicated merely that the subject was the appointment of a land surveyor. After months or even years, when the whole matter was nearly forgotten in the village, department B sent the empty folder back for completion. But because the original decree could not be found, the village mayor simply repeated that there was no need for a land surveyor. An extensive correspondence ensued between the mayor and department B, where a mistrustful official, who was not satisfied with any of the information, looked into the matter himself. Even so, the origin of the confusion could not be determined, so department B had no choice but to send secretaries to the village to determine whether a land surveyor was or was not needed. After long debates, the town council stated that no land surveyor was needed. By then, however, a supervisory department, C, had discovered that years earlier, a letter from department A had gone unanswered. This correspondence was now repeated, and the mayor replied as he had in the past—this was now the third time—that there was no need whatsoever for a land surveyor. Several more years passed by, until one evening, a stranger suddenly appeared at the Bridge Inn and—astonishingly—introduced himself as the land surveyor who had been appointed by the castle.[32]

Several months after writing this episode of the novel, Kafka received a letter from the Prague-Žižkov tax office, dated September 25, 1922, reference number Rp 38/21, in which he was summoned to appear at the bureau and explain when the last capital contributions had been made at the First Prague Asbestos Works, of which he was a partner. Kafka replied immediately that he was quite ill and was therefore unable to appear in person, but he assured them that since 1914—the year in which his brother-in-law Paul Hermann had joined as copartner—there had been no additional accumulation of capital, and that the business in question had been removed from the company register in 1917 and had thus ceased to exist five years earlier. After a few days, Kafka received another letter from the tax office, asking him what his message meant, and stating that they had no knowledge of an inquiry dated September 25 or of a reference number Rp 38/21. Kafka was baffled, but relieved; he had already paid plenty of supplementary taxes for the factory and had even had to request payment in installments and debt relief. Now he could finally consider the matter settled because if the official file was missing, there was certainly no official awaiting his response. That turned out to be wrong. About a month later, on November 3, the Prague-Žižkov tax office sent another letter: "You are requested to answer this letter, dated September 25, 1922, Rp 38/21 within eight days, otherwise we will press charges at the Prague financial district office for the purpose of imposing a fine."

CHAPTER TWENTY-FOUR

Retiree and Hunger Artist

All reasonably large snail shells make good sounding boards....

—*Brehms Tierleben*

"IN MY BUREAU, THINGS ARE CALCULATED AS THOUGH MY LIFE were not beginning until tomorrow, yet I am at the end."[1] Of course, there are also *internal* bureaus as impenetrable as Austro-Hungarian administrations, and quite some time can pass before they take note of reality. But when Kafka returned from three weeks in Spindelmühle—he had spent several days there without his doctor—he recognized that there were other, far more efficient bureaus, among them the Workers' Accident Insurance Institute, and in his absence there had been quite a bit of judicious calculation.

Kafka's vacation in the Riesengebirge had already necessitated a further extension of his sick leave, and this time he had not had much to offer beyond the hope for recovery and a "gradual" resumption of his normal workload. This did not sound convincing, and after the medical officer had recommended that Kafka retire months earlier, it was clear to all concerned that this situation was precarious. It is quite likely that at the very time Kafka was working away at his new novel, discussions were going on at the institute on the question of how to retirement that began on July 1, a relatively beneficial payment plan was approved: 10,608 Czech kronen annually, plus a 1,920 Czech kronen cost-of-living allowance, in all about 60 percent of his previous income. Kafka knew that he would have to get by on that, most likely forever.[5]

Robert Klopstock noticed that Kafka had grown more withdrawn and less outgoing as the months went on. The medical student, who was still in the High Tatras, knew Kafka only as a convalescent, far from his daily obligations. Their relationship was cordial. Kafka confided in Klopstock and proved to be an attentive listener and adviser for other guests, as well. His helpfulness was astonishing; even months after leaving Matliary, Kafka was still running from one office to the next to obtain benefits for Klopstock and enable him to move to Prague. Of course he was not writing nearly as often or in as much detail as Klopstock, who was thirsting for conversation, would have liked. Particularly when it came to Kafka's own problems, including his health setbacks, every little detail had to be coaxed out of him. Kafka sent only one card from Spindelmühle, and when he received yet another demanding telegram from Klopstock after his return, he defiantly handed it to his mother to answer.

Klopstock did not understand this; he was disappointed, and he faced the looming estrangement by stepping up his efforts to curry favor with Kafka while reproaching him. He complained that everything had been so different in Matliary. Kafka denied that this was the case; the idealized "phantom" that Klopstock was now making out of him existed only in the letters. "You will quite easily see that it does not exist, but only a man who is hard to put up with, who is buried in himself and locked away within himself with a strange key, but who has eyes to see and will rejoice at every step forward that you take and at your great encounter with the world that rushes to meet you."[6]

Klopstock was of course not content with these vague generalities, and when he finally came to Prague in April 1922 to enroll at the German University and continue his medical studies, his fears were confirmed. Although Kafka was as helpful as ever, and had prepared Klopstock's move as best he could and had even gotten him a little job in the laboratory of Dr. Hermann, he did not wish to see Klopstock every day.[7]

Klopstock now had to learn what Brod had struggled to internalize for two decades: a friendship with Kafka was possible only if his need to be alone was respected unconditionally and at all times, especially when his retreats seemed totally unexpected and unmotivated. It would take the medical student some time to grasp the fact that this rule was not a personal slight. When Kafka once insisted on putting off seeing him to the following day, Klopstock reacted like a spurned lover and sent several unhappy and possibly accusatory notes to his home. He evidently felt that he was being held at arm's length only because Kafka, a writer and chief secretary, was no longer dependent on him in Prague and because he considered Klopstock "inferior." That was so far from the truth that Kafka was compelled to respond:

> This alleged "inferiority" is that we are desperate rats who hear the footsteps of the master of the house and flee in various directions, for instance to women, you to this one or that one, I to literature. But it is all in vain; our very choice of refuges sees to that, the choice of particular women, etc. That is the inferiority.[8]

That did not sound especially kind, but Klopstock's behavior, and hints he kept dropping in his letters, had given Kafka the uneasy feeling that Klopstock was in Prague solely on his account. Of course, there were reasons (which they had discussed at length in Matliary) that Klopstock was unable to continue his studies in Budapest: The anti-Semitically charged atmosphere was unbearable there; all Hungarian universities had already introduced admissions quotas for Jews (this was the first country in Europe to do so), and Klopstock even feared for his life if he were stuck in Hungary without a passport. The German University in Prague was not free of anti-Semitic aggression either, as he would soon learn. In the summer and fall of 1922, there were riots by German National students who refused to receive their diplomas from the hands of a Jewish rector. But the very fact that a Jew would even be chosen to be the rector and then placed under special protection by the government would have been unthinkable in Hungary.[9] Klopstock was also greatly relieved to meet more than a thousand Hungarian-speaking fellow students in Prague: Hungarians who had become citizens of Czechoslovakia after the war, when the borders were shifted, and Hungarian Jews who were refused permission to study in Budapest.

There were good reasons for him to pick Prague, but in Matliary they had never discussed the idea that Kafka's presence might be a decisive factor, let alone the sole criterion in Klopstock's decisions about where his life was heading. This was not what they had agreed to, Kafka stated curtly, only to concede that he could no longer assume a responsibility like that for anyone. His fear was too great:

> [F]ear of any indissoluble bond at present—I am not talking about the future—a bond emphatically, outrightly (I leave aside tacit agreements), magnificently planted before heaven and adorned with all the sacraments of inseparability. It is as unattainable for me with men as it is with women. What's the use of such grand things on this pilgrimage, in this state of begging? Every moment brings inescapable, delightedly seized opportunities for the most shameless kind of boasting. Why look for still more opportunities? And anyway, the loss may not be as great as it sometimes seems: If one feels some sort of shared direction, there is bond enough in that. May the rest be left to the stars.[10]

Kafka was not mincing words, and even though Klopstock was certainly not the man for "tacit agreements," he must have begun to realize that although the boundary drawn by Kafka had to be respected, it was also porous under certain conditions. This boundary line was essentially drawn under the watchful eyes of the "ghosts," the "opposing side" that Kafka did not want to provoke with any ostentatious claim to happiness. But in the seclusion of the moment, in the spontaneity of the conversation, there was enough room remaining to defy even "heaven."

For Klopstock, it was surely comforting to know that the "shared direction" Kafka was offering was not just a meaningless phrase. There *were* shared interests, and Klopstock's role was not restricted to that of disciple and devotee. He still maintained intellectual contacts at the Hungarian capital, and he knew several authors in the milieu of the leading literary journal, *Nyugat* (The west), and this was how Kafka learned about the dawn of modernity in Hungarian literature, especially the work of the prominent poet Endre Ady, whom he read in German translation (a gift from Klopstock). Not only was Klopstock well-read, but he also tried his hand at translation from the Hungarian. Kafka looked over his drafts and added his own suggestions for revision. Klopstock's linguistic competence must have won him over early on, and in the fall of 1922 he entrusted Klopstock with his own works. He had found out that in Košice, Hungary, two unauthorized translations—of "The Judgment" and "The Metamorphosis"—had been published, and he asked Kurt Wolff Verlag (which had evidently failed to notice these publications) to reserve future translation rights for Robert Klopstock. The publisher did not respond, so Kafka repeated his request in the spring of 1923, this time successfully. Klopstock was apparently planning not only publications of Kafka's texts in *Nyugat* but also—and this was a striking parallel to Milena Pollak—a selection of Kafka's works in book form. This book project was never completed, but several translations he later published in the *Prágai Magyar Hírlap* ("Prague Hungarian Newspaper"): "Up in the Gallery," "Absent-Minded Window-Gazing," "The Trees," and "A Fratricide," published in 1925, show that Klopstock took this project seriously and had already begun work on it.[11]

But all this was not enough for Klopstock, because he did not have the kind of literary friendship Max Brod enjoyed with Kafka, a friendship in which each could glimpse the work of the other. Kafka did say on occasion that he was trying his hand at writing again after years of silence, but he used statements of that sort only in order to excuse his own absence. Writing, he explained, was now "the most important thing in the world to me . . . the way a madman's delusion is important to him . . . or a woman's pregnancy to her."[12] He did not let Klopstock peer inside his writing process, and there is no evidence that he ever read parts of his new novel to him. That remained the privilege of his old friends, especially Brod, who even took a notebook of *The Castle* home with him and could clamor for more, the way he had for so long. But even Brod must have been taken aback when he learned that Kafka, who was constantly feverish, was not only working intensely on his greatest literary creation to date—he produced sixteen chapters in a space of only four months—but was also finding time for other projects.

One of the small notebooks that Kafka had carried up to the Hradčany every day during the war to write in from Ottla's tiny cottage contains a long fragment that seems to emanate from an exotic literary world. "The Great Wall of China" was Kafka's title for this text, which is somewhere between a story and a legend, political reflection and fictional memoir, and it is unclear what the first-person narrator is driving at. Evidently he is interested primarily in the function of the emperor, who unites the vast Chinese population as a ubiquitous symbol—without any direct communication between "above" and "below"; in fact this communication does not function even on the rare occasions when those "above" desire it. Embedded in this text is a parable that illustrates this idea. Kafka later published this parable separately, as "An Imperial Message," which was yet another variation on his key metaphor, the hierarchy of authorities thrust between people and their destinies as an impenetrable obstruction. Kafka, who was pausing here on his path from *The Trial* to *The Castle*, seemed to be realizing for the first time that this metaphor had a dark underside: the gate remains closed to us not only because the doorkeeper refuses to open it but because the key is missing on the other side—which makes the situation far more dire.

"The Great Wall of China," however, begins with a narrative detour, focusing not on the emperor, but on the Great Wall, which takes generations to build and supposedly requires a special technique to give it a lasting quality. It is constructed not as a single entity but rather in individual sections far apart from one another, each only several hundred yards in length. Between them there are gaps that are filled in little by little, but their number and extent remain unknown to the workers and even to the local site managers. Hence, no one apart from those in the top command can say with any certainty how far the construction has progressed; it is not even clear whether the wall will really have all the gaps filled in when the work is done. It is never completed, and remains a fragment made up of fragments.

Readers cannot help but be reminded of Kafka's creative process and of the bits and fragments with which he filled his notebooks. And didn't *The Trial* originate in this very manner? Kafka wrote the first chapter, then the last. Afterwards he tried to close the "gap," not in a linear manner, the way a bridge is built, but rather with loosely connected chapters, with something evidently happening in between, something that the author skipped over and might add later. What is more, Kafka kept putting *The Trial* aside to work on other projects, and the resultant stories were "In the Penal Colony, "The Village Schoolmaster," and "Memories of the Kalda Railway." An additional step back reveals the outlines of a comprehensive life's work that is hinted at in fragments and even more in gaps, a meta-structure that has been characterized as "Kafka's world" or "Kafka's universe."

This world of the imagination can seem oppressively sealed off and self-referential. It has the structure of a myth, which explains why readers get the odd feeling that they either do or do not have access, and that no amount of interpretation can force the issue. On the other hand, this imaginary world is also manifold and far-flung; Kafka inevitably failed at the attempt to capture it in a single work, although there is some indication that he clung to this utopia of literary creation down to the end but was foiled by a technical problem that stood in the way of achieving this utopia: every text that recounts something is carried by a plot, by characters and places, and this foundation is resilient only to a point and cannot be expanded at will later on. No single work can envelop everything. For instance, Kafka would surely have undermined the mysterious, parabolic, or allegorical structure of *The Castle* if he had had his protagonist appear explicitly as a Jew or a writer, although this double experience of exclusion clearly underlay his dogged battle for village and castle: the isolation of the western European Jew who is cut off from his own tradition and who is even refused the right to be a guest ("we do not need guests"), and the voluntary seclusion of the author, who emigrates from the ordinary life and strives for something "higher," no matter what the cost, even if it means losing his family, friends, and loved ones. But because these two themes were plaguing Kafka once again, especially once he knew that he had reached the end of the road as a professional and thus also as an upstanding member of society, he came upon a solution that he had employed successfully in the past: he opened up more construction sites apart from the novel, new segments of the Great Wall; they were not joined together, but they all lay along the same line.

"First Sorrow" is the title of a miniature narrative for which he had already interrupted his work on the novel back in March. It is the portrait of a childlike trapeze artist, dependent on his impresario, his life utterly replaced by art: he avoids touching the ground, lives contentedly on his trapeze, and the first and only sorrow that his profession poses comes from his sudden wish to work with *two* trapeze bars. Kafka sent a copy of this story to Hans Mardersteig, the editor of *Genius*, a bibliophile journal of literature and art that was published twice a year by Kurt Wolff Verlag.[13] Mardersteig had asked him several times, both cordially and insistently, to send a contribution to the journal, and had even said he would be willing to print a fragment, no matter what the length; Kafka would not, of course, entertain the thought of doing so. But it was now quite awkward that Kafka's final offer—there would be just a single issue of the journal still to be published—was responded to not by Mardersteig himself, but by Wolff, to whom Kafka had owed an answer for months. We cannot tell whether he was able to bring himself to send a few noncommittal words of thanks to the publisher this time, but the prospect of being pestered, on and on, displeased Kafka in the extreme. He would be happy, he wrote to Brod, if he "could take the repulsive little story out of Wolff's desk drawer and wipe it out of his memory; it is impossible for me to read his letter."[14]

That would not happen to him again. He now came up with a far better and more radical version of art's hostility to life as embodied by the performer in a story he called "A Hunger Artist." Even Kafka regarded this gem of a story, for which he had interrupted his work on the novel for a day or two, as "tolerable," the highest grade he bestowed on any of his own texts. Even so, Wolff did not hear about it at first—instead, the story went via Max Brod to a competitor, Rudolf Kayser, who had become the editor in charge of *Die neue Rundschau* early that year.

The reputation of this S. Fischer Verlag publication had again risen markedly after the nationalist delirium of 1914–1915, and while the numerous more recent journals, which had placed far too much emphasis on Expressionism, disappeared one by one (among them Schickele's *Die weissen Blätter*), *Die neue Rundschau* became established as the platform for the progressive democratic and European-minded intelligentsia. Now that Brod had introduced Kafka in a major essay, the opportunity to be published here became a greater temptation for Kafka than ever—greater, at any rate, than the prospect of being put off again for years with production difficulties by Kurt Wolff, who would have instantly claimed the manuscript for himself. Kafka was clearly aware that this publication in Berlin was almost an affront after all the encouraging letters he had received from his publisher. Nevertheless, "A Hunger Artist" was printed in *Die neue Rundschau* in October 1922, and the lesser piece, "First Sorrow," in *Genius* in early 1923. This was an unambiguous signal from Wolff's perspective. Hadn't Kafka kept telling him that he had nothing to offer? And now that he had obviously returned to his true calling, the benefits were being reaped elsewhere. A few years earlier, Wolff would not have hesitated to suggest a separate publication of the two texts to Kafka, in an additional slim volume in large print. But this time he said nothing.

It was the kind of landscape that Kafka now loved. A wide valley, a calm river with tree-lined shores and sandy spots that seemed perfect for swimming, with pastures, gently rising hillsides, and silent woods all around. A simple landscape that was situated not in the shadow of imposing mountaintops but out in the open under a big sky. The village of Planá, the popular summer resort at the Lužnice River in southern Bohemia, just a hundred kilometers from Prague.

Ottla and Josef David had rented a modest apartment here in the house of a craftsman. It had two rooms on the second floor, one bright and warm, with two windows and a lovely view of the river and woods, and the other a small, sloped attic room with a view of the garden, plus a large kitchen. Ottla and Věra (who was now fifteen months old) would spend the summer here, and Ottla's husband would come to Planá on the weekends and for a brief vacation. This idyll was an irresistible temptation for Kafka. It brought back memories of Zürau, his happiest time. Never had he been as well cared for as there. Now that Ottla was free of the tough agricultural work and the daily struggle for food, she might be able to take care of her brother as well as her child. A maid came with them to Planá, and thus everything could work out even better than it had on the farm. The Davids were fine with the idea of Franz moving in; the attic room would not be in use a good bit of the time anyway, and if he shared in the rent, everyone would come out ahead.

Even so, it was a decision that required some courage on Ottla's part, and, as she knew from experience, some sacrifice. It could be quite fun to live right next door to Franz—in Prague there was also just one story between them—but it also meant that she would have to play the nurse, keeping an eye on what he was eating and coping with the peevish behavior he was even more prone to display since the onset of his fever and insomnia in Zürau. But what would become of him, where would he turn to get some light and air for his ailing body in the summer? He could no longer afford a long stay at a health resort, as he had in Merano, and spending the nicest part of the year alone on Altstädter Ring—his parents were in Franzensbad, Elli at the Baltic Sea, Weltsch in Schelesen, and Klopstock back in the High Tatras now that the semester had ended—would have gone against the doctor's advice and been depressing. So on June 23, one week before his official retirement, he took an express train heading south. The last stop of this train was Vienna, a destination that was now far beyond his horizon. Just one and a half hours later, he got out in Tábor and changed to a local train for a few kilometers until he reached Planá, then he need to take just a few steps to get where he would be staying, Příčná ulice no. 145. The tracks leading to Vienna were right nearby, but the long-distance trains did not stop here. For a full three months, they rode through Kafka's field of vision, but he did not know how often Milena Pollak was in them.

He wrote to Klopstock that Planá was "extraordinarily beautiful." But was it all right to say that? Wouldn't it arouse the opposing side and entice the ghosts? Of course: there they were! Evidently they had come from Prague on the slow train, and on the second day they brought up their weapons. It was the old familiar arsenal, which Kafka knew all too well from Zürau, Matliary, and Spindelmühle, but the ghosts had now rearmed, and he was soon subjected to their merciless clever attacks from all sides: a boy practicing his French horn, a large family that tedded the hay right under his window, and wood being chopped for hours under the other window. A few hundred yards away, there was a sawmill with an electrical buzz saw; hammering and clanking chains from the railway station, where the logs brought in on the river are loaded; and a winch that was usually pulled "by sensible horses" but, on occasion, by dimwitted oxen that needed constant goading with cries of "*gee* and *ho* and *sakramentská pakáž*."[15] And most cunningly of all, whole groups of children, some from the neighborhood and others relatives of the landlady, turned up in the front garden of the house at eight in the morning and romped around with a handcart. What could be done about the children? They had no other place to play, and the racket they were making was an expression of the most innocent high spirits. "*Mařenka*!" Kafka shouted in desperation when he saw the thirteen-year-old leader of the group. "Why don't you go pick mushrooms?"[16]

More than once, he thought about whether the big apartment in Prague, which was absolutely quiet in the summer, might not have been the better solution. But he did not want to abandon Ottla, who was trying hard to keep down the noise level. Sometimes she went down with little Veruška in her arms and bribed the children with candy to make them go away for a while. But Kafka was ashamed, especially when he saw that the neighbor, a millworker who did shift work and desperately needed his siesta, sometimes had no choice but to send his own seven children over to the small fenced yard in front of Kafka's window. And he was even more ashamed when Josef David, who would have greatly preferred to sleep in the big room, was ushered into the cool attic by Ottla. The three of them spent cramped weekends there, while the writer took over almost the entire rest of the apartment. And they had to be quiet because he slept so little, and when he was not sleeping, he usually sat in front of his notebooks, coughing, with earplugs in his ears.

There were also peaceful times. Almost every evening, as dusk approached, Kafka took a long walk, accompanied by the landlady's black spotted dog. He crossed the river to a forested area adjacent to a neighborhood with new, luxurious villas that were rented out during the summer months. The previous year, even the governor had stayed there, far from the sawmill and the loading ramps at the railway station. President Beneš and other prominent politicians from Prague also spent time here, and even actors, singers, and directors of the Nationaltheater could be spotted. Kafka walked past the villas into the woods, and the quiet of the evening under the trees now seemed to him the best thing the world had to offer. At the edge of the woods, there was a bench with a wonderful view. Sometimes he went a few miles downstream, watching the farmers return home from the fields and having a look at the Soukeník mill near the former fortress in Sedlec, and when he turned around, he could see Tábor in the distance. How lovely it would be to live on *this* side of Lužnice, on one of those well-kept properties ... a thought that evidently provoked the ghosts all over again because one dreadful day, Kafka heard "hellish noise" at the edge of the woods. This noise came from two hundred children from Prague who were spending the night at a campground nearby, "a scourge of humanity."[17]

He was exaggerating, and he knew it. It was not always that bad, and he did not let on to his friends that on some days he even contributed to the noise by chopping wood for the cool evenings. But how else was he to explain his hyperexcitable state to his friends, a state that was bringing him closer to insanity than anything they knew from personal experience? Brod was also starting to struggle with insomnia and the torture of nocturnal obsessive thoughts that drove him to jealous homicidal fantasies. Felix Weltsch was sometimes tormented beyond endurance by his wife. And Klopstock was suffering from feelings of inferiority that bordered on depression. But the sufferings of these people came from the fact that they were living and loving, and their losses were nothing but the consequence of risks they willingly assumed, risks of life and of love. Kafka, by contrast, aimed more and more at *avoidance*, and the dead silence he craved symbolized this avoidance. He tried to limit any movement or change, like a wounded man who fears pain so much that he stays in whatever position he is in, no matter how uncomfortable.

He had lost the fight for Milena, but back then—about two years earlier—he had fought for the decision as long as his strength held out, and down to the end he had remained in charge of his decisions. His friends respected that, even though they considered his resignation premature. But what was he fighting for now? Oskar Baum had suggested he come to Georgenthal in Thuringia to spend a few summer weeks with him and his family; Baum had looked into suitable accommodations, and even reserved a quiet room for Kafka with a balcony and lounge chair. But at the last moment, after yet another sleepless night, Kafka begged off, claiming that he was too afraid of traveling and could not bring himself to make *any* change in the life he had grown accustomed to in Planá: "This will mean," he wrote to Brod, "that from now on I cannot go out of Bohemia; before long, I will be confined to Prague, then to my room, then to my bed, then to a certain position in bed, then to nothing more."[18]

Two months later—it was now the fall—Kafka had a chat with Frau Hnilička, the landlady, who had not been especially cordial to him in the past. Kafka told her that he was quite pleased with Planá and would like to stay on, perhaps even through the winter. But if Ottla was no longer there, he would have to fend for himself at the inn, and that would not be the right thing to do. Frau Hnilička remarked that he seemed to be afraid of being alone, but Kafka made light of this idea, whereupon she offered to cook for him and told him he could stay as long as he liked. What would he say to that? Kafka could hardly believe his ears, and he thanked her again and again without thinking it over. He could not imagine anything better; it would not be expensive, he would not have to eat meat, the surroundings were familiar and pleasant, the noise from the children would let up in the winter, and once the Lužnice River was frozen over and there were no more timber rafts, the buzz saw would fall silent as well. He turned and went into the house, but as he climbed the winding staircase, he started to panic. He knew that he would not be able to sleep a wink until he took back this spontaneous decision. But how? Kafka was relieved when Ottla dismissed the idea on medical grounds: the air was too chilly, and the valley was often foggy in the winter. The next morning, she took the matter with the landlady into her own hands, which required no more than a few words, while Kafka stood there gaping "like Gulliver listening to the giant women conversing."[19]

This was hardly the first time Kafka had had feelings of this sort; he had experienced agitation bordering on a loss of psychological control in the past, but the new element was that it did not take much to bring on these "breakdowns," as he called them, and they lasted for days on end. Occasional disruptions and pressures threw him into a state of panic, while he was readily able to carry out very concrete tasks, even unpleasant ones, provided that they did not require him to make decisions. In mid-July, for instance, he received a telegram from his mother begging him to come home: his father had developed an umbilical hernia that pinched off his intestines; he had been transported to Prague and needed an operation the same evening. Kafka spent quite a number of hours at his father's sickbed and found he could accept without complaint the interruption of his summer vacation (and thus also of his novel) and observe the events in his family, especially the interesting phenomenon of his helpless father, rather matter-of-factly.

Max Brod, whom he kept informed with detailed letters, felt of course that Kafka's sufferings were caused by his calculated suppression of his erotic desires. "You avoid women," he wrote, "you try to live without them. And that doesn't work." Kafka readily admitted to avoiding women and suppressing his sexual desire, but Brod seemed to believe that Kafka did so out of a penchant for asceticism, and hence on ideological grounds. Brod felt that he needed to emerge from this defensive position, meet new people, take a trip through Germany, visit his publisher, enjoy a theater premiere in Berlin, maybe even accept a concrete journalism assignment. These nice illusions were based on the assumption that Kafka had a choice, that it was just a matter of pulling himself together. But the fact was that his irritability was like an open wound. Even women in summer clothing in the big city—a sight that was certainly nothing new to him—suddenly seemed "half-naked" to him; they brought his agitation to an almost painful level and made him hasten back to the country.[20]

It was most likely Brod himself who had understandably become the victim of suppression: the deeper his entanglements in erotic anguish, the more he assumed that his friend—particularly since the episode with Milena—was out to avoid emotional pain. But Kafka was now facing a threat of an entirely different dimension. His hypersensitivity (now bordering on pathological), insomnia, and increasing fear of being alone were brought on not by suppression but by recognition of his plight. His very insight instilled fear of the imminent catastrophe. There is no record of any frank conversations he had about this matter in Planá, but it is certain that Ottla sensed instinctively what was at stake, no matter how dismissive of medical advice her brother appeared to be. She was well aware while taking care of him that there might not be many more opportunities to do so. And when she noticed that her upcoming departure in early September brought him near the point of desperation, she offered to stay on a few more weeks.

Brod was probably also misled about the gravity of the situation by Kafka's intense work on *The Castle* over the previous six months. How could someone become desperate when looking ahead to the prospect of publishing this novel? There were also the new contacts with Berlin, as well as the forthcoming printing of "A Hunger Artist," which might open up new opportunities. And didn't it seem as though Kafka's self-awareness as an author had grown? At first he had been almost ashamed to show Brod the first chapters of the novel, regarding them as boring and tedious. Brod begged to differ and called it a "very entertaining, colorful book"—he underlined the word "colorful" twice. Kafka kept on writing, and he considered the later chapters he finished in Planá more successful. It seemed highly unlikely to Brod that Kafka would be held back by any pettishness during such a creative phase that was utterly free of professional obligations. Even when Kafka wrote to him on September 11 that more than two weeks had gone by since he had made progress on the novel, and he would "evidently have to drop [it] forever," Brod was not prepared to accept the bad news. He replied merrily that he could only regard Kafka's message as "fabricated sensationalism" and advised Kafka to write more about the matter at hand, "that is, about continuing on with work."[21]

The final pages of the *Castle* manuscript, in Castle Notebook VI (which was not published in its entirety until 1982), show unmistakable traces of his trials and tribulations. The plot begins to unravel, various attempts and variants compete with one another, the deletions get longer and more complicated, and it is obvious that Kafka was working against strong resistance, as though he were rolling an ever-growing mass uphill. By some point in late August, it was over; he had reached an impasse.

What had happened? Was it another depressive "breakdown," as he intimated to Brod, or was it a visit to his parents in Prague that distracted him for too long and caused irreparable damage to the literary web he was weaving? It was certainly not an issue of uncertainty about the direction and endpoint of the novel, because Kafka's papers show that he had set his sights on a specific conclusion. He probably could have written the final chapter even before completing the novel, as he had for *The Trial*, since he had already determined the fate of his protagonist:

> The ostensible land surveyor gains at least partial satisfaction. He does not slacken in his struggle, but dies of exhaustion. The community gathers around his deathbed, and just then the decision comes down from the castle that although he has no legal claim to live in the village, considering certain circumstances, he is permitted to live and work there.

Before Max Brod published the novel he found in Kafka's literary estate, he sketched out the finale Kafka had planned as an unquestionable, but not unconditional, defeat.[22] It was a credible ending, characteristic of Kafka's thinking: the castle evidently *cannot* grant the desired legitimization as long as it is of any use for the petitioner, any better than the doorkeeper of the law can clear the way as long as the man who wants to get in is still able to do so. But this obvious mirroring of a well-considered motif did not help Kafka along, because contrary to his initial impression, and presumably even contrary to his original plans, he had come up against daunting narrative problems in writing *The Castle* that went well beyond the technical demands of *The Trial*. The longstanding construction principle in "The Great Wall of China"—the system of piecemeal construction—did not work here, and the linear principle of episodic drama, in which the author can work through the planned stages in virtually any order, was even less possible. Even though *The Castle* focuses almost exclusively on encounters, while the people the defendant Josef K. talks to, and all the other minor characters in *The Trial*, show up as if out of a fog and disappear again, *The Castle* develops a whole network of social relationships that introduces more and more characters and eventually includes even the castle bureaucracy from which individual officials come forth and make their mark. All these characters have their own stories; they forge alliances and foster hostilities, despise or love one another, and because these subepisodes affect the fate of the land surveyor, Kafka needed to follow them through to the end and to tie them together plausibly.

What, for example, becomes of Barnabas's family, whose story is presented to the reader over several chapters? How does the relationship between Frieda and the former "assistant" Jeremias develop? What happens to the ambitious chambermaid Pepi when she has to go back to her menial job after Frieda returns to the Gentry Inn? Then there are the land surveyor's numerous budding relationships, some of which remain vague, but others assume the concrete form of plans for future get-togethers. It is likely that Kafka was planning another encounter between K. and the mysterious Amalia. K. is also supposed to meet with a "girl from the castle," the mother of the boy Hans. The landlady of the Gentry Inn wants something from him, which presents yet another issue we expect to get resolved. Pepi talks K. into spending the winter in the basement of the Gentry Inn in a tiny cubbyhole and in the beds of three girls, and eventually the family of the peasant Gerstäcker also makes an appearance, and, suprisingly, offers K. a little job. As small as this world is, the exhausted land surveyor could use an appointment calendar; in the end, he loses control and, it would seem, so does the author. He is like a juggler who had learned how to keep a certain number of objects in motion and in the air, but everything topples if just a single one is added.

It must have been a depressing, even anguishing experience to fail with his third and—as he knew—final novel project, after more than half a year of intense work on it. A decade earlier, after breaking off his work on *The Man Who Disappeared*, he had briefly kept up hope that he would regain his powers of imagination and finish that novel, and then, too, he had had a concrete and visual notion of how the story would end. Kafka might have been able to resume his work even on *The Trial* as long as the struggle surrounding his possible marriage to Felice dragged on, and thus as long as the biographical constellation out of which the novel was born did not undergo any fundamental changes. But with *The Castle*, Kafka failed as a writer: he had put himself up to a task that he found narratively overwhelming, and he was unable to reconcile the creative process and the wealth of his imagination with the practical requirements of literary composition.

The letters and documents from Planá show that Kafka did not react to this defeat with laments, as he typically had in the past, but instead made it the subject of intense reflection and attempts to integrate it into his self-perception. Earlier this year, he was still defining himself as an émigré turning his back on life to move into an unknown extraterrestrial desert, and he prided himself on daring to do something that others denied themselves, and governing a whole empire that others could not even enter. However, Kafka's shorter texts indicated that this image of his personal myth, stemming from his reawakening desire to write literature, would not endure. The trapeze artist who lives and works high above the heads of his audiences in "First Sorrow" is anything but an admirable character, even though we learn right at the beginning that his art is one of the most difficult, that he is "an extraordinary, irreplaceable artist," and that he therefore has to subordinate all his personal needs to striving for perfection. Even if this sad person were to regard the narrow trapeze as his own home, it would not be a domain of freedom.

And the hunger artist? He, too, is a gypsy leading a rootless existence. In this text, Kafka was playing with an elusive definition of "art," which, when applied to the world of the circus and vaudeville, was always questionable. The physical specialization of the performer contains an element of absurdity and potential peril (even when he survives his performances), and for this very reason he never misses an opportunity to invoke the aura of life as an artist, whereas the audience knows quite well how to draw the distinction. A second-rate writer, painter, or musician is generally better known and enjoys a higher reputation than a first-class performer—not to mention sword swallowers, knife throwers, strongmen—or "hunger artists," whose art is nothing but a failure to act and hence positively invites fraud. Kafka, who was well informed about the working conditions of performance artists,[23] was describing a profession that was contentious even among circus people and was carried out not in the spotlight of menageries but in the twilight of sideshows. By the end of the nineteenth century, this skill was regarded as so deleterious and superfluous that impresarios had to make a pretext of furthering scientific aims, and by the onset of the hunger catastrophes of the war and the postwar period, this type of performance seemed somewhat obscene. Kafka was not justifying, let alone idealizing, the life of the hunger artist. At most, he made the reader feel his suffering and granted a final word of defense to the artist, who claims that he simply could not find the food he liked, otherwise he would not have "raised a fuss" and eaten like everyone else. But even if that were so, his hunger act would still be senseless, grounded in a merely individual sensibility, perhaps even a delusion. Hence it may be sad but not, strictly speaking, tragic that the public loses interest in the hunger artist long before his death and that life moves beyond him. At the end of the story, Kafka devoted a whole paragraph to the young panther that has now replaced the "artist" in his cage, with rapt spectators crowded around him.

The dubious nature of the artistic endeavor could hardly be illustrated more graphically, and the connection to Kafka's greatest literary undertaking is quite clear. The lengthier and more unwieldy the manuscript of his novel grew, the more he was assailed by doubts about the meaning of this work. He started to believe that it was actually a form of escapism, an abuse of a readily available drug, which, like any other chronic intoxication, culminates in the pain of withdrawal and destruction. It took Kafka no more than a few weeks after writing "A Hunger Artist" to fold this new pessimistic understanding of authorship into his personal myth, which is not a desert or a summit but more akin to a chasm into which he is being sucked, with the *opposing side* and the *powers* pulling him down.

> Last night, as I lay sleepless and had everything go back and forth between my aching temples again and again, what I had almost forgotten during the last relatively quiet time became clear to me: what frail or even nonexistent ground I live on, over a darkness from which the dark power emerges according to its will and, heedless of my stammering, destroys my life. Writing sustains me, but isn't it more accurate to say that it sustains this kind of life? By this I don't mean, of course, that my life is better when I don't write. In fact, it is much worse then and wholly unbearable and has to end in madness. But that, granted, only follows from the condition that I am a writer, which is actually true even when I am not writing, and a nonwriting writer is a monster inviting madness. But what about being a writer itself? Writing is a sweet and wonderful reward, but for what? In the night it became clear to me, as clear as a child's visual instruction, that it is the reward for serving the devil. This descent to the dark powers, this unshackling of spirits bound by nature, these dubious embraces and whatever else may take place down below, which is unknown to those up above, writing

The *Castle* notebooks in his suitcase were full of crossed-out pages. We cannot tell whether he brought himself to read aloud from them again—though it is likely, because Oskar Baum, to whom Kafka still felt indebted, had to rely on being read aloud to if he wanted to know what his friends were working on. And Kafka had woven a wonderful little twist into his manuscript that was most likely intended more for his friends than for a general audience.

The plot twist comes in the thirteenth chapter, when the land surveyor resorts to dubious methods in trying to enter the castle through some side door. He dupes an innocent child, Hans Brunswick, whose Madonna-like mother comes from the castle and is therefore irresistible to the land surveyor. The plan is for Hans to pave the way for K. to get to his mother. But what reason might the sickly woman have to agree to see K., to contend with his problems, and in doing so risk quarreling with her husband? Her illness would be a good reason, K. answers brazenly, because he, the land surveyor, knows a thing or two about medical care. And as though that were not enough, he adds that he has sometimes succeeded where doctors failed. At home he is even known as "the bitter herb" because of his healing powers.

Only readers well versed in the literary scene of the time would have realized on whose behalf the land surveyor was talking, and that he is even saying something true—in a sense. In May 1922, not long before Kafka wrote this scene, Franz Blei had published his spectacular *Bestiary of Modern Literature*, featuring a satirical lexicon in which he portrayed contemporary writers and intellectuals as exotic creatures. Blei seemed to have been extraordinarily well informed about the fondnesses, foibles, and phobias of the individuals he highlighted. His entry on Kafka reads as follows:

The Kafka is a very rare magnificent moon-blue mouse that does not eat meat but feeds on herbs. It is a fascinating sight because it has human eyes.[26]

CHAPTER TWENTY-FIVE

The Palestinian

The acts that had smashed all boundaries flowed back and left emptiness behind.

—Heimito von Doderer, *Der Grenzwald*

Dear Max, this time I really may not get up again, the onset of pneumonia is certainly likely after the month of pulmonary fever, and not even writing it down will keep it at bay, although the writing has a certain power.

In this case, then, my last will regarding all my writings:

Out of everything I have written, the only ones that count are these books: Judgment, Stoker, Metamorphosis, Penal Colony, Country Doctor, and the story Hunger Artist. (The few copies of Meditation can remain, I don't want to make anyone go to the trouble of pulping them, but nothing from it is to be reprinted.) When I say that those five books and the story count, I don't mean that I have any wish for them to be reprinted and passed on to the future; on the contrary, if they should disappear completely, it would be in accordance with my real wish. But since they're there, I'm not preventing anyone from keeping them if he wants to.

However, everything else of mine in writing (publications in journals, manuscripts or letters) is *without exception*, insofar as it can be obtained or recovered from the recipients (you know most of the recipients, the main ones being Frau Felice M, Frau Julie née Wohryzek, and Frau Milena Pollak; and in particular don't forget the few notebooks that Frau Pollak has)—all this is *without exception and preferably unread* (I won't stop you from looking at it, I'd prefer it if you didn't, but in any case nobody else must see it)—all this is without exception to be burned, and I ask you to do so as soon as possible,

Franz[1]

Kafka had known the significance of contracting pneumonia since being stricken with the Spanish flu in October 1918. This time he was in luck; the fever went down and there were no further complications. He could not handle another convalescence with his uncle Siegfried in Triesch (Třešť), Moravia, although the arrangements had been made—the family now made sure that Franz remained under its supervision—but it was doubtful whether the country doctor could have contributed anything beyond the standard wisdom.

Kafka did not hand the second set of provisions for his will to his friend, either, but instead kept it in his drawer. There would not have been much point in trying to justify it. Brod had already asked whether he could discreetly dispose of several sets of letters and notes he had hidden in the office if tragedy should strike, largely because of his wife Elsa. Still, chances were slim that Kafka's last will would be followed point by point, even though he had spelled out his wishes in detail, because no one shared his strict notion of an author's exclusive power of disposition. But even if Brod were to save the three unfinished novels from the fire—which was virtually certain—maybe he would at least show some consideration when it came to the letters and diaries? It was at least worth a try to articulate his own will clearly, while he was of sound mind but in fear of the end of his life approaching, and it was also a matter of self-respect. Some still argue today that Kafka should not have entrusted his friend and impresario with such a strict act of destruction if he meant it seriously, but that view overlooks the pragmatic reality that no one besides Brod even had access to the papers designated for destruction. Brod was related to Felice Marasse (née Bauer), Milena Pollak respected him, he himself was in possession of several of Kafka's manuscripts, and Kafka's family would not withhold the pertinent papers (this did turn out to be true). Brod became the executor of Kafka's will because no one else could have executed this will. Paradoxically, it is the huge number of letters and manuscripts collected by Brod that bore out Kafka's reasoning.

Would he have formulated his will this same way the following year, or the year after that? It is surprising that the story "First Sorrow," which he had intended to publish himself and would even include in his final book later, is missing from the list of the "valid" works. And we have no way of telling why he did not destroy the manuscript of *The Castle* and other notebooks from the previous months himself—or at least some of them. We can therefore conclude that the novel project, at any rate, was alive, and Kafka was undecided about what to do with the hundreds of pages he had written in Spindelmühle and Planá; his will to destruction was not steady enough to wipe out the achievement of an entire year of his life. But he had no doubts about "A Hunger Artist"; its publication in *Die neue Rundschau* and in the *Prager Presse* was a first visible indication that he was finally returning to his true profession. The family must have been astonished to learn that this story was even being reprinted in German-language papers in the United States. It was an odd idea, and perhaps the first to make the Kafkas think in terms of something as improbable as "fame." In this faraway place, there were actually people who cared about stories thought up by *our Franz*.[2]

The most striking change in Kafka was a new form of social (though not psychological) approachibility. In earlier years, when he was still free to spend time in coffeehouses whenever he liked or to wander about for hours in evening discussions, he had carefully shielded his parents' apartment as a retreat. Only his closest friends got to see his bed and desk. His room seemed quite uninviting, and even here he did not always take off his suit and tie. But this clean division between public and private space could not be maintained now that he was suffering from a chronic illness. Patients don't *make* visits; they *are* visited. By the fall of 1921, after he returned from Matliary, it had become more difficult to get Kafka to venture out of the house; he could not leave the apartment in cold or damp weather or if it was too hot outside. Sometimes his fever made it impossible to go out for weeks on end. In time it became routine for people to visit him at home without much fanfare, and sometimes the maid let in whole groups of visitors. On occasion Kafka had people over whom he had never seen before, such as the dramatist Georg Kaiser, whom Brod simply brought along with him.

It was thus a special, though not exceptional, occasion in mid-November when Franz Werfel came to visit Kafka (who was stricken with fever yet again) at his parents' apartment. Werfel was probably feeling a bit shy in Kafka's presence: he had underestimated him for a long time, and had later attempted to make up for his prior lack of praise by paying ecstatic tribute to him, but he evidently failed to find any deep connection to his work, and no pertinent "influences" can be found in Werfel's texts. Kafka, in turn, had been one of Werfel's earliest admirers, and even though his wide-eyed receptivity had largely evaporated—the war had seen to that—he was still astounded by the way things that others could not achieve, no matter how much effort they put into them, seemed to fall into this person's lap. Werfel did not seem tormented by having missed out on life; he wrote the way others breathed. In Kafka's eyes, Werfel embodied a utopian literary life that was not compromised even by weaker achievements. He found an "abundance of vitality" in Werfel's highly emotional drama *Mirror Man* (1920), despite its pathos and stylistic limitations, and he admired the author of the *Goat Song* (1921) as a "great swimmer," which, in Kafka's imagery was a term of the highest regard.[3]

But now he was quite tense when the writer traveled in from Vienna and came to see him. He had seen Werfel's latest drama, *Schweiger*, an odd blend of cheap sensationalism and a drama of ideas that Werfel had made nearly unpalatable with its flood of escalating and crisscrossing motifs: spiritualism, the priesthood, social democracy, anti-Semitism, psychiatry and psychoanalysis, abortion, murder and suicide, tragic love, and a death onstage. That was too much, and, Kafka wrote to Brod, if there was anything to admire in this play, it was "having the strength to wade through these three acts of sludge." But that was not all there was to it; Kafka was disappointed not only on a literary level, but also from the overwhelming feeling of having suffered a personal slight, even an insult.

> If it had been an ordinary dislike, it might possibly have been easier to formulate and moreover might have been so unimportant that I might have had no problem keeping it to myself. But it was a horror, and justifying that is difficult; one seems stubborn and tough and unruly, where one is only unhappy. You are surely one of the leaders of this generation, which is not meant as flattery and cannot serve as flattery of anyone, for many a man can lead this society in the mires, which is why you are not only a leader but something more . . . and one follows your course with fierce suspense. And now this play. It may have every possible merit, from the theatrical to the highest, but it is a retreat from leadership; there is not even leadership there, rather a betrayal of the generation, a concealment, an anecdotization, and therefore a degradation of its sufferings.[4]

It is not known whether Kafka stated his opinion in person; he appears to have couched it in polite turns of phrase, and Werfel defended himself with his usual eloquence. Kafka needed several running starts—a letter resulted from the third go-around—to make the point that he regarded Werfel's play not only as a literary mishap but as a moral debacle. The case of the watchmaker Franz Schweiger would have been well-suited as a template for a Kafka story, but Werfel brutally deconstructed the case of Schweiger—a man who is out of step with the world, alienated from his fellow man, and tormented by something he can neither recall nor articulate, and who cannot be saved even by the selfless love of his wife—by reducing him to a psychiatric case in point. Schweiger had suffered a schizophrenic episode, we later learn, and shot at children, in a textbook case of mental derangement. And for good measure, Werfel brings in the character of an insane lecturer named Ottokar Grund, an undisguised and rather malicious caricature of Otto Gross, who had lost his grip on reality. "You invent the story of child murder," Kafka wrote to Werfel, almost overwhelmed by his own anger. "I regard that as a debasement of the sufferings of a generation. Anyone who does not have more to say on this than psychoanalysis should not be tackling the subject."[5]

Werfel was a high-strung individual, though generally conciliatory, and he knew how to keep critical remarks about his work, which his lover, Alma Mahler, leveled at him in a very different tone, apart from personal feelings. He realized that it was better to put off his next visit to Kafka for a while,[6] but that did not stop him from inviting his ailing friend and critic to Semmering once again, and he even suggested they stay together in Venice. Of course Kafka's criticisms were downright savage, compared to his usual restraint, and the fact that Werfel had indulged in a little joke at Gross's expense hardly justified his behavior—even though the three of them had considered launching a journal together years earlier. Werfel's opinion about the "case" of Otto Gross had changed since then. And hadn't Max Brod always claimed that it was one of Kafka's outstanding and exemplary habits that he acknowledged any earnest effort and looked for the good intention in failures, and even for the good in malice?

This habit was easy to misconstrue. As a reader, Kafka was not simply good-natured; he related to literary and even to theoretical works as though they were living people whose story he was open to hearing even if their fate might not matter to him. He was therefore able and willing to take in mediocre things and to recommend writings to others regardless of negative reviews. After all, he wrote to Brod, art should ultimately be understood as an attempt at communication, as "enabling the exchange of truthful words from person to person."[7] This attitude of taking literature strictly personally often led Kafka to make astonishingly lenient judgments, especially when he was friendly with the author and had had a role in creating the work in question. But Werfel now learned that for the same reasons and with the same tenacity, the very opposite could occur. Kafka reacted as though *Schweiger* was addressed directly to him and held up a mirror to him, and in this mirror he saw the face of a man who was a mystery to himself, who was infinitely remote from his fellow man and was therefore incapable of reciprocating love. That was Franz Schweiger. Werfel had aimed his arrow straight into an open wound and hit a bull's-eye.

Even so, Kafka wavered on the question of whether he was entirely correct. He was confident of his critical judgment, perhaps more confident than ever before, and he was gratified to see that Werfel's play was given short shrift in the press. Nonetheless, he had lingering doubts about the radius of general acceptance a judgment of this kind could claim. While Kafka used the word "generation" twice in the drafts of the letters to Werfel to make it clear that he was not speaking merely on his own behalf, he readily admitted in a message to Brod that his feeling about *Schweiger* was "so personal that perhaps it may apply only to me": "it hit me hard, affects me horribly on the most horrible level."[8]

This uncertainty about his literary judgment was nothing new for Kafka; it vexed him throughout his life. He was capable of describing the effect of a work of art as impressively as though he were describing the magnetism of a person, but he kept coming up short when applying binding standards and bringing his impressions into line with criteria that would apply across the board. A freelance writer's life of the kind Kafka had often imagined during his years of employment would have been virtually inconceivable without an ability to be objective, and that was still the case. In any of the avocations Kafka would have needed to pursue to get by outside Prague—as a reviewer, journalist, editor, or freelance editor for a publishing company—the ability to make competent and comprehensible judgments was rewarded with higher pay than submissions that hinged on pure linguistic facility. But Kafka had such a hard time crafting full-fledged appraisals that he rarely tried his hand at them. In the end, he had had to give up a critique of Hans Blüher's anti-Semitic pamphlet *Secessio Judaica* after just two or three paragraphs, even though all his friends knew and were discussing this brochure (which would have enabled him to seek advice and guidance in conversations), and he felt, as they all did, that Blüher's attack could not go unanswered.[9]

This failing was especially worrisome now that he could look forward to the freedom of "provisional retirement." As a critic or essayist, Kafka would not have had much trouble finding opportunities to publish; he was well known and respected as a literary author. And even though he could not contemplate writing a series or contributing articles on assignment in the way Max Brod had for months in the *Prager Presse*, Kafka could likely have improved his financial situation substantially while retaining free rein over topics and submission deadlines. This option seems to have been discussed among his friends from time to time, as well. In August 1922, Brod and Weltsch came up with the strange idea of recommending that Kafka take over the editorship of *Der Jude* from Martin Buber, who had decided to relinquish this post for the time being. Kafka replied that they must be joking. "How could I think of such a thing, with my boundless ignorance of things, my complete lack of connection with people, the absence of any firm Jewish ground under my feet? No, no."[10]

There is no doubt that the responsibility for a journal would have been too much for Kafka. His illness and chronic lack of sleep would have been enough to stand in the way of a commitment of this kind, but his meticulousness with texts and the uncontrollable dependency on moods and outside influences would have posed an even greater problem. But why invoke a lack of Judaism? Kafka's protest did not sound very convincing. While it was true that he was not conversant with Jewish rituals—he was mainly interested in the carnivalistic Purim festival because it offered something for children[11]—he did have a solid grounding in the political and cultural history of Judaism and had been following the discussions about Zionism for a good decade. He read *Selbstwehr* and *Der Jude*, and seems to have been acquainted with *Die jüdische Rundschau*, which had been launched in 1919. Although he was no expert, he did have a wide-ranging overview and a keen sense for topical Jewish subjects. He was pleased to find that in the Zionist-minded journals, abstract debates about "Jewish identity" and "Jewish ethnicity" were gradually falling out of favor; the focus was now on the concrete cultural and political work of the kind being done in the Jewish Home in Berlin, and on the Jewish settlement of Palestine, which raised a whole host of economic, political, religious, and ethnic problems. Kafka considered that far more interesting than expansive reflections on cultural and religious history of the sort found in Brod's two-volume "denominational book," *Paganism, Christianity, Judaism* (1921). He even had an ironic response to this attempt at proving the superiority of Jewish over Christian religiosity.

At the same time, Kafka grasped the true import of frontal attacks on the Jewish people, such as Hans Blüher's. It was not the intellectual depth or any surprising points in Blüher that made Kafka take up his pen but rather the fact that Blüher was attacking a vulnerable spot. He was describing Judaism with the same vocabulary of decadence and mimicry[12] that the Zionists and Kafka himself used to characterize the western European Jews. Every Jew, Blüher wrote, was "in essence sick, which is not the case with any other people." Despite the intellectual obtuseness of Blüher, who had picked up this way of fiddling with empirically unverifiable "substances" from Weininger, this anti-Semite's sure instinct in attacking the Jews on their sore point—their lingering doubt about whether they could be anything but tolerated lodgers anywhere on this planet—by threatening a "world pogrom" was chilling. "Germany will be the only land that will recoil from murder," he added.[13]

Kafka's interest in everything pertaining to the future of Judaism grew quite a bit in the last years of his life. A great variety of factors, some personal, others from the world around him, reinforced one another, factors that cannot all be reconstructed now, only the broad outlines of their order of importance and chronology. Kafka, like every Jew, was certainly disappointed and depressed about the uninterrupted persistence of anti-Semitism throughout the world. The new political order that had been awaited at the end of the war and the disappearance of autocratic systems of government achieved absolutely nothing in this regard; it even seemed as though wherever democracy was giving it new latitude, anti-Semitism had just become more visible and aggressive. In Germany there was fear of the mob of "swastika wielders" who fought for power not in parliament but on the streets, and the murder of Walter Rathenau on June 24, 1922, dashed any last hope that these were only the birth pangs of the republic: "Incomprehensible that they let him live as long as they did," Kafka commented with a cynicism borne of resignation.[14] The organized anti-Semites were clearly unwilling to recognize the power monopoly of the state even under stable political circumstances, which meant that Jews were not only not safer in a democratically governed land but were actually in a more precarious situation than under the regime of a kaiser. And was it any better in Prague? No one needed to fear a revolt from the right, but the police had to keep putting down anti-Semitic violence, and the atmosphere at the German University—which Kafka was keeping his eye on for Klopstock's sake—was incurably poisoned. Wherever you looked, the old familiar menaces were rising up again, vehemently and vociferously. And it made no sense, and was also hard to reconcile with any claim to truthfulness, to flee into regression from a world like this.

A writer cannot just sit back and read the paper and pursue his dreams. He has to react to what is brewing in the world by writing while keeping a keen eye on events or by distancing himself deliberately. Even in phases of his own literary standstill, Kafka was watching closely how other German Jewish authors were positioning themselves, and as usual, he could be fascinated by and admire their stances even if he did not agree with them. Of course, it was a sign of decadence to deny one's own cultural and historical roots and adopt an ironic or indifferent stance, and the anti-Semitism that confronted assimilated western European Jews served them right, according to Brod and for a while, in even more radical form, to Kafka, as well. But ideas about what an individual could do to remedy this shameful situation were few and far between. Naturally one could join a Zionist group, learn Hebrew, go to temple every now and then, and make donations for Palestine. Those outward acts might ease the pain but could not mend the severed roots. This was what Kafka had in mind when he reminded Werfel of the sufferings of their generation, sufferings that issued not from the usual conflict between the generations but from a rupture that went far deeper: from the realization that the assimilated Judaism of their fathers was an utterly illusory and untenable matter lacking historical legitimacy and subject to imminent destruction, and from the equally harrowing recognition that one could not just simply decide to drop out of this "Western" Judaism.

> In this case I prefer another approach over psychoanalysis, namely the realization that this father complex that some draw on for intellectual sustenance applies not to the innocent father, but to the father's Jewishness. Most young Jews who began to write German wanted to leave Jewishness behind them, generally with a vague approval by their fathers (this vagueness was the outrageous part); but with their hind legs they were still glued to their father's Jewishness and they found no new ground for their front legs. Their despair became their inspiration.[15]

Kafka had clearly recognized the implications of this dilemma for the writer for quite some time, but his view was diametrically opposed to the inferences Max Brod drew for his own work. Brod advocated instruction; he believed that the Jewish author who had already recognized that assimilation was a dead end had to pass along this knowledge and show possible alternatives and positive counterimages, which is why Brod's novels and stories included the words "Jew" and "Jewish" in unexpected contexts—even in a mundane discussion about jealousy. Kafka, by contrast, insisted that literary writing was irreconcilable with propaganda. Instead of discussing experiences, the writer should *represent* them in as pure a form as possible—in "self-forgetfulness," as he wrote to Brod, leaving aside intellectual censorship and even, for the most part, the reality principle. In his own texts, Kafka's aesthetic ideal aimed at leaving open the question of which parts were personal, which Jewish, and which merely "human," which meant that anything explicitly Jewish was taboo. The word "Jewish" never appears in his literary work. Even so, he achieved a depth of focus that far surpassed Zionist-inspired literature.

Kafka's tendency at times to give absolute priority to the *form* of a work of art over what the author says or thinks had quite paradoxical consequences. With these criteria, it no longer mattered whether the writer was even striving to achieve a vivid, eloquent portrayal of the tragedy of western European Jews but rather that his work become a persuasive *expression* of this tragedy, irrespective of what he had set out to do, and possibly even against his will. It was, above all, the name Karl Kraus that marked the precise point at which Kafka steered away from literary criticism and chose a different route. While Brod and Werfel, who had not come off well in the confrontation with the editor of *Die Fackel*, gradually lost interest in Kraus—a factual debate seemed utterly out of the question here—Kafka continued to read him quite eagerly and was not even put off by the incomparable broadside that Kraus delivered in his aggressive satire *Literature, or We'll See about That* and the attacks directed at his circle. What did Kafka find appealing about reading matter like this? He tried to justify it to Brod.

> My impression at the time, which of course has faded quite a bit by now, was that it was extraordinarily piercing, piercing straight to the heart. In this small world of German-Jewish literature, he is really dominant—or rather the principle represented by him, to which he has so admirably subordinated himself that he has actually confused himself with it and brought others into his confusion.

> I think I am distinguishing fairly well between the elements in the book that are pure wit (albeit magnificent wit), pitiful whimpering, and, finally, truth, at least as much truth as there is in this hand with which I write, just as distinct and frighteningly physical. The wit principally consists of Yiddish-German *mauscheln*; no one can *mauscheln* like Kraus, although in this German-Jewish world hardly anyone can do anything but *mauscheln*. This *mauscheln*—taken in the broadest sense of the term, and that is the only way it should be taken—is a brash, or implicit, or self-tormenting appropriation of someone else's property, something not earned, but stolen in a (relatively) fleeting grasp, while remaining someone else's property, even if there is not even the slightest hint of a gaffe, for here the whispering buzz of conscience verifies the whole crime in a penitent hour. This is not to say anything against *mauscheln*; *mauscheln* in itself is even lovely, an organic compound of written German and pantomime . . . a product of a sensitive feeling for language that has recognized that in German only the dialects are really alive, and apart from them, only the most highly personal High German, while all the rest, the linguistic middle ground, is nothing but embers that can be brought to a semblance of life only when excessively lively Jewish hands rummage through them. That is a fact that can be regarded as amusing or horrifying; but why are the Jews so irresistibly drawn to this language? German literature existed before the emancipation of the Jews and attained great glory; it was, as far as I can see, generally no less varied than today—in fact, it may even have lost some of its variety today. And the fact that all this and Jewishness as such are related, or rather young Jews and their Jewishness, to the frightful inner predicament of these generations, is something that Kraus in particular recognized, or rather, this was something that came to light in regard to him.[16]

The final sentence is the crux of the matter; it no longer mattered whether Karl Kraus had truly "recognized" and understood the crisis (and he had *not*, in Kafka's view[17]), and it made no real difference whether Kraus judged the protagonists in this crisis fairly. The essential point was that his enormous opus represented the Western Jewish crisis, in an overwhelming and doubly comical manner. Kafka was praising the *Fackelkraus*, the Western Jewish writer par excellence, the rigid defender of the language who regarded any incorrect use of the dative case as a personal affront, the celebrated elocutionist who heaped ridicule on his rivals for sprinkling in Yiddish, as a master of *mauscheln*. This was a crucial point, the penetrating force of which even Brod could not ignore, since it reinforced his oft-repeated credo that no one could leave Judaism.[18]

But was it really necessary to tolerate Kraus to understand that? Kafka's old friends had trouble understanding why he kept both *Die Fackel* and *Selbstwehr* on his desk and read both journals with equal enthusiasm although they were from incompatible linguistic and ideological worlds. Kafka stated his reason frankly to his younger, impartial friend Robert Klopstock, with whom he had pored over *Die Fackel* and most likely also Kraus's *Literature, or We'll See about That* (which Kraus called his "magical operetta") in Matliary: "I do not want to deny myself this tasty dessert made up of all the good and bad instincts," he wrote from Planá when he had been waiting for the latest issue of the journal for months, and later he even talked about "enervating orgies" that he had indulged in "for evenings on end" with *Die Fackel*, as Klopstock was well aware. Brod learned nothing more about these sins.[19]

Kafka had himself shown that the horrors of assimilation could be depicted quite vividly without putting an actual name to it. His "Report to an Academy," delivered by a trained "apeman," made even confessed Zionists cringe. In the fall of 1922, just after stopping work on *The Castle*, Kafka returned to this theme, but this time in far more subtle form. "Investigations of a Dog" is the title (added by Brod) of a fairly polished text, which, if it had been completed, might have reached the length of "The Metamorphosis" or even of a short novel, yet it dispensed almost entirely with a structuring plot.[20] It is the autobiographical report of a dog who spends years investigating phenomena of life as a dog, through observation and persistent questioning, but also by experimenting on himself. His curiosity is piqued by the exciting appearance of seven "music dogs" observed by the canine narrator as a child; these dogs danced, jumped, walked on their hind legs, and made music in some mysterious way. The question of what these creatures are all about soon leads the young observer to further reflections that encompass both everyday and abnormal phenomena, such as the question of where dog food comes from, and legends about so-called airborne dogs that are said never to touch the ground.

Even though this text remained a fragment as well, Kafka achieved a work of art so ingenious that Kafka researchers were thrown off course and led astray for decades. The first things readers wanted to know was who was really meant here. Since dogs generally do not write autobiographies and since it was surely not Kafka's intention to make a contribution to behavioral science, his story clearly belongs in the tradition of the animal fable. It is a human community, these are human habits that are being researched and reported here, and it is not very difficult to figure out who is meant. "No species, to my knowledge," the narrator muses, "lives as widely dispersed as we dogs do ... we who want to stick together—and again and again, in spite of everything, we do succeed ... in exuberant moments—we are the very ones who live far apart from one another." These are the Jews—who else? This description fits them to a tee, as do other elements in the story. Airborne dogs (*Lufthunde*) bring to mind the famous *Luftmenschen*, impractical dreamers who are not "grounded" in reality, either because they are deracinated socially or because they bury themselves in the ancient scriptures. The fact that Kafka was portraying eastern European Jewish actors—who had provided him a form of revelation—in the Café Savoy in the form of music dogs—is also clear; even atmospheric descriptions in "Investigations of a Dog" accord with the corresponding passages in his 1911 diary. And thus it is not surprising that "Investigations of a Dog" mentions two types of food: the kind found on earth, and food that comes "from above," food for thought (religion, art, and history), without which no people could survive, the Jews least of all.

It is difficult to find a persuasive alternative to this interpretation, yet it functions only in looking at the story as a whole, and many individual details remain as baffling as ever. Why, for example, is there such an emphasis on the fact that the airborne dogs are small and weak? What is meant by the "hodgepodge of timber" in which the narrator finds himself while listening to the music dogs? Also the encounter with another dog who is supposedly hunting and therefore wants to—and must—drive away the narrator remains incomprehensible if dogs stand for Jews here. The equation comes *close* to working out, but the unexplained remainder is too substantial to dismiss it as mere narrative padding.

The little jest that Kafka indulges in with his readers here is without parallel in his entire oeuvre. "Investigations of a Dog" calls for interpretation, as do all of Kafka's texts, and the fact that its very theme is investigation reinforces this directive and makes it irresistible. But the only way to figure out what the narrator is all about is by taking him at his word and dispensing with metaphorical interpretations. Astonishingly, the text remains readable even when you assume there are no other layers to unearth, that this is simply one dog living among other dogs. In this case, the little airborne dogs way on high (who reproduce in some unknown way) are nothing but lapdogs. The dog with no choice but to clear away the obstacles to his hunt is a trained hunting dog under orders from his master, and the dog's dark threat that the narrator should back away now before he is forced to run can only mean that his master is nearby with a gun. The hodgepodge of timber in which the narrator is wedged when he is watching the music dogs perform are the legs of the many chairs on which the actual audience is sitting and the fact that it is "a bit hazy" indicates that people are smoking up there—while the music dogs are not, of course, "conjuring forth" the music but are trained animals responding to a man-made melody. And the food? From the perspective of domesticated dogs, food almost always comes from above, and it is not an observation of some sort of "canine science," as the narrator pompously states, but only natural that the food is often snapped up as it is still flying through the air, while a dog who remains passive has to pick it up from the floor. Kafka's pleasure in narrative jesting is almost palpable here, particularly in regard to the investigating dog's obliviousness to a key element. "What else is there besides dogs?" he asks. "Who else can you appeal to in this vast empty world?" What about people? They are never mentioned a single time in his report. If he would finally notice them and realize that the dogs are a dependent minority group living under the sway of an overpowering majority, the mysteries of his little universe would be solved on their own and he could call a halt to his scientific activity. The dogs' blind spot prevents them from understanding why they live in such isolation even though they greatly prefer to gather in packs. They do so because they have to. Like the Jews.[21]

An extraordinary event brought new life to the Jewish community of Prague in the fall of 1921, an event that would have been almost unthinkable just a few years earlier. An eighteen-year-old girl from Jerusalem appeared in their midst. She was not visiting her old homeland; rather, she had been *born* in Palestine and was coming to Europe for the first time in her life. The community in Prague had had to become more open after the wave of refugees and the attendant misery of the war years. A great many people were coming and going, and everyone had gotten used to the idea of fellow Jews from far corners of the world dropping in, exotic and mostly uneducated people who got by in broken Yiddish, Polish, Russian, or Hungarian. But Puah Ben-Tovim, the traveler from Jerusalem, was an altogether different case. She spoke a modern and pure Hebrew—not the kind from the aforementioned textbook by Professor Rath but learned personally from Eliezer Ben-Yehuda, known as the father of Modern Hebrew[22]—and she also spoke passable German, which she had learned at a missionary-led high school in Jerusalem. Her knowledge of these languages also brought her together with Hugo Bergmann, the founder and director of the library of the Hebrew University of Jerusalem, and Bergmann in turn helped her get established in Prague, where she enrolled at the German University to study mathematics. Bergmann wrote a letter of recommendation for her to Dr. Brody, the chief rabbi, and Puah moved into a room at the home of Bergmann's mother.

She had come in order to learn, but something happened that she had not foreseen: the Jews of Prague—especially the most highly educated among them—were eager to learn from *her*. She was handed around, spent a good number of evenings with the teenagers in the Blue-White Jewish youth group, taught in the small Jewish community school, took part in seminars by Isidor Pollak, the professor of Middle Eastern Studies, and was invited by members of the B'nai B'rith, to which Felix Weltsch belonged. Everyone was delighted by her Hebrew, and once the word had gotten around that she could teach not the vocabulary of the Torah but reliable *ivrit* from a native speaker, she was in high demand as a language teacher.

Kafka sought her out as well. It has not been established when and where he met Puah. He may have met her with his mother, who was well acquainted with Frau Bergmann, or possibly by way of Brod or Weltsch, who had no intention of letting this precious opportunity to learn about daily life in Palestine from a non-European perspective slip away. For the Zionists in Prague, most of whom could only dream of Palestine, Puah embodied nothing less than the future of Judaism: a Jewish self-awareness that was no longer dependent on mimicry, that knew the constraints of assimilation only from history class, and that regarded the old continent not in nostalgic memory but rather with the curiosity of a tourist. Kafka's questions about Palestine were unending; what he learned from Puah sounded incomparably livelier and more vivid than the political updates in *Selbstwehr* and was more authentic and current than even newspaper reports by a clever observer like Arthur Holitscher, whose *Journey through Jewish Palestine* had been published a few months earlier.[23] It was also "the little Palestinian," as he called her, who revived Kafka's interest in the Hebrew language. In 1922, probably after Kafka returned from Planá, Puah began to come to his apartment on Altstädter Ring twice a week to give him lessons.

Judaism, youth, and femininity—for Kafka those were three good reasons to focus his interest on and even idealize Puah. In her later years, Puah Ben-Tovim recalled that he never failed to compliment her on a new skirt or on her overall appearance. "There is no question that he was attracted to me, but it was more to an ideal than to the actual girl that I was, and to the image of a Jerusalem far away. He was constantly picking my brain about Jerusalem, and wanted to come with me when I went back." She also wrote that at times he seemed like a man who was drowning emotionally and would grasp at any straw.[24] She could not, of course, return these feelings. To Puah, Kafka was a remarkable man, but he was twenty years older and in poor health. It is unlikely that she would have been able to make sense out of "Investigations of a Dog," which he was writing at the same time as these

Hebrew lessons—although a look at his manuscript would have made it easier for her to understand why he was so keen about certain word families, for example for *lahkor*, meaning "investigate."

Kafka knew how to put the educational opportunity that had come his way to good use. His vocabulary notebooks show that he did not regard Puah's visits (for which he was certainly paying a good fee) as Palestinian teatimes; he prepared intensively and in writing. Some 350 pages with Hebrew notes were found in his papers. Evidently there was less emphasis on grammar than on Hebrew conversation. Kafka tried to learn whole lexical fields so that he could express himself in everyday situations, similar to the kind of instruction given by native speakers these days. He also noted numerous expressions that were too new or too colloquial to be included in his dictionary. Georg Langer, in a sense Puah's predecessor as a language teacher, reported that at some point Kafka spoke Hebrew "fluently" and with pride—the result of extraordinary persistence—because in spite of the coughing, which was bound to disturb the instruction all the time, and in spite of some interruptions necessitated by his fever, Kafka continued his intensive lessons with Puah until mid-1923.[25] And he surely would have stayed with it longer had not the excessive erotic and other forms of harassment to which Puah Ben-Tovim was subjected in Zionist circles in Prague,[26] coupled with the constant focus on Jewish topics, made her change her plans: against her parents' will, and to Kafka's disappointment, she broke off her academic studies and went to Berlin to devote herself to social and pedagogical work with Jewish children.

It is difficult to tell how serious Kafka was about going to Palestine. His plans at first were certainly not as far from reality as he later saw them. Still, they were not an outgrowth of Zionist belief but rather—just as ten years earlier, when he first met Felice Bauer—they arose from personal relationships and remained dependent on them. The idea of settling in Palestine and being helped out by a young confidante was a pipe dream he clung to for months. This goal seemed to move into sight when, in April 1923, Hugo Bergmann and his wife Else came to Prague and encouraged Kafka in his plans to emigrate. They were probably alarmed by the change in his appearance. They had last seen him three years earlier, just before they moved to Jerusalem; now he was weak and gaunt, and his aura of youthfulness was gradually draining from his face as the tuberculosis took over. Else Bergmann was so worried that she invited Kafka to live with them, in spite of their cramped living space and her husband's insistence that it was too great a responsibility to assume and could compromise the well-being of their daughter and two sons.[27]

Did Kafka have any idea what would be in store for him in Eretz Israel? He certainly did not share the committed Zionists' widespread illusion that Palestine revolved around—or at least soon *would* revolve around—Jewish life. Even the propaganda film Kafka saw in October 1921, *Shivat Zion* (Return to Zion), about building a Jewish Palestine, left no doubt as to the actual majority, especially in regard to urban life; this was an unmistakably Eastern, multiethnic setting.[28] In the fall of 1922, only 11 percent of the three million people living in Palestine were Jews, and the notion that Jews would reclaim Palestine with their hands—namely by acquiring and cultivating land—was no more than a collective myth. Only 3 percent of the landed property was in Jewish hands, and only about a thousand people lived in kibbutzim. The Jewish immigrants who came later crowded into the cities and even misstated their professions so that they would not be sent to the country.[29] The problem was the same as during the Ottoman Empire: settlement required the acquisition of land, but the overwhelming majority of immigrants came with nothing but their manpower. They were dependent on credit from the Jewish National Fund and the Keren Hayesod (Foundation Fund), which, in turn, drew its finances from donations from around the world.

The primary goal of the lecture tour Hugo Bergmann took in the spring of 1923 was to raise money for the Keren Hayesod. He was a skilled and persuasive speaker, as Kafka had known for a long time, but by now Bergmann had seen with his own eyes what he was talking about. He was the most prominent man in Prague to have taken the big leap, and he had developed into a Jewish authority. When he spoke before a large audience in Prague about "The Situation in Palestine" on April 26, 1923—Brod, Weltsch, and Baum were of course also in attendance—Kafka was so excited that he raced behind the curtain afterwards to announce to Bergmann: "You gave this lecture just for me."[30] He might easily have added: You sent Fräulein Puah here just for me as well.

Bergmann had no reason to dampen his audience's enthusiasm. It was fine with him that people in Prague had very optimistic visions of life in Palestine, particularly in Jerusalem, and it certainly worked to the benefit of his list of donors. In conversations in more intimate settings—for instance, when the Bergmanns and the Brods spent an evening with the Kafkas—the actual oppressive conditions did come up. After all, everyone who read the newspapers knew that the tensions between the Arabs and the Jews were steadily rising and had already exploded into violence, and there were Zionists who had already given up hope for peaceful coexistence, although no one was saying as much out loud.[31] Palestine was not, as people had hoped, placed under the responsibility of the League of Nations or the United States but instead had been left by mandate to the local victorious power, Great Britain. But British policy in the Middle East was not targeted to the concerns of the Jews, as some Zionist dreamers had expected after the sensational Balfour Declaration in 1917. Instead, the government in London operated according to the standard patterns of colonial power politics, that is, altogether pragmatically and with the goal of controlled pacification. Local problems were left to the initiative of Jewish and Arab civil servants, and attempts were made to keep relations with the Arab nationalists, who were now well-organized, as free of conflict as possible, especially by a considerable reduction of the region that had originally been intended for Jewish settlement, and by making a point of remaining impartial.[32] Jewish interests were given an overall framework delimiting boundaries, but otherwise there was effectively self-rule. The Jews also had to protect themselves from Arab attacks for the most part, although they were barred from engaging in paramilitary training and stockpiling arms. The British were an occupying power, and despite their close cooperation with the Zionist executive—the first British high commissioner for Palestine, Herbert Samuel, was Jewish and a moderate Zionist—they made it clear that they considered the numerous Jewish petitions and appeals just as bothersome as the Arab ones.

Bergmann himself also suffered from this inauspicious turn of events and did not come across as a happy man who had fulfilled his dreams. He appeared more serious than before, and he and his family were living in conditions that were harsher in every regard—materially, culturally, and socially—than in Prague. In 1922, he wrote to Leo Hermann, the former managing director of *Selbstwehr*, "How will we drag ourselves from one land to another and from one outlook to another, from hope to doubt? I have now been in the country for more than two years, but I'm still far fom finding my path here. I feel quite alien, have no friends, don't go to any social gatherings, and apart from my work in the library, I don't see any task ahead for me."[33] An experience of isolation that every immigrant from the West went through, especially in Jerusalem. It was necessary to speak Arabic to fit in here, and bourgeois etiquette was not exactly helpful in coping with everyday life. The German-speaking Jews, known as *yeckes*, in particular tended to remain among themselves and suffer from nostalgia, and were sniggered at or even openly scorned by the majority of the eastern European immigrants, most of whom were petit bourgeois or proletarian. Bergmann's title, "director of the Hebrew National Library," sounded impressive only to the ears of cultural Zionists, but his actual work revolved around repairing damaged books and labeling file cards.

Kafka had written to Klopstock that the average lawyer would "first be ground to dust" before reaching Palestine, "because Palestine needs earth but it does not need lawyers."[34] By this point, Kafka was retired. Palestine had even less need of retired lawyers, and none at all of tubercular patients. Of course, he could now verify a steady source of income that made him independent of the job market in Palestine and Jewish charity—his pension was actually higher than Bergmann's meager and uncertain income. But this advantage was outweighed by the fact that young healthy people who were able to work were given preference in immigration, and the agreement between the British and the Zionists stipulated that to whatever extent possible, a preliminary selection should be made in the countries of origin accordingly. In some instances, Jewish immigrants with tuberculosis were not even allowed on land in Jaffa and were sent back on the same ship.[35] Kafka was evidently willing to assume this risk. He had planned to learn an easy craft, and if working the land was a top priority in Palentine—as he still believed—he might be able to make himself useful with his knowledge of gardening. He would have been able to afford the trip, even without the aid of his indignant parents; he knew more Hebrew than most German immigrants; he had someone to accompany him;

and there was an address in Jerusalem where he was expected. His prospects looked good, the only thing missing was a couple of visas, and he could have tried to do it. But Palestine remained a dream that his body ultimately destroyed. In July 1923, when Else Bergmann, who was leaving for Palestine soon and pressed him to make a decision, he had to acknowledge to himself and to her that it was too late:

> I know that now I shall certainly not go—how could I go—but that along with your letter the ship virtually docks at the threshold of my room and that you are standing there asking me, and asking me as you do, which is no small thing. . . . It would not have been a voyage to Palestine, but in the spiritual sense something like a voyage to America by a cashier who has embezzled a large sum of money. And that the voyage would have been undertaken with you would have greatly increased the spiritual criminality of the case. No, I could not go that way, even if I had been able—I repeat, and "all berths are already taken," you add. And once again the temptation beckons, and again the absolute impossibility answers. That is how it is, no matter how sad, but in the final analysis nevertheless quite right. The hope persists for later, and you are kind and do not dash it.

A few months later, the Bergmanns took in another emigrant: the brilliant young Gerhard Scholem. All that was left of Kafka, whom they never saw again, was a portrait photograph. They framed it and displayed it on the piano.[36]

CHAPTER TWENTY-SIX

Dora

No one is averse to listening when urged to eat or to stay alive.

—Petronius, *Satyricon*

A HOT-WATER BOTTLE, TWO BLANKETS, A DOWN QUILT. THE ROOM kept heated by the maid. Ten years earlier, when Kafka had slept with an open window even in the winter, an atmosphere like this would have seemed like a hellish burden. Overheated rooms were always metaphors for a lack of freedom and renunciation of life in his literary works. Now he lay covered in several layers, shivering and afraid of coming down with pneumonia.

In the winter of 1922/1923, there were many days like this. Sometimes it got even worse, and Kafka was tormented for hours on end by stomach and intestinal cramps. Was that part of the tuberculosis too? Max Brod hurried off to the Kafkas' family doctor physician and confirmed his suspicion: Yes, it was quite possible, said Dr. Hermann (none too discreetly) that the infection had already spread to the intestines. This was the first time a physician was admitting that the limits of therapeutic treatment might already be hopelessly exceeded. That would not prove to be true quite yet, but complications of this kind certainly compromised Kafka's chances of recovering. And they did not leave him enough strength to concentrate on his two most important tasks—literature and Hebrew—at the same time. He opted for the latter, and "Investigations of a Dog" was abandoned for good.

At times, it was not only his room but the entire apartment that felt like a hospital ward. Kafka's mother was taking a long time to recover from an operation that was, as he wrote, "extraordinarily grave," and entailed "extremely painful procedures."[1] The situation did not improve until the spring, when Kafka's fever disappeared altogether for several months, and apart from new bouts of insomnia, which he even took medicine to combat on occasion, he was strong enough again by April to go outside. In early May, he decided to go to a Prague summer resort for a few days, to Dobřichovice, which was a half hour away by train and which he liked as much as he had Planá. He could not expect a drastic improvement in such a brief period of time, of course, but the trip could serve to prove that he was still able to travel and was not an invalid. He was probably also thinking that it would be better to be out of the way when Ottla gave birth to her second child, and the due date was coming soon. But it turned out to be impossible to stay in the country for long because Dobřichovice was so expensive, he wrote to Milena, "it is really just for spending one's last days before death."[2] And so, just a day or two after the happy birth of his niece Helene, he was back in Prague.

Now Ottla also had to recover for a while, but that was possible only at home, and there was no way he could plan on a summer vacation with her and her newborn baby until at least August. Kafka was not interested in traveling by himself again until then, especially considering the risk of winding up bedridden in some hotel and needing to be brought home at great effort and expense. He was even less interested in traveling to the High Tatras with Klopstock to live among the ailing. So where should he go? Kafka's sister Elli was going on vacation with her three children—Hanna, the youngest, was only three—but to the Baltic Sea, and his doctor had actually advised against this bracing northern climate. Nevertheless, the family decided that this solution was probably the best one and that Franz should go with Elli. He needed someone close to help out in case of an emergency, and, his parents felt, he needed some distraction from his plans for Palestine, which were starting to take on threatening proportions under the coaxing of his friends in Prague. But this strategy backfired in a positively hilarious way because, as it happened, some beaches at the Baltic had plenty of people who dreamed of Palestine, and the family had unwittingly selected one of these places.

One of the reasons Kafka agreed to this expedition was that it would take him through Berlin. He had not seen this city since those unhappy days at the Askanischer Hof. Nine years had gone by since then, but the indescribable misery, the enormous upheavals that Berlin had suffered in the interim were very much on Kafka's mind. In sharp contrast to Vienna, the former center of power of his universe, which appealed to Kafka only briefly and only as Milena's home turf, Berlin had remained a locus of intellectual refuge and orientation, and not merely a larger or accelerated version of Prague but something completely different. Kafka's enthusiasm was of course rather naive, and his friends, who knew Berlin far better from their own experience, found it touching. He had once written to Felice that Berlin hung over Prague like the sky over the earth.[3] He still felt that way. The image did not pertain to Felice; it came from a recurring dream of the kind prisoners have, a liberation fantasy. Berlin was to Kafka what the big wide world is to children. He was justified in feeling that Berlin represented the "world"—the world of the future, the dawn of modernity—in a way that was utterly different from Vienna, with its makeshift democracy, and even from Prague. In Berlin, all social, ethnic, cultural, and intellectual conflicts were fought out more openly, articulately, and vigorously. The pulse here was quicker and stronger. Brod, who was utterly exhausted after just a few days in Berlin, wrote, "They work like crazy." Kafka replied that he grew "hot" at the sound of that, and confessed that he would never have been able to resist a serious "offer" from Berlin.[4]

But it had been Max Brod who had not only received an offer of this kind but jumped at the chance to accept it. He went to Berlin as often as he could, awaited by a lover who begged him to come even more frequently. Over the course of two and a half years, Brod kept telling Kafka that Kafka simply had to meet Emmy, and that she wanted to meet him too, and because he could not invite her to Prague, Kafka would just have to go to Berlin. He would have liked nothing better, but his illness and weakness prevented him from doing so. The trips that Kafka could undertake had become shorter and shorter. But now he could actually go. He celebrated his fortieth birthday in Prague, then set off for Germany. This trip would exceed his wildest expectations.

On the afternoon of July 5, Kafka said goodbye to his sister at the Anhalt railway station in Berlin. Elli continued on toward Rostock so she could reach the Baltic seaside resort of Müritz that same evening, and Kafka took a hotel room in Berlin. He had come up with a plan that brought him the greatest pleasure he had felt in a long time. Of course, he wanted to see Brod's girlfriend Emmy Salveter at long last, after exchanging postcards with her from time to time. She already knew quite a bit about him. But Puah Ben-Tovim was also in Berlin; she had just begun her training in social pedagogy in the country with Jewish refugee children from Poland and Ukraine who were housed in a residence. The Jewish community in Eberswalde, about an hour northeast of Berlin by train, had agreed to take in these children for a month, and Puah, who had never worked with children before, was their counselor.[5]

Kafka wanted to see this place with his own eyes, and Emmy had agreed to travel out to Eberswalde with him—which made for a truly awkward situation, as he was well aware. Emmy had not only been courted for months by a young supporter of Hitler, but she herself had anti-Semitic leanings, particularly in regard to eastern European Jews, which Brod had been able to tone down little by little. Unfortunately, only the first part of the plan worked out. When Kafka and Emmy Salveter were barely halfway there, they realized that the time they had allotted for the excursion was far too tight, and that they would not be able to return until night. For Kafka, who had been on the road since the early morning, that was too much of a strain, so they got out in Bernau, went for a walk, and traveled back.

Nevertheless, Kafka was in high spirits, and delighted with this new acquaintance. "She is charming," he wrote to Brod. "And focused entirely on you. Whatever the subject, she managed to refer it to you. . . . A truly intense originality, directness, seriousness, a dear and childlike seriousness." Evidently their mutual trust grew so quickly that they were able to address sensitive issues, as well. She remarked several times that it was strange "how we adopt the views of someone we love, even when they are opposed to the ones we used to have." It was clear that Emmy had been catching on. "She was very nice to me," Kafka said in summary.[6]

This sounded (as Kafka intended) as though he had been with a nursemaid, not a lovely young woman. But of course Brod got a report from Emmy as well (undoubtedly a more detailed one), and their meeting and little trip together appeared in a somewhat different light. "I almost felt like kissing him," Emmy wrote to Prague with childlike gravity. If she had, she would have found that his cheek was hot. Kafka was running a slight fever on that day, July 5, 1923.

> Haus Glückauf, Guesthouse, tel. 29. Built in 1909. In a quiet, dry, wooded area at a high elevation, situated 8 minutes from the lovely Baltic Sea beach, the jetty, the spa facilities, and the extensive swimming beach, shielded from wind from the East and North. Bright, tastefully furnished, airy rooms, nearly all with a veranda or canopied balcony. Open view of the sea. Renowned for fine cuisine. Reasonable prices. Meals served at small tables in a friendly, spacious dining room. Electric light. Running water. Flush toilets. Further information gladly supplied. Free brochure. Tel./Address: Glückauf. Baltic Seaside Resort in Müritz. Karl Schütt, Jr.

Kafka had not spent time at the sea for ten years, and it seemed to him that it had grown more beautiful in all this time. He was happy to see it even though he could not just dive in whenever the spirit took him, as he had in the past. It now depended on the temperature—his own, that is, which he took daily like clockwork.

It is not entirely clear how the Kafkas had come across the Baltic seaside resort in Müritz. Perhaps someone had recommended it to Elli when she had taken a vacation the previous year in Brunshaupten, which was thirty kilometers west; maybe she had visited the place on that occasion. Or someone in the family had seen the advertisement for the guesthouse in Glückauf, and Kafka was especially taken with the "small tables" where meals were served. A crucial factor was the advantageous location of Müritz, which travel guides confirmed and which also helped to allay the fears of the family doctor: Müritz was both a seaside resort and a health resort, located at the edge of the

Rostocker Heide, a vast woodland that extended nearly to the dunes on the beach. The contrast of two worlds within a small geographical area offered Kafka a near-ideal combination: peak season on the beach, with comfortable wicker chairs, men playing soccer, women exchanging gossip, and children frolicking. It was right by the edge of an old mixed woodland that offered complete silence, and the deeper one went into the woods, the wilder and more varied the woods became. The seaside resort was therefore quite rightly recommended expressly for convalescents, and it boasted the first professionally run convalescent homes.

Most of the inns and hotels were situated right next to the woods. They were villa-like buildings in the resort architectural style that was typical for the turn of the century, with numerous weather-protected balconies and verandas, some of them enclosed for use year-round. Kafka had one of these rooms, on the third floor, facing away from the street, with a view of the small garden and the woods, which were just a few steps away. His daily path to the beach (which was then called Badeweg, but is now Franz-Kafka-Weg) took him under a canopy of oak and beech leaves, and it was only when he reached the walkway along the dunes that he was out in the open air and suddenly among droves of strolling summer guests. Behind that were bathing areas for women, men, and families, where the beach life (which was then still separate from the dressing rooms) was most colorful. Kafka rented a covered wicker beach chair with the initials F. K. shaped out of pine cones—presumably put together by ten-year-old Gerti and eleven-year-old Felix.

Yet another surprise was in store for him in Müritz. When Kafka opened the balcony door, he heard the voices of children—an unusually large number of them. This brought back unhappy memories of the throngs of youngsters making a racket under his windows in Planá that had brought him to the brink of despair. But the sounds here were quite different. There was singing—evidently they were rehearsing songs—and the voices of adult counselors could be heard in two or three languages. Through the leaves of the trees Kafka could make out the group, which was housed in a building about fifty yards away, almost in the woods. He soon realized that he was not hearing German folk songs. These were Yiddish songs—no doubt about it—in the sing-song chanting style of the Hasidim.

It was such an improbable stroke of fate that on the day before his arrival, Kafka came close to visiting a colony of eastern European Jewish children, then took up quarters in Müritz right next to a vacation spot for the Jewish Home in Berlin, that he must have regarded it not just as a sign of fate but as a summons. There had been a time that the home in Berlin interested him far more than all the cultural offerings in Prague. He had urged Felice Bauer to volunteer there, he had given donations, but he had never seen this place of his dreams with his own eyes. In the seven years that had now gone by, a great deal had changed, and the days of Werfel reading Polish refugee children poems to acquaint them with the high points of Western culture were long over. Zionism had now found numerous young enthusiasts in the Scheunenviertel section of Berlin, and the Home was being led by the Young Jewish Hiking Group, which focused on producing pioneers for Palestine rather than educated workers and merchants. Everything was geared to fostering a Jewish community spirit, and the celebrations and singing were intended not just for pleasure but to break down the barriers between the various native tongues and milieus. Everyone called the others *chaverim* (friends), as though they were already on a kibbutz. And of course Hebrew was taught.

Seeing them back then would have entailed a full day's trip to Berlin; now he was just a few steps away. Kafka had to go over to the children and make sure once and for all that this was no dream. And the opportunity to do so soon arose because the other side had taken note of his presence as well, most likely because Felix and Gerti told everyone on the beach that the rail-thin, frail gentleman with the rather dark skin who showed up every day was their famous uncle, the writer Dr. Franz Kafka. One of the girls from the Jewish Home, sixteen-year old Tile Rössler, explained to her *chaverim* who he was. She was an apprentice at a bookshop and had held "The Stoker" in her hands. She idolized Kafka right from the start and sought a private conversation with him. Kafka was happy to oblige and listened to long stories of her hardships at home. Tile arranged for him to be invited to the next Sabbath dinner.[7] A big event for all concerned. The very same day, he got himself a *siddur* (Hebrew prayer book) and asked which verses would be read. He wanted to be prepared, so as not to stand out with his lack of knowledge. Kafka had never been at a Sabbath celebration like this, with blessings, Hasidic music, and an opulent feast in a hall decorated for the occasion.

On the evening of July 13, one week after his arrival, Kafka headed there with the prayer book in his pocket. Through a window on the ground floor, he peered into the kitchen, where a young woman with medium-length, thick, curly hair, round cheeks, and full lips was hard at work. She was holding a knife in her hand and scaling fish for the big meal. Kafka stopped in his tracks at the sight of her and waited until she looked up before coming inside. "Such tender hands," he said, "and they have to do such bloody work."[8]

Dymant, Dimont, Dymand, Diament, Dimant, Diamant. First name: Dvojne, Dworja, or Dora. The haziness surrounding the family name, which appears in six different spellings in the scanty documentation, was an indicator of their alien status. These are transliterations of Hebrew characters into Yiddish and German. The young woman belonged to both worlds. To the German authorities, she was Dora Diamant. She later signed a dedication in a copy of *A Country Doctor* as "Dora Dymant-Kafka."

"I came from the East," she recalled, "a dark creature."[9] She was born on March 4, 1898, in Pabianice, an industrial town near Łódź. A Polish state did not exist at this time, so her parents—Herschel Aron and Frajda (whose Yiddish name was Friedel, and who was not even twenty when she married)—were subjects of the tsar. Eight children were born of their marriage. The first two lived only a few months, and of the surviving two girls and four boys, Dora was the second child. Their mother died young; it may have been the last childbirth in 1905 that took her life, or the cause may have been tuberculosis.[10]

Herschel and his children moved to Będzin in Upper Silesia, a predominantly Jewish town in a coal mining region. He set up a factory that manufactured suspenders and garters, and prospered as Herschel *der Shleikesmacher* (the shoulder-strap maker). But by the time he left for work in the morning, he had already spent several hours reading and praying. Herschel was a model of learned Hasidism, who had his own comprehensive library, read ancient Hebrew, spoke Yiddish and German in addition to Polish, and strictly observed not only the religious rituals but also the ultra-Orthodox Jewish guidelines for everyday conduct—including a commitment to generous support for and hospitality to destitute families. His long-standing spiritual mentor was the "wonder rabbi" of Ger (Yiddish name: Góra Kalwaria), head of an extremely conservative Hasidic "court" that was influential throughout Poland.

Dora grew up in a world in which every strong emotion and every daily activity was infused with symbolic significance but was also reined in by a tight net of religious rules. Individuals could not shape their own destinies here, least of all women, and it took quite a bit of willpower, coupled with extraordinary circumstances, to leave the prescribed path without facing social ostracism. It took two catastrophic events to open up Dora's world. One was the early death of her mother, which forced her to gain a degree of independence even before puberty, and which probably also held her father back from calling the marriage broker, since he needed someone to run the household. The second catastrophe was the beginning of the world war, which resulted in thousands of strangers showing up in Będzin and barriers between the various Jewish milieus breaking down at long last. Here, too, political Zionism took hold, especially among young people, and suddenly girls from ultra-Orthodox, conservative, and fully assimilated families were enrolled in the same Hebrew courses.

Dora worked her way through the classics of Zionism, especially the writings of Herzl. She learned Hebrew, went to the eastern European Jewish theater, and even acted in several performances, a scandal that posed a most distressing dilemma for her father because his highest spiritual authority, the rabbi of Ger, threatened all Jews who did not immediately pull their children out of Zionist circles that they would be excluded from the community; the influential Herschel had no choice but to concur. He decided it would be expedient to get his daughter out of town, away from Będzin and her large circle of friends. He brought her to Krakow and placed her in an Orthodox Jewish boarding school that had the rebbe's blessing. It was the first Bais Yaakov school, founded with the mission of training teachers who would abide by religious law. But it was too late; Dora was already nineteen years old, and the anti-Semitic furor she experienced in the Polish metropolis only fueled her dream of Palestine. She fled Krakow and got as far as Breslau, where her father caught up with her and brought her back, but after her second escape, he gave up and mourned for her as though she had died.

She remained in Breslau (in German Silesia)—presumably as a registered refugee—for about a year. She worked in a children's home and quickly picked up the German language. The highly educated, Zionist-minded Badt family in Breslau appears to have given her the idea of moving to Berlin, and there she became a governess in the home of one of the sons, Hermann Badt, who was a representative of the SPD party and a leader in the Jewish community. She also took part in political rallies. One of Dora's acquaintances in Breslau, a medical student named Ludwig Nelken, even recalled seeing her in Berlin onstage with the prominent communist Angelica Balabanoff.[11] But in 1920, she was referred to a place that would prove more significant for her life: the Jewish Home. A young woman who had a command of all the important languages spoken here, who was used to austere living conditions, experienced at working with difficult children, and able to cook. Dora Diamant must have been an incredible godsend for the Jewish Home. It is not known when she first traveled with the refugee children, but in Müritz she seemed to be in charge of everything: she was the chef, housekeeper, and singing and language teacher.

The friendly, somewhat boyish gentleman from the guesthouse had already caught Dora's eye. He was usually in the company of a woman and several children, and this family struck her as so odd—she even wondered whether he was a "half-breed American Indian"—that she once followed them down the street.[12] Then she found out that he was a bachelor from Prague, a Jew, *and* the writer everyone had been eagerly awaiting. A very modest writer, as it turned out, one who did not like to talk about himself at all but rather wanted to learn, like everyone else here. She liked that, and was impressed. From then on they saw each other as often as her many duties allowed.

Kafka kept his silence about this momentous encounter for a long time, even more consistently than he usually did. He wrote about his enthusiasm for the Jewish Home, for the "cheerful, healthy, spirited children," and commented to Bergmann, "It is not that I'm happy when I'm among them, but I'm at the threshold of happiness"—the happiness of identification, the kind he had felt back in Prague when he looked through the windows of the Jewish Town Hall and saw, spellbound and excited, the eastern European Jewish refugee children who were temporarily housed there and felt that his greatest wish was to be one of them. Only to Klopstock did he admit that this dream vision entailed the pain of disillusionment. The vacation camp in which he was now spending nearly every evening was "the most important thing in Müritz and beyond Müritz," yet he remained no more than a guest, "and not even clearly a guest, which pains me; not clearly because a personal relationship cuts across the general relationship."[13] Still, he did try to maintain the other relationships he had established. He spoke to the jealous Tile Rössler and later even sent a long, serious letter to her in Berlin. And he was even able to offer the *chaverim* a surprise that boosted his reputation even further: a quick visit from his friend and teacher Puah Ben-Tovim, a real Palestinian. She was a sensation in Müritz.

In early August, Elli's husband, Karl Hermann, also arrived to spend a few days at the seaside, but he was out of luck; the weather turned bad, and a sudden drop in temperature cleared off the beach and sent many guests packing. For Kafka, this meant that the hours he was spending with Dora in the warm sand amongst the children and often reading Hebrew texts came to an abrupt end. The Hermanns decided to leave early, with or without Franz. They agreed that Franz should leave the Baltic Sea and spend a few days in Marienbad with his parents, who were staying at the health resort there as they did once a year. But overnight the weather turned so unpleasant there, too, that this plan was scrapped. The Hermanns went home, and Kafka was free to think about what to do.

From a health point of view, the beach vacation in Müritz had been a failure. His insomnia and headaches had not let up, nor had the feeling of constant fatigue and weakness, and he had even lost weight.

Here, of all places, where everyone else felt so energetic, he finally realized that he was not up to the physical challenge of Palestine. But making plans with Dora was also difficult under these circumstances. She could not travel with him now because the Jewish children's vacation was still in full swing, but she was hoping against hope that he would go to Berlin, and she was prepared to make life easy for him there, to the best of her ability. Of course, no one in Prague would understand the idea that a man suffering from tuberculosis would willingly spend the winter in Berlin, which was cold, plagued by inflation, and socially chaotic. A fight was sure to follow.

Even so, he took the first step. Without telling his sister and brother-in-law what he had in mind, he left them in Berlin and stayed in a hotel for three nights. He wanted to size up the situation, and he appears to have studied the housing market in the *Berliner Tageblatt* and visited the neighborhoods Dora recommended. He stopped in on at least one acquaintance in Berlin: Tile Rössler. On his very first afternoon there, he rattled at the door of the Jurovics Bookstore in Charlottenburg, where she worked. He had probably noticed that some stores had started to close rather early in the day; no one wanted to sell anything at the prices before the stock market closed—not even books. But finally, after he had knocked several times, a surprised and delighted Tile opened the door. Kafka handed her a bouquet of violets and asked her if she would like to go to the German Theater with him that evening to see Schiller's *The Robbers*. He told her that she could bring along girlfriends from the camp if she liked.

In the evening, Kafka took the subway to Oranienburger Tor, then went to the theater with three teenaged girls. He was dead tired and found it hard to follow this play, which he had known since his schooldays, but at one point he nudged Tile, leaned over, and whispered, "Listen to that, Tile, the scoundrel is named Franz!"

There was no mistaking the fact that Kafka had lost weight recently. He now looked as thin and frail as he had three years earlier. He weighed in at 54.5 kilograms, which meant that nothing remained of the outward success of the course he had pursued so determinedly in the dining rooms in Merano and Matliary, and his parents, who were still using Franz's weight as an indicator of hope, rightly asked how things would go on from here. Of course, it could not have been Elli's job to supervise his eating, but someone had to tackle the problem. After all, the days of hardship and the black market were long over, and in contrast to Germany, the markets in Bohemia carried everything; he just had to eat and give no thought to the prices. In the end, it was once again Ottla who helped out. On many occasions, she had proved to be a master of "fattening him up," even under the most trying circumstances, and she was feeling adventuresome because her second pregnancy had made it impossible for her to go on a vacation. It was therefore decided that Kafka would go to a summer resort with Ottla for a while, as he had the year before, but this time to Schelesen, which would be close enough for Josef David to make occasional visits.

Kafka stayed for five weeks. There is little documentation as to how the siblings spent their time in a merchant's house there, but Kafka could hardly have picked a better spot. For one thing, he was quite familiar with Schelesen and would not have to encounter any surprises; the wistful memory of the cheerful walks with Julie Wohryzek and the struggles he faced in writing the "Letter to His Father" (how far away all that now seemed!) must have strengthened his conviction that Dora's appearance in his life was nothing short of miraculous, and that his new plans were far more realistic and more autonomous than anything he had defended so fiercely a few years earlier. For another, Ottla was the only person to whom he could reveal decisions with such far-reaching implications. When it came to matters of the heart, she showed understanding even if they were the diametric opposite of her own experience, and she knew and accepted the fact that her brother could easily do without the well-meaning advice the family typically doled out.

Kafka had arranged with Dora that she would find suitable lodgings for him in Berlin and provide him with all the necessities after the move (he told Tile that Dora was his "housekeeper"). The prospect that this could become a permanent move, and that keeping house together might turn into the actual life together with a woman he had yearned for with every fiber of his being for such a long time, seemed so overwhelming to Kafka that he did not even dare to put the idea into words: "I must be a very precious possession of those counterforces," he wrote to Brod, "they fight like the devil, or are the devil."[14] But Kafka did not tell even Brod that he was actually planning on leaving Prague and his family; only Ottla knew about the preparations and the near-daily correspondence between Schelesen and Berlin. In late August, Dora found an affordable furnished room way out in Steglitz, and Kafka sent the written confirmation in secret.

He appears not to have informed his parents about his departure until the last possible moment, so that there would be no time left for long debates. Since Ottla had rented her place in Schelesen until mid-August, the Kafkas naturally assumed that Franz would stay there as long as the weather permitted. But suddenly, on September 21, he appeared in Prague and announced that he would travel to Berlin two days later, alone, no matter what the doctors said. He had put on a little weight under his sister's supervision—his weight gain was visible if you gave him a good hard look, and it owed in large part to the beneficial effect of fresh farm butter. But that butter was not available in Berlin, and many other items could only be had at astronomical prices, so how would he feed himself? Kafka was unconcerned about his future diet; instead, he spent hours packing his suitcase to ensure that it held as few clues as possible to his plans. No winter clothes, for example; this was just an excursion. There was no more cash than for a week or two in the house anyway. Well, his parents would send it. The point now was simply to leave.

It was the night before taking the big plunge. Kafka spent it awake because the ghosts of Prague had united to launch one final major attack. Sleeping pills were useless; he had to fight, and his fear was overwhelming. No, he would not go. Dora would understand, and he would send a telegram to the landlord in Steglitz to cancel the room. The only thing he needed was a credible explanation. Kafka began frantically to formulate the text of this telegram, but he could not finish it. Finally it was light outside, his sister was making breakfast, and his luggage was all packed. Ottla's husband came upstairs to say goodbye. Josef David could not understand how someone could go to Berlin at a time like this. Kafka's father grumbled a bit but did not seem to mean anything by it this time, and he may even have been impressed by his son's sudden determination. His mother gazed at him sadly. Kafka thought about what he had discussed with Ottla, and the devoted way she had prepared him for this big journey. No, there was no going back; there would be no telegram. He turned away, got into the elevator, the doors closed, and for the first time ever, he did not say when he would be coming back.

CHAPTER TWENTY-SEVEN

The Edge of Berlin

I suffer about many things that others merely pity.

—Lichtenberg, *Sudelbücher*

> It seems to me that the minute two people marry in order to be happy together, they rob themselves of the chance to do so.... The only good reason for two people to get married is if it is impossible for them not to marry. If they simply cannot live without each other. Without any romance, sentimentality, tragedy: it happens.

MILENA POLLAK PUBLISHED THIS UNSENTIMENTAL STATEMENT IN early 1923, in an essay called "The Devil at the Hearth." Kafka not only read this text but studied and commented on it in detail, almost sentence by sentence.[1] It was obvious that Milena was drawing on her own experience as a married woman, especially when it came to the discrepancy between grand convictions and the mind-numbing quarrels about trivial matters she had endured for years. She wrote that it was pointless to make promises that could not be kept; it would be far better for the partners to accept each other as they were, and to behave with "human decency" even when daily aggravations piled up. Kafka had held this view for a long time. It was not enough to replace the conventional obligations of marriage and family, which were a matter of course to his parents, with vows of everlasting love and passion. A never-ending quest for the "ideal" partner was not the answer. He had insisted time and again to Felice that only the deep feeling of belonging together could sustain and justify a marriage, regardless of the living arrangement one might choose. There was an aspect of existential pathos in this standpoint, but Kafka's determination to dispense with the romantic vocabulary of the heart also had an element of pragmatism, even of objectivization, that Felice would have had to go along with. Regrettably, the only examples he could come up with were middle-class married couples; anything beyond that was the stuff of fantasy and literature.

In the course of the decade that followed, however, Kafka had made the acquaintance of self-confident Czech women, and Ottla herself had been forging her own path for years. The unwritten laws governing "reputation" and "good name" were becoming more and more porous. War and the breakdown of social constraints had cemented his conviction that these once-inviolable procedures of planning a bourgeois life were not only forbidding but also anachronistic. It no longer made sense to plan for decades, let alone generations. And Kafka was now older. Even by the standards of his parents, who continued influence him, against his own better judgment, a forty-year-old was no longer obliged to embark on "engagement expeditions," and hiring detective bureaus to spy on the family of the prospective bride was now increasingly considered shady even within the bourgeois middle class.

This development brought Kafka a new form of serenity that he could not have imagined just a few years earlier. Of course, he had lost the battle for marriage as well as the battle *against* a marriage—Milena's—and if marriage was the institution that represented life, he, the eternal bachelor, was not only a loser but also a social revenant, which was even worse. For a while, Kafka was actually determined to accept this consequence and to drift out of life—not into actual death, which his tuberculosis was threatening anyway, but into literature. And he had to wonder whether this urge to flee was even the impetus behind his plans for Palestine, whether even those plans were ultimately only a way of racing away from defeat.

But now, quite late in the game, he began to understand that many possibilities had stayed out of reach precisely because he had forced the issues. The phrase "attempt at marriage" was telling. He had not meant it ironically, yet it sounded more like the achievement of a high jumper or a student taking an examination than an intimate social act, and ideas like these underscored the extent to which he had internalized the traditional list of obligations. But what was the alternative if one did not want to lapse into social irresponsibility, the way Otto Gross had? Paradoxically, it was the very fear of these kinds of examinations—a fear that grew with each "failing grade"—that finally helped Kafka find a way out. He decided that in order not to make an issue of human relationships, there would be no more "sacraments of inseparability," or "bond . . . magniloquently laid before heaven," as he wrote to Klopstock, to put a damper on his onslaught of friendliness. But if this resolution were applied to life with a woman, he was saying exactly what Milena had called for in her essay: the end of forced, destructive demands on oneself and others.

It may never have crossed Kafka's mind that someone like himself, who had never spent a single day with a lover in a shared apartment, might one day adopt such a calm attitude that was concerned only with the present, and not only for himself but together with a woman, yet this is what happened in 1923. With Dora Diamant, he did not have to talk about wedding plans, or family planning, or the role of parents, or even about the question of how to label their relationship for the outside world. All this would work itself out at some point. Both wanted to spend a great deal of time together, and both knew that this was possible under three conditions: Kafka had to leave Prague and thus the sphere of his family's influence; Dora had to see to his everyday needs; and finally—the least problematic part—he would have to share his pension benefits with her. That was their agreement.

On a basis like that, they could safely leave aside the question of whether a relationship between a twenty-five-year-old Eastern Jewish woman and a forty-year-old Western Jewish man who suffered from tuberculosis could "work out." It turned out to be a remarkably happy setup. Kafka was impressed and moved by the energy with which Dora had blazed her own trail while still being deeply affected by the fate of others, and he was surely reminded of his youngest sister. Dora had wrested herself from the social bonds of Orthodox Judaism, and had even accepted the inevitable rift with her own family in the quest for freedom, yet she remained true to her heritage, in sorrow and in pride—an attitude he had also marveled at and admired in Yitzhak Löwy. For Dora, Kafka represented a human ideal. He had affirmed his Jewish identity while absorbing and refining everything that fascinated her about the West: education, individualism, a fine sense of humor, and a social commitment extending beyond his own group. She even admired the way Kafka paid close attention to unremarkable, ordinary things, which reminded her of the "sanctification" of life that Hasidism preached and she had internalized. Nothing escaped his attention. The simplest things made him happy, and even when he was provoked into offering resistance and criticism, he was never disrespectful.

Even his approach to literature was guided by this quest for immediacy. During the first few evenings in the holiday camp in Müritz, he was greeted as a writer, a prominent man deserving of special honor. But that was exactly what he did not want. As important as the written word was to him, the idea that literature could put him on a social pedestal frightened him, even though he knew—and if he forgot, his friends reminded him—that once he released his writings to the public, they developed an autonomy in space and time far beyond the horizons of his own life. But he had great trouble reconciling that reality with the intimate act of writing.

"When it came to literature," Dora Diamant recalled, "he was not open to negotiation or compromise. His entire existence was at stake. He not only wanted to *get to* the bottom of things; he *was* at the bottom."[2] That was a perfect summation (it may even have been Kafka's own wording) and confirmed Dora's view that literary language could not be isolated from its author any more than a significant gesture or a facial expression could. She read and listened to Kafka's notations as though they were personal messages and sought out what applied to her, figuring that since these were texts from the hand of the man she loved, these were messages *to* her. She eventually came to modify this view (which would pose great difficulties for Max Brod in publishing Kafka's literary estate) but continued to insist that it was altogether impossible for an outsider to understand Kafka solely on the basis of his published works, or the works without his presence. The idea that a distinguished writer was a giant of intellectual history who also happened to have a physical and personal life would have seemed absurd to her, and there is every indication that it was not Kafka's literary achievement but only his personal appeal that captivated her.

It had to be a quiet place to live, far from the noise of the city, with good air, stores nearby, and a reasonably convenient mode of transportation to the center. That was a tall order, but Dora had chosen well. When Kafka first saw his new lodgings in Steglitz, which he had known about only from descriptions in her letters, he was greatly relieved. It was a large, nicely furnished room with bay window, and there was an option of using the balcony belonging to the landlords, a merchant and his wife who were living in a rental apartment at Miquelstrasse 8 (which is called Muthesiusstrasse today, at the corner of Rothenburgstrasse). It was a petit bourgeois, peaceful ambiance, typical for this outlying district: a bank official, a craftsman, an engineer, another merchant, and three retirees were the neighbors. Kafka found the local area charming, and he thought right away of spending the winter here. It was outside central Berlin, with tranquil, tree-lined boulevards that seemed to have changed little since the days when Steglitz was a village. Only in the past two decades had Berlin begun to expand out this way, and Steglitz had been incorporated as a municipal district, but Miquelstrasse, Kafka wrote, was the last one with an urban character. When he walked just a few steps away from the city, he was surrounded by gardens and country villas: "If I go outside on these warm evenings, a fragrance comes to me from the lush old gardens that is more delicate and strong than I think I have ever sensed anywhere else, not in Schelesen, not in Merano, not in Marienbad."[3] Somewhat farther out of town, about a half hour by foot, there was Grunewald, and if that was too far, Kafka could relax at the New Botanical Garden in Dahlem, less than a mile away. Right around the corner was Schlossstrasse, which was also beginning to develop into a regional center of retail trade, and this was also the location of the Steglitz town hall and a stop on the Number 6 streetcar line, which went downtown. Short paths leading everywhere, the amenities of the big city, and the fragrance of a Mediterranean health resort—even if Kafka may have been exaggerating a bit to appease his family in Prague, he had happened upon a far better situation than he could have expected with his limited means.

His letters to his family revealed nothing about Dora. It is likely that his parents had yet to hear of her,[4] so one of the greatest advantages of the apartment in Steglitz, namely the fact that "lady visitors" were permitted here—though not overnight—went unmentioned. But Kafka did not dare to think about really living together with Dora anyway. He would not have been able to manage this twofold exodus, which he had fought for over the space of so many years—from his hometown to the faraway metropolis, and from self-sufficient bachelorhood to sharing a home with a woman—all at the same time. Dora, who had a room or some other place to sleep in the Scheunenviertel neighborhood, traveled the long way out to Steglitz nearly every day to get Kafka everything he needed. Kafka made small purchases himself; every morning he dressed in a suit and tie and went off with his milk can to get it refilled. The landlords prepared his breakfast. But Dora took care of everything else, and because they could afford to go to restaurants only once or twice a month, she also made his hot meals, using two portable "spirit stoves" and a thermally insulated "cooking box" in which the food finished cooking. Then they went on walks together. In the afternoons, Kafka took siestas, and he often read aloud to her—Grimms' fairy tales, E.T.A. Hoffmann, or Kleist—sometimes late in the evening while she lay on the couch. Or they made shadow plays with their hands, at which Kafka proved to be adept. The room was rather dimly lit; there was no electricity, and so they had to make do with gas light, but Dora was able to construct a large petroleum lamp out of parts she borrowed and purchased, so that Kafka had a tolerable degree of light, at least for reading and writing. This idyll in Steglitz had only one fault, but it was an ominous one, and even Dora could not do anything about it: It cost 500 billion marks a month.

"How are you?" "Rotten, times the index number." Berliners had a sassy saying for almost everything.[5] But what had been playing out since the fall of 1921 in the markets, department stories, groceries, and banks put even the sharpest Berlin tongue to the test. The daily list of index numbers—exchange rates and wholesale prices in which people's real disposable income was reflected—started sliding, then accelerated, and eventually exploded. The dollar exchange rate was consulted every morning like an oracle, even by people whose income came in a pay envelope and had never in their lives dealt with foreign currency. Before the war, everyone knew that one dollar was worth four marks and twenty pfennigs. In January 1922, it had risen to two hundred marks; in August, to one thousand; and by July 1923, people were calculating in millions, then in billions.

This situation was unparalleled in history, and even economists who had warned about a collapse of the German currency after the war could not have imagined the bizarre circumstances under which this catastrophe would actually unfold. Of course, any newspaper reader could point to the cause of the debacle, namely the staggering indebtedness of the German state, which had waged its war of conquest not with increased tax revenues but on credit. And the high reparations imposed by the victors in Europe—France the most relentless—who insisted that the damage incurred be paid for over the long term. Neither at the Spa Conference (in July 1920) nor in other negotiations was the German government able to achieve a significant reduction or at least an extension of the payment cycles—tangible assets were the only acceptable substitute. The diplomatic watchword was: *We are willing to pay, but we cannot*. The reply from Paris read: *If the reparations are not forthcoming, we will come and take them*. It was hard to imagine how they could make good on this threat because whether or not there was a military occupation, where could the economically devastated Germany get more than two billion gold marks a year? But France was now determined to make an example and, in January 1923, occupied the Ruhr region, carting off coal and industrial goods and issuing a bill for the cost of this occupation. This misguided decision went against all economic logic. For years, Germany had been blamed for deliberately weakening its own currency and fueling inflation, and now the country really was doing so on a self-destructive scale. To offset the losses and to support the population of the Ruhr region in its "passive resistance" to the occupiers, the Reichsbank printed immense quantities of banknotes that were not covered by anything but assurances.

Prices spiked, and the salary and wage increases with which the furious victims of this monetary policy had to be appeased were paid with paper fresh from the mint. By July 1923, there was no stopping this carousel. The mark was losing in value on a daily basis, and in August, the German currency system went completely out of control. On September 21, two days before Kafka's arrival in Berlin, the first banknotes with a face value of one billion marks were introduced. And that was not the end.

There could hardly have been a worse time to move to the German capital. The social disparities were most pronounced here, the consequences of the hyperinflation the most devastating. Berlin was suffering from hunger as it had in the final weeks of the monarchy, the difference being that this time, the consumer goods they were longing for did exist and were sometimes displayed provocatively in shop windows. Anyone who had banked on war bonds, savings books, or a pension was left with nothing, regardless of the amount of the previous income, but those who had opted for material assets exchanged them for dollars, and they could be used to purchase almost anything at off hours. This blatant inequity brutalized the public sphere even more than during the war. Aggressive begging, holdups in broad daylight, spontaneous mobs and looting, and violent confrontations with the police were now reported on a constant basis, along with daily spontaneous strikes and protest marches; the ban on organized gatherings that had been enacted months earlier did nothing the prevent them. In mid-October, the situation intensified dramatically once again when the city of Berlin stopped issuing bread ration stamps once it was no longer able to carry the costs of producing and distributing them and thus did away with "municipal bread rolls" as the last affordable food. In the inner-city neighborhoods, many businesses stopped opening altogether or opened only with police protection. Armored vehicles patrolled the streets, and armed force was the only way to ward off the populace from staging an attack on city hall in Berlin.

It was as if Kafka had set up house at the edge of a minefield. It was still relatively peaceful out there in the neighborhoods that had only recently become part of Greater Berlin; but he thought it better to find out what was going on downtown by reading the *Steglitzer Anzeiger*, which was openly displayed on Schlossstrasse, than to see the situation with his own eyes. He went into the city once or at most twice a week, and always with the fear of the disabled not to be able to bear up under the hectic pace and the turmoil. He got together with Brod at Café Josty, he visited Puah, who was working in a home for girls, he had passport photos taken at Wertheim Department Store, then he came home "feeling miserable and profoundly grateful to be living in Steglitz."[6] But here, too, he remained true to his practice of keeping his complaints to himself when everyone else was affected as well. Even in his communications with Brod, who was kept steadily informed about the situation in Berlin by Emmy, Kafka limited himself to hints, and his letters give no indication that he was living in a metropolis at the brink of social anarchy or civil war. But even his family, whom he told only about practical concerns, but never about political issues, read the graphic reports in the *Prager Tagblatt*. Fortunately, they had no idea that he had a special connection to the most severely affected area, the Scheunenviertel, but newspaper commentaries, such as those by Alfred Döblin, provided deeply unsettling reading for the people of Prague and left no doubt in his parents' minds that unlike his previous convalescences in mountain valleys, summer resorts, and sanatoriums, this one would be a kind of purgatory:

> The sight was astounding even for a Berliner. Grenadierstrasse and Dragonerstrasse, where the Eastern Jews live, have been cordoned off by police troops; the streets are all dark. On the corners there are powerful, pushy mobs, smashed windows and stores. Cursing and whispered conversations could be heard. Münzstrasse has been a center of the dangerous riffraff, and police patrols are the order of the day. Now they are evidently all jumping in, the gentlemen with their neckbands and jaunty caps. But foreign men, looking utterly bourgeois, are there as well, and many women. One look reveals that anti-Semitism is a matter of indifference to most of them; they're here to loot.[7]

It was hard to compete with eyewitness statements like these, but Kafka's parents had a vulnerable spot that Kafka was very experienced at using to his advantage: their inclination to push things out of their minds. If they were kept busy with some clear-cut problem that could not be solved too easily but would require practical resources, they threw themselves into it headlong and put aside the far more serious problems they—or anyone else, for that matter—had no power to fix. And that is how it worked out this time, as well.

Nineteen letters and postcards that Kafka sent to his parents from Berlin have been preserved; almost all talk about prices and exchange rates, clothing and household needs, and of course concerns about food, which were undeniable but, in his description, quite tolerable. He claimed that there was enough to eat, and the bread was even better than in Prague; only the butter was inedible. Maybe they could send him a little? There were also eggs, he wrote; the only problem was their price. Eggs had cost the equivalent of half a Czech krone apiece, but now the price had skyrocketed to 1.60 kronen. Kafka did not need to calculate that the nominal price for a single egg was actually three billion marks; it was obvious that under circumstances like these he might be able to cover the cost of food for a healthy person, but not for someone with tuberculosis. For his mother that was reason enough to send off regular packages with Ottla's help. The first packages contained food, then came winter clothing and small household objects. But none of his letters gives any indication that his parents asked about his medical care, and on only one occasion did his father bring himself to ask the obvious question about the point of the whole enterprise. He wanted to know whether Franz had "a future for later" in Berlin.[8]

Kafka was used to financial woes, since he was no longer receiving a full salary, but he was now living at the brink of poverty and more than once contemplated breaking off the experiment before he faced complete ruination. To save postage, he sent postcards with messages in tiny print (which still cost 36 billion) instead of letters. He could not afford a daily newspaper, a night at the movies, a ticket to the theater, an unnecessary streetcar ride, or of course any medications. Once the precious alcohol for the cooker was used up, Dora sometimes warmed up his food with candle stumps, and she put off going to the laundry service as long as possible. Kafka had no reserves to work with; if his pension did not arrive from Prague on time, he had to borrow money—most likely for the first time in his life. Buying books was out of the question. Almost every book on his shelf came from the suitcase he had brought from Prague: a sorry sight. In an odd twist of fate, the telephone—a machine that irritated Kafka more than ever—was one of the few amenities whose cost remained behind that of the overall inflation. The *Vossische Zeitung* had reported right at the start of the economic landslide that it made sense to make as many telephone calls as possible, because at least you would get something for your money. This was not especially helpful advice for Kafka. Still, his tiny household in Steglitz could be reached by telephone, although anyone calling his number generally got Dora on the line.

The fact that Kafka remained solvent at the height of the hyperinflation, between September and early December 1923, and did not suffer from hunger was primarily because he received his income in Czech currency. Paradoxically, this was also the very reason that he was not much better off than a German retiree because although he was entitled to a monthly sum of approximately one thousand kronen, this money was paid out in Prague, and in order for him to spend it, he not only had to transfer it to Berlin, which entailed enormous fees, but what was worse, he had to change it to paper marks because German retailers and landlords were prohibited from billing in foreign currency (with which he could have cleaned out the stores in Berlin). All that took up time, and time now meant a loss of money that could be calculated to the penny. Kafka was beside himself when he learned that his parents, who were naive in monetary matters, had sent him a check in the amount of several hundred kronen, but issued in marks and calculated at the exchange rate of the day it was posted. Three days later, when Kafka took receipt of the payment, it had already lost a third of its value because of the raging inflation; the bank that executed the transaction registered the difference as a profit. "I would rather lose money on my own," Kafka wrote angrily, "than on a detour through banks."[9] It was far safer simply to send the Czech banknotes by letter, and later the Kafkas prevailed upon friends and acquaintances who happened to be heading to Berlin and could bring large sums of money for their son, in which case Franz had to take a streetcar somewhere to pick up the money. These were inconveniences and aggravations no matter what the arrangements, and Kafka was far from happy about his continued dependence on his parents for packages of butter and now even for his meager finances.

Meanwhile, it was far from certain that these sums would be paid out to his family. Strictly speaking, Kafka was not an early retiree; he was simply in "provisional retirement," which meant that the Workers' Accident Insurance Institute was still entitled to call him back to work. A spontaneous recovery from tuberculosis would have meant his return to the office—or the withdrawal of his pension. The institute was also under no obligation to accept automatically his residency abroad, where it no longer had access to him. Kafka had not considered this problem at all; his hectic departure from Prague had not even left him time to pore over the pertinent regulations and find out what legal measures he had to take to ensure the continuation of the pension payments. He figured that he had no need to justify a little trip to anyone. But three months later, when he had decided to spend the winter in Berlin, it was high time to come clean with the director. Ottla took care of this by heading straight to the institute, where she was given a cordial reception. Kafka followed up with a detailed letter describing his health and financial situation, and in order not to put off Odstrčil with any linguistic lapses, he asked his brother-in-law, Josef David, to translate it into perfect Czech first.

The main point he had to justify was how a stay in Berlin would serve to restore his ability to work, because the institute would not put up with having a semiretired employee willfully ruin his health for long. Kafka wrote that this decision was well considered and rational. For one thing, he was hoping for a favorable effect on his "neurological condition" (which was the bureaucratic expression for "ghosts"), and for another, Steglitz, as his doctor had assured him, was "somewhat favorable" for his lung ailment; after all, it was a "semirural suburb," where he had the help of friends. His financial situation was the only aspect that was turning out to be more problematic than he had anticipated, and he was therefore requesting that his pension payments continue to be sent to his parents. It is easy to picture the quizzical look on the director's face when he read this diplomatic letter. The idea that Berlin was a health resort was certainly news to him, and Kafka's inclusion of the word "garden" five times in a single (run-on) sentence did not make it any more credible. But Kafka's state of health had worsened in Prague, as well, as was amply clear from the letter, and it was therefore probably for the best to let him make such momentous decisions on his own. On December 31, Kafka's request to draw retirement benefits while living abroad was officially approved. Odstrčil replied generously that all he needed to do was to assign power of attorney to his parents and to submit a "certificate of life" once a month or so, certified by the police. "If, however, you should wish to settle *permanently* in Germany or any other place abroad, you would be required to inform us and request a further remittance of your uncurtailed retirement benefits."[10]

Kafka did not mention that he would need a good bit of luck to hang on to his place in the garden city of Steglitz. The cost of his lodgings was a substantial hurdle, and problems with his landlady made him lose hope that things would work out. He had rented the room in August for the equivalent of 28 Czech kronen. By the time he arrived in Berlin, this price had tripled, and the amount owed for October was six or seven times that, plus heating costs, which in the cool autumn temperatures and with doors and windows that did not close tightly climbed even more quickly and were eventually just as expensive as the rent itself. It is difficult to establish how often he was hit by steep increases, but it can be assumed that by late October, the rent had to be renegotiated continually. On the night of October 31 alone, the German mark lost half its value, and in the following night even more than half once again. At about this time, Kafka wrote a letter to his parents (unfortunately it was undated) that he was now paying a half trillion, but even that could not be the end of the escalation, because by November 7 this mountain of money had the equivalent value of a single American dollar.[11]

Landlord complaints were a daily theme in the German business news. Rents lagged behind the inflationary increases of other costs of living because they had to be paid in advance, in the monetary value on the payment date, so that it was usually the renter who had the advantage. The disputes that inevitably resulted were legion, and thus the unpleasant discussions Kafka had to have on Miquelstrasse more and more frequently did not necessarily mean that he was being taken advantage of. But obviously the landlady had pictured the economic status of a retired official with a doctorate differently, especially a renter who had money in a foreign currency and was always dressed so very properly. During their first conversation, she had asked him about his income and received a truthful reply. This—Kafka later suspected—

had been his crucial error, because back in September, one thousand kronen a month had been a substantial sum of money, which virtually invited rent increases. There were also possible tensions because of Dora's frequent presence. The atmosphere quickly deteriorated. In early November, things fell apart altogether, and Kafka was told to leave the apartment.

He was relieved. As a parting shot, Kafka decided to give Frau Hermann of Miquelstrasse 8 a place in literary history. "A Little Woman" was the title of a highly ironic portrait Kafka wrote near the end of the year. It was a depiction of anger—even hatred—without any identifiable reason, an anger that resisted conciliation. "This little woman is very unhappy with me, she always finds fault with me, I am always doing the wrong thing to her, I annoy her at every step." To mollify the woman, he even makes "some changes" in himself, the first-person narrator reports in comic resignation and equally comic indeterminacy, but it is all in vain. "Her unhappiness with me, as I am now aware, is a fundamental one; nothing can eliminate it, not even the elimination of myself; if she heard that I had committed suicide, her rage would be boundless." But if the suffering of this nameless lady could not even be put to rest with the ultimate sacrifice, one might as well go on living with a clean conscience. "So however I consider the matter," this strange prose piece, in which *nothing* really happens, says at the end, "it appears, and I will stick to this, that if I keep my hand over it, even quite lightly, I will be able to go on quietly living my life for a long time to come, untroubled by the world, despite all the outbursts of the woman."[12]

And that is exactly what Kafka himself did. He found a new place to live, only two blocks away, but did not reveal his moving date to the indignant landlady until the last minute. On the morning of November 15, he left the house and went downtown. When he returned at about 6 P.M.—much later than he had planned—and rang the doorbell in the front yard of his new abode, a villa at Grunewaldstrasse 13, two comfortably arranged rooms on the second floor were waiting for him. Dora had seen to the move all on her own. She had carried over the little that he owned, and nothing was left for him to do. The perfect moving experience. And the "little woman" was left empty-handed.

We have no more than a hazy image of Kafka's daily life in Berlin, and the pieces of the puzzle that the strategically formulated letters to his family provide are too few and far between to fill in the gaps between them with anything but mere speculation. Even the question of whether Kafka and Dora Diamant "lived together" cannot be given a simple answer. Dora's memoirs blend the months they spent together in Berlin into a single, quasi-timeless state, to an epoch of their life: *We* lived in Steglitz, she writes, "first in one room, and later we had two." But in doing so, she was remaining within the confines of psychological experience; the outward circumstances were not those of "cohabiting." Also, an erotic relationship with Kafka seems to have developed only gradually, although the barriers of the utmost discretion that he set up even to his friends have resulted in little more than a smattering of clues for posterity. A letter Kafka wrote in early January 1924 contains a postscript in Dora's hand, and we infer that she was now spending the night in Steglitz.[13] But two months earlier, just before the move to Grunewaldstrasse, Kafka was still seriously considering the idea of subletting one of the two rooms to save money—to his uncle Siegfried, the country doctor. Kafka would hardly have tolerated this outpost of the family in Prague at the height of an erotic passion right under his nose—particularly because his two rooms were separated by the landlady's bedroom, which would have meant a fairly unorthodox arrangement even in tolerant Berlin. In mid-January, Dora still had her own place in Berlin, yet Kafka's messages to his parents—who by now did know about the woman he loved in Berlin—took for granted that he would be living together with Dora no matter where they wound up. We do not know what erotic intensity this life developed or perhaps could have developed later, whether Dora got to know his "fear" and the extent to which Kafka's increasing physical weakness limited the opportunity for sexual experience. He wrote to Tile Rössler that Dora was "a wonderful person"[14]—an indirect declaration of love, but he could not reveal more here, either. Dora and he shared their lives and, in a sense, also lived together because it was impossible for them *not* to live together. That was the way Milena's publicly formulated criterion had read, and Kafka was certainly aware that for the first time, and contrary to all expectations, he was meeting this criterion.

They lived in seclusion, but they were not cut off from the world. Kafka's lack of participation in the cultural life of Berlin was a symptom first of his financial situation, then of his medical condition, but word soon got around that he was living in Berlin and could even be reached by telephone. A whole series of literary emissaries came out to Steglitz: Rudolf Kayser from *Die neue Rundschau*; Willy Haas; the writer Ernst Blass; Ernst Weiss, who was also impoverished; Kafka's friend and admirer Ludwig Hardt; Egon Erwin Kisch and Jarmila Haas (who were now a couple); and even Werfel, who still refused to accept Kafka's rejection and left in tears this time.[15] Brod also visited Kafka's home several times and was not surprised to find his room as bare and almost as impersonal as his earlier one in Prague, not to mention the uncomfortable cold. But he found that Dora, who addressed him with the familiar *du* right off the bat, was a model of humane behavior. Brod admired her touching devotion to Kafka, and in spite of severe financial difficulties, she was able to put a meal of goulash, eggs, and salad on the table for their guest from Prague.

It was a little odd, and no one could have predicted that Kafka would now have far more occasion to speak to Emmy Salveter than to Brod himself, who did not get away from Prague for weeks on end at times and had to keep using his job as a pretext. Every so often the situation became so tense that Emmy headed for Kafka's home for no other purpose than to seek advice and encouragement. Brod was telling her—Kafka learned to his astonishment—that only "duty" was keeping him in the marriage. But no one was buying that excuse. Emmy, who had just explained that she was prepared to accept the monthly visits of her lover, now suddenly demanded that Brod get a divorce, and the letters and telegrams between Berlin and Prague became so fraught that Kafka gave her the serious (and, as it turned out, the only sensible) advice to simply keep silent and leave the solution of the problem to the next time they got together in person.[16]

It goes without saying that one of Kafka's visitors was the "little bookshop girl," the effusive Tile. It took some time for her to understand the role of the jealous and rather dismissive Dora—and several times Tile brought her young painter friend along to introduce him to a real writer. Dora surely enjoyed and learned more from another

For foreigners living in Germany, the immediate consequence of the currency reform of December 1923 was the elimination of a privilege. Even if they were able to change their foreign currency without incurring a loss and to spend it on the spot, and even if they paid with dollars in secret, there was no longer an advantage over holders of the new mark. They now had to struggle as much as the locals with the now stable—albeit high—costs of living, and these costs were considerable in comparison with Austria or Czechoslovakia. Kafka was also not helped much by the fact that the supply of goods had now multiplied within weeks, and that the lines in front of the stores in Berlin vanished virtually overnight. That made for a more relaxed atmosphere, but the new price signs quickly made him aware that he would not survive here for long without outside support. Kafka's dependence on supplies from Prague continued to increase—even though he was still denying that in early January. His parents sent him advance payments on his pension money that would be coming in over the following months, and he also got several hundred kronen from Ottla and Elli. The title of a brief article in the *Prager Tagblatt* read "The Poor Foreigners in Berlin," and it seemed like a cruel joke that the Kafkas used this very page to wrap a stick of butter in for Franz and Dora.[23] His Berlin doppelgänger, a second Franz Kafka, who had also moved to Berlin in 1923 but had bought the house in which he lived on the spot, was in significantly better shape. The Berlin telephone book listed his profession as "proprietor." Enviable.[24]

His parents had given him fair warning: *A future for later*, yes or no; that was the crucial question. Kafka had replied that that was a touchy subject because "as of now, there is not the least indication of a prospect of my earning money."[25] This matter-of-fact disclosure was not unexpected but nonetheless deeply unsettling. Hadn't Franz kept telling them in earlier years that he would have to reside in Berlin to be able to make a living as a writer? Had he now given up on his literary plans? If that was the case, it was impossible to understand why he continued to cling to this economically devastated, violent metropolis.

It was probably a wise decision not to give his parents any unfounded hopes, as he had done too often and too hastily in the past to keep peace in the family. Dodging uncomfortable questions was something he had learned from his parents, one of those disingenuous

mental inhibitions he had wanted to cast off with his abrupt departure.
Eventually he would begin to believe his own vague promises, so it was better to understate the case a little and to hold off revealing good news until the news had assumed concrete form. There was certainly an "indication" of future earnings, even though he did not mention anything of the kind in his many letters to Prague.

Months earlier, Kafka had established a connection to Die Schmiede, a new and evidently financially solid publisher in Berlin. It is unclear how he did so; Max Brod reports that he was the one to have introduced Kafka to Georg Salter, the head of the company, but the publisher had drawn up a written agreement back on August 1, 1923, which was when Kafka had spent a day in Berlin while traveling to Müritz. It is therefore far more likely that he had made this contact by letter while in Prague.

Kurt Wolff was probably not surprised to learn that Kafka had been seriously entertaining offers from other publishers that came his way every now and then. Theirs had not been an especially fruitful connection. Of course, Wolff had recognized Kafka's unique status, and some of the most prominent readers—from Prague and well beyond—had confirmed this judgment. "I have never read a single line by this author that did not touch or amaze me in its own peculiar way," Rilke wrote to Wolff in 1922, and asked him to "make a point of" reserving a copy for him of everything that was published by Kafka.[26] Ludwig Hardt similarly affirmed to Wolff that he regarded Kafka's texts as something quite extraordinary. But Wolff had never gone out of his way to establish a more personal, ongoing communication with Kafka. The thin thread kept snapping during the years of breaks between the publications, and by the early 1920s, Wolff had quite clearly lost interest. The wonderful novels Kafka had written, which Brod kept raving about, even in public, had never been completed, and without a novel, this author was not marketable. The dismal sales figures allowed for no other conclusion.

By the time Kafka endured the long-drawn-out production of *A Country Doctor*, he was also wondering whether Kurt Wolff Verlag was still the right place for him. His publisher's cordial words made for an odd contrast with all the ongoing incomprehensible carelessness, such as the publisher's insistence on sending letters to Kafka's earlier office address despite Kafka's repeated complaints, and the lack of response to Robert Klopstock's interest in the Hungarian translation rights. In the fall of 1923, Kafka received two letters from the publisher that must have reinforced his resolve: royalties were sent to him from an outfit called Kloppstock Company, and he was informed that the publisher had closed his royalty account in the absence of sales. He would be receiving no further payment, but in lieu of money, he would be entitled to several books of his choosing. Kafka selected a few, only to find himself in the awkward position of sending a reminder after several weeks of waiting in vain for these books to arrive.[27]

It was no secret in literary circles that many other Wolff authors were also turning their backs on the publisher, who no longer promoted new German-language literature with the same verve as he had before the war. Wolff felt that the creative force of Expressionism had ebbed. "I find more and more," he wrote to Werfel, "that your generation, which I may also call my own, has no young creative successors; at least I am unable to spot any, despite my keenest attentiveness over a broad spectrum."[28] Sure enough, he was vacating quite a bit of the literary terrain that had been identified with the name Kurt Wolff for the past decade. His "New Novel" series had now opened to European literature. The demise of the avant-garde book series *Der jüngste Tag* was a clear signal that times had changed: in 1920, there were four volumes published; in 1921, the number was down to three, all of them lesser literary works, and volume 86 was the final publication. This forum was no longer an option for the publication of *A Hunger Artist* as a stand-alone volume. It was also blatantly obvious that Wolff's ambitions were increasingly directed at the visual arts.

The galloping inflation in Germany in the early 1920s was the primary factor in the publishing industry's plunge into chaos. Bankruptcies, newly formed companies, and mergers resulted in author rights traveling from house to house. Local literary milieus split apart, and the old networks were no longer functional. Even long-time authors were now inclined to switch to financially sound publishers, with disputes about terms of payment and late royalties (which had only a fraction of the original purchasing power) dominating the correspondence. Many publishers were accused of using the crisis to fatten their own wallets at the expense of their authors; while the list price of books was multiplying, the actual income of the authors was sinking drastically. On occasion, even a play that enjoyed success throughout Germany did not earn its creator a penny, because the playwright had neglected to ensure reasonable adjustments for inflation. "All parties involved agree," wrote Herbert Eulenberg, a successful playwright, "that of all the businesses in postwar Germany, the publishers have gone the furthest in exploitation." Kurt Wolff Verlag was also suspected of cheating, and even Kafka felt that Wolff must have earned a "truly enormous amount of money" from the inflation.[29]

Disputes also hinged on exchange rates. German-language authors who lived in Austria or Czechoslovakia gained little from the paper marks they received. Even Werfel, whose works were more successful than ever before, earned so little from Wolff that he decided to part with his former mentor and sign a contract with Zsolnay Verlag, which paid in Austrian kronen. But the standard advances were far too low in Germany, as well, in relation to the rising cost of living the author had to expect in the months after the contract was signed and up until the time that his book was actually in bookshops. Kafka learned about this problem directly from people he knew well: first from Max Brod, who was receiving minuscule royalties from Munich, then from Ernst Weiss, who had switched from S. Fischer to Kurt Wolff in 1921.

Weiss told his new publisher in the fall of 1922 that he had completed a short novel, and in order for him to be able to buy clothing for the winter, he was forced to ask for an advance of seventy to eighty thousand marks, which was what another publisher was offering him.[30] But Wolff did not want to go along with this. Weiss's claim would have hinged on prepayment for several thousand copies, and it seemed unlikely that Weiss had received such a generous offer. It turned out, though, that this was no mere negotiation tactic, but the intervention of a serious competitor, the Berlin publisher Die Schmiede. Ernst Weiss's novel *The Trial by Fire* was in fact published by Die Schmiede, in an edition that impressed even the bibliophile Kurt Wolff. There were 675 numbered copies, illustrated by Ludwig Meidner and printed with a hand press on exquisite stock. How was that possible; where did such a new publisher get these kinds of resources?

Die Schmiede, founded in the fall of 1921, stood out by the following year with a list that was both comprehensive and highly literary, in large part titles from Roland Verlag in Munich, which had been taken over in its entirety: works by Alfred Wolfenstein, Georg Kaiser, Oskar Loerke, Arnold Zweig, Heinrich Mann, and others. Its profile strongly resembled Kurt Wolff's. Several of Wolff's authors, among them Carl Sternheim and even Wolff's associate and occasional editor, Walter Hasenclever, consequently switched over to Die Schmiede. Literary critics applauded the publisher's rapid expansion, and it fueled authors' hopes. Die Schmiede was soon reputed to be paying generous royalties.

It took a while for people to realize that this strategy of acquisition and wooing away authors was essentially based on mismanagement. Die Schmiede had been founded as an offshoot of a profitable theater agency, and the owners were using the agency's assets to cover the book publisher's deficits. The details can no longer be reconstructed, but it is evident that blurring the boundaries between the two areas resulted in major miscalculations. As long as the profits flowed out of the theater agency, there was no need to worry about the fate of individual book projects. The motto was: Buy the rights and commit the authors, and everything else will follow.

These connections were obscured for quite some time, and Kafka had no way of knowing about them. Like many others, Kafka found the concrete offer so enticing that he did not give any further thought to a long-term association with an inexperienced publisher. He had only two stories to offer initially—"A Hunger Artist" and "First Sorrow"—but in combination with "A Little Woman," there were the makings of a compact volume of narrative prose, for which he negotiated a new contract in February that yielded him an advance of approximately eight thousand Czech kronen,[31] which was a considerable sum in the eyes of his parents, as well, although it came too late to be of use to Kafka in defending his outpost in Berlin. Kafka most likely realized later that Die Schmiede was a shady outfit. The production of the book was oddly protracted, and several inquiries went unanswered, but only his literary executor, Max Brod, actually witnessed the swift decline. Complaints about irregular royalty payments started pouring in, and by 1925, Die Schmiede was essentially bankrupt. Not a single one of the list of prominent authors with whom Die Schmiede had created a short-lived sensation stayed with this publisher longer than his contract required. And Brod saw to it that this was true of Kafka, as well.

On the afternoon of December 24, 1923, Dora returned from the city, where she had run some errands to prepare for the holidays. The weather had been freezing for several days, and Dora was looking forward to a hot cup of tea. But she was in for a nasty surprise when she got back to Grunewaldstrasse: Kafka, who had been in good shape in the morning, lay in bed shivering and was running a high fever. This had never happened before, and although he had spoken several times about earlier bouts of fever that had gone on for weeks, they had neglected to make precautionary arrangements. Where could they get a doctor now, on Christmas Eve? Dora, in a panic, called Lise Weltsch, who promised to get her help quickly and got in touch with a relative who was a tuberculosis specialist. But this man bore the title of Associate Professor, and she could only imagine what kind of fee he would charge. So what could she do? Dora, who knew just how touchy Kafka could be on the subject of his family's interventions, felt she had no choice but to call Prague and beg Elli for money. Late that evening, a doctor did come all the way out from the city. Luckily, he was a somewhat more reasonably priced assistant, but his examination did not yield any tangible results; he recommended continued bed rest and waiting for the fever to pass. This visit cost twenty marks. And although Dora was later able to bargain it down to half that amount, this evening signified a crucial turning point: Kafka had to acknowledge that the independence he had fought so hard to maintain was hanging by a thread.[32]

Independence above all from his family's judgments. Kafka's letters were cordial, but he set unequivocal boundaries. A letter to Ottla, written months earlier, asked her to visit him in Berlin alone if at all possible:

> You know the tone in which people sometimes speak about matters pertaining to me, when they are obviously under Father's influence. There is nothing mean-spirited about it; it is more like sym-

> pathy, understanding, pedagogy, and the like; it is nothing mean, but it is the Prague that I not only love but also fear. To see and to hear directly such judgments, no matter how good-natured, no matter how friendly, would seem to me like Prague's reaching all the way out here to Berlin for me, would be harmful to me and disturb my nights.[33]

The reference was to "Pepa," Ottla's husband, who of course was not pleased at the prospect of her taking this trip, because of the children. But Ottla, who had experienced similar things in the past—she had not forgotten the food packages to Zürau that were weighted down with well-meaning advice—knew quite well what her brother was afraid of, and did come to Berlin alone in late November. Once she had met Dora, she understood his situation much better. She was the only one in the family who had a concrete idea of the life Kafka was now leading, and she was probably the first to tell the family (to her parents' horror) that he was living with a young eastern European Jewish woman and was *nonetheless* well taken care of. There were some discussions about his parents going to Berlin, but they never set a specific travel date. It seems as though Kafka was not even particularly eager for a visit from Robert Klopstock, who spent time at the Kafkas' apartment and was therefore almost a part of "Prague."

This detachment was not intended personally, and Kafka was not afraid of being swayed in his course of action. He was doing what he considered right, living in a foreign city and defending the measure of freedom that his illness had given him. But he did fear that the ghosts of the past assembled in Prague could "reach all the way out" into his new life and into his nights, which had become peaceful since Dora's appearance, and he was doing his utmost to prevent that from happening. In mid-January, he wrote to Brod that his parents were acting "quite delightfully," by which he meant that they were being generous with their money, but in the same breath he rejected a suggestion to move to Schelesen, to "warm, well-fed Bohemia": "Schelesen is out of the question; Schelesen is in Prague, besides, I had warmth and good feeding for forty years, and the result does not tempt me to go on trying them." He rejected the very idea of going to Vienna, because this route would have taken him through Prague, and just stopping off there—and thus, as we read between the lines, subjecting Dora to his family and his earlier life—was "too risky" for the time being.[34]

It was above all his fear of new encroachments by his family that made him conceal the threatening developments in his illness for weeks. The shivering fit that Kafka had suffered at Christmas had not recurred, but this time he waited in vain for a true recovery. He now had an elevated temperature on an almost daily basis, and because the central heating functioned inadequately with the constant frost, he spent half the day in bed. The coughing was now returning little by little—which was unpleasant especially at night, right next to the sleeping landlady—and he had to collect his sputum in a jar with a top to obviate the danger of contagion, as in Matliary. Kafka's physical condition apparently deteriorated quite rapidly in January 1924; he continued to lose weight, and by the end of the month he had to stop attending the academy.

Now, of all times, the landlady decided to augment her earnings by renting out the entire floor instead of just the two rooms. But what would Kafka and Dora Diamant do with three rooms? They could not afford that and were therefore given immediate notice, for the second time—as "poor foreigners who cannot pay high rents," he reported sarcastically to Brod.[35] Of course, there were plenty of unoccupied apartments in Berlin now that landlords no longer took billmarks (which were still officially valid), but only goldmarks; an ad placed by Dora announced that a supposedly "older gentleman" was seeking a new residence also brought in a good number of responses. But despite the numerous offers, Kafka had still failed to find an affordable apartment just days before he had to move out, and thus he had no choice but to consider the unaffordable ones and to count on Dora's negotiating skills.

Late in the evening of January 28, a woman named Dr. Busse called from Zehlendorf, an affluent residential area in the southwestern part of the city, with an offer of the upper floor of her house, one large and one small room, with stove heating and veranda, at Heidestrasse 25–26. Kafka leafed through the telephone book: *Busse, Carl.* He knew the name. Busse was a writer who had once made a name for himself with imitations of Detlev von Liliencron but was better known as a conservative critic with a jaundiced view of literary modernity, and especially of German Jewish authors. Ought Kafka to subject himself to *this* kind of nuisance after all the trouble he had been through? He decided to take his chances and visit the apartment. The next day, when he came face to face with the landlady—probably alone at first, without his "housekeeper," whose accent could have queered the deal—it turned out that the adversary he was expecting was in actuality someone with whom he had shared a medical history. In late 1918, Carl Busse, who was then forty-six years old, had come down with the Spanish flu, but unlike Kafka, he did not survive. Frau Paula Busse was a widow, and only her teenaged daughter lived with her.

Just three days later, on February 1, it was time to make the dreaded move. It was quite a strain on Dora; since Kafka was unable to carry his belongings himself, she had to ride the train to Zehlendorf several times on her own, laden with luggage. Toward evening it turned windy and rainy, as well, and there was no choice but to take a taxi. Unfortunately, the new apartment was not only farther from the center of Berlin than the lodgings in Steglitz but even farther away from public transportation. It took at least fifteen minutes to get from Heidestrasse (now called Busse-Allee) to the Zehlendorf train station, which was a serious obstacle for Kafka. In the months of February and March, he was not even able to produce the required police "certificate of life," so it is doubtful that he ever got beyond the immediate vicinity of the Busse villa.

It must have struck him as a stroke of fate that on the very day of his move, his family in Prague was attending a reading by Ludwig Hardt, while two days later he himself had to stay home when the elocutionist read Kafka's "Report to an Academy" at the Meistersaal in Berlin on Potsdamer Platz. Kafka was running a fever, as he did nearly every evening, and Dora had to attend this event alone, as well. Still, she was able to convince Hardt to come out for a visit to Zehlendorf, and presumably this was the occasion at which Hardt gave Kafka a little private performance. Hardt was planning a trip to Italy, and feeling somewhat helpless in view of Kafka's desolate situation, he suggested that Kafka accompany him. It was nothing more than a gesture. How could Kafka even think of a trip to the south that would last several weeks if the train station was not within his reach and a taxi was too expensive? And since he had trouble simply saying "no," he replied with a gesture of his own by giving Hardt a book he had recently read, a description of Siberia, and inscribed it: "in preparation for a trip together to Italy."[36] Siberia, Italy, Palestine . . . all these parts of the world were beyond the horizon of immense Berlin—all equally far and unreachable.

Frau Busse was unexpectedly friendly to her odd renters, perhaps because she was keeping a secret of her own: she, too, was from a Jewish family and had later converted to Christianity. It is highly unlikely that she was afraid of what the neighbors in the semirural environment of Zehlendorf might say, or that Kafka himself, as her daughter Christine later reported, would try to pass as an "Aryan." Even if he had been able to pull off this deception, Dora's eastern Jewish background would have been impossible to hide, as was her status as a lover, and neither could be reconciled with the fictional character of the respectable chemist "Dr. Kaesbohrer," as Kafka appears to have called himself. But it is more plausible that Paula Busse was concerned about sharing a residence with someone who was clearly quite ill with tuberculosis. His coughing could be heard in the morning and at night, sometimes for hours on end, and she must have noticed that he was constantly expelling large quantities of phlegm. At times, Kafka spat into the backyard from the terrace—once directly onto a little arbor where Christine was enjoying some private time with a girlfriend. After this deeply embarrassing incident, the arbor was temporarily off limits to the girls.[37]

Fever, coughing, phlegm—Kafka had had these symptoms for years, and because the onset of spring typically gave him some relief, he thought that he would be able to go without medical treatment this time, as well. What could a conventional doctor do for him? If the patient really insisted on waiting out the end of the cold in Berlin, then it was best for him to stay in bed or, as Kafka now tried every once in a while, wrapped in blankets in a rocking chair at the open window. No doctor was needed for advice of this kind. Dora was alarmed by Kafka's increasing weakness and wanted to seek out help once again. She contacted Ludwig Nelken, the medical assistant she knew from Breslau, who was now working at the Jewish Hospital in Berlin, and implored him to make a house call. "He was not lying in bed when I entered his room," Nelken later recalled. "But he was in terrible shape." Of course, Nelken could do little but prescribe medicine to lower his temperature and calm his cough—and confirm to Kafka that doctors' fees were a waste of money.[38]

A fever slightly over 100, night after night—it could not go on like this. Max Brod, who had last seen Kafka shortly before he moved, was also quite worried, and because Kafka's parents "liked to feel safe," as he noted, he urged Ottla to do something about the situation. For the past few weeks, Julie's brother, Siegfried Löwy ("the country doctor"), had been living with the Kafkas for several weeks, and he had already offered money to support Franz. But now it had become far more urgent to get a clear picture of the situation. It was probably another secret cry for help on Dora's part—to either Brod or Kafka's sisters—that made the decision: Löwy, who actually had different travel plans, was summoned to Berlin by the Kafkas, and because this visit was sure to arouse Kafka's suspicions, Kafka was not let in on the news until the very last minute. He was incensed by his family's continued meddling. He had also been suggesting that his uncle and mother visit him sometime—not in subfreezing temperatures (the icy weather showed no intentions of easing up that year), of course, but later in the spring, when he was back on his feet and looked a bit better. But when he picked up the telephone on February 21 to head off the invasion, he learned that his uncle was already on the train to Berlin.

Siegfried Löwy did not write any recollections of his nephew, and there are no more than a few lines in his hand from Berlin, on a postcard, reporting that Franz was "in very good hands" here.[39] But Löwy must have been shocked. Even the last known posed photograph of Kafka in Berlin, with severe facial features that no longer looked boyish, made the advanced state of his illness readily apparent, and if, as is likely, this passport photograph was the one he had taken back in October 1923, he probably looked significantly worse by February, after numerous feverous nights and further weight loss. Löwy commented that it was out of the question for Kafka to stay on in Berlin under private care; he needed better air, better food, and professional help, which was available only in specialized sanatoriums. This perspective made Kafka so depressed that for the first time, he spent time denying even the most obvious facts. "The quiet, open, sunny, airy apartment," he wrote to his parents, "the pleasant housekeeper, the lovely area, the proximity to Berlin, the beginning of spring—I should leave all that just because I have a slightly elevated temperature as a result of this unusual winter and because my uncle was here during bad weather and saw me in the sun only once, but otherwise in bed, several times, just the way it was in Prague the previous year. I would be quite reluctant to leave, and giving notice would be a difficult decision for me."[40]

Blaming it on the weather was not going to set his parents's mind at ease. Even though Kafka was not continually bedridden, he had been unable to leave the house for weeks, and while Siegfried Löwy had a little look at the cultural life of Berlin, Kafka was incapable of keeping him company, not even for a reading by Karl Kraus, who was making guest appearances in Berlin at this time. It was like a final test of Kafka's mobility. On four different evenings, they could have gone to see Kraus together, but Kafka was unable to travel downtown on any of them, so Löwy went with Dora, and while they enjoyed the rhetoric of the "Karl Kraus theater" (as the Social Democratic *Vorwärts* called it), Kafka lay in bed and had to make do with the latest issue of *Die Fackel*, which he had just gotten from Klopstock. This was certainly not just a matter of the weather.[41]

Löwy, who stayed more than a week, brought his medical authority to bear and persuaded, or at least intimidated, Dora. Kafka eventually gave in and promised to try a sanatorium again in spite of his aversion to the "eating requirements" he would be sure to face. His family would come up with the money somehow, and Dora assured him she would be nearby, no matter what place he chose. The only thing the two of them feared was a confrontation with Kafka's parents, which would reawaken the ghosts of Prague and provoke disparaging remarks about the eastern Jews, to which his father in particular was prone. Kafka could not bear to face this kind of turmoil. His uncle suggested avoiding Prague altogether and traveling directly to a sanatorium, but it had been half a year since Kafka had last seen his parents,[42] so it was decided that he would stay in Prague for two or three days while Dora dissolved the household. Then they would see each other again—somewhere else, on neutral territory.

Since Kafka was no longer able to take the trip to Prague by himself, somebody had to be lined up to accompany him first. On March 14, Max Brod arrived in Berlin and gave Dora a big suitcase for Kafka's belongings. While they were packing in Zehlendorf, Brod went to see

> ventures that evolved quite rapidly, appropriate to the particular rhythm of a doll's life. After a few days, the child had forgotten the real loss of her toy and thought only of the fiction she had been offered as a substitute. Franz wrote every sentence of the novel with such attention to detail and sparkling wit that the doll's situation became quite tangible. The doll grew up, went to school, and met other people. She kept assuring the child of her love, but alluded to the complications in her life, other obligations, and other interests that did not permit her to resume her life with the little girl for the time being. The little girl was asked to reflect upon this, and in this way was prepared for the inevitable loss of the doll.
>
> The game lasted at least three weeks. Franz was terribly afraid when he pondered how to bring it to an end.... He thought long and hard, and finally decided to marry off the doll. He started by describing the young man, then the engagement party, the wedding preparations, then, in great detail, the newlyweds' house: "You can see for yourself that we will have to give up the idea of getting back together." Franz had solved a child's small conflict by means of art—the most effective method he had for bringing order into the world.[45]

This moving, bittersweet story has often been retold. Brod correctly noted that the story recalls Hebel's *Treasure Chest*, the moral of which exemplifies the true meaning of human kindness. It also presents Kafka as an emblematic, virtually timeless figure in this phase of his life. The story certainly typified his approach to literature: his love of playfulness and invention, consistency and responsibility in the fiction he created, and last but not least, his ability to lend the imaginary the impact of the real. But Kafka knew that the lure of the imaginary exacts a price. He granted the child the relief of having dulled the pain of loss by means of the powers of imagination that the letter invoked, but not himself. And we may be sure that the epistolary novel he wrote in Steglitz, which is likely gone for good, did not contain even a glimmer of a factitious, unfulfillable hope.[46]

Another story from Kafka's time in Berlin, far less well known but equally impressive, lacks a moral hero and hence is not edifying, yet has the invaluable advantage of being available to readers in Kafka's own words, in a letter Kafka wrote to his sister Elli in 1923. Elli could not have gauged its significance for the future, but she surely never forgot it.

> Recently I had an amorous escapade. I was sitting in the sun in the Botanical Garden . . . when the children from a girls' school walked by. One of the girls was a lovely long-legged blonde, boyish, who gave me a coquettish smile, turning up the corners of her little mouth and calling out something to me. Naturally I smiled back at her in an overly friendly manner, and continued to do so when she and her girlfriends kept turning back in my direction. Until I began to realize what she had actually said to me. "Jew" is what she had said.[47]

CHAPTER TWENTY-EIGHT

Last Sorrow

When I die, just keep playing the records.

—Jimi Hendrix

"I HAVE SET UP MY BURROW AND IT SEEMS TO HAVE COME OUT well." This self-assured line is spoken by one of Kafka's many narrating animals, as he recounts and loses himself in his own story, which in Kafka's work assumes such manifold forms. This animal is a successor to Red Peter, who evolves from an ape into a man; the jackals in need of redemption; and a dog who conducts research. It is the opening line of "The Burrow," a story written in December 1923 with black ink on the pages of an ordinary graph paper pad.

"The Burrow" is a striking example of Kafka's late literary style, which moved further and further from the prose of his novels. It is still a narrative text, but its highly unspectacular surface story and tone of a slowly unfolding monologue ensnare the reader step by step in its paranoid logic. It is contemplative, discursive prose in which every question, every option, even every nagging doubt exerts the persuasive pressure of cogent discourse, while the absurdity of the assumptions on which everything rests is increasingly lost sight of. The reader faces the same situation as in "Investigations of a Dog": the moment the reader concedes that the amazingly eloquent first-person narrator is a rational being, the narrator's questions become the reader's own, and the temptation to join his quest for meaning becomes almost overwhelming. The key to breaking the spell is the realization that the narrator is deluding himself, and hence us.

"The Burrow" adheres to this pattern, but the unmasking process is incomparably more difficult here. An animal (possibly a badger) that usually lives underground has spent years of painstaking labor digging an extensive system of passages, secured from the outside by various types of camouflage, with the inside fully stocked at all times, physically equipped to repel intruders and mentally equipped with tactical emergency plans. The builder's smugness is unmistakable, but since he seems to avoid relationships with other members of his species and his thoughts revolve exclusively around his own plans, readers need to be wary of his claims. How credible is such an isolated narrator? The attentive reader realizes that this burrow, the tidiness and silence of which is praised again and again, is actually a cave populated by small animals and stinking of the decaying flesh of his prey. It is inherent in the logic of the animal story that human notions of cleanliness do not apply. The animal's clearly exaggerated need for security does not necessarily indicate delusion; after all, even the creator of the burrow concedes that he may have overdone it and that there is no such thing as absolute security. He even dreams of coming to an understanding with an adversary who might turn up, and tolerating that adversary's presence even though the tomb-like seclusion of the burrow does not allow for an "audible neighbor." It turns out that security was not the only point of the burrow, and may never have been the point at all.

> When I stand on the castle plaza, surrounded by my supply of meat piled high, my face turned to the ten passages that radiate from here, each one sunken or raised, elongated or rounded, widening out or tapering in accordance with my master plan, and all equally silent and empty and ready, each in its way, to lead me on to the many plazas, and all of these, too, silent and empty—then the thought of security is far from my mind, then I know without a doubt that here is my castle, which I have wrested from the intractable ground by scratching and biting, stomping and shoving, my

> castle, which can never belong to anyone else in any way and that is so very mine that here I can calmly accept even the mortal wound from my enemy in the end, for my blood seeps into my own soil here and will not be lost.[1]

The manuscript reveals that Kafka first used the word "home" and only later replaced this word with "castle." This is at heart an issue of belonging, an identification that runs deeper and is more lasting because the animal does not rely on any collective (which is the least complicated way to gain an identity), but rather can point to an achievement of his own. *This is what I am*: a human kind of pride that no one can deprecate as delusional per se. The animal displays his life's work, and no matter how bizarre the details, the reader has to concede that accomplishing one's life's work is not the meanest fate that might befall someone.

One element of the formal refinement of this story is that the actual test of the animal's sense of reality does not take place until he has gained a certain respect for his wondrous undertaking. The silence of the burrow is suddenly broken by a noise that goes on day and night without a stop: "[I]t always sounds unvaryingly thin, with regular pauses, at times like hissing, at others more like piping." Is it a mighty adversary digging its way toward him? Is the noise actually intensifying, or does it just seem to be? The avalanche of speculations it triggers does not lead to a tangible result but allows the reader to step outside the first-person narrator's overly confined perspective. If, as we are told, the eerie noise sounds equally loud at any place in the huge burrow, it would appear to be coming from the animal himself. The very fact that the animal does not hit upon this obvious idea makes it even more compelling. A hissing and piping with regular pauses that the animal hears is its own sound of life, its own breath; the animal itself is the ultimate source of the disquiet that continually disturbs the perfect silence of its creation.

We do not know what end Kafka had in mind for the panic-stricken animal keeping to his burrow. The manuscript breaks off mid-sentence, although this break occurs on a page that is filled with writing down to the bottom, which indicates that the text may well have continued beyond what has been preserved.[2] But this story has no need for a real conclusion; its actual, terrible core is biographical and can be inferred not from the text but from the circumstances under which it originated. The question of whether it is an enemy from without that threatens the burrow or whether the constant noise is a danger from within is of no consequence for someone suffering from tuberculosis. The noise of his own breath, which kept getting shorter, this sign of life that is always there but is fearful only to a sick man; this noise *is* the adversary.[3] Kafka did not invent this metaphor but rather adapted it, and readers who take it literally come closest to understanding his text.

The same applies to Kafka's final work, "Josefine, the Singer or the Mouse Folk," a story that brings the old familiar alias "Josef" right into the title. Once again, the story is told by an animal—this time, a mouse assuming an air of complete objectivity and erudition in a morose sort of way—and once again the focus is on the true meaning of a noise that Josefine, the mouse diva, passes off as art, although it is actually a "soft, somewhat hissing piping," a "characteristic expression of life" that can be made by any other mouse just as well, and without any special effort; hers is a "nothing of a voice," a "nothing of an achievement."[4] This raises the question of why she attracts any audience at all (it turns out that some audience members have been summoned to attend), and why Josefine's artistic superciliousness is tolerated as much as it is. The narrator devotes quite a bit of discussion to this mystery and concludes that it is not the art but the staging that provides the aura to keep the crowd momentarily spellbound, and that any demands that extend beyond the temporal or spatial confines of the performance are justifiably rejected by the mouse folk. Art or non-art: no one stands outside the law. The social privileges Josefine demands—especially that she be excused from all physical labor—are flatly denied, and her threat to cut back on her artistic performances betrays a downright delusional misjudgment of her actual status. For the first time, Kafka was bringing the two central motifs of his late years quite close together, so close that it was tantamount to a short circuit. One was an absolute claim to truth, which only the art of the autonomous individual could fulfill (while sacrificing one's life), and the other was a yearning for community, for a concrete social and physical connection to one's own group. The fact that they are mutually exclusive was the heroic essence of Kafka's personal myth right from the start. Now, at the end of the road, he seemed to move away from this position, and the battle of his life appeared in the light of irony. In the end, the diva disappears from view. Whatever the status of her claim to produce art, the other members of her species can live quite well without her. Her performances will live on in anecdotes for now, but future generations will forget her, and then it will be as though Josefine had never existed.

It is difficult to imagine how Kafka could have continued to develop from a literary standpoint if he had recovered from tuberculosis. Max Brod even considered it possible that he might opt for complete silence and social self-sacrifice: "Many things he has told me suggest this."[5] On the other hand, the closing sentences of the "Josefine" story are marked by unmistakable sorrow, not relief, at having finally escaped a life-threatening insanity. If literature—as Kafka believed at the end of his life—is the attempt to pave the way for "a true word from one human being to another," "Josefine" cannot have been his last word but, at most, his departure from the myth of the loner, from all the suppressed sons, accused men, and land surveyors whose narcissism is so voluble, yet so lonely.

Kafka had thought he would stay in Prague for just a few days, then go to a sanatorium—to Davos in Switzerland, which was probably his best option, but certainly the most expensive one. This suggestion came from his uncle, and evidently Kafka had already booked lodgings because on March 19, after only two days in Prague, Kafka told the institute director that he would be leaving soon. For some reason, though, this plan fell through (presumably the entry permit did not come in time), and inquiries had to be sent to different sanatoriums. To be on the safe side, Kafka applied for a passport that would allow him to travel to several countries: Germany, Austria, Italy, and Switzerland—a sign that he was only now looking into practical alternatives and that for the moment he was stuck in Prague.

As it turned out, Kafka was in for hard times. On about March 20, when he was just about to complete the Josefine story and was running a constant fever, Kafka noticed that something was wrong with his throat, as well. He felt a slight burning in his larynx, especially when he drank fruit juice, and he seemed to have more trouble speaking; his voice had a hint of hoarseness. "I think," he wrote to Klopstock in reference to Josefine, who was sometimes hoarse, "I started investigating animal piping at the right time."[6] It could have been an ordinary sore throat, but the symptoms got worse and bothered him even while eating. It is difficult to determine whether Kafka was aware of the imminent danger he was facing, but he did know from conversations with fellow patients and doctors that tuberculosis often caused secondary infections, although he generally tried not to think about that. Max Brod, whom Kafka summoned for daily visits in an imperious tone, was surely more anxious about Kafka's poor health and rattling breath than about the decrease in his vocal power, which was barely perceptible at first. But the fact that the doctor who was summoned for a house call did not even bother to have a look at Kafka's larynx made no sense at all. This man, Kafka later wrote, was simply too lazy to bring along his laryngeal mirror.[7] What about going to one of the real laryngologists in Prague? Instead of bringing Kafka to a specialist, the family decided he should go to the Wienerwald sanatorium in Lower Austria to resume a systematic convalescence. Löwy knew one of the two attending physicians there, who were also the owners of the sanatorium, and this connection seemed to offer both support and a 10 percent discount.

We have no information about his departure from Prague and from his family. It was his final departure; he would never again see his parents or his hometown. One little scene, recorded by the journalist and poet Michal Mareš, is all that remains for posterity. Mareš had known Kafka for many years, and ran into him on the street on a lovely spring day shortly before Kafka left. Kafka was holding a big colorful ball in his hands, which he threw to his niece Věra. Ottla was standing nearby and watching the game. "Would you like to have lunch with us?" Kafka asked with a smile. But Mareš had other plans, and he left. This scene was on Altstädter Ring, on the sidewalk, at the entrance to a funeral home.[8]

The Wienerwald sanatorium, which specialized in lung disorders, enjoyed an international reputation. It was a five-story building with the dimensions of a luxury hotel, incorporating architectural designs from Davos, and boasted a solarium, lounges, reading and music rooms, treatment rooms for radiation therapy, and even its own operating room. The building was at the top of a hill, with a lovely view to the south, and was surrounded by a spacious park, with nothing beyond but miles of woods. The sanatorium was in an isolated spot at the end of a narrow valley, and the next town, Ortmann (today a part of Pernitz), was a good hour's walk away. The journey there was difficult; the seventy kilometers from Vienna required several changes of vehicle, and in the end, a traveler needed to spend several hours on the quaint Gutenstein railway, which chugged its way upward at an agonizingly slow pace. Kafka may have completed this "endless journey" all alone.[9]

Dora waited impatiently to see Kafka again. The few days of separation she had expected had now turned into nearly three weeks. He wrote to her regularly, but Kafka still dreaded the idea of Dora meeting his family, and the excitement and frictions that meeting would entail, so he implored her to stay in Berlin. No sooner had the day of his departure been decided, however, than Dora made her way to Austria. She got to Vienna in a single day of travel and took a hotel room there. She probably called the Kafkas on the telephone to get the exact address of the sanatorium, and while he was still trying to postpone Dora's arrival, she was already on her way to him. On April 8, she arrived in Ortmann, took a room in a farmhouse near the sanatorium, and came to Kafka's sickroom.

He felt extremely ill at ease at the Wienerwald, and later even called it a "nasty, oppressive" sanatorium. He appears to have suffered from the abrupt change from the practical assistance, tailored to his own needs, he had enjoyed for months to the large and impersonal health resort with an international clientele in Ortmann. He did not find that he was getting any special treatment from the two chiefs of staff, and neither seemed trustworthy: "one is tyrannical and the other submissive, but both believe in conventional medicine and are helpless when you need them most."[10] Kafka spent most of his time in bed, listening to the chitchat from the neighbors' balconies; his increasing hoarseness precluded him from joining in. But the worst part was that no one was willing to tell him what could be done long-term. His treatment was limited to alleviating the symptoms: liquid Pyramidon to reduce the fever, an ineffective medicine to suppress the coughing, and lozenges with an anesthetic to make it easier to swallow. "Probably the larynx is the chief problem," Kafka wrote to Klopstock; that much was now certain. "I don't learn anything definite when discussing it, since in talking about tuberculosis of the larynx, everybody drops into a shy, evasive, glassy-eyed manner of speech. But 'swelling at the back,' 'infiltration,' 'not malignant,' but 'we cannot yet say anything definite'—all that in connection with very malignant pain is probably enough."[11] It was the first time Kafka had complained about severe pain, and Klopstock knew what this meant as well as anyone else in the medical profession. If it really was not cancer (but how could the doctors at the Wienerwald know this without tissue samples?), then the rapidly increasing level of pain, the edema, and the infiltration were sure signs that Kafka's tuberculosis had spread to the larynx.

It was presumably his reluctance to present himself in such a helpless and ill-humored state that made him hesitate to admit how bad things were, even to Dora. She had things to take care of in Berlin, she could not live abroad without an income, and as much as he was looking forward to her visit, he thought it was out of the question for her to leave her familiar surroundings just for his sake, but the very moment Dora saw Kafka, she must have known that she would be staying here for quite some time. He now weighed less than fifty kilos, his voice was altogether different, and the relaxed, often even cheerful mood in Berlin had evaporated under the pressure of the pain. Within just three weeks, he had become a person in need of constant care whom she could not just leave behind, even if Kafka thought otherwise. On April 9, he wrote to his parents that Dora was with him for a few days, and would then return home, but Dora wrote below his message, "It is not sure yet whether I'll go home." He was far more direct in a card to Brod he wrote the same day, asking Brod to offer the Josefine story to the *Prager Presse* and then to a publishing company, Die Schmiede, because he needed money urgently: "It's evidently the larynx after all." Dora noted underneath: "If it can somehow be arranged, I will be staying here and not in Vienna. We shall see." Then she added a second postscript without Kafka's knowledge: "Please, Max, sell whatever is possible. I have to stay here, whatever the cost. I need incredibly little, so it will be possible. His condition is very, very grave."[12]

often made patients worse.[16] Surgery did not seem imperative yet. The possibility of "artificial pneumothorax" therapy (temporarily collapsing a lung to promote healing), which Klopstock kept recommending, was weighed, but in Kafka's bad overall state of health, this procedure would have been risky. It was decided first to reduce the pain and coughing, which could be achieved relatively easily with menthol spraying of the larynx. The Wienerwald might have come up with this idea. Sure enough, Kafka's trouble swallowing was alleviated within a matter of days, and he was once again able to eat adequate amounts of food. His gratitude probably would have made him submit to the strict medical routine for a while, had his mistrust of medicine not been confirmed in a most brutal way.

For the first time in his life, he was sharing a room with complete strangers—ailing strangers—and it was the first time that even his most basic needs for sleep, food, and conversation were subject to a strict schedule. At 5:30 A.M. the patients were awakened, then one after another, they used a bowl and running warm water to wash up. Next there was breakfast, and at 6:30 everyone was back in their freshly made beds, ready for the doctor's visit. Visiting hours were limited to 2 P.M. to 4 P.M., and although Dora ignored this rule and regularly showed up an hour early, Kafka found these limitations hard to bear. Even so, he quipped to his parents, the daily routine was still a "very small and weak belated substitute for the military life that I missed out on."[17]

This was a major understatement. Kafka saw things in this large, sunny shared room that he certainly would have been spared in the barracks. The bed next to his was occupied by a married shoemaker from the Waldviertel region of Lower Austria, also suffering from laryngeal tuberculosis, and the doctors had had to resort to a tracheotomy to keep him from suffocating. Although this man, Josef Schrammel, now had a breathing tube, he was in good spirits, had a big appetite, and seemed to take it in his stride that no one came to visit him; his family was too poor to travel. Kafka was surely reminded of the lonely Czech man with the terrible mirrors and of others he had met in Matliary. Klopstock had twice reported to him the death of a former fellow patient, and to Kafka's dismay, they were the very ones who had seemed most optimistic and robust. The affable Schrammel, who had never dealt with doctors his whole life, was blissfully unaware of the gravity of his situation, and Kafka observed angrily that the staff neglected him. "They killed the man beside me," he later noted. "They let him walk around with pneumonia, 106 temperature. Wonderful the way all the assistants were sound asleep in their beds at night and only the priest with his acolytes was there."[18] The following morning, Schrammel's bed was empty, and Kafka was inconsolable. He kept bursting into tears, and for the first time in days, his fever rose.

Of course, it was easy to predict that he could not recover in such a psychologically stressful environment, and the resolutely cheerful cards he sent his parents did not fool anyone. A whole chain of friends and family sprang into action. Elli's husband Karl Hermann came on behalf of the family to cover the finances; Felix Weltsch, who also visited Kafka, inquired into sanatoriums in the vicinity. Max Brod alerted Werfel, who lived in Vienna, and Werfel in turn wrote a letter to Professor Hajek. He also asked a doctor he knew to come to the clinic and intercede on Kafka's behalf, and to the patient himself he sent roses and a signed copy of his newly published novel, *Verdi*. "Someone named Werfel writes me," Professor Hajek is said to have remarked sarcastically, "that I should do something for someone named Kafka. I know who Kafka is; he's the patient in no. 12; but who is Werfel?" This anecdote is a nice little invention. The fact of the matter is that Hajek authorized Kafka's transfer to a single room within a matter of days. Hajek was firmly opposed to releasing Kafka from the clinic, claiming that "everything needed for recuperation, emergencies, and convalescence was on hand" in his hospital, and that this was Kafka's "only option."[19] But it was too late. Kafka had decided to leave the hospital. On April 19, a bright and sunny day, Dora flung open the windows and packed his few belongings. He had been able to fend off a visit from Werfel to this death chamber. The final entry in his medical file read, "Released into home care." That was not exactly the case.

Without the "Sanatorium" sign at the front of the building, Dr. Hugo Hoffmann's private sanatorium in the village of Kierling, near Klosterneuburg, fifteen kilometers from Vienna, could easily be mistaken for a modest inn. It was a plain building on a country road, with a ground floor, two upper stories, a veranda in the back, and a small garden in the front. There were only twelve rooms, which were sometimes used by visitors, and the patients' medical care lay in the hands of Dr. Hoffmann, his assistant, and a nurse. The technical equipment consisted of an inhalation device and a sunlamp, and medical histories were not even recorded because the staff knew their patients' data by heart. It was a family business, and Professor Hajek would not have rated what was offered here as much higher than "home care."

From Kafka's perspective, however, the Hoffmann sanatorium offered invaluable advantages that far outweighed its medical backwardness: Dora could now stay in the house as long as she wanted, and could even use the kitchen. Personal requests were invariably granted; the doctor was only a few steps away, even at night; and patients' wishes to be left undisturbed for specified periods were also honored. Kafka moved into a single room upstairs, which was simple and furnished entirely in white, with a sunny balcony and a lovely view of rose beds, a brook, vineyards, and woods. He felt greatly relieved after all those months of being cooped up, and the shock of the final days in Vienna gradually faded away in the spring landscape full of aromas and colors. Kafka spent as much time as he could outdoors; he even managed to take a little walk into town, and one day Dora rented a one-horse carriage for a few hours to be driven through the vicinity of Kierling with Kafka nestled in cozy cushions. Kafka had not experienced this kind of pleasure since Planá.

The question was whether this arrangement was also the most sensible from a medical point of view. What did well-to-do Austrians do in a comparably precarious situation? If they were no longer able to travel, they moved into a private sanatorium in Vienna and top specialists were called in to treat them. Klopstock had strongly urged Kafka to do the same—to get away from the clinic, but not from Hajek, and not to try any experiments in alternative medicine. Klopstock, who was back in the High Tatras and could weigh in only by mail, was horrified to learn that Dora had contacted a naturopathic doctor. He wrote to Ottla that Dora was taking wonderful care of the patient, but the family absolutely had to dissuade her from pursuing this course of therapy. Luckily, this disagreement soon became superfluous because Dr. Hoffmann had no faith in naturopathy and would not hear of alternative treatments taking place in his little sanatorium.

But of course he had no objection to one of the prominent specialists coming out to Kierling from Vienna. It was all a matter of good connections and having the means to afford the specialist's fee. Once again, Kafka's friends lost no time in smoothing the way for Dora: Werfel informed his friend, Professor Tandler, who served on the city council in Vienna and oversaw the public health service; Max Brod wrote several letters of introduction; the laryngologist Kurt Tschiassny was willing to treat Kafka for free if he was unable to pay; a Dr. Glas, a follower of Rudolf Steiner, was summoned to Kierling; Felix Weltsch knew Oscar Beck, a lecturer in otiatry (medical treatment of the ears) at the university clinic; and finally even Beck's superior, Professor Heinrich Neumann, the "king of the Viennese pulmonologists," was mobilized and, to Kafka's amazement, also charged nothing but the night taxi to Kierling.[20] This lineup of top-notch physicians—the Hoffmann sanatorium had probably never experienced anything of the kind—needed first and foremost to determine what to do about the pain, which was intensifying and could no longer be controlled with menthol. This pain was making eating torture for Kafka, and now drinking was becoming more difficult as well. His complete lack of appetite, which he had to overcome with every bite, was bad enough, but when he was no longer able to swallow the soft and tasty food prepared by Dora—noodles, sweet rice pudding, and eggs—how could he ever regain the physical stability required for the operation that might rescue him? And even the lovely spring weather did not ease the pain, which grew worse with each passing day.

No written report by Professors Neumann and Tschiassny has been preserved, but there is a detailed statement by Dr. Beck, written after his visit with Kafka to fill in Felix Weltsch on the situation. While all the correspondence between family and friends is marked by strategic considerations—even Klopstock complained that there was no reliable, objective information available about Kafka's condition—Beck's letter is the only document to offer an unvarnished picture of the situation. It is likely that Weltsch did not show this letter to anyone but Max Brod, for good reason.

> Yesterday I was called to Kierling by Fräulein Diamant. Herr Kafka had very sharp pains in his larynx, particularly when he coughed. When he tries to eat, the pains increase to the point that swallowing becomes almost impossible. I was able to confirm that there is a decaying tubercular action that also includes a part of the epiglottis. In such a case an operation is not even conceivable, and I have given the patient alcohol injections in the *nervus laryngeus superior*. Today Fräulein Diamant called me up again to tell me that the success of this treatment was only temporary and the pains had come back with all their former intensity. I advised Fräulein Diamant to take Dr. Kafka to Prague, since Professor Neumann, too, estimated that he could be expected to live about three more months. Fräulein Diamant rejected this advice because she thinks it would make the patient aware of the seriousness of his illness. It is your duty to give his relatives a full account of the seriousness of the situation. From a psychological point of view, I can quite understand that Fräulein Diamant, who is looking after the patient's interests in a self-sacrificing and touching fashion, and feels she ought to call a number of specialists to Kierling for a consultation. I therefore had to make it clear to her that Dr. Kafka's lungs and larynx were in such a state that no specialist could help him any more, and the only thing one can do is to relieve pain by administering morphine or Pantopon.[21]

This devastating medical prognosis put an enormous strain on Dora Diamant. Her suffering about the impending loss ran too deep for her simply to surrender to her fate without putting up a fight, but there was no one in Kierling to whom she could speak her mind. Telling Kafka that the doctors felt he had no chance of survival was out of the question. She was convinced that this would have destroyed any remaining powers of self-healing that lay dormant within him, and announcing the sentence would have been tantamount to carrying it out. But the situation now became even more complicated because Kafka was delegating more and more of his communication with his family to Dora. When he had sent postcards home to Prague from Vienna, she had added brief remarks or just sent her regards, but now the proportions were reversed: Dora wrote to Kafka's parents, and if there was space at the bottom, Franz added a couple of sentences. She also corresponded with Elli and Ottla—Kafka was not privy to these letters—and she had to take frequent calls from Prague, sometimes daily, from people she had never met and whose reactions she had trouble gauging. At one point, Ottla came to Kierling for a few hours, and at another, his rather strict uncle, Siegfried—these were the only opportunities she had to communicate with Kafka's family in any detail. And while Dora tried to bolster her own courage and that of her beloved Franz, she needed to choose her words carefully when writing to his relatives because each member of this family could handle a different dose of truth. On May 19, she wrote to Kafka's parents that his sore throat was "quite insignificant" and there was "absolutely no reason to worry." Two weeks earlier, she had confessed to Elli that her brother could sleep only when he was given injections to relieve the pain and that there was nothing left to be done for him.[22]

But medical procedures were not the only subject that needed to be discussed; their financial problems were also weighing on her mind, and they required a good measure of diplomacy because if there really was "no reason to worry," why did Kierling bring him a steady stream of specialists, a growing number of anesthetics, and many costly night visits? Then there were Dora's daily needs to be considered; she had no source of income and was utterly dependent on the Kafkas' support. All this was difficult to communicate. Even though his family in Prague had enough money put aside, and had even come into an inheritance from the estate of the "Madrid Uncle" Alfred Löwy,[23] it was unthinkable to enumerate the actual expenditures to Kafka's parents. Dora also begged Kafka's sisters to get Robert Klopstock to come, since he had experience with tubercular patients. Klopstock did not have money for even a ticket, and thus also needed financial support from Prague. But evidently arrangements could be made very quickly, and just a few days after Dr. Beck's terrible disclosures, Klopstock arrived in Kierling, moved into a small room in the sanatorium, and took over some of the routine medical tasks, and—to Dora's great relief—also some of the correspondence and telephone calls to Prague.

Kafka was shielded from most of these problems so that he would not reject a medical consultation or medication to save money. If he insisted on details, Dora gave him only vague information, and she did not shrink back from painting the situation as she saw fit. She told him that his family had sent so much money that they would get by for the next five months. This was an astonishing gift—assuming there was any truth to it. Kafka not only had complete faith in Dora but had put his life entirely in her hands, and once Klopstock was also helping out and taking care of him day and night, Kafka felt secure in what he liked to refer to as his "little family." Presumably it was nothing but Kafka's will to uphold his dignity in this situation of childlike helplessness that held him back from allowing Klopstock, who was overly informal, to use the familiar form of address with him.

It might appear odd that there is more ample documentation of this muted period in Kafka's life, which he spent in a quiet, sunny, white sickroom in which nothing seemed to move, than of all the previous months Kafka had spent with Dora. The reason is, paradoxically, a medical one—namely, the therapeutic directive that he had to speak as little as possible, at most with the doctor, and even then at a whisper. This "silence cure," aimed at immobilizing the swollen and usually inflamed larynx, was one of the standard (though useless) measures in treating tuberculosis that required enormous self-control from patients. Kafka was unable to stick to a regimen of total silence, and he often noted down words, phrases, and brief sentences to convey his messages or questions. Klopstock collected these slips of paper, and Brod later published a selection of the notes.[24] These moving documents capture individual moments in virtually undistilled form, fragments of a conversation in which Kafka's insistence on sublime linguistic form is far less in evidence than in his letters. Moreover, the conversation slips reveal that as Kafka's interest was retreating from the world—anything outside the sanatorium almost always appears as a reference to the past—his attention to his immediate surroundings was growing in the same proportion. As we might expect, many of the notes relate to physical conditions: eating, drinking, and medication. But he was also concerned that someone might step on pieces of broken glass lying on the floor, and it bothered him that his visitors might be disturbing the rest period of people on the neighboring balconies, although he had no contact with the other patients in the sanatorium. He enjoyed the flowers that people kept bringing him, but he wanted them arranged so that each individual one stood out, and he wanted to make sure that they were treated properly: "Do you have a moment? Then please spray the peonies a little."

Of course, these conversation slips address no more than a cross-section of his life in Kierling. His relationship with Dora is almost entirely absent; Kafka could not jot down things that were meant for her alone (or at least not on the slips that Klopstock collected), and it seems logical that in the final weeks, he was far more dependent on Dora's devotion than the fragmentary notes reveal. But the only extant conversation slip that addressed the issue of their life together indicates that Kafka was fully aware of what he was asking of her. "How many years will you be able to stand it? How long will I be able to stand your standing it?" There is not a word about the many plans they had made in Berlin, about the possible places they might share their future: Vienna, Brno, some small town in Bohemia, Lake Garda. And not a word about another plan—the most important one of all, which was hatched within the "little family" but kept secret from the "big one." Only Max Brod learned about this plan firsthand, and told about it in his memoirs:

> He wanted to marry Dora, and had sent her pious father a letter in which he explained that although he was not a practicing Jew in her father's sense, he was nevertheless a "repentant one, seeking 'to return,'" and therefore might perhaps hope to be accepted into the family of such a pious man. The father took the letter and went to the man he honored most, whose authority counted most, the "rabbi of Ger." The rabbi read the letter, put it aside, and said nothing more than a curt "no." No further explanation. He tended never to give explanations.[25]

It was the third time Kafka was asking for a woman's hand in marriage, and this time, too, he began with an "although . . . nevertheless" and did not want to go against the will of the family. But for the first time, the answer was "no." Herschel Diamant was convinced that there was no point in "repenting" and "returning"; the rabbi of Ger saw beneath the surface, and so Dora's father made this "no" his own. Kafka was sad to learn this, but he was also impressed. If he were healthy, he might have said that this "no" was shortsighted, but in the state he was in, he read it as a bad omen.

On May 3, Max Brod had a visit from Kafka's sister Elli. The letter from Dr. Beck had not yet arrived in Prague, but Elli had already learned its contents from Dora. *Unstoppable*, Brod noted. He had to go to Kierling. But he had never taken such a long journey just to see Kafka, not even during the long months in Matliary, and if he did so this time, he would be robbing his friend of his last hope. Brod came up with a white lie, claiming that he had been invited to lecture in Vienna, and this was a good opportunity to come by for a visit.

He had expected to be confronted with the emotional and physical misery of a dying man. But Kafka was delighted to see him again; he was fully alert and did not even seem to be in an especially bad frame of mind, although he was running a fever, was unable to speak much, and on this very day was coping with the rude response from Dora's father. It seemed close to impossible to Brod that his friend, who was so lively, was a medically hopeless case, and he began to talk about the next time they would get together when he traveled to Italy in the coming summer, almost buying into this story as he spoke. He had tried to mislead Kafka, but he was now misleading himself.

For Kafka, Max Brod was not just a longtime close friend who had come to his sickbed. He also represented a world that had remained impassable to him despite his best efforts. Brod was married; he was a politician, journalist, and writer; he gave public lectures; he traveled a great deal; and his ability to work seemed limitless. In the previous year, he had begun work on a new historical novel, *Reubeni: Prince of the Jews*, which would become his greatest success after *Tycho Brahe*, and the parts that Kafka knew of it had impressed and even "delighted" him. In addition, Brod was able to lend his support; he helped many people, he had connections, and he had had no trouble arranging for two of Kafka's stories, "A Little Woman" and "Josefine, the Singer," to be published in Prague newspapers at Easter.[26] And almost as an afterthought, Brod held down a steady job as an editor at the *Prager Tagblatt*, and for the past few months he had been publishing an article every two or three days, mostly reports about theater performances or concerts he had attended the previous evening. And this man was now visiting him in the sanatorium in Kierling, so shouldn't Kafka at least maintain a little dignity? When they parted for the final time, their thoughts went in markedly different directions. Brod's hopes rose ever

so slightly, but Kafka was dejected about the image he had projected.
He wrote to his distraught friend that he had "wretchedly spoiled" this visit, which had turned so "dismal," and that he should have acted "somewhat more human."[27]

Kafka's final weeks were one long bout of pain. He had learned in Matliary that not everyone suffering from tuberculosis died in a state of euphoria, the way the literary cliché would have us believe. The end was likely to be quite different. After witnessing his neighbor there deteriorate wretchedly, he had made Klopstock promise to give him a morphine injection rather than artificially prolong the torture. His recent experience in the hospital in Vienna made him start to realize that he could fare even worse than his fellow sufferer, who had eventually thrown himself out of a train.

Even Professor Hajek, whom Klopstock now brought to Kierling despite the many depressing diagnoses on which every doctor essentially agreed, was surprised at how far the destruction of the tissue had progressed since he had last seen Kafka some four weeks earlier. Like Dr. Beck, he attempted to block the upper laryngeal nerve by injecting alcohol. The minor success he achieved was short-lived, but without these terribly unpleasant injections, which Kafka endured on a regular basis (preferably without anyone looking on), it was absolutely unbearable. Even the slightest movement in his larynx brought on fierce pain, and coughing was torture. Even drinking was now possible in only tiny sips. Kafka was constantly thirsty; he dreamed about all sorts of drinks and relished the sight of people gulping down a glass of water in front of him. He forced down a small glass of wine a day, and sometimes a little beer; even water had to be warmed up before he could sip at it. "Have you also tried the latest wine here?" he asked his father. "I would really love to drink it with you sometime in nice big swigs because even though my ability to drink is not great, I am second to none in being thirsty. That's the way I've bared my drinking soul." A day or two after these jocose remarks, Kafka learned fom Klopstock that his survival could be ensured only with artificial feeding. "He is so distraught about this procedure," Klopstock wrote, "that I cannot say; he's having a hard time wrapping his mind around it."[28]

Dora later wrote about Kafka, "He really demanded a great deal of respect. If he was met with due respect, everything was all right, and he didn't care a thing about formalities. But if he wasn't met with respect, he was very annoyed."[29] This helps explain some of his surprising gruffness. Even his most devastating pronouncements about himself gave no one the right to speak about him as if he was not there. But Kafka's quirk had an equally important flip side: The awareness that he had to earn this respect never left him, and he had strong doubts that a forty-year-old man who no longer had the most natural reflexes and had to be artificially fed to stay alive could present a respectable image.

The same applied to his capability for mental effort. Kafka had long since resigned himself to the fact that his reserves were waning. The illness, the weakness, the pain he endured, and the struggle between fear and hope all wore him out. "The natural state of my eyes is being closed," he wrote to Brod, who had sent him some Reclam books, "but playing with books and magazines makes me happy." He was making painfully slow progress in Werfel's *Verdi* novel[30] and preferred to leaf through the *Prager Tagblatt*, which the family sent him regularly. He was grateful that Dora and Klopstock had taken over much of his daily correspondence, but he was disturbed by the psychological side effects of his medications. "Even if I really were to recover a little from it all, I certainly wouldn't recover from the narcotics," he noted. He found the alcohol injections, which had to be repeated in briefer and briefer intervals, particularly objectionable because they clouded his thinking and compromised his ability to express himself: one could have respect for a weary man, or even for a man condemned to silence by the doctors—but not for a man injected with alcohol. Kafka even thought he might prefer the pain to the loss of control and self-respect.

He anxiously awaited the galleys for the *Hunger Artist* story collection. There was no doubt that as long as he remained conscious, he would do the revisions by himself and with the usual attention to detail. Brod urged the publisher to begin typesetting the book as soon as possible, citing Kafka's critical condition, but Die Schmiede was still waiting for "Josefine, the Singer," the fourth story it was told to expect. Finally, in mid-May, Kafka received the first galley proof. By this point, his stamina was already sharply reduced, and he often slept during the day as well. "Now I want to read it," he noted nonetheless. "It will rile me up too much, perhaps, because I have to experience it anew." For the first and only time, Kafka felt something like fear of his own texts, and one in particular: the title story, "A Hunger Artist," about a man who no longer *wished* to eat, written by a man who no longer *could* eat. For Kafka, whose works had so often used metaphors of food and refusing food, this cruel paradox was hard to bear. While reading the story, he could not hold back his tears, and even Klopstock, who was utterly devoted to Kafka during these final days, found the situation "really eerie."[31] Even so, Kafka insisted on reading through the final proofs, which arrived in late May, and he was still working on them the day before he died.

It was as though he was refusing to lay claim to any mental break, and even in the face of his own death, he tried to remain at the height of his thinking ability and to retain an intellectually respectable posture. The conversation slips clearly reveal that he rejected attempts at calming him down or cheering him up that were not based in fact: "We're always talking about my larynx," he wrote, "as though it could only take a turn for the better, but that's not true." Another time, he commented, "If it is true—and it seems probable—that the quantity of food I consume at present is insufficient for the body to mend of its own accord, then there's no hope, apart from miracles." When Klopstock broke a tongue depressor, Kafka noted, "If I should go on living, you'll break another ten on me." Of course Klopstock assured him that he would certainly go on living, and Kafka replied, "I wanted to hear that even though I don't believe it."

Kafka longed for words of comfort, as anyone in his situation would. His will to survive was still unbroken in mid-May, and any sign of real hope got him so worked up that he was able to forget his condition for the moment. "When I started to eat," he noted, "something in the larynx dropped, which made me feel wonderfully free, and I was already thinking of all sorts of possible miracles, but the feeling was soon gone." Professor Tschiassny, who came to Kierling once a week, once surprised Kafka with the observation that his throat was looking better than the last time. When Dora came in, Kafka was in tears. He embraced her again and again, and declared that he had never wished for life and good health as much as he did now.[32] Another note—"When are we going for the operation?"—even suggests that in May, Kafka still believed in the possibility of surgical relief.

Those were just flashes of optimism. By and large, he knew that his prospects for the future—which goes unmentioned in his last known statements—were relentlessly shutting down. And his fear did not let up. It was not so much fear of the end of life or of passing into an unknown darkness but rather the fear of an agonizing death that threatened him, as Kafka well knew, even though everyone who spoke with him strictly avoided the topic. But the hard facts of his case were unequivocal, as were Kafka's observations in the hospital in Vienna. Swellings on the larynx, particularly in the area of the glottis, meant death by suffocation. If he chose not to place himself in the care of Professor Hajek again, this time for the inevitable tracheotomy, he would suffocate in Kierling.

> Dearest Parents, Now about the visits you sometimes mention. I think about that every day, for it is very important to me. It would be so nice; we have not been together for such a long time—I'm not counting my stay with you in Prague, which just introduced confusion into the household, but rather I mean spending a few days together peacefully in a beautiful area, alone—I don't remember when the last time was: perhaps once for a few hours in Franzensbad. And then drinking "a good glass of beer together," as you write, from which I see that Father doesn't think much of this year's wine, and I'll agree with him there as far as the beer is concerned as well. In the past, as I often remember during heat spells, we used to have a drink together quite often, many years ago, when Father would take me along to the Civilian Swimming Pool.
>
> That and many other things argue in favor of the visit, but there is too much that argues against it. First of all, Father probably will not be able to come because of passport difficulties. Naturally that robs the visit of a large part of its meaning, but above all, Mother, no matter who else accompanies her, will be concentrating too much on me, will be too dependent on me, and I am still not very nice to look at, not at all worth seeing. You know about the problems of the early period around here and in Vienna; they got me down somewhat; they interfered with the rapid lowering of the

fever, which ate away at my strength. The shock of the business with the larynx during the early period weakened me more than it should have, objectively speaking.

Only now am I beginning to work my way out of all these weakening factors, with the help I am getting from Dora and Robert—absolutely inconceivable from a distance (what would I be without them). There are disruptions in my progress even now, such as, for example, an intestinal grippe these last few days, which I've yet to rally from completely. The upshot is that in spite of my wonderful helpers, in spite of good air and food, almost daily sunbathing, I still have not properly recovered, in fact on the whole am not even so well as I was recently in Prague. If you also consider that I am allowed to speak only in whispers, and even that not too often, you will gladly postpone the visit. Everything is at the best of beginnings—recently a specialist announced that the larynx was significantly improved, and although I [cannot fully believe] this extremely kind and unselfish man—he comes out here once a week in his own automobile and charges almost nothing—his words were still a great comfort to me. Everything is, as I said, at the best of beginnings, but even the best beginnings don't amount to much. Since I cannot show the visitors—and what is more, such visitors as you two would be—major, undeniable progress, measurable even by lay eyes, I think we should rather let it be. So shouldn't we let it be for now, dear parents?[33]

Kafka wrote this letter the day before he died. He was fully in control, and right to the end, he remained a master of language, the medium of his life. He wanted to make his peace, even with his father. His thoughts were focused on the past, on the few bright spots of memory. He even told Dora about how he once got to drink a glass of beer with his father. But in order for him to make peace, he had to be left in peace. A visit from his mother had already been discussed, but now his parents wrote that they both wanted to come. He had no idea why, but it was because Julie Kafka had asked Klopstock for a medical prognosis for her son, and Klopstock had met this request with silence.

Kafka must have discussed the question of this visit with Dora. The very notion of having his parents stay in the guest room of the sanatorium was appalling. Perhaps they could regard the trip as a visit to a summer resort and find lodgings in a bed and breakfast nearby, taking excursions and stopping by the sanatorium once a day? Kafka was seriously considering this option, but the shock would be too great—not only his own, but also that of his parents, who would inevitably reflect it back to him. No, that was not an option. "Everything is at the best of beginnings."

Monday, June 2, 1924 was a warm, sunny day. Kafka was lying on the balcony reading the proofs for his last book. Later Klopstock came back from Vienna after doing some shopping—he bought strawberries and cherries. Kafka inhaled their fragrance again and again before eating them slowly. Later he started work on the letter to his parents, which grew longer and longer, and he was too exhausted to finish writing it. "I took the letter from his hand," Dora added to the same page. "It was quite an effort. Only a few more lines, but what he is asking seems very important:" Her sentence ended with a colon, then stopped. Perhaps he had fallen asleep.

There is only indirect information about the events of the following day, which was June 3. There are reports by Klopstock that Brod recounted in his memoirs of Kafka, and the oral report of a nurse, which Willy Haas recorded. These recollections are somewhat contradictory, but taken together, they flesh out the picture.

At four in the morning, Dora rushed to Klopstock's room and woke him up to tell him that Kafka was having trouble breathing. Klopstock threw on some clothing, looked in on his friend, and alerted the doctor, who was on call that night in the sanatorium. Kafka was given an injection of camphor to stimulate the respiratory center and an ice pack was placed on his throat. None of this helped. Kafka was short of breath and in pain. Hours passed.

At some point in the morning, Kafka gave the nurse a brusque sign that she was to leave the room. He then demanded a lethal dose of morphine from Klopstock. "You've been promising it to me for four years." Klopstock, who had been fearing this responsibility for weeks, balked and objected, but Kafka, who was now dependent on the decisions of others more than ever before, suddenly turned belligerent and accused Klopstock of being a murderer if he refused this final act of loyalty. "You are torturing me; you have always been torturing me. I am not talking to you any more. I will die all on my own." Klopstock injected Pantopon, an opiate, which was nearly as numbing as morphine. Kafka remained skeptical. "Don't cheat me; you're giving me an antidote." But when he felt his pain subsiding, he insisted on having more. Klopstock gave him more—we do not know how much.

Klopstock had agreed to send Dora into town under some pretext so that she would not witness this struggle. But in Kafka's final minutes, he missed her, and a maid was sent to get Dora back. She raced back in, out of breath, and sat at Kafka's bedside. She spoke to him and held a few flowers up to his face for him to sniff. And Kafka, who had appeared to be unconscious, raised his head one last time.

Kafka was forty years and eleven months old. In the registry of the Jewish community, the cause of death is listed as "cardiac arrest." Siegfried Löwy and Karl Hermann, who rushed to Kierling, took care of the formalities. Two days later, Kafka's body was transported to Prague in a soldered metal coffin. In the same train, in a compartment with Klopstock, Löwy, and Hermann, sat Dora Diamant, who would now be seeing Kafka's hometown for the first time. His parents and sisters gave her the welcome she deserved. "Only someone who knows Dora can know what love means," Klopstock had written to Elli that day after Kafka's death.

In the days that followed, several obituaries were published in Prague, all written by close friends: Max Brod in *Prager Tagblatt*, Rudolf Fuchs in *Prager Abendblatt*, Oskar Baum in *Prager Presse*, Felix Weltsch in *Selbstwehr*, and Milena Jesenská in *Národní Listy*. All were clearly in shock, and, seeking superlatives to express the extent of their loss, resorted to the high tone and the conventions of a posthumous tribute.[34]

Kafka was buried in the New Jewish Cemetery on the outskirts of Prague, a few miles from where he had lived. The Jewish burial ceremony took place on June 11, in muggy weather, at about four in the afternoon. Fewer than a hundred people joined the funeral procession. No representative of the political or cultural institutions of Prague attended, either German or Czech.

Eight days later, on June 19, a memorial service for Kafka was held at the Prague German Chamber Theater, arranged by Max Brod and

Hans Demetz, the theater director of the Prague German Playhouse. Every last seat in the auditorium was filled. Brod spoke, as did Johannes Urzidil, a twenty-eight-year-old writer and journalist. An actor recited texts by Kafka, including "A Dream," "Before the Law," and "An Imperial Message."

The words spoken by Urzidil were published shortly thereafter. Urzidil had met Kafka several times and had observed him in coffeehouses in group settings. His eulogy does not reveal any personal closeness; it contains catchwords such as "fanatic of the truth within himself," "noble but unpretentious . . . artist," and "wondrous genius." Then again, he also included a statement with which Urzidil, probably as the first after Kafka's death, drew people's attention to the vital issue: "If ever there was a perfect instance of the congruence of life and artistry, it applies to Franz Kafka."[35]

Later, in his recollections of the German literary scene in Prague, Urzidil returned to this issue, the mystery of congruence. He wrote that Kafka's friends were all in agreement that Kafka's prose was extraordinarily "deep," regardless of whether the friends' orientations were literary, like Max Brod's and Oskar Baum's; philosophical, like Felix Weltsch's; or religious and historical, like Hugo Bergmann's. But they all sought the key to the ultimate door. "They did know how to explain what Kafka may have meant[,] and one could agree with their interpretations or offer one's own. But how it happened that Kafka said what he said; how it happened that he said it the way he said it; how it happened that one never came into conflict with what he said or with him himself, that no one could explain."[36]

How it happened. That ought to be the starting point.

EPILOGUE

PARTICULARLY IN THE EARLY YEARS OF KAFKA'S WORLDWIDE renown, his work, his achievement as a writer, was insistently categorized as "prophecy." Kafka, it was said, was one of the first to predict and envision the anonymous violence of the twentieth century, and that was the primary reason for his overwhelming resonance. But this view overlooks the fact that Kafka was himself witness to the devastations of utterly depersonalized, technologically based violence, which was already claiming victims in his day. This lethal alliance of violence and bureaucracy burst onto the scene in August 1914 and was later called the "great seminal catastrophe" of the century. The world war was unthinkable without typewriters, files, index cards, and official seals—he knew that better than any of his writer friends. But imagining the inferno that would descend on his social and even his most personal milieu just a decade and a half after his death was not in his power—or anyone's.

All three of Kafka's sisters died in gas chambers, Elli and Valli in Chelmo, Ottla in Auschwitz. Kafka's uncle, Siegfried Löwy, the country doctor, avoided imminent deportation by committing suicide. Elli's son, Felix, probably died in a French concentration camp. Marie Wernerová, who had served the Kafkas for decades as a housekeeper, was also deported and did not return.

Of the four women with whom Kafka had the most sustained relationships, two died in concentration camps: Julie Wohryzek was killed in Auschwitz, and Milena Jesenská died as a political prisoner in

Ravensbrück. Grete Bloch was also murdered in Auschwitz. Kafka's friend Yitzhak Löwy died in Treblinka, Otto Brod (Max Brod's only brother) in Auschwitz. Ernst Weiss committed suicide in Paris because once the Germans entered the city, there was no escaping. Kafka's school friend Ewald Felix Přibram died on a ship that was bombed by the Germans.

This list is incomplete. If one were to include Kafka's larger circle of acquaintances—friends from his college days, acquaintances from Zionist circles, colleagues from the Workers' Accident Insurance Institute, eastern European Jewish actors, doctors who treated him, friends Kafka made in sanatoriums, artists, authors, and journalists in Prague, and finally the people Dora Diamant associated with—the list of the victims would be quite a bit longer. An all-too-typical case was the fate of the poet Ernst Feigl: he survived in Prague thanks to his non-Jewish wife, but three of his siblings were killed in concentration camps.

Jews in Prague who had no lifeline like Feigl's had only two ways of escaping murder: dying in time or fleeing in time. Hermann Kafka did not live long enough to experience the rise of the Nazis, but Kafka's mother, Julie, who survived her husband by three years and died in September 1934, did. Oskar Baum would certainly have been deported had he not died in 1941 of complications from an operation. His wife, Margarete, however, spent the last days of her life in the Theresienstadt concentration camp.

Many others who were close to Kafka survived by fleeing the country. Felice Bauer emigrated to the United States with her husband, Moritz Marasse, and their two children, as did her sisters, Erna and Else (but two of Felice's aunts took their own lives just before being deported). The Brods and Weltsches made their escape from the German troops entering Prague at the last possible moment, and got to Palestine. Dora Diamant first lived in the Soviet Union at the side of her husband, Ludwig Lask, but after he was sentenced to imprisonment in a labor camp, she managed to emigrate. During the war, she spent a brief period in an internment camp in England, then remained in London until her early death in 1952. Kafka's niece, Marianne Steiner, also escaped to England, as did the writers Otto Pick and Rudolf Fuchs and Milena's first husband, Ernst Pollak. Robert Klopstock immigrated to the United States and became a successful pulmonologist. Georg Langer, Puah Ben-Tovim, and Tile Rössler went to Palestine. A good number of prominent emigrants who had known Kafka were scattered over several continents: Franz Werfel, Willy Haas, Egon Erwin Kisch, Johannes Urzidil, Albert Ehrenstein, Martin Buber, and others.

The world in which Kafka grew up—a familiar milieu and existential center, yet never, even after he had lived there for decades, a true home—was gripped by two waves of destruction. The first was World War I, which may have spared his family and friends physically but brought about a social, cultural, and even moral transformation that forced Kafka to reorient himself completely. He felt uprooted, and more vulnerable than ever as a Jew, and it was hard for him to reconcile the Czech-dominated Prague of the 1920s with the Prague he remembered.

Kafka was spared the second wave of violence, initiated by the Nazi regime in Germany, but the occupation of Czechoslovakia, the German terror, the genocide of the Jews, and World War II tore apart his world. The fate of many people he was close to was sealed, and countless traces of Kafka's life that were left behind in the collective memory were wiped out. Letters, photographs, literary estates, even entire archives were destroyed. The violence that gripped the era often made it impossible to identify what was lost, and even to ascertain *that* it was lost. If Kafka had had the double good fortune of surviving the tuberculosis and then a concentration camp, he would not have recognized anything left after the end of this catastrophic blow to civilization. His world no longer exists. Only his language lives.

ACKNOWLEDGMENTS

WHILE WRITING THIS BIOGRAPHICAL STUDY, I WAS IN CONTINUOUS contact with Ulrike Greb, Ursula Köhler, Jochen Köhler, and Anna Boskamp. Their patient reading of and contributions to this work over the years resulted in numerous linguistic and factual improvements, solutions to problems of presentation, and, last but not least, encouragement at critical phases.

My special thanks go to Hans-Gerd Koch. He provided access to an abundance of documents, information, and the fruits of his research; without these materials, many a biographical connection would have remained unrelatable or unilluminated.

For conversations, references, and factual assistance, I would like to thank Hartmut Binder, Klas Daublebsky, Theodor Gheorghui, Michael Haider, Jan Jindra, Waltraud John, Věra Koubová, Leo A. Lensing, Naděžda Macurová, Henry D. Marasse, Judita Matyosová, Michael K. Nathan, Reinhard Pabst, Wolf-Detlef Schulz, Václava Vyhnalová, and Klaus Wagenbach.

The extensive research for this volume of the Kafka biography again swelled beyond the original time frame and scope. Generous funding by the S. Fischer Foundation made it possible for me to see this work through to its conclusion without compromise to the contents.

Once again, I am especially grateful to Shelley Frisch, an extraordinary translator, who was undeterred by the length and complexity of this task. Our work together has been an informative pleasure.

TRANSLATOR'S NOTE

English-language readers seeking a standard edition of Kafka's complete writings will find that no such edition exists in the English language. In translating *Kafka: The Years of Insight* into English, then, I have provided new renditions of all passages from Kafka's prose texts, diary entries, letters, and other writings that are quoted in this book.

This volume was translated with the support of the Banff International Literary Translation Centre (BILTC) at The Banff Centre, Banff, Alberta, Canada, and the Europäisches Übersetzer-Kollegium in Straelen, Germany; a three-week residency in each of these writers' havens proved invaluable in bringing this book to a timely completion. I would also like to express my gratitude to Geisteswissenschaften International in Germany for its financial backing of the translation.

KEY TO ABBREVIATIONS

Franz Kafka's literary works, letters, and diaries are quoted according to the German critical edition published by S. Fischer Verlag in Frankfurt and edited by Gerhard Neumann, Malcolm Pasley, and Jost Schillemeit. All texts by Kafka have been newly translated from the German for this volume, apart from three quotations from *Office Writings*, a volume compiled by Stanley Corngold, Jack Greenberg, and Benno Wagner, and translated by Eric Patton with Ruth Hein. Wherever possible, letters are quoted according to their manuscript form, but reference is always provided to the volumes of letters that have been published to date as part of the critical edition.

References to the critical edition are noted with the appropriate abbreviation from the list below, followed by the page number (for example, "B2 416" refers to the volume *Briefe 1913–1914*, page 416). The notation "App" appended to an abbreviation refers to the critical apparatus accompanying that volume (for example, "V App 153" refers to page 153 of the critical apparatus for the novel *The Man Who Disappeared*).

Letters written in the years 1921–1924, for which the critical edition is still forthcoming, are quoted according to the original or the manuscript of the final volume of letters (B5). Letters from this period that have already been published in full elsewhere contain a reference to the publication in question, especially in the case of Kafka's correspondence with Max Brod, Robert Klopstock, his sister Ottla, and his parents.

The following abbreviations are used in this book:

AS	*Amtliche Schriften* [Office writings], ed. Klaus Hermsdorf and Benno Wagner. Frankfurt: S. Fischer, 2004.
AS	Mat *Materialien auf CD-ROM* [Materials on CD-ROM], included with the critical edition of the *Amtliche Schriften*.

B1	*Briefe 1900–1912* [Letters, 1900–1912], ed. Hans-Gerd Koch. Frankfurt: S. Fischer, 1999.
B2	*Briefe 1913–1914* [Letters, 1913–1914], ed. Hans-Gerd Koch. Frankfurt: S. Fischer, 2001.
B3	*Briefe 1914–1917* [Letters, 1914–1917], ed. Hans-Gerd Koch. Frankfurt: S. Fischer, 2005.
B4	*Briefe 1918–1920* [Letters, 1918–1920], ed. Hans-Gerd Koch. Frankfurt: S. Fischer, 2013.
B5	Briefe 1921–1924 [Letters, 1921–1924], forthcoming.
D	*Drucke zu Lebzeiten* [Writings published during his lifetime], ed. Wolf Kittler, Hans-Gerd Koch, and Gerhard Neumann. Frankfurt: S. Fischer, 1994.
NSF1	*Nachgelassene Schriften und Fragmente I* [Unpublished writings and fragments I], ed. Malcolm Pasley. Frankfurt: S. Fischer, 1993.
NSF2	*Nachgelassene Schriften und Fragmente II* [Unpublished writings and fragments II], ed. Jost Schillemeit. Frankfurt: S. Fischer, 1992.
P	*Der Process* [The trial], ed. Malcolm Pasley. Frankfurt: S. Fischer, 1990.
S	*Das Schloss* [The castle], ed. Malcolm Pasley. Frankfurt: S. Fischer, 1982.
T	*Tagebücher* [Diaries], ed. Hans-Gerd Koch, Michael Müller, and Malcolm Pasley. Frankfurt: S. Fischer, 1990.
V	*Der Verschollene* [The man who disappeared/Amerika], ed. Jost Schillemeit. Frankfurt: S. Fischer, 1983.

NOTES

Prologue: The Ants of Prague

1. On the history of war exhibitions in the German Reich, which set an example for Austria and grew increasingly elaborate, see Britta Lange, *Einen Krieg ausstellen: Die "Deutsche Kriegsstellung" 1916 in Berlin* (Berlin: Verbrecher Verlag, 2003).

2. The actual deposit of the 2,000 kronen on November 6, 1915, cannot be verified with absolute certainty, but the daily published lists contain the following remark for the final day the third war bond was offered for sale: "Dr. K. 5000 K" (*Prager Tagblatt*, Nov. 7, morning edition, p. 5). It is likely that this abbreviated name refers to Kafka. For one thing, the amount was pledged at the Bohemian Discount Bank, the German bank of the Prague Workers' Accident Insurance Institute. For another, Kafka's parents had already invested 3,000 kronen in his name (though without his knowledge; see T 771), and in cases of this kind, the total sum was generally entered in the published lists of names. Evidently Kafka did not want to see his full name printed in this context; he was probably a bit embarrassed at the amount. Kafka's lawyer, the well-to-do Dr. Robert Kafka, pledged 8,000 kronen on the same day; Egon Erwin Kisch pledged 2,000 kronen the previous day; and the Zionists Robert Weltsch and Hans Kohn each pledged 500 kronen.

Chapter 1: Stepping Outside the Self

1. Letter to Felice Bauer, presumably May 3, 1915 (B3 132–33).

2. Cynthia Ozick, "The Impossibility of Being Kafka," *New Yorker*, Jan. 11, 1999, pp. 80–87.

3. Letter to Felice Bauer, Oct. 31, 1912 (B2 201).

4. Max Brod to Kafka, Jan. 19, 1921; Kafka to Max Brod, late Jan. 1921. In Brod/Kafka, *Briefwechsel*, vol. 2 of *Max Brod, Franz Kafka: Eine Freundschaft*, ed. Malcolm Pasley (Frankfurt am Main: S. Fischer, 1989) (hereafter Brod/Kafka, *Briefwechsel*), pp. 302, 310.

5. Letters to Felice Bauer, November 1–2, 1914; April 20, 1915; and early March 1916 (B3 106–7, 129, 154).

6. Diary, May 4, 1915 (T 743). The abbreviation "E." likely refers to Kafka's sister Elli, with whom he had taken a trip to Hungary about ten days before this note and on this occasion probably spoke in detail about his worries; see chapter 35, "No-Man's Land" in Reiner Stach, *Kafka: The Decisive Years*, trans. Shelley Frisch (New York: Harcourt, 2005), pp. 508–16.

7. P 48; Diary, August 3, 1914 (T 544).

8. Julie Kafka to Anna Bauer, August 7, 1914, in Franz Kafka, *Briefe an Felice und andere Korrespondenz aus der Verlobungszeit*, ed. Erich Heller and Jürgen Born (Frankfurt am Main: S. Fischer, 1967), pp. 613–14.

9. A term from Kafka's letter to Felice Bauer, October 19, 1916 (B3 261).

10. See chapter 14, "The Lives of Metaphors: 'The Metamorphosis'" in Stach, *Kafka: The Decisive Years*, pp. 192–205.

11. Letter to Grete Bloch, June 11, 1914 (B3 85).

12. Postcard to Ottla Kafka, Feb/March 1915 (B3 125).

13. NSF2 590–91, 592. In this passage, too, there is a revealing correction that shows Kafka wavering at the height of his reflection: instead of "it gives me untold pleasure, and what is more, it soothes me," he first wrote "it gives me untold pleasure, though it is quite tarnished by anxieties."

14. Letter to Grete Bloch, Oct. 15, 1914 (B3 104–5.). What Grete Bloch intimated about Felice Bauer cannot be deduced from the extant documents, but Kafka's mention of his unhappiness about Felice's self-deception certainly suggests that there was talk of a permanent decision to forgo marriage and family—if the contact to Kafka were to break off for good. Felice Bauer had already expressed this intention during an oral confrontation with Kafka; see his letter to Grete Bloch on March 2, 1914 (B2 338).

15. On this *manifest* content of Kafka's letter to Grete Bloch, the imagination of an internal court, see Stach, *Kafka: The Decisive Years*, pp. 494ff.

16. All quotations from the diary entry of October 15, 1914 (T 678–80).

17. Letter to Felice Bauer, May 3, 1915 (B3 133).

18. Letter to Felice Bauer, January 18, 1916 (B3 150–51).

19. Diary, Feb 22, March 13, March 23, April 27, May 3, May 14, 1915 (T 728, 732, 733, 734, 742, 745).

20. Letter to Felice Bauer, April 20, 1915 (B3 129).

21. Diary, Feb. 25, 1915 (T 729).

22. Letters to Felice Bauer, May 26 and 27, 1915 (B3 136, 137; Diary, May 27, 1915 (T 745).

23. Letter to Felice Bauer, Aug. 9, 1915 (B3 140).

Chapter 2: No Literary Prize for Kafka

1. T App 44.

2. See Brod's correspondence with Hans-Joachim Schoeps, which contains several references to mailing Kafka manuscripts; in Julius H. Schoeps, ed., *Im Streit um Kafka und das Judentum*. In 1935, Brod gave a manuscript page of *The Man Who Disappeared* to Stefan Zweig as a gift, and wrote his own note on the blank reverse side of the page; see V App 43.

3. See Malcolm Pasley, "Die Handschrift redet."

4. Letter to Felice Bauer, probably mid-Feb. 1916 (B3 152).

5. Carl Sternheim to Thea Sternheim, August 15, 1915. In Carl Sternheim, *Briefe II*, p. 175.

6. Georg Heinrich Meyer to Max Brod, July 7, 1916; quoted in Joachim Unseld, *Franz Kafka: A Writer's Life*, trans. Paul F. Dvorak (Riverside, CA: Ariadne Press, 1994), p. 153. Max Brod to Kafka, August 1, 1919, in Brod/Kafka, *Briefwechsel*, p. 267. Georg Heinrich Meyer to Franz Werfel, Feb. 28, 1915; quoted from Wolfram Göbel, *Der Kurt Wolff Verlag, 1913–1930: Expressionismus als verlegerische Aufgabe*, special ed. from *Archiv für Geschichte des Buchwesens*, vols. 15 and 16 (Frankfurt am Main, 1976, 1977), col. 715.

7. For the organizational links between *Die weissen Blätter*, the Verlag der Weissen Bücher, and Kurt Wolff Verlag, see Stach, *Kafka: The Decisive Years*, pp. 405–6. Schickele's contact to Kafka and Brod had evidently broken off because Schickele had relocated to Switzerland for political reasons and changed his place of residence several times in rapid succession.

8. Georg Heinrich Meyer to Kafka, Oct. 11, 1915 (B3 738–39). The enclosed card from Carl Sternheim has not been preserved, and no other biographical sources indicate that Sternheim had given any special thought to Kafka's work. A diary entry by Thea Sternheim on March 3, 1947 implies that Sternheim never mentioned either Kafka or the conditions of the presentation of the prize even to her.

9. Letter to René Schickele, April 7, 1915 (B3 128).

10. Letter to Georg Heinrich Meyer, Oct. 25, 1915 (B3 145).

11. Letter to Georg Heinrich Meyer, Oct. 15, 1915 (B3 142).

12. Letter to Georg Heinrich Meyer, Oct. 20, 1915 (B3 144).

13. Otto Stoessl to Kafka, probably Jan. 30, 1913; quoted in a letter from Kafka to Felice Bauer, Jan. 31/Feb. 1, 1913 (B2 72).

14. Evidence of that—as well as a trace of Kafka's dismissive reaction—is found in a letter from Brod to Kafka on Dec. 18, 1917: "Werfel thinks . . . that you are the greatest German writer. . . . That has been my view for a long time as well, as you know. My own misgivings center on what you have taught me about being wary of such flamboyant language—but they do not come from the heart" (B3 782).

15. Letter to Felice Bauer, September 2, 1913 (B2 275).

16. Franz Werfel to Franz Kafka, Nov. 10, 1915 (B3 740–41).

Chapter 3: "Civilian Kavka"

1. The roughly approximate prices in today's currency are: fifty-five cents for an egg, fifteen dollars for a pound of butter, and fifteen dollars for a pound of meat (as per purchasing power in 2000).

2. One of the oddest instances of this mentality came from the influential secretary of state of the Imperial German Naval Office, Grand Admiral Alfred von Tirpitz, who in 1912 was still insisting on equipping warships with rams,

although it was obvious that future naval battles would be fought with torpedos and heavy artillery—that is, from miles away.

3. Letter to Felice Bauer, May 3, 1915 (B3 133).

4. Petition from the Workers' Accident Insurance Institute to the Austro-Hungarian military command in Prague, June 10, 1915; notification by the military command dated June 21, 1915; see AS Mat 860–863.

5. Postcard to Felice Bauer, probably July 20, 1915; letter to Felice Bauer, Aug. 9, 1915 (B3 138, 141).

6. The numbers come from the "Report by the Worker's Accident Insurance Institute for the Kingdom of Bohemia in Prague about Its Activities in the Period from January 1 to December 31, 1914" (AS 306–437), most of which was written by Kafka.

7. Postcard to Felice Bauer, May 31, 1916 (B3 166).

8. Postcard to Felix Weltsch, July 26, 1915 (B3 138).

9. Diary, Dec. 25, 1915 (T 775). "I can't give notice now, because of my parents and the factory," Kafka wrote. He apparently expected to be held liable as a debtor with the looming bankruptcy of the Kafkas' asbestos company, of which he was a partner. If he had resigned in 1915 and given up a steady income, he would have shifted the responsibility to his parents.

10. The gist of Kafka's conversation with Marschner can be reconstructed from his diary entry on the same day (T 785–86) and from a letter to Felice Bauer (B3 159ff.), which he appears to have written three days later. These documents recount the incident in nearly identical terms. But Kafka made a remarkable error in the diary—one that he himself picked up on. Instead of writing "Request ... that the claim be withdrawn" he initially wrote: "Request ... the claim"—the exact *opposite*.

11. Rainer Maria Rilke, *Possibility of Being: A Selection of Poems*, trans. J. B. Leishman (New York: New Directions, 1977), p. 107.

12. Rainer Maria Rilke to Axel Juncker, Oct. 19, 1914. In Rilke's *Briefe zur Politik*, pp. 97–98. Juncker's inquiry was in reference to the two collections he planned as *New War Songs*, which were published in 1914–1915 without Rilke's cooperation, after which Rilke consistently refused to contribute even one item to a second Insel Verlag war almanac. He also refused to allow performances of a musical rendition of his Cornet poetry cycle, rightly fearing that these would be misused for propagandistic purposes; see his letter to Kurt Stieler on June 15, 1915, ibid., pp. 112–13.

13. Rainer Maria Rilke to Helene von Nostitz, July 12, 1915, ibid., pp. 125–26; to Erica Yvette Hauptmann-von Scheel, Aug. 18, 1915, ibid., p. 134.

14. Stefan Zweig, *Die Welt von Gestern* (Frankfurt am Main: S. Fischer, 1970), p. 228. On Zweig's chauvinism and his opportunistic, politically disingenuous behavior, even to his friend Romain Rolland, see Hans-Albert Walter, *Deutsche Exilliteratur 1933–1950*, vol. 1.1 (Stuttgart: J. B. Metzler, 2003), pp. 520ff; on Zweig's reaction to the atrocities of the first months of the war, see Stach, *Kafka: The Decisive Years*, pp. 457–58.

15. *Hofmannsthal/Beer-Hofmann: Briefwechsel*, ed. Rudolf Hirsch and Eugene Weber (Frankfurt am Main: S. Fischer, 1972), p. 134. Hofmannsthal, *Briefwechsel mit Ottonie Gräfin Degenfeld und Julie Freifrau von Wedelstadt*, ed. Marie Therese Miller-Degenfeld, 2nd ed. (Frankfurt am Main: S. Fisher, 1986), p. 314.

16. Diary, May 11, 1916 (T 786).

17. Not one of the people in question ever expressed a wish of this kind. The only known case of resistance was, once again, Rilke, who refused to engage in *Heldenfrisieren*. Hofmannsthal, by contrast, did not balk even at stylizing Trakl's suicide in the face of the horror of the Battle of Grodek as a hero's death, although there is clear evidence that he knew better (see Eberhard Sauermann, *Literarische Kriegsfürsorge: Österreichische Dichter und Publizisten im Ersten Weltkrieg* [Vienna: Böhlau, 2000], pp. 60–61).

18. On Kafka's reaction to the beginning of the war, see Stach, *Kafka: The Decisive Years*, pp. 459–463.

19. One significant example of the censors' rear guard actions is the article "Die Wirkung der Gasbomben" (The effect of gas bombs) published in the *Prager Tagblatt* on June 3, 1915, the day of Kafka's physical examination. This coverage of the first German chloric gas attack on French troops in Flanders (on April 22) portrays the physical symptoms of poisoning realistically but denies that a lethal mass impact of the new weapon is intended. A mere three casualties are mentioned, "of which two had tubercular conditions." It is unclear even today how many victims the successful German attack really claimed.

20. See the eyewitness reports in *Die weissen Blätter* 2, no. 3 (March 1915), pp. 269–84. On Kafka's trip to Sátoralja-Ujhely, see the closing chapter of Stach, *Kafka: The Decisive Years*.

21. Excerpts from a list of "uses for the disabled" in the Viennese journal *Der Arbeitsnachweis: Zeitschrift für Arbeitslosigkeit, Arbeitsvermittlung, Auswanderung und innere Kolonisation* 9 [1915], pp. 272–79.

22. Robert Marschner, *Die Fürsorge der Frauen für die heimkehrenden Krieger* (Prague: Deutscher Verein zur Verbreitung gemeinnütziger Kenntnisse in Prag, 1916), p. 4.

23. Diary, May 11, 1916 (T 786).

24. Letter to Ottla Kafka, after June 16, 1918 (B4 45).

25. "An die Leitung der Kanzlei der Staatlichen Landeszentrale für das Königreich Böhmen zur Fürsorge für heimkehrendde Krieger", progress report by the Prague Workers' Accident Insurance Institute for 1917 and 1918 (AS Mat 752–59).

26. "Ein grosser Plan der Kriegsfürsorge verlangt Verwirklichung, Gründung einer Nervenheilanstalt in Deutschböhmen" in *Rumburger Zeitung*, Oct. 8, 1916 (AS 494–98). The article is signed by "Chief Inspector Eugen Pfohl," but was definitely written by Kafka; see the commentary in AS 894ff. This English translation of Kafka's text is taken from *Kafka: The Office Writings*, ed. Stanley Corngold, Jack Greenberg, and Benno Wagner; trans. Eric Patton with Ruth Hein (Princeton: Princeton Univ. Press, 2008), p. 336.

27. On October 9, 1917, in an article called "Wunderbare Heilungen: Der Stumme spricht, der Taube hört, der Lahme geht," the morning edition of the Prague newspaper *Bohemia* detailed the purported successes of Dr. Wiener. Kafka appears not to have known that various forms of therapeutic torture were widely used before 1917 as well—for example, in Vienna's Garrison Hospital No. 2, headed by Julius Wagner-Jauregg, the future Nobel Prize winner and National Socialist "racial hygienist." Credible reports on this subject did not appear in daily newspapers until the war had ended, after former patients had filed complaints (details in K. R. Eissler). In several parts of the German Reich, such as Bavaria, the "Kaufmann cure" was banned even during the war.

28. AS 498–501; Kafka wrote this text in late October 1916. This English translation of Kafka's text is taken from Corngold, Greenberg, and Wagner, *Kafka: The Office Writings*, pp. 339–40.

29. All quotations are from the lengthy article "Helfet den Kriegsinvaliden! Ein dringender Aufruf an die Bevölkerung," which also provides exhaustive details about the tasks and the early successes of the Public Crownland Agency (AS 506–13); this article was published (without a byline) on December 16, 1916, in both the *Prager Tagblatt* and the *Bohemia*. Another briefer and more matter-of-fact appeal that was published in the *Bohemia* on May 10, 1917, was most likely also by Kafka (AS 513–14). Quotations here are in Corngold, Greenberg, and Wagner, *Kafka: The Office Writings*, p. 347.

30. Enclosure with a letter to Felice Bauer, Oct. 30, 1916 (B3 615ff.).

31. Karl Dittrich, owner of the Rumburg sanatorium and textile manufacturer in the neighboring town of Schönlinde (Krásná Lípa), also attended the inaugural meeting and signed Kafka's appeal to the "fellow countrymen." The fact that Kafka's rousing article about the *Kriegszitterer* was published in the *Rumburger Zeitung* weeks before the association was launched suggests that this sanatorium had been chosen quite early in the process.

32. At the second general meeting of the "Deutscher Verein" on May 12, 1918, it was announced that the association's assets (including state subsidies) had now reached 1.5 million kronen, with more than 1,600 members. It is unclear to what extent Kafka still had a part in this ongoing success.

33. Diary, May 11, 1916 (T 785).

34. Austrian citizens who resided in the German Reich could be excused from military service by German military authorities, provided that they could furnish evidence of cultural activity "in the interest of the German public," along with documentation to that effect from a third party, such as a German publisher or a newspaper editor. It is unclear whether Kafka ever learned of this agreement between the Central Powers. "I should have left in 1912," he wrote to Felice Bauer on Dec. 21, 1915, without further elaboration (B3 148).

35. Diary, Oct. 5, 1915 (T 769).

36. Postcard to Felice Bauer, May 27, 1915; letter to Felice Bauer, Aug. 9, 1915 (B3 137, 141).

37. Postcard to Felice Bauer, April 14, 1916 (B3 156).

38. "Was empfindet man beim Bajonettkampf? Psychologisches von der Front," in *Prager Tagblatt*, May 8, 1915, morning edition, p. 4.

39. *Die Schaubühne*, July 1, 1915, p. 26. This is a quotation from the June 1915 issue of *Süddeutsche Monatshefte*.

40. Albert Anzenbacher to Kafka, Apr. 17, 1915 (B3 738). Anzenbacher, the only colleague with whom Kafka used the informal *Du* form of address, was stabbed to death by a Russian bayonet in 1916 at Przemyśl.

41. Letter to Felice Bauer, June 8–16, 1913 (B2 210).

42. Letter to Felice Bauer, Feb. 11, 1915 (B3 120).

43. Letter from the Public Crownland Agency for Returning Veterans in Prague to police headquarters, Oct. 9, 1918; telegram from police headquarters to the foreign police stations, Oct. 16, 1918; letter from police headquarters to the head office in Prague, Oct. 22, 1918 (AS Mat 864–65).

Chapter 4: The Marvel of Marienbad

1. Diary, Nov. 3, 1915, and June 2, 1916 (T 769, 787).

2. Diary, Sept. 13, 1915 (T 751).

3. Diary, Nov. 21 and Dec. 25, 1915 (T 774–75). The December entry comes right after the November entry in the diary.

4. See the collective postcard to Egon Erwin Kisch on Dec. 28, 1915, which was signed by Kafka as well as Max and Elsa Brod, Franz Werfel, and Heinrich and Mimi Mann (B3 149). There were most likely additional get-togethers of this kind, because Heinrich Mann stayed in Prague for an extended period of time. On January 11, he read his essay on Zola and his novella "Die Unschuldige" at the Palace Hotel, and Kafka definitely attended this reading.

5. Kafka's correspondence with Ernst Weiss has not been preserved, but we do have a copy of "The Metamorphosis" with Kafka's handwritten dedication "To my dear Ernst 20/XII 15 Franz" alongside Ernst Weiss's name as the owner of the book.

6. Hans Sahl, "Erinnerungen an Ernst Weiss," *Weiss-Blätter*, no. 2 (Aug. 1973), p. 4.

7. Postcards to Felice Bauer, April 19 and May 11, 1916 (B3 156, 159).

8. Ernst Weiss to Rahal Sanzara, June 27, 1916, and Jan. 10, 1917 (Deutsches Literaturarchiv, Marbach).

9. Soma Morgenstern, letter to Peter Engel on Apr. 22, 1975, in Soma Morgenstern, *Kritiken, Berichte, Tagebücher*, ed. Ingolf Schulte (Lüneburg: Zu Klampen Verlag, 2001), pp. 564–65. Ernst Weiss, "Bemerkungen zu den Tagebüchern und Briefen Franz Kafkas," *Mass und Wert* 1 (1937/38), pp. 319–25; reprinted in Jürgen Born, ed., *Franz Kafka: Kritik und Rezeption zu seinen Lebzeiten 1912–1924* (Frankfurt am Main: S. Fischer, 1979), p. 443. Weiss's

essay contains additional critical statements that harp on Kafka's self-referentiality.

10. In a letter to Milena Pollak on June 10, 1920 (B4 171).

11. Letter to Felice Bauer, May 28, 1916 (B3 164).

12. The revised novel was published in 1919, again with S. Fischer Verlag, bearing this better-known title. But a factor in determining the new title that may have outweighed the influence of Kafka was the attempt to play down military associations—most readers had quite enough of them for the moment.

13. Letter to Felice Bauer, Aug. 9, 1915 (B3 139–40). Kafka's remark that the third "suffering" was "even in print" refers to the prose piece "The Bachelor's Unhappiness," published in the volume *Meditation*.

14. Letters to Felice Bauer, Dec. 5 and 26, 1915, Jan. 18 and early March 1916 (B3 146–47, 148, 150, 154). The telegram dated Apr. 6, 1916 (B3 155) is the reply to Felice Bauer's suggestion to meet at the home of Brod's sister Sophie Friedmann in Waldenburg (Breslau district), just a few miles from the Bohemian border. But Kafka's police record contains no application for a passport for the time period in question.

15. The disconcerting key term "excess salary" is evidently not Doderer's invention but is adopted from an Austrian regulation, which Doderer cites in his novel *The Lighted Windows*: "Should an official [civil servant] whose salary is being paid on a quarterly basis become entitled to a higher salary during a given quarter, then this will be taken into account at the next payment of his wages, by arranging in each case for restitution to be made in monthly installments equivalent to the excess salary accumulated" (Heimito von Doderer, *The Lighted Windows; or, the Humanization of the Bureaucrat Julius Zihal*, trans. John S. Barrett [Riverside, CA: Ariadne Press, 2000], p. 30).

16. See the postcard to Felice Bauer dated April 19, 1916 (B3 156). The neurologist recommended "electrical treatments," which Kafka refused in writing. Two weeks earlier, on April 3, Ottla had written to Josef David: "He is really not well, and I sometimes have to be patient with him."

17. Postcard to Felice Bauer, May 15, 1916 (B3 161); letter to Felice Bauer, May 28, 1916 (B3 163).

18. Letter to Felice Bauer, May 28, 1916 (B3 164).

19. Two postcards to Felice Bauer, May 31, 1916 (B3 165–66).

20. The wedding of a cousin, the attorney Dr. Robert Kafka, to Elsa Robitschek. Kafka's aloofness also comes through in his postcard to Max Brod on July 5, where, oddly, he describes the event as his "brother-in-law's wedding" (B3 168).

21. See his diary entry dated April 19, 1916 (T 777). A few days later, Kafka began writing a story about children who are pulled through a door against their will (the "Hans and Amalia" fragment, T 780–84).

22. Diary, July 3, 1916 (T 790).

23. Diary, July 5 and 6, 1916 (T 791–92) The dash before the words "poor Felice" probably indicates that they were added later.

24. Two postcards to Max Brod, July 8, 1916 (B3 169).

25. Letter to Max Brod, July 12–14, 1916 (B3 172–73).

26. Diary, probably July 10, 1916 (T 795). Kafka's concern about discretion is evident in his closing sentence to Brod: "This letter can of course be shown to Felix [Weltsch], but not at all to women."

27. This is one of Kafka's "conversation slips" (see chapter 28, "Last Sorrow"): "She was not beautiful, but had a slender, fine body, which she has kept, according to reports (Max's sister, her girlfriend)" (Franz Kafka, *Briefe 1902–1924* [Frankfurt am Main: S. Fischer, 1958], p. 491).

28. Letter to Max Brod, July 12–14, 1916 (B3 174). A hint of the old conflicts with Felice Bauer is evident in his repeated references to the "dark sides" of being together, and in a later remark to Felice that in Marienbad he had gone down one of their "old paths," the "parade of sulks and secrets"—a reference to the two main accusations that were leveled at Kafka in 1914 and that were evidently discussed once again in Marienbad.

29. Diary, Jan. 29, 1922 (T 896–97).

30. Letter to Felice Bauer, presumably mid-Feb. 1916 (B3 152).

31. The sources clearly show that all this talk of "hedonism" was essential propaganda and not an outpouring of piety. The governments of the Central Powers endeavored to put this oft-bemoaned notion to good use in covering up the disastrous nature of the war itself. The major war exhibition in Vienna, which attracted 60,000 visitors on the first weekend (it was July 2, 1916, the day Kafka traveled to Marienbad), ran its own movie theater. The main feature was *Vienna at War: Four Amusing Acts*. There were also war toys: for a while, the war welfare office in Prague sold a puzzle called "Russian Death" for 3.60 kronen. And in 1915, the war relief agency of the ministry of the interior in Vienna published *Let's play world war! A picture book in keeping with the times for the younger set*, "to benefit the Red Cross, the war welfare office, and the war relief agency."

32. To Felice Bauer, July 20, 1916 (B3 184–85).

Chapter 5: What Do I Have in Common with Jews?

1. Postcard to Felice Bauer, July 18, 1916 (B3 182).

2. Letter to Felice Bauer, Jan. 20–21, 1913 (B2 51).

3. Max Brod, *Über Franz Kafka* (Frankfurt am Main: S. Fischer, 1974), p. 137. Werfel, who also went on a pilgrimage to Žižkov with Langer, had a very similar reaction ("a psychopath") and regarded the "indifference to dirt" he observed there as mentally compromising; see Werfel's diary entries in *Zwischen oben und unten*, pp. 696–97.

4. Diary, Sept. 14, 1915 (T 752).

5. Sátoralja-Ujhely in Hungary, where Kafka stayed briefly in April 1915, also had this kind of widely influential Hasidic court, but the diary entries do not reveal whether he knew about it.

6. Letter to Max Brod, July 17–18, 1916 (B3 180).

7. Julius Elias, "Marienbad" in *Berliner Tageblatt*, July 20, 1916, evening edition, p. 2.

8. On Feb. 6, 1916, a polemical article by Abraham Kohane in the Zionist weekly *Selbstwehr* had taken direct aim at the rabbi of Belz and portrayed his regime as corrupt.

9. Postcards to Felice Bauer, July 20, 26, 16, 1916 (B3 185, 189, 176).

10. Postcards to Felice Bauer, Aug. 18 and 25, 1916 (B3 204, 212).

11. A few years earlier, Kafka had said that Feigl's comments about art did not interest him very much, but he did care about Feigl's life: "But all I wanted . . . to hear, again and again, was how he has been married for a year, is happy, works all day, lives in two rooms in a house with a garden in Wilmersdorf, and other things of that nature, which give rise to envy and strength." (Letter to Felice Bauer, Nov. 28, 1912 [B1 282])

12. Letter to Felice Bauer, Sept. 12, 1916 (B3 222).

13. See the postcard to Felice Bauer, Aug. 5, 1916 (B3 195).

14. Postcard to Felice Bauer, Aug. 2, 1916 (B3 194).

15. Letter to Felice Bauer, Sept. 12, 1916 (B3 222–24).

16. Siegfried Lehmann, "Die Stellung der westjüdischen Jugend zum Volke," *Der Jude* 4, no. 5 (1919), pp. 207–15, this passage is on p. 211.

17. Letter to Felice Bauer, Sept. 11, 1916 (B3 219).

18. Lehmann later wrote about the Jewish Home in Berlin: "the grand experience of once again experiencing the *Volk* as a source of strength for one's own life by living in close proximity with the *Volk* inevitably failed to materialize because Jewish people who leave their homeland and seek a new life in the cities of Europe are no longer *Volk*. They are withered particles that are no longer sustained by the *Volk* and are thus not fit to convey the grand experience of '*Volk*' to those in search of it" ("Von der Strassenhorde zur Gemeinschaft," *Der Jude* 2 [special issue, 1926], p. 23). Lehmann went to Lithuania in 1920 to establish a children's home for returning Jewish refugees. In 1927 he founded the Ben Shemen youth village near Lod in Palestine.

19. See Gustav Landauer, "Christlich und christlich, jüdisch und jüdisch," *Der Jude* 1 (1916/17), pp. 851–52.

20. Letters to Felice Bauer, Sept. 11 and 16, 1916 (B3 220, 227). Gerhart Hauptmann's novel *Der Narr in Christo Emanuel Quint* was also a gift from Kafka, on the occasion of Felice Bauer's twenty-eighth birthday in November 1915. The student Abraham Grünberg had come from Krakow to Prague as a war refugee and had joined the Zionist group here; see the diary entry dated Nov. 6, 1915 (T 772–73). Grünberg presented his slender self-published work,

Ein jüdisch-polnisch-russisches Jubiläum (Der grosse Progrom von Siedlce im Jahre 1906), to Kafka in November 1916 with this dedication: "To the Esteemed Dr. and Writer Franz Kafka . . ."

21. Diary, Jan. 8, 1914 (T 622).

22. *Selbstwehr*, vol. 9, no. 34 (Sept. 7, 1915), pp. 2–3.

23. Martin Buber to Kafka, Nov. 22, 1915 (B3 741); letter to Martin Buber, Nov. 29, 1915 (B3 146).

24. Max Brod to Martin Buber, May 9, 1916, in Martin Buber, *Briefwechsel aus sieben Jahrzehnten*, ed. Grete Schaeder (Heidelberg: L. Schneider, 1972), vol. 1, p. 433.

25. Max Brod to Martin Buber, June 21, 1916 (copy in Max Brod Archives, Tel Aviv). "Unsere Literaten und die Gemeinschaft" was published in Oct. 1916 in *Der Jude*; Brod's remarks about Kafka are on pp. 463–64 of that essay.

26. Buber had initially agreed to Brod's suggestion, but changed his mind once he had read Kafka's text. His rejection letter has not been preserved. Kafka initially regarded it as "more honorable . . . than an ordinary acceptance could have been" (postcard to Felice Bauer, Sept. 23, 1916 [B3 232]). Brod was of course aware of the close connection between "The Dream" and the fragment of *The Trial* that Kafka established by giving the protagonist the identical name, "Josef K.," but Buber and the readers of the Jewish anthology, which was published on Dec. 15, 1916 and in the *Prager Tagblatt* on Jan. 6, 1917, would not have noticed this. ("A Dream" was published at virtually the same time in the *Almanach der neuen Jugend auf das Jahr 1917* [Verlag Neue Jugend, Berlin] under the aegis of Wieland Herzfelde.)

27. Letter to Felice Bauer, Oct. 7, 1916 (B3 250). Kafka is referring to the review essay "Phantasie" by Robert Müller in the October issue of *Die Neue Rundschau*, which contains this remark about "The Metamorphosis": "It is pleasing as an ingenious, assiduous, and flawlessly conceived game, but the demands it makes are excessive. . . . Kafka's normally ingenuous narrative art, which is quintessentially German in a laudably tractable manner and is masterfully told, is deformed by hypothetical patches on its beautiful material garb."

28. M. G., "Rasende Motore," *Deutsche Montags-Zeitung*, Nov. 20, 1916.

29. *Das Tagebuch* (Berlin) 11, no. 18 (May 3, 1930), p. 726.

30. Max Brod to Martin Buber, June 21, 1916 (copy in Max Brod Archives, Tel Aviv).

31. Max Brod to Martin Buber, Jan. 20, 1917, in Martin Buber, *Briefwechsel aus sieben Jahrzehnten*, ed. Grete Schaeder (Heidelberg: L. Schneider, 1972), vol. 1, p. 461.

32. Letter to Max Brod, late June 1921, in Brod/Kafka, *Briefwechsel*, pp. 356–60. Brod's immediate reply, dated July 4, 1921, has been preserved (pp. 362–64 of this same volume) but contains no reaction to Kafka's unusually detailed and pointed linguistic commentary. Later, Brod saw how easily

11. Postcard to Felice Bauer, Dec. 7, 1916 (B3 277). Unfortunately there is no clear evidence as to whether Rilke attended Kafka's reading, but Rilke's unpublished appointment book, which has "Franz Kafka evening at Goltz," clearly shows that Rilke's statement was made in direct conversation with Kafka and was not told to him after the fact. (Rilke Archives, Gernsbach)

12. Postcard to Felice Bauer, Nov. 21, 1916 (B3 274). An additional indication that the verbal sparring in Munich cannot have been altogether harmless is the fact that Kafka's first postcards after this incident are missing from the bundle of letters; according to his own statement, these messages dealt with "the quintessence of living together" (ibid.). Evidently Felice Bauer did not want rehashings of oral confrontations to see publication. In February 1914, when similar incidents had occurred, the pertinent letters are missing as well; see Stach, *Kafka: The Decisive Years*, pp. 396ff., esp. n. 12.

13. Postcard to Felice Bauer, Nov. 24, 1916 (B3 276).

14. A letter from Kafka to Ottla on Aug. 29, 1917, shows that this impression does not stem merely from a fragmentary documentation. Referring to Felice, he wrote: "Recently I've been suffering dreadfully from the old delusion again; incidentally, last winter was the longest hiatus to date in these five years of suffering" (B3 309).

Chapter 7: The Alchemist

1. Postcards to Felice Bauer, Dec. 9 and 14, 1916 (B3 279).

2. Letter from Ottla Kafka to Josef David, Dec. 3, 1916. German translation of the Czech letter in Hartmut Binder, "Kafka und seine Schwester Ottla," *Jahrbuch der deutschen Schillergesellschaft* 12 (1968), p. 426. Stern (Hvězda) is a star-shaped castle west of the Prague Castle, with a large zoo, then a popular place for outings.

3. Postcard to Felice Bauer, Dec. 14, 1916 (B3 279).

4. Stürgkh was shot to death on October 21, 1916, in a hotel restaurant in Vienna. The thirty-seven-year-old assassin, Friedrich Adler, was the editor-in-chief of the Social Democratic journal *Der Kampf* and a confirmed Marxist. His father, Viktor Adler, was a member of the Reichstag and party leader of the Austrian Social Democrats. Even the conservative daily newspapers (such as the *Reichspost*, on October 22) were surprised that the target was not someone who could have shouldered a concrete share of the blame for World War I. The semiofficial German-language newspaper *Pester Lloyd* warned that "in enemy foreign countries" it should not be assumed that the assassination had anything to do "with issues pertaining to food."

5. Julie Kafka to Felice Bauer, Oct. 8, 1916. In Kafka, *Briefe an Felice*, p. 721.

6. In the middle or latter part of November 1916, a letter from Felice Bauer to Kafka was rejected and returned—presumably because of statements about the food situation in Berlin. In this letter, she once again proposed that they

get together at Christmas, which Kafka continued to be against; see the card to Felice Bauer on Dec. 4, 1916 (B3 276). See also Julie Kafka's letter to Anna Bauer dated Dec. 31, 1916: "I think d[ear] Felice will surprise us on Christmas with her lovely visit" (Kafka, *Briefe an Felice*, p. 748).

7. To Ottla Kafka, Jan. 1, 1917 (B3 282); evidently a message Kafka left for Ottla at Alchimistengasse.

8. Quotation from an unpublished diary excerpt (Max Brod Archives, Tel Aviv).

9. For a detailed discussion of the massive and distorting interventions with which Brod attempted to bring the chaos under control and to scrape together "reader friendly" bits of text from Kafka's octavo notebooks, see the monograph by Annette Schütterle, *Franz Kafkas Oktavhefte: Ein Schreibprozess als "System des Teilbaues"* (Freiburg im Breisgau: Rombach, 2002), pp. 268–83.

10. NSF1 384–93. In the manuscript, he initially wrote "nobodies," then "jesters," then "nobodies" again, then "jesters" once again, and finally "windbags" (NSF1 App 324). Kafka clearly had difficulties with invectives.

11. In the late 1920s, Oskar Baum recalled that Kafka completed a drama called "The Grotto" or "The Crypt" on Alchimistengasse, but that he flatly refused to read aloud from it and retorted ironically: "The only thing about this play that is not amateurish is that I am not reading it aloud." Baum was obviously referring to "The Warden of the Tomb," which according to all available documentation was never completed and in its manuscript form was untitled (the title by which it is known today was added by Brod). And the fact that Kafka's typed copy is folded in such a way as to facilitate reading aloud does not really jibe with Baum's recollections, which are unreliable in other ways as well. See Oskar Baum, "Rückblick auf eine Freundschaft" in Koch, "*Als Kafka mir entgegenkam . . .* ," pp. 71–75. The surviving typescript, which may be incomplete, was published in NSF1 290–303.

12. The following prose pieces from the winter of 1916–17 exist only in their printed versions: "A Country Doctor," "Up in the Gallery," "The Next Village," "A Fratricide," "Eleven Sons," "The Cares of a Family Man," and "A Visit to a Mine." Evidently these works were written in additional octavo notebooks that have not been preserved, but their dates of composition can be ascertained to the nearest month (and may have formed part of a larger group of works and fragments that are unknown to us). In a letter to Ottla on April 19, 1917 (B3 296–97), Kafka claimed he used "manuscripts" to light fires on Alchimistengasse—an additional indication that the full scope of his productivity exceeds even what the extant manuscripts substantiate.

13. One of the variants of "The Warden of the Tomb" contains a characterization of the inexperienced prince that bears a remarkable resemblance to Karl I. Since the latter's initial steps in office were on everyone's mind during the very weeks in which "The Warden of the Tomb" was written, this influence can hardly be coincidental. "The prince appears in a double guise. The one

deals with matters of government and wavers absentmindedly in public, disregarding his own privileges. The other admits to searching quite painstakingly for the reinforcement of its foundations. It searches in the past, delving ever deeper into the past." (NSF1 255)

14. For the first—but by no means the last—time on Dec. 10, 1916, as a letter Ottla wrote Josef David documents. The coal crisis (which stemmed primarily from the lack of railway cars on account of the war) escalated so sharply that in mid-February, Karl I ordered the military to stand by to ensure the coal supply in Prague.

15. This did not apply only to the beginning of his new writing phase; the prose piece "An Old Manuscript" was written just a few days after the lost power struggle and the abdication of the Russian tsar in mid-March 1917—an event of colossal proportions in its time.

16. Letter to Felice Bauer, Nov. 24, 1916 (B3 276).

Chapter 8: Ottla and Felice

1. Letter to Felice Bauer, Nov. 24, 1916 (B3 276).

2. Letter to Felice Bauer, Jan.–Feb. 1917 (B3 290). It is not entirely clear whether Kafka actually sent this long and important letter, which is the only one that been preserved from the winter of 1916/1917. His literary estate contains a typewritten copy, but the original is missing from the bundle sold by Felice Bauer.

3. In old buildings, even those referred to as "manorial," bathrooms were the exception rather than the rule. The previous tenant in the big apartment that Kafka was initially offered in the Palais Schönborn had installed a bathroom at his own expense (which took up half the hall). The elegant Fuchsschlössl in Rodaun (Austria), in which Hugo von Hofmannsthal and his family had been living since 1901, had no bathroom until the end of the war, and the upper floor did not even have running water.

4. Letter to the Workers' Accident Insurance Institute, Feb. 5, 1917 (B3 285–86). The request was denied; only a raise in the "regular cost-of-living allowance" was granted, which yielded Kafka an annual increase of a mere six hundred kronen—which, however, was enough to cover the rent for the apartment in Schönborn.

5. Ottla Kafka to Josef David, Oct. 20, 1916; quoted in Binder, "Kafka und seine Schwester Ottla," p. 439.

6. A draft of a letter by Kafka asked for advice on this matter for Ottla. The intended recipient of this letter appears to have been Moriz Schnitzer, the fanatical vegetarian and founder of numerous associations for naturopathy who lived in Warnsdorf in northern Bohemia. Kafka had been "examined" by Schnitzer in April 1911. The swearword "scoundrel" is documented in Kafka's letter to Ottla dated April 19, 1917 (B3 296). Kafka's "Letter to His Father"

conveys the severity of the conflict between Ottla and her parents (NSF2 170 and 178–79).

7. Channa Meisel, "Landwirtschaftliche Mädchenerziehung," *Jüdische Rundschau* 22, nos. 8 and 9 (Feb. 23 and Mar. 2, 1917). It is certain that this article was debated in Ottla's club, particularly as it was rare to hear concrete details about the lives of Jewish women in Palestine. Kafka, who was a regular reader of the *Jüdische Rundschau*, is likely to have known the essay and discussed it with his sister.

8. For a discussion of the family conflicts surrounding the Prague Asbestos Works, see Stach, *Kafka: The Decisive Years*, pp. 125ff. It was removed from the company register on July 16, 1918.

9. Letter to Ottla Kafka, Apr. 19, 1917 (B3 296).

10. Letter to Ottla Kafka, May 16, 1917 (B3 299–300).

11. Irma Weltsch was so furious about Kafka's inquiry, which she evidently interpreted as a sign of the rudest sort of mistrust, that she not only scolded her husband for bringing "friends" of this kind into their home but also wrote quite an aggressive letter to Kafka himself (as we learn from Weltsch's unpublished diaries). Kafka did not receive this letter until after his return from Budapest, whereupon he sent an immediate apology that was both profuse and diplomatic (on July 20, 1917 [B3 302–3]).

12. A letter from Julie Kafka to Felice Bauer, dated March 26, 1917, reveals that this visit was already planned for the spring.

13. Brod, *Über Franz Kafka*, p. 140. Brod's remark that in the summer of 1917 "a flat was taken for the young couple" and that furniture was bought is clearly a memory lapse on his part.

14. Postcard to Ottla Kafka, July 28, 1917 (B3 304).

15. The writer Rudolf Fuchs, whom Kafka met in Vienna on his way home, reported in his memoirs: "He started dropping hints to me back in Prague that once he reached Budapest he would decide whether to keep or break up the engagement. In Vienna he told me he had broken up with his fiancée. Kafka was quite calm about this. He even seemed to feel good" (Rudolf Fuchs, "Kafka und die Prager literarischen Kreise" in Koch "*Als Kafka mir entgegenkam . . .*," p. 110). It is unlikely that Kafka was that unequivocal, but this piece of the puzzle does fit, to a certain extent. Felice Bauer's journey on to Arad is mentioned in Brod's biography of Kafka, but there is no clear evidence to support that she went there. Although Arad was no longer facing a military threat, the sisters may have decided to meet in Budapest.

Chapter 9: The Country Doctor Ventures Out

1. Letter to Felice Bauer, Dec. 20, 1916 (B3 280).

2. "A Dream," in *Prager Tagblatt*, Jan. 6, 1917, Entertainment Supplement, p. 1.

3. In the first six issues of the monthly *Die schöne Rarität* (July through December 1917), Kafka was named on the masthead, but he did not publish in this journal. Toward the end of 1917, Kafka withdrew in response to his changed circumstances (B3 390). His brief association with *Donauland* is mentioned in two letters to Josef Körner, dated Dec. 8–10 and 16, 1917 (B3 376–77, 380–81).

4. In this case, though, the initiative ultimately also came from Feigl, who had asked Kafka for support at Kurt Wolff Verlag back in the fall of 1916. Kafka complied with this request (letter to Georg Heinrich Meyer, Sept. 30, 1916 [B3 243]), but his efforts were unsuccessful.

5. See Felix Weltsch to Kafka, Oct. 1917: "the personification of an uncomplicated nature" (B3 762–63); and Kafka's reply on Oct. 19–21, 1917: "he cannot be so easily dismissed" (B3 354).

6. Gross was arrested on Nov. 9, 1913; on Dec. 20, both *Die Aktion* (Berlin) and *Revolution* (Munich) published special issues on Otto Gross with several articles attacking his father personally. The behind-the-scenes and probably illegal cooperation between the Berlin police and the Austrian professor of criminal law sparked bitterness. It is quite possible that Kafka had this affair in mind eight months later when writing the opening sequence of *The Trial*.

7. Letter to Milena Pollak, June 25, 1920 (B4 196). "He used a passage from the Bible to explain his theory," Kafka explained. "[H]e would not stop picking apart this passage, would not stop adding new material, would not stop demanding my agreement." It is likely that Gross's remarks that night were drawn from his essay "Die kommunistische Grundidee in der Paradiessymbolik" (*Sowjet* 1 [1919], pp. 12–17), because this is the only one of his texts in which he undertook an extensive exegesis of Genesis. Kafka had attended lectures by Hans Gross during the winter semester of 1903–1904 to the winter semester of 1904–1905 and also enrolled in a seminar. He attended the lecture "History of the Philosophy of Law" (summer semester 1904) together with Brod.

8. Letter to Max Brod, Nov. 14, 1917 (B3 364).

9. Martin Buber to Max Brod, Jan. 15, 1917, in Buber, *Briefwechsel aus sieben Jahrzehnten*, p. 459.

10. See Franz Werfel, "Die christliche Sendung: Ein offener Brief an Kurt Hiller," *Die neue Rundschau* 28 (1917), pp. 92–105; and Max Brod, "Franz Werfels 'christliche Sendung,'" *Der Jude* 1 (1916–17), pp. 717–24.

11. Martin Buber, "Vorbemerkung über Franz Werfel," *Der Jude* 2 (1917–18), pp. 109–12. Buber could prove his point by citing a personal note from Werfel dated Jan. 31, 1917: "Just take my hand now, and my avowal (which may be of no importance) that I feel utterly 'national' as a Jew and take all the bad this implies as well as the little that is good" (Buber, *Briefwechsel aus sieben Jahrzehnten*, p. 468). For a statement of Buber's distrust of outward political successes, see his letter to Siegmund Kaznelson dated July 9, 1917: "The out-

ward sign of the situation is the current 'success' of Zionism; there are very few Zionists who share or even understand the pain it is causing me" (ibid., p. 502).

12. Max Brod to Martin Buber, Apr. 7, 1917 (Jewish National and University Library, Jerusalem). Max Brod himself had a piece in this issue of *Der Jude*, an essay on the horrors of Taylorism ("Two Worlds").

13. Letter to Martin Buber, May 12, 1917 (B3 299).

14. Note in Octavo Notebook G, Oct. 19, 1917 (NSF2 30). Initially, instead of "the calm exterior outside," Kafka had written "the calm view of the onlooker" (NSF2 App 199).

15. In the winter of 1916–1917, Hugo Bergmann had asked Buber to broaden his scope from Jewish topics to "subjects of general human interest" (Buber, *Briefwechsel aus sieben Jahrzehnten*, p. 488, n. 1).

16. Buber had printed a propaganda text in the very first issue of *Der Jude*, in which western European Jews were characterized as opportunists and parasites: "We have an adaptability, which developed in *galut* [exile], to process the products of others' lives according to our mentality and to use the fruits of their labor to make delicacies for our palates" (A. D. Gordon, "Arbeit," in *Der Jude*, 1 (1916–17), pp. 37–43; this quotation is on pp. 39–40).

17. For selected examples, see Julius H. Schoeps and Joachim Schlör, eds. *Antisemitismus: Vorurteile und Mythen* (Munich: Piper, 1995), pp. 21ff. Kafka was sure to have known Adalbert Stifter's story "Abdias," which tells of "dirty Jews" living in close proximity with jackals.

18. Max Brod, "Literarischer Abend des Klub jüdischer Frauen und Mädchen (am 19. Dezember, 1917)" in *Selbstwehr*, Jan. 4, 1918.

19. Letter to Martin Buber, Apr. 22, 1917 (B3 297).

20. Kurt Wolff to Kafka, July 3, 1917 (B3 745).

21. Kurt Wolff to Kafka, Sept. 1, 1917 (B3 748).

22. Kurt Wolff to Kafka, Aug. 1, 1917 (B3 747).

23. Letter to Kurt Wolff, Sept. 4, 1917 (B3 312).

24. See Kafka's letter to Kurt Wolff, Aug. 20, 1917 (B3 306–7).

25. Additional details about the numous errors and delays at Kurt Wolff Verlag can be found in Unseld, *Franz Kafka: A Writer's Life*, pp. 182–84 and 187–98. "A Homicide" was published in Wolff's almanac *Die neue Dichtung* in late 1917; the newer version ("A Fratricide") had already appeared in the biblio phile Expressionist bimonthly *Marsyas* (vol. 1, no. 1, July–August 1917).

26. Wolff's correspondence with Franz Werfel's father on this matter (Oct. and Nov. 1917) forms part of the Kurt Wolff Archives in the Beinecke Rare Book and Manuscript Library at Yale University.

27. Letter to Josef Körner, Dec. 16, 1918 (B3 381).

28. Unfortunately we have no record of Kafka's letter to Wolff, but he described it to Brod as an "ultimatum letter" (Letter to Max Brod, March 26 or 27, 1918 [B4 33]). "I do not advise you to leave Wolff," Brod replied on March

29. "The booksellers are saying that disorganization is rampant among all publishers right now." (Brod/Kafka, *Briefwechsel*, p. 249).

29. *Sagen polnischer Juden*, ed. and trans. Alexander Eliasberg (Munich: Georg Müller, 1916. This volume is in the portion of Kafka's library that has been preserved. The two quoted stories are the "Resurrection of the Dead Bride" (pp. 40–44) and "Swift Trip to Vienna" (pp. 182–184). In another short piece, "Rabbi Moshe Leib's Funeral Music" (p. 195), horses make their way to their destination on their own, galloping "over hill and dale" with a carriage.

30. For a discussion of the dating of the publication, see Unseld, *Franz Kafka: A Writer's Life*, p. 203. The only review of *A Country Doctor* during Kafka's lifetime was published on Oct. 31, 1920 in *Prager Tagblatt*: R[udolf] Th[omas], "Drei Prager Autoren."

Chapter 10: *Mycobacterium tuberculosis*

1. Letter to Ottla Kafka, Aug. 29, 1917 (B3 308–9).

2. Since the initial hemorrhage also goes unmentioned in his descriptions to Ottla and Felice Bauer, it is likely that Kafka kept this information from his friends as well. It was not until three years later, on July 28, 1920, that he told Milena Pollak about it, with an unmistakable undertone of a queasy conscience: "If I had gone straight to the doctor—everything would have probably happened exactly as it did without the doctor; the only thing is that back then, no one knew about the blood—actually I didn't even know about it myself—and no one was worried" (B4 257). These kinds of blood seepages were in and of themselves not a typical symptom of tuberculosis, but of course they were alarming in combination with the subsequent hemorrhaging.

3. Card to Ottla Kafka, Sept. 4, 1917 (B3 313).

4. Card to Max Brod, Aug. 29, 1917 (B3 310).

5. NSF1 401 (Oktavheft E).

6. It was widely believed that delicately built, unathletic people with a flat rib cage—the so-called *habitus phthisicus*, which somewhat resembled Kafka's body type and was considered hereditary—were predisposed to tuberculosis. Although empirical data had called this hypothesis into question, it was still taught at medical schools during the war. It was not until the 1920s that all *habitus* and constitution theories were abandoned, and the only factor that continued to be highlighted in both heredity and tuberculosis was the efficiency of the immune system. Sander Gilman's 1995 monograph, *Franz Kafka: The Jewish Patient*, reads Kafka's medical history and self-diagnosis against the backdrop of contemporary tuberculosis theories, particularly in regard to the *habitus phthisicus* and the widespread notion at the time that Jews had an unusual constitution. Although Gilman brings in extraordinarily rich materials from the history of medicine, the significance of these kinds of eugenic ideas

for Kafka's own interpretation remains speculative, because we are not aware of any statements by Kafka that link his illness directly, or causally, to his Jewish heritage or the *habitus phthisicus*.

7. A few years later, it was discovered that the routinely prescribed (and frequently effective) arsenic compounds significantly increased the risk of skin cancer.

8. Letter to Ottla Kafka, Aug. 29, 1917 (B3 309).

9. David Epstein, *Diagnostisch-therapeutisches Taschenbuch der Tuberkulose: Ein Leitfaden für den praktischen Arzt* (Berlin: Zerban & Schwarzenberg, 1910), p. 85.

10. Max Brod to Kafka, Sept. 24, 1917 (B3 751).

11. Felix Weltsch to Kafka, Oct. 5, 1917 (B3 757). The Yiddish term *chochmeh* means both "witticism" and "wisdom," somewhat like the double meaning of *wit*.

12. Letter to Felix Weltsch, Oct. 11, 1917 (B3 344–45).

13. Card to Ottla Kafka, Sept. 4–5, 1917 (B3 313).

14. Letter to Kurt Wolff, Sept. 4, 1917 (B3 312).

15. Years later, Kafka drew this paradoxical conclusion in so many words: "It would be easy to ask for a leave if I could tell myself and others that the illness was somehow brought on or aggravated by the office, but actually the opposite is true; the office kept the illness in check" (letter to Ottla David, April 1921, in Franz Kafka, *Briefe an Ottla und die Familie*, ed. Hartmut Binder and Klaus Wagenbach [Frankfurt am Main: S. Fischer, 1974], p. 119).

16. Kafka described his conversations in the Workers' Accident Insurance Institute in two cards to Ottla, dated Sept. 6 and 7, 1917 (B3 315–16) and in a letter to Felice Bauer, dated Sept. 9, 1917 (B3 317).

17. This quotation and the other information about Kafka's departure are taken from an unpublished diary excerpt by Max Brod. Kafka had informed Felice Bauer about his tuberculosis five days before his departure, but because of the long postal delivery time during the war, the correspondence card in question could not have been written in reaction to his prior message. Brod noted in his diary, "Despairing letter from her, although she does not know anything yet."

Chapter 11: Zürau's Ark

1. Letter to Oskar Baum, late Nov. 1917 (B3 370).

2. According to a census conducted in February 1921 (*Statistický lexikon obci v Čechách*, Prague: Bursík & Kohout, 1924, p. 254). Siřem (as it is called today) now has fewer than 100 inhabitants.

3. In the district of Podersam (Podbořany), to which Zürau belongs, there was a higher-than-average incidence of tuberculosis even before the war (see

Brod, "Die jüdische Kolonisation in Palästina," *Die neue Rundschau* 28, no. 9 (Sept. 1917), pp. 1267–76. When Brod wrote this essay, which attested to the "steady continued existence of Turkish rule and the insight of Turkish statesmen," the Turkish government had already begun the forced evacuation of Jewish settlements.

7. Letter to Max Brod, Feb. 9, 1918 (B4 28).

8. Some of the texts in *A Country Doctor* are self-reflexive even in their form, which most likely did not come through to contemporary readers. Malcolm Pasley has argued persuasively that "A Visit to a Mine" and "Eleven Sons" are nothing but literature about literature ("Drei literarische Mystifikationen Kafkas" in Jürgen Born et al., eds., *Kafka-Symposium* [Berlin: Klaus Wagenbach, 1965], pp. 21–37). This view is confirmed by a statement by Kafka, as quoted by Brod: "The eleven sons are quite simply eleven stories I am working on this very moment" (*Über Franz Kafka*, p. 122).

9. Max Brod to Franz Kafka, Oct. 4, 1917 (B3 754); letter to Max Brod, Oct. 7–8, 1917 (B3 343).

10. NSF2 40–42, 38. Both texts were untitled in the original; the titles commonly used today are from Brod.

11. Max Brod's diary, Dec. 26, 1917 (unpublished); letter to Max Brod, March 26 or 27, 1918 (B4 33).

12. NSF2 30, 44, 55, 61, 68, 73, 91, 100–101.

13. In the fall of 1920, Kafka incorporated a modified version of "aphorism" 69 into a letter to Brod without marking it as a quotation—an indication that Brod had not seen the Zürau slips of paper even years after they were composed (letter to Max Brod, Aug. 6, 1920, B4 285; see the original version in NSF2 65, 128).

14. Diary, Sept. 25, 1917 (T 838).

15. Franz Kafka, *Beim Bau der chinesischen Mauer: Ungedruckte Erzählungen und Prosa aus dem Nachlass, ed. Max Brod and Hans-Joachim Schoeps* (Berlin, 1931; reprint, Hildesheim: G. Olms, 2008); the meditations are on pp. 225–49 in this volume. A typewritten copy (not by Kafka) that contained several distortions was used as a manuscript given to the typesetter; see NSF2 53.

16. See Max Brod, *Franz Kafkas Glauben und Lehre*, in *Über Franz Kafka*.

17. Particularly on the stage. But during the war, Kafka evidently did not attend any Jewish theater performances. In January 1917, a Jewish theater troupe was performing at Hotel Schwan, just down the block from Kafka's office; and on January 18, there was an evening in honor of the actress Flora Krug, whom Kafka knew from Yitzhak Löwy's ensemble. But even these events do not seem to have prompted him to interrupt his work on Alchimistengasse. The only contact he maintained for a while was to Yitzhak Löwy, whose memoirs, "On the Jewish Theater," he had promised to edit (see NSF1 424ff., 430ff.). On Kafka's encounter with Jewish theater from the East, see Stach, *Kafka: The Decisive Years*, pp. 54ff.

18. Moses Rath, *Lehrbuch der hebräischen Sprache für Schul- und Selbstunterricht*, 2nd ed. (Vienna: n.p., 1917).

19. Miriam Singer, "Hebräischstunden mit Kafka" in Koch, "*Als Kafka mir entgegenkam* . . . ," pp. 151–54; this remark appears on p. 152. The deficient knowledge of Hebrew on the part of the Prague Zionists planted seeds of discord for years to come; see Oskar Epstein, "Die Prager Zionisten und das Hebräische," *Selbstwehr* 14, no. 42 (Oct. 22, 1920).

20. Postcard to Max Brod, Sept. 21, 1918 (B4 53).

21. NSF2 29; this note is dated Oct. 19, 1917.

22. Letter to Robert Klopstock, June 1921 (unpublished).

23. The only notable exception is found in two diary entries dated July 20, 1916, in which Kafka speaks directly to God (T 798–99). But even these statements—written in the exceptional psychological circumstances of Marienbad—are anything but submissive: "If I am condemned, then I am not only condemned to die but also condemned to struggle until I die."

24. "According to God, the immediate consequence of eating from the Tree of Knowledge ought to be death; according to the serpent (or at least it could be understood this way), becoming like God. Both were wrong in similar ways" (NSF2 73).

25. NSF2 124; see also NSF2 58.

26. NSF2 94 and NSF2 App 230; NSF2 62.

27. NSF2 354.

28. Letter to Ottla Kafka, Sept. 4–5, 1917 (B3 313). This statement is also documented in Brod's diary dated the same day. In Wagner's opera, it reads "I would have thought *you* more refined!" (Richard Wagner, *Die Meistersinger von Nürnberg*, act 2, scene 4)

29. These statements were made on Feb. 28, 1920; see Brod, *Über Franz Kafka*, p. 71. Brod must have had later regrets about letting the public know about this conversation, since it impeded his effort to stylize Kafka as a Jewish thinker. He ultimately took refuge in the assertion that Kafka was stripping all hope only from secularized Western Jews—a qualification that is clearly refuted by the context of the statement. (Brod, *Franz Kafkas Glauben und Lehre*, in *Über Franz Kafka*, p. 246)

30. Max Brod to Kafka, Oct. 10, 1917 (B3 758).

31. Letter to Max Brod, Oct. 13, 1917 (B3 346).

32. "Queasiness after too much psychology," Kafka wrote in Octavo Notebook F (NSF1 423). The entry cannot be dated precisely, but seems to have been written shortly before Brod's letter.

33. Letter to Felice Bauer, Oct. 16, 1917 (B3 348–49).

34. NSF1 402, 407, 403 (Octavo Notebook E).

35. Letter to Max Brod, Nov. 14, 1917 (B3 363).

36. Søren Kierkegaard, *Buch des Richters: Seine Tagebücher 1833–1855 im Auszug aus dem Dänischen von Hermann Gottsched* (Jena: Eugen Diederichs, 1905),

p. 160. Kafka quoted this passage in detail in a letter to Max Brod written March 26 or 27, 1918 (B4 35–36).

37. NSF2 97–98. The text was written on Feb. 25, 1918.

Chapter 13: Spanish Influenza, Czech Revolt, Jewish Angst

1. Richard Katz, "Im Prager Literaten-Café," *Prager Tagblatt*, June 11, 1918, morning edition, p. 3.

2. Letter to Max Brod, late March/early April 1918 (B4 38).

3. By the beginning of the war, even Masaryk was accusing Jews of being highly active as informers; see Stach, *Kafka: The Decisive Years*, pp. 456–57. Although this intractable rumor could not be confirmed in government files that were opened up after 1918, acts of revenge against alleged Jewish informers set off anti-Semitic rioting, particularly in the suburbs of Prague.

4. The term was used explicitly by a board member named Kohner. He demanded that "the authorities proceed against the pests with all due severity." Quoted in Martin Welling, "Von Hass so eng umkreist," in *Der Erste Weltkrieg aus der Sicht der Prager Juden* (Frankfurt am Main: Peter Lang, 2003), p. 203.

5. B. R., "Hass ringsum," *Selbstwehr* 12, no. 31 (Aug. 16, 1918), p. 1. At this time, fewer than six thousand Jewish refugees were still living in Prague, which represented a decline of about two-thirds.

6. On Jan. 18, 1918, and evidently on the following day as well, the fancy goods store was closed, because all the employees were taking part in a general strike (letter from Irma Kafka to Ottla Kafka, Jan. 18, 1918).

7. We know about the existence of this letter, which was written about a week before Kafka's departure from Zürau, from a letter written by Irma, complaining about "what Franz did to me with his letter to his father" (Irma Kafka to Ottla Kafka, April 25, 1918). Two days later, Ottla wrote to her boyfriend, Josef David: "I'm getting along well with my brother again; I'm glad that there is nothing wrong between us." This could indicate that there had been differences of opinion about the tone and contents of the letter with Ottla as well.

8. On March 18, 1918, Ottla wrote to Josef David, "they don't let me write, mainly Franz; you know, it is my room, and I could throw them out, my brother and the girl [one of the maids], but he promises to be quiet, and anyway, I'm happy when he's happy." (Quoted in Binder, "Kafka und seine Schwester Ottla," p. 443).

9. Herbert Elias, "Grippe," *Volksgesundheit im Krieg*, part 2 (Vienna: Hölder-Pichler-Tempsky, 1926), pp. 55–56.

10. The terms "Spanish illness" and "Spanish influenza" evidently took root only because the Spanish press, which was not subject to war censorship,

was the first to provide detailed coverage of the epidemic. The Spanish king Alfonso XIII fell ill with the disease.

11. Even today, there is no definitive explanation for this statistically verifiable phenomenon. It was thought at the time that older people who had gone through the flu epidemic of 1889 were immunized by it. Today we are more inclined to believe that many deaths were caused by a severe autoimmune reaction, which meant that, paradoxically, well-nourished middle-aged patients whose immune systems reacted most vigorously also ran the highest risk.

12. Letter to Max Brod, ca. Oct. 14, 1918 (B4 56).

13. In a letter to Eugen Pfohl, dated Nov. 25, 1918 (B4 58), Kafka wrote "as high as 107.6." The clinical reports of the day indicate that fevers ranging from 102 to 104 were the norm, and there were few cases in which they rose above 105, so Kafka's pneumonia appears to have been unusual even for this epidemic.

14. See *Prager Tagblatt*, Oct. 10, 1918, p. 3.

15. Quoted in Richard Georg Plaschka, Horst Haselsteiner, and Arnold Suppan, *Innere Front: Militärassistenz, Widerstand und Umsturz in der Donaumonarchie 1918*, vol. 2: *Umsturz* (Munich: Verlag für Geschichte und Politik, 1974), p. 145.

16. "Die Erfahrungen eines Tages" in *Prager Tagblatt*, Oct. 15, 1918, p. 1. Eduard von Zanantoni, commanding officer in Prague, noted in his war memoirs that orders had come from Vienna to avoid bloodshed in the downtown area of Prague (manuscript p. 464, Vienna War Archives).

17. There were several spots in the city where eruptions of violence were narrowly avoided. On the blockaded Charles Bridge, two machine guns were trained on a Czech crowd forcing its way over to the Kleinseite. The military command was stationed just a few hundred yards away, and a bloodbath would have been virtually inevitable if the Czechs had actually moved forward onto the bridge.

18. A letter from Max Brod to Leo Hermann, a Prague Zionist working in London, which was mailed on Oct. 18, 1918, just a few days before the anticipated end of the monarchy, shows just how concrete this anxiety was. Brod proposed using a secret telegram code so that he would be able to inform Hermann without delay in the event of anti-Semitic riots. "Congratulations on your wedding" meant "pogrom has already erupted in Prague," "vacation time granted" meant "the military is taking action against the Jews," and so on. Brod suggested that if Hermann received a telegram of this kind, he should convey the news to sympathetic British and American politicians, who then could exert pressure on the Czech national council by telegraph. See Max Brod, *Streitbares Leben: Autobiographie 1884–1968* (Frankfurt am Main: Insel, 1979), pp. 236ff.

19. The full text of the memorandum co-authored by Brod can be found in Leon Chasanowitsch and Leo Motzkin, eds., *Die Judenfrage der Gegenwart: Dokumentensammlung* (Stockholm: Judäa, 1919), pp. 51–55.

20. Brod translated the libretti of five Janáček operas into German (beginning with *Jenůfa*, 1917), which made it possible to perform them in metropolises such as Berlin and Vienna. While the composer was still alive, Brod published a first brief biography of Janáček in 1925 (*Leoš Janáček: Leben und Werk*). Brod and Janáček encountered opposition primarily from Zdeněk Nejedlý, an influential musicologist who lived in Prague, who referred to Janáček's operas as folklore.

21. The first exploratory talks between Zionists in Prague (including Brod) and Czech members of parliament had taken place back in the latter part of 1917. Karel Baxa was one of the participants in these discussions on the Czech side. Baxa, an aggressive anti-Semite, was one of the people chiefly responsible for the escalation of the "ritual murder trial" against Leopold Hilsner. After the change of government, Baxa became the mayor of Prague and remained in this position until 1937, so he must have had quite a few additional meetings with Brod. The Czech media also treated Brod far more considerately than the other representatives on the Jewish national council.

22. Medical journals published in 1920 frequently claimed that the Spanish flu would *not* have a negative impact on the course of pulmonary tuberculosis, which was obviously a premature assessment, determined after too brief a period of observation. Over the course of the subsequent decades, the opposite view began to prevail. In the case of Kafka, it appears likely (though it is of course impossible to verify) that the inflammatory process made the lung tissue encystments that had already developed break open again, so the tuberculosis virus was able to circulate freely in his body again.

23. Letter to Felice Bauer, Oct. 23, 1916 (B3 265).

24. Letter to Eugen Pfohl, Nov. 25, 1918 (B4 58–59). Perhaps Kafka was thinking of Brod, who put in only sporadic appearancess at his own job at the post office.

25. Letter to Ottla Kafka, Sept. 3, 1918 (B4 51).

26. Beginning in the early part of December 1918, the German Bohemian territories were gradually occupied by the Czech military; Friedland was occupied on December 16–17. Looting had begun there in November.

27. In August 1902, Kafka and his family stayed in nearby Liboch (Liběch). Most likely he also knew the village of Schelesen from visits to Oskar Baum, who spent several summer vacations here.

28. Postcard to Max Brod, Dec. 17, 1918 (B4 63).

29. Letter to Max Brod, Nov. 29, 1918 (B4 60).

Chapter 14: The Pariah Girl

1. See the medical certificate issued by Dr. Josef Popper on Jan. 8, 1919 (B4 460).

2. Kafka immediately took steps to firm up his Czech, probably for fear of losing his job. In 1919, he even began subscribing to the magazine *Naše řeč: Listy pro vzdělávání a tříbení jazyka české* (Our language: Magazine for research on and cultivation of the Czech language).

3. The Czech attacks on Pfohl did not stop even after his death. On October 26, 1919, the *Národní Listy* called him a "major schemer" and an "evil spirit." Marschner and Pfohl were accused of making "unethical" agreements with German and Austrian businessmen, while Czech businessmen were said to have been the victims of blatant discrimination during the war (AS Mat 766ff.). Marschner's and Pfohl's extant personnel files indicate that both could speak Czech fluently (Státní ústřední archiv, Prague).

4. The civil servant Václav K. Krofta reported decades later that after the war, he reviewed Kafka's personnel file in his capacity of "revolutionary councilor" and recommended keeping him on "because he had not done anything wrong to the Czech people during his tenure" (V. R. Krofta, "Im Amt mit Franz Kafka," in Koch, "*Als Kafka mir entgegenkam . . .*," p. 99). There is no documentation to substantiate this version, however. Because Krofta was only twenty-three at the time in question, it hardly seems likely that his judgment was significant for the further course of Kafka's career.

5. By 1985, Hermine Beck, née Pomeranz, was eighty-six years old, and had only a spotty memory of her encounter with Kafka; see Koch, "*Als Kafka mir entgegenkam . . .*," pp. 157ff.

6. Letter to Max Brod, Feb. 8, 1919 (B4 71).

7. Diary, Aug. 20, 1912 (T 341).

8. Reliable information about Julie Wohryzek and her family did not emerge until the 1990s; see Anthony Northey, "Julie Wohryzek, Franz Kafkas zweite Verlobte," *Freibeuter* (Berlin) 59 (1994), pp. 3–16; also Hartmut Binder, "Puder und Schleier, Glanz und Genuss: Eine Entdeckung; Kafkas spate Verlobte Julie Wohryzek," *Neue Zürcher Zeitung*, April 28–29, 2001, p. 49.

9. Letter to Max Brod, March 2, 1919 (B4 78).

10. Letter to Käthe Nettel, Nov. 24, 1919 (B4 86–93). This letter was first published in 1947, in Hugo Siebenschein et al., *Franz Kafka a Praha: Vzpomínky, Úvahy, Dokumenty* (Prague: Vladimir Zikes, 1947). This volume reproduces one page in facsimile form to authenticate it, but the handwritten original of the letter is missing today.

11. Kafka wrote to Ottla on Nov. 13, 1919 (B4 86), "You write nothing about Fräulein W." This is the only extant indication that Kafka had introduced the woman he loved to anyone at all. Even Max Brod had no memories of Julie Wohryzek to report when he wrote his biography of Kafka. He explained this omission by claiming that in 1919, Kafka was "not in Prague for the most part," which was clearly untrue (Brod, *Franz Kafkas Glauben und Liebe*, in *Über Franz Kafka*, pp. 273–74).

12. This information about the Klaus brothers is from *Prager Profile: Vergessene Autoren im Schatten Kafkas*, ed. Hartmut Binder (Berlin: Mann, 1991). (Hans Klaus's statement about Kafka's behavior is on pp. 62–63.) Victor Klaus died on Oct. 12, 1919, after a botched operation on his lungs. Hans Klaus, like his brother, got his degree in chemistry.

13. Letter to Robert Klopstock, mid-Sept. 1921, in Hugo Wetscherek, ed. *Kafkas letzter Freund: Der Nachlaß Robert Klopstock (1899–1972)* (Vienna: Inlibris, 2003), p. 15. See also the letter to Milena Jesenská dated Sept. 6, 1920: "[O]h, the poet was there for maybe two hours and has now run off crying" (B4 336).

14. The first version was published in 1951 in German, and an expanded edition with ostensibly newly discovered material in 1968. Since numerous chronological errors have now been identified in these publications, the notes on which Janouch was basing his text can hardly have been taken at the time of his conversations in Kafka's office.

15. "Conversations about his books were always very brief." Gustav Janouch, *Conversations with Kafka*, 2nd ed., trans. Gornwy Rees (New York: New Directions, 2012), p. 31.

16. Janouch first met Hans Klaus in Kafka's office, but although he inundated Klaus's literary circle with his own lyrical creations, he was never really taken seriously by this group and was eventually excluded from it. Janouch's short text that Kafka helped him place in *Selbstwehr* (vol. 14, no. 13)—a review of Oskar Baum's novel *The Door into the Impossible*—was written in a vague and breathless language that even in 1920 must have seemed like a parody of Expressionism.

17. Diary, June 27, June 30, and July 6, 1919 (T 845).

18. This and the following quotations appear in Kafka's letter to Käthe Nettel, Nov. 24, 1919 (B4 86–93).

19. "Brief an den Vater" (NSF2 205).

20. "Brief an den Vater" (NSF2 206).

21. D 57. The second edition of *The Judgment* was published in the fall of 1919, and the dedication "For F." was retained, which suggests that once again, Kafka had been surprised by his publisher and did not have an opportunity to proofread the text.

22. Unpublished excerpt from Max Brod's diary, entry dated Sept. 23, 1919.

23. Letter to Ottla Kafka, Nov. 7, 1919 (B4 84).

24. "Brief an den Vater" (NSF2 158).

25. Letter to Milena Pollak, June 10, 1920 (B4 173).

26. "Brief an den Vater" (NSF2 208).

27. Letter to Käthe Nettel, Nov. 24, 1919 (B4 92, 90).

1. Olga Stüdl's brief sketch of Kafka was published in 1931 under the pseudonym "Dora Geritt"; see Koch, "*Als Kafka mir entgegenkam . . .*," pp. 155–56.

2. A characteristic episode took place on May 30, 1919, two weeks before the elections. Brod was a guest at a German Social Democratic electoral meeting. When he explained that the Jewish national council truly represented the interests of the Jewish people as a whole, people shouted at him: "Profiteers!" (*Selbstwehr*, June 5, 1919, p. 2) In the same week, German stores in Prague were again looted.

3. Max Brod to Kafka, Nov. 11, 1919 (B4); letter to Ottla Kafka, Nov. 7, 1919 (B4 84).

4. Letter to Hermann and Julie Kafka (B4 44). The editor of Kafka's letters dates this fragment as "presumably late May 1918" but concedes that an even earlier date of composition is conceivable. The letter fragment begins with the salutation "Dear Parents," but only Kafka's father is actually addressed.

5. Ottla Kafka to Josef David, Oct. 14, 1918 (privately owned).

6. Card to Ottla Kafka, Dec. 11, 1918 (B4 62).

7. Kafka himself cited a curious example of this linguistic confusion. His father had wanted to tell Josef David that he was "on a friendly footing" with someone, but he translated this figure of speech into Czech literally: *na přátelské noze stojí*. David was astonished to hear that Hermann Kafka was standing on someone's foot in a friendly way. (Letter to Ottla Kafka, Feb. 20, 1919, B4 72)

8. Julie Kafka to Ottla Kafka, Dec. 1, 1918, and Feb. 5, 1919 (privately owned).

9. Julie Kafka to Ottla Kafka, March 14, 1919 (privately owned). Robert Kafka himself had national Czech sympathies, which may have been one reason for his enthusiastic endorsement of Josef David.

10. Julie Kafka to Ottla Kafka, March 20, 1919 (privately owned).

11. See Kafka's letter to Ottla, ca. April 30, 1920 (B4 124), where explicit mention is made of Ottla's "hesitation" about marriage.

12. This single yet unequivocal indication that Ottla was still thinking about emigrating just a few months before her wedding is found in Kafka's letter to Max Brod, presumably early March 1920 (B4 109).

13. Kafka made one of his remarkably frequent slips in this correspondence. On February 20, 1919, he wrote, "How do you intend to look for the job and why must you talk with Mother first? I don't fully understand that." In her reply, Ottla evidently stated that life was too short to keep up these kinds of tensions between mother and daughter without setting limits, whereupon Kafka wrote on February 24: "[T]he fact that life is short is an argument just as much for the journey as against it." He meant the opposite, of course: "just as much against the journey as for it" (B4 73, 74).

14. "Brief an den Vater" (NSF2 143, 145).

15. Brod, *Über Franz Kafka*, p. 30; Klaus Wagenbach, *Franz Kafka: Eine Biographie seiner Jugend 1883–1912* (Bern, 1958. Reprint, Berlin: Wagenbach, 2006), p. 10; Heinz Politzer, *Franz Kafka, der Künstler* (Frankfurt am Main: S. Fischer, 1965), pp. 439–450; Margarete Mitscherlich-Nielsen, "Psychoanalytische Bemerkungen zu Franz Kafka." *Psyche* 31, no. 1 (1977), pp. 60–83; Ernst Pawel, *The Nightmare of Reason: A Life of Franz Kafka* (New York: Farrar, Straus & Giroux, 1984), p. 384.

16. Letter to Milena Pollak, July 4–5, 1920 (B4 202).

17. Compare, for example, Kafka's stated childhood memories of his father, always presented in a tone of moral accusation ("Brief an den Vater," NSF2 169), with the corresponding passages in the diary dated Dec. 26, 1911 (T 323–24).

18. Letter to Max Brod, Nov. 14, 1917 (B3 363).

19. "Brief an den Vater" (NSF2, 200, 210).

20. Letter to Felice Bauer, Oct. 19, 1916 (B3 262); diary, Oct. 18, 1916 (T 808). The words "without going mad" were added to the diary entry later. In referring to their argument about Yitzhak Löwy, Kafka also used the word "hatred," but more in the sense of an atmospheric disturbance: "I should not have written it down, for I have really written myself into a hatred of my father" (Diary, Oct. 31, 1911 [T 214–15]). After a quarrel about the asbestos factory, he wrote, in a similar vein, "I hate them all, one after the other" (letter to Max Brod, Oct. 7–8, 1912 [B1 180]). On one of the notepads Kafka used before the war, there is this remark in shorthand: "My hatred of my father" (T App 68).

21. Brod, *Über Franz Kafka*, p. 30.

22. Diary, Jan. 23, 1922 (T 887).

23. A Czech translation of Benjamin Franklin's autobiography *The Life of Benjamin Franklin* (1868).

24. Letter to Max Brod, March 26–27, 1918 (B4 33).

25. "Please do not forget the dedication of the whole book 'To My Father'" (letter to Kurt Wolff Verlag, Oct. 1, 1918 [B4 55]). "The title and the dedication page were missing from the *Country Doctor* book" (letter to Kurt Wolff Verlag, late Feb. 1919 [B4 76]).

26. Friedrich Thieberger, "Kafka und die Thiebergers" in Koch, "*Als Kafka mir entgegenkam . . .* ," p. 134.

27. Paul Federn, *Zur Psychologie der Revolution: Die vaterlose Gesellschaft* (Leipzig: Anzengruber, 1919), p. 7.

28. Otto Gross, "Zur Überwindung der kulturellen Krise," *Die Aktion* 3, no. 4 (April 2, 1913), columns 386–87.

29. Diary, Oct. 8 and 16, 1916 (T 804–5). See the letter to Max Brod dated Dec. 10, 1917, in which Kafka wrote, with explicit reference to Foerster, that the "pedagogy of self-restraint" struck him as "more and more helpless" (B3 379).

30. Only three of these letters have survived (May to August 1921), but several statements reveal that the pedagogical correspondence between Kafka and his sister Elli was more extensive.

31. Quoted in Thomas Nitschke, *Die Gartenstadt Hellerau als Pädagogische Provinz* (Dresden: Hellerau-Verlag, 2003), p. 75.

32. Peter de Mendelssohn, *Hellerau, mein unverlierbares Europa* (Dresden: Hellerau Verlag, 1993), p. 54; diary, Jan. 17, 1920 (T 851).

33. Letter to Elli Hermann, ca. July 10, 1922 (unpublished). It is not entirely clear why the Hermanns ultimately decided not to send their daughter to Hellerau after talking to Lilian Neustätter, but it is likely that their discussion focused on the politically unstable situation and the school's financial problems that made its continued existence precarious. In 1924, Neill returned to England to found the Summerhill School, and in 1925, the Neue Schule Hellerau closed down. Not long afterwards, Edwin and Willa Muir, teachers Neill had hired in Hellerau, became two of the first of Kafka's translators into English.

34. "Brief an den Vater" (NSF2 178).

35. Brod, *Über Franz Kafka*, p. 23.

36. Letters to Milena Pollak, June 21 and July 4–5, 1920 (B4 192, 202).

37. Diary, Jan. 13, 1920 (T 849).

Chapter 16: Merano, Second Class

1. Letter to Hermann, Julie, and Ottla Kaka, May 4, 1920 (B4 128). Sick leaves had to be formally approved by the management committee of the institute.

2. Letter to Käthe Nettel, Nov. 24, 1919 (B4 95).

3. *Internationales Bäderhandbuch* (Berlin: Hugo Steinitz, 1914), p. 286. After the suppression of the Munich Soviet Republic (1919), Partenkirchen was one of the few Bavarian health resorts at which Jewish guests were explicitly welcome. There is no documentation as to whether Kafka was aware of this fact.

4. Letter to Minze Eisner, April 1, 1920 (B4 114).

5. Letter to Ottla Kafka, April 5, 1920 (B4 114–15).

6. Letter to Milena Jesenská, Apr. 12, 1920 (B4 120). At this time, Kafka did not know that shortly after his departure from Prague, a letter had arrived from Milena and had been saved for him in the mailroom of the Workers' Accident Insurance Institute.

Chapter 17: Milena

1. Willy Haas, *Die literarische Welt: Erinnerungen* (Munich: List, 1957), pp. 36–37.

2. Quoted in a letter from Kafka to Milena Pollak, ca. May 12, 1920 (B4 134–35).

3. The father of Milena Hejzlarová was the Czech educator František Hejzlar, who was appointed regional superintendent in 1886 and moved to Prague with his family. Hejzlar's publications included a chemistry textbook that was used in both German and Czech schools.

4. Greek and Latin were required courses at the Minerva school. German, French, and English were offered as electives. Records indicate that Milena attended German classes; see her letter to her teacher, Albína Honzáková, in the spring of 1915: "The other day I had German at ten . . ." in her volume of letters edited by Alena Wagnerová (*"Ich hätte zu antworten tage- und nächtelang": Die Briefe von Milena* [Mannheim: Bollmann, 1996], p. 30).

5. The term is from Hartmut Binder, who pieced together what little is known about Pollak in his portrait "Ernst Polak—Literat ohne Werk: Zu den Kaffeehauszirkeln in Prag und Wien," *Jahrbuch der Deutschen Schillergesellschaft* 23 (1979), pp. 366–415. The Czech spelling "Polak" dated from the years of emigration, beginning in 1938.

6. Egon Erwin Kisch's name for Café Arco; see Kisch, *Briefe an den Bruder Paul und an die Mutter 1905–1936* (Berlin: Aufbau, 1978), p. 135.

7. Milena Jesenská, "Wien" in Milena Jesenská, *"Alles ist Leben": Feuilletons und Reportagen 1919–1939*, ed. Dorothea Rein (Frankfurt am Main: Verlag Neue Kritik, 1984), pp. 11–12. Published in the Czech original as "Víden̆" in the Prague *Tribuna* dated Dec. 30, 1919.

8. She wrote to Willy Schlamm in the late 1930s that during her early years in Vienna, the Czech journalist Josef Kalmer was the only one who had supported her unselfishly: "[He] may have saved my life, or at least saved me from streetwalking" (quoted in Alena Wagnerová, ed., *Milena Jesenská: "Alle meine Artikel sind Liebesbriefe": Biographie* [Mannheim: Bollmann, 1994], p. 70).

9. In a letter Kafka wrote to Milena Pollak on Sept. 15, 1920 (B4 343), three of her activities are mentioned: "carrying wood, carrying luggage, the piano." She had already described how difficult it was to gather and sell wood in her first published essay ("Wien") but did not mention that this was her way of earning money. The reference to the piano might indicate that she also did occasional work as a musician in nightclubs.

10. Gina Kaus, *Und was für ein Leben: Mit Liebe und Literatur, Theater und Film* (Hamburg: Albrecht Knaus, 1979), p. 56. Milena once stole from Kaus herself; see ibid., pp. 55–56.

11. The stalwart Paní Kohler, who must have quite a major role in the lives of the Pollaks as "maid, cook, housekeeper, lady-in-waiting, laundress, seamstress, washerwoman, liaison." Milena portrayed her in two articles: "Meine Freundin" and "Scheiden tut weh" in *"Alles ist Leben,"* pp. 27–32 and 50–54. In the Czech original, the titles were "Moje přítelkyně" and "Loučení, loučení," and they were published in the *Tribuna* on Jan. 27 and Aug. 17, 1921 under the

name A. X. Nessey. Kafka probably met Paní Kohler during his stay in Vienna. On July 10 or 11, 1920, he sent her a telegram asking about Milena's state of health, but he did not receive a reply. On July 15, he sent her an envelope with money to give to Milena.

12. Kaus, *Und was für ein Leben*, p. 75. Gina Kaus, the lover of Franz Blei, enjoyed success in 1920 at the Burgtheater in Vienna with her comedy *Thieves in the House* (using the pseudonym Andreas Eckbrecht). In the same year, she was awarded the Fontane Prize for her story "The Ascent."

13. Article 2 of the declaration of the republic, dated Nov. 12, 1918, stated, "German Austria is part of the German Republic." However, this union was prevented by the Allies, and in October 1919, the new state had to be renamed Republic of Austria. At this time, about 6.5 million people were Austrian citizens; 2 million of them lived in Vienna.

14. Letter to Milena Pollak, ca. May 6, 1920 (B4 132).

15. Letter to Milena Pollak, ca. May 19, 1920 (B4 145). On the quality of Milena Pollak's translations, and on Kafka's commentaries, see Marek Nekula, *Franz Kafkas Sprachen* (Tübingen: Max Niemeyer, 2003), pp. 243ff.

16. "Zpráva pro jistou akademii" (A report to an academy) in *Tribuna*, Sept. 26, 1920, pp. 1–4. The published texts from *Meditation* are as follows: "Náhlá procházka" (The sudden walk), "Výlet do hor" (Excursion into the mountains), "Neštěstí mládence" (The bachelor's unhappiness), "Kupec" (The businessman), "Cesta domû" (The way home), and "Ti, kterí bezí mimo" (The passers-by), all in *Kmen*, Sept. 9, 1920. An additional piece in *Meditation* was published in the *Tribuna* on July 16, 1920: "Nešt'asný" (Unhappiness). Milena Pollak's translation of "The Judgment" appeared in the journal *Cesta* 5, no. 26/27 (Dec. 1923/Jan. 1924).

17. Letters to Milena Pollak, ca. May 19 and Oct. 22, 1920 (B4 144, 360). On Oct. 24, 1920, "Před zákonem" (Before the law) in the Sunday supplement to *Právo lidu* (Rights of the people), a daily newspaper with a Social Democratic leaning, in a translation by Milena Illová. She was the wife of one of Kafka's schoolmates, Rudolf Illový, who wrote him a letter about this translation just a few days before its publication.

Chapter 18: Living Fires

1. Letter to Milena Pollak, ca. May 5, 1920 (B4 131).

2. Letter to Milena Pollak, ca. May 12, 1920 (B4 135).

3. "Not a single word that was not carefully considered": Kafka was quoting Milena in Czech: *ani jediné slovo které by nebylo velmi dobře uváženo*. Letter to Milena Pollak, June 10, 1920 (B4 170).

4. "If you are able," she wrote to Max Brod shortly after Kafka's death, "would you kindly arrange for my letters to Franz to be burned; I confidently

entrust them to you; though the matter is not important" (Jesenská, "*Ich hätte zu antworten tage- und nächtelang*" [Frankfurt: S. Fischer, 1999] p. 52). It is uncertain whether Brod carried out this request or whether he even found the letters in Kafka's literary estate at all.

5. Letter to Milena Pollak, June 11, 1920 (B4 176). This appears to refer to a remark Kafka made on June 1: "You are so kind to worry, you miss my letters, yes, there were a few days last week when I didn't write" (B4 158).

6. Letter to Milena Pollak, May 31, 1920 (B4 157).

7. Letter to Milena Pollak, June 10, 1920 (B4 170).

8. Letter to Milena Pollak, June 6, 1920 (B4 165).

9. Max Brod to Franz Kafka, June 9, 1920 (B4 730–31); letter to Milena Pollak, June 12, 1920 (B4 179). Brod's report contains a few inaccuracies: Jarmila Reinerová was still in Prague at the time, and Haas was not the manager, but the editor of the *Film-Kurier* in Berlin. The story of the girlfriends' alleged similarity in appearance is probably explained by the fact that Jarmila tried to imitate Milena for a while.

10. Letter to Milena Pollak, June 20, 1920 (B4 189).

11. Letter to Max Brod, June 12, 1920, or shortly thereafter (B4 180).

12. Letters to Milena Pollak, June 12 and 13, 1920 (B4 180, 183–84).

13. Letter from Max Brod to Kafka, May 24, 1921, in Brod/Kafka, *Briefwechsel*, p. 348. Brod went on to report that in the course of this conversation, Milena even confessed her "instinctive hatred" of his wife. Kafka explained that this was more likely a function of Elsa Brod's tone of admiration toward her husband, which Milena found "submissive." "M[ilena] hates almost all Jewish women," he added shortly thereafter. (Letters to Max Brod, late May and mid-June 1921, ibid., pp. 350, 357).

14. The essay in question, "Nový velkoměstský typus" (The new urbanite), was published in the *Tribuna* on August 7, 1920. Remarkably, this text mentions "nouveaux riches" and "war profiteers" but not Jews. See Marek Nekula's German translation and Kafka's letter to Milena Pollak dated Aug. 10, 1920 (B4 300–301).

15. Letter to Max Brod, April 6–8, 1920 (B4 117–18).

16. Letter to Max Brod, after May 16, 1920 (B4 142). In the same year, Otto Pick provided an illustration of what Kafka meant by the "innocence of anti-Semitism" in a fictitious piece called "Conversation about Anti-Semitism" in *Selbstwehr*. One passage, which certainly drew on his own experience, reads: "Despite the fact that I was born a Jew, I am typically not taken to be a Jew because of my looks or my way of talking, so I have often experienced Christians indulging in blatant anti-Semitic remarks in my presence. . . . When I revealed that I was a Jew, they took the news with the conciliatory comment that I was just an exception to the rule (because I don't look Jewish?!) and if all Jews were like me, there wouldn't be any anti-Semitism" (Dec. 24, 1920, p. 1).

17. Letter to Ottla David, March 16, 1921, in Kafka, *Briefe an Ottla und die Familie*, p. 116.

18. Point 4 of the "twenty-five point program" of the National Socialist German Workers' Party, which Hitler read out on February 24, 1920, at the Hofbräuhaus, stated: "Only those who are our fellow countrymen can become citizens. Only those who have German blood, regardless of creed, can be our countrymen. Hence no Jew can be a countryman."

19. Buber gave this speech on March 27, 1920, in Prague; Max Brod and Hugo Bergmann were also present. The entire text was printed in *Selbstwehr* on April 2, 1920, pp. 6–7.

20. Letter to Max Brod, after May 16, 1920 (B4 141). Kafka had *Selbstwehr* sent to him regularly in Merano; he could of course assume that Brod knew Buber's essay.

21. Letter to Milena Pollak, Nov. 17 and 20, 1920 (B4 370–71). The rioting, which was initially fueled by anti-German sentiment, went on for several days. The two German-speaking theaters were occupied, as well as several coffeehouses and the editorial offices of the *Prager Tagblatt* and the *Bohemia*. Once again, Baxa, the anti-Semitic mayor of Prague, made sure that most of the apprehended perpetrators were quickly released from custody.

22. In Merano, at Hotel Emma, Kafka had spoken with a Jewish man from Prague who struck him as a classic example of opportunism. His son had also switched schools: "now he won't know either German or Czech, so let him bark" (letter to Max Brod, April 6–8, 1920 [B4 117]). The rioting in November 1920 demonstrated that renaming themselves did nothing to help the Jews: the nameplates that were destroyed by the dozens bore almost exclusively Czech names—but names that *sounded* Jewish.

23. Letter to Ottla Kafka, May 16, 1920, or shortly thereafter (B4 139).

24. Letter to Milena Pollak, May 31, 1920 (B4 156).

25. Letter to Milena Pollak, June 23, 1920 (B4 194).

26. In a letter to Grete Bloch, whom he also pressured to leave Vienna as soon as possible, Kafka called the city a "decaying mammoth village" even before the war began (April 8, 1914, B3 19).

27. Milena Pollak, letter to Max Brod, Jan./Feb. 1921 in Jesenská, "*Ich hätte zu antworten tage- und nächtelang*," p. 46. The term "burned" means "tanned" here, an Austrianism that Kafka used on occasion.

28. Letter to Milena Pollak, July 15, 1920 (B4 228).

29. Letter to Milena Pollak, Aug. 9, 1920 (B4 298).

30. Letters to Milena Pollak, Aug. 8–9 and July 29, 1920 (B4 295, 261).

31. Letter to Max Brod, after May 16, 1920 (B4 142).

32. Letter to Milena Pollak, July 5–6, 1920 (B4 208).

1. Letter to Milena Pollak, July 5–6, 1920 (B4 207–8).

2. Letter to Milena Pollak, June 10, 1920, and to Ottla Kafka, June 11, 1920 (B4 172, 175).

3. Letter to Milena Pollak, May 31, 1920 (B4 154). A letter from Milena Pollak to Max Brod indicates that she had talked to Kafka about Felice Bauer: "If you ask him why he loved his first fiancée, he replies, 'She was so good at business,' and his face begins to beam with reverence" (Jesenská, "*Ich hätte zu antworten tage- und nächtelang*," p. 42; Kafka's words were in German in the original letter). Kafka himself had an ironic take on this information: he sent Milena a copy of Grillparzer's *Poor Fiddler*, in part "because he loved a girl who was good at business" (July 4–5, 1920, B4 203).

4. Telegram to Milena Pollak, July 5, 1920. This telegram has not been preserved, but Kafka repeated its contents in a letter to Milena Pollak dated July 5–6, 1920 (B4 207).

5. Letter to Milena Jesenská, July 4–5, 1920 (B4 203). Born, *Franz Kafka: Kritik und Rezeption*, p. 85.

6. Letter to Milena Pollak, July 24, 1920 (B4 247).

7. See the letter to Milena Pollak dated July 10, 1920 (B4 218).

8. Heimito von Doderer later went so far as to claim that Pollak and some of his Viennese acquaintances had formed a "Kafka cult" at the Café Central ("Nicht alle zogen nach Berlin," *Magnum* 9 [1961], p. 61).

9. As luck would have it, decades later, Pollak would be one of the first to read the entire bundle of letters. Willy Haas, to whom Milena had entrusted the letters in 1939, asked Pollak in 1946, a year before Pollak's death, for advice on how to go about possibly getting them published. So it was not Max Brod who decided to publish Kafka's letters to Milena, but the very two people who had most to fear a compromising situation—Pollak because of his questionable role as a husband, and Haas because of his influence on the fate of Jarmila and Josef Reiner, which the letters comment on repeatedly and severely. The result of their work on the letters was a truncated edition prepared by Haas himself (1952), which contained the passages relating to Pollak, but suppressed the complete Haas-Jarmila episode. "Unfortunately, certain parts of the letters had to be deleted in this edition in consideration of people who are still alive," Haas wrote in his afterword. "The editor regrets this particularly because these happen to include passages of the letters in which his own name appears repeatedly. Future editors should be advised that he personally has no objections to their publication, as far-fetched and bizarre certain conclusions were that Kafka came to concerning a certain tragic incident." Haas's first wife, Jarmila, was still alive at the time; she had a successful career as a journalist and translator, and died in 1990 at the age of ninety-four.

10. Letter to Milena Pollak, May 25–29, 1920 (B4 148).

11. Letter to Milena Pollak, July 8, 1920 (B4 213–14).

12. Letter to Milena Pollak, July 18, 1920 (B4 233).

13. Letter to Milena Pollak, Aug. 13, 1920 (B4 308).

14. Letter to Milena Pollak, Sept. 27, 1920 (B4 350).

15. Letter to Milena Pollak, July 18, 1920 (B4 236).

16. Letter to Milena Pollak, Aug. 4, 1920 (B4 280).

17. Letter from Milena Pollak to Max Brod, in Jesenská, "*Ich hätte zu antworten tage- und nächtelang*," p. 42. Dating the letter as "early August 1920" appears suspect: at this time no definite decision had been reached about Kafka's trip to Vienna, but Milena wrote "I really needed it *at the time*" (emphasis added).

18. Letter to Milena Pollak, Aug. 2, 1920 (B4 275).

19. Letters to Milena Pollak, May 31 and July 12, 1920 (B4 157, 219).

20. Letter to Milena Pollak, July 9, 1920 (B4 215).

21. Letter to Milena Pollak, Aug. 13, 1920 (B4 308).

22. The term "angel of death" is found in a letter to Milena Pollak, dated Sept. 3–4, 1920 (B4 335). Kafka's comments were unusually aggressive after his first meeting with Staša: "she has probably been extinguished by her husband. She is tired and dead and doesn't know it. When I want to imagine hell I think of her and her husband" (letter to Milena Pollak, July 13, 1920, B4 222). Kafka does not appear to have known that Staša Jílovská worked as an editor, translated from several languages, and was acquainted with a good number of German-language authors, particularly the younger ones.

23. See the description of his conversation with Vlasta Knappová in the letter to Milena Pollak dated Sept. 3–4, 1920 (B4 331–34). Kafka's correspondence mentions Milena's favorite restaurant, the "Weisser Hahn" at Josefstädter Strasse 24, several times, which indicates that he knew it from personal experience. Kafka confirmed that he had also addressed the subject of Pollak's debts in another letter, dated Sept. 15, 1920 (B4 342–43). The Pollaks' financial situation did not improve over the following years. In a letter Milena wrote to Karel Horch on March 5, 1924, in which she spoke of her impending divorce, she said, "I will give up my apartment and sell my furniture—my husband has substantial debts, and I want to pay them off before I go" (Jesenská, "*Ich hätte zu antworten tage- und nächtelang*," p. 68).

24. Letter to Milena Pollak, Sept. 10, 1920 (B4 339). The text of Milena Pollak's telegram has not been preserved (apart from the words "at once"), but its tone and contents can be inferred from Kafka's subsequent letters.

25. See NSF2 254–57 and the accompanying textual variants in the critical apparatus volume. The critical Kafka edition dates the fragment as Aug. 28, 1920 (see NSF2 App 68ff.); the finals of the swimming competitions in Antwerp took place August 24 to 26. It is unclear how well informed Kafka was about the competitions, because in light of the local Olympic Committee's bankruptcy, journalists were given scant information, and not even a final of-

ficial bulletin was published. The German-language newspapers also provided very little coverage, because both Germany and Austria had been excluded from the Summer Olympic Games.

26. Franz Kafka, *Beim Bau der chinesischen Mauer*; idem, *Beschreibung eines Kampfes: Novellen, Skizzen, Aphorismen aus dem Nachlass* (Prague: Heinrich Mery Sohn, 1936). All these titles are by Brod, with the exception of "The Problem of Our Laws."

27. Letter to Milena Pollak, July 8, 1920 (B4 214). The prose piece "The City Coat of Arms" was written about two months later.

28. Peter Panter (pen name of Kurt Tucholsky), "In der Strafkolonie," *Die Weltbühne*, June 3, 1920; idem, "Der Prozess," *Die Weltbühne*, March 9, 1926; idem, "Auf dem Nachttisch," *Die Weltbühne*, Feb. 26, 1929. See Born, *Franz Kafka: Kritik und Rezeption zu seinen Lebzeiten 1912–1924*, p. 96; and idem, *Franz Kafka: Kritik und Rezeption 1924–1938* (Frankfurt am Main: S. Fischer, 1983), pp. 110, 206.

29. NSF2 334.

30. Letters to Milena Pollak, July 21 and Aug. 9, 1920 (B4 241, 297).

31. Letter to Milena Pollak, Aug. 26, 1920 (B4 318–19).

32. Milena Pollak to Max Brod, Jan. or Feb. 1921, in Jesenská, "*Ich hätte zu antworten tage- und nächtelang*," p. 48. It is not known whether Kafka ever got to see these letters, though it would be conceivable, given Brod's usual lack of discretion.

33. Letter to Milena Pollak, Oct. 21 or 22, 1920 (B4 358).

34. Letters to Milena Pollak, Sept. 25 and 27, 1920 (B4 348, 351).

Chapter 20: Escape to the Mountains

1. Letter to Milena Pollak, Aug. 10, 1920 (B4 299). The term "greatest day of glory" refers to the fact that this letter was written on Milena's twenty-fourth birthday.

2. "I know very well that I have lost nothing; have you lost your cars or something of the sort since the wedding? And since you still have them, may I no longer play with them? Well, then" (Postcard to Ottla David, July 25, 1920 [B4 249]).

3. Letter to Milena Pollak, Aug. 31, 1920 (B4 326).

4. Medical report by Dr. Odolen Kodym, Oct. 14, 1920 (B4 658–59).

5. Letter to Milena Pollak, Oct. 21 or 22, 1920 (B4 359).

6. Rooms in the Grimmenstein sanatorium ran about three hundred Austrian crowns a day and up, including meals and medical care; that was the equivalent of about sixty Czech kronen, which meant that Kafka would have had to spend two full monthly salaries for every month in the sanatorium.

7. Letter to Milena Pollak, Dec. 2, 1920 (B4 374).

1. Max Brod to Kafka, Jan. 6, 1921, in Brod/Kafka, *Briefwechsel*, p. 293; letter to Max Brod, Jan. 13, 1921, ibid., p. 300.

2. Letter to Max Brod, late Jan. 1921, ibid., p. 308.

3. Letters to Max Brod, Jan. 13 and late Jan. 1921, ibid., pp. 296, 307, and facsimile p. 306.

4. Letter to Max Brod, Dec. 31, 1920 (B4 382). The Shulchan Aruch ("set table") is a compendium of Jewish ritual laws and legal provisions; the author is the rabbi and cabbalist Joseph ben Ephraim Karo (1488–1575). Because later editions of the text were overrun with copious commentary, compact summaries of the Shulchan Aruch were popular beginning in the nineteenth century.

5. All quotations are from Klopstock's brief oral recollections recorded at Schocken Verlag in New York and published as "Mit Kafka in Matliary," in Koch, "*Als Kafka mir entgegenkam . . .*," pp. 164–67. Klopstock's description of their first meeting, in which he claimed to have had Kierkegaard's *Fear and Trembling* with him and that Kafka was reading this work at the same time, is evidently a memory lapse on his part, because it was Kafka who sent home for his own copy of this book to lend it to Klopstock about two weeks later.

6. Klopstock, "Mit Kafka in Matliary," p. 166.

7. Ludwig Hardt, "Der Autor und sein Rezitator," in Koch, "*Als Kafka mir entgegenkam . . .*," p. 216.

8. Letter to Max Brod, early Feb. 1921, in Brod/Kafka, *Briefwechsel*, p. 315. For information about Klopstock's early years, see Wetscherek, *Kafkas letzter Freund*; wherever possible, Kafka's letters to Klopstock are quoted according to this volume. In exile in America, Klopstock became a member of the Episcopal Church.

9. Letter to Max Brod, early May 1921, in Brod/Kafka, *Briefwechsel*, p. 343.

10. Letters to Ottla David, March 16 and ca. Feb 10, 1921, in Kafka, *Briefe an Ottla und die Familie*, p. 115, 108; letter to Max Brod, late April 1921, in Brod/Kafka, *Briefwechsel*, p. 339.

11. Letters to Ottla David, April 1921, and May 6, 1921, in Kafka, *Briefe an Ottla und die Familie*, pp. 118, 122. The article that was published in the *Karpathen-Post* on April 23, 1921, bore the title "Aus Matlárháza" (D 443).

12. See the letters to Max Brod, late Jan. and April 13–14, 1921 in Brod/Kafka, *Briefwechsel*, pp. 309, 335.

13. Letter to Max Brod, early May 1921, in Brod/Kafka, *Briefwechsel*, p. 343. The answers to Brod's "questionnaire" dated June 12, 1921, consisted of the following information: "Objective condition of the lungs? The doctor's secret, supposedly favorable. Temperatures? In general free of fever. Breathing? Not good; on chilly evenings almost as bad as in winter" (see the facsimile, ibid, p. 361).

14. In June, Kafka wrote to Brod "if I were well, I would find lung disease in someone near me very upsetting, not only because of the constant danger of infection but above all because this continual illness is filthy, filthy, this contradiction between the appearance of the face and the lungs, all of it filthy." (Brod/Kafka, *Briefwechsel*, p. 357). In the summer of 1921, Milena Pollak was living in a sanatorium on the Spitzberg (Špičák) near Eisenstein (Železná Ruda).

15. Letter to Max Brod, early March 1921, in Brod/Kafka, *Briefwechsel*, p. 320. In a similar vein, Kafka wrote to Director Odstrčil about his "helplessness in regard to the lung disease, the real importance of which I have come to recognize only here, where I am living among lung patients" (letter in German dated April 3, 1921, in Kafka, *Briefe an Ottla und die Familie*, p. 202).

16. Max Brod found these first provisions for Kafka's will when he was sifting through Kafka's papers after his death. The folded sheet contains Brod's mailing address (Brod/Kafka, *Briefwechsel*, p. 365).

Chapter 22: The Internal and the External Clock

1. Thomas Mann, "Ludwig Hardt," in *Essays II: 1914–1926*, ed. Hermann Kurzke (Frankfurt am Main: S. Fischer, 2002), pp. 303–5. The text was first published in the Munich professional journal *Wort und Ton* on April 17, 1920, just six days after Hardt's reading, which Mann and his son Klaus had attended. This reading was not sold out. The review was reprinted in the Prague *Bohemia* on Nov. 17, 1922.

2. E. Dietrichstein, "Berliner Podium," *Deutsche Zeitung Bohemia* (Prague), Nov. 21, 1920.

3. H. St., "Vortragsabend," in *Vossische Zeitung* (Berlin, March 10, 1921); reprinted in Born, *Franz Kafka Kritik und Rezeption zu seinen Lebzeiten*, pp. 130–31. Hardt's recitation in Berlin on March 9, 1921, is the earliest in which Kafka is known to have been on the program. Later, Hardt wrote that before he got to know Kafka personally, he had been reciting his works "for years." This was certainly a memory lapse (Hardt, "Der Autor und sein Rezitator" in Koch, "*Als Kafka mir entgegenkam . . .*," p. 215). On many of his recitation evenings in Prague in January and February 1921, he did *not* read texts by Kafka.

4. Soma Morgenstern, "Franz Kafka [2]," in Morgenstern, *Kritiken, Berichte, Tagebücher*, pp. 453–54.

5. Credible information on this subject in Janouch, *Conversations with Kafka*, p. 98.

6. On June 11, 12, and 14, Karl Kraus had performed in the Mozarteum, and on the first two evenings his recitations included excerpts from *The Last Days of Mankind*. At this time, Kafka was in Merano. Kraus was extremely dissatisfied with Hardt's style of presentation, and after hearing him on May 12, 1922, at a performance in Vienna, he announced that he would be forbidding

any reading from his works by people other than himself ("Due to the behavior of an actor in Berlin . . ."); see *Die Fackel*, nos. 595–600, p. 80). His satirical poem, "Der neue Rezitator," clearly targeted Hardt (*Die Fackel*, nos. 622–32, June 1923, pp. 7475).

7. Max Brod's report for the *Prager Abendblatt* spoke of a "storm of applause": "Der Rezitator Ludwig Hardt (Vortragsabend im Mozarteum)," Oct. 4, 1921; reprinted in Born, *Franz Kafka: Kritik und Rezeption zu seinen Lebzeiten*, p. 133). Brod was not pleased, of course, that this evening's offerings included works by his archenemy, Karl Kraus (as indicated in an anonymous short review in the *Prager Tagblatt* on the same day). He wrote that Hardt's program was "perhaps somewhat too varied."

8. Letter to Ludwig Hardt, Oct. 5, 1921 (unpublished).

9. Hardt, "Der Autor und sein Rezitator," pp. 213–14.

10. We can infer from a remark by Kafka that Klopstock could finance his more than one-year stay in Matliary only by taking on temporary local medical jobs: "By the way, what is your situation with the position in Matliary? How is it? And is it secure for the long term?" (letter to Robert Klopstock, Nov. 1921, in Wetscherek, *Kafkas letzter Freund*, p. 26). In an unpublished letter to Julie Kafka, written about May 17, 1924, Klopstock stated that he had "worked a great deal in large pulmonary sanatoriums . . . for about 4 years."

11. The engineer Hugo Georg Klopstock (born 1891) had been taken captive by the Russians and sent to a camp near Krasnojarsk (Siberia), but he then appears to have remained in Russia voluntarily, which must have made him an object of suspicion for the Horthy regime, which was anti-Semitic, nationalistic, and adamantly anticommunist. It was therefore crucial to warn him in time of the dangers that would face him if he returned to Hungary. In 1923, he risked doing so anyway; it is not known whether he actually faced reprisals when he and his Russian wife arrived in Budapest. Robert Klopstock's fear of internment was not unfounded. The tensions between the Czechoslovak Republic and Hungary assumed menacing proportions after the second unsuccessful attempted coup of the last kaiser, Karl I, in mid-October 1921. Military maneuvers were carried out at the Slovakian border to Hungary, and there were temporary internments of Hungarian journalists in Slovakia who were suspected of advocating a return of Hungary to a monarchy. On October 26, Prime Minister Beneš declared in the Prague parliament that the issue was not only to repulse the ambitions of Karl I but also to implement democracy throughout central Europe—a statement that Hungarians took as a threat of war.

12. Milena Pollak to Max Brod, July 27, 1924, in Jesenská, "*Ich hätte zu antworten tage- und nächtelang*," p. 52.

13. Letter to Robert Klopstock, Oct. 4, 1921, in Kafka, *Briefe 1902–1924*, p. 360. Letter to Robert Klopstock, Oct. 8, 1921, in Wetscherek, *Kafkas letzter Freund*, p. 24.

14. "Maybe I'll take it along to Gmünd," he wrote on Aug. 9, 1920 (B4 293). Kafka must have thought long and hard about this plan; on the original draft of his "Letter to His Father," there is the beginning of a penciled explanation intended for Milena (which had the incidental effect of making it impossible to give it to his father later; see NSF2 App 55). Moreover, in the summer of 1920, Kafka had a typewritten copy made, evidently so that he could keep one for himself. Some of the typical misreadings of what he had written (such as mistaking the word "friends" [*Freunde*] for the similarly spelled "strangers" [*Fremde*]) show that he did not type the letter himself, but it cannot be established to whom he entrusted this work. (It does not appear to have been Julie Kaiser, to whom Kafka had dictated for years and who also visited him in Zürau, because she left the Workers' Accident Insurance Institute in mid-May of 1920 while Kafka was still in Merano.)

15. The only extant documentation of this question is found in his diary entry dated Jan. 19, 1922 (T 882), but the context makes it very likely that it was directed squarely at Milena—in person, because four days later he wrote in his diary that he had "told" her something (T 888).

16. Diary, Dec. 1, 1921 (T 874).

17. We learn this from a letter Milena Pollak wrote to Brod in the early part of 1921. The volume, which the Prague publishing company F. Borový planned for the winter of 1921–1922 (Edition "Verven"), was also to contain a translation of "The Metamorphosis," as well as a foreword by Max Brod. Because the publication was delayed (and ultimately abandoned altogether, for unknown reasons), Milena Pollak suggested that Brod publish his completed foreword elsewhere. It therefore seems likely that Brod's essay in *Die Neue Rundschau*, which was published in November 1921, was an expanded version of this same foreword, originally addressed to Czech readers. (Jesenská, "*Ich hätte zu antworten tage- und nächtelang*," pp. 49–51)

18. Thomas Mann's diary states that Hardt read him prose pieces by Kafka on August 1, 1921, and first made him aware of this author. On September 22, he wrote: "have developed considerable interest in the writings of Franz Kafka, recommended to me by the monologist Hardt" (Thomas Mann, *Diaries: 1918–1939* [New York: Harry N. Abrams, 1982], p. 120). However, Kafka did not live long enough to read Mann's public recommendation in the *Prager Tagblatt* to read the "remarkable" *Trial* (in response to the question: "Which books are you giving as Christmas presents?" Nov. 29, 1925, in Thomas Mann, *Essays II*, p. 1053). In a letter to Kafka on Nov. 29, 1921, F. A. Brockhaus asked for "a brief outline of your life and works for lexical purposes" (unpublished).

19. Letter to Robert Klopstock, Sept. 1921, in Kafka, *Briefe 1902–1924*, p. 357. The French writer Fred Bérence, who seems to have had a long talk with Kafka on this evening at Café Edison, wrote an essay about it ("Zwei Abende mit Franz Kafka" in Koch, "*Als Kafka mir entgegenkam . . .*," pp. 168–72). They got together at Café Edison after Ludwig Hardt's performances as well; see

Johannes Urzidil, *There Goes Kafka*, trans. Harold A. Basilius (Detroit: Wayne State University Press, 1968), p. 24.

20. Kurt Wolff to Kafka, Nov. 3, 1921, in Wolff, *Briefwechsel eines Verlegers*, pp. 54–55.

21. Max Brod, "Der Dichter Franz Kafka" in *Die neue Rundschau*, Nov. 1921, pp. 1210–16. Although Kafka surely disapproved of this eulogy, it was published shortly thereafter in an anthology, *Juden in der deutschen Literatur*, ed. Gustav Krojanker (Berlin: Welt-Verlag, 1922), pp. 55–62.

22. Kurt Wolff to Kafka, March 1, 1922, in Wolff, *Briefwechsel eines Verlegers*, p. 55. Kurt Wolff used the phrases "quite depressed" and "jittery" in a letter to Brod on January 30, 1922, one day after another encounter with Ludwig Hardt, who was most likely still in contact with him by mail at this time (Max Brod Archives, Tel Aviv).

23. Diary, Oct 30, 1921 (T 872). He wrote to Brod in early May 1921: "When you speak to her [Milena] about me, speak as you would of someone dead, I mean as far as my 'externality' is concerned, my 'extraterritoriality.'" (Brod/Kafka, *Briefwechsel*, p. 342) The use of the term "extraterritoriality," which was unusual for Kafka, is an allusion to the writer Albert Ehrenstein, whom he mentioned in the very next sentence. In 1911, Ehrenstein had published "Ansichten eines Exterritorialen," about a cosmic, "extraterrestrial" visitor to the earth (in *Die Fackel*, no. 323, May 18, 1911, pp. 1–8).

24. Letters to Robert Klopstock, Nov. 1921 (Wetscherek, *Kafkas letzter Freund*, p. 27) and Sept. 1921: "Incidentally, I'm too weak to show anyone around town" (Kafka, *Briefe 1902–1924*, p. 357).

25. Letter to Robert Klopstock, Sept. 23, 1921, in Kafka, *Briefe 1902–1924*, p. 353. On this day, Kafka had to stay home from work because of his fever. In September 1921, one hundred Czech kronen could be exchanged for only five or six Swiss francs, which made traveling to former "enemy" or neutral countries quite expensive (when the Czech currency was introduced in the spring of 1919, it had been more than thirty francs).

26. Medical report by Dr. Otto Hermann, Nov. 1921; quoted in Franz Kafka, *Amtliche Schriften*, ed. Klaus Hermsdorf (Berlin: Akademie-Verlag, 1984), p. 438. "Egophony" (from the Greek, meaning "goat sound") designated a nasal voice with a slight bleating quality, a symptom of lung disease. "Fremitus" is a palpable (tactile) vibration of the chest while speaking; increased fremitus indicates thickened lung tissue.

27. This can be deduced from an undated message to Brod: "Dear Max, I'm not coming; I have to eat at 7 or else I can't sleep. The threat of injections is effective." (in Brod/Kafka, *Briefwechsel*, p. 366) Arsenic injections are probably meant here.

28. Kafka, *Amtliche Schriften*, p. 438.

29. Letters to Ottla David, March 9 and mid-June 1921, in Kafka, *Briefe an Ottla und die Familie*, p. 111, 127.

30. Diary, Jan. 16, 1922 (T 877–78).
31. Diary, Jan. 21, 1922 (T 884).
32. Diary, Jan. 23, 1922 (T 887–88).
33. Diary, Oct. 21, 1921 (T 869).

Chapter 23: The Personal Myth

1. S App 115–17.

2. Diary, Jan. 27, 1922 (T 892). Kafka used the term "periods of insanity" in a letter to Robert Klopstock in March 1922 (unpublished).

3. Diary, Jan. 27, 1922 (T 393).

4. See S 67, line 24, and S App 185. For the corresponding scene in *The Trial*, the defendant's fling with the "nurse," Leni, see P 146.

5. "Then I jumped up, abandoning all sense of prudence, and actually made a grab for my gnarled walking stick . . ." (S App 125).

6. A note in the so-called Hunger Artist Notebook (NSF2 373).

7. Diary, Oct. 15 and 16, 1921 (T 863–64).

8. Diary, Jan. 20, 1922 (T 883).

9. Diary, Jan. 18–20, 1922 (T 879–82). Kafka first wrote *Ges* (the first three letters of *Geschlecht*, the German word for "sex"), then reduced this abbreviation to the initial *G*.

10. Letter to Max Brod, early May 1921, in Brod/Kafka, *Briefwechsel*, p. 342.

11. See Hartmut Binder, *Kafka-Kommentar zu den Romanen, Rezensionen, Aphorismen und zum Brief an den Vater* (Munich: Winkler, 1976).

12. This information comes from Pepi, the barmaid (S 488). Kafka's attempt to walk to a bridge is noted in a diary entry dated Jan. 29, 1922 (clearly the "Jubiläumsbrücke" at Weisswasser; no other place matches the geographical description). The corresponding scene in the first chapter of *The Castle* must have been written just after that (T 894). In Spindelmühle, Kafka read *An Arctic Robinson* by Einar Mikkelsen (Leipzig: Brockhaus, 1922). He probably acquired the book while he was in Spindelmühle, and it was found in his literary estate.

13. Frieda mentions the possibility of emigrating to the South of France or to Spain, an idea that K. rejects on the spot. And he is told that many visitors from neighboring villages came to a fire brigade festival (S 24, 215).

14. S 18. Additional, and controversial, models that have been proposed, including the castles in Friedland (here, too, there is a bridge from which the castle can be viewed) and in Wossek, his father's birthplace. Details in Klaus Wagenbach, *Franz Kafka: Biographie seiner Jugend 1883–1912* (Bern, 1958; reprint, Berlin: Wagenbach, 2006), appendix: "Wo liegt Kafkas Schloss?" pp. 265–80.

15. He is likely to have gotten the idea from Božena Němcová's *Babička* (The grandmother), a popular novel Kafka had read to his sisters when he was

a student. Here, too, as in the Amalia episode, a castle official is rejected by a furious woman in the village.

16. Letters from Max Brod to Kafka, Jan. 6 and 19, 1921, in Brod/Kafka, *Briefwechsel*, pp. 294 and 301–2. Max Brod, "Liebe als Diesseitswunder: Das Lied der Lieder," in *Heidentum Christentum Judentum: Ein Bekenntnisbuch* (Munich: Kurt Wolff Verlag, 1921), vol. 2, pp. 5–65; this quotation is on p. 11. Kafka had read this work in manuscript form back in the summer of 1920 and was quite critical, as a letter dated Aug. 7 documents (Brod/Kafka, *Briefwechsel*, p. 282); he had known Brod's view of the erotic "marvel this side of the beyond" for a long time. Most likely Kafka saw Georg Langer's book *Die Erotik der Kabbala* in manuscript form as well; the Talmud quotation is on p. 25 of that book.

17. Letters to Max Brod, Jan. 13 and late Jan. 1921; letter from Max Brod to Kafka, Jan. 19, 1921; in Brod/Kafka, *Briefwechsel*, pp. 297–98, 310, 301.

18. Letter to Max Brod, Aug. 16, 1922, in Brod/Kafka, *Briefwechsel*, p. 411.

19. Letter to Max Brod, Aug. 16, 1922, in Brod/Kafka, *Briefwechsel*, p. 412. A note in Brod's diary indicates that the first open discussion with his wife occurred in early 1924, although she had long known about his lover. The relationship between Brod and Emmy Salveter, who really did find her way into the theater in 1925 (she performed under the stage name Änne Markgraf), lasted into the early 1930s. For additional documents, see Leonhard M. Fiedler, "'Um Hofmannsthal': Max Brod und Hugo von Hofmannsthal; Briefe, Notizen," *Hofmannsthal-Blätter* 30 (August 1985), pp. 23–45.

20. Later editions bore the shortened title *A Second-Class Love*. Kafka knew the biographical background of this novel quite well. He sent it to Milena Pollak in the early part of 1923, evidently at her request. He probably anticipated the former "Minervist's" reaction, as his explanatory and almost apologetic remarks demonstrate (letter to Milena Pollak, Jan./Feb. 1923 in Kafka, *Briefe an Milena* [Frankfurt am Main: S. Fischer, 1983], p. 315). In *Leben mit einer Göttin* (1923) and *Mira: Ein Roman um Hofmannsthal* (1958), Brod also portrayed the conflicts with Emmy Salveter.

21. S 60, 138, 25. The underhandedness with which K. tries to bring about a visit to that "girl from the castle" is the object of "Frieda's Reproof" (the title of chapter 14). For a detailed study of female typology in Kafka's work (and its relationship to Weininger), see Reiner Stach, *Kafkas erotischer Mythos. Eine ästhetische Konstruktion des Weiblichen* (Frankfurt am Main: S. Fischer, 1987).

22. Letter to Milena Pollak, Sept. 2, 1920 (B4 329).

23. The manuscript of *The Castle* documents this tendency to obscure the picture later on. Especially revealing is the episode about the log that Klamm's secretary, Momus, prepares about K.'s behavior. When Momus refuses to let K. look at this log, K. uses gentle force to take it and does not encounter the least resistance; in fact, he is shown the particular page he needs to read. Kafka quotes this page word for word. It charges K. with being a calculating charac-

ter with no feelings for his fiancée, Frieda. It is the only time in any of Kafka's works that his protagonist gets a glimpse of the files, the only direct look at the activities of the authorities the reader is ever given. But Kafka immediately recognized this inconsistency and deleted the entire passage, which extends to several pages in the manuscript—much to the chagrin of Brod, who complained that this log would make the land surveyor's guilt plain to the reader. Perhaps this was why Kafka had the innkeeper at the Bridge Inn and Frieda level these accusations against K. almost verbatim (see S App 272–73; S 243ff.; and the letter from Max Brod to Kafka dated July 24, 1922, in Brod/Kafka, *Briefwechsel*, p. 390).

24. The fact that they remain passive and function like gigantic echo chambers is something the authorities in *The Trial* and *The Castle* have in common. K.'s profession, which only serves him as a pretext, is confirmed by the castle on the telephone the very evening of his arrival (S 12). The two assistants who are to arrive—another white lie on the part of K.—are assigned to him by the castle as substitutes (S 31, 367). K.'s dismissal as a school janitor is rendered invalid simply because K. does not accept it (S 239–40), and although looking into the castle files is prohibited, he is not prevented from doing so (see the preceding note). After Frieda has left K. and returns to work at the bar of the Gentry Inn, an official asks K. to send his fiancée back to the Gentry Inn (S 427–28). Moreover, the "punishment" of Amalia and her family initially comes from the villagers, and then from her own sense of guilt; the castle, however, does not intervene. The official who has been dismissed disappears from the village radar (see the chapters "Amalia's Punishment" and "Petitioning," S 319–45.

25. Letter to Felice Bauer, April 26, 1914 (B3 45); letter to Grete Bloch, June 8, 1914 (B3 83); diary, Feb. 5, 1922 (T 902); letter to Milena Pollak, late March 1922, in Kafka, *Briefe an Milena*, p. 302.

26. Diary, Oct. 17 and 30, 1921 (T 866, 872).

27. Diary, June 12, 1923 (T 926).

28. Diary, Jan. 29, 1922 (T 897).

29. Diary, Jan. 16, 1922 (T 878).

30. Diary, Jan. 24, 28, 29, 1922 (T 890, 893, 895–96).

31. Roberto Calasso, *K.*, trans. Geoffrey Brock (New York: Knopf, 2005), p. 9.

32. This description by the village mayor is far more exhaustive in *The Castle*; see S 96–111.

Chapter 24: Retiree and Hunger Artist

1. Diary, Feb. 12, 1922 (T 906).

2. Excerpts of these medical reports in Kafka, *Amtliche Schriften*, pp. 438–39. On June 7, 1922, Dr. Kodym contributed this rather vague opinion: "For

the foreseeable future, even with uninterrupted spa treatment, no substantial improvement can be expected. There might be a degree of improvement after repeated appropriate treatment."

3. In a letter Kafka wrote to Hans Mardersteig in early May 1922, he mentions having been at the office a few days earlier, for the first time in three months (unpublished).

4. Letter to the Workers' Accident Insurance Institute, June 7, 1922 (AS Mat 837–38). See also the "Service Chart II" with Kafka's earnings (AS Mat 871–73).

5. Kafka's request to make his salary as chief secretary the basis of the calculation was accepted by the Workers' Accident Insurance Institute ("exceptionally accorded"; see AS Mat 875). But the common practice of including, as time served, the months or years that the retired official would have needed for the "automatic" attainment of the next salary level was rejected; in Kafka's case that would have been January 1, 1926. Kafka's notes on the 1920 tax return are reprinted in Nekula, *Franz Kafkas Sprachen*, pp. 358–59.

6. Letter to Robert Klopstock, late March 1922, in Wetscherek, *Kafkas letzter Freund*, p. 43.

7. In the files of the German University in Prague, where Klopstock matriculated on May 8, 1922, his "temporary" place of residence was listed as Kafka's address on Altstädter Ring (see the facsimile in Rotraut Hackermüller, *Kafkas letzte Jahre: 1917–1924* [Munich: Kirchheim, 1990], p. 83). Later, Klopstock took rooms on Bolzanogasse and on Kleinseitner Ring.

8. Letter to Robert Klopstock, April 1922 (unpublished).

9. The rector was the historian Samuel Steinherz (1857–1942), who had been chosen as rector of Charles University for purely formal reasons (he was the senior member of the faculty). The German National attacks continued into the following semester, and on November 15, they occupied the university building and declared a strike. Steinherz offered to leave his post in February 1923, but the minister of education and culture refused to accept his resignation. Steinherz was murdered in Theresienstadt.

10. Letter to Robert Klopstock, April 1922 (unpublished).

11. For additional details on Klopstock's and Kafka's interest in Hungarian literature, see the biographical essays by Christopher Frey and Leo A. Lensing in Wetscherek, *Kafkas letzter Freund*, pp. 83–84 and 275–77.

12. Letter to Robert Klopstock, April 1922 (unpublished).

13. Hans Mardersteig had been the production manager at Kurt Wolff Verlag since the early part of 1917, and in this capacity he was responsible for the technical layout and typographic design of Kafka's *A Country Doctor*. The journal *Genius*, which under Mardersteig's influence devoted far more room to the visual arts than to literature, was published from 1919 until early 1923 (its subtitle was "Journal für Werdende and Alte Art"; the second editor was

Carl Georg Heise). The print run started at 4,000 copies, and each issue ran between 145 and 185 pages.

14. Letter to Max Brod, June 26, 1922, in Brod/Kafka, *Briefwechsel*, p. 370.

15. The Czech phrase means: "you goddamned beasts." See the card to Robert Klopstock dated June 25, 1922 (unpublished) and the letter to Max Brod dated July 12, 1922 (in Brod/Kafka, *Briefwechsel*, p. 386).

16. This and other details from Kafka's situation in Planá according to research by Josef Čermák: "Pobyt Franze Kafky v Plané nad Lužnicí (Léto 1922)," *Světová Literatura* 34 (1989), pp. 219–37.

17. Letter to Max Brod, July 12, 1922, in Brod/Kafka, *Briefwechsel*, p. 384.

18. Letter to Max Brod, July 5, 1922, in Brod/Kafka, *Briefwechsel*, p. 379.

19. See the letter to Max Brod dated Sept. 11, 1922, in Brod/Kafka, *Briefwechsel*, pp. 415–17.

20. Letter from Max Brod to Kafka, Sept. 14, 1922; letter to Max Brod, Aug. 13, 1922, in Brod/Kafka, *Briefwechsel*, pp. 420, 407.

21. Letter to Max Brod, Sept. 11, 1922; letters from Max Brod to Kafka, July 24, 1922 and Sept. 14, 1922, in Brod/Kafka, *Briefwechsel*, pp. 415, 390, 421. In his letter to Hans Mardersteig in early May 1922, Kafka had denigrated the novel in harsh terms, calling it "pathetic stuff, a dreary knitting project, trivial, amateurish work pieced together mechanically." In the letter to Brod on September 11, however, he conceded that "the part written in Planá is not quite as bad as the part you know."

22. Max Brod, advance publication of his afterword to the first edition of *The Castle*, in *Berliner Tageblatt*, Dec. 1, 1926.

23. The realistic details in "First Sorrow" and "A Hunger Artist" clearly stem from his reading of journals in this field. Kafka was acquainted with the trade journal *Der Artist: Central-Organ der Circus, Variété-Bühnen, reisenden Kapellen und Ensembles*, and he even had the less important *Proscenium* sent to Zürau in 1917. Only the fact that the hunger artist is put on display in an animal cage is Kafka's own invention, which obviously allows for the appearance of the panther at the end of the story. Just before "A Hunger Artist," Kafka's manuscript notebook has the beginning of another story from the world of the circus, about an act called "the ride of dreams" and its inventor, who had died of "consumption" long ago (NSF2 383–84). Kafka was still preoccupied with this subject in the final months of his life. Although "A Hunger Artist" had already been published, he wrote a scene in the spring of 1924 in which the hunger artist is visited by a former playmate who is now his diametric opposite, a "cannibal" (NSF2 646–49). For further details, see the essays by Walter Bauer-Wabnegg, "Monster und Maschinen, Artisten und Technik in Franz Kafkas Werk" and Gerhard Neumann, "Hungerkünstler und Menschenfresser: Zum Verhältnis von Kunst und kulturellem Ritual im Werk Franz Kafkas"; both are in *Franz Kafka: Schriftverkehr*, ed. Wolf Kittler and Gerhard Neumann (Freiburg: Rombach Verlag, 1990).

24. Letter to Max Brod, July 5, 1922, in Brod/Kafka, *Briefwechsel*, pp. 377–79.

25. Letter from Max Brod to Kafka, July 9, 1922, in Brod/Kafka, *Briefwechsel*, p. 380.

26. Franz Blei, *Das große Bestiarium der modernen Literatur* (Berlin: Rowohlt, 1922) p. 42. The cited passage in *The Castle* (inserted later by Kafka) can be found on S 229. There are very few chapters in *The Castle* for which dates of composition can be pinned down, but there is no mistaking that this one drew on Blei's characterization. Kafka wrote chapter 8 in early April 1922, and chapter 16 in mid-June. Chapter 13, with its allusion to Blei, was most likely written in May, the same month that the *Bestiary* was published. Blei's book also features entries on "The Brod" and "The Werfel."

Chapter 25: The Palestinian

1. The provisions for his will were dated Nov. 29, 1922, and placed in an envelope labeled "Max." Quoted from Brod/Kafka, *Briefwechsel*, pp. 421–22.

2. "A Hunger Artist" was published in *Die neue Rundschau* in early October 1922, in *Prager Presse* on October 11, in *Sonntagsblatt der New Yorker Volkszeitung* on November 5, in *Wochenblatt der New Yorker Volkszeitung* on November 11, and in *Vorbote: Unabhängiges Organ für die Interessen des Proletariats* (Chicago) on November 15.

3. Letter to Milena Pollak, Oct. 20, 1920, in Kafka, *Briefe an Milena*, p. 283. Letter to Robert Klopstock, Nov. 1921, in Kafka, *Briefe 1902–1924*, p. 363.

4. Letter to Franz Werfel, late Nov. 1922, in Kafka, *Briefe 1902–1924*, pp. 424–25.

5. Draft of a letter to Franz Werfel, after mid-November 1922 (unpublished).

6. Werfel went home without seeing Kafka again. But less than two months later, he returned to Prague for the world premiere of *Schweiger* at the New German Theater on January 6, 1923. It is certain that Kafka did not attend this event, but there is no indication as to whether Kafka and Werfel continued their conversation, aside from an indirect remark in Max Brod's diary dated January 1923: "K. does not like a play by Werfel." Arthur Schnitzler's diary shows that he, like Alma Mahler, considered Werfel's *Schweiger* a complete failure. On December 12, a discussion between Werfel and Schnitzler evidently ran along the lines of Werfel's debate with Kafka in the previous month (see Arthur Schnitzler, *Tagebuch*, vol. 7: *1920–1922* [Vienna: Verlag der Österreichischen Akademie der Wissenschaften, 1995], p. 388). The audience reaction was more positive, and the productions in 1923 were well attended (including one on Königgrätzerstrasse in Berlin, with Werfel's childhood friend Ernst Deutsch in the leading role).

7. Letter to Max Brod, Oct. 22–24, 1923, in Brod/Kafka, *Briefwechsel*, p. 435.

8. Letter to Max Brod, Dec. 1922, in Brod/Kafka, *Briefwechsel*, p. 422.

9. Hans Blüher, *Secessio Judaica: Philosophische Grundlegung de historischen Situation des Judentums und der antisemitischen Bewegung* (Berlin: Der Weisse Ritter Verlag), 1922. In June 1922, Kafka studied this brochure, which was only sixty-six pages in length despite its pompous title, and he attempted to write a review, possibly for *Selbstwehr*, during the week before he left Planá (T 923–24). After failing to complete it, he suggested Klopstock as a reviewer, although Klopstock was not well versed in Jewish history (letter to Robert Klopstock, June 30, 1922, in Wetscherek, *Kafkas letzter Freund*, p. 45). Eventually Oskar Baum took on the assignment: "Philosophischer Antisemitismus: Bemerkungen zu Blühers 'Secessio Judaica,'" in *Selbstwehr* 16, no. 50. On March 7, 1923, Baum also gave a speech about Blüher's work, which Kafka apparently attended.

10. Max Brod to Kafka, Aug. 6, 1922; letter to Max Brod, Aug. 7, 1922; in Brod/Kafka, *Briefwechsel*, pp. 397, 402.

11. On March 12, 1922, Kafka went to a Purim celebration; his niece, Marianne Pollak, was also there. Yet in early 1923, he was still unaware that a bar mitzvah always takes place on the Sabbath; see his letter to Oskar Baum, mid-January 1923, in Kafka, *Briefe 1902–1924*, p. 428.

12. The term "mimicry," which was popularized by Darwinism, was adopted by anti-Semites and Zionists alike to characterize the way in which Jews "camouflaged" themselves in an environment that was "alien in nature" to them; Max Nordau and Theodor Herzl also used the term mimicry in derogatory sense. See Ritchie Robertson, *Kafka: Judaism, Politics, and Literature* (Oxford: Clarendon Press, 1985), pp. 165–66.

13. Blüher, *Secessio Judaica*, pp. 20, 57.

14. Letter to Max Brod, June 30, 1922, in Brod/Kafka, *Briefwechsel*, p. 372.

15. Letter to Max Brod, June 1921, in Brod/Kafka, *Briefwechsel*, p. 360.

16. Letter to Max Brod, June 1921, in Brod/Kafka, *Briefwechsel*, pp. 358–59.

17. Further evidence is a remark Kafka made to Brod: "Karl Kraus locks the Jewish writers into his hell, guards them well, and keeps them under strict discipline. The only thing he forgets is that he belongs in this hell with them" (Brod, *Über Franz Kafka*, p. 70).

18. Kraus used the terms *mauscheln* and *jargon* primarily in reference to a sloppy blend of High German and Yiddish words or intonation, but he never attacked the Yiddish language as such. Kraus even took pleasure in the deliberate use of Yiddishisms in Jewish vaudeville, and he called the performances of the Budapest Orpheum Society some of the best offerings on the Viennese stage. "When there is *mauscheln* in the Burgtheater, that doesn't prove anything. In art, it depends on who is doing the *mauscheln*." (*Die Fackel*, nos. 343–44, p. 21). In Franz Blei's *Bestiary*, Karl Kraus was presented as "The Fackelkraus";

Kraus himself went on to print this rather mean-spirited portrait with commentary (*Die Fackel*, nos. 601–7, pp. 86ff.).

19. Letters to Robert Klopstock, June 30, 1922, and Feb. 29, 1924, in Wetscherek, *Kafkas letzter Freund*, pp. 45, 68. For further details about Kafka's opinions about *Die Fackel*, see Lensing, "'Fackel'-Leser und Werfel-Verehrer," pp. 267–92.

20. NSF2 423–82, 485–91.

21. Ritchie Robertson was the first to demonstrate this literal interpretation of "Investigations of a Dog"; see his *Kafka: Judaism, Politics, and Literature*, pp. 275ff. For the quotations from "Investigations," see NSF2 425–26, 441.

22. Eliezer Ben-Yehuda (born 1858) was a friend and neighbor of Puah's parents, who had emigrated from Russia to Palestine back in the 1880s. In 1911, the first complete Modern Hebrew dictionary, written by Ben-Yehuda, was published in Berlin. Puah did not see him again, because he died on December 16, 1922, during her stay in Prague.

23. In late June 1922, Kafka compiled an order list for Ewer, a Jewish bookstore in Berlin, to give to his sister Elli; the list included Holitscher's book on Palestine, from which Kafka was about to read an excerpt in *Die neue Rundschau* in advance of the book's publication. But Holitscher's coverage (which contained fifteen photographs) did not convey any current information about Palestine because at the time of publication, his trip was already two years in the past.

24. Puah Menczel-Ben-Tovim, "Ich war Kafkas Hebräischlehrerin," in Koch, "*Als Kafka mir entgegenkam . . .* ," p. 178. For further details, see the preface to the volume Puah Menczel-Ben-Tovim edited: *Leben und Wirken: Unser erzieherisches Werk; In memoriam Dr. Josef Schlomo Menczel, 1903–1953* (Jerusalem: Gedächtnisstiftung Dr. J. S. Menczel, 1983), and Pawel, *Nightmare of Reason*, pp. 428–31.

25. Georg Mordechai Langer, "Etwas über Franz Kafka," in Koch, "*Als Kafka mir entgegenkam . . .* ," p. 136. See Hartmut Binder, "Kafkas Hebräischstudien: Ein biographisch-interpretatorischer Versuch," in *Jahrbuch der deutschen Schillergesellschaft* 11 (1967), pp. 527–56.

26. In a conversation with Ernst Pawel, which was published in the *New York Times* on August 16, 1981, Puah Ben-Tovim explained this reason for leaving as follows: "too many proposals, and too many propositions. I was no prude, but I must say that the sexual attitudes and behavior of many Prague intellectuals—whom I otherwise greatly admired—seemed to me shockingly primitive. This by the way remained true later on, when many of them found themselves transplanted to Israel."

27. Hugo to Else Bergmann, early August 1923, Hugo Schmuel Bergmann, *Tagebücher und Briefe* (Königstein: Jüdischer Verlag bei Athenäum, 1985), vol. 1, pp. 170–71. According to Martin S. Bergmann (oral statement, 1997) the family often discussed the danger of contagion.

28. For details about this film, see Hanns Zischler, *Kafka Goes to the Movies*, trans. Susan H. Gillespie (Chicago: University of Chicago Press, 2002), pp. 109ff.

29. Tel Aviv, a settlement that was not founded until 1909, was originally planned as a "garden city" and was mockingly referred to as the "Grunewald of Palestine," in reference to an upscale leafy neighborhood in Berlin. In the 1920s, the number of residents rose from 3,000 to 50,000—a third of the Jewish population of Palestine.

30. Hugo Bergmann, "Schulzeit und Studium," in Koch, "*Als Kafka mir entgegenkam . . .*," p. 29.

31. David Ben Gurion, who later became Israel's first prime minister, stated in June 1919: "Not everybody sees that there's no solution to [the problem in relations between the Jews and the Arabs]. There is no solution! . . . There's a national question here. We want the country to be ours. The Arabs want the country to be theirs" (quoted in Tom Segev, *One Palestine, Complete: Jews and Arabs under the British Mandate*, trans. Haim Watzman [New York: Metropolitan Books, 2000], p. 116).

32. Even before July 24, 1922, the day on which the mandate for Palestine approved by the League of Nations went into effect, the British government had decided to limit Jewish settlement to the territories west of the Jordan, which was about half of the settlement area the Zionists had hoped for. "Transjordan," which was also part of the mandate territory, by contrast (roughly the area that is now Jordan) became a semiautonomous emirate, with the British de facto deciding on the borders alone.

33. Hugo Bergmann to Leo Hermann, July 19, 1922, in Bergmann, *Tagebücher und Briefe*, vol. 1, p. 174. A letter to Robert Weltsch (ibid., p. 171) indicates that Bergmann was undergoing psychoanalytic treatment at this time.

34. Letter to Robert Klopstock, Dec. 1921, in Wetscherek, *Kafkas letzter Freund*, p. 30.

35. The immigration quotas were negotiated privately between the British and the Zionists, but the local Zionist organizations in the countries of origin were the ones to issue the appropriate certificates—Zionist visas, in a manner of speaking. (For Kafka, accordingly, the Zionist district committee in Prague would have been responsible.) This procedure worked out nicely for the British, since they were by and large in agreement as to which people would be excluded—prostitutes, alcoholics, communists, and people with infectious diseases—but it remained a bone of contention among the Jews who were hoping to immigrate, many of whom were not confirmed Zionists. Historical details on this extremely complex question can be found in Segev, *One Palestine, Complete*, pp. 227ff.

36. Letter to Else Bergmann, July 1923, in Kafka, *Briefe 1902–1924*, p. 438. This letter also indicates that Kafka's parents disapproved of his plans to emigrate. Kafka made ironic reference to the "Palestinian danger" that his mother

saw in these plans. A trip from Prague to Jaffa (second class) cost about 3,500 Kč, which amounted to Kafka's income for three and a half months. British, Italian, Yugoslavian, and Austrian visas were required. The information about the portrait photograph is from an oral statement by Martin S. Bergmann.

Chapter 26: Dora

1. Letter to Minze Eisner, winter 1922–1923 (unpublished). The specifics of her operation are unknown.

2. Card to Milena Pollak, May 9, 1923, in Kafka, *Briefe an Milena*, p. 318.

3. Letter to Felice Bauer, Feb. 9, 1914 (B2 328).

4. "Nothing but great weakness and poverty kept me from Berlin, and so prevented the 'offer,' but never would have prevented me from succumbing to the 'offer.'" Letter to Max Brod, Dec. 31, 1920 (B4 380); see Max Brod to Kafka, Dec. 27, 1920 (B4 734–36).

5. For details, see Puah Menczel, "In memoriam Emma und Salomon Goldschmidt: Eine deutsche jüdische Familie," in Puah Menczel-Ben-Tovim, *Leben und Wirken*, pp. 62–63.

6. Letter to Max Bod, July 10, 1923, in Brod/Kafka, *Briefwechsel*, p. 427.

7. Tile (Tilla) Rössler later wrote quite sentimental recollections of Kafka that are not consistently reliable and understandably highlight her own role. Excerpts of these writings were published under the title "'Hörst du, Tile, Franz heisst die Kanaille!' Tile Rösslers Begegnungen mit Franz Kafka," in Koch, "*Als Kafka mir entgegenkam . . .* ," pp. 180–93. Still, these notes are an important source, because Kafka's own correspondence from Müritz was quite sparse. Also, the feature of Kafka that she emphasized, namely the way he took the emotional and practical conflicts of teenagers seriously, was witnessed and documented elsewhere, such as in his letters to Minze Eisner. Beginning in the mid-1920s, Tile Rössler studied modern dance at the Palucca School in Dresden; later she worked as a choreographer in Israel.

8. Dora Diamant, "Mein Leben mit Franz Kafka," in Koch, "*Als Kafka mir entgegenkam . . .* ," p. 194.

9. Ibid., p. 195. For a long time, very little was known about Dora Diamant's early years. Much of the information included here draws on Kathi Diamant's pioneering work in her book *Kafka's Last Love: The Mystery of Dora Diamant* (New York: Basic Books, 2003).

10. An indication that tuberculosis caused her death is found in one of the "Conversation Slips" Kafka wrote in the last month of his life: "Tell me again how your mother drank . . . Did she never have a complication that made it forbidden for her to drink for a while?" (Kafka, *Briefe 1902–1924*, p. 486) Since Kafka did not address anyone besides Dora with the familiar *du* while he was in Kierling, and the slip uses that form of address, it is evident that Frajda Diamant is meant here.

11. Ludwig Nelken, "Ein Arztbesuch bei Kafka," in Koch, "*Als Kafka mir entgegenkam . . . ,*" p. 211.

12. Diamant, "Mein Leben mit Franz Kafka," p. 194.

13. Letter to Hugo Bergmann, July 1923; letter to Robert Klopstock, early August 1923; in Kafka, *Briefe 1902–1924*, pp. 436, 441. On Kafka's observation of the refugee children in the Jewish Town Hall in Prague, see his letter to Milena Pollak dated September 7, 1920: "[I]f someone had told me last night I could be whatever I wanted, I would have chosen to be a small Jewish boy from the East" (B4 338).

14. Card to Max Brod, Aug. 29, 1923, in Brod/Kafka, *Briefwechsel*, p. 429.

Chapter 27: The Edge of Berlin

1. Milena Jesenská, "Ďábel u krbu," in *Národní Listy*, Jan. 18, 1923, pp. 1–2. A German translation, by Kurt Krolop, is printed in the appendix to Kafka, *Briefe an Milena*, pp. 394–401; this quotation is on pp. 394–95. For Kafka's remarks, written in January or February, see ibid., pp. 309–13.

2. Dora Diamant, "Mein Leben mit Franz Kafka," in Koch, "*Als Kafka mir entgegenkam . . . ,*" p. 199.

3. Card to Ottla David, Oct. 2, 1923 in Kafka, *Briefe an Ottla und die Familie*, pp. 134–35.

4. Dora was not even mentioned in the postcards to Ottla before December, although his sister did know the circumstances; evidently Kafka wanted to ensure that these cards could be shown to their parents.

5. Kafka quoted this saying in a letter to Valli Pollak, Nov. 12–15, 1923, in Kafka, *Briefe 1902–1924*, p. 463.

6. Letter to Max Brod, Oct. 22–24, 1923, in Brod/Kafka, *Briefwechsel*, p. 435.

7. Alfred Döblin, "Während der Schlacht singen die Musen," in *Prager Tagblatt*, Nov. 11, 1923, pp. 3–4.

8. Quoted in Kafka's letter to his parents dated Nov. 20, 1923, in Kafka, *Briefe an die Eltern aus den Jahren 1922–1924*, p. 42.

9. Letter to Ottla David, Nov. 22, 1923 (unpublished).

10. See his letter to Ottla and Josef David in mid-December 1923, in which Kafka formulated his Czech letter to Bedřich Odstrčil in German, in Kafka, *Briefe an Ottla und die Familie*, pp. 149–51. Kafka characterized his place of residence here as follows: "Steglitz is a semirural suburb of Berlin, rather like a garden city; I am living in a small house with a garden and glass veranda; half-hour walk between gardens takes one to Grunewald; the great botanical garden is ten minutes away, there are other parks in the neighborhood, and every street away from mine leads through gardens" (ibid., p. 150). It seems highly implausible that Kafka's family doctor approved this area in advance, because

the move to Steglitz was not decided on until Kafka was in Schelesen, and after that he spent just one day in Prague. The German-language version of the director's reply, dated December 31, 1923, is in Franz Kafka, *Briefe an die Eltern aus den Jahren 1922–1924*, p. 103.

11. Letter to Hermann and Julie Kafka, late October/early November 1923, ibid., p. 35. On November 22, Kafka wrote to Ottla that he had to "spend 31 trillion as quickly as possible" before it lost even more of its value (unpublished).

12. D 322, 328, 333. Dora Diamant's memoirs confirm that this really is a portrait of the landlady in Steglitz; see "Mein Leben mit Franz Kafka" p. 198.

13. Letter to Ottla David, Jan. 3 or 4, 1924, in Kafka, *Briefe an Ottla und die Familie*, p. 154. The lines in Dora's hand read as follows: "Just very, very warm regards. So tired! I'm already asleep. Goodnight."

14. Letter to Tile Rössler, Aug. 3, 1923, in Kafka, *Briefe 1902–1924*, p. 439.

15. "Werfel came by once to read to Kafka from his latest book. After they had been together for a long time, I saw Werfel leave in tears. When I entered the room, Kafka was sitting there utterly shattered. He murmured to himself several times, 'To think that there can be something so terrible!' He, too, was weeping. He had let Werfel go away without being able to say a single word about his book" (Diamant, "Mein Leben mit Franz Kafka," p. 202). It is not known which text Werfel was reading from. Kafka's meeting with Kisch and his lover, Jarmila Haas, is documented in the memoirs of Nico Rost, a Dutch journalist who was living in Berlin at the time and witnessed the encounter ("Persoonlijke ontmoetingen met Franz Kafka en mijn Tsjechische vrienden" in *De Vlaamse Gids* 48 (Feb. 1964), pp. 75–97). Kafka did not invite the three of them to his home, however, but instead arranged to meet with them on a park bench in Steglitz, without Dora. Another possible visitor was Manfred Georg (later known as Manfred George), an attorney, writer, and journalist who subsequently funded *Aufbau*, an emigrants' journal in New York. Dora Diamant had met Georg in Breslau, where he was working as a correspondent for the *Vossische Zeitung*. In 1923, he returned to Berlin and wrote theater reviews for the *Berliner Volkszeitung*. Kafka's chance meeting with the Dadaist Raoul Hausmann, about which the latter later wrote, may be fiction (see Hausmann, "Begegnung mit Franz Kafka 1923 in Berlin" in Koch, "*Als Kafka mir entgegenkam . . .* ," pp. 206–10).

16. Letter to Max Brod, Nov. 5, 1923, in Brod/Kafka, *Briefwechsel*, p. 443.

17. Lise Weltsch can be seen together with Kafka on the famous photograph with the airplane display (Vienna, 1913); see Stach, *Kafka: The Decisive Years*, illustration 39.

18. Postcard to Robert Klopstock, Dec. 19, 1923, in Kafka, *Briefe 1902–1924*, p. 470. In an interview with Ernst Pawel (*New York Times*, Aug. 16, 1981), Puah Ben-Tovim explained that she even helped with the housework: "Dora didn't know much about keeping house, so I did some sewing and laundry for

them." Since one of Dora Diamant's jobs that year was as a seamstress in a Jewish orphanage, it is rather unlikely; all other evidence indicates that she was actually a skilled housekeeper.

19. Yosef Haim Brenner, *Breakdown and Bereavement* (Tel Aviv: Shtiebel, 1920). The contents of the first three chapters, which Kafka definitely read, can be found in Binder, "Kafkas Hebräischstudien," p. 550. Brenner was killed at the age of forty in May 1921 during the Arab riots in Jaffa, a fact of which Kafka was surely aware.

20. Postcard to Robert Klopstock, Dec. 19, 1923, in Kafka, *Briefe 1902–1924*, p. 470.

21. On December 21, 1923, in a postcard to his sister Elli, Kafka sent a list of destitute Jews to a Jewish women's organization in Prague that sent food packages to Germany. This list included Ernst Weiss and an auditor at the Jewish Academy (with the remark "kosher"). Of the teachers whose lectures Kafka attended, only one is identifiable: Rabbi Julius Grünthal. Leo Baeck was also a lecturer at the Hochschule, but there is no documentation of a meeting with Kafka.

22. According to a note written by Dora Diamant; see Kathi Diamant, *Kafka's Last Love*, pp. 77–78.

23. Hella Rohm, "Die armen Ausländer in Berlin," in *Prager Tagblatt*, Dec. 21, 1923, p. 3.

24. Kafka's namesake, who was first listed in the Berlin address book in 1924, lived in the Schöneberg neighborhood, at Würzburer Strasse 4.

25. Postcard to Hermann and Julie Kafka, Nov. 30, 1923 (unpublished).

26. Rainer Maria Rilke to Kurt Wolff, Feb. 17, 1922 in Wolff, *Briefwechsel eines Verlegers*, p. 152. Rilke had received a set of new publications from Wolff and read Kafka's *A Country Doctor* first.

27. See Kafka's wish list in a letter to Georg Heinrich Meyer in late November 1923, as well as the complaint (his last known letter to the publisher) dated December 31, 1923, in Wolff, *Briefwechsel eines Verlegers*, pp. 59–60.

28. Kurt Wolff to Franz Werfel, Aug. 24, 1921, in Wolff, *Briefwechsel eines Verlegers*, p. 344.

29. Herbert Eulenberg, "Unsre Verleger" in *Die Weltbühne* 20, no. 2 (Jan. 10, 1924), p. 48. One telling example was an ongoing dispute between Arthur Schnitzler and his publisher Samuel Fischer, which centered in part on the allocation of currency payments and almost resulted in their parting ways. Fischer even offered to pay for Schnitzler's train ride to Berlin so that he could have a look at the accounting records. See Samuel Fischer and Hedwig Fischer, *Briefwechsel mit Autoren*, ed. Dierk Rodewald and Corinna Fiedler (Frankfurt am Main: S. Fischer, 1989), pp. 134ff. Kafka's statement comes from a letter to Max Brod, Nov. 2, 1923, in Brod/Kafka, *Briefwechsel*, p. 441.

30. Ernst Weiss to Kurt Wolff, Sept. 11, 1922 in Wolff, *Briefwechsel eines Verlegers*, pp. 381–82.

31. The contract that was drawn up by Die Schmiede on March 7, 1924, provided an advance of 750 goldmarks, payable in two installments, which came to about 6,300 Kč at that time. In mid-March, Kafka wrote to his sister Elli that Dora would follow Brod's advice to renegotiate this sum to raise it to 8,000 Kč (unpublished). It is quite likely that Kafka actually received this higher advance, because according to the contract, 2,000 copies of *A Hunger Artist* were to be paid in advance, but 3,000 copies were printed.

32. The physician who was a relative of Lise Weltsch was Professor Eugen Kisch, who taught at the Hohenlychen tuberculosis sanatorium in Berlin and also published articles about tuberculosis. Dora finally confessed to Kafka a few days later that she had called Elli, but she appears not to have let on that she had asked for money because when Elli sent 500 kronen (about 60 marks) in January without any explanation, Kafka could not figure out why he was getting this gift. See his letter to Elli Hermann dated December 28, 1923 (unpublished), and to Hermann and Julie Kafka, January 28, 1924, in Kafka, *Briefe an die Eltern aus den Jahren 1922–1924*, p. 54.

33. Letter to Ottla David, October 8, 1923, in Kafka, *Briefe an Ottla und die Familie*, p. 137.

34. Letter to Max Brod, ca. Jan. 14, 1924, in Brod/Kafka, *Briefwechsel*, p. 450.

35. Ibid. He used the same wording in a postcard to Felix Weltsch, Jan. 28, 1924, in Kafka, *Briefe 1902–1924*, p. 475.

36. Since Hardt wrote that on this occasion he was seeing Kafka for the last time, the dedication was presumably written in February 1924. And his memory of reciting poems by Matthias Claudius at Kafka's "sickbed" refers to this time. See Hardt, "Der Autor und sein Rezitator," pp. 213–14.

37. See the recollections of Christine Geier (née Busse) in Heike Faller, "Die Suche," in *Die Zeit* (2001), sec. 2 ("Life"), p. 4. Kafka's landlady, Paula Busse, later survived the Theresienstadt concentration camp.

38. Nelken refused to send a bill, however, so Kafka gave him a copy of Georg Simmel's essay on Rembrandt, which he had himself received gratis from Kurt Wolff Verlag. The date of the doctor's visit is unclear. Nelken reports it was in early May 1924, but it is unlikely that Dora Diamant would have waited until just before Kafka was preparing to leave Berlin to ask for help from this doctor, whom she knew personally. See Nelken, "Ein Arztbesuch bei Kafka," pp. 211–12.

39. Postcard to Julie Kafka, Feb. 23, 1924, in Kafka, *Briefe an die Eltern aus den Jahren 1922–1924*, p. 63.

40. Postcard to Hermann and Julie Kafka, March 1, 1924, in ibid., p. 64.

41. Between February 21 and March 21, 1924, Karl Kraus gave a total of twelve readings at the Lustspielhaus in Berlin. The programs are listed in *Die Fackel*, nos. 649–56, pp. 74–75. For details on Kafka's readings in *Die Fackel*, see his postcard to Robert Klopstock, Feb. 29, 1924, in Wetscherek, p. 68.

42. In view of this prolonged separation, Siegfried Löwy's suggestion was astonishing, and would appear to indicate that he wanted to spare the Kafkas the sight of their ailing son, who looked startlingly different. See Kafka's letter to Robert Klopstock, early March 1924 in Kafka, *Briefe 1902–1924*, p. 479.

43. Letter to Hermann and Julie Kafka and to Ottla David, Jan. 5–8, 1924, in Kafka, *Briefe an die Eltern aus den Jahren 1922–1924*, p. 52.

44. Only after Dora Diamant had confessed to Brod in April 1933 that the notebooks had not been lost until this search of her home did he turn to the writer Camill Hoffmann, who was then cultural attaché at the Czech embassy in Berlin. Hoffmann's attempt to get Kafka's papers back from the Gestapo was unsuccessful. Ludwig ("Lutz") Lask (born 1903) was suspected of being involved in the production and distribution of the banned *Rote Fahne*; he was in Gestapo custody in 1933, as were his mother and two brothers. He was tortured and interned in a camp for several months. In 1934 he fled to the Soviet Union via Prague; four years later, he was arrested there on spying charges and was sentenced to prison camp in Siberia. He died in East Berlin in 1973.

45. Diamant, "Mein Leben mit Franz Kafka," pp. 196–198. The version provided by Max Brod contains several deviations: Kafka claims to have seen and spoken to the doll (which is more plausible than the story of getting a letter), and he ends the matter by giving the child another doll before leaving Berlin (which is highly unlikely, because if that were so, he would have maintained contact with the girl in Steglitz from his apartment in Zehlendorf). See Brod, *Über Franz Kafka*, pp. 338–39.

46. In 1959, a call was put out in Steglitz to attempt to locate the girl in the park and thus Kafka's doll letters. Kafka translator Mark Harman repeated this attempt in 2001, but he was also unsuccessful.

47. Letter to Elli Hermann, Oct. 4, 1923 (unpublished).

Chapter 28: Last Sorrow

1. NSF2 600–601. The story is untitled in the manuscript.

2. However, the idea that "The Burrow" was completed, as Dora Diamant later claimed to recall, is unlikely. If that had been the case, Kafka, who was in desperate need of money, would have offered the text for publication and included it in the contract with Die Schmiede. Analyses of the manuscript have shown that Kafka's work on "The Burrow" was interrupted by the severe bouts of fever he suffered in late December 1923; see NSF2 App 142ff.

3. Even the inconsistent description of the noise in "The Burrow" supports this reading. At first, we are told, "it is not even constant, the way such noises tend to be; there are long pauses," but the text later speaks in terms of "brief pauses" instead (NSF2 607, 624).

4. D 352, 362. The fact that Kafka picked an animal species so unlike humans seems to have stemmed from his devoted reading of the *Fackel*. Since

December 1922, Karl Kraus had been using the polemical term "Little Mouse" (taken from Mechthilde Lichnowsky), which he defined as follows: "if something makes a grand gesture of something but displays nothing but a total failure in showing it off, one must plant oneself in front of it with arms crossed, let it play out, look thoughtful, and in a whisper, so as not to interrupt, simply say: 'Little Mouse!'" (*Die Fackel*, nos. 608–612, p. 71). See Lensing, "'Fackel'-Leser und Werfel-Verehrer," pp. 280ff.

5. Max Brod, *Über Franz Kafka*, p. 339.

6. Kafka, *Briefe 1902–1924*, p. 521; D 367.

7. Postcard to Hermann and Julie Kafka, Apr. 13, 1924, in Kafka, *Briefe an die Eltern aus den Jahren 1922–1924*, p. 71.

8. Michal Mareš, "Kafka und die Anarchisten," in Koch, "*Als Kafka mir entgegenkam . . .*," p. 90.

9. Postcard to Hermann and Julie Kafka, Apr. 7, 1924, in Kafka, *Briefe an die Eltern aus den Jahren 1922–1924*, p. 67. Siegfried Löwy, who was originally intending to bring Kafka to Davos, had been in Venice for the past two weeks and was therefore unavailable as a travel companion. According to Dora Diamant's memoirs, one of Kafka's sisters went with him, but if that was the case, it would seem odd that Kafka kept pointing out the great distance between Vienna and the sanatorium to his parents, as though that were news to them.

10. Letter to Max Brod, Apr. 20, 1924, in Brod/Kafka, *Briefwechsel*, p. 454. Postcard to Hermann and Julie Kafka, Apr. 21, 1924 in Kafka, *Briefe an die Eltern aus den Jahren 1922–1924*, p. 74.

11. Letter to Robert Klopstock, Apr. 7, 1924, in Wetscherek, *Kafkas letzter Freund*, p. 69.

12. Postcard to Hermann and Julie Kafka, Apr. 9, 1924, in Kafka, *Briefe an die Eltern aus den Jahren 1922–1924*, pp. 67–68. Postcard to Max Brod, Apr. 9, 1924, in Brod/Kafka, *Briefwechsel*, p. 453.

13. Brod, *Über Franz Kafka*, p. 178. The story that Dora Diamant stood up throughout the hours of the journey to Vienna to protect Kafka from the rain (as Brod reports here) is probably a legend. It is highly unlikely that the renowned Wienerwald sanatorium would have allowed patients to be treated this way. It would appear that Kafka was in an open car for only the three miles it took to get to the train station in Ortmann, which was bad enough in his condition.

14. Robert Klopstock to Ottla David, mid-April 1924 (Archiv Kritische Kafka-Ausgabe, Wuppertal). Markus Hajek (1862–1941) was a student of Johann Schnitzler, a renowned laryngologist and the father of Arthur Schnitzler. Hajek worked at the polyclinic in Vienna as an attending physician at the same time as Arthur Schnitzler and later became his brother-in-law. Hajek was a contributor to the first *Clinical Atlas of Laryngology* (1895), and a pioneer in the field of endonasal surgery. He founded an outpatient clinic for voice and speech disorders at the Laryngological Clinic in Vienna.

15. See the facsimiles in Hackermüller, *Kafkas letzte Jahre*, pp. 111–13.

16. See Markus Hajek, *Pathologie und Therapie der Erkrankungen des Kehlkopfes, der Luftröhre und der Bronchien* (Leipzig: C. Kabitzsch, 1932), p. 263.

17. Postcard to Hermann and Julie Kafka, Apr. 16, 1924, in Kafka, *Briefe an die Eltern aus den Jahren 1922–1924*, p. 73.

18. A note evidently intended for Klopstock on one of the "conversation slips" in Kafka, *Briefe 1902–1924*, p. 487. On Josef Schrammel, see Hackermüller, *Kafkas letzte Jahre*, pp. 114ff. Kafka could not have known that Sigmund Freud almost bled to death a year earlier after being operated on by Hajek, also because of the staff's negligence. See Peter Gay, *Freud: A Life for Our Time* (New York: W. W. Norton, 2006), p. 419.

19. Franz Werfel to Max Brod, ca. Apr. 27, 1924 (Archives of the Kafka Critical Edition, Wuppertal). Hajek's supposed statement quoted in Brod, *Über Franz Kafka*, p. 178. It is impossible for Hajek, who got together with his brother-in-law Arthur Schnitzler quite often, not to have heard of Werfel, who was famous in Vienna. Schnitzler's diary indicates that Hajek went to the theater with Schnitzler at least once, and that he saw Schnitzler on another day shortly before Schnitzler attended a performance of Werfel's *Mirror Man* (May 25, 1922, and March 10, 1923; see Arthur Schnitzler, *Tagebuch 1920–1922*, p. 311; *Tagebuch 1923–1926*, pp. 32–33).

20. See the postcard to Hermann and Julie Kafka dated April 25, 1924, in Kafka, *Briefe an die Eltern aus den Jahren 1922–1924*, p. 76. Julius Tandler, the city councilman Werfel brought in, might have been able to get Kafka a bed at a reduced price (or even free) at the Grimmenstein sanatorium in Lower Austria, but Kafka did not follow through, because he did not feel that he was able to undertake the journey or to endure the hustle and bustle of a large sanatorium.

21. Oscar Beck to Felix Weltsch, May 3, 1924; quoted in Brod, *Über Franz Kafka*, p. 179.

22. Dora Diamant and Kafka to Hermann and Julie Kafka, ca. May 19, 1924, in Kafka, *Briefe an die Eltern aus den Jahren 1922–1924*, p. 78. Dora Diamant to Elli Hermann, May 5, 1924 (Archives of the Kafka Critical Edition, Wuppertal).

23. When Alfred Löwy died in Madrid on February 28, 1923, a rumor circulated in Prague that the Kafkas had inherited an immense fortune. After Alfred's sister, Julie Kafka, went to Paris in September 1923 to clarify the legal and tax questions, Kafka wrote to Brod, "The truth is that the estate amounts to about 600,000 crowns gross, and three uncles have a claim to it in addition to my mother. Even so, that would still be pretty good, but unfortunately the chief participants are the French and Spanish governments and the notaries and lawyers of Paris and Madrid" (letter to Max Brod, Nov. 2, 1923, in Brod/Kafka, *Briefwechsel*, p. 441). It is not known when and in what amount the inheritance was finally paid out.

24. See Kafka, *Briefe 1902–1924*, pp. 484–91, and D App 395–96.

25. Brod, *Über Franz Kafka*, p. 181. A jocular remark by Kafka that has been preserved on one of the conversation slips may contain a veiled reference to this marriage plan: "we want to live there, and you're already starting with the gossip." That can logically refer only to where her father lived or to Breslau.

26. The texts in question were the first publications of the two stories "Josefine, the Singer" in *Prager Presse*, Apr. 20, 1924; and "A Little Woman," in *Prager Tagblatt*, Apr. 20, 1924 (abridged version). *Reubeni: Prince of the Jews* was published by Kurt Wolff in 1925. Brod read Kafka the beginning of the novel in May 1923 and noted in his diary: "He is delighted."

27. Letter to Max Brod, May 20, 1924, in Brod/Kafka, *Briefwechsel*, p. 456. In January 1924, Brod switched from the semiofficial *Prager Presse* over to the *Prager Tagblatt*, where he published far more than a hundred articles a year until 1939. See Peter Doležal, pp. 131ff.

28. Letter to Hermann and Julie Kafka, ca. May 19, 1924, in Kafka, *Briefe an die Eltern aus den Jahren 1922–1924*, p. 79. Robert Klopstock to Elli Hermann, ca. May 20, 1924 (Archives of the Kafka Critical Edition, Wuppertal).

29. Quoted in Brod, *Über Franz Kafka*, p. 185.

30. On a slip of paper in Klopstock's literary estate, there is this remark by Kafka, "Read the episode in Werfel's novel as well. Once again, it affects me as deeply as *Schweiger*; I can't say anything about it" (Wetscherek, *Kafkas letzter Freund*, p. 74). Werfel's *Verdi* was certainly not the last book Kafka read, because in addition to the books from Brod, Die Schmiede also sent him a package of books that appears to have arrived in Kierling in early May (see D App 393). Kafka received another (unnamed) book on May 20, which he had requested, and which Brod arranged for him to get from a bookstore in Prague (see Brod/Kafka, *Briefwechsel*, p. 456). The message to Brod is from a letter dated Apr. 28, 1924, in ibid., p. 455.

31. Kafka, *Briefe 1902–1924*, p. 520.

32. Brod, *Über Franz Kafka*, p. 182.

33. Letter to Hermann and Julie Kafka, June 2, 1924, in Kafka, *Briefe an die Eltern aus den Jahren 1922–1924*, pp. 80–82.

34. A German translation of Milena Jesenská's obituary is found in Hackermüller, *Kafkas letzte Jahre*, pp. 158–59. The German-language obituaries are reprinted in Born, *Franz Kafka: Kritik und Rezeption 1924–1938*, pp. 16ff.

35. Urzidil, *There Goes Kafka*, pp. 201, 202, 200.

36. Urzidil, *There Goes Kafka*, 187.

BIBLIOGRAPHY

Works on Kafka

Alt, Peter-André. *Franz Kafka: Der ewige Sohn.* Munich: C. H. Beck, 2005.

Anz, Thomas. "Jemand musste Otto G. verleumdet haben ... Kafka, Werfel, Otto Gross und eine 'psychiatrische Geschichte.'" *Akzente* 31, no. 2 (1984), pp. 184–91.

Baioni, Giuliano. *Kafka: Literatur und Judentum.* Stuttgart: Metzler, 1994.

Baudy, Nicolas. "Entretiens avec Dora Dymant, compagne de Kafka." *Evidences* (Paris) 8 (February 1950), pp. 21–25.

Bauer-Wabnegg, Walter. "Monster und Maschinen, Artisten und Technik in Franz Kafkas Werk." *Franz Kafka: Schriftverkehr.* Ed. Wolf Kittler and Gerhard Neumann. Freiburg: Rombach Verlag, 1990, pp. 316–82.

Benjamin über Kafka: Texte, Briefzeugnisse, Aufzeichnungen. Ed. Hermann Schweppenhäuser. Frankfurt am Main: Suhrkamp, 1981.

Binder, Hartmut. "Franz Kafka und die Wochenschrift 'Selbstwehr.'" *Deutsche Vierteljahresschrift für Literaturwissenschaft und Geistesgeschichte* 41 (1967), pp. 283–304.

———, ed. *Kafka-Handbuch.* Vol. 1: *Der Mensch und seine Zeit.* Vol. 2: *Das Werk und seine Wirkung.* Stuttgart: Kröner, 1979.

———. *Kafka-Kommentar zu den Romanen, Rezensionen, Aphorismen und zum Brief an den Vater.* Munich: Winkler, 1976.

———. *Kafka-Kommentar zu sämtlichen Erzählungen.* Munich: Winkler, 1975.

———. "Kafka und seine Schwester Ottla." *Jahrbuch der deutschen Schillergesellschaft* 12 (1968), pp. 403–56.

——— "Kafkas Briefscherze: Sein Verhältnis zu Josef David." *Jahrbuch der deutschen Schillergesellschaft* 13 (1969), pp. 536–59.

———. "Kafkas Hebräischstudien: Ein biographisch-interpretatorischer Versuch." *Jahrbuch der deutschen Schillergesellschaft* 11 (1967), pp. 527–56.

———. *Kafkas "Verwandlung": Entstehung, Deutung, Wirkung.* Frankfurt am Main: Stroemfeld, 2004.

———. "Puder und Schleier, Glanz und Genuss: Eine Entdeckung; Kafkas späte Verlobte Julie Wohryzek." *Neue Zürcher Zeitung,* April 28–29, 2001, p. 49.

Born, Jürgen, ed. *Franz Kafka: Kritik und Rezeption zu seinen Lebzeiten 1912–1924*. Frankfurt am Main: S. Fischer, 1979.

———, ed. *Franz Kafka: Kritik und Rezeption 1924–1938*. Frankfurt am Main: S. Fischer, 1983.

———. *Kafkas Bibliothek: Ein beschreibendes Verzeichnis*. Frankfurt am Main: S. Fischer, 1990.

Born, Jürgen, Ludwig Dietz, Malcolm Pasley, Paul Raabe, and Klaus Wagenbach, eds. *Kafka-Symposion*. Berlin: Klaus Wagenbach, 1965.

Brod, Max. "Der Dichter Franz Kafka." *Die neue Rundschau* 32 (1921), pp. 1210–16.

———. *Über Franz Kafka*. Frankfurt am Main: S. Fischer, 1974. (This volume contains the following book-length works: *Franz Kafka: Eine Biographie*, *Franz Kafkas Glauben und Lehre*, and *Verzweiflung und Erlösung im Werk Franz Kafkas*.)

Calasso, Roberto. *K*. Trans. Geoffrey Brock. New York: Knopf, 2005.

Canetti, Elias. *Kafka's Other Trial: The Letters to Felice*. Trans. Christopher Middleton. New York: Schocken Books, 1974.

Caputo-Mayr, Maria Luise, and Julius Michael Herz, eds. *Franz Kafka: Internationale Bibliographie der Primär- und Sekundärliteratur; Eine Einführung*. 2nd ed. 2 vols. Munich: K. G. Saur, 2000.

Čermák, Josef. *Franz Kafka: Výmysly a mystifikace*. Prague: Odeon, 2005.

———. "Pobyt Franze Kafky v Plané nad Lužnicí (Léto 1922)." *Světová Literatura* 34, no. 1 (1989), pp. 219–37.

Diamant, Kathi. *Kafka's Last Love: The Mystery of Dora Diamant*. New York: Basic Books, 2003.

Dietz, Ludwig. *Franz Kafka: Die Veröffentlichungen zu seinen Lebzeiten (1908–1924); Eine textkritische und kommentierte Bibliographie*. Heidelberg: Stiehm, 1982.

Gelber, Mark H., ed. *Kafka, Zionism, and Beyond*. Tübingen: De Gruyter, 2004.

Gilman, Sander. *Franz Kafka, the Jewish Patient*. New York: Routledge, 1995.

Grözinger, Karl Erich. *Kafka and Kabbalah*. Trans. Susan Hecker Ray. New York: Continuum, 1994.

Grözinger, Karl Erich, Stéphane Mosès, and Hans Dieter Zimmermann, eds. *Kafka und das Judentum*. Frankfurt am Main: Athenäum, 1987.

Gruša, Jiři. "Die Verlockung auf dem Dorfe oder 'Die Jungfrau und das Ungeheuer.'" *Nach erneuter Lektüre: Franz Kafkas "Der Process."* Ed. Hans Dieter Zimmermann. Würzburg: Königshausen & Neumann, 1992, pp. 251–67.

Hackermüller, Rotraut. *Kafkas letzte Jahre: 1917–1924*. Munich: Kirchheim, 1990.

Hermes, Roger, Waltraud John, Hans-Gerd Koch, and Anita Widera, comp. *Franz Kafka: Eine Chronik.* Berlin: Klaus Wagenbach, 1999.

Janouch, Gustav. *Conversations with Kafka.* Trans. Gornwy Rees. 2nd ed. New York: New Directions, 2012.

Kafka, Franz. *Amtliche Schriften.* Ed. Klaus Hermsdorf. Berlin: Akademie-Verlag, 1984. Excerpts of Kafka's office writings have been compiled into an English translation, edited by Stanley Corngold, Jack Greenberg, and Benno Wagner, and translated by Eric Patton with Ruth Hein: *Kafka: The Office Writings.* Princeton: Princeton University Press, 2008.

———. *Beim Bau der Chinesischen Mauer: Ungedruckte Erzählungen und Prosa aus dem Nachlass.* Ed. Max Brod and Hans-Joachim Schoeps. Berlin, 1931. Reprint, Hildesheim: G. Olms, 2008.

———. *Beschreibung eines Kampfes: Novellen, Skizzen, Aphorismen aus dem Nachlass.* Prague: Heinrich Mery Sohn, 1936.

———. *Briefe 1902–1924.* Frankfurt am Main: S. Fischer, 1958.

———. *Briefe an die Eltern aus den Jahren 1922–1924.* Ed. Josef Čermák and Martin Svatoš. Frankfurt am Main: S. Fischer, 1990.

———. *Briefe an Felice und andere Korrespondenz aus der Verlobungszeit.* Ed. Erich Heller and Jürgen Born. Frankfurt am Main: S. Fischer, 1967.

———. *Briefe an Milena.* Frankfurt am Main: S. Fischer, 1983.

———. *Briefe an Ottla und die Familie.* Ed. Hartmut Binder and Klaus Wagenbach. Frankfurt am Main: S. Fischer, 1974.

Karl, Frederick R. *Franz Kafka: Representative Man.* New York: Ticknor & Fields, 1991.

Kilcher, Andreas. "Franz Kafkas 'hebräische Kraftanstrengung.'" *Neue Zürcher Zeitung,* April 8, 2000.

Koch, Hans-Gerd, ed. *"Als Kafka mir entgegenkam . . .": Erinnerungen an Franz Kafka.* Expanded ed. Berlin: Klaus Wagenbach, 2005.

———. *Kafka in Berlin: Eine historische Stadtreise.* Berlin: Klaus Wagenbach, 2008.

———. "Kafkas Max und Brods Franz: Vexierbild einer Freundschaft." *Literarische Zusammenarbeit.* Ed. Bodo Plachta. Tübingen: Max Niemeyer, 2001, pp. 245–56.

Koch, Hans-Gerd, and Klaus Wagenbach, eds. *Kafkas Fabriken.* Marbach am Neckar: Schillergesellschaft, 2002.

Lensing, Leo A. "'Fackel'-Leser und Werfel-Verehrer: Anmerkungen zu Kafkas Briefen an Robert Klopstock." *Kafkas letzter Freund: Der Nachlaß Robert Klopstock (1899–1972).* Ed. Hugo Wetscherek. Vienna: Inlibris, 2003, pp. 267–92.

Max Brod, Franz Kafka: Eine Freundschaft. Ed. Malcolm Pasley. Vol. 1: *Reiseaufzeichnungen.* Vol. 2: *Briefwechsel.* Frankfurt am Main: S. Fischer, 1987, 1989.

Mitscherlich-Nielsen, Margarete. "Psychoanalytische Bemerkungen zu Franz Kafka." *Psyche* 31, no. 1 (1977), pp. 60–83.

Morgenstern, Soma. "Franz Kafka [1]," "Franz Kafka [2]," "Wer ist Franz Kafka?" *Kritiken, Berichte, Tagebücher.* Ed. Ingolf Schulte. Lüneburg: Zu Klampen, 2001, pp. 443–48, 449–54, 455–80.

Mülerová, Radana. "Franz Kafka a Siřem." *Sborník okresního archivu v Lounech* 10 (2001), pp. 199–228.

Murray, Nicholas. *Kafka.* New Haven: Yale University Press, 2004.

Nekula, Marek. *Franz Kafkas Sprachen.* Tübingen: Max Niemeyer, 2003.

Neumann, Gerhard. "Hungerkünstler und Menschenfresser: Zum Verhältnis von Kunst und kulturellem Ritual im Werk Franz Kafkas." *Franz Kafka: Schriftverkehr.* Ed. Wolf Kittler and Gerhard Neumann. Freiburg im Breisgau: Rombach Verlag, 1990, pp. 399–432.

Northey, Anthony. "The American Cousins and the Prager Asbestwerke." *The Kafka Debate.* Ed. Angel Flores. New York: Gordian, 1977, pp. 133–46.

———. "Julie Wohryzek, Franz Kafkas zweite Verlobte." *Freibeuter* (Berlin) 59 (1994), pp. 3–16.

———. *Kafka's Relatives.* New Haven: Yale University Press, 1991.

Ozick, Cynthia. "The Impossibility of Being Kafka." *New Yorker*, January 11, 1999, pp. 80–87.

Pasley, Malcolm. "Die Handschrift redet." *Marbacher Magazin* (Marbach am Neckar) 52 (1990), pp. 69–72.

Pawel, Ernst. "Kafka's Hebrew Teacher." *New York Times,* August 16, 1981.

———. *The Nightmare of Reason: A Life of Franz Kafka.* New York: Farrar, Straus & Giroux, 1984.

Politzer, Heinz. *Franz Kafka, der Künstler.* Frankfurt am Main: S. Fischer, 1965.

Robert, Marthe. *As Lonely as Franz Kafka.* Trans. Ralph Manheim. New York: Harcourt Brace Jovanovich, 1982.

Robertson, Ritchie. *Kafka: Judaism, Politics, and Literature.* Oxford: Clarendon Press, 1985.

Rost, Nico. "Persoonlijke ontmoetingen met Franz Kafka en mijn Tsjechische vrienden." *De Vlaamse Gids* 48 (Feb. 1964), pp. 75–97.

Schoeps, Julius H., ed. *Im Streit um Kafka und das Judentum: Max Brod, Hans-Joachim Schoeps, Briefwechsel.* Königstein im Taunus: Jüdischer Verlag bei Athenäum, 1985.

Schütterle, Annette. *Franz Kafkas Oktavhefte: Ein Schreibprozess als "System des Teilbaues."* Freiburg im Breisgau: Rombach, 2002.

———. "Franz Kafkas 'Tropische Münchhausiade': Eine Lesung in München." *Freibeuter* 75 (1998), pp. 153–56.

Siebenschein, Hugo, et al. *Franz Kafka a Praha: Vzpomínky, Úvahy, Dokumenty.* Prague: Vladimir Zikes, 1947.
Stach, Reiner. *Kafka: The Decisive Years.* Trans. Shelley Frisch. New York: Harcourt, 2005.
———. *Kafkas erotischer Mythos: Eine ästhetische Konstruktion des Weiblichen.* Frankfurt am Main: S. Fischer, 1987.
Stoelzl, Christoph. *Kafkas böses Böhmen: Zur Sozialgeschichte eines Prager Juden.* Munich: Edition Text + Kritik, 1975.
Tismar, Jens. "Kafkas 'Schakale und Araber' im zionistischen Kontext betrachtet." *Jahrbuch der deutschen Schillergesellschaft* 19 (1975), pp. 306–23.
Unseld, Joachim. *Franz Kafka: A Writer's Life.* Trans. Paul F. Dvorak. Riverside, CA: Ariadne Press, 1994.
Urzidil, Johannes. *There Goes Kafka.* Trans. Harold A. Basilius. Detroit: Wayne State University Press, 1968.
Voigts, Manfred. *Kafka und die jüdisch-zionistische Frau: Diskussionen um Erotik und Sexualität im Prager Zionismus.* Würzburg: Königshausen & Neumann, 2007.
Wagenbach, Klaus. *Franz Kafka: Pictures of a Life.* Trans. Arthur S. Wensinger. New York: Pantheon Books, 1984.
———. *Franz Kafka: Eine Biographie seiner Jugend 1883–1912.* Bern, 1958. Reprint, Berlin: Wagenbach, 2006.
———. *Kafka's Prague.* Trans. Shaun Whiteside. Woodstock, NY: Overlook Press, 1996.
Wagnerová, Alena. *"Im Hauptquartier des Lärms": Die Familie Kafka aus Prag.* Berlin: Bollmann, 1997.
Weiskopf, F. C. *Das Slawenlied.* Berlin: Dietz Verlag, 1960.
Weiss, Ernst. "Bemerkungen zu den Tagebüchern und Briefen Franz Kafkas." *Mass und Wert* 1 (1937/38), pp. 319–25.
Wetscherek, Hugo, ed. *Kafkas letzter Freund: Der Nachlaß Robert Klopstock (1899–1972).* With an annotated first publication of 38 letters by Franz Kafka, with contributions by Leonhard M. Fiedler and Leo A. Lensing. Vienna: Inlibris, 2003.
Zischler, Hanns. *Kafka Goes to the Movies.* Trans. Susan H. Gillespie. Chicago: University of Chicago Press, 2002.

Literature by and about Kafka's Contemporaries

Amann, Klaus, and Armin A. Wallas, eds. *Expressionismus in Österreich.* Vienna: Böhlau, 1994.
Binder, Hartmut, ed. *Brennpunkt Berlin: Prager Schriftsteller in der deutschen Metropole.* Bonn: Kulturstiftung der deutschen Vertriebenen, 1995.

———. "Ernst Polak—Literat ohne Werk: Zu den Kaffeehauszirkeln in Prag und Wien." *Jahrbuch der Deutschen Schillergesellschaft* 23 (1979), pp. 366–415.
———, ed. *Prager Profile: Vergessene Autoren im Schatten Kafkas*. Berlin: Mann, 1991.
Blei, Franz. *Das große Bestiarium der modernen Literatur*. Berlin: Rowohlt, 1922.
Brenner, Josef Chaim. *Breakdown and Bereavement*. Tel Aviv: Shtiebel, 1920.
Brod, Max. "Gerhart Hauptmanns Frauengestalten." *Die neue Rundschau* 33 (1922), pp. 1131–41.
———. *Das grosse Wagnis*. Leipzig: Kurt Wolff Verlag, 1918.
———. *Leben mit einer Göttin*. Munich: Kurt Wolff Verlag, 1923.
———. *Mira: Ein Roman um Hofmannsthal*. Munich: Kindler, 1958.
———. "Die neue Zeitschrift." *Die weissen Blätter* 1 (1913–14), pp. 1227–30.
———. *Der Prager Kreis*. Frankfurt am Main: Suhrkamp, 1979.
———. *The Redemption of Tycho Brahe*. Trans. Felix Warren Crosse. London: Knopf, 1928.
———. *Rëubeni, Fürst der Juden: Ein Renaissanceroman*. Munich: Kurt Wolff Verlag, 1925.
———. *Streitbares Leben: Autobiographie 1884–1968*. Frankfurt am Main: Insel, 1979.
Buber-Neumann, Margarete. *Milena: Kafkas Freundin*. Munich: Langen Müller, 1963.
Černá, Jana. *Milena Jesenská*. Frankfurt am Main: Neue Kritik, 1985.
Corino, Karl. *Robert Musil: Leben und Werk in Bildern und Texten*. Reinbek: Rowohlt, 1988.
Dietz, Ludwig. "Kurt Wolffs Bücherei 'Der jüngste Tag': Seine Geschichte und Bibliographie." *Philobiblon* 7 (1963), pp. 96–118.
Doderer, Heimito von. *The Lighted Windows; or, the Humanization of the Bureaucrat Julius Zihal*. Trans. John S. Barrett. Riverside, CA: Ariadne Press, 2000.
———. *Die Strudlhofstiege oder Melzer und die Tiefe der Jahre*. Munich: dtv, 1995.
Doležal, Pavel. *Tomáš G. Masaryk, Max Brod und das "Prager Tagblatt" (1918–1938)*. Frankfurt am Main: Peter Lang, 2004.
Fiala-Fürst, Ingeborg. *Der Beitrag der Prager deutschen Literatur zum deutschen Expressionismus: Relevante Topoi ausgewählter Werke*. St. Ingbert: Röhrig Universitätsverlag, 1996.
Fiedler, Leonhard M. "'Um Hofmannsthal': Max Brod und Hugo von Hofmannsthal; Briefe, Notizen." *Hofmannsthal-Blätter* 30 (August 1985), pp. 23–45.

Fischer, Samuel, and Hedwig Fischer. *Briefwechsel mit Autoren*. Ed. Dierk Rodewald and Corinna Fiedler. Frankfurt am Main: S. Fischer, 1989.
Göbel, Wolfram. *Der Kurt Wolff Verlag 1913–1930: Expressionismus als verlegerische Aufgabe*. Special ed. from *Archiv für Geschichte des Buchwesens*, vols. 15 and 16, cols. 521–1456. Frankfurt am Main, 1976, 1977. Reprint, Munich: Buch & Media, 2000.
Gold, Hugo, ed. *Max Brod: Ein Gedenkbuch 1884–1969*. Tel Aviv: Alamenu, 1969.
Goldstücker, Eduard. *Weltfreunde: Konferenz über die Prager deutsche Literatur*. Berlin: Luchterhand, 1967.
Haas, Willy. *Die literarische Welt: Erinnerungen*. Munich: List, 1957.
Hauptmann, Gerhart. *Tagebücher 1914 bis 1918*. Ed. Peter Sprengel. Berlin: Propyläen Verlag, 1997.
Hermann, Frank, and Heinke Schmitz. "Avantgarde und Kommerz: Der Verlag *Die Schmiede* Berlin 1921–1929." *Buchhandelsgeschichte* 4 (1991), pp. B129–50.
Heydemann, Klaus. "Der Titularfeldwebel: Stefan Zweig im Kriegsarchiv." *Stefan Zweig 1881/1981: Aufsätze und Dokumente*. Ed. Dokumentationsstelle für neuere österreichische Literatur (*Zirkular*, special issue 2, Oct. 1981).
Hockaday, Mary. *Kafka, Love and Courage: The Life of Milena Jesenská*. Woodstock, NY: Overlook Press, 1997.
Hugo von Hofmannsthal / Richard Beer-Hofmann: Briefwechsel. Ed. Rudolf Hirsch and Eugene Weber. Frankfurt am Main: S. Fischer, 1972.
Hofmannsthal, Hugo von. *Briefwechsel mit Ottonie Gräfin Degenfeld und Julie Freifrau von Wedelstadt*. Ed. Marie Therese Miller-Degenfeld. 2nd ed. Frankfurt am Main: S. Fischer, 1986.
Jesenská, Milena. *"Alles ist Leben": Feuilletons und Reportagen 1919–1939*. Ed. Dorothea Rein. Frankfurt am Main: Verlag Neue Kritik, 1984.
———. Jesenská, *"Ich hätte zu antworten tage- und nächtelang."* Frankfurt am main: S. Fischer, 1999.
Jungk, Peter Stephan. *Franz Werfel: A Life in Prague, Vienna, and Hollywood*. Trans. Anselm Hollo. New York: Grove Weidenfeld, 1990.
Kaus, Gina. *Und was für ein Leben: Mit Liebe und Literatur, Theater und Film*. Hamburg: Albrecht Knaus, 1979.
Kayser, Werner, and Horst Gronemeyer. *Max Brod*. Hamburger Bibliographien, vol. 12. Hamburg: Christians, 1972.
Kisch, Egon Erwin. *Briefe an den Bruder Paul und an die Mutter 1905–1936*. Berlin: Aufbau, 1978.
———. *Briefe an Jarmila*. Ed. Klaus Haupt. Berlin: Verlag Das neue Berlin, 1998.

Kraus, Karl. *Die letzten Tage der Menschheit: Tragödie in 5 Akten mit Vorspiel und Epilog.* Frankfurt am Main: Suhrkamp, 1992.

———. *Literatur oder Man wird doch da sehn: Magische Operette in 2 Teilen.* Vienna: Verlag Die Fackel, 1921.

Krolop, Kurt. *Reflexionen der Fackel: Neue Studien über Karl Kraus.* Vienna: Verlag der Österreichischen Akademie der Wissenschaften, 1994.

Kudszus, Winfried. "Erzählung und Zeitverschiebung in Kafkas 'Prozess' und 'Schloss.'" *Deutsche Vierteljahresschrift für Literaturwissenschaft und Geistesgeschichte* 38, no. 2 (1964), pp. 192–207.

Mann, Thomas. *Diaries: 1918–1939.* Ed. Hermann Kesten. Trans. Richard and Clara Winston. New York: Harry N. Abrams, 1982.

———. "Ludwig Hardt." *Essays II: 1914–1926.* Ed. Hermann Kurzke. Frankfurt am Main: S. Fischer, 2002, pp. 303–5.

Morgenstern, Soma. *Kritiken, Berichte, Tagebücher.* Ed. Ingolf Schulte. Lüneburg: Zu Klampen Verlag, 2001.

Musil, Robert. *Briefe 1901–1942.* Ed. Adolf Frisé. Reinbek: Rowohlt, 1981.

———. *Tagebücher.* Ed. Adolf Frisé. Reinbek: Rowohlt, 1983.

Pazi, Margarita. *Fünf Autoren des Prager Kreises.* Frankfurt am Main: Peter Lang, 1978.

———, ed. *Max Brod 1884–1984: Untersuchungen zu Max Brods literarischen und philosophischen Schriften.* New York: Peter Lang, 1987.

———. *Staub und Sterne: Aufsätze zur deutsch-jüdischen Literatur.* Göttingen: Wallstein Verlag, 2001.

Pazi, Margarita, and Hans Dieter Zimmermann, eds. *Berlin und der Prager Kreis.* Würzburg: Königshausen & Neumann, 1991.

Pulver Max. *Erinnerungen an eine europäische Zeit.* Zurich: Orell Füssli Verlag, 1953.

Raabe, Paul, ed. *Expressionismus: Aufzeichnungen und Erinnerungen.* Olten: Walter, 1965.

Rilke, Rainer Maria. *Briefe zur Politik.* Ed. Joachim W. Storck. Frankfurt am Main: Insel Verlag, 1992.

Sahl, Hans. "Erinnerungen an Ernst Weiss." *Weiss-Blätter*, no. 2 (August 1973), p. 4.

Šrámková, Barbora. *Max Brod und die tschechische Kultur.* Wuppertal: Arco Verlag, 2010.

Schamschula, Walter. "Franz Werfel und die Tschechen." *Die österreichische Literatur: Ihr Profil von der Jahrhundertwende bis zur Gegenwart (1880—1980).* Ed. Herbert Zeman. Graz: Akademische Druck- und Verlagsanstalt, 1989, pp. 343–59.

———. "Max Brod und die tschechische Literatur." *Max Brod 1884–1984: Untersuchungen zu Max Brods literarischen und philosophischen*

Schriften. Ed. Margarita Pazi. New York: Peter Lang, 1987, pp. 233–49.

Schnitzler, Arthur. *Tagebuch*. Vol. 7: *1920–1922*. Vol. 8: *1923–1926*. Vienna: Verlag der Österreichischen Akademie der Wissenschaften, 1993, 1995.

Steenfatt, Margret. *Milena Jesenská: Biographie einer Befreiung*. Hamburg: Europäische Verlagsanstalt, 2002.

Sternheim, Carl. *Briefe II: Briefwechsel mit Thea Sternheim, Dorothea und Klaus Sternheim*. Ed. Wolfgang Wendler. Darmstadt: Luchterhand, 1988.

Sternheim, Thea. *Tagebücher 1903–1971*. Ed. Thomas Ehrsam and Regula Wyss. Vol. 3: *1936–1951*. Göttingen: Wallstein, 2002.

Timms, Edward: *Karl Kraus: Apocalyptic Satirist*. New Haven: Yale University. Press, 2005.

Ungern-Sternberg, Christoph von. *Willy Haas 1891–1973: "Ein großer Regisseur der Literatur."* Munich: Edition Text + Kritik, 2007.

Wagenknecht, Christian. "Die Vorlesungen von Karl Kraus: Ein chronologisches Verzeichnis." *Kraus-Hefte* 35–36 (1985), pp. 1–30.

Wagnerová, Alena, ed. *"Ich hätte zu antworten tage- und nächtelang": Die Briefe von Milena*. Mannheim: Bollmann, 1996.

———. *Milena Jesenska: "Alle meine Artikel sind Liebesbriefe"; Biographie*. Mannheim: Bollmann, 1994.

Walter, Hans-Albert. *Deutsche Exilliteratur 1933–1950*. Vol. 1.1: *Die Mentalität der Weimardeutschen / Die "Politisierung" der Intellektuellen*. Stuttgart: J. B. Metzler, 2003.

Weiss, Ernst. *Die Feuerprobe*. Berlin: S. Fischer, 1923.

———. *Franziska*. Berlin: S. Fischer, 1919.

———. *Der Kampf*. Berlin: S. Fischer, 1916.

———. *Schweiger: Trauerspiel in 3 Akten*. Munich: Kurt Wolff Verlag, 1922.

———. *Spiegelmensch: Magische Trilogie*. Munich: Kurt Wolff Verlag, 1920.

———. *Verdi: Roman der Oper*. Vienna: Zsolnay, 1924.

Werfel, Franz. *Zwischen Oben und Unten: Prosa, Tagebücher, Aphorismen, Literarische Nachträge*. 2nd ed. Munich: Langen Müller Verlag, 1975.

Wolff, Kurt. *Autoren, Bücher, Abenteuer: Betrachtungen und Erinnerungen eines Verlegers*. Berlin: Wagenbach, 1965.

———. *Briefwechsel eines Verlegers 1911–1963*. Expanded ed. Ed. Bernhard Zeller and Ellen Otten. Frankfurt am Main: S. Fischer, 1980.

Zweig, Stefan. *Briefe 1914–1919*. Ed. Knut Beck, Jeffrey B. Berlin, and Natascha Weschenbach-Feggeler. Frankfurt am Main: S. Fischer, 1998.

———. *Tagebücher.* Frankfurt am Main: S. Fischer, 1984.
———. *Die Welt von Gestern.* Frankfurt am Main: S. Fischer, 1970.

Philosophy, Sociology, Psychology, and Pedagogy

Blüher, Hans. *Die Rolle der Erotik in der männlichen Gesellschaft: Eine Theorie der menschlichen Staatsbildung nach Wesen und Wert.* 2 vols. Jena: Diederichs, 1917–19.

Federn, Paul. *Zur Psychologie der Revolution: Die vaterlose Gesellschaft.* Nach Vorträgen in der Wiener Psychoanalytischen Vereinigung und im Monistenbund. Leipzig: Anzengruber, 1919.

Foerster, Friedrich Wilhelm. *Jugendlehre: Ein Buch für Eltern, Lehrer und Geistliche.* Berlin: Reimer, 1904.

Gay, Peter. *Freud: A Life for Our Time.* New York: W. W. Norton, 2006.

Gross, Otto. "Die kommunistische Grundidee in der Paradiessymbolik." *Sowjet* 1 (1919), pp. 12–27.

Hoschek, Maria. *Friedrich Wilhelm Foerster (1869–1966): Mit besonderer Berücksichtigung seiner Beziehungen zu Österreich.* Frankfurt am Main: Peter Lang, 2002.

Kierkegaard, Søren. *Buch des Richters: Seine Tagebücher 1833–1855 im Auszug aus dem Dänischen von Hermann Gottsched.* Jena: Eugen Diederichs, 1905.

———. *Stages on Life's Way.* Ed. and trans. Howard U. Hong and Edna H. Hong. Princeton: Princeton University Press, 1988.

Landauer, Gustav, and Fritz Mauthner. *Briefwechsel 1890–1919.* Ed. Hanna Delf and Julius H. Schoeps. Munich: C. H. Beck, 1994.

Mitscherlich-Nielsen, Margarete. "Psychoanalytische Bemerkungen zu Franz Kafka." *Psyche* 31, no. 1 (1977), pp. 60–83.

Tagger, Theodor. *Das neue Geschlecht: Programmschrift gegen die Metapher.* Berlin: Verlag Heinrich Hochstim, 1917.

Weltsch, Felix, and Max Brod. *Anschauung und Begriff: Grundzüge eines Systems der Begriffsbildung.* Leipzig: Kurt Wolff, 1913.

Judaism

Abeles, Otto. *Jüdische Flüchtlinge: Szenen und Gestalten.* Vienna: Verlag Löwit, 1918.

Bajohr, Frank. "Unser Hotel ist judenfrei." *Bäder-Antisemitismus im 19. und 20. Jahrhundert.* Frankfurt am Main: S. Fischer, 2003.

Bärsch, Claus-Ekkehard. *Max Brod im Kampf um das Judentum: Zum Leben und Werk eines deutsch-jüdischen Dichters aus Prag.* Vienna: Passagen, 1992.

Benjamin, Walter, and Gershom Scholem. *Briefwechsel*. Frankfurt am Main: Suhrkamp, 1980.
Bergmann, Hugo. *Jawne und Jerusalem: Gesammelte Aufsätze*. Berlin, 1919. Reprint, Königstein: Jüdischer Verlag bei Athenäum, 1981.
Bergman[n], Hugo Schmuel. *Tagebücher und Briefe*. Ed. Miriam Sambursky. Vol. 1: *1901–1948*. Königstein: Jüdischer Verlag bei Athenäum, 1985.
Blüher, Hans. *Secessio Judaica: Philosophische Grundlegung der historischen Situation des Judentums und der antisemitischen Bewegung*. Berlin: Der Weisse Ritter Verlag, 1922.
Brenner, Michael. *The Renaissance of Jewish Culture in Weimar Germany*. New Haven: Yale University Press, 1996.
Brod, Max. "Franz Werfels 'christliche Sendung.'" *Der Jude* 1 (1916–17), pp. 717–24.
———. *Heidentum Christentum Judentum: Ein Bekenntnisbuch*. 2 vols. Munich: Kurt Wolff Verlag, 1921.
———. *Sozialismus und Zionismus*. Berlin: Löwit, 1920.
———. "Unsere Literaten und die Gemeinschaft." *Der Jude* 1 (1916–17), pp. 457–64.
Buber, Martin. *Briefwechsel aus sieben Jahrzehnten*. Ed. Grete Schaeder. Vol. 1: *1897–1918*. Heidelberg: L. Schneider, 1972.
———. "Die Eroberung Palästinas." *Der Jude* 2 (1917–18), pp. 633–34.
———. "Vorbemerkung über Franz Werfel." *Der Jude* 2 (1917–18), pp. 109–12.
Chasanowitsch, Leon, and Leo Motzkin, eds. *Die Judenfrage der Gegenwart: Dokumentensammlung*. Stockholm: Judäa, 1919.
Cohen, Gary B. "Jews in German Society: Prague, 1860–1914." *Jews and Germans from 1860 to 1933: The Problematic Symbiosis*. Ed. David Bronsen. Heidelberg: Carl Winter Universitätsverlag, 1979, pp. 306–37.
Eliasberg, Alexander, ed. and trans. *Sagen polnischer Juden*. Munich: Georg Müller, 1916.
Fromer, Jakob. *Der babylonische Talmud*. Berlin-Charlottenburg: Reichel, 1909.
Graetz, Heinrich. *History of the Jews*. 6 vols. Philadelphia: Jewish Publication Society of America, 1891–98.
Gronemann, Sammy. *Hawdoloh und Zapfenstreich: Erinnerungen an die ostjüdische Etappe 1916–18*. Berlin: Jüdischer Verlag, 1924.
Grözinger, Karl Erich. *Jüdisches Denken: Theologie, Philosophie, Mystik*. Vol. 2: *Von der mittelalterlichen Kabbala zum Hasidismus*. Frankfurt am Main: Campus Verlag, 2005.
Grünberg, Abraham. *Ein jüdisch-polnisch-russisches Jubiläum (Der grosse Pogrom von Sedlice im Jahre 1906)*. Prague: Selbstverlag, 1916.

Hackeschmidt, Jörg. "Jüdische Orthodoxie und zionistische Jugendkultur im frühen 20. Jahrhundert." *Janusfiguren: "Jüdische Heimstätte," Exil und Nation im deutschen Zionismus*. Ed. Andrea Schatz and Christian Wies. Berlin: Metropol, 2006, pp. 81–101.

Haumann, Heiko. "Zionismus und die Krise jüdischen Selbstverständnisses." *Der Traum von Israel: Die Ursprünge des modernen Zionismus*. Weinheim: Beltz Athenäum, 1998, pp. 9–64.

Herzog, Andreas, ed. *Ost und West: Jüdische Publizistik 1901–1928*. Leipzig: Reclam, 1996.

Holitscher, Arthur. *Reise durch das jüdische Palästina*. Berlin: S. Fischer, 1922.

Das jüdische Prag. *Eine Sammelschrift*. Prague: Selbstwehr, 1917.

Kieval, Hillel J. *The Making of the Czech Jewry: National Conflict and Jewish Society in Bohemia, 1870–1918*. New York: Oxford University Press, 1991.

Kreppel, J. *Juden und Judentum von heute: Ein Handbuch*. Zurich: Amalthea-Verlag, 1925.

Krojanker, Gustav, ed. *Juden in der deutschen Literatur*. Berlin: Welt-Verlag, 1922.

Kuděla, Jiři. "Die Emigration galizischer und osteuropäischer Juden nach Böhmen und Prag zwischen 1914–1916/17." *Studia Rosenthaliana* 23 (1989), pp. 119–34.

———. "Galician and East European Refugees in the Historic Lands: 1914–16." *Review of the Society for the History of Czechoslovak Jews* 4 (1991–92), pp. 15–32.

Landauer, Gustav. "Christlich und christlich, jüdisch und jüdisch." *Der Jude* 1 (1916/17), pp. 851–52.

Langer, František. "My Brother Jiří." *Nine Gates*. By Jiří Langer. New York: D. McKay Co., 1961, pp. vii–xxxii.

Langer, Georg. *Die Erotik der Kabbala*. Prague: J. Flesch, 1923.

Langer, Jiři [Georg]. *Devět bran*. Prague: Evropský literární klub, 1937.

Lappin, Eleonore. *Der Jude 1916–1928: Jüdische Moderne zwischen Universalismus und Partikularismus*. Tübingen: M. Siebeck, 2000.

Lehmann, Siegfried. "Jüdische Volksarbeit." *Der Jude* 1 (1916/17), pp. 104–11.

———. *Das jüdische Volksheim Berlin: Erster Bericht, Mai–Dezember 1916*. Berlin: n.p., 1916.

———. "Von der Strassenhorde zur Gemeinschaft." *Der Jude* 2 (special issue, 1926), pp. 22–36.

Menczel-Ben-Tovim, Puah, ed. *Leben und Wirken: Unser erzieherisches Werk; In memoriam Dr. Josef Schlomo Menczel, 1903–1953*. Jerusalem: Gedächtnisstiftung Dr. J. S. Menczel, 1983.

Meyer, Michael A., and Michael Brenner, eds. *German-Jewish History in Modern Times*. Vol. 3: *Integration in Dispute 1871–1918*. New York: Columbia University Press, 1998.
Míšková, Alena. "Die Lage der Juden an der Prager Deutschen Universität." *Judenemanzipation, Antisemitismus, Verfolgung in Deutschland, Österreich-Ungarn, den Böhmischen Ländern und in der Slowakei*. Ed. Jörg K. Hoensch et al. Essen: Klartext-Verlagsgesellschaft, 1999, pp. 117–29.
Naor, Mordecai. *The Twentieth Century in Eretz Israel: A Pictorial History*. Cologne: Könemann, 1998.
Nekula, Marek, and Walter Koschmal. *Juden zwischen Deutschen und Tschechen: Sprachliche und kulturelle Identitäten in Böhmen 1800–1945*. Munich: Oldenbourg, 2006.
Rath, Moses. *Lehrbuch der hebräischen Sprache für Schul- und Selbstunterricht*. 2nd ed. Vienna: n.p., 1917.
Rechter, David. *The Jews of Vienna and the First World War*. London: Littman Library of Jewish Civilization, 2001.
Rozenblit, Marsha L. *Reconstructing a National Identity: The Jews of Habsburg Austria during World War I*. New York: Oxford University Press, 2001.
Rychnovsky, Ernst, ed. *Masaryk und das Judentum*. Prague: Marsverlagsgesellschaft, 1930.
Schoeps, Julius H., and Joachim Schlör, eds. *Antisemitismus: Vorurteile und Mythen*. Munich: Piper, 1995.
Scholem, Gershom. *Tagebücher*. Vol. 1, part 1: *1913–1917*. Ed. Karlfried Gründer and Friedrich Niewöhner. Frankfurt am Main: Jüdischer Verlag im Suhrkamp Verlag, 1995.
———. *Von Berlin nach Jerusalem: Jugenderinnerungen*. Expanded ed. Frankfurt am Main: Suhrkamp, 1997.
Schuster, Frank M. *Zwischen allen Fronten: Osteuropäische Juden während des Ersten Weltkrieges (1914–1919)*. Cologne: Böhlau, 2004.
Segev, Tom. *One Palestine, Complete: Jews and Arabs under the British Mandate*. Trans. Haim Watzman. New York: Metropolitan Books, 2000.
Sieg, Ulrich. *Jüdische Intellektuelle im Ersten Weltkrieg: Kriegserfahrungen, weltanschauliche Debatten und kulturelle Neuentwürfe*. Berlin: Akademie-Verlag, 2001.
Stölzl, Christoph. "Die 'Burg' und die Juden: T.G. Masaryk und sein Kreis im Spannungsfeld der jüdischen Frage; Assimilation, Antisemitismus und Zionismus." *Die "Burg": Einflussreiche politische Kräfte um Masaryk und Beneš*. Ed. Karl Bosl. Vol. 2. Munich: Oldenbourg, 1974, pp. 79–110.

Verein jüdischer Hochschüler Bar-Kochba in Prag, ed. *Vom Judentum: Ein Sammelbuch*. Leipzig: Kurt Wolff Verlag, 1913.

Wassermann, Jakob. *Mein Weg als Deutscher und Jude*. Berlin: S. Fischer, 1921.

Welling, Martin. "Vom Hass so eng umkreist." *Der Erste Weltkrieg aus der Sicht der Prager Juden*. Frankfurt am Main: Peter Lang, 2003.

Weltsch, Felix, ed. *Dichter, Denker, Helfer: Max Brod zum fünfzigsten Geburtstag*. Moravian Ostava: Julius Kittls Nachfolger, Keller & Co., 1934.

Werfel, Franz. "Die christliche Sendung: Ein offener Brief an Kurt Hiller." *Die neue Rundschau* 28 (1917), pp. 92–105.

Zechlin, Egmont. *Die deutsche Politik und die Juden im Ersten Weltkrieg*. Göttingen: Vandenhoeck u. Ruprecht, 1969.

History: Political, Social, Cultural

Biersack, Werner. *Der Fremdenverkehr im Kurort Meran*. Innsbruck: Wirtschafts- und sozialwissenschaftlicher Arbeitskreis, 1967.

Binder, Hartmut. *Wo Kafka und seine Freunde zu Gast waren: Prager Kaffeehäuser und Vergnügungsstätten in historischen Bilddokumenten*. Prague: Vitalis, 2000.

Biwald, Brigitte. *Von Helden und Krüppeln: Das österreichisch-ungarische Militärsanitätswesen im Ersten Weltkrieg*. 2 vols. Vienna: ÖBV & HPT, 2002.

Bosl, Karl, ed. *Aktuelle Forschungsprobleme um die Erste Tschechoslowakische Republik*. Munich: Oldenbourg, 1969.

Böss, Gustav. *Die Not in Berlin: Tatsachen und Zahlen*. Berlin 1923. Reprinted in Christian Engeli, ed. *Gustav Böss: Oberbürgermeister 1921–1930; Beiträge zur Kommunalpolitik*. Berlin: Kohlhammer, 1981, pp. 1–32.

Breiter, Marion. "Hinter der Front: Zum Leben der Zivilbevölkerung im Wien des Ersten Weltkriegs." PhD diss., University of Vienna, 1991.

Brod, Max. *Leoš Janáček: Leben und Werk*. Vienna: Wiener Philharmonischer Verlag, 1925.

Butschek, Felix. *Statistische Reihen zur österreichischen Wirtschaftsgeschichte: Die österreichische Wirtschaft seit der industriellen Revolution*. Vienna: Böhlau, 1993.

Čapek, Karel. *Gespräche mit Masaryk*. Stuttgart: Rogner & Bernhard, 2001.

Doležal, Pavel. *Tomáš G. Masaryk, Max Brod und das* Prager Tagblatt *(1918–1938): Deutsch-tschechische Annäherung als publizistische Aufgabe*. Frankfurt am Main: Peter Lang, 2004.

Eissler, K.R. *Freud und Wagner-Jauregg vor der Kommission zur Erhebung militärischer Pflichtverletzungen.* Vienna: Locker, 1979.
Epkenhans, Michael. "Kriegswaffen—Strategie, Einsatz, Wirkung." *Der Tod als Maschinist: Der industrialisierte Krieg 1914–1918.* Ed. Rolf Spilker and Bernd Ulrich. Catalogue for the exhibition in the Museum of Industrial Culture, Osnabrück, May 17–August 23, 1998.
Godefroid, Annette. *Geschichte der Berliner Verwaltungsbezirke.* Vol. 7: *Steglitz.* Ed. Wolfgang Ribbe. Berlin: Colloquium Verlag, 1989.
Glatzer, Ruth, ed. *Berlin zur Weimarer Zeit: Panorama einer Metropole 1919–1933.* Berlin: Siedler, 2000.
Graham, Frank D. *Exchange, Prices, and Production in Hyper-Inflation: Germany 1920–1923.* Princeton 1930. Reprint, New York: Russell & Russell, 1967.
Hanisch, Ernst. *Der lange Schatten des Staates: Österreichische Gesellschaftsgeschichte im 20. Jahrhundert.* Vienna: Böhlau, 1994.
Hirsch, Ernst. *Der Wehrpflichtige.* Vienna: Perles, 1913.
Hirschfeld, Magnus, ed. *Sittengeschichte der jüngsten Zeit: Eine Darstellung der Kultur, Sittlichkeit und Erotik des zwanzigsten Jahrhunderts.* Leipzig: Verlag für Sexualwissenschaft Schneider & Co., 1930–32.
Hoensch, Jörg K. *Geschichte Böhmens: Von der slavischen Landnahme bis zur Gegenwart.* 3rd ed. Munich: C. H. Beck, 1997.
Holtfrerich, Carl-Ludwig. *Die deutsche Inflation 1914–1923: Ursachen und Folgen in internationaler Perspektive.* Berlin: Walter de Gruyter, 1980.
Hösch, Edgar. *Geschichte der Balkanländer: Von der Frühzeit bis zur Gegenwart.* Munich: C. H. Beck, 1999.
Internationales Bäderhandbuch. Berlin: Hugo Steinitz, 1914.
Keegan, John. *The First World War.* New York: Knopf, 1999.
Kleindel, Walter. *Österreich: Daten zur Geschichte und Kultur.* Vienna: Österreichischer Bundesverlag, 1995.
Kunz, Andreas. "Verteilungskampf oder Interessenkonsensus? Einkommensentwicklung und Sozialverhalten von Arbeitnehmergruppen in der Inflationszeit 1914 bis 1924." *Die deutsche Inflation: Eine Zwischenbilanz.* Ed. Gerald D. Feldman et al. Berlin: Walter de Gruyter, 1982, pp. 347–84.
Lange, Britta. *Einen Krieg ausstellen: Die "Deutsche Kriegsausstellung" 1916 in Berlin.* Berlin: Verbrecher Verlag, 2003.
Lemberg, Hans. "1918: Die Staatsgründung der Tschechoslowakei und die Deutschen." *Wendepunkte in den Beziehungen zwischen Deutschen, Tschechen und Slowaken.* Ed. Detlev Brandes, Dušan Kováč, and Jiři Pešek. Essen: Veröffentlichungen der Deutsch-Tschechischen und Deutsch-Slowakischen Historikerkommission 2007, pp. 119–35.

——, ed. *Universitäten in nationaler Konkurrenz: Zur Geschichte der Prager Universitäten im 19. und 20. Jahrhundert.* Munich: Oldenbourg, 2003.

Linnenkohl, Hans. *Vom Einzelschuss zur Feuerwalze: Der Wettlauf zwischen Technik und Taktik im Ersten Weltkrieg.* Koblenz: Bernard & Graefe, 1990.

Mamatey, Victor S., and Radomir Luža, eds. *A History of the Czechoslovak Republic, 1918–1948.* Princeton: Princeton University Press, 1973.

Marschner, Robert. *Die Fürsorge der Frauen für die heimkehrenden Krieger.* Prague: Deutscher Verein zur Verbreitung gemeinnütziger Kenntnisse in Prag, 1916.

Mendelssohn, Peter de. *Hellerau, mein unverlierbares Europa.* Dresden: Hellerau Verlag, 1993.

Mentzel, Walter. "Kriegsflüchtlinge in Cisleithanien im Ersten Weltkrieg." PhD diss., University of Vienna, 1997.

Mommsen, Hans, Dušan Kováč, and Jiří Malíř, eds. *Der Erste Weltkrieg und die Beziehungen zwischen Tschechen, Slowaken und Deutschen.* Essen: Klartext-Verlagsgesellschaft, 2001.

Nitschke, Thomas. *Die Gartenstadt Hellerau als Pädagogische Provinz.* Dresden: Hellerau-Verlag, 2003.

Ostwald, Hans. *Sittengeschichte der Inflation: Ein Kulturdokument aus den Jahren des Marktsturzes.* Berlin: Neufeld & Henius, 1931.

Pawlowsky, Adolf. *Einjähriger Präsenzdienst (Einjährig-Freiwilligendienst).* Prague: A. Haase, 1910.

Pichlík, Karel. "Zur Kritik der Legenden um das Jahr 1918." *Aktuelle Forschungsprobleme um die Erste Tschechoslowakische Republik.* Ed. Karl Bosl. Munich: Oldenbourg, 1969, pp. 79–92.

Plaschka, Richard Georg, Horst Haselsteiner, and Arnold Suppan. *Innere Front: Militärassistenz, Widerstand und Umsturz in der Donaumonarchie 1918.* Vol. 2: *Umsturz.* Munich: Verlag für Geschichte und Politik, 1974.

Rauchensteiner, Manfred. *Der Tod des Doppeladlers: Österreich-Ungarn und der Erste Weltkrieg.* Graz: Styria, 1993.

Redlich, Joseph. *Austrian War Government.* New Haven: Yale University Press, 1929.

Ribbe, Wolfgang, ed. *Geschichte Berlins.* Vol. 2: *Von der Märzrevolution bis zur Gegenwart.* Munich: C. H. Beck, 1987.

Rott, Wenzel. *Der politische Bezirk Podersam.* Prague: A. Haase, 1902–1905.

Rumpler, Helmut. *Eine Chance für Mitteleuropa: Bürgerliche Emanzipation und Staatsverfall in der Habsburgermonarchie.* Vienna: Ueberreuter, 1997.

Salfellner, Harald. *Das Goldene Gässchen.* Prague: Vitalis Verlag, 1998.

Saltarino, Signor. *Fahrend Volk: Abnormitäten, Kuriositäten und interessante Vertreter der wandernden Künstlerwelt.* Leipzig: Weber, 1895.

Sandgruber, Roman. *Ökonomie und Politik: Österreichische Wirtschaftsgeschichte vom Mittelalter bis zur Gegenwart.* Vienna: Ueberreuter, 1995.

Sauermann, Eberhard. *Literarische Kriegsfürsorge: Österreichische Dichter und Publizisten im Ersten Weltkrieg.* Vienna: Böhlau, 2000.

Schmitz, Walter, and Ludger Udolph. *"Tripolis Praga": Die Prager "Moderne" um 1900. Katalogbuch.* Dresden: Thelem, 2001.

Slapnicka, Helmut. "Recht und Verfassung der Tschechoslowakei 1918–1938." *Aktuelle Forschungsprobleme um die Erste Tschechoslowakische Republik.* Ed. Karl Bosl. Munich: Oldenbourg, 1969, pp. 93–111.

Spann, Gustav. "Zensur in Österreich während des 1. Weltkrieges 1914–1918." PhD diss., University of Vienna, 1972.

Spector, Scott. *Prague Territories: National Conflict and Cultural Innovation in Franz Kafka's Fin de Siècle.* Berkeley: University of California Press, 2000.

Statistický lexikon obci v Čechách. Prague: Bursík & Kohout, 1924.

Teichova, Alice, and Herbert Matis, eds. *Österreich und die Tschechoslowakei 1918–1938: Die wirtschaftliche Neuordnung in Zentraleuropa in der Zwischenkriegszeit.* Vienna: Böhlau, 1996.

Ulrich, Bernd, and Benjamin Ziemann, eds. *Frontalltag im Ersten Weltkrieg: Wahn und Wirklichkeit.* Essen: Klartext, 2008.

Urban, Otto. *Die tschechische Gesellschaft 1848–1918.* 2 vols. Vienna: Böhlau, 1994.

Wetzel, Jürgen. *Zehlendorf.* Geschichte der Berliner Verwaltungsbezirke. Vol. 12. Ed. Wolfgang Ribbe. Berlin: Colloquium Verlag, 1988.

Žipek, Alois. "Zásobování Prahy v r. 1918 až do převratu." *Domov za války: Svědectví účastníků.* Vol. 5. Ed. Alois Žipek. Prague: Pokrok, 1931.

History: Medical

Bochalli, Dr. "Grippe und Tuberkulose." *Münchener Medizinische Wochenschrift* 66, no. 12 (1919), p. 330.

Derblich, Wolfgang. *Die simulirten Krankheiten der Wehrpflichtigen.* Vienna: Urban & Schwarzenberg, 1878.

Deusche, Gustav. "Grippe und Tuberkulose." *Münchener Medizinische Wochenschrift* 66, no. 17 (1919), pp. 464–64.

Dinges, Martin, ed. *Medizinkritische Bewegungen im Deutschen Reich (ca. 1870 – ca. 1933).* Stuttgart: Steiner, 1996.

Dörbeck, Franz. "Die Influenzaepidemie des Jahres 1918." *Deutsche Medizinische Wochenschrift* 45, no. 26 (1919), pp. 716–18.

Eisenstaedt, Karl. "Gibt es äussere Anzeichen einer phthisischen Konstitution?" *Zeitschrift für Tuberkulose* 55 (1929), pp. 27–40.

Elias, Herbert. "Grippe." *Volksgesundheit im Krieg*. Part 2. Ed. Clemens Pirquet. Vienna: Hölder-Pichler-Tempsky, 1926, pp. 55–66.

Epstein, David. *Diagnostisch-therapeutisches Taschenbuch der Tuberkulose: Ein Leitfaden für den praktischen Arzt*. Berlin: Zerban & Schwarzenberg, 1910.

Ghon, Anton, and R. Jaksch-Wartenhorst, eds. *Die Tuberkulose und ihre Bekämpfung: Nach dem Stande vom Jahre 1921*. Vienna: Haim, 1922.

Hajek, Markus. *Pathologie und Therapie der Erkrankungen des Kehlkopfes, der Luftröhre und der Bronchien*. Leipzig: C. Kabitzsch, 1932.

Hoffmann A., and E. Keuper. "Zur Influenzaepidemie." *Deutsche Medizinische Wochenschrift* 45, no. 4 (1919), pp. 91–94.

Jütte, Robert. *Geschichte der alternativen Medizin: Von der Volksmedizin zu den unkonventionellen Therapien von heute*. Munich: C. H. Beck, 1996.

Kolata, Gina. *Flu*. New York: Touchstone, 2001.

Kretschmar, Jörg-Michael. *Die Pathologie und Therapie der Kehlkopftuberkulose im 19. und 20. Jahrhundert*. PhD diss., Dresden University of Technology, 2001.

Ladek, E. "Lungenkranke und 'Spanische Grippe.'" *Wiener klinische Wochenschrift* 31, no. 51 (1918).

Langerbeins, Ingeborg. *Lungenheilanstalten in Deutschland (1854–1945)*. PhD diss., University of Cologne, 1979.

Leitner, Philipp. "Über die Ätiologie, Symptomatologie und Therapie der pandemischen Influenza (Spanische Grippe)." *Wiener klinische Wochenschrift* 31, no. 43 (1918), pp. 1155–58.

Lesky, Erna. *Meilensteine der Wiener Medizin*. Vienna: Maudrich, 1981.

Maak, Ernst. *Über Lungenkomplikationen bei Grippe, mit einleitenden Bemerkungen über einige epidemiologische Besonderheiten bei Grippe*. PhD diss., University of Hamburg, 1920.

Mentrup, Ludger. *Die Apotheke in der Inflation 1914–1923*. Stuttgart: Deutscher Apotheker Verlag, 1988.

Nicol, Kurt, and G. Schröder. *Die Lungentuberkulose: Lehrbuch der diagnostischen Irrtümer*. Munich: Verlag der Ärztlichen Rundschau Otto Gmelin, 1927.

Radkau, Joachim. *Das Zeitalter der Nervosität: Deutschland zwischen Bismarck und Hitler*. Munich: Carl Hanser, 1998.

Rickmann, Dr. "Grippe und Lungentuberkulose." *Deutsche Medizinische Wochenschrift* 45, no. 2 (1919), pp. 39–40.

Riedesser, Peter, and Axel Verderber, eds. *"Maschinengewehre hinter der Front": Zur Geschichte der deutschen Militärpsychiatrie*. Frankfurt am Main: S. Fischer, 1996.

Vorschrift für die ärztliche Untersuchung der Wehrpflichtigen. Vienna: Hof- und Staatsdruckerei, 1912.

PHOTO CREDITS

1, 4, 6, 10, 27, 34, 38, 57, 60, 63, 64: © Archiv Klaus Wagenbach, Berlin

3, 13, 46, 52, 59: Archives of the Kafka Critical Edition, Wuppertal

14, 22, 29, 45, 50: Archives of the Kafka Critical Edition Archives/ BL Oxford, Wuppertal

5, 30, 70: © Archiv S. Fischer Verlag, Frankfurt am Main

7, 8, 21, 48, 55, 56, 68: Hans-Gerd Koch, Hagen

11, 12: The Schwadron portrait collection, The Jewish National and University Library, Jerusalem

15: Jiří Gruša

16, 66: Facsimile of "The Country Doctor." In *Franz Kafka. Ein Landarzt. Faksimile-Reprint der Erstausgabe von 1919*. Supplement to the historical-critical Franz Kafka Edition. Ed. Roland Reuss and Peter Staengle. A publication by the Institut für Textkritik e.V., Heidelberg 2006, Stroemfeld Verlag, Frankfurt am Main and Basel. Reprinted with the kind permission of the publisher.

17: Internationale Otto Gross Gesellschaft e.V., Hannover

18: Ullstein Bild, Berlin, photograph by Genja Jonas

20, 33: Jan Jindra, Prague

23: Profimedia, Pardubice

24: Vojenský ústřední Archives, Prague

25, 26, 35: Museum of Czech Literature, Prague

28, 32, 40, 42, 54: Hartmut Binder Archives, Ditzingen

31, 62: Ullstein Bild, Berlin

36, 37: Verlag Neue Kritik Archives, Frankfurt am Main

39: Österreichische Nationalbibliothek, Vienna, picture archives, 111084-D

58: Franz Kafka Museum, Prague

61: Ullstein Bild, Berlin, Archiv Gerstenberg

65: Collections of the Medical University, Vienna, picture archives

INDEX

Page numbers in *italic* type refer to photographs in the photograph section.